Sanjaya Hettihewa

SAMS
Teach Yourself
Active Server
Pages 2.0
in 21 Days

SAMS

201 West 103rd St., Indianapolis, Indiana, 46290 U

D1210892

Sams Teach Yourself Active Server Pages 2.0 in 21 Days

Copyright © 1999 by Sams Publishing

International Standard Book Number: 0-672-31333-2

Library of Congress Catalog Card Number: 98-84934

Printed in the United States of America

First Printing: *November, 1998*

00   99   98   4   3   2   1

Trademarks

Warning and Disclaimer

EXECUTIVE EDITOR
Bradley L. Jones

ACQUISITIONS EDITOR
Kelly Marshall

DEVELOPMENT EDITOR
Scott Parker

MANAGING EDITOR
Jodi Jensen

PROJECT EDITOR
Lisa M. Lord

INDEXER
Johnna VanHoose

PROOFREADER
Mona Brown

TECHNICAL EDITOR
Erik Johnson

SOFTWARE DEVELOPMENT SPECIALIST
Dan Scherf

TEAM COORDINATOR
Carol Ackerman

INTERIOR DESIGN
Gary Adair

COVER DESIGN
Aren Howell

LAYOUT TECHNICIANS
Brian Borders
Marcia Deboy
Susan Geiselman

Contents at a Glance

Contents

Dedication

This book is dedicated to you, the reader, for deciding to embark on a fascinating journey of discovery and exploration so that you can implement innovative Internet and intranet solutions to solve problems one Active Server Page at a time!

Acknowledgments

I would first like to thank Kim Spilker for getting me started writing books for Macmillan Computer Publishing and for being such a wonderful friend.

Brad Jones is the executive editor for this book, and I'd like to thank him for helping me complete this project. Brad is also the development editor, and he did a wonderful job of guiding me through this project, refining my work, and making this a better book. Special thanks also go out to Kelly Marshall for helping me stay on track and complete this book. Lisa Lord is the project editor of this book, and she is one of the nicest people with whom I've had the pleasure of working. She did a remarkable job of thoroughly going over all my chapters and ensuring the book is easy to read. Her technical skills really complement her language skills, and I'm so happy she worked on this project! If this book is easy to read, it's because of all of Lisa's efforts. Erik Johnson is the technical editor of this book. Erik did a superb job of analyzing and going over the book's technical content and making sure all the topics covered are technically accurate. His suggestions and queries made this a better, more comprehensive book. I'd like to also thank Scott Parker for helping out with author review and development.

Books are a result of the collective efforts of many people who work behind the scenes. I'd like to thank the highly skilled staff at Macmillan Computer Publishing who are involved with the tasks of indexing, proofreading, and production of this book. Books like this would never be possible if not for all the hard work and dedication of everyone at Macmillan Computer Publishing.

Writing a book can be a long process, and it can easily isolate you from the rest of the world. I'd like to thank Michael Morgan, Mary Jelacic, Marie Mikulak, Brian Ashton, Jennifer Perry, and Katherine DePasquale for their friendship and being so wonderful to me. I'd also like to thank Herbert and Carol Traxler for organizing the Viennese Waltz classes at the Austrian Embassy. I thoroughly enjoy the classes and look forward to waltzing at the beautiful ballroom of the Austrian Embassy each week.

Special thanks go out to Jerry and Monique Feffer for all their support and friendship, and to my parents for giving me the tools to discover and explore the stimulating and fascinating world of computer science. I appreciate all that you've done for me!

About the Author

SANJAYA HETTIHEWA is an accomplished Webmaster and a consultant specializing in integrating Windows NT–based information systems on the Internet. He has lived in the Washington, D.C., area for the past eight years and is the Web Architect for TeraTech, Inc., a Web and Visual Basic consulting company in Rockville, Maryland, and specializes in projects that integrate capabilities of ASP, IIS, VB, and related technologies. Sanjaya is the author of *Windows NT 4 Web Development* and has co-authored seven books, including *Designing and Implementing Internet Information Server*, *Teach Yourself Active Server Pages in 14 Days*, *Internet Explorer Unleashed*, and *Internet Information Server Unleashed*, all by Macmillan Computer Publishing. You can reach Sanjaya at `http://www.NetInnovation.com/Sanjaya/` (or, if you prefer the old-fashioned way, you can send e-mail to `sanjaya@NetInovation.com`).

Tell Us What You Think!

As the reader of this book, *you* are our most important critic and commentator. We value your opinion and want to know what we're doing right, what we could do better, what areas you'd like to see us publish in, and any other words of wisdom you're willing to pass our way.

As the Executive Editor for the Advanced Programming Team at Macmillan Computer Publishing, I welcome your comments. You can fax, e-mail, or write me directly to let me know what you did or didn't like about this book—as well as what we can do to make our books stronger.

Please note that I cannot help you with technical problems related to the topic of this book, and that due to the high volume of mail I receive, I might not be able to reply to every message.

When you write, please be sure to include this book's title and author as well as your name and phone or fax number. I will carefully review your comments and share them with the author and editors who worked on the book.

Fax:	317-817-7070
E-mail:	`adv_prog@mcp.com`
Mail:	Bradley L. Jones
	Executive Editor
	Advanced Programming Team
	Macmillan Computer Publishing

Introduction

Active Server Pages is revolutionizing the way Web applications are developed, almost the same way Windows NT 4.0 revolutionized client/server computing. Thanks to Active Server Pages, Web developers can now easily make a Web site interactive and offer dynamic, compelling information to users browsing the site.

Before Active Server Pages, developing a typical interactive Web application meant compiling an executable application using a traditional application development environment, such as Visual C++. After the application was compiled, it was copied to a CGI directory of the Web server. Even the slightest change to the application meant recompiling the entire application and replacing the previous version of the executable file. This process is unnecessarily resource intensive in a production environment. Active Server Pages solves this problem by offering an easier, more direct way to create Web applications.

All that's required to take advantage of Active Server Pages is familiarity with Visual Basic or a Web scripting language, such as JScript/JavaScript or VBScript. Active Server Pages simplifies the lives of Web application developers by offering a way to create sophisticated Web applications with a familiar scripting language, such as VBScript, JScript/JavaScript, or Perl.

Teach Yourself Active Server Pages in 21 Days comprehensively covers all aspects of Active Server Pages in an easy-to-understand format.

How This Book Is Organized

This book is organized into days and weeks. The first week introduces you to Active Server Pages and covers the basics of ASP application development. The second week delves into more complex topics, such as database application development and using ASP objects and components. The third and final week covers advanced topics such as building custom ASP components with Visual Basic, complex client/server applications, and ASP security.

After reading this book, you will be able to use the capabilities of Active Server Pages to truly activate your Internet applications, one Active Server Page at a time.

 Note

> Please refer to the Week in Review and Week at a Glance sections for more information about the topics covered each day.

Why This Book Is Special

The World Wide Web has experienced phenomenal growth during the past few years. More and more Web sites are relying on Microsoft Windows NT for setting up Internet and intranet Web servers. Active Server Pages, an integral part of IIS, makes it easier to develop powerful Web applications using industry standard technologies, such as DAO, ODBC, OLE, COM, and ActiveX. This book covers all aspects of developing ASP applications in a straightforward, easy-to-understand manner.

Who Should Read This Book

This book teaches you everything that's needed to begin developing sophisticated ASP applications. Even if you have little previous knowledge about Web application development, you can easily follow this book. The topics covered are all explained in clear terms. Screen shots and diagrams are used extensively to explain concepts and to help you visualize the demonstrations and examples.

This book should be read by anyone who wants to make use of the power of Active Server Pages to create a dynamic Web site. The Web is made up of a diverse group of people. Likewise, this book has been written for an equally diverse audience. Specifically, this book is for the following:

- Web application developers
- Web site administrators
- Information systems architects
- Windows NT system administrators

Web Application Developers

Although the Web was originally used mostly for distributing information, it is increasingly being used for more sophisticated tasks. The Web is no longer about simply distributing static HTML files. It is about providing dynamic content to millions of users when they want it. If you are a Web application developer, it is crucial that you stay on top of new Web publishing tools, and know how and when to use them. Active Server Pages is Microsoft's preferred application development environment for developing Web applications. The tips and techniques in this book can be used by Web application developers to make the best use of this powerful new Web technology.

Web Site Administrators

The role of Web site administrators is becoming more and more complicated as new Web development applications and technologies are invented. This book can help Web site administrators learn about the issues related to developing and deploying ASP applications.

Information Systems Architects

This book is of particular value to information systems architects who have been delegated the task of establishing a Web presence and exploring the options available for developing Web applications. With the aid of this book, information systems architects can learn the benefits of using Active Server Pages to develop Web applications.

Windows NT System Administrators

Active Server Pages is an integral part of IIS 4.0. Although system administrators might not be directly responsible for publishing information on the Internet, they need to have a working knowledge of integral Web publishing technologies, such as Active Server Pages. They also need to be familiar with issues such as security that arise when Web applications are published on the Internet. With the help of this book, Windows NT system administrators can quickly become familiar with Active Server Pages and learn how to effectively deploy ASP applications on the Web.

WEEK 1

At a Glance

You must be eager to get started with this book. Before you turn the page to the first day, please take the time to read this section before beginning your tutorial, especially those of you who never read the introduction section of a book! By reading this section, you will have a better understanding of how this tutorial is structured and how you can make the best use of it.

Over the next three weeks, you will embark on a journey of discovery, learning how to unleash the potential of Active Server Pages and build richly interactive, dynamic Web applications. All that's required is a Web browser, a text editor (yes, even Windows Notepad will do), a Web server that implements ASP 2.0, and your time.

Many real-world ASP applications will be presented to you throughout this tutorial. At times, it will seem that a lot of material is covered in one day. The book does indeed cover a lot of material. However, we've made every effort to present the material in a manner that is clear, concise, and easily understood. At the end of each day, a small workshop is offered, complete with quiz questions and exercises. Answers to the quiz questions are supplied in Appendix A, "Answers to Questions," and answers to almost all the exercises are given on the MCP Web site at www.mcp.com.

You can learn all about Active Server Pages by reading this book; however, if you really want to master Active Server Pages, you should take the time to experiment with the applications presented in this book. By following this 21-day tutorial, you are perfectly capable of mastering ASP at the end of the third week. All I ask that you do to make this a reality is carefully go over the material offered on each day and invest the time to modify and experiment with the code that's supplied.

Feedback

At the end of the third week, I encourage you to write to me and let me know how this book has helped you with ASP development. If you have any suggestions for improvement, please let me know so I can incorporate your suggestions in the next edition. My e-mail address is `Sanjaya@NetInnovation.com`. I look forward to hearing from you.

Where You Are Going...

The first week covers the fundamental topics of Active Server Pages (ASP). Day 1, "Getting Started with Active Server Pages," goes over the basics of using ASP to implement Web projects. Day 2, "Web Development with Active Server Pages," shows you the structure and core components of an ASP application. Upcoming lessons depend on information given in the first two days, so be sure to take the time to carefully go over them. You learn how to build effective Web user interfaces that use HTML forms, input and message boxes, ActiveX controls, and Java on Day 3, "Interacting with Your Users," and on Day 4, "Building and Processing Web Forms," you learn how to process information you retrieve through Web forms. Data validation and processing is also covered on Day 3, so be sure to experiment with the ASP code presented in that lesson. The next three days of the week focus on how to use scriptlets to componentize your ASP code and how to use two of the built-in ASP components, the `Request` object and the `Response` object. Day 5, "Using Scriptlets to Componentize ASP," shows how to build your own scriptlets and use them in ASP applications. On Day 5, you also learn how to work with local files. At the end of Day 5, you will be able to create your own scriptlet library. Day 6, "Getting Information About HTTP Requests with the `Request` Object," shows you how to use the `Request` object to get information about an HTTP transaction. It is important that you spend the time to thoroughly understand the `Request` object because you will use it often. Day 7, "Responding to Client Requests with the `Response` Object," shows you how to customize HTTP responses (including cookies and URL redirects) sent to Web browsers with the `Response` object.

Okay, It's Time to Get Started!

Enough talking already! Want to master Active Server Pages? Turn the page, and let your three-week journey of discovery begin. Soon you will discover the rewards and joy of implementing complex Web projects and see them come alive with users who depend on your application to get their work done.

WEEK 1

DAY 1

Getting Started with Active Server Pages

Today, you are introduced to Active Server Pages (ASP) and shown how you can benefit from some of its unique features and capabilities. ASP makes it easy to develop interactive Web applications. After you read this book, you will find ASP to be one of the most powerful weapons in your arsenal of Web development tools. The purpose of today's tutorial is to quickly get you up to speed with ASP by providing a quick overview of it and related technologies. Today, you cover the following:

- Learn what ASP is.
- Review the benefits of using ASP.
- Discover what you need to know to get started with ASP.
- See the hardware and software resources you need.
- Understand how ASP compares with other Web development technologies and tools.

Today's tutorial concludes by teaching you how to build not one, but several, simple ASP applications!

What Is Active Server Pages?

Active Server Pages (ASP) is Microsoft's most recent Web server application development technology, designed to make it easier for Web application developers to create sophisticated Web applications.

Take a look at Figure 1.1 to help you better understand the role ASP plays in Web application development and where ASP fits in with other server-side Web application development technologies. As you can see in Figure 1.1, ASP is one of many technologies available for developing Web server applications. At the end of today's lesson, you will understand why ASP is better suited for developing most Web applications you build.

FIGURE 1.1.

The role ASP plays in Web development.

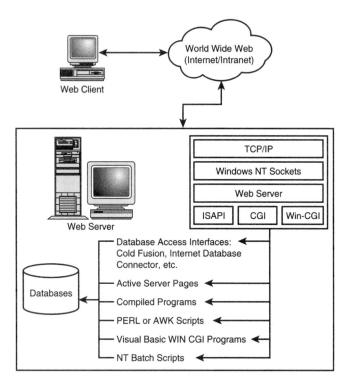

Active Server Pages enables Web application developers to easily leverage their existing investments on Windows application development tools and technologies to the Internet. ASP is designed to make it easier to develop interactive Web applications and work with industry-standard Windows technologies, such as Object Linking and Embedding (OLE) Automation, ActiveX, Active Data Objects (ADO), VBScript, JavaScript, Visual Basic, Open Database Connectivity (ODBC), Component Object Model (COM), and so on.

What Do I Need to Know to Get Started?

1

You are probably familiar with (or have at least heard of) JavaScript and VBScript. ASP is a similar technology, except that ASP applications are exclusively executed on the server side. Because ASP supports VBScript, JScript, Perl, and other scripting languages, Web developers don't need to learn an entirely new language. ASP has been designed to make use of the existing knowledge of Web application developers.

You will be happy to know that ASP has a smooth learning curve. As long as you are familiar with the Windows environment, HTML, and VBScript (or Visual Basic), you'll have no trouble with this tutorial. Before long, you'll be an expert in ASP!

By default, Active Server Pages supports only VBScript and JScript/JavaScript. Support for additional scripting languages such as Perl can be added, as demonstrated in Day 19, "Exploiting ASP: Tips and Advanced Topics."

ASP simplifies the lives of Web application developers by providing a mechanism for creating sophisticated Web applications with a familiar scripting language such as VBScript, JScript/JavaScript, or Perl. Because VBScript is so easy to learn and use, all the ASP examples in this tutorial are in VBScript.

Understanding Where ASP Fits into Microsoft's Active Platform

ASP is an integral part of the Active Platform, Microsoft's core Internet strategy. The Active Platform is a common set of languages, standards, and services that can be used to develop either Active Desktop (client-side) or Active Server (server-side) applications. The Active Platform paradigm makes it easier and more cost-effective for developers to leverage their skills to develop a broad spectrum of applications that run on the server and the client. It also makes it very easy to transform a desktop application to a full-blown client/server application.

ASP is actually a DLL component installed on your Web server. This component processes files that end with the extension .asp and transmits the result to the client that requested the ASP file. This does not mean that ASP applications render technologies such as Internet Server Application Programming Interface (ISAPI) obsolete. Rather, ASP applications compliment Web application technologies like ISAPI.

Benefits of Using ASP

There are many benefits in using ASP that make it one of the most powerful tools available for developing sophisticated Web applications. Here are some of the benefits:

- ASP complements client-side scripting.
- ASP development is easy to learn.
- With the ASP development environment, you can easily leverage existing investments and skills.
- ASP development is compile-free.
- The ASP environment is extensible.
- ASP protects proprietary business algorithms and information.

ASP Complements Client-Side Scripting

ASP applications don't replace client-side scripting languages. Rather, they complement client-side scripting languages by offering yet another powerful tool that can be used by Web site developers to develop richly interactive, compelling Web sites.

You can add a new level of interactivity to your Web pages by using client-side scripting. For example, before data in an HTML form is submitted to a Web server for processing, a VBScript subroutine can examine the data and point out errors to the user. However, some Web browsers don't support client-side scripting. When it isn't possible to use client-side scripting, server-side scripting can be used to give users a rich, interactive experience—even if they use technologically challenged Web browsers.

ASP Development Is Easy to Learn

ASP can be used to easily add a new level of interactivity to a Web site. All you need to start building ASP applications is familiarity with a Web scripting language, such as JScript/JavaScript or VBScript. Because VBScript resembles BASIC in many ways, it is easy to learn, even if you are new to programming. If you are familiar with C/C++, you will be happy to learn that the syntax of JScript/JavaScript is similar to the C/C++ syntax. Both VBScript and JavaScript offer ASP developers the ability to access and manipulate the events, objects, and methods exposed to ASP applications.

NEW TERM An *event* is created to indicate that a certain action has occurred.

NEW TERM An *object* is an entity that implements certain functionality, using a well-defined interface and behavior.

NEW TERM   A *method* is simply a subroutine that can be executed by calling its method
name.

Leveraging Existing Investments and Skills

Chances are you have already made significant investments in productivity and database
applications such as Microsoft Office. ASP helps you leverage your investments to the
Internet. As demonstrated in Day 10, "Programming Web Databases," Day 11, "Building
Database Applications Using ActiveX Data Objects," and Day 12, "Database
Development Illustrated: Building a User Registration System," ASP's database features
can be used to interface with databases already installed on your system. ASP makes use
of the industry-standard technologies and database access interfaces you are most likely
already familiar with, such as ODBC, OLE, ActiveX, and COM.

What does all this mean to you? It means you do not have to make additional investments in tools and training to leverage your existing investments to the Internet. ASP
allows you to easily work with applications and tools you are already using.

ASP Development Is Compile-Free

Before ASP, developing a typical interactive Web application required compiling an executable application by using a traditional application development environment, such as
Visual C++. After the application was compiled, it was copied to the Web server's CGI
directory. Even the slightest change to the application required recompiling the entire
application (or a code module) and replacing the previous version of the executable file.
This process is unnecessarily resource-intensive in a production environment. ASP solves
this problem by offering a more direct and easier way to create Web applications. After
you develop an ASP application, you do not have to compile it. Simply save the file with
the .asp extension, and the ASP DLL then processes the file when it is requested by a
user.

NEW TERM   *Compiling* is the process of creating an executable program that can be directly
run without having its source code processed at runtime. Compiled programs run
faster because they are in a format that can be understood and directly executed by your
computer without any additional processing. Interpreted languages such as VBScript and
JScript, on the other hand, are interpreted line by line at runtime, making them less efficient for applications having many complex calculations. Rest assured that for most Web
applications you build, the performance hit of using an interpreted language is barely
noticeable. In Day 20, "Building Custom ASP Components with Visual Basic," you learn
how to build custom ASP components that are compiled (for better performance).
Custom ASP components are ideal for performing complex calculations for your ASP
applications.

The ASP Environment Is Extensible

ASP is fully extensible and ships with several built-in components that can be used for tasks such as allowing database access and creating rotating advertisement banners. You can develop your own custom components and extend the capabilities of ASP, as shown in Day 20.

ASP Protects Proprietary Business Algorithms and Information

One disadvantage of using client-side scripting languages is that it exposes proprietary business algorithms and information. In a payroll application, for example, an employer might use a complicated formula to determine an employee's bonus by taking into account factors such as employee evaluations. For various reasons, the employer might not want to make public the criteria used to calculate the bonus. If the bonus calculation is implemented with a client-side scripting language, such as VBScript, anyone looking at the source code of the Web page can observe proprietary business algorithms used by the employer. On the other hand, if the employer uses ASP, possibly along with a custom ASP component or two, users no longer have access to proprietary business algorithms and information because ASP code is executed on the server. Only the output is sent to the user.

How ASP Compares with Similar Web Development Technologies

At the time this book goes to press, Active Server Pages has been around for about two years and is rapidly becoming a widely used Web development technology. To give you a better understanding of existing Web application development technologies, here is a list of commonly used ones:

- Common Gateway Interface (CGI)
- Internet Server Application Programming Interface (ISAPI)
- Internet Database Connector (IDC)
- Windows CGI (WinCGI)
- Practical Extraction and Report Language (commonly called *Perl*)
- Internet features of productivity and database applications
- Cold Fusion

The following sections compare ASP with these technologies.

Common Gateway Interface (CGI)

CGI is perhaps the oldest Web application development technology in existence. It was designed to give Web application developers the opportunity to build programs executed on the server each time a Web user requests that application through a URL. The CGI program can get input from the user (if needed), process data, and send output back to the user. CGI worked quite well in the early days. However, it has an inherent resource usage problem. Each time the CGI application is executed, a new process has to be created on the server, which can be quite resource-intensive for the server—especially when several users try to execute the same application simultaneously. With millions of new users signing on to the Internet every month, CGI is not a very efficient solution for Web server applications because it isn't scalable.

Internet Server Application Programming Interface (ISAPI)

ISAPI is a high-performance Web application development technology. ISAPI applications are compiled applications, so they are very efficient and ideal for high-performance Web sites. However, ISAPI applications are more complicated and not as easy to build and deploy as ASP applications. By using ASP with custom ASP components you build with Visual Basic, you can realize some of the benefits of ISAPI without learning a more complex application development language, such as C++.

Internet Database Connector (IDC)

IDC is Microsoft's first Web database application development framework. It enables Web application developers to build Web database applications by creating special template files that insert and retrieve information from databases. IDC has limited capabilities when it comes to interfacing with multiple databases and processing data before it is presented to the user. ASP solves the limitations of IDC by providing a powerful and extensible Web application development framework.

Windows CGI (WinCGI)

WinCGI, pioneered by O'Reilly Associate's Web Site Web server, makes it easy to build and deploy Web solutions using the power and flexibility of Visual Basic. However, WinCGI doesn't offer Web application developers the flexibility offered by ASP, such as the ability to use the scripting language of your choice.

Practical Extraction and Report Language (Perl)

Perl is a powerful scripting language widely used by Web application developers (particularly in the UNIX world). Active Server Pages supports Perl, so if you're familiar with it, you can build your ASP applications using all the powerful features of Perl. If you aren't familiar with Perl, you can always learn it later, and then use your Perl skills when building ASP applications. This book does not cover building complex ASP applications with Perl. Instead, in Day 19, you are shown how to extend your ASP development environment by adding support for Perl.

Cold Fusion

Cold Fusion is a database markup language primarily used to build database applications easily. Since its first release, Cold Fusion has become a powerful tool for developing all sorts of database applications. If you are familiar with Cold Fusion, you might want to continue using it for your database projects until you learn how to build database applications with ASP in Day 10. Although Cold Fusion works well for building database applications, ASP is more integrated with IIS and gives you a more flexible, robust, and scalable platform for building and deploying sophisticated database applications.

New Term *Live data* is data that is online. If the data changes at the source, then the data that's displayed is automatically updated with the new data. Live data is essential for certain Web applications, such as real-time stock stickers.

New Term *Static data* is a snapshot of data at a certain point in time. If your data changes only at certain intervals, it might make more sense for you to build static HTML pages using your data when the data changes.

Internet Features of Productivity and Database Applications

You are probably already familiar with the Internet features of the productivity and database applications you use, such as Microsoft Word, Access, SQL Server, PowerBuilder, and so forth. The Internet features of these applications allow you to easily publish information on the Internet as static (HTML pages) or live data (ASP or IDC applications).

Note
Although built-in Internet features of productivity applications can be a substantial timesaver, often the "cookie cutter" ASP code generated by applications needs to be customized to meet the unique needs of the application you are building. Without the knowledge of ASP, you can't maintain the ASP applications that are automatically built by your database and productivity applications.

Drawbacks to Using ASP for Web Development

Unlike most other Web application development tools, there are few drawbacks to using Active Server Pages, mostly because it is not a specific programming language. Rather, it's a framework for developing and deploying Web applications on the Internet using a multitude of tools and technologies available to Windows developers, such as Visual C++, Delphi, Visual Basic, Perl, and so on. Virtually any Web project you can imagine can be effectively implemented with Active Server Pages. With Active Server Pages, you can easily mix and match features of different programming languages and application development tools to build your Web application.

Requirements for ASP Development

The basic software and hardware requirements for developing ASP applications are listed here. Although some requirements are optional, meeting or exceeding the listed recommended requirements will make your life as an ASP developer more pleasant!

- 486 processor (a Pentium-based computer is highly recommended).
- 32MB of RAM (48MB or higher recommended).
- About 150MB of free hard-drive space.
- Windows NT Server 4.0, Windows NT Workstation 4.0, or Windows 98/Windows 95 with TCP/IP networking support properly installed and configured.

Note

Although Windows NT Server, Windows NT Workstation, Windows 98, and Windows 95 can be used to develop ASP applications, when deploying ASP applications on the Internet—especially mission-critical ones—I recommend that you use Windows NT Server because of its security, performance, and application-integration capabilities. For additional information, see the next section, "Do You Really Need Windows NT Server 4.0?"

- A Web server that supports ASP 2.0 (such as Internet Information Server 3.0 or later; if you are using Windows NT Server, IIS 4.0 is recommended) or Microsoft Personal Web Server (PWS) is required if you are using Windows 98/Windows 95, and Microsoft Peer Web Services is required if you are using Windows NT Workstation. Because the ASP component is actually an ISAPI application, you should be able to develop ASP applications with any ISAPI-compliant Web server by simply downloading the ASP component of IIS 3.0 and installing it. However, you are likely to have better ASP integration with IIS and PWS/Peer Web Services.

- A database that supports ODBC (such as Microsoft Access or Microsoft SQL Server). You will be unable to build Web database applications later in Day 10, Day 11, and Day 12 if you do not have a database that supports ASP.
- Microsoft Visual InterDev 6.0 is highly recommended, but not required.

Do You Really Need Windows NT Server 4.0?

Windows NT used with IIS and ASP gives you a powerful platform for developing and deploying Web applications. If you are simply learning ASP, then Windows 98, Windows 95, or Windows NT Workstation will suffice for most of your needs. However, if you will be deploying ASP solutions on the Internet, I highly recommend that you use Windows NT Server for the following reasons:

Do

DO use Windows NT Server to deploy your ASP solutions on the Internet. Windows NT Server offers superior scalability and security and a robust environment for deploying ASP applications. You can, of course, use Windows NT Workstation, Windows 98, or Windows 95 to develop your ASP applications.

- Windows NT Server yields better performance.
- Windows NT Server is more secure.
- Windows NT Server allows for easy integration with enterprise-quality applications, such as Microsoft SQL Server.

 Note

This book focuses on teaching you how to make the best use of Active Server Pages, and it doesn't matter whether you use Windows NT Server/Workstation or Windows 98/Windows 95. If you are using Windows NT Workstation or Windows 98/Windows 95, you will be able to follow the exercises in this book with no problem. However, discussions about Windows NT security and Internet Information Server will not apply to you.

Windows NT Server Yields Better Performance

Windows NT Server has been optimized to provide the best performance for network-intensive server applications. On the other hand, Windows 95 and Windows NT

Workstation have been optimized to offer the best performance for productivity applications. Therefore, Windows NT Server yields better performance when hosting ASP applications.

Windows NT Server Is More Secure

Because IIS uses NTFS security when it's run under Windows NT Server 4.0, Windows NT Server is a more secure platform for hosting ASP applications. Because Windows 98 and Windows 95 use Microsoft Personal Web Server, a watered-down version of IIS, you can't implement security with NTFS (NT File System, used by Windows NT) security permissions unless you use Windows NT.

Easy Integration with Enterprise-Quality Applications

Enterprise-quality applications, such as those in the Microsoft BackOffice Suite (Microsoft SQL Server, Microsoft Exchange Server, and so on), require Windows NT Server. Therefore, choosing to develop your ASP applications with Windows NT Server makes it easier for you to integrate your ASP applications with components of BackOffice to develop sophisticated Web applications.

Web Browser Requirements

As you'll learn in upcoming chapters, although Active Server Pages is a Microsoft technology, it is a cross-platform/browser technology and does not tie you down to any particular Web browser. In fact, you will learn how to create ASP applications that can actually produce customized output for virtually any Web browser. It doesn't matter whether the user is using Netscape 2.0, Internet Explorer running on Windows CE, or the latest version of Internet Explorer or Netscape Navigator. ASP applications can effectively communicate with all these Web browsers. Therefore, it is up to you, the ASP developer, to take advantage of this cross-browser capability when developing ASP applications.

Do
DO make sure your ASP applications can be comfortably browsed with an	older Web browser, such as Netscape Navigator 2.0.

Internet Explorer 4.0 is used for almost all the examples in this book. However, Netscape Navigator 4.0 or similar Web browsers also work fine. At a minimum, the Web browser you use should support tables. This requirement isn't very difficult because tables have been supported by Web browsers for more than two years.

For some of the examples in more advanced chapters toward the end of the book, you need a Web browser that supports Java and ActiveX.

DON'T

DON'T depend on Web browsers that support ActiveX when building ASP applications unless you will be deploying your ASP application in an intranet environment, where you have control over the Web browser used by your users.

Getting ASP

If you are an IIS user, ASP is already installed as part of IIS. So if you are using IIS 4.0, you don't have to do anything special to download or install it. If you are using IIS 3.0 or earlier, consider upgrading to IIS 4.0 (or the current version of IIS available when you read this). This book assumes you are using IIS 4.0 or higher. If you use Windows 95 or Windows 98, you can develop ASP applications by installing Personal Web Server (PWS) software.

Note

For the latest information about IIS, visit the Microsoft IIS Web site at
http://www.Microsoft.com/IIS/.

If you will be using a different Web server with this tutorial, please make sure it supports ASP 2.0 the same way PWS/IIS 4.0 supports ASP 2.0, and you won't have any problems with the exercises. Because of the many Web servers in use, it's beyond the scope of this book to discuss and analyze different ASP implementations used by other Web servers. Instead, this book focuses on ASP 2.0 as implemented by IIS 4.0 and PWS.

Tools for Developing ASP Applications

Now that you understand what ASP and related technologies are all about, you're ready to begin developing ASP applications—after a quick overview of tools that can be used to build ASP applications.

Notepad and Other Text Editors

To develop applications with ASP, you need a plain text editor that can edit ASCII text files. Notepad (Notepad.exe, affectionately referred to by the development community as Visual Notepad) works just fine; however, as you begin developing complex ASP applications, you can greatly benefit from an integrated ASP development environment (such as Microsoft Visual InterDev) that is optimized for developing ASP applications.

Microsoft FrontPage 98

Microsoft FrontPage 98 is a wonderful Web page design and layout tool. Unfortunately, some of its features make life a bit complicated for ASP developers because it sometimes insists on formatting the ASP code you enter. Although Microsoft FrontPage 98's ASP support has greatly improved over that of FrontPage 97, it still has a tendency to do certain things to ASP applications that you rather wish it didn't. For most of the applications you build in this tutorial, you can use FrontPage 98 with few problems. However, as your ASP applications become more and more complex, keep in mind the possibility that FrontPage 98 might modify your ASP code.

 Note

FrontPage 98's purpose in life is not ASP development. Rather, FrontPage 98 is Microsoft's "end-user" Web page design and layout tool. For Web application developers (such as yourself!), Microsoft has created, and suggests using, the Visual InterDev tool. If you will be using FrontPage 98 for ASP development, bear in mind that FrontPage 98 is not intended to do hardcore ASP development.

Using Microsoft FrontPage 98 for ASP Development

It's easy to use Microsoft FrontPage 98 for simple ASP development. Just open the ASP file you want to work on and select the HTML tab so you can edit the HTML code, as shown in Figure 1.2.

FIGURE 1.2.

FrontPage 98 can be used to work on ASP applications.

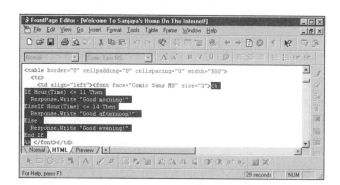

Refer to Figure 1.3 for the output of the ASP code shown in Figure 1.2. This should give you a basic idea of how ASP code is processed and how ASP applications display output to Web browsers.

FIGURE 1.3.

Output of the ASP code in Figure 1.2.

When Can Microsoft FrontPage 98 Be Used?

FrontPage 98 is acceptable for simple ASP applications that are composed of only a few blocks of ASP code. However, a plain text editor or a tool designed especially for ASP, such as Microsoft Visual InterDev, is more suitable for developing complex ASP applications. When you're trying to debug a complex ASP application with pages and pages of code, the last thing you want to worry about is whether your editor made changes to your code!

Note

> Although FrontPage 98 is a wonderful Web page design and layout tool, it is not the tool of choice for ASP development. As long as your ASP applications are simple and don't include more than a few ASP code blocks, the FrontPage 98 editor works okay. However, as your ASP applications become more and more complex, you'll notice the FrontPage 98 editor making unwanted modifications to your ASP code.

Microsoft Visual InterDev

Microsoft Visual InterDev is a Rapid Application Development (RAD) tool for developing ASP applications, but it isn't required for this tutorial. You can easily develop complicated Web applications with Microsoft Visual InterDev because it simplifies developing and debugging ASP applications. The ability to easily create ASP database applications is one of the best, most productive features of Visual InterDev. You will be happy to know that Visual InterDev 6.0 uses Microsoft's IntelliSense technology to aid ASP development, as shown in Figure 1.4.

If the Visual InterDev application window shown in Figure 1.4 looks too complicated, don't worry. Although the development environment might look complicated at first, it really is very easy to use, especially if you have used another Microsoft visual tool (Visual C++, Visual Basic, and so forth) before. If you haven't, learning Visual InterDev makes it easier for you to master other Microsoft visual tools. Coverage of Visual InterDev 6.0 is included in Day 17, "Building ASP Applications with Visual InterDev 6.0."

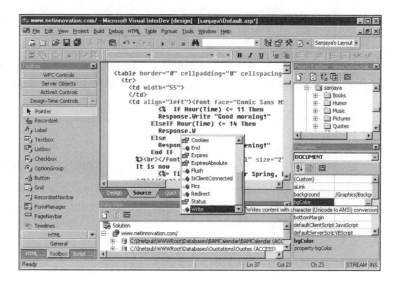

FIGURE 1.4.

Visual InterDev uses Microsoft's IntelliSense technology to aid ASP development.

Microsoft Visual Basic

Microsoft Visual Basic is a wonderful Windows application development tool that complements ASP very nicely. In Day 20, "Building Custom ASP Components with Visual Basic," you learn how to use Visual Basic's powerful, easy-to-use features to extend ASP's capabilities.

The Three Different Code Delimiters

ASP code is simply inserted between HTML statements of a Web page. The ASP Interpreter separates ASP code from the rest of the Web page by using special ASP code delimiters. There are three different types of ASP code delimiters you can use:

- The delimiters used to separate blocks of ASP code from the rest of a Web page.
- The delimiters used to display the value of an ASP expression.
- The delimiters that define ASP script blocks while specifying the scripting language being used.

This section briefly introduces you to the concept of using ASP script delimiters. This topic is revisited again tomorrow, when you see an example that uses all three scripting delimiters. The following sections examine when you should use each code delimiter.

Separating Blocks of ASP Code from the Rest of a Web Page

Use the following ASP code delimiter to separate ASP code written in the default scripting language (which is VBScript). The syntax for this code delimiter is very simple:

```
<%
<Your ASP statements go here>
%>
```

Displaying the Value of an Expression or Variable

The next script delimiter is used only to display results of calculations or variables in the middle of HTML code. Don't use it to separate several ASP statements or carry out complex calculations. Use it exclusively to display values of expressions and variables within HTML code. Here's the format for this code delimiter:

```
<%= <Expression to display> %>
```

The purpose of this script delimiter will make more sense to you after you see an example of how it is used. The following line of ASP code uses the script delimiters <%= and %> to display the current date:

```
<%= FormatDateTime(date,vbLongDate) %>
```

Note that the following ASP statement creates exactly the same effect:

```
<% Response.Write FormatDateTime(date,vbLongDate) %>
```

Defining ASP Script Blocks and Specifying the Scripting Language

The script delimiters <% and %> work in most cases. As mentioned earlier, ASP allows you to use multiple scripting languages, even on the same page. If you want to use a scripting language that is different from the default scripting language (VBScript), you can use the following script delimiters to separate your ASP code and specify the scripting language you want to use:

```
<SCRIPT RUNAT = SERVER LANGUAGE=VBScript>

<Your ASP statements go here>

</SCRIPT>
```

Of course, before you use a different scripting language, such as Perl, you need to install support for it. You find out how to do this in Day 19.

1

Specifying Directory Permissions

Before you can execute ASP applications on your Web server, you have to make sure the directory containing your ASP applications has script execute permissions. The exact procedure for assigning execute permissions for a directory depends on the Web server you are using. Consult your Web server's documentation for all the details.

If you are using IIS 4.0, open the Microsoft Management Console's IIS folder, select the directory, click the right mouse button, and select Properties from the pop-up menu. When the Directory Properties dialog box is displayed (see Figure 1.5), make sure the directory has Script or Execute (including script) permissions enabled.

FIGURE 1.5.

A directory needs Script or Execute permission before ASP applications in that directory are executed.

Hello World, Active Server Pages!

Enough talking already! Now that you understand what ASP is all about and how you can benefit from this powerful Web application development technology, it's time to develop your first ASP application.

Hello World, the Simplest ASP Application in the World!

The Hello World application developed in Listing 1.1 displays the current date and time and displays the string "Hello World!" using different font sizes.

Tip

> Use the VBScript code continuation character (the underline character _) to
> break down long VBScript statements into multiple lines.

LISTING 1.1. HELLO WORLD, ACTIVE SERVER PAGES!

```
 1: <%@ LANGUAGE=VBScript %>
 2: <HTML>
 3: <HEAD>
 4: <TITLE>Hello World, Active Server Pages!</TITLE>
 5: </HEAD>
 6: <BODY>
 7:
 8: <H1><FONT face=Arial size=5>Welcome To The
 9: <FONT style="BACKGROUND-COLOR: #ffe4b5">Exciting</FONT>
10: World of ASP Development!</FONT></H1>
11:
12: It is now <%= Time & " on " & FormatDateTime (date,vbLongDate) %>.
13:
14: <HR>
15:
16: <%
17:
18: Dim LineCount
19:
20: For LineCount = 1 to 7
21:   Response.Write ("<FONT size=" & LineCount & _
22:     "> Hello World! </Font> <BR>")
23: Next
24:
25: %>
26:
27: <HR>
28:
29: </BODY>
30: </HTML>
```

ANALYSIS Line 1 of Listing 1.1 states that the default scripting language used for this ASP
page is VBScript. Unless otherwise specified, using the <SCRIPT> tag, all ASP
code contained in the ASP page is assumed to be in VBScript. Line 12 uses the VBScript
string concatenation operator to display the current date and time and uses the VBScript
function FormatDateTime() to format the current date. The for next loop in lines
20–23 displays the string "Hello World!" using increasing font sizes. The
Response.Write() statement, used in line 21 of Listing 1.1, simply displays a given text
expression.

Figure 1.6 shows the Web page generated by the ASP application in Listing 1.2.

Note

If the long date format specified for your computer in the Control Panel is different, the format of the date displayed in the Web page in Figure 1.6 will be slightly different.

FIGURE 1.6.

The output of the Hello World application.

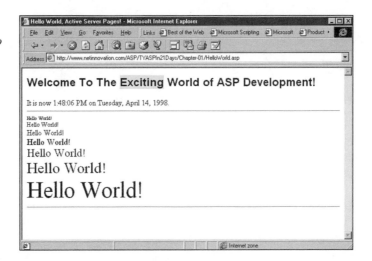

Listing 1.2 contains the HTML code generated by the ASP application in Listing 1.1. Notice how the ASP statements in Listing 1.1 have been replaced by HTML statements.

LISTING 1.2. THE HTML CODE GENERATED BY THE ASP APPLICATION IN LISTING 1.1.

```
<HTML>
<HEAD>
<TITLE>Hello World, Active Server Pages!</TITLE>
</HEAD>
<BODY>

<H1><FONT face=Arial size=5>Welcome To The
<FONT style="BACKGROUND-COLOR: #ffe4b5">Exciting</FONT>
World of ASP Development!</FONT></H1>

It is now 1:48:06 PM on Tuesday, April 14, 1998.

<HR>

<FONT size=1> Hello World! </Font> <BR>
```

continues

LISTING **1.2.** CONTINUED

```
<FONT size=2> Hello World! </Font> <BR>
<FONT size=3> Hello World! </Font> <BR>
<FONT size=4> Hello World! </Font> <BR>
<FONT size=5> Hello World! </Font> <BR>
<FONT size=6> Hello World! </Font> <BR>
<FONT size=7> Hello World! </Font> <BR>

<HR>

</BODY>
</HTML>
```

Developing a Birthday Countdown Timer

Although the ASP application you develop in this section is somewhat complex for Day 1, it will help you understand how ASP applications are built and how they communicate with the user. Don't worry if you don't understand entirely how the code works. At this point, as long as you have a general idea about how the code functions, you are fine. At the end of Day 3, "Interacting with Your Users," you will fully understand how the birthday countdown timer ASP application functions.

The Birthday Countdown Application

The birthday countdown application, shown in Listing 1.3, displays a form used to get a birth date from the user. The application then calculates and displays when the user's next birthday is and how many days away it is. Although that might sound a bit complicated, you will have no trouble understanding the source code of the birthday countdown application as long as you are familiar with VBScript.

LISTING **1.3.** THE SOURCE CODE FOR THE BIRTHDAY COUNTDOWN APPLICATION.

```
 1: <%@ LANGUAGE=VBScript %>
 2: <HTML>
 3: <HEAD>
 4: <META NAME="GENERATOR" Content="Microsoft Visual Studio 6.0">
 5: <TITLE>Birthday Countdown Application</TITLE>
 6: </HEAD>
 7: <BODY>
 8:
 9: <P><FONT face=Verdana size=5><STRONG>
10: The ASP Birthday Countdown Application<BR>
11: <FONT face="Times New Roman" size=4 style="BACKGROUND-COLOR:
    ➥#fafad2">
12: (Professional Version!)</FONT>
13: </STRONG></FONT></P>
```

```
14:
15: <%
16:
17: ' Declare variables that will be used later in the program.
18:
19: Dim UserDay
20: Dim UserMonth
21: Dim UserYear
22: Dim BirthdayString
23: Dim NextBirthdayDate
24: Dim UserAge
25:
26: ' If the user did not fill in the form completely,
27: ' display the form to the user.
28:
29: If (Request.Form ("BirthdayMonth") = "") AND _
30:   (Request.Form ("BirthdayDay") = "") AND _
31:   (Request.Form ("BirthdayYear") = "") Then
32:
33: %>
34:
35: <P><FONT face=Arial><STRONG>
36: Use it to find out how long you have to wait until your
37: next birthday.
38: </STRONG></FONT></P>
39:
40: <FORM method=post action=BirthdayCountdown.asp
41:   id=DataEntryForm name=DataEntryForm>
42:
43:
44: <P>Please enter the month of your birthday
45: <INPUT name=BirthdayMonth size=2><BR>
46:
47: Please enter the day of your birthday
48: <INPUT name=BirthdayDay size=2><BR>
49:
50: Please enter the year of your birthday
51: <INPUT name=BirthdayYear size=4><BR></P>
52: <P>
53:
54: <INPUT type=submit value="How long do I have to wait for my
    ➥birthday?"
55:   name=BirthdayFormSubmitButton>
56: </P>
57:
58: </FORM>
59: <%
60: ' If the user did fill in the form, calculate how many
61: ' days are left until the user's next birthday and display the
62: ' result.
```

continues

LISTING 1.3. CONTINUED

```
63:
64: Else
65:
66: ' Get input from the user. The Request.Form() method
67: ' can be used to get data from HTML forms submitted via the
68: ' POST method.
69:
70:    UserMonth = Request.Form ("BirthdayMonth")
71:    UserDay   = Request.Form ("BirthdayDay")
72:    UserYear  = Request.Form ("BirthdayYear")
73:
74:    BirthdayString = DateValue (UserMonth & "/" & UserDay & "/" &
       ➥UserYear)
75:
76:    Response.Write ("<P>The Birthdate you entered is: " & _
77:      BirthdayString & "</P>")
78:
79: ' Determine the user's current age.
80:
81:    UserAge = (DateDiff("yyyy", BirthdayString, Now))
82:
83: ' Add one to the user's age if the user's birthday has already
84: ' occurred for this year so you can calculate the number of days
       ➥until
85: ' the user's next birthday (next year).
86:
87:    If CInt(UserMonth) < (Month(date)) Then
88:      UserAge = UserAge + 1
89:    ElseIf (CInt(UserMonth) = (Month(date)) AND (CInt(UserDay) <
       ➥Day(Date))) Then
90:      UserAge = UserAge + 1
91:    End If
92:
93:    NextBirthdayDate = DateSerial (UserYear+UserAge,UserMonth,UserDay)
94:
95:    Response.Write ("<P>Your next Birthday is on: " & _
96:      NextBirthdayDate & "</P>")
97:
98:    Response.Write ("<P>You have to wait ")
99:
100: ' Calculate and display the number of days until the user's
101: ' next birthday.
102:
103:    Response.Write (DateDiff("d", Now, NextBirthdayDate))
104:    Response.Write (" days until your birthday!</P>")
105:
106: End If
107: %>
108:
```

```
109:
110: </BODY>
111: </HTML>
```

When the application is first invoked, the If statement in line 29 of Listing 1.3 makes sure the user has filled out the form completely. If the user has not, the data entry form shown in Figure 1.7 is displayed.

FIGURE 1.7.

Data is entered for the Birthday Countdown application.

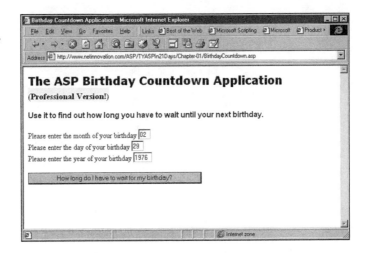

After the user clicks the Submit button, the If statement in line 29 detects that the form has been filled out completely and executes its Else clause, which starts on line 64. After calculating the information, the user is shown the Web page in Figure 1.8. The application correctly handles a leap year—without any special instructions from you—because you used built-in VBScript functions for all date calculations.

Tip

Whenever possible, use built-in VBScript functions for your calculations. Doing so makes your code less bug prone and more compact and efficient.

Note

This application doesn't use the most efficient ASP code, and it also needs more error checking. However, in the interest of keeping the ASP code as simple as possible, comprehensive error checking has been sacrificed. I encourage you to add error checking to this application, using the Visual Basic date and time functions as an exercise.

FIGURE **1.8.**

*Notice how the
application correctly
handles a leap year
birthday.*

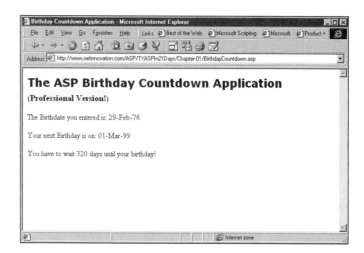

You can add special comments to your programs to explain what each section of code
does by using either the Rem statement or the apostrophe (') and following it with your
comments, as shown in line 17.

> **Tip**
>
> Use comments in your code to explain what your code is doing. Both you
> and the people who maintain your code in the future will really appreciate
> it! Although you might understand perfectly well what each segment of
> code in your application does, it's very likely that the next time you look at
> the code, perhaps six months from now, you will have trouble understand-
> ing what the code does. Proper commenting can prevent hours of wasted
> time.

Summary

ASP can be used to easily add a new level of interactivity to your Web site. Traditional
server-side application development environments are not optimized for developing interactive Web applications and producing information formatted in HTML.

You are now aware of the unique features and capabilities of ASP and how you can use
them to develop interactive Web applications. The pace of this book will increase considerably, so get some rest and get ready for the next three weeks (or 20 days). By this time
next week, you will be wondering how you ever got along without ASP!

I encourage you to take some time to search for information on Active Server Pages
using one of the popular search engines when you have some free time. A wealth of
information is out there on the Internet about Active Server Pages.

Q&A

Q **I am already familiar with JavaScript and prefer to use it to code Active Server Pages. Why does this book use VBScript to code Active Server Pages?**

A It really doesn't matter which scripting language you use. What matters is that at the end of the 21-day tutorial, you have a comprehensive understanding of Active Server Pages and how you can best use this technology to build sophisticated Web applications. This book uses VBScript for all its examples because VBScript is a lot easier to learn than JavaScript. If you are a JavaScript programmer who has never used VBScript, you should have little or no trouble understanding VBScript. Don't think you are learning VBScript just so you can script ASP applications—although that by itself is reason enough! After you learn VBScript, you can leverage your VBScript skills to develop Windows applications and custom ASP components using Visual Basic, and extend the power and capabilities of Microsoft Office and other applications by using Visual Basic for Applications. You can also use VBScript to program client-side VBScript applications executed on the Web browser.

Q **Is Microsoft Visual InterDev required to develop ASP applications?**

A No. Microsoft Visual InterDev is a RAD (Rapid Application Development) tool for creating ASP applications.

Q **Can ASP applications be developed with scripting languages other than VBScript?**

A Yes. ASP 2.0 supports ECMAScript/JavaScript right out of the box. Scripting engines for additional languages (such as Perl and Python) can be installed to work with ASP.

Workshop

The quiz questions and exercises are provided for your further understanding. Please refer to Appendix A, "Answers to Questions," for the answers to the quiz questions; the answers to the exercises are on the MCP Web site.

Quiz

1. How can you break down VBScript statements that are too long?
2. True or False: You should be careful about putting business logic into ASP code because users browsing your Web site can see the ASP code.
3. How can you add special comments to your ASP applications to explain what the code segments do?

4. True or false: Users have to use Internet Explorer to browse Web pages generated with ASP code.

5. Which ASP statement is equivalent to the effect of the `<%= %>` delimiter?

Exercises

1. Modify the Birthday Countdown application to also display how many days have passed since the user's last birthday. ·

2. Modify the Birthday Countdown application so that it tells you on what day of the week the user's next birthday falls. (Hint: Use the `DatePart()` function to find out which day of the week a certain date falls on. You can use a `Select/Case` statement to convert the integer return value of the `DatePart()` function to a value the user can understand.)

3. Visit your favorite Web search engine and search for information on Active Server Pages. Bookmark interesting URLs you find so you can visit them later.

WEEK 1

DAY 2

Web Development with Active Server Pages

Today you learn the fundamentals of ASP application development. Read this chapter carefully because information presented in upcoming days builds on the information you get today. This chapter gives you a more in-depth overview of Active Server Pages (ASP) and covers the fundamental ASP topics you need to understand the information in the rest of this tutorial. Today, you are covering quite a few fundamental ASP topics. Although the list of topics covered today might look a bit daunting at first, have no fear! They are very straightforward and easy to understand. You'll be done with today's tutorial and exercises in no time! Today, you cover the following:

- Understand the structure of an ASP application.

- How and when to use server-side includes (SSI).

- Learn about the purpose of the `global.asa` file.

- Learn about the ASP object model and ASP components.

- Find out how to use different scripting languages to program ASP applications.

- Learn about special considerations when developing Web applications.

How ASP Pages Work

All ASP code is executed on the Web server. This means each time a user visits an ASP page, its code is actually executed on the Web server and the results are sent back to the Web browser. Unlike static HTML pages, ASP pages can easily offer dynamic content to users browsing a Web site because the page's contents are created dynamically, on-the-fly.

So how does the Web server determine whether a Web page is a static HTML page or an ASP page? It simply looks at the file's extension to determine whether it should process a file as an ASP page. If a file ends with the .asp extension, the file is treated as an ASP file and executed on the Web server, and the output is sent to the Web browser. On the other hand, files ending with the .html extension are treated as plain old static Web pages and their contents are sent to the Web browser without any further processing.

ASP code can be written with a number of scripting languages. Primarily, ASP applications are written using JavaScript, JScript, or VBScript. Any of these scripting languages is suitable for creating Active Server Pages. For the exercises and examples in this book, however, I am using VBScript because it's easier to learn.

Understand the Structure of an ASP Application

You already know what an ASP application looks like. In fact, you saw several simple ASP applications yesterday. Before you develop more complex ones, it is important that you understand the structure of an ASP application.

An ASP application is simply one or more Web pages with additional scripting commands executed on the server. An ASP application is composed primarily of the following elements:

- Server-side includes (optional)
- HTML code
- Script delimiters
- Script code
- ActiveX components (optional)
- ASP objects (optional)

The only difference between a typical Web page and an ASP application is the presence of ASP script delimiters. Listing 2.1 illustrates a typical ASP application with ASP script delimiters. Figure 2.1 shows the output of that ASP application.

Note

An ASP application is a text file that contains script commands executed by the Web server. The ASP application is parsed and executed by the Web server's ASP interpreter, allowing the generation of dynamic content. ASP statements are embedded between ASP delimiters. Additionally, server-side ActiveX components can be instantiated and natively accessed.

2

Note

You will notice line numbers in the code listings. They are there solely to make it easier to refer to different lines of code.

LISTING **2.1.** COMPONENTS OF A TYPICAL ASP APPLICATION.

```
 1: <%@ LANGUAGE="VBSCRIPT" %>
 2:
 3: <SCRIPT RUNAT=SERVER LANGUAGE=VBSCRIPT>
 4:
 5: Sub SayHello ()
 6:
 7:   Response.Write("<H1>Hello! Today's date is " & Date & " </H1>")
 8:
 9: End Sub
10:
11: </SCRIPT>
12:
13: <HTML>
14: <HEAD>
15:
16:
17: <TITLE>Syntax of ASP Applications</TITLE>
18: </HEAD>
19: <BODY bgcolor="#DBFFBF" link="#0000FF" vlink="#800080">
20:
21: <!-- Insert HTML here -->
22:
23: <%= "<H2>This line of text is displayed as output </H2>" %>
24:
25: <%
26:
27:   Call SayHello ()
28:   Response.Write ("<HR>")
29:
30: %>
31:
32: </BODY>
33: </HTML>
```

FIGURE 2.1.

The output of the ASP application in Listing 2.1.

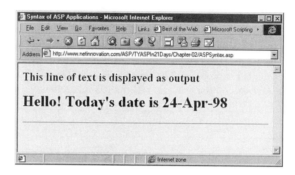

ANALYSIS The scripting language used by the ASP application is specified by using the statement `<%@ LANGUAGE="VBSCRIPT" %>`. This statement is placed at the beginning of the ASP application, as shown in line 1. The LANGUAGE keyword can be set equal to any supported scripting language, such as JScript.

ASP subroutines can be enclosed between the delimiters `<SCRIPT RUNAT=SERVER LANGUAGE=VBSCRIPT>` and `</SCRIPT>`. The scripting language of the subroutine(s) is specified with the LANGUAGE argument. Refer to lines 3–11 for an example of using the `<SCRIPT>` delimiter to define an ASP subroutine. The subroutine defined in lines 3–11 is executed by the ASP statement in line 27. Line 23 uses a special ASP script delimiter to display a string of text on the Web browser window.

Note

Subroutines and functions can also be placed directly in your server-side code between the `<%` and `%>` delimiters. Server-side code is not exclusive to the `<SCRIPT>` tags. If you enclose server-side code between the `<%` and `%>` delimiters, the default scripting language (VBScript) is assumed for the ASP code.

Note

The RUNAT=SERVER statement is required to indicate that the script commands should be executed on the server. Otherwise, the commands are embedded in the HTML file sent to the Web browser.

You can easily display any expression by enclosing it between the delimiters `<%=` and `%>`. For example, to display the string of text `This line of text is displayed as output` on the Web page, the following statement is used in line 23:

```
<%= "<H2>This line of text is displayed as output </H2>" %>
```

You can also use the statement Response.Write to display the value of an expression. Use Response.Write when you need to display a value in the middle of a subroutine. Use the delimiters <%= and %> when you need to quickly display the value of an expression in the middle of HTML code.

Inline ASP statements are placed between the delimiters <% and %>, as shown in lines 25–30. Think of inline ASP expressions as inline images you include in Web pages. The only difference is that instead of the image being displayed, the output of the ASP statements is displayed.

 Note

> Use Response.Write to display the value of an expression within an ASP script block (ASP script blocks are enclosed between the delimiters <% and %>). Include only ASP expressions (not statements) between the script delimiters <%= and %>.

Using Server-Side Includes

Server-side includes (SSI) are a powerful feature when they are used properly. They can be used with Active Server Pages. If you are familiar with C/C++, think of SSI as preprocessor directives. Server-side includes can be used to include ASP subroutines contained in other files. You might want to create a separate file containing your favorite ASP subroutines and include that file in other ASP applications using SSI. SSI can also be used to implement certain company policies. For example, a subroutine in an SSI file can calculate a sale price, using a certain formula. Later, if the formula used to calculate the sale price is changed, only one file needs to be updated. Other ASP applications that use the SSI file automatically use the new formula to calculate sale prices after the SSI file is updated with the new formula.

When you create a server-side include file, you should give it a useful name. Additionally, you should use the extension .inc. There are two ways in which you can include SSI files in ASP applications: virtual pathnames and relative pathnames.

Using Virtual Pathnames

You can include files relative to the path of the virtual root directory of the Web server by using the following statement:

```
<!--#INCLUDE VIRTUAL="/VIRTUAL/Path/Of/File.inc"-->
```

Use virtual pathnames to implement global policies and subroutines that are common to many applications.

Using Relative File Pathnames

Files relative to the path of the current file can be included by using the following statement:

```
<!--#INCLUDE FILE="Relative/Path/Of/File.inc"-->
```

Use relative pathnames to implement policies and subroutines unique to the application being developed.

Understanding the ASP Objects and Object Model

Although you might not have noticed it, you have already used an ASP object to interact with the user. Remember the `Response.Write()` statement you used yesterday to display output to the user? The `Write()` function is actually a method of the `Response` object, which is one of six objects shipped with ASP 2.0. Refer to Figure 2.2 for a diagram of all six built-in ASP objects.

FIGURE 2.2.

The six built-in ASP objects.

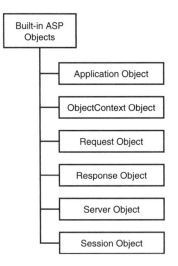

All the built-in ASP objects are covered comprehensively on Days 6, "Getting Information About HTTP Requests with the `Request` Object," 7, "Customizing HTTP Responses with the `Response` Object," and 8, "Processing Web Data with the `Server`, `Session`, and `Application` Objects." For now, it's enough that you understand that when you use a statement such as `Response.Write("I Love ASP!")` you are actually using a method of one of the built-in ASP objects. Table 2.1 lists the purpose of each of these objects, and on which day it's covered.

TABLE 2.1. THE SIX BUILT-IN ASP OBJECTS.

Name of Object	Purpose	On Which Day the Object Is Covered
Application object	Share information between users of an ASP application	Day 8
ObjectContext object	Commit or abort a transaction that is managed by Microsoft Transaction Server	Day 8
Request object	Used to retrieve information passed to the Web server by the Web browser	Day 6
Response object	Sends text output to the Web browser	Day 7
Server object	Manage server objects, HTML streams, and URLs	Day 8
Session object	Store temporary information used during the course of a user session	Day 8

Understanding ASP Components

ASP *components* as prepackaged modules of code you can use to perform certain predefined tasks. You can use them to extend the capabilities of ASP and have them perform various tasks for you (such as rotating an advertisement banner). For example, the Browser Capabilities component, which you learn about in Day 9, "Using ActiveX Components Built for ASP," can be used to display custom HTML text based on the Web browser being used.

By the end of the third week, you will know how to build your own sophisticated ASP components. For now, it's enough that you understand their purpose and realize you will master them in a few weeks.

Understanding the `global.asa` File

The `global.asa` file is a special file. It is not directly executed, like other ASP applications. Instead, it holds information, procedures, objects, and type libraries used by the Active Server Pages in an ASP application. The `global.asa` file defines your Web application. It is always called the first time a user interacts with your site and a new user session is started.

 A *type library* is simply a file that contains information about constants and data types used by an object. Type libraries are covered in Day 19, "Exploiting ASP: Tips And Advanced Topics."

Declaring Procedures in the `global.asa` File

Procedures defined in the `global.asa` file are executed when applications are started or shut down, or when a new user session is started or ended. The following procedures can be defined in the `global.asa` file:

- `Application_OnStart`—The block of script defined in this procedure is executed the very first time a user executes a page of the ASP application. It is a good place to define or initialize variables and resources you use in various sections of your application.

- `Application_OnEnd`—This procedure is executed only when your application is shut down. It is a good place to perform any cleaning up (deleting temporary files, and so forth) your application has to do before it is shut down.

- `Session_OnStart`—Each time a new user session is started, the code contained in this procedure is executed.

- `Session_OnEnd`—Each time a user session times out (or is explicitly ended), the code in this procedure is executed.

> **Note**
> The `global.asa` file must be placed in the root directory of your application.

> **Note**
> You could cause the current user session to timeout by calling the `Session` object's Abandon method from within your ASP code. You learn more about the `Session` object in Day 8.

Declaring Objects in the `global.asa` File

You can also define objects that have session or application scope from within the `global.asa` file. ASP objects are used to interact with users browsing the Web site as well as resources of the Web server, such as text files and databases. You can define objects inside the global.asa file with Application and Session scope by using the following syntax:

```
<OBJECT RUNAT=Server
        SCOPE=<ScopeOfObject>
        ID=<NameSpecifiedForObject>
        {PROGID="<progID>"¦CLASSID="<ClassID>"}>

</OBJECT>
```

The italicized text in angle brackets are placeholders and should be replaced with the arguments outlined in Table 2.2.

TABLE 2.2. ARGUMENTS USED TO DECLARE OBJECTS.

Name of Placeholder	Value of Placeholder
<ScopeOfObject>	Specifies whether the object has Application or Session scope.
<NameSpecifiedForObject>	Specifies the name given to the object being instantiated. This name is used by ASP scripts to refer to the object.
<progID>	Refers to the ID of the object you are creating. The syntax of <progID> values take the format [Vendor.]Component[.Version]. For example, PROGID="MSWC.AdRotator" refers to the Ad Rotator component shipped with ASP. You need to specify a value for either <progID> or <ClassID>—but not both!
<ClassID>	Refers to the unique class identifier of the object you are creating (this is usually a long string of numbers and letters that you can get from the Registry). You need to specify a value for either <progID> or <ClassID>—but not both!

NEW TERM   *Instantiation* is the process of creating an instance of a certain object. You can think of an object as a blueprint that defines how the object interfaces with your application and how it processes data. By instantiating an object, you are bringing to life an instance of an object.

Making Modifications to the global.asa File

If you make changes to your global.asa file and save it, the changes do not take place immediately. The Web server waits until all current application requests are processed. When that is done, the global.asa file is recompiled. While this is happening, the Web server responds to additional requests with an error message. The error message states that the application is being restarted.

Do	Don't
DO make necessary modifications to the global.asa file when the Web server is not under heavy load.	**DON'T** constantly make modifications to your global.asa file when the server is under a heavy load because that might disrupt the activities of your users.

Specifying the Scripting Language

As you found out yesterday, one of ASP's many beneficial features is its ability to support several scripting languages. In fact, at press time, scripting support for about half a dozen scripting languages is available for Active Server Pages. It is beyond the scope of this book to cover all these scripting languages, but you can build ASP applications using VBScript, JScript, JavaScript, or even PerlScript.

Note   Although all the examples in this book use VBScript, you are free to use any other supported scripting language, including JavaScript. To keep things simple, I suggest you use VBScript while reading this book.

ASP is flexible, so it allows you to use multiple scripting languages in the same ASP application, but it's your responsibility to use this feature responsibly.

Tip   Do not try to mix and match scripting languages just because you can. Doing so can make your code unnecessarily complex and error prone, and make the task of debugging even more complicated.

Using JScript/JavaScript to Script Active Server Pages

ASP applications can use JScript to script various commands. The application in Listing 2.2 illustrates using JScript to declare a subroutine within an ASP application. See Figure 2.3 for the output of the ASP application in Listing 2.2.

LISTING 2.2. JSCRIPT VERSION OF THE CLASSIC HELLO WORLD! APPLICATION.

```
 1: <%@ LANGUAGE="VBSCRIPT" %>
 2:
 3: <SCRIPT RUNAT=SERVER LANGUAGE=JSCRIPT>
 4:
 5: function  UserDefinedJScriptFunction ()
 6: {
 7:   var DateObject = new Date()
 8:   Response.Write("<H2>UserDefinedJScriptFunction has been
      ➥called.<BR>")
 9:   Response.Write("The current time is " + DateObject.getHours() + " :
      ➥" +
10:                   DateObject.getMinutes() + " : " +
                      ➥DateObject.getSeconds())
11: }
12:
13: </SCRIPT>
14:
15: <HTML>
16: <HEAD>
17:
18:
19: <TITLE>Document Title</TITLE>
20: </HEAD>
21: <BODY bgcolor="#DBFFBF" link="#0000FF" vlink="#800080">
22:
23: <% Call UserDefinedJScriptFunction %>
24:
25: </BODY>
26: </HTML>
```

ANALYSIS Lines 3–13 of Listing 2.2 declare a JScript subroutine that displays the current time. The JScript subroutine is then executed with the statement in line 23. The output of the ASP application can be found in Figure 2.3. As shown in Listing 2.2, you can easily leverage your JScript skills to the Internet when developing ASP applications.

FIGURE 2.3.

The output of the ASP application in Listing 2.2.

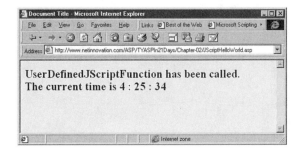

Mixing Scripting Languages

It is possible to mix scripting languages in an ASP application, as demonstrated in Listing 2.3. If you mix scripting languages, you should develop subroutines that use only one scripting language with clearly defined input and output.

Do	Don't
DO stick to one scripting language to avoid possible confusion.	DON'T mix scripting languages unless you have a very good reason for doing so (such as the need to use a powerful feature of each scripting language).

LISTING 2.3. MIXING SCRIPTING LANGUAGES.

```
 1: <%@ LANGUAGE="VBSCRIPT" %>
 2:
 3: <SCRIPT RUNAT=SERVER LANGUAGE=VBSCRIPT>
 4:
 5: Sub UserDefinedVBScriptFunction ()
 6:
 7:    Response.Write("<H2>UserDefinedVBScriptFunction has been
       ➥called.<BR>")
 8:    Response.Write("Today's date is " & Date )
 9:
10: End Sub
11:
12: </SCRIPT>
13:
14:
15: <SCRIPT RUNAT=SERVER LANGUAGE=JSCRIPT>
16:
17: function  UserDefinedJScriptFunction ()
18: {
19:    var DateObject = new Date()
20:    Response.Write("<H2>UserDefinedJScriptFunction has been
       ➥called.<BR>")
21:    Response.Write("Today's time is " + DateObject.getHours() + " : " +
22:                   DateObject.getMinutes() + " : " +
                      ➥DateObject.getSeconds())
23: }
24:
25: </SCRIPT>
26:
27: <HTML>
28: <HEAD>
```

```
29:
30:
31: <TITLE>Mixing Scripting Languages</TITLE>
32: </HEAD>
33: <BODY bgcolor="#DBFFBF" link="#0000FF" vlink="#800080">
34:
35: <H1>About to call VBScript subroutine</H1>
36: <% Call UserDefinedVBScriptFunction %>
37:
38: <H1>About to call JScript subroutine</H1>
39: <% Call UserDefinedJScriptFunction %>
40:
41: </BODY>
42: </HTML>
```

ANALYSIS Lines 3–12 declare a VBScript subroutine, and lines 15–25 declare a JScript subroutine. The two subroutines are called in lines 36 and 39. Figure 2.4 shows the output of Listing 2.3.

FIGURE 2.4.

The output of the ASP application in Listing 2.3.

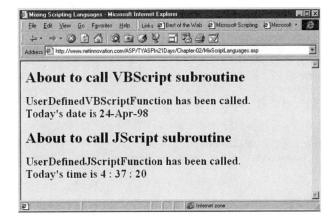

Loops and Control Structures Fundamental to ASP Development

It's important that you have a solid understanding of how ASP control structures and loops function to understand the material presented in upcoming chapters. Loops and control structures add intelligence to ASP applications by defining how many times and when certain blocks of code should execute. The following topics related to using loops and controls structures are covered next:

- How to use a loop within an ASP application.
- When to use which loop structure.
- How to control the flow of an ASP application.
- How to use a control structure within an ASP application.
- When to use which control structure.

Using Loops for Repetitive Tasks

Loops can be used to execute iterative statements. The application in Listing 2.4 demonstrates using a loop within an ASP application to add some flair to the classic Hello World! application.

LISTING 2.4. USING LOOPS FOR REPETITIVE TASKS.

```
 1: <%@ LANGUAGE="VBSCRIPT" %>
 2:
 3: <HTML>
 4: <HEAD>
 5:
 6:
 7: <TITLE>Hello World!</TITLE>
 8: </HEAD>
 9: <BODY bgcolor="#DBFFBF" link="#0000FF" vlink="#800080">
10:
11: <FONT SIZE=3 FACE="ARIAL">
12:
13: <%
14: Greeting = "HELLO WORLD!"
15: For RowCount = 1 to Len(Greeting)
16: %>
17:
18: <TABLE>
19: <TR>
20: <TD BGCOLOR=000000 WIDTH=<%= (RowCount^2)+(RowCount*15)%>>+</TD>
21: <TD><%= Left(Greeting,1) %></TD></TR>
22: </TABLE>
23:
24: <%
25: Greeting = Right(Greeting, Len(Greeting)-1)
26: Next
27: %>
28:
29: </FONT>
30:
31: <HR>
32:
```

```
33: <B>The time now is <%= Time %> on <%= Date %>.</B>
34:
35: </BODY>
36: </HTML>
```

ANALYSIS The loop in lines 15–26 displays the string `Hello World!` one character at a time, followed by a table with increasing width (the background color of the table is set to black). The output of the application is shown in Figure 2.5.

FIGURE 2.5.

A loop is used to add flair to the classic Hello World! application.

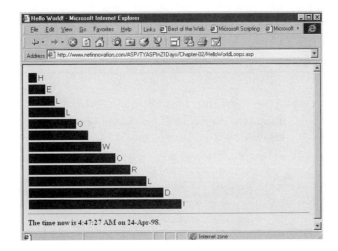

Using Conditional Statements for Flow Control

Conditional statements can be used to control the flow of an ASP application. The application in Listing 2.5 uses an `If...Then...Else` control structure to display a greeting based on the time of day the Web page is invoked (see Figure 2.6 for the output).

LISTING 2.5. USING CONDITIONAL STATEMENTS FOR FLOW CONTROL.

```
 1: <%@ LANGUAGE="VBSCRIPT" %>
 2: <HTML>
 3: <HEAD>
 4:
 5:
 6: <TITLE>Conditional Statements</TITLE>
 7: </HEAD>
 8: <body bgcolor="#DBFFBF" link="#0000FF" vlink="#800080">
 9: <H1> Hi! </H1>
10: <FONT Face="Comic Sans MS" Size=6>
```

continues

LISTING 2.5. CONTINUED

```
11: <%
12: If (Hour(Time) < 12) Then
13:   Response.Write "Good morning!"
14: ElseIf (Hour(Time) < 15)  Then
15:   Response.Write "Good afternoon!"
16: Else
17:   Response.Write "Good evening!"
18: End If
19: %>
20: </FONT>
21: <HR>
22: The current time is <%= Time %>.
23: </BODY>
24: </HTML>
```

ANALYSIS Line 12 checks whether the current hour is less than 12. If it is, a "Good morning!" message is displayed. If the current hour is greater than 12 but less than 3:00 PM (15:00 hours), a "Good afternoon!" message is displayed. Otherwise, line 17 displays a "Good evening!" message.

FIGURE 2.6.

Conditional statements are used to display a special message based on the time of day.

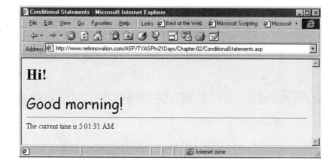

The Three Script Delimiters Revisited

ASP supports three different script delimiters. It is important that you know how and when to use each of them. Listing 2.6 contains an example that uses all three of ASP's script delimiters.

LISTING 2.6. AN EXAMPLE USING THE THREE SCRIPT DELIMITERS.

```
1: <%@ LANGUAGE=VBScript %>
2: <HTML>
3: <HEAD>
```

```
 4: <TITLE>The ASP Script Delimiters</TITLE>
 5: </HEAD>
 6: <BODY bgColor=lightgoldenrodyellow>
 7:
 8: <P><STRONG><FONT color=#006633
 9: face="Comic Sans MS" size=5 style="BACKGROUND-COLOR:
    ➥#ccff99"> Using ASP
10: Code Delimiters </FONT></STRONG> </P>
11:
12: <P>
13: <%
14:
15: Response.Write ("This line of text is displayed by the " & _
16:     "Response.Write () ASP statement.")
17:
18: %>
19:
20: <HR>
21:
22: <%= "This line of text is displayed by the ASP text output
    ➥delimiters." %>
23:
24: <HR>
25:
26: <SCRIPT RUNAT = SERVER LANGUAGE=VBScript>
27:
28: Response.Write ("This line of text is also displayed by the " & _
29:     "Response.Write () ASP statement. However, this time, from " & _
30:     "within a SCRIPT block.")
31:
32: </SCRIPT>
33:
34: <P></P>
35:
36: </BODY>
37: </HTML>
```

ANALYSIS The ASP statements in Listing 2.6 display strings of text. However, in place of strings of text, you can include variables and expressions—and perhaps even combine the two. For example, the VBScript string concatenation operator & can be used to join the value of an expression (FormatDateTime(date,vbLongDate)) to a string ("Today's date is: ") to form the string Today's date is: Tuesday, April 14, 1998 and display it using this ASP statement:

```
<%= "Today's date is: " & FormatDateTime(date,vbLongDate) %>
```

Figure 2.7 presents the output of the code in Listing 2.6.

FIGURE 2.7.

*Output of the ASP
code in Listing 2.6.*

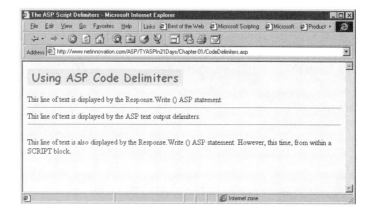

FIGURE 2.7.

*Output of the ASP
code in Listing 2.6.*

Understanding the Web's Stateless Nature

HTTP is a *connectionless* and stateless protocol. After the user downloads a Web page,
no information about the previous connection is retained.

 A *connectionless protocol* is one that does not need a persistent connection.
When a Web server receives an HTTP request, the Web server processes the
HTTP request and sends data to the client. When the requested data has been transmitted,
the connection is closed.

> **Note**
>
> The HTTP 1.1 protocol addresses a drawback of the original HTTP 1.0 proto-
> col specification that does not allow persistent connections. As long as both
> your Web browser and Web server support persistent connections, Web
> browsers do not have to go through the resource-wasting task of creating a
> new connection for each object that is part of a Web page.

Web servers listen for incoming HTTP requests and when one is received, the requested
data is sent to the client. If information requested by a client is simply a Web page con-
sisting of plain text, a few images, sound, or other objects, the Web server simply transmits these objects at the request of the client. More work is involved, however, when
dynamic content must be provided by executing an ASP script on the Web server. See
Figure 2.8 for a graphical representation of how a Web server executes an ASP script and
sends its output back to the user. Notice that after the output is sent to the user, no information about the transaction that just took place is retained.

FIGURE 2.8.

After the execution of an ASP script, no information about the transaction that just transpired is retained.

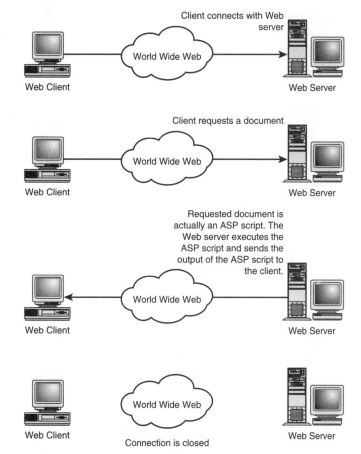

Client connects with Web server

Web Client — World Wide Web → Web Server

Client requests a document

Web Client — World Wide Web → Web Server

Requested document is actually an ASP script. The Web server executes the ASP script and sends the output of the ASP script to the client.

Web Client ← World Wide Web — Web Server

Web Client   World Wide Web   Web Server

Connection is closed

When a user accesses a page at a Web site, usually more than one HTTP connection is made. Generally, a separate connection is made for each object, such as a graphics file or Java applet, that's embedded in the Web page being accessed. If you type the Windows NT command `netstat` at the command prompt when someone is accessing your Web site, you will notice that usually more than one connection is made by the user accessing your Web site.

Importance of Tracking User Sessions

If the HTTP protocol does not by default keep track of user sessions, you might wonder how Web applications are built to allow hundreds of thousands of users to navigate a Web site, place orders, and keep all those transactions separate. For the Web applications you build in the next few days, the stateless nature is really not a big issue because you do not need to keep track of user sessions. However, as you build more complex Web applications, especially those that interface with a database, the need to keep track of user sessions becomes more and more important.

An online shopping cart application is an example of an application that uses user sessions. The ASP `Session` object can be used to easily build a shopping cart application. It is used to keep track of merchandise selected for purchase by the user.

You will be happy to know that ASP gives you an easy way to keep track of user sessions with the `Session` object. You learn more about using the `Session` object to keep track of user session in Day 8.

Summary

You now understand the structure of an ASP application. ASP applications are composed of server-side includes (optional), HTML code, script delimiters, script code, ActiveX components, and ASP objects (optional).

Server-side includes can be used to easily insert text from other files to ASP applications. They can also be used to call VBScript subroutines in another file.

Components and objects are really the foundation of ASP because they allow you to interact with other objects on the server and process information. You now have a good understanding of what objects and components are all about.

The `global.asa` file is instrumental in carrying out actions at critical stages of the life of a session or an application. The `global.asa` file also defines resources that can be used by other ASP applications.

Loops can be used to perform repetitive tasks within ASP applications. It is easy to add intelligence to ASP applications by using conditional statements for flow control.

The three script delimiters, which you learned about yesterday, were revisited today and you were shown how an ASP application can use all three ASP script delimiters at the same time. Yesterday, you found out that you can develop ASP applications with JavaScript. Today, you got to see an actual ASP application that uses JavaScript and how you can mix scripting languages in an ASP application.

By default, the HTTP protocol is a stateless protocol and does not retain any information between HTTP sessions. This makes things a bit complicated for Web application developers. However, ASP provides Web application developers with two powerful tools that can be used to retain information between HTTP sessions: the `Session` object and methods to manipulate cookies. These powerful tools are covered in detail later in this book.

Q&A

A Can the name for a server-side include file be created dynamically by using ASP code?

Q No. You cannot use an ASP statement to generate the name of a file to include as an SSI because ASP statements are processed after all external files are included.

Q How does IIS/PWS determine whether a certain Web page is an ASP application?

A IIS/PWS determines whether a certain Web page is an ASP application by examining the file extension of the Web page. If the file extension is `.asp`, the Web page is executed on the server as an ASP application.

Q So to publish an ASP application on the Internet, all that's needed is to save the file with the extension .asp?

A Not quite. You also need to make sure the directory in which the file is saved is given execute permissions. You were shown how to do this yesterday.

Q What is the easiest way to display the value of the variable InterestRate in the middle of a table cell?

A Use the statement `<TD> <%= InterestRate %> </TD>`.

Q I anticipate that I will call a subroutine from several other ASP applications. Should I include this subroutine in a virtual or a relative SSI file?

A You should use a virtual SSI so that other applications can easily refer to the subroutine without being concerned about the directory structure of your application.

Workshop

The quiz questions and exercises are provided for your further understanding. Please refer to Appendix A, "Answers to Questions," for the answers to the quiz questions; the answers to the exercises are on the MCP Web site.

Quiz

1. Name two benefits of using server-side includes.
2. Name the six built-in ASP objects.
3. Of these six objects, which object did you use yesterday? (Hint: It is the same object that you used the most today.)
4. What is the purpose of the `Request` object?
5. Why shouldn't you make changes to the `global.asa` file when the server is under heavy load?

Exercises

1. Visit the following Microsoft Web page to learn about custom ASP components that you can download from Microsoft's Web site and use in your own ASP applications:

   `http://backoffice.microsoft.com/downtrial/moreinfo/iissamples.asp`

2. Create a new file and move the subroutine `SayHello()` in Listing 2.1 to that file. Use a server-side include to include the file you just created. Call the `SayHello()` subroutine from the ASP application using the file you just created.

3. Write an ASP application that displays the multiplication table from 5×1 to 5×15.

4. Modify the application you created in Exercise 3 to also display the multiplication tables for 6, 7, and 8. (Hint: Use a table to format the values and use a nested loop.)

WEEK 1

DAY 3

Interacting with Your Users

Today, you learn the different ways ASP applications can interact with users browsing a Web site. There are several ways an ASP application can get user input: message boxes, input boxes, ActiveX controls, and HTML form fields. Depending on the application and circumstances, you have to select the best method. Today, you cover the following:

- Learn how to display a window on the user's screen and get text input from the user.
- Display a message on the user's screen with one or more buttons the user can click to respond.
- Get input using data-entry controls, such as text boxes, selection lists, and check boxes, on an HTML form.
- Interact with users by using ActiveX controls.
- Understand how to interact with users by using Java applets.

How ASP Applications Interact with Users

Nearly all Web applications interact with users browsing a Web site. Sometimes this interaction is indirect. For example, depending on the time of day, a Web application might greet the user with "Good morning!" or "Good evening!" Although the greeting is displayed on the user's Web browser, the interactive, dynamic nature of the Web page is not always obvious because the user did nothing special to execute the Web application. At other times, the interaction between the Web application and the user is visible and direct, as in the case of a calculator application used for an online mortgage payment.

It is important you understand that nearly all user input occurs on the client side. One of the key features of using Active Server Pages is that your ASP files can determine what is sent to the client's browser. To take advantage of this feature, you should be aware of the limitations of certain Web browsers. For example, if a Web browser does not support VBScript, you can't use the InputBox() and MsgBox() functions. Additionally, not all browsers support technologies such as ActiveX controls or VBScript.

Even if most of your users don't use a Web browser that supports ActiveX or VBScript, your ASP applications can still interact with users. Using ASP, you can send them animated images or Java applets instead.

Some of the key ways to interact with users are to have your ASP files send the following:

- HTML forms
- VBScript functions, such as InputBox()
- VBScript procedures, such as MsgBox
- ActiveX controls
- Java applets

Before covering each of these topics, you should first understand how to design effective interfaces for your users.

Guidelines for Developing Effective Web User Interfaces

Web user interfaces are quite different compared with the user interfaces of traditional applications. They are especially different from Windows applications.

The following are some guidelines for building effective user interfaces for your ASP applications:

- Develop Web-based wizard-style user interfaces
- Streamline forms to make data entry easier
- Optimize for limited bandwidth
- Use colors effectively
- Use fonts effectively
- Use the capabilities of the "intelligent client"

Note

> The user interfaces of Windows applications are always "connected" to the Windows application itself. However, because of the stateless nature of HTTP, Web applications are not directly connected to their Web interfaces. This poses some significant challenges to Web application developers.
>
> For example, as soon as a Web page is downloaded, the connection between the Web browser and the Web server is terminated. A new connection is established if the user requests another Web page from the same Web server.

3

Developing Web-Based Wizard-Style User Interfaces

If you have installed or worked with a Windows application you are probably familiar with wizard-style user interfaces. Your ASP applications can use similar wizard-style user interfaces to get input from users. Tomorrow, in Day 4, "Building and Processing Web Forms," you learn how to build a Web-based wizard-style user interface to get information from users.

Wizard-style user interfaces make it easier for users to enter information because they guide the user step by step through the entire data entry process. A *wizard-style user interface* is simply a series of dialog boxes (or windows) that guide and help the user enter data. Instead of displaying a single window or dialog box containing many data entry controls (which might overwhelm the user), it is often better to spread the data entry controls across several dialog boxes or windows and then step the user from one to the next.

An example of using a wizard-style user interface for Web-based data entry is the user interface for a Web application used by a car rental agency to rent cars. In some states, to rent certain cars, you have to be over 25 years old. Rather than show a list of all the types of vehicles available for renting, the ASP application can first display an HTML form that gets certain information from the user. This information can include the user's name, driver's license number, date of birth, whether the user currently has insurance, and so forth. Based on the information entered by the user, the ASP application can then display a list of vehicles the user is qualified to rent.

Streamlining Forms to Make Data Entry Easier

When building data entry forms, you should streamline them for ease of data entry. You can do this by trying to organize data entry fields into a logical order. Fields that are most likely to be filled in should be near the top of the form so they can be filled out without the need to skip a lot of fields.

Design your interface so that the reader does not have to scroll off the screen. Depending on the information, it might be better to offer a way to continue to a second screen instead of forcing the user to scroll down.

You should specify default values for HTML data entry controls. By supplying the most common default values, you help the user complete the form easily and quickly.

A final suggestion for entry forms is to clearly mark any fields that are required. By marking these fields, you show users exactly what they must enter.

| | It is good programming practice to include default data values to guide the user toward entering valid data. |

Optimizing for Limited Bandwidth

Watch the size of your files when building data entry forms. No matter how well your Web forms are designed, they serve little purpose if they take too long to load and display on a Web browser. Web users are not always as patient as you would like them to be. If a page does not load within about 30 seconds, the user might move somewhere else (and fill in someone else's form!). Watch out for the following when designing Web forms to ensure the Web form loads quickly:

- Avoid using large graphics in Web forms. In fact, most Web forms really do not require any graphics. Use graphics only if you have to.

- Use Java applets and ActiveX controls only if you have to. Java applets and ActiveX controls can be used to add some flair to Web forms; however, they add to the form's file size and, in some cases, affect the time it takes to render the Web form.

- Avoid using complex background graphics in Web forms. They take longer to load and add to the total file size of the Web form. Plain white backgrounds are fine for most Web forms. If you must do something fancy, select a two-color Web graphic with a left-hand border.

- Avoid complex form controls. For example, avoid using a drop-down list with many selection items. Each item you add to a drop-down list must be downloaded with the form. If you have several drop-down lists with many items, then this can begin to add up in size.

Try not to add more than about 50 items to a selection list.

When browsing the Web some time ago, I came across a data entry form that seemed to take forever to load. When I examined the form's HTML code, I noticed that it contained several drop-down lists for selecting data and each drop-down list had dozens of items! The amount of data in the lists was increasing the time it took the form to load.

Use Colors Effectively

Colors can be used to make your Web forms more interesting and visually appealing. There is a flip side to using colors, however. Ineffective use of colors can make your Web forms unattractive and difficult to use.

When using colors, stick to a limited number of very dark and light colors. If you are using a light color for the text, use a dark color for the background to add contrast. Here are some guidelines for using colors more effectively:

- Don't overuse colors. Keep the number of colors on your page to a minimum.

- Don't assume the reader is using a monitor that supports a high number of colors. Browse your Web page with a browser running on a computer with only 256 colors. This is especially important if you are using images on your page.

- Use colors only when necessary. A good use of colors is to display the labels of required data fields in red.

After building a Web form that uses colors, ask someone else to give you feedback on your color scheme.

Use Fonts Effectively

Fonts can be used to add a professional touch to your Web forms. When using fonts in Web pages (as well as Web forms), it's best to stick to fonts that are available in virtually all computers, such as

- Arial
- Courier
- Times Roman

Fonts, like colors, should not be overused. You should limit the number of different fonts used to as few as possible.

Note For more information about using fonts in Web pages, please visit the following URL: http://www.microsoft.com/typography/

Using Capabilities of the "Intelligent Client"

When designing a Web site, you need to determine what browsers will be used to access your site. In addition to considering which browsers, you need to consider which versions. By knowing which browsers and versions are accessing your site, you can add more functionality to your pages by taking advantage of the browsers' built-in functionality.

For example, if you know that both Netscape Navigator and Microsoft Internet Explorer browsers are going to be used and if you know that you want to use scripting, then you should design your pages with JavaScript rather than VBScript. JavaScript is supported by both browsers, so your code will be portable. If you use VBScript, the Netscape browsers might not be able to run your scripts.

You can use the browser's intelligence to help design more user-friendly applications. With client-side scripting, you can create a more effective Web user interface by giving the user instant feedback if a data entry field is not filled in properly. Client-side validation is not a substitute for server-side data validation, however. You still need to plan on validating data on the server by using an ASP subroutine. Client-side data validation complements server-side data validation. It is not a substitute.

Note

Microsoft FrontPage can automatically generate JavaScript code that validates the form data on the client side. To do this, select a data entry field in the FrontPage editor by right-clicking and then selecting Form Field Validation. Use the Text Box Validation dialog box shown in Figure 3.1 to specify data validation parameters.

FIGURE 3.1.

Use client-side data validation.

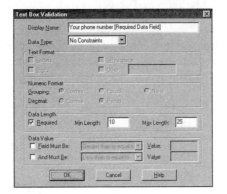

Getting Input from HTML Forms

Virtually all Web browsers support HTML forms, so ASP applications can use HTML forms to communicate with almost anyone browsing your Web site. HTML forms are used to transfer data entered by users to an ASP application.

There are primarily two ways in which HTML forms send data to the Web server:

- Using the GET method.

  (This is specified in the <FORM METHOD="GET" ... HTML tag of the data entry HTML form.)

- Using the POST method.

  (This is specified in the <FORM METHOD="POST" ... HTML tag of the data entry form.)

The following two sections examine how the same HTML form can send data to the Web server by using either the GET method or the POST method. Notice that most of the application remains unchanged except for where the Form method is specified and where the ASP application retrieves form data from the Request object.

Using the GET Method to Get Input

When using a form to get data, you can use the GET method. The GET method is ideal for forms that return no more than a few dozen bytes of data. It is limited to around 2,044 bytes of data because the data submitted with it appears as a query string in the Web browser's URL text box.

When the GET method is used in an HTML form, an ASP application can easily determine the value of HTML form variables by using the Request.QueryString() method, as shown in this example:

```
Request.QueryString("UserName")
```

This line returns the value of the "UserName" HTML form data entry field. Listing 3.1 presents an ASP application that uses the HTML GET method.

LISTING 3.1. AN ASP APPLICATION THAT USES THE HTML FORM GET METHOD FOR DATA INPUT (FormGetMethod.asp).

```
 1: <%@ LANGUAGE=VBScript %>
 2: <HTML>
 3: <HEAD>
 4:
 5: <TITLE>Using The HTML Form GET Method For Data Entry</TITLE>
 6: </HEAD>
 7: <BODY>
 8: <P><FONT face="Comic Sans MS" size=4 style="BACKGROUND-COLOR:
    ➡#99ff00">
 9: Using The HTML Form GET Method For Data Entry</FONT></P>
10:
11: <P><FONT face=Georgia>This HTML form
12: uses the HTML Form Get method to transfer the HTML Form data to
    ➡the ASP
13: application. The ASP form retrieves the data using the Request.
    ➡QueryString
14: method.</FONT></P>
15: <P>
16: <HR>
17: <P>
18: <%
19:
```

```
20: If Request.QueryString ("UserName") = "" Then
21:
22: %>
23:
24: <FORM method=get action=FormGetMethod.asp id=DataEntryForm
25:   name=DataEntryForm>
26:
27:   <FONT face=Verdana><STRONG>Please enter your name</STRONG></FONT>
28:   <INPUT id=UserName name=UserName value=Sanjaya ><BR>
29:
30:   <INPUT type=submit value="Submit name to ASP application"
31:     id=SubmitButton name=submit1>
32:   <INPUT type=reset value="Reset Form"
33:     id=ResetButton name=reset1><BR>
34:
35: <% Else %>
36:
37: <P><FONT size=4>Thanks for submitting the HTML Form! </FONT></P>
38: <P><STRONG><FONT face=Arial size=5 style="BACKGROUND-COLOR: #ffff66">
39:
40: <%= "Hello ," & Request.QueryString ("UserName") & "!" %>
41:
42: </STRONG></FONT></P><P><A href="FormGetMethod.asp">
43: Please select this link if you wish to restart the application.</A>
44:
45: <% End If %>
46:
47:   </P>
48:
49: </FORM>
50: </P>
51: <HR>
52:
53:
54: </BODY>
55: </HTML>
```

ANALYSIS When the ASP application in Listing 3.1 is invoked, the Web page shown in Figure 3.2 is displayed. The form in this Web page is associated with the ASP application that generated the HTML form. After the Submit Name to ASP Application button is clicked, the name entered in the text box is sent to the ASP application `FormGetMethod.asp`.

The `If` statement in line 20 of Listing 3.1 checks whether the HTML form has been filled in. If it has not, the HTML statements in lines 23–33 are displayed. If the HTML form has been filled in, the `Else` clause defined in lines 37–43 is displayed. Notice how line 40 uses the `Request.QueryString()` method to get the value of the HTML form data entry field `UserName`.

FIGURE 3.2.

An HTML form data entry field is used to type in a value.

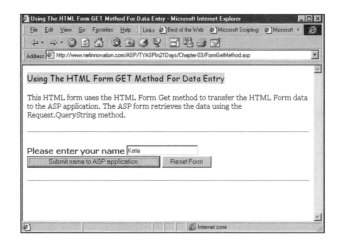

When the HTML form in Figure 3.2 is submitted with data, the ASP application in Listing 3.1 generates the Web page shown in Figure 3.3. Notice how the data from the HTML form is submitted to the ASP application as part of the URL address string:

```
http://www.netinnovation.com/ASP/TYASPIn21Days/Chapter-
➥03/FormGetMethod.asp?UserName=Kate&submit1=Submit+name+to+ASP+application.
```

Pay particular attention to the `UserName=Kate` string because it sends the form's data to the ASP application.

Note

When the user submits the HTML form, the data in the HTML form is sent to the ASP application. A connection is established with the Web server to transfer the data only when the form's Submit button is clicked. ASP parses that data and gives you access to it by using the `Request` object.

Using the POST Method to Get Data

When you need to send large amounts of data, you should not use the GET method. Instead, use the POST method.

When the POST method is used in an HTML form, an ASP application can easily determine the value of HTML form variables by using the `Request.Form()` method, as in this example that returns the value of the `"UserName"` HTML form data entry field:

```
Request.Form("UserName")
```

Listing 3.2 presents an ASP application that is very similar to Listing 3.1, except that the POST method is used instead of the GET method.

FIGURE 3.3.

The value of the HTML form field is sent to the ASP application.

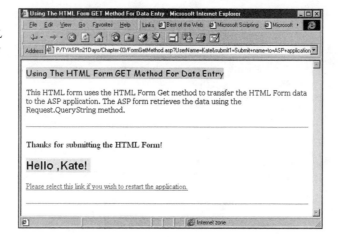

LISTING 3.2. AN ASP APPLICATION THAT USES THE HTML FORM POST METHOD FOR DATA INPUT (FormPostMethod.asp).

```
 1: <%@ LANGUAGE=VBScript %>
 2: <HTML>
 3: <HEAD>
 4:
 5: <TITLE>Using The HTML Form POST Method For Data Entry</TITLE>
 6: </HEAD>
 7: <BODY>
 8: <P><FONT face="Comic Sans MS" size=4 style="BACKGROUND-COLOR:
    ➥#99ff00">
 9: Using The HTML Form POST Method For Data Entry</FONT></P>
10:
11: <P><FONT face=Georgia>This HTML form
12: uses the HTML Form POST method to transfer the HTML Form data to
    ➥the ASP
13: application. The ASP form retrieves the data using the Request.Form
14: method.</FONT></P>
15: <P>
16: <HR>
17: <P>
18: <%
19:
20: If Request.Form ("UserName") = "" Then
21:
22: %>
23:
24: <FORM method=POST action=FormPostMethod.asp id=DataEntryForm
25:    name=DataEntryForm>
26:
27:    <FONT face=Verdana><STRONG>Please enter your name</STRONG></FONT>
```

continues

3

LISTING 3.2. CONTINUED

```
28:    <INPUT id=UserName name=UserName value=Sanjaya ><BR>
29:
30:    <INPUT type=submit value="Submit name to ASP application"
31:      id=SubmitButton name=submit1>
32:    <INPUT type=reset value="Reset Form"
33:      id=ResetButton name=reset1><BR>
34:
35: <% Else %>
36:
37: <P><FONT size=4>Thanks for submitting the HTML Form! </FONT></P>
38: <P><STRONG><FONT face=Arial size=5 style="BACKGROUND-COLOR: #ffff66">
39:
40: <%= "Hello ," & Request.Form ("UserName") & "!" %>
41:
42: </STRONG></FONT></P><P><A href="FormPostMethod.asp">
43: Please select this link if you wish to restart the application.</A>
44:
45: <% End If %>
46:
47:   </P>
48:
49: </FORM>
50: </P>
51: <HR>
52:
53:
54: </BODY>
55: </HTML>
```

ANALYSIS When the ASP application in Listing 3.2 is invoked, the Web page shown in Figure 3.4 is displayed. The form in this Web page is associated with the ASP application that generated the HTML form. After the Submit Name to ASP Application button is clicked, the name entered in the text box is sent to the ASP application.

Note

You should understand at this point that ASP works with GET and POST data slightly differently. You use two distinct methods within the Request object—QueryString and Form, respectively—to access data. You'll learn more about this procedure later.

FIGURE 3.4.

The HTML form uses the POST method to transfer data to the ASP application.

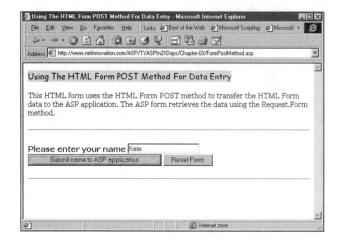

The If statement in line 20 of Listing 3.2 checks whether the HTML form has been filled in. If it has not, the HTML statements in lines 24–33 are displayed. If the HTML form has been filled in, the Else clause defined in lines 37–43 is displayed. Notice how line 40 uses the Request.Form() method to get the value of the HTML form data entry field UserName. When the HTML form in Figure 3.4 is submitted, the ASP application in Listing 3.2 generates the Web page shown in Figure 3.5. Notice how the data from the HTML form is submitted to the ASP application without modifying the URL address string:

```
http://www.netinnovation.com/ASP/TYASPIn21Days/Chapter-
➥03/FormGetMethod.asp
```

FIGURE 3.5.

The value of the HTML form field is sent to the ASP application.

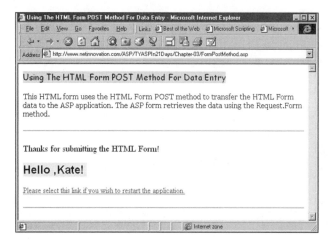

Using the `InputBox()` Function

The `InputBox()` function can also be used to get data from a user on an Web page. It is displayed by a client-side VBScript subroutine along with the text passed to the `InputBox()` function. Because the `InputBox()` function is a feature of VBScript, you should make sure your users' Web browsers support VBScript before you use this function. The `InputBox()` function gets input from the user by presenting a dialog box with a data entry field. The syntax of the `InputBox()` command is as follows:

```
InputBox(<Prompt>,[Title],[Default],[X],[Y])
```

Here's what the variables in the syntax mean:

- `<Prompt>` is the dialog box prompt.
- `[Title]` is the title of the dialog box.
- `[Default]` is the default input value.
- `[X]` is the horizontal position, in number of twips, from the left side of the screen.
- `[Y]` is the vertical position, in number of twips, from the top of the screen.

NEW TERM   A *twip* is $\frac{1}{20}$ of a printer's point, which is $\frac{1}{1,440}$ of an inch.

Using the `InputBox()` Function

The ASP application in Listing 3.3 demonstrates how an ASP application can get input from a user through the `InputBox()` function. It is used by the ASP application to get the user's name and the height of a tree drawn by the application.

LISTING 3.3. THE `InputBox()` FUNCTION IS USED TO GET INPUT BY AN ASP APPLICATION (`InputBox.asp`).

```
 1: <%@ LANGUAGE="VBSCRIPT" %>
 2: <SCRIPT LANGUAGE="VBSCRIPT" RUNAT=SERVER>
 3: Sub DrawTree ()
 4:
 5:   TreeHeight = Request.QueryString("TreeHeight")
 6:   UserInput = Request.QueryString("Name")
 7:
 8:   Response.Write "<PRE>"
 9:   For LoopCountVariable = 0 To (TreeHeight - 1)
10:     Response.Write "Hello " & UserInput & "!"
11:     For AsterisksCountVariable = 0 To (TreeHeight-LoopCountVariable)
12:       Response.Write " "
13:     Next
14:     For AsterisksCountVariable = 0 To (LoopCountVariable*2)
```

```
15:        Response.Write "*"
16:      Next
17:      Response.Write "<BR>"
18:    Next
19:    For LineCountVariable = 0 To ((TreeHeight / 3) - 1)
20:      For SpaceCountVariable = 0 To ( 7 + Len(UserInput) + (TreeHeight))
21:        Response.Write " "
22:      Next
23:      Response.Write "***<BR>"
24:    Next
25:    Response.Write "</PRE><HR>"
26:    Response.Write "<A HREF=InputBox.asp>Click here to start over.</A>"
27:
28: End Sub
29: </SCRIPT>
30: <HTML>
31: <HEAD>
32:
33: <META HTTP-EQUIV="Content-Type" content="text/html; charset=
    ➥iso-8859-1">
34: <TITLE>Using The InputBox Function For User Input</TITLE>
35: </HEAD>
36: <BODY BGCOLOR="FFFFFF">
37: <B>
38:
39: <%
40:    If NOT (IsEmpty(Request.QueryString("TreeHeight"))) Then
41:      Call DrawTree
42:    Else %>
43:      <FORM ACTION="InputBox.asp" METHOD="GET" NAME="DataForm">
44:          <INPUT TYPE=HIDDEN NAME="Name">
45:          <INPUT TYPE=HIDDEN NAME="TreeHeight">
46:      </FORM>
47:      <SCRIPT LANGUAGE="VBScript">
48: <!--
49:
50: Sub window_onLoad()
51:
52:    Name = InputBox ("Please enter your name and press enter", _
53:                "The InputBox function is used to get your name", _
54:                "Please type your name here", 300, 200)
55:    Do
56:      TreeHeight = InputBox ("Please enter the height of your tree", _
57:                  "Please enter the height of your tree (1-20)", _
58:                  "Please type the height of your tree here",200,200)
59:      If NOT((TreeHeight>=1) AND (TreeHeight<=20)) Then
60:        MsgBox "Please enter a height between 1 and 20."
61:      End If
62:    Loop Until ((TreeHeight>=1) AND (TreeHeight<=20))
63:
64:    DataForm.Name.value=Name
```

3

continues

LISTING 3.3. CONTINUED

```
65:    DataForm.TreeHeight.value=TreeHeight
66:    DataForm.Submit
67:
68: end sub
69: -->
70:    </SCRIPT>
71: <%
72:    End If
73: %>
74:
75:    </B>
76: </BODY>
77: </HTML>
```

Note

The VBScript subroutine `window_onLoad()` is always executed before the user can manipulate elements of the Web page. Therefore, `InputBox()` statements should be placed inside the `window_onLoad()` subroutine, as shown in lines 50–68 of Listing 3.1, to ensure the input boxes are displayed as soon as the Web page is loaded.

ANALYSIS When the Web page in Listing 3.3 is invoked, it displays the input box shown in Figure 3.6 to get the user's name. This input box is created by lines 52–54 in Listing 3.3.

FIGURE 3.6.

The ASP application uses the InputBox() *function to get the user's name.*

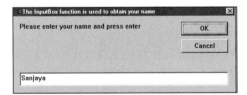

After the user types his or her name and presses Enter, the input box shown in Figure 3.7 is displayed. This input box, generated by lines 56–58, is used to get the height of the tree drawn by the ASP application.

FIGURE 3.7.

An input box is used to get the height of the tree.

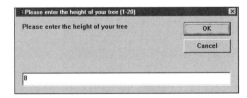

The Do...Loop Until iterative structure, defined in lines 55–62, ensures that a number between 1 and 20 is entered as the height of the tree. If an invalid number is entered, the message box shown in Figure 3.8 is displayed, and the user is returned to the input box shown in Figure 3.7.

FIGURE 3.8.

Invalid tree heights are rejected by the Do...Loop Until *iterative structure.*

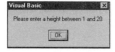

After the user's name and the height of the tree is obtained, the ASP application generates the Web page shown in Figure 3.9.

FIGURE 3.9.

The Web page generated by the ASP application.

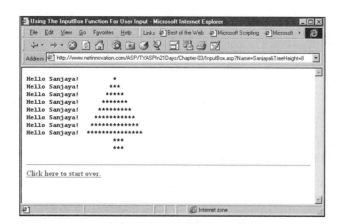

The ASP application in Listing 3.3 demonstrates how the InputBox() function is used to get user input. Notice how lines 64–66 populate the HTML form variables with values and then submit the HTML form to the ASP application. The two HTML form variables used to transfer the user's name and the tree height are declared in lines 44 and 45 as hidden HTML form variables. This is a trick that can be used to send information to an ASP application if the information was not directly obtained from an HTML form.

> **Tip**
>
> You can simply declare a hidden HTML form variable and use it to send information to ASP applications.

The `MsgBox` and `Alert()` Functions

The `MsgBox` function is a VBScript routine that displays a message box. Although using the `MsgBox` function might seem a bit complicated at first, it can add a professional touch your ASP application. The syntax of the `MsgBox` command is as follows:

`MsgBox <MessageBoxPrompt>,<ButtonStyle>,<Title>`

In this syntax, here's what the variables mean:

- `<MessageBoxPrompt>` is the prompt of the message box.
- `<ButtonStyle>` is a value from Table 3.1 that determines which button style is displayed (optional).
- `<Title>` is the title of the message box (optional).

TABLE 3.1. MESSAGE BOX CODES.

Button Type	Button Description
0	OK
1	OK and Cancel
2	Abort, Retry, and Ignore
3	Yes, No, and Cancel
4	Yes and No
5	Retry and Cancel
16	Critical Message icon (see Figure 3.10)
32	Warning Query icon (see Figure 3.11)
48	Warning Message icon (see Figure 3.12)
64	Information Message icon (see Figure 3.13)
256	Second button is default
512	Third button is default
4096	Message box always appears on top of all other windows until the user responds to the message box

For your reference, Figures 3.10 through 3.13 show the types of message boxes that can be created with the `MsgBox` function.

FIGURE 3.10.

The Critical Message box.

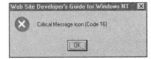

FIGURE 3.11.

The Warning Query box.

FIGURE 3.12.

The Warning Message box.

FIGURE 3.13.

The Information Message box.

3

Tip

The MsgBox function is a feature of VBScript. If your users' Web browsers don't support VBScript, you might want to consider using the JavaScript function Alert() instead. Here is its syntax:

window.alert(<"*Alert Message*">)

Listing 3.4 demonstrates how an ASP application can display a message box on the user's desktop by using the MsgBox function. ASP applications can use the MsgBox function to display critical information to users. For example, the application in Listing 3.4 demonstrates how the MsgBox function can be used to remind users that the information they are about to see is confidential (see Figure 3.14).

LISTING 3.4. THE MsgBox FUNCTION IS USED BY AN ASP APPLICATION.

```
 1: <%@ LANGUAGE="VBSCRIPT" %>
 2:
 3:     <SCRIPT LANGUAGE="VBScript">
 4: <!--
 5:
 6: Sub window_onLoad()
 7:
 8:   MsgBox "The information you are about to see is confidential!", _
 9:          16 ,"Confidential information - keep it private!"
10:
11: end sub
12: -->
13:     </SCRIPT>
14:
```

continues

LISTING 3.4. CONTINUED

```
15: <HTML>
16: <HEAD>
17: <TITLE>Using The MsgBox Function</TITLE>
18: </HEAD>
19: <BODY BGCOLOR="FFFFFF">
20:
21: <H1>Confidential information goes here!</H1>
22:
23: </BODY>
24: </HTML>
```

FIGURE 3.14.

The message box displayed by the ASP application in Listing 3.4.

There are many practical applications of the MsgBox function. For example, you can use the ever-so-popular Windows "Abort, Retry, or Ignore" message box in an ASP application if a certain action cannot be immediately performed. Users can then decide whether they want to retry the action, ignore the action, or abort the task.

Using ActiveX Controls for Data Entry

As long as the Web browser supports ActiveX, ActiveX controls can be used by ASP applications to get input from users on the client side. The application in Listing 3.5 demonstrates how ASP applications can communicate with users through the use of ActiveX controls. Because ActiveX controls are not directly supported by HTML forms, a small trick is used to transfer the values of ActiveX controls to an ASP application. When the information is submitted for processing, a VBScript subroutine copies the values of the ActiveX controls to hidden HTML form variables. The HTML form is then submitted to the ASP application.

LISTING 3.5. AN ASP APPLICATION THAT USES ACTIVEX CONTROLS FOR DATA INPUT.

```
1: <%@ LANGUAGE="VBSCRIPT" %>
2:
3: <SCRIPT LANGUAGE="VBScript">
4: <!--
5: Sub SubmitButton_onClick()
6:
```

```
 7:     DataForm.Name.value=UserName.Value
 8:     DataForm.Submit
 9:
10: end sub
11: -->
12: </SCRIPT>
13:
14: <HTML>
15: <HEAD>
16:
17: <TITLE>Using ActiveX Controls For Data Entry</TITLE>
18: </HEAD>
19: <BODY BGCOLOR=FFFFFF>
20:
21: <H1>
22: <%
23:   If NOT (IsEmpty(Request.QueryString("Name"))) Then
24:     Response.Write ("Hi " & Request.QueryString("Name") )
25:   Else %>
26:     Please enter your name <BR>
27:     <OBJECT ID="UserName" WIDTH=300 HEIGHT=37
28:      CLASSID="CLSID:8BD21D10-EC42-11CE-9E0D-00AA006002F3">
29:         <PARAM NAME="VariousPropertyBits" VALUE="746604571">
30:         <PARAM NAME="BackColor" VALUE="8454143">
31:         <PARAM NAME="Size" VALUE="7938;979">
32:         <PARAM NAME="Value" VALUE="Please type your name here">
33:         <PARAM NAME="BorderColor" VALUE="0">
34:         <PARAM NAME="FontName" VALUE="Comic Sans MS">
35:         <PARAM NAME="FontHeight" VALUE="315">
36:         <PARAM NAME="FontCharSet" VALUE="0">
37:         <PARAM NAME="FontPitchAndFamily" VALUE="2">
38:     </OBJECT>
39:     <FORM ACTION="ActiveXInput.asp" METHOD="GET"
40:           NAME="DataForm">
41:         <INPUT TYPE=HIDDEN NAME="Name">
42:         <INPUT TYPE=Button Name=SubmitButton
43:                VALUE="Submit name to ASP application">
44:     </FORM>
45: <%
46:   End If
47: %>
48: </H1>
49:
50: </BODY>
51: </HTML>
```

ANALYSIS When the ASP application in Listing 3.5 is invoked, the Web page shown in Figure 3.15 is displayed. The user uses the text box ActiveX control shown in Figure 3.15 to interact with the ASP application by supplying his or her name.

FIGURE 3.15.

An ActiveX control is used to get input from the user.

After the Submit Name to ASP Application button is clicked, the name entered by the user is sent to the ASP application through the use of a hidden form field. Line 7 copies the value entered by the user to the hidden HTML form field. The ASP application then generates the Web page shown in Figure 3.16.

FIGURE 3.16.

The value of the ActiveX control is sent to the ASP application.

Tip

When inserting ActiveX controls to your Web pages, you can use a tool such as Microsoft ActiveX Control Pad to automate the process of inserting the class ID string and other values associated with ActiveX controls. You can download the ActiveX Control Pad from Microsoft's Web site. Both Microsoft Visual InterDev and FrontPage also support the easy insertion of ActiveX controls.

Using Java Applets

Java applets can be used to spice up your ASP applications and create more compelling user interfaces on the client side. Because Java is supported by almost all Web browsers currently in use, you can use Java to add a new level of interactivity to your ASP applications.

Figure 3.17 is an example of an ASP application that uses a Java applet to display information dynamically. Each time a user visits the Ballroom at Maryland home page, an ASP application accesses a database to determine the time of the next dance and uses a Java applet to count down in real time. You can browse the actual Web page in Figure 3.17 by visiting this site:

`http://www.NetInnovation.com/Ballroom/`

FIGURE 3.17.

A Java countdown timer is used to dynamically display data generated by an ASP application.

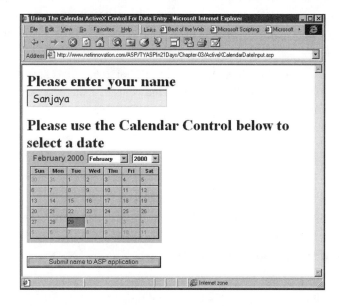

Using Java does not mean that Web browsers not supporting Java are in the dark. Any ASP statements or HTML text that you place between the <APPLET>...</APPLET> tags (used to define a Java applet) are displayed by Web browsers that do not support Java. Web pages can be designed so that you can offer the same information (perhaps not so dynamically) to Web browsers that do not support Java.

Platform Compatibility Issues

For you to interact with users using ActiveX controls, Java applets, VBScript, or any other specific technologies, you need to make sure your users use a Web browser that supports the technology. This can be accomplished more easily in an intranet environment where you have some control over your users' Web browsers.

When building Internet applications used by the general public, it is not recommended that you rely solely on ActiveX controls or any of the other technologies to interact with users. By doing so, you are shutting out all the people who use browsers that are not compatible. For example, Netscape Navigator (which is roughly about 50 percent of the Internet population!) doesn't support ActiveX controls.

Summary

Nearly all Web applications interact with users to get and display information. Today you learned that before creating a Web site, you should think about how you are going to interact with users. You should also consider such factors as appropriate color and font use, browser compatibility, and bandwidth when designing your Web site.

You also learned how to use ASP with HTML forms to interact with users. You reviewed using message boxes, input boxes, ActiveX controls, and HTML form elements to interact on the client side with users browsing your Web site. Use ActiveX controls to interact with users when you are certain they use a Web browser that supports ActiveX; ActiveX controls offer additional control over the attributes of data entry objects.

Q&A

Q How can an ASP application get input from users?

A ASP applications can get input from users through the use of message boxes, input boxes, ActiveX controls, and HTML form fields.

Q If I'm not sure whether a Web browser supports ActiveX or VBScript, how can my ASP application get input?

A Almost all Web browsers can handle HTML forms. Your ASP application can use an HTML form to get data. In later days, you learn how to use ASP to figure out some of the features supported on the user's browser.

Q How can I transfer a value obtained from an input box to an ASP application.

A A VBScript or JavaScript subroutine can transfer the value to a hidden HTML form variable and submit the HTML form to the ASP application.

Q Why should I use server-side data validation when I can do it on the client side using JavaScript?

A Remember, not every single Web browser out there supports JavaScript, so you should not rely on JavaScript to do your data validation. Another reason for using server-side validation is that users can modify client-side data validation subroutines. For example, a Web-based banking application might use a client-side data validation subroutine to ensure the user is not trying to transfer more than $1,500 at a time. If you rely solely on client-side data validation, a user (possibly with not-so-good intentions) can simply edit the HTML form, change the limit in the client-side script to $1,500,000, and completely bypass a policy the bank wants to enforce.

Q Do I have to build my own Java applets if I want to use Java applets to get input from my users?

A Not necessarily. If your needs are basic, chances are someone has already written a Java applet that does what you want it to do and has made it freely available on the Internet. Just visit your favorite search engine and execute a search for "Java Applets" and you'll find many Web sites with Java applets.

Q Today's lesson covered keeping the amount of information sent to the client at a minimum, yet you said to use JavaScript to validate information on the client. Wouldn't it be better to save bandwidth and do all the validation on the server?

A It's true that client-side scripting makes Web pages slightly larger. However, the penalty you pay by making a Web page slightly larger because of client-side scripting is almost always well worth the expense. Users make mistakes when entering data. It makes more sense to catch these mistakes by using the capabilities of the Web browser instead of using resources of the Web server to inform the user that a mistake was made.

Workshop

The quiz questions and exercises are provided for your further understanding. Please refer to Appendix A, "Answers to Questions," for the answers to the quiz questions; the answers to the exercises are on the MCP Web site.

Quiz

1. Name five methods you can use to interact with your users.

2. You are developing an intranet Web application. All your users use Windows NT, Windows 95, or Windows 98. Is it okay to use VBScript and ActiveX controls on the client side?

3. You are developing an extranet Web application. All your users use Windows NT, Windows 95, or Windows 98. However, some of your clients use Macintosh computers and even Windows CE–based handheld computers. Is it okay to use VBScript and ActiveX controls on the client side?

4. Is it a good idea to use client-side data validation as a substitute for server-side data validation?

5. Why should you not use the GET method to send large amounts of data from HTML forms to the Web server?

6. Which VBScript subroutine is always executed before the user can manipulate elements of a Web page? If you decide to use JavaScript instead, for the benefit of those who use Netscape, what would be the answer to the question?

7. What is the JavaScript equivalent of the MsgBox function?

Exercises

1. Visit some of your favorite Web search engines and search for Web sites that distribute Java applets. Bookmark Web sites that you find particularly interesting for future reference.

2. Download the ActiveX Control Pad from Microsoft's Web site by visiting http://www.microsoft.com/intdev/sdk/dtctrl/dcsdkdl.htm and install it on your computer. Read the online documentation to become familiar with how to use the ActiveX Control Pad to insert ActiveX controls to Web pages.

3. Build an ASP application that uses the Calendar ActiveX control to get a valid date from the user.

4. **ON YOUR OWN:** Create an HTML form that interacts with the user. On this form, collect the first name, last name, and birth date. After it's captured, display this information back to the user.

DAY 4

Building and Processing Web Forms

Yesterday, you learned the ways in which an ASP application can interact with users browsing a Web site. Today, you learn more about using forms to get input from users as well as how to process data entered by users. By the end of today, you will be an expert in building Web applications that interact with users and in processing and validating user input. Today, you cover the following:

- Build a generic form handler capable of handling input from any HTML form.
- Learn to validate numbers.
- Learn to validate dates and times.
- Perform arithmetic with dates and times.
- Compare date and time values.
- Build wizard-style user interfaces.
- Store data in files.
- Retrieve data from files.

There is a lot to learn today! By the end of today, you will be an expert in building Web user interfaces and validating data entered by users. You also learn how to store data obtained from users in text files on the Web server.

Building a Generic Form Handler

Sometimes, ASP applications need to be able to process HTML forms without knowing the names of all the form variables. As the application in Listing 4.1 demonstrates, you do not need to know the names of HTML form data entry fields in advance to find out their values.

LISTING 4.1. THIS ASP APPLICATION CAN EXTRACT INPUT FROM ANY HTML FORM (HTMLFORMVARIABLESREVISITED.ASP).

```
 1: <%@ LANGUAGE=VBScript %>
 2: <HTML>
 3: <HEAD>
 4:
 5: <TITLE>HTML Form Variables Revisited</TITLE>
 6: </HEAD>
 7: <BODY>
 8: <P><FONT face="Comic Sans MS" size=4 style=
    ➥"BACKGROUND-COLOR: #99ff00">
 9: HTML Form Variables Revisited: Iterating Through Form Data</FONT></P>
10:
11: <%
12:
13: 'This variable is used to iterate through the Form data collection.
14: Dim FormKey
15:
16: ' First check to see if any form data has been filled in.
17: If (Request.Form.Item = "") Then
18:
19: %>
20:
21: <P><FONT face=Georgia>This ASP
22: application processes any HTML Form data entry field that you see
    ➥below. Try it
23: out about adding a Form data entry field or two of your own and
    ➥submitting the
24: Form!</FONT></P>
25:
26: <FORM method=post action=HTMLFormVariablesRevisited.asp
27:    id=DataEntryForm name=DataEntryForm>
28: <P>
29:    <FONT face=Verdana><STRONG>Please enter your first name
       ➥</STRONG></FONT>
```

```
30:    <INPUT id=UserName name=FirstName value=Sanjaya ><BR>
31:
32:    <FONT face=Verdana><STRONG>Please enter your last name
33:    <INPUT id=LastName name=LastName
       ➥value=Hettihewa><BR></STRONG></FONT>
34:
35:    <FONT face=Verdana><STRONG>Please enter your city
36:    <INPUT id=City name=City value="Silver Spring"><BR></STRONG></FONT>
37:
38:    <FONT face=Verdana><STRONG>Please enter your State
39:    <select id=State name=State>
40:    <OPTION id=MD name=Maryland >Maryland</OPTION>
41:    <OPTION id=DC name=WashingtonDC >Washington DC</OPTION>
42:    <OPTION id=VA name=Virginia >Virginia</OPTION>
43:    <OPTION id=WV name=WestVirginia >West Virginia</OPTION>
44:    <OPTION id=WA name=WashingtonState >Washington State</OPTION>
45:    <OPTION id=OT name=Other >Other. Please specify:</OPTION>
46:    </select>
47:    Other
48:    <INPUT id=OtherState name=OtherState><BR>
49:    Which computer platforms do you use?</STRONG></FONT><BR>
50:    <input type="checkbox" id=Prehistoric name=Prehistoric>Prehistoric
51:    <input type="checkbox" id=Abacus name=Abacus>Abacus
52:    <input type="checkbox" id=Pentium name=Pentium>Pentium
53:    <input type="checkbox" id=PentiumII name=PentiumII>PentiumII
54:    <input type="checkbox" id=PentiumPro name=PentiumPro>PentiumPro
55:    <input type="checkbox" id=DECAlpha name=DECAlpha>DEC Alpha<BR>
56:    <FONT face=Verdana><STRONG>Please enter any comments below<BR>
57:    </STRONG></FONT>
58:    <TEXTAREA cols=40 id=Comments name=Comments rows=4>
59:      Any comments you type here will be
60:      properly retrieved by the ASP
61:      application using the Form
62:      collection.</TEXTAREA>
63: <P><BR>
64:
65:    <INPUT type=submit value="Submit name to ASP application"
66:      id=SubmitButton name="Submit Button">
67:    <INPUT type=reset value="Reset Form"
68:      id=ResetButton name=reset1><BR>
69: </FORM>
70:
71: <% Else %>
72:
73:
74: <P><FONT size=4>Thanks for submitting the HTML Form! The Form you
75: submitted contains the data fields you see below (as reported by the
76: Form Collection):</FONT></P>
77:
```

4

continues

LISTING 4.1. CONTINUED

```
78: <TABLE border=2 width=500>
79: <TR bgColor=#ccffff>
80: <TD><FONT face=Verdana><STRONG>Form Data Key</STRONG></FONT></TD>
81: <TD><FONT face=Verdana><STRONG>Form Data Item
82:                 Value</FONT></STRONG></TD>
83: </TR><STRONG>
84:      <%
85:
86: ' Values of all the HTML form data entry fields are displayed
87: For Each FormKey in Request.Form
88:    Response.Write "<TR><TD>" & FormKey & "</TD>"
89:    Response.Write "<TD>" & Request.Form.Item (FormKey) & "</TD></TR>"
90: Next
91:
92: %>
93:      </STRONG>
94: </TABLE>
95:
96: <P><A href="HTMLFormVariablesRevisited.asp"><STRONG>
97: Please select this link if you wish to restart the
     ➥application.</STRONG></A>
98: <% End If %>
99:
100:  </P>
101:
102: </BODY>
103: </HTML>
```

ANALYSIS Although it might look a bit complex, the ASP application in Listing 4.1 is really very simple. Line 17 checks whether the form has been filled in. If none of the data entry fields have been filled in, it displays the HTML form shown in Figure 4.1 so that the user can fill it in. If the form is filled in, the Else clause defined in lines 71–98 displays the information entered by the user, as shown in Figure 4.2. The information is displayed using a For Each loop that uses the Request.Form collection. The Request.Form.Item() method returns the values from the collection created by the form submission. You learn more about methods of the Request object in Day 6, "Getting Information About HTTP Requests with the Request Object."

Validating Data

When you use forms in your applications to gather information, you are leaving it to the user to enter valid data. If you do not pay attention to data validation, you could get *GIGO* ("Garbage In, Garbage Out"). You should always make sure the user's input is valid.

FIGURE 4.1.

A Web page with HTML form data entry fields.

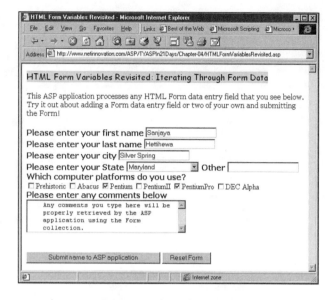

FIGURE 4.2.

The ASP application displays the values of all the HTML form data entry fields.

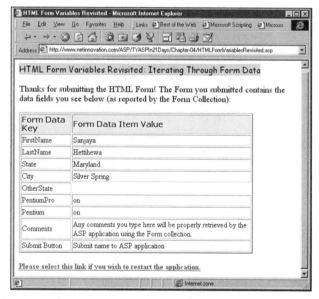

Figure 4.3 illustrates how a form can be used by an ASP application to interact with the user. You should note that the connection between the Web server and the Web browser is terminated after the form is transmitted to the Web browser. At this point, the user interacts with the form and submits it to the Web server for processing.

Figure 4.3.

An HTML form is used by an ASP application to interact with the user.

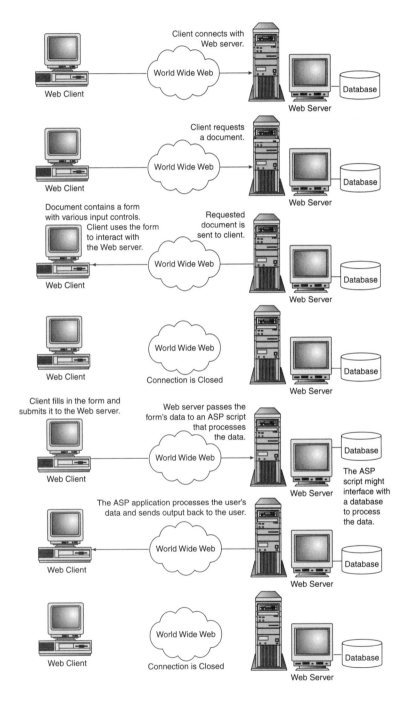

You can add client-side scripting subroutines to make your application more user-friendly and perform data validation on the client side before the form is actually submitted to the Web server for processing. This addition cuts back on your server load and bandwidth requirements because the user does not have to contact the Web server to determine that a data entry field has been improperly filled in. After the form data is accepted by the Web server, it is passed to an ASP application that processes the data. After the data is processed, the output of the ASP application is sent to the Web browser. The ASP application validates data before doing anything with it.

Tip

> Use JavaScript for client-side data validation because Netscape does not yet support VBScript. If you are certain your users use only Internet Explorer, however, you can use VBScript for client-side data validation.

Refer to Figure 4.4 for a typical data validation flowchart. The user sees a dialog box or data entry form. After the form is filled in, a client-side or server-side subroutine checks the form's data values and then flags invalid data values. The data is processed only after the data is validated.

FIGURE 4.4.

A typical data validation flowchart.

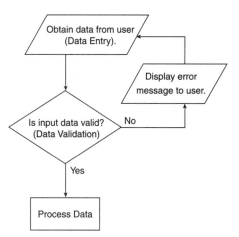

The following quotation should give you some inspiration (and perhaps some humor) when building data validation into your ASP applications.

"Nothing is foolproof to a sufficiently talented fool."

—Anonymous

Your mission is to make your ASP applications foolproof—yes, even to sufficiently talented fools! The next few sections demonstrate how to validate, from within your ASP applications, information entered by users.

Do	Don't
DO use client-side data validation to help users supply valid data to your ASP application.	**DON'T** solely depend on client-side data validation. Client-side data validation compliments server-side data validation, but does not replace it.

Validating Numbers

When accepting numbers as input from users, first make sure the user actually entered a number. Afterward, make sure the number is within the upper and lower bounds defined by your application. Make sure you validate numbers entered by users before processing them.

You can determine whether a number is valid by using the IsNumeric() function, which is demonstrated in the application in Listing 4.2.

LISTING 4.2. VALIDATING NUMBERS (VALIDATINGNUMBERS.ASP).

```
 1: <%@ LANGUAGE=VBScript %>
 2: <HTML>
 3: <HEAD>
 4:
 5: <TITLE>Validating Numbers</TITLE>
 6: </HEAD>
 7: <BODY>
 8: <% If (Request.Form.Item ("UserNumber") ="") Then %>
 9:
10: <P><STRONG><FONT face=Arial
11: style="BACKGROUND-COLOR: #99ff99">This ASP application
12: determines if the string you enter below is a valid number.
13:   </FONT></STRONG> </P>
14:
15: <P><form method=POST action="ValidatingNumbers.asp" id=DataEntryForm
16:    name=DataEntryForm>
17: <FONT face=Verdana>Please enter a valid number
18:    <INPUT id=UserNumber name=UserNumber ><BR>
19:    <INPUT type=submit value="Please validate this number"
20:      id=SubmitButton name=SubmitButton>
21: </FONT>
22: </form></P>
23:
```

```
24:
25: <% Else %>
26:
27: <P><STRONG><FONT face=Arial
28: style="BACKGROUND-COLOR: #99ff99">Thanks for submitting the
29: form!
30: </FONT></STRONG> </P>
31: <%
32:     If IsNumeric(Request.Form.Item ("UserNumber")) Then
33:       Response.Write ("Congratulations! Your input is a valid
          ↪number.")
34:     Else
35:       Response.Write ("I am sorry but your input is <B>NOT</B>" _
36:         & " a valid number.")
37:     End If
38:     Response.Write ("<BR>Your input is = <B>" & _
39:       Request.Form.Item ("UserNumber") & "</B><BR>")
40:   End If %>
41:
42: <HR>
43: This Web page was generated at <%= Date %> on <%= Time %>. <BR>
44: <A HREF="ValidatingNumbers.asp">
45: Please select this link to run this application again.</A>
46:
47: </BODY>
48: </HTML>
```

ANALYSIS   Line 8 checks whether the user has filled in the data entry form. If not, the HTML form shown in Figure 4.5 is displayed. If the form has been filled in, the Else clause defined in lines 25–40 is executed. The result of the data validation code is displayed to the user. If the user enters a valid number, the Web page shown in Figure 4.6 is displayed. If an invalid number is entered, the Web page shown in Figure 4.7 is displayed. The If statement defined in line 32 uses the IsNumeric() function to determine whether the user has entered a valid number. The statement Request.Form.Item("UserNumber") returns the value entered by the user.

If the data validation code in your ASP application detects invalid input, always echo back the invalid data entered by the user, as shown in Figure 4.7. Add an explanation of why the data was invalid and give the user a chance to enter a correct value without having to enter all the form data. You should not make your users type the same information over and over again.

FIGURE 4.5.

A number is entered for validation.

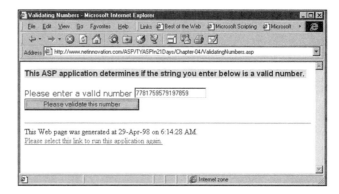

FIGURE 4.6.

The number entered by the user is valid.

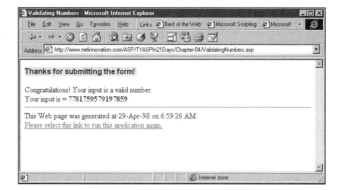

FIGURE 4.7.

The number entered by the user is invalid and is echoed back to the user.

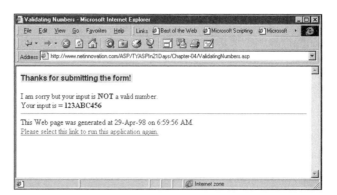

Caution

When working with numbers, keep an eye on division calculations that use a user-supplied number as the denominator. Make sure the denominator is never 0.

Validating Dates

In addition to numbers, you should always validate dates. Fortunately, as you will find out soon, the task of validating dates is made easy thanks to the IsDate() function. If an HTML form field requests a date, you should use the IsDate() function to check whether a date was entered. Additionally, you should validate that the date is in the proper range. For example, birthdays should be before the current date. If an entered birth date is after the current date, you know it is wrong.

The IsDate() function takes a value as an argument and returns true if the value is a valid date. For example, IsDate("February 29, 1976") returns true and IsDate("I Love ASP") returns false. The ASP application in Listing 4.3 validates a given date.

Note

> Billions of dollars have been spent on the "Year 2000" problem, which is a result of programmers not thinking of the full consequences of using ambiguous two-digit years. Although using two-digit dates saved memory, it's now posing a problem. A date such as 04/29/98 can be April 29th in any century! You should avoid such ambiguity in your ASP applications by using a four-digit year, especially when storing date values in databases so that your ASP applications are year 2000 compliant.

4

LISTING 4.3. VALIDATING DATES (VALIDATINGDATES.ASP).

```
 1: <%@ LANGUAGE=VBScript %>
 2: <HTML>
 3: <HEAD>
 4:
 5: <TITLE>Validating Dates</TITLE>
 6: </HEAD>
 7: <BODY>
 8: <%
 9:
10:    Dim DateString
11:
12:    If (Request.Form.Item ("UserDay") = "" OR _
13:        Request.Form.Item ("UserMonth") = "" OR _
14:        Request.Form.Item ("UserYear") = "" ) Then %>
15:
16: <P><STRONG><FONT face=Arial
17: style="BACKGROUND-COLOR: #99ff99">This ASP application
18: determines if the value you enter below is a valid date.
19:   </FONT></STRONG> </P>
20:
```

continues

LISTING 4.3. CONTINUED

```
21: <P><form method=POST action="ValidatingDates.asp" id=DataEntryForm
22:    name=DataEntryForm>
23: <FONT face=Verdana>Please enter a valid Month
24:    <INPUT id=UserNumber name=UserMonth ><BR>
25: <FONT face=Verdana>Please enter a valid Day
26:    <INPUT id=UserNumber name=UserDay ><BR>
27: <FONT face=Verdana>Please enter a valid Year
28:    <INPUT id=UserNumber name=UserYear ><BR>
29:    <INPUT type=submit value="Please validate this date"
30:     id=SubmitButton name=SubmitButton>
31: </FONT>
32: </form></P>
33:
34: <% Else %>
35:
36: <P><STRONG><FONT face=Arial
37: style="BACKGROUND-COLOR: #99ff99">Thanks for submitting the
38: form!
39: </FONT></STRONG> </P>
40: <%
41:     DateString = Request.Form.Item ("UserMonth") & "/" & _
42:                  Request.Form.Item ("UserDay") & "/" & _
43:                  Request.Form.Item ("UserYear")
44:
45:     If IsDate(DateString) Then
46:       Response.Write ("Congratulations! Your input is a valid date.")
47:     Else
48:       Response.Write ("I am sorry but your input is <B>NOT</B>" _
49:         & " a valid date.")
50:     End If
51:     Response.Write ("<BR>Your input is = <B>" & _
52:       DateString & "</B><BR>")
53:   End If %>
54:
55: <HR>
56: This Web page was generated on <%= Date %> at <%= Time %>. <BR>
57: <A HREF="ValidatingDates.asp">
58: Please select this link to run this application again.</A>
59:
60: </BODY>
61: </HTML>
```

ANALYSIS Lines 12–14 check whether the user has filled in the data entry form. If not, the HTML form shown in Figure 4.8 is displayed. If the form has been filled in, the Else clause defined in lines 34–53 is executed. The result of the data validation code is displayed to the user. If the user enters a valid date, the Web page shown in Figure 4.9 is displayed. If an invalid date is entered, the Web page shown in Figure 4.10 is displayed.

The If statement defined in line 45 uses the IsDate() function to determine whether the user has entered a valid date.

FIGURE 4.8.

A date is entered for validation.

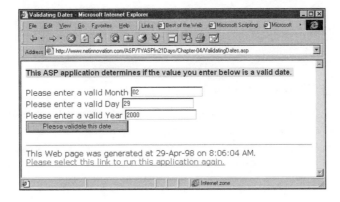

FIGURE 4.9.

The date entered by the user is valid.

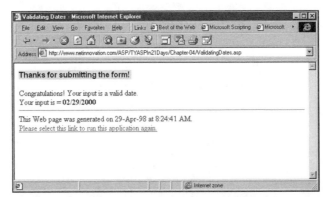

FIGURE 4.10.

The date entered by the user is invalid and is echoed back to the user.

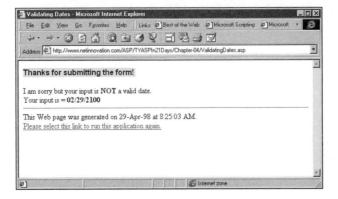

> **Note**   In Microsoft Windows, note that the range of dates from January 1, 100 through December 31, 9999 are considered valid dates by the IsDate() function. This holds true regardless of which Web browser is being used because the IsDate() function is executed on the Web server (that is running Windows).

Validating Leap Years

Be sure to correctly deal with leap years in your applications. A leap year is any year divisible by four except for years divisible by 100, unless those years are divisible by 400. For example, 2000 and 2400 are leap years; however, the years 2100, 2200, 2300, and 2500 are not leap years.

Look back at Figures 4.9 and 4.10 and notice how the ASP application from Listing 4.3 uses the IsDate() function to correctly validate February 29 on a leap year.

> **Note**   For an informative, thorough, and interesting discussion of calendar dates, including leap year issues, visit the following Web page:
>
> http://www.pip.dknet.dk/~pip10160/calendar.html

Validating Four-Digit Years

When getting dates from the user, you might want to separately get month, day, and year values if it makes it easier for you to validate and process dates. For example, if you are looking for a date between 2010 and 2020 and not a date between 1910 and 1920, by getting the year separately, you can make sure the user enters a four-digit year, not an ambiguous 04/29/10, which might be 04/29/1910, 04/29/2010, or perhaps even a date in another century!

> **Note**   IsDate() considers 2/29/00 a valid date—which it is!

Validating Time Values

It is also important to validate values entered for a time. Before asking for a time from the user, it is a good idea to let the user know whether you use the a.m./p.m. clock or the 24-hour clock. Additionally, make sure the time is within range. If you are writing a Web application that allows users to make appointments with you through a Web page, you might want to design your Web page so that users can make appointments only at times when you are available.

The ASP application in Listing 4.4 demonstrates how to get and validate a time from the user. It also shows how you can simplify your code with a user-defined subroutine.

LISTING 4.4. VALIDATING TIME VALUES (VALIDATINGTIMES.ASP).

```
 1: <%@ LANGUAGE=VBScript %>
 2: <HTML>
 3: <HEAD>
 4:
 5: <TITLE>Validating Times</TITLE>
 6: </HEAD>
 7: <BODY>
 8: <%
 9:
10:    Sub ValidateTime
11:      If   (Request.Form.Item ("UserHours") >= 0 And _
12:            Request.Form.Item ("UserHours") <= 23) AND _
13:           (Request.Form.Item ("UserMinutes") >= 0 And _
14:            Request.Form.Item ("UserMinutes") <= 59) AND _
15:           (Request.Form.Item ("UserSeconds") >= 0 And _
16:            Request.Form.Item ("UserSeconds") <= 59) Then
17:        Response.Write ("Congratulations! Your input is a valid time.")
18:      Else
19:        Response.Write ("I am sorry but your input is <B>NOT</B>" _
20:          & " a valid time.")
21:      End If
22:    End Sub
23:
24:    Dim TimeString
25:
26:    If (Request.Form.Item ("UserHours") = "" OR _
27:          Request.Form.Item ("UserMinutes") = "" OR _
28:          Request.Form.Item ("UserSeconds") = "" ) Then %>
29:
30: <P><STRONG><FONT face=Arial
31: style="BACKGROUND-COLOR: #99ff99">This ASP application
32: determines if the value you enter below is a valid time.
33:   </FONT></STRONG> </P>
34:
35: <P><form method=POST action="ValidatingTimes.asp" id=DataEntryForm
36:    name=DataEntryForm>
37: <FONT face=Verdana>Please enter a valid time (HH:MM:SS)
38:    <INPUT id=UserNumbers name=UserHours size=2 maxlength=2> :
39:    <INPUT id=UserNumbers name=UserMinutes size=2 maxlength=2> :
40:    <INPUT id=UserNumbers name=Userseconds size=2 maxlength=2>
```

continues

LISTING 4.4. CONTINUED

```
41:    <INPUT type=submit value="Please validate this time"
42:       id=SubmitButton name=SubmitButton>
43: </FONT>
44: </form></P>
45:
46: <% Else %>
47:
48: <P><STRONG><FONT face=Arial
49: style="BACKGROUND-COLOR: #99ff99">Thanks for submitting the
50: form!
51: </FONT></STRONG> </P>
52: <%
53:     TimeString = Request.Form.Item ("UserHours") & ":" & _
54:                  Request.Form.Item ("UserMinutes") & ":" & _
55:                  Request.Form.Item ("UserSeconds")
56:
57:     If  (NOT IsNumeric (Request.Form.Item ("UserHours"))) OR _
58:        (NOT IsNumeric (Request.Form.Item ("UserMinutes"))) OR _
59:        (NOT IsNumeric (Request.Form.Item ("UserSeconds"))) Then
60:       Response.Write ("INVALID INPUT: Only numeric data is accepted.")
61:     Else
62:       Call ValidateTime
63:     End If
64:     Response.Write ("<BR>Your input is = <B>" & _
65:        TimeString & "</B><BR>")
66:   End If %>
67:
68: <HR>
69: This Web page was generated on <%= Date %> at <%= Time %>. <BR>
70: <A HREF="ValidatingTimes.asp">
71: Please select this link to run this application again.</A>
72:
73: </BODY>
74: </HTML>
```

ANALYSIS   Lines 26–28 check whether the user has filled in the data entry form. If not, the
HTML form shown in Figure 4.11 is displayed. If the form has been filled in, the
Else clause defined in lines 46–66 is executed. The result of the data validation code is
displayed to the user. If the user enters a valid time, the Web page shown in Figure 4.12
is displayed. If an invalid time is entered, the Web page in Figure 4.13 is displayed. The
If statement defined in lines 11–16 determines whether the user has entered a valid time.
Notice how part of the time validation code has been moved to a user-defined subroutine
(defined in lines 10–22) to make the code less cluttered.

FIGURE 4.11.

A time is entered for validation.

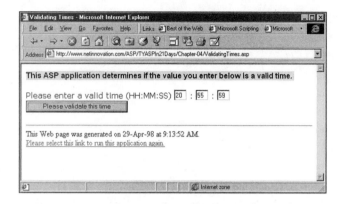

FIGURE 4.12.

The time entered by the user is valid.

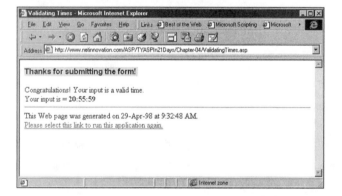

> **Tip**
>
> Never write blocks of ASP statements that are more than a page long. If they are longer, break them down into code blocks that perform well-defined tasks. Next, create a subroutine for each code block. You can then call the subroutines you created. These steps greatly simplify debugging and maintaining ASP applications.

Processing Dates and Times

Now that you know how to get valid date and time values, you can easily perform arithmetic operations with time and date values by using VBScript time and date functions, such as the following:

- `DateSerial()`—Used to perform arithmetic on dates and to return a `Date` when a year, month, and date is specified.

FIGURE 4.13.

*The time entered by
the user is invalid and
is echoed back to the
user.*

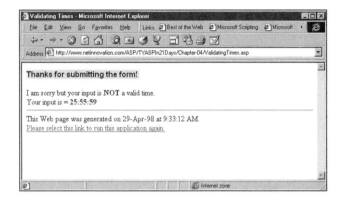

- DateValue()—Takes a value such as "Feb 29, 2000" or "02/29/2000," converts the value to a VB Date, and returns it.

- CDate()—Takes a value such as "Feb 29, 2000" or "02/29/2000," converts the value to a VB Date, and returns it. The difference between the CDate() function and the DateValue() function is that CDate() also converts the time portion of an expression, but the DateValue() function ignores the time portion of an expression.

- Date()—Returns the current date from the system clock.

- Day()—Takes a valid date as the argument and returns a number between 1 and 31 representing the day.

- Month()—Takes a valid date as the argument and returns a number between 1 and 12 representing the month.

- Year()—Takes a valid date as the argument and returns a number representing the year.

- Weekday()—Used to determine the day of the week, such as "Monday," "Tuesday," and so forth.

- Time()—Returns the current time from the system clock.

- Hour()—Takes a valid time as the argument and returns a number between 0 and 23 representing the number of hours in the time.

- Minute()—Takes a valid time as the argument and returns a number between 0 and 60 representing the number of minutes in the time.

- Second()—Takes a valid time as the argument and returns a number between 0 and 60 representing the number of seconds in the time.

- Now()—Returns the current date and time from the system clock.

- `TimeValue()`—Converts a string, given to the function as an argument, to a valid time.

Formatting Data

After you process the data, it is important that you properly format the data displayed to the user. How you present information has a lot to do with whether users are comfortable using your application. No matter how hard you work on the internals of your ASP application, users will not be comfortable with it unless it has a user-friendly, consistent look and feel. Properly formatting data promotes these goals.

 Tip Be consistent in formatting data. This consistency adds a professional touch to your applications and makes them more user-friendly.

VBScript includes many functions for formatting data just the way you want it to look. Table 4.1 is a list of useful VBScript data formatting functions. For more information about using data formatting functions, please refer to Appendix B.

TABLE 4.1. USEFUL DATA FORMATTING FUNCTIONS.

Function	Decription
`FormatDateTime()`	This function is useful for formatting date and time values.
`FormatCurrency()`	Use this function to format currency values. You can determine how to specify negative values (that is, inside parentheses), how to group digits, whether to include a leading 0, and how many decimal points should be used.
`FormatNumber()`	A useful function for formatting numbers in your applications.
`FormatPercent()`	Useful for formatting percentage values. The value passed to the function is multiplied by 100 and returned with a trailing % character.

Building a Web-Based Data Entry Wizard

Wizard-style user interfaces simplify data entry by guiding the user through complex questions. Another benefit of using wizard-style user interfaces is that they help the user concentrate on one set of questions before moving on to the next set of questions. Also, based on the answers to a previous set of questions, subsequent questions can be customized.

 Caution
> Web-based wizard-style user interfaces are a wonderful, compelling way to interact with your users. However, be sure to use this tool only when you need it. Wizard-style user interfaces are not particularly efficient for building simple data entry forms. Use wizard-style user interfaces when you need to build a complex Web interface in which questions you ask the user depend on answers to questions you previously asked.

A Web-based data entry wizard is not an entirely simple Web application to build. However, as long as you follow the steps outlined in the next section, you will have little trouble building your own Web-based data entry wizards. Of course, you can use the data entry wizard you build in the next section as a model when building your own data entry wizards.

Steps in Creating a Web-Based Data Entry Wizard

By following the seven simple steps outlined in this section, you can build your own Web-based data entry wizards. If the following steps do not make a lot of sense to you at first, don't worry. You will understand their purpose when you build an actual ASP application that uses a Web-based wizard-style user interface for data entry in the following sections.

1. Create a flowchart. As you build more complex Web-based user interfaces, you can minimize confusion by drawing a flowchart of exactly how your user interface is going to function.

   Figure 4.14 is a flowchart of the wizard-style user interface presented in the next section. As you can see in the figure, the ASP application first gets some general information about the user. The user then selects a type of vehicle—a car or a sport utility vehicle (SUV). Depending on the type of vehicle selected, the ASP application displays a different form containing only the type of vehicles selected by the user. After the user selects a specific vehicle, the ASP application processes all the information entered by the user. Notice how the `Session` object is used for temporary data storage.

Figure 4.14.

The flowchart of the Web-based data entry wizard you are building.

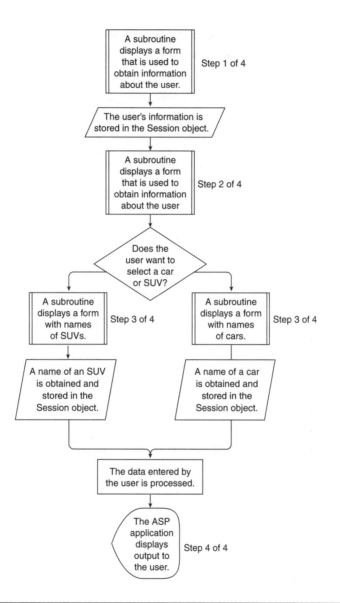

The Session object is covered in detail in Day 8, "Processing Web Data with the Server, Session, and Application Objects." For now, all you need to know is that you can temporarily store data in the Session object and each time a new user visits your Web site, a new session is created for that user. Users who continue to browse your Web site use the same Session object until the user session expires.

2. Create all the data entry forms. After you create a flowchart, the next step is actually creating all the HTML forms that are part of the data entry wizard you are building.

Tip

> When creating a sequence of HTML forms that are part of a data entry wizard's user interface, maintain a consistent layout and color scheme. Additionally, you can make users feel at home by making your HTML form actually look like familiar Windows dialog boxes. (Look at Figures 4.15 through 4.18 for examples.)

3. Create a subroutine for each data entry form. Move each HTML form to a separate subroutine that displays the data entry form.

4. Use a hidden HTML form variable to keep track of the current page. Add a hidden HTML form variable that keeps track of the current data entry form the user is filling out. A data entry wizard could have several data entry forms. Your ASP application uses the hidden HTML form variable to determine which data entry form the user is currently on.

5. Use a `Select Case` statement to display the correct data entry form. A `Select Case` statement can be used to send the user from one data entry form to another data entry form. When all the data entry forms of the data entry wizard are filled in, the `Select Case` statement can trigger a subroutine that processes the data entered by the user.

6. Use the `Session` object to store user data. When a user goes from one data entry form to another, the `Session` object can be used to store data already entered by the user.

7. After the user has entered all the data, retrieve the data by using the `Session` object and then process it.

Tip

> If your data entry wizard has more than two steps and each step displays a different data entry form, label each data entry form so that the user knows how many more forms need to be filled in. For example, at the top of each data entry form, the user sees a message such as "Step 3 of 4." Notice how this useful information is supplied in the application you build in the next section.

Building a Web-Based Data Entry Wizard

The ASP application in Listing 4.5 demonstrates how to build an ASP application that uses a wizard-style user interface to interact with the user. The purpose of the ASP application is simple. First, it gets some basic information about the user, and then, to provide some work inspiration, gives the user a chance to select either a car or a sport utility vehicle. Depending on the type of vehicle selected, the ASP application displays a different data entry form. After the user selects a vehicle, the ASP application processes all the data entered by the user and displays a summary of that data.

ON THE WEB

You can experiment with the application in Listing 4.5 by downloading the code distribution file for this book from the MCP Web site at www.mcp.com, copying the file /Chapter-04/DataEntryWizard.asp to your Web server and executing it with a Web browser.

LISTING 4.5. AN ASP APPLICATION WITH A WIZARD-STYLE USER INTERFACE (DATAENTRYWIZARD.ASP).

```
 1: <%@ LANGUAGE=VBScript %>
 2: <HTML>
 3: <HEAD>
 4:   <TITLE>Data Entry Wizard: Active Work Inspiration 1.0</TITLE>
 5: </HEAD>
 6: <BODY>
 7:
 8: <%
 9:
10: ' ##### Begin Display Luxury Cars #####
11:    Sub DisplayLuxuryCars %>
12:
13:    <CENTER><TABLE border=1 cellpadding=3 cellspacing=0 width=410>
14:    <TR>
15:    <TD bgColor=#004080><P align=center><STRONG>
16:      <FONT color=#ffffff>Select Your Choice Of A Premium Luxury Car
17:    </FONT></STRONG></P></TD>
18:    </TR>
19:    <TR>
20:    <TD bgColor=#e1e1e1><P align=right><FONT face=Verdana>
21:      <STRONG>Step 3 of 4</STRONG></FONT></P>
22:    <P><form method=POST action="DataEntryWizard.asp"
23:        id=DataEntryForm name=DataEntryForm>
24:      <INPUT id=VehicleSelected name=VehicleSelected
25:        value="Lexus LS400" type=radio checked>Lexus LS 400<BR>
26:      <INPUT id=VehicleSelected name=VehicleSelected
```

continues

LISTING **4.5.** CONTINUED

```
27:            value="Infiniti Q45" type=radio>Infiniti Q45<BR>
28:         <INPUT id=VehicleSelected name=VehicleSelected
29:            value="Acura 3.5 RL" type=radio>Acura 3.5 RL<BR>
30:         <INPUT id=VehicleSelected name=VehicleSelected
31:            value="Jaguar XJ8" type=radio>Jaguar XJ8<BR>
32:         <INPUT id=VehicleSelected name=VehicleSelected
33:            value="Mercedes 600SL" type=radio>Mercedes 600SL<BR><BR>
34:         <INPUT type=hidden name=NextPage value=4><BR>
35:         <input type="submit" value="Next ->" id=NextButton
36:           name=NextButton>
37:         </form>
38:         </P></TD>
39:    </TR>
40: </TABLE>
41: </CENTER>
42:
43: <%
44: ' ##### End Display Luxury Cars #####
45:    End Sub
46:
47:
48: ' ##### Begin Display Initial Page #####
49:    Sub DisplayInitialPage %>
50:
51:    <TABLE border=1 cellpadding=3 cellspacing=0 width=410
52:      bordercolor=#808080 align=center>
53:    <TR>
54:    <TD bgColor=#004080><P align=center><STRONG><FONT color=#ffffff>
55:    Welcome To Active Work
56:            Inspiration Version 1.0</FONT>
57:    </STRONG></P></TD>
58:    </TR>
59:    <TR>
60:    <TD bgColor=#e1e1e1><P align=right>
61:    <FONT face=Verdana><STRONG>Step 1 of 4</STRONG></FONT></P>
62:       It's 3:00 in the morning and you are still
63:       busy working on your latest ASP application... It's time
64:       for some work inspiration (and perhaps a cup of Espresso).
65:       Active Work Inspiration, the result of millions of dollars
66:       in R&amp;D, has been designed to motivate you to get back
67:       to work in just four simple steps using a Wizard Style user
68:       interface (<EM>as seen on Teach Yourself Active Server
69:       Pages In 21 Days!</EM>).</P>
70:       <form method=POST action="DataEntryWizard.asp"
71:         id=DataEntryForm name=DataEntryForm>
72:         <P>Please enter your first name
73:            <INPUT id=FirstName name=FirstName> <BR>
74:         Please enter your last name
75:            <INPUT id=LastName name=LastName> <BR>
```

```
76:            Please enter your city
77:               <INPUT id=City name=City> <BR>
78:            Please enter your state
79:               <INPUT id=State maxLength=2 name=State size=2> <BR>
80:            Please enter your e-mail address
81:               <INPUT id=Email name=Email><BR>
82:               <INPUT type=hidden name=NextPage value=2><BR>
83:               <input type="submit" value="Next ->" id=NextButton
84:                  name=NextButton>
85:         </form>
86:      </TD>
87:   </TR></TABLE>
88:
89: <%
90: ' ##### End Display Initial Page #####
91:    End Sub
92:
93:
94: ' ##### Select vehicle type to display #####
95:    Sub SelectVehicleType %>
96:
97:      <CENTER><TABLE border=1 cellpadding=3 cellspacing=0 width=410>
98:      <TR>
99:      <TD bgColor=#004080><P align=center><STRONG><FONT color=#ffffff>
100:     Select Your Choice Of A New Vehicle Type</FONT></STRONG></P></TD>
101:     </TR>
102:     <TR>
103:     <TD bgColor=#e1e1e1><P align=right><FONT face=Verdana><STRONG>
104:     Step 2 of 4</STRONG></FONT></P>
105:     <P>What type of a new vehicle would you like to have?</P>
106:     <P><form method=POST action="DataEntryWizard.asp"
107:         id=DataEntryForm name=DataEntryForm>
108:      <INPUT id=VehicleType name=VehicleType value=LuxuryCar
109:      type=radio checked>Premium luxury car<BR>
110:      <INPUT id=VehicleType name=VehicleType value=LuxurySUV
111:      type=radio>Luxury SUV<BR><BR>
112:      <INPUT type=hidden name=NextPage value=3><BR>
113:      <input type="submit" value="Next ->" id=NextButton
114:            name=NextButton>
115:      </form>
116:      </P></TD>
117:      </TR>
118:      </TABLE>
119:      </CENTER>
120:
121: <%
122: ' ##### End select vehicle type to display #####
123:    End Sub
124:
```

4

continues

LISTING 4.5. CONTINUED

```
125:
126: ' ##### Begin Luxury SUVs #####
127:    Sub DisplayLuxurySUVs %>
128:
129:      <CENTER><TABLE border=1 cellpadding=3 cellspacing=0 width=410>
130:      <TR>
131:      <TD bgColor=#004080><P align=center><STRONG><FONT color=#ffffff>
132:      Select Your Choice Of A Luxury SUV</FONT></STRONG></P></TD>
133:      </TR>
134:      <TR>
135:      <TD bgColor=#e1e1e1><P align=right><FONT face=Verdana>
136:      <STRONG>Step 3 of 4</STRONG></FONT></P>
137:      <P><form method=POST action="DataEntryWizard.asp"
138:          id=DataEntryForm name=DataEntryForm>
139:        <INPUT id=VehicleSelected name=VehicleSelected
140:          value="Lexus RX300" type=radio checked>Lexus RX300<BR>
141:        <INPUT id=VehicleSelected name=VehicleSelected
142:          value="Lexus LX470" type=radio>Lexus LX470<BR>
143:        <INPUT id=VehicleSelected name=VehicleSelected
144:          value="Infiniti QX4" type=radio>Infinity QX4<BR>
145:        <INPUT id=VehicleSelected name=VehicleSelected
146:          value="Mercedes ML320" type=radio>Mercedes ML320<BR>
147:        <INPUT type=hidden name=NextPage value=4><BR>
148:        <input type="submit" value="Next ->" id=NextButton
149:          name=NextButton>
150:        </form>
151:        </P></TD>
152:      </TR>
153:      </TABLE>
154:      </CENTER>
155: <%
156: ' ##### End Luxury SUVs #####
157:    End Sub
158:
159:
160: ' ##### Begin Display Summary #####
161:    Sub DisplaySummary
162: %>
163:
164: <CENTER><TABLE border=1 cellpadding=3 cellspacing=0 width=410>
165:    <TR>
166:      <TD bgColor=#004080><P align=center><STRONG><FONT color=#ffffff>
167:      Time To Get Back To Work</FONT></STRONG></P></TD>
168:    </TR>
169:    <TR>
170:      <TD bgColor=#e1e1e1><P align=right>
171:      <FONT face=Verdana><STRONG>Step 4 of 4</STRONG></FONT></P>
172:      <p><strong><font face="Arial">
173:        You typed in the following information:</font></strong></p>
```

```
174:
175:     <TABLE>
176:     <TR bgcolor=#ffffcc><TD>Data Field</TD><TD>Your Input</TD></TR>
177:     <TR  bgcolor=Beige><TD>First name</TD>
178:       <TD> <%=Session.Value("FIRSTNAME")%></TD></TR>
179:     <TR bgcolor=Beige><TD>Last name</TD>
180:       <TD> <%=Session.Value("LASTNAME")%></TD></TR>
181:     <TR bgcolor=Beige><TD>State you live in</TD>
182:       <TD> <%=Session.Value("STATE")%></TD></TR>
183:     <TR bgcolor=Beige><TD>City you live in</TD>
184:       <TD> <%=Session.Value("CITY")%></TD></TR>
185:     <TR bgcolor=Beige><TD>Your e-mail address</TD>
186:       <TD> <%=Session.Value("EMAIL")%></TD></TR>
187:     </TABLE>
188:
189:     <P><strong><font face="Arial">And the vehicle you selected is:
190:       <%=Session.Value("VEHICLESELECTED")%>.</font></strong></P>
191:
192:     It's time to get back to work so you can get
193:         your work done, and perhaps start saving money!
194:     </TD>
195:   </TR>
196: </TABLE></CENTER>
197:
198: <%
199: ' ##### End Display Summary #####
200:    End Sub
201:
202:
203: ' ##### Begin StoreUserDataInSessionObject #####
204:    Sub StoreUserDataInSessionObject
205:
206:      Dim FormKey
207:
208:      For Each FormKey in Request.Form
209:        Session(FormKey) = Request.Form.Item (FormKey)
210:      Next
211:
212: ' ##### End StoreUserDataInSessionObject #####
213:    End Sub
214:
215:
216:    Dim CurrentPage
217:
218:    If Request.Form.Item("NextPage") = "" Then
219:      CurrentPage = 1
220:    Else
221:      CurrentPage = Request.Form.Item("NextPage")
222:    End If
```

4

continues

LISTING 4.5. CONTINUED

```
223:
224:    Call StoreUserDataInSessionObject
225:
226:    Select Case CurrentPage
227:      Case 1 : Call DisplayInitialPage
228:      Case 2 : Call SelectVehicleType
229:      Case 3 : If Request.Form.Item("VehicleType") = "LuxuryCar" Then
230:                   Call DisplayLuxuryCars
231:               Else
232:                   Call DisplayLuxurySUVs
233:               End If
234:      Case 4 : Call DisplaySummary
235:    End Select %>
236:
237: <BR><HR>
238: <A HREF="DataEntryWizard.asp">
239: Please select this link to restart this application</A>.<BR>
240: It is now <%= Date %> at <%= Time %>.
241:
242: </BODY>
243: </HTML>
```

ANALYSIS Lines 10–200 define subroutines that display forms that are part of the data entry wizard. Look at a single subroutine (see lines 10–45) and notice how HTML form code is encapsulated in a user-defined subroutine. The Select Case structure defined in lines 226–235 displays the correct data entry form to the user based on the data entry form just filled in. The application keeps track of this information by using the hidden HTML form variable NextPage. Notice how lines 218–222 examine the value of this NextPage variable to determine which data entry form should be displayed to the user when using the Select Case structure in line 226. When moving from one data entry form to another, the subroutine defined in lines 203–213 uses the Session object to store data entered by the user. Finally, the subroutine defined in lines 160–200 uses the same Session object to display a summary of all the data entered by the user.

Basic information about the user is supplied to the ASP application using the data entry form in Figure 4.15. Notice how the wizard's data entry forms look somewhat like Windows dialog boxes to make the user feel more at home.

The data entry form in Figure 4.16 is used to specify the type of vehicle the user is interested in. The user has selected to have an SUV. Lines 95–123 of Listing 4.5 generate the form in Figure 4.16.

FIGURE 4.15.

Step 1 of the data entry wizard gets information about the user.

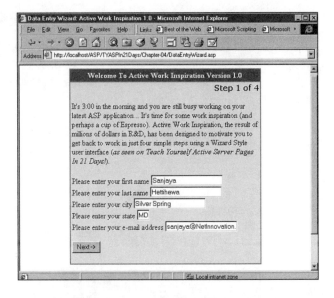

FIGURE 4.16.

Step 2 of the data entry wizard gets the type of vehicle the user wants.

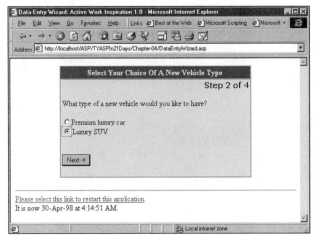

4

The user selects the type of SUV using the data entry form in Figure 4.17. Had the user chosen to have a car in the previous data entry form, the ASP application would have displayed a different data entry form containing only cars.

After the user has entered all the information, the ASP application processes the data entered by the user and displays a summary of it, as shown in Figure 4.18.

FIGURE 4.17.

In step 3 of the data entry wizard, the user selects a specific vehicle.

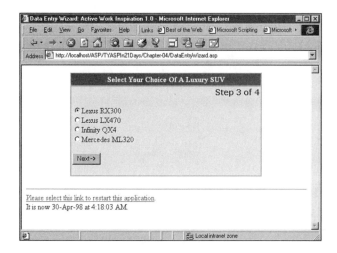

FIGURE 4.18.

In step 4 of the data entry wizard, data entered by the user is displayed.

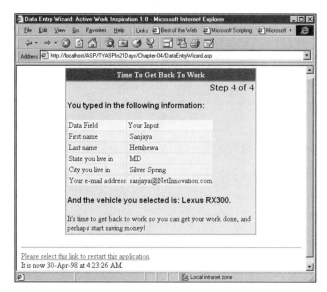

Tip

If your form is complex, consider using a separate ASP file for each page of the data entry wizard.

Working with Local Text Files on the Server

It is important that you understand how to work with files on the server. Although a database is ideal for storing information in most cases, sometimes all you need is a simple plain text file to store some information. In such cases, you can use the Text Stream component to work with local files on the server.

Caution

> Don't use local files to store large amounts of data. Using a database is more efficient and less error prone.

The Text Stream Component

By using the Text Stream component, ASP applications can access the server file system. The Text Stream component was designed to make it easy to manage text streams within ASP applications.

 NEW TERM A *text stream* is used to read or write data from a data source. Some data sources, such as a disk file, allow reading and writing of data, but other data sources, such as a keyboard, allow only reading of data. When I talk about text streams in this section, I refer to files stored on the hard drive.

The Text Stream component uses the `FileSystem` object to read and write text streams to files. The `FileSystem` object has two methods that can be used to manipulate text streams:

- `CreateTextFile`—Creates a text file and returns a `TextStream` object that can be used to read or write text.
- `OpenTextFile`—Can be used to read from a text file or append text to it.

Note

> It is possible to have two or more instances of the same application running at the same time. When you're building ASP applications, anticipate this happening. If a previous instance of an ASP application is writing to a file, that file might be unavailable for writing at that time.

Before methods of the `FileSystem` object can be used, the object must be instantiated with the following ASP statement:

```
Set FileStreamObject = CreateObject("Scripting.FileSystemObject")
```

4

After the `FileSystem` object is instantiated, you can use either the `CreateTextFile` method or the `OpenTextFile` method to manipulate text streams.

Properties of the `TextStream` Object

When reading a text stream, properties of the `TextStream` object (listed in Table 4.2) can be used to monitor your current position in the file.

TABLE 4.2. PROPERTIES OF THE TEXTSTREAM OBJECT.

Property	Description
AtEndOfLine	Used to determine whether you are at the end of the line when reading characters from a text stream. This property is useful when you read a file one character at a time using the Read method.
AtEndOfStream	Used to determine whether you are at the end of the text stream. This property is useful when you read a file an entire line at a time using the ReadLine method.
Column	Used to determine how many characters you have currently read from the beginning of the line.
Line	Used to determine how many lines you have read so far.

Methods of the `TextStream` Object

In addition to the `Close` method, the `TextStream` object has methods that can be used to read, write, and skip text. Table 4.3 lists the methods of the `TextStream` object.

TABLE 4.3. METHODS OF THE TEXTSTREAM OBJECT.

Method	Stream Type	Description
Read	Input	Used to read text one character at a time.
ReadAll	Input	Causes the contents of the entire TextStream to be loaded into memory. This method should not be used for very large files.
ReadLine	Input	Used to read an entire line of text.
Write	Output	Writes a string of characters to the output stream. (A carriage return is not included at the end of the line.)
WriteLine	Output	Writes a string of characters to the output stream and follows it with a carriage return.
WriteBlankLines	Output	Used to insert blank lines. The number of blank lines can be specified as a parameter.
Skip	Input	Skips the specified number of characters.
SkipLine	Input	Skips the current line and proceeds to the next line.

Using the `CreateTextFile()` Method

The `CreateTextFile()` method is used to create a text file. After the text file is created, the `CreateTextFile()` method returns a `TextStream` object that can be used to read or write text. Its syntax is as follows:

```
Set FileStreamObject = CreateObject("Scripting.FileSystemObject")
FileStreamObject.CreateTextFile (<NameOfFile>,<Overwrite>, <Unicode>)
```

In this syntax, here's what the variables mean:

- *<NameOfFile>* is the name of the file to be created.
- *<Overwrite>* contains a Boolean value. If the value is TRUE, existing files are overwritten. If the value is FALSE, existing files are not overwritten.
- *<Unicode>* contains a Boolean value. If the value is TRUE, the file is created as a Unicode file. If the value is FALSE, the file is created as an ASCII file. If you omit this argument, a file type of ASCII is assumed. For most purposes, the ASCII file type works fine. Use Unicode only if the range of the ASCII character set is not enough to store your text.

The ASP application in Listing 4.6 creates a text file named `TextFile.txt` and writes the string `Hello World!`.

LISTING 4.6. USING THE CREATETEXTFILE METHOD.

```
1: Set FileStreamObject = CreateObject("Scripting.FileSystemObject")
2: Set WriteStream = FileStreamObject.CreateTextFile("TextFile.txt", True)
3: WriteStream.WriteLine("Hello World!")
4: WriteStream.Close
```

Using the `OpenTextFile()` Method

The `OpenTextFile()` method can be used to read from a text file or to append text to it. Its syntax is as follows:

```
Set FileStreamObject = CreateObject("Scripting.FileSystemObject")
Set TextStream = FileStreamObject.OpenTextFile (<FileName>,
<Mode>,<Create>)
```

Note

The parameters *<Mode>* and *<Create>* are optional.

In this syntax, here's what the variables mean:

- *<FileName>* is the name of the file to be opened.

- *<Mode>* is an optional argument used to specify the input/output mode of the text stream. Files can be opened in either input or output mode. Replace *<Mode>* with ForReading to open the file for reading (input) and ForAppending to open the file for appending (output).

- *<Create>* is an optional Boolean argument that determines whether a new file should be created if the specified *<FileName>* does not exist. Replace *<Create>* with TRUE to create a new file if *<FileName>* does not exist. Replace *<Create>* with FALSE, otherwise.

 Caution

> When writing to files or creating files, make sure your file access permissions are set up correctly. The user account should have write permissions to the directory where you are creating or writing to the file. If a user does not have write permissions for the directory structure, you can get errors.

The ASP application in Listing 4.7 creates a text file named TextFile.txt and writes the string Hello World!. Afterward, it reads and displays the contents of TextFile.txt. See Figure 4.19 for the output of this application.

LISTING 4.7. USING THE TEXTSTREAM OBJECT.

```
 1: <%@ LANGUAGE=VBScript %>
 2: <HTML>
 3: <HEAD>
 4:
 5: <META HTTP-EQUIV="Content-Type" content="text/html; charset=iso-8859-
    ➥1">
 6: <TITLE>Manipulating Text Streams</TITLE>
 7: </HEAD>
 8: <BODY bgColor=#ffffff>
 9:
10: <H2><FONT face=Arial size=4 style="BACKGROUND-COLOR: #99ff00">
11: The FileSystemObject can be used to manipulate text streams. </FONT>
12: </H2>
13:
14: <H3><FONT style="BACKGROUND-COLOR: #ccffff">Now creating
15: &quot;TextFile.txt&quot; ... </FONT>
16: </H3>
17: <%
18:   Set FileStreamObject = CreateObject("Scripting.FileSystemObject")
19:
```

```
20: ' ### NOTE ###
21: ' You may have to modify the following statement based on the
22: ' directory structure and permissions of your system.
23: ' The directory you specify MUST have WRITE access permissions
24: ' and the IIS account must also have write access permissions to
25: ' the directory. If the IIS account does not have write access
26: ' permissions to the directory specified below, the following line
27: ' of code will fail with a file permission error.
28:
29:   Set WriteStream = _
30:     FileStreamObject.CreateTextFile(Server.MapPath _
31:       ("/ASP/TYASPIn21Days/Chapter-04") & "\TextFile.txt", True)
32:   WriteStream.WriteLine("Hello World!")
33:   WriteStream.Close
34:
35: %>
36:
37:
38: <H3><FONT style="BACKGROUND-COLOR: #ffff99">Now reading and
39: displaying the contents of &quot;TextFile.txt&quot; ... </FONT>
40: </H3>
41:
42: <%
43:
44: ' ### NOTE ###
45: ' You may have to modify the following statement based on the
46: ' directory structure of your system.
47:
48:   Set ReadStream = FileStreamObject.OpenTextFile ( _
49:    Server.MapPath ("/ASP/TYASPIn21Days/Chapter-04") _
50:     & "\TextFile.txt", 1)
51:
52:   While not ReadStream.AtEndOfStream
53:     Response.Write ReadStream.Readline
54:     If not ReadStream.AtEndOfStream Then
55:       ReadStream.SkipLine()
56:     End If
57:   Wend
58:   Set ReadStream=Nothing
59: %>
60:
61: <p></p>
62: <HR>
63:
64: This Web page was generated on <%= Date %> at <%= Time %>.
65:
66: </BODY>
67: </HTML>
```

4

ANALYSIS Line 18 defines an instance of `FileSystemObject`. This object is used by lines 29–31 to create a text file. Line 32 writes to the text file that is created and line 33 closes the text file. Lines 48–50 open the text file that was just created, and the `While...Wend` loop defined in lines 52–57 displays the contents of the text file.

> **Tip**
>
> `FileSystemObject` creates new files in the current directory. Chances are you do not know the current directory of your computer at any given time (try guessing your computer's current directory!). To avoid looking all over your hard drive(s) for files you create, use the `Server.MapPath()` method to specify a pathname in relation to the document root directory of your Web server. Refer to lines 30–31 of Listing 4.7 for an example of how the `Server.MapPath()` method is used to specify the path of the text file `TextFile.txt`.

FIGURE 4.19.

Output of the ASP application in Listing 4.6.

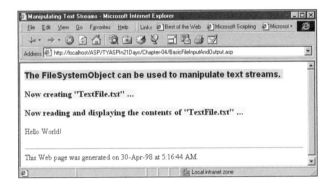

Summary

Data validation is an important aspect of building an ASP application. You should always validate information entered by users before processing it. ASP applications can easily validate almost any type of data, including numbers, dates, and time values, as well as strings. Consider using client-side scripting to compliment server-side data validation to make your user interfaces more efficient and user-friendly. Text streams can be manipulated in ASP applications through the use of the Text Stream component. Using the Text Stream component, you can create files on the server and then read them at a later time.

Q&A

Q Should you use ASCII mode or Unicode mode to create a regular text file?

A The ASCII mode is recommended for regular text files.

Q **Do I have to learn JavaScript if I want to add client-side data validation sub-routines?**

A Although it would certainly help if you learn JavaScript, you don't have to learn it to add simple client-side data validation subroutines to your Web forms. You can use a tool such as Microsoft FrontPage 98 that automatically generates client-side JavaScript code to validate data. You can also get freeware JavaScript data validation subroutines from the Web. Of course, you can use VBScript for client-side data validation. However, if you decide to do this, be aware that Netscape Navigator, which accounts for about 40%–50% of Web browsers in use today, does not support VBScript.

Q **When should I use a database and when should I use text files to store data?**

A Generally, when you need to store structured information (such as a user's contact information), use a database so that you can easily store and retrieve the data. On the other hand, if you are generating a report that will be e-mailed to the reader, it makes more sense to use a text file to create the report, e-mail the text file, and later delete it. Text files are great for temporary storage of text, and databases are more suitable for structured data storage.

Workshop

The quiz questions and exercises are provided for your further understanding. Please refer to Appendix A, "Answers to Questions," for the answers.

Quiz

1. Which ASP statements should you use to create a text file called `NumVisits.txt` if the file does not already exist?

2. How do you determine a leap year?

3. What dates are considered valid by the `IsDate()` function?

4. What are the benefits of building Web-based wizard-style user interfaces?

5. Which method of the `FileSystem` object can be used to append text?

Exercises

1. Modify the ASP application in Listing 4.1 so that a radio button is used to specify whether the application should display the values of HTML form data entry fields with null values. For example, as it is, if you do not fill in the first name before you submit the form, you see that data entry field listed in the table even though it

has no value. Modify the application so that you can use a radio button to toggle whether the ASP application displays data entry fields with null values.

2. Add additional data entry controls to the HTML form in Listing 4.1. Run the ASP application, fill in the data entry form, and submit it. Notice how the ASP application properly processes data submitted with the new data entry controls you added.

3. Modify the ASP application in Listing 4.2 so that it verifies that a valid number between 1 and 250 is entered by the user. (Hint: Add an If...Then...Else statement inside the If clause defined in line 32 of Listing 4.2.)

DAY **5**

Using Scriptlets to Componentize ASP Code

Today, you learn all about scriptlets and how you can use them in your ASP applications. This lesson covers the following topics:

- Learn about scriptlets.
- Understand the difference between server and client scriptlets.
- Discover the benefits of using scriptlets.
- Install support for scriptlets.
- Build your own scriptlet.
- Use the Microsoft Scriptlet Wizard.
- Incorporate scriptlets into ASP applications.

At the end of today's tutorial, you will be able to build your own scriptlets and use them in your ASP applications.

Introduction to Scriptlets

Scriptlets are self-contained code components you build with a familiar scripting language, such as VBScript, JavaScript, JScript, Perl (PERLScript and Pscript), Python, and ECMAScript. They are "non-compiled" Component Object Model (COM) components you build using a scripting language that supports the Microsoft ActiveX Scripting Interfaces.

 ECMAScript is a standard, general-purpose, cross-platform scripting language based on JScript 2.0 and JavaScript 1.1. JavaScript 3.1 supports the ECMAScript standard. For all the details about ECMA-262, the specification on which ECMAScript is based, visit the following URL:

```
http://www.ecma.ch/stand/ecma-262.htm
```

There are two main kinds of scriptlets: Server and Dynamic HTML scriptlets (DHTML scriptlets). *Server scriptlets* can be instantiated and used by ASP applications after they are properly registered on the Web server. This tutorial concentrates only on server scriptlets. *Dynamic HTML scriptlets* are used to create HTML-based controls that can be used in containers that support DHTML scriptlets, such as Microsoft Visual Basic 6.0 and Microsoft Internet Explorer 4.0.

Note

> Scriptlets use the server scriptlet runtime DLL found in the file `scrobj.dll`.

You have now been introduced to scriptlets and know that there are two different types. Before you go any further, it is important that you understand the difference between them, which is illustrated in the next section.

Difference Between Server and Client Scriptlets

The difference between server and client scriptlets is very simple. Server scriptlets are components that run on the Web server. Clients have no access to the code of server scriptlets. Client scriptlets, on the other hand, are executed on the client side. This section focuses only on server scriptlets and how to use them from within ASP code. You would run DHTML scriptlets on the client side and server scriptlets on the Web server.

Benefits of Using Scriptlets

Before developing scriptlets, it is important that you understand some of the benefits of using them. You can then make use of scriptlets to their full potential when developing ASP applications. Some of the benefits of developing scriptlets include the following:

- Centralized code management
- The black box model
- Mix-and-match programming languages
- Ease of alteration
- Code reuse
- Small and efficient to use
- Ease of distribution

Centralized Code Management

When business logic is implemented as an ASP component, you can centrally manage the business logic code without being concerned about everyone having access to the code's latest revision. When you make a change to a scriptlet's code, the next time it is instantiated by an ASP application, the newly modified code is used.

Scriptlets allow the developer to write commonly used ASP subroutines only once in the form of a scriptlet. When the subroutines are needed, the developer just needs to instantiate the scriptlet once to use its subroutines. This method saves time because the developer does not need to copy and paste a certain subroutine into every ASP page; instead, the developer can instantiate the scriptlet once and use the subroutines in the scriptlet anywhere.

The Black Box Model

NEW TERM Scriptlets support the *black box model*, which refers to an object that operates predictably and consistently when proper input is provided. An object implemented according to the black box model encapsulates features in the form of properties, methods, and events. The user need not know the code's internal implementation details. All the user needs to use the object is an understanding of its interfaces and how it processes input.

For example, to use a radar detector, the driver just needs to know how to turn it on and how to supply the power. The logic required to detect laser and radar from police speed-detection equipment is contained in the radar detector unit, and the user doesn't need to know how the technology works to use the device. Likewise, scriptlets hide details of

5

implementation from the user. All the user needs to know to use a scriptlet is what the scriptlet does and how to provide input. The logic required to process the input is contained in the scriptlet.

Mix-and-Match Programming Languages

Because any language capable of creating an ActiveX control can be used to develop a scriptlet, scriptlets can make the best use of features of many languages, such as VBScript, JavaScript/ECMAScript, Perl, and so on. This is a major benefit of using scriptlets; almost no other Web component development technology gives more freedom in selecting the language you use to develop custom components. See Listing 5.1 for an example of how to use multiple scripting languages in a scriptlet.

LISTING 5.1. HOW TO USE MULTIPLE SCRIPTING LANGUAGES IN A SCRIPTLET.

```
 1: <SCRIPTLET>
 2:
 3: <REGISTRATION
 4:     Description="Utilities Scriptlet"
 5:     ProgID="Scriptlet.Utilities"
 6:     Version="1"
 7:     ClassID="{2b8e29d0-fbbb-11d1-a8d4-00a0cc20afd1}">
 8:
 9: <SCRIPT LANGUAGE="VBScript">
10:
11:    Dim PropertyName1, InternalVariableName
12:
13:    Function Register()
14:      Msgbox "The Scriptlet.Utilities Scriptlet is " & _
15:                 "successfully registered."
16:         End Function
17:
18:         Function Unregister()
19:      Msgbox "The Scriptlet.Utilities Scriptlet is " & _
20:                 "successfully unregistered."
21:    End Function
22:
23: </SCRIPT>
24: </REGISTRATION>
25:
26: <IMPLEMENTS ID=automation TYPE=Automation>
27:    <PROPERTY NAME="UserName"/>
28:    <PROPERTY NAME="AccountBalance" INTERNALNAME="UserAccountBalance"/>
29:    <METHOD NAME="GetRandomNumber"/>
30:    <METHOD
31:        NAME="DateAndTime"
32:        INTERNALNAME="GetDateAndTime">
```

```
33:    </METHOD>
34: </IMPLEMENTS>
35:
36: <SCRIPT LANGUAGE="VBScript">
37:
38: Dim UserName, UserAccountBalance
39:
40: ' Initialize the properties
41: UserName = "Default User"
42: UserAccountBalance = 0
43:
44: ' ----------------------------------------------------------------
45:
46: Function GetRandomNumber (LowerBound,UpperBound)
47:
48:    Randomize ()
49:    GetRandomNumber = Int((upperbound-lowerbound+1) * Rnd + lowerbound)
50:
51: End Function
52:
53: ' ----------------------------------------------------------------
54:
55: </SCRIPT>
56:
57: <SCRIPT LANGUAGE="JavaScript">
58:
59: // ----------------------------------------------------------------
60:
61: Function GetDateAndTime () {
62:
63: // Create an object with the current date and time and
64: // specify the format of the date and time
65:
66:    dateObject = new Date("month day, year [hours:minutes:seconds]")
67:
68: // Return the date and time
69:    return dateObject.getDate()
70:
71: }
72:
73: // ----------------------------------------------------------------
74:
75: </SCRIPT>
76:
77: </SCRIPTLET>
```

5

ANALYSIS Lines 26–55 implement VBScript code, and lines 57–75 implement JavaScript code. Don't be confused about the rest of the code elements. They are explained to you shortly.

Ease of Alteration

Scriptlets can be easily modified when business formulas and conditions change. Think of an online storefront (which happens to sell ASP T-shirts) implemented with Active Server Pages. Every week, the store puts certain ASP T-shirts on sale. The percentage to subtract is calculated by using a business formula. If the formula is included in each ASP page, any slight change to the formula requires several pages to be updated. On the other hand, if the formula is contained in a scriptlet used by the ASP pages, it can be easily altered in one place. By their very nature, scriptlets promote and aid centralized code management.

Code Reuse

Scriptlets promote code reuse. If you find yourself using certain subroutines and functions over and over again, it is a good idea to combine all the ones you use frequently and create a scriptlet. You can then easily reuse your favorite subroutines and functions without having to hunt all over your hard drive for the source code.

Small and Efficient to Use

By building a scriptlet, you are actually creating a COM component that is both small and efficient. Scriptlets are ideal for performing middle-tier business logic, which includes manipulating database records.

> **Note**   Scriptlets are ideal for packing subroutines and functions you commonly use into small, efficient COM components.

Ease of Distribution

Scriptlets can be easily distributed after they are created. All that's required to use a scriptlet in a new computer after it is developed is to register the scriptlet on the new server. A scriptlet can be registered using either the command-line tool regsvr32.exe or the Microsoft Scriptlet Wizard. The next section explains how to install support for scriptlets.

Installing Support for Scriptlets

Downloading and installing support for scriptlets is very straightforward. First, visit the following Web page:

```
http://msdn.microsoft.com/scripting/default.htm?/scripting/scriptlets/
➥server/serverdown.htm
```

After downloading the Server Scriptlet Technology distribution file, execute it to install support for scriptlets. The installation wizard also installs the Microsoft Scriptlet Wizard for registering scriptlets you create. You are shown how to use the Microsoft Scriptlet Wizard at the end of today's lesson in the section "Using the Microsoft Scriptlet Wizard," but first, you will go step by step through building a scriptlet.

How to Build a Scriptlet

It is very easy to build a scriptlet. The following steps outline the process:

1. Locate the ASP code that will be in the scriptlet.

2. Create the scriptlet file and save it on your hard drive. Scriptlets end with the file extension .sct.

3. Register the scriptlet file on your computer.

 Note A scriptlet is actually a plain text file that you register using the Microsoft Scriptlet Wizard or the command-line utility regsvr32.exe.

4. That's it! You can now instantiate and use the scriptlet from within your ASP applications.

Now go through the steps, in more detail, of building an actual scriptlet and using it in an ASP application.

5

Building and Locating the Scriptlet's Code

The first step is to either build or locate the code that will be in the scriptlet. If the code already exists for the scriptlet's subroutines, simply locate the subroutines you want you use. Otherwise, you have to build the subroutines by yourself. The subroutines used in the scriptlet you're building today are provided for you in Listing 5.2. The scriptlet you create in this section uses the three functions GetRandomNumber(), GetLongDate(), and GetLongTime().

LISTING 5.2. ASP CODE OF THE SCRIPTLET YOU'RE CREATING.

```
 1: <% Option Explicit %>
 2: <!DOCTYPE HTML PUBLIC "-//W3C//DTD HTML 3.2 Final//EN">
 3:
 4: <HTML>
 5: <HEAD>
 6:    <TITLE>This file contains code of the scriptlet we create in Day
       ➥ 05</TITLE>
 7: </HEAD>
 8:
 9: <%
10:
11: ' ---------------------------------------------------------------
12:
13: Function GetRandomNumber(LowerBound,UpperBound)
14:
15:    Randomize()
16:    GetRandomNumber = Int((upperbound-lowerbound+1) * Rnd + lowerbound)
17:
18: End Function
19:
20: ' ---------------------------------------------------------------
21:
22: Function GetLongDate (DateToFormat)
23:
24:    GetLongDate = FormatDateTime (DateToFormat,1)
25:
26: End Function
27:
28: ' ---------------------------------------------------------------
29:
30: Function GetLongTime (TimeToFormat)
31:
32:    GetLongTime = FormatDateTime (TimeToFormat,3)
33:
34: End Function
35:
36: ' ---------------------------------------------------------------
37:
38: %>
39:
40: <BODY>
41:
42: Random Number = <%= GetRandomNumber (1,10) %><BR>
43: Long Date = <%= GetLongDate (Date) %><BR>
44: Long Time = <%= GetLongTime (Time) %><BR>
45:
46:
47: </BODY>
48: </HTML>
```

The code in Listing 5.2 is very simple. Lines 13–18 define a function that returns a random number between two given numbers. Notice how the `Randomize()` function is used in line 15 to *seed* the random number generator before the `Rnd()` function is used to get a random number. The two functions `GetLongDate()` and `GetLongTime()`, defined in Listing 5.2, use the function `FormatDateAndTime()` to format date and time values.

> **Note**
>
> Unlike humans, computers have a hard time wearing a tuxedo and picking a random number from a tall black hat with the wave of a magician's wand. Instead, they have to rely on a complex formula to generate pseudo-random numbers. Before generating a random number, you first have to seed the random number generator. By "seeding" it, you are planting an initial number in the random number generator that determines which numbers are returned each time you call the `Rnd()` function. A call to the `Randomize()` function without an argument seeds the random number generator with a number obtained from the system timer (internal clock).

Refer to Figure 5.1 for the output of the ASP application in Listing 5.2.

FIGURE 5.1.

Output of the functions in Listing 5.2.

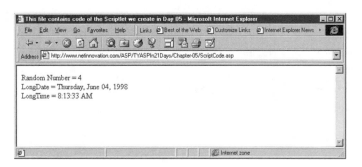

Creating the Scriptlet File

Now that you have the ASP code for the scriptlet you will be building shortly, the next step is actually creating the scriptlet's text file, which is an XML (Extensible Markup Language) file. An XML file is very much like an HTML file, but with additional elements that define how the scriptlet functions. Before you go ahead and create the scriptlet's text file, it is important you understand the syntax and format of elements of the scriptlet's XML file; they are defined in Table 5.1.

TABLE 5.1. ELEMENTS OF THE SCRIPTLET'S XML FILE.

Element	Description
SCRIPTLET	The SCRIPTLET element encloses the entire scriptlet.
REGISTRATION	The scriptlet's REGISTRATION element contains registration information, such as the scriptlet's PROGID, DESCRIPTION, VERSION, and CLSID. The information in the REGISTRATION element is used to register the scriptlet as a COM automation object.
IMPLEMENTS	The IMPLEMENTS element defines the COM interface handler used by the scriptlet. The COM interface handler determines the scriptlet's COM component type. Interfaces of the scriptlet you are creating (such as the scriptlet's properties, functions, and subroutines) are defined in the scriptlet's SCRIPT element.
SCRIPT	The SCRIPT element contains all the subroutines, functions, and properties implemented by the scriptlet. You can mix and match scripting languages by grouping subroutines written in different scripting languages in different SCRIPT elements.

Creating the SCRIPTLET Element

The SCRIPTLET element is easy to define because it simply encloses the entire code of the scriptlet. The first line of a scriptlet file is <SCRIPTLET> and the last line is </SCRIPTLET>. Listing 5.1 gives you an example of how the SCRIPTLET element is used.

Creating the REGISTRATION Element

Before a scriptlet can be instantiated in an ASP application, it has to be registered by an application that places the scriptlet's registration information in the Windows Registry. Refer to Listing 5.3 for the syntax of a scriptlet's REGISTRATION element.

LISTING 5.3. SYNTAX OF A SCRIPTLET'S REGISTRATION ELEMENT.

```
1: <REGISTRATION
2:   ProgID="ProgID"
3:   ClassID=GUID
4:   Description="Description"
5:   Version="Version" >
6: </REGISTRATION>
```

Simply replace the italicized placeholders in Listing 5.3 with the values in Table 5.2.

TABLE 5.2. ARGUMENTS OF THE SCRIPTLET'S REGISTRATION ELEMENT.

REGISTRATION *Element Arguments*	*Description*
ProgID	Specifies the name of the scriptlet; it's used by ASP applications to instantiate the scriptlet.
GUID	Specifies the scriptlet's Class ID. If you do not specify a Class ID, one is assigned. However, this is not recommended because each time you register the scriptlet, it then has a different Class ID complicating the task of maintaining different versions and scriptlet distribution. This is an optional argument.
Description	Contains the scriptlet's description. This is an optional argument.
Version	Contains the scriptlet's version number. This is an optional argument.

Note

When creating the REGISTRATION element, version numbers cannot contain decimal points.

Listing 5.4 shows the REGISTRATION element of the scriptlet you are building.

LISTING 5.4. THE REGISTRATION ELEMENT OF THE SCRIPTLET.

```
1: <REGISTRATION
2:     Description="Utilities Scriptlet"
3:     ProgID="Scriptlet.Utilities"
4:     Version="1"
5:     ClassID="{2b8e29d0-fbbb-11d1-a8d4-00a0cc20afd1}">
6: </REGISTRATION>
```

5

ANALYSIS You will not have any trouble understanding where the values in Listing 5.4 came from, with the exception of the Class ID value in line 5. The globally unique Class ID value was obtained using a command-line utility called uuidgen, as shown in Figure 5.2. You can simply cut and paste the result into the scriptlet's REGISTRATION element.

FIGURE 5.2.

The uuidgen
*command-line utility is
used to get a globally
unique Class ID.*

When you register the scriptlet later, it is convenient if the scriptlet lets you know whether it was successfully registered on the computer. You can implement two functions to inform you whether it was successful, as shown in Listing 5.5.

LISTING 5.5. RUNNING CODE DURING SCRIPTLET REGISTRATION AND UNREGISTRATION.

```
 1: <REGISTRATION
 2:    Description="Utilities Scriptlet"
 3:    ProgID="Scriptlet.Utilities"
 4:    Version="1"
 5:    ClassID="{2b8e29d0-fbbb-11d1-a8d4-00a0cc20afd1}">
 6:
 7: <SCRIPT LANGUAGE="VBScript">
 8:
 9:   Function Register()
10:     Msgbox "The Scriptlet.Utilities Scriptlet is " & _
11:        "successfully registered."
12:   End Function
13:
14:   Function Unregister()
15:     Msgbox "The Scriptlet.Utilities Scriptlet is " & _
16:        "successfully unregistered."
17:   End Function
18:
19: </SCRIPT>
20:
21: </REGISTRATION>
```

ANALYSIS The VBScript subroutine defined in lines 9–12 is executed when the scriptlet is successfully registered; the subroutine in lines 14–17 is executed when the scriptlet is successfully unregistered. You then see the dialog box generated by these subroutines when you register the scriptlet.

Creating the IMPLEMENTS Element to Define Properties and Methods

The IMPLEMENTS element is used to define the interface handler as well as properties and methods of a scriptlet. See Listing 5.6 for the syntax of a scriptlet method definition.

LISTING 5.6. THE SYNTAX OF A SCRIPTLET METHOD DEFINITION.

```
1: <IMPLEMENTS TYPE=Automation ID=automation>
2:    <METHOD
3:       NAME="NameOfPublicMethod"
4:       INTERNALNAME="InternalNameOfPublicMethod">
5:    </METHOD>
6: </IMPLEMENTS>
```

ANALYSIS   The public method defined in line 3 is used by ASP applications to invoke the scriptlet method specified in line 4. If the internal scriptlet method is the same as the public method defined in line 3, you do not have to specify the INTERNALNAME as shown in line 4. The INTERNALNAME argument is optional.

Listing 5.7 gives the syntax of a scriptlet property definition.

LISTING 5.7. THE SYNTAX OF A SCRIPTLET PROPERTY DEFINITION.

```
1: <IMPLEMENTS ID=automation TYPE=Automation>
2:    <PROPERTY NAME="PropertyName1"/>
3:    <PROPERTY NAME="PropertyName2" INTERNALNAME="InternalVariableName"/>
4: </IMPLEMENTS>
```

ANALYSIS   Scriptlet properties are defined as shown in lines 2 and 3. Scriptlet properties simply link an identifier to a variable contained in the scriptlet. If the variable's internal name is the same name as the public property name, you do not have to use the INTERNALNAME as shown in line 3. The INTERNALNAME argument is optional.

Defining scriptlet properties will be clearer after you see an example. Listing 5.8 shows an example that defines the methods and properties of the scriptlet you are building.

5

LISTING 5.8. HOW TO DEFINE THE METHODS AND PROPERTIES OF A SCRIPTLET.

```
 1: <IMPLEMENTS ID=automation TYPE=Automation>
 2:    <PROPERTY NAME="UserName"/>
 3:    <PROPERTY NAME="AccountBalance" INTERNALNAME="UserAccountBalance"/>
 4:    <METHOD NAME="GetRandomNumber"/>
 5:    <METHOD
 6:       NAME="LongTime"
 7:       INTERNALNAME="GetLongTime">
 8:    </METHOD>
 9:    <METHOD
10:       NAME="LongDate"
11:       INTERNALNAME="GetLongDate">
12:    </METHOD>
13: </IMPLEMENTS>
```

ANALYSIS Line 2 defines a property named `UserName`. Because an internal name is not specified, it is linked to a variable in the `SCRIPT` element by the same name. Line 3 defines a property named `AccountBalance` that is linked to the variable `UserAccountBalance` defined in the `SCRIPT` element. The methods of the scriptlet are defined in lines 4–12. The `GetRandomNumber()` method in line 4 is linked to the function `GetRandomNumber()` defined in the `SCRIPT` element. The `LongTime()` method in line 6 is explicitly linked to the function `GetLongTime()` defined in the `SCRIPT` element. The `LongDate()` method in line 10 is explicitly linked to the function `GetLongDate()` defined in the `SCRIPT` element.

Linking Scriptlet Properties to Functions

In the previous section, you learned how to link a scriptlet property to a variable defined in the `SCRIPT` element. You can also link a scriptlet property to a function defined in the `SCRIPT` element. Doing this allows you to have more control over how a property of the scriptlet can be modified at runtime.

Refer to Listing 5.9 for the syntax of a scriptlet property definition that uses functions.

LISTING 5.9. HOW TO DEFINE THE PROPERTIES OF A SCRIPTLET USING FUNCTIONS.

```
1: <IMPLEMENTS ID=automation TYPE=Automation>
2:    <PROPERTY
3:       NAME="NameOfProperty">
4:       <GET INTERNALNAME="getFunctionName"/>
5:       <PUT INTERNALNAME="putFunctionName"/>
6:    </PROPERTY>
7: </IMPLEMENTS>
```

ANALYSIS Line 3 defines the name of the property being created. Line 4 defines the function that handles requests to retrieve information contained in the property `NameOfProperty`. Line 5 defines the function that handles modifications to the property. The functions are defined outside the `IMPLEMENTS` element inside the scriptlet's `SCRIPT` element. The property value to be modified is passed to the function as an argument.

> **Tip**
> Link properties of scriptlets to functions to enforce the data integrity of scriptlet properties. If you expose a scriptlet variable as a property, anyone can modify it to any value he or she wants. If a function is used to modify a scriptlet variable, the function can ensure the integrity of the variable's data. For example, if the variable stores only integer values, a function can see to it that the user does not mistakenly try to assign a string value to the variable.

Creating the SCRIPT Element to Implement Properties and Methods

The SCRIPT element implements all the functions and properties of the scriptlet. Listing 5.10 shows the SCRIPT element of the scriptlet you are building.

LISTING 5.10. THE SCRIPT ELEMENT OF THE SCRIPTLET.

```
 1: <SCRIPT LANGUAGE="VBScript">
 2:
 3: Dim UserName, UserAccountBalance
 4:
 5: ' Initialize the properties
 6: UserName = "Default User"
 7: UserAccountBalance = 0
 8:
 9: ' -------------------------------------------------------------
10:
11: Function GetRandomNumber (LowerBound,UpperBound)
12:
13:    Randomize ()
14:    GetRandomNumber = Int((upperbound-lowerbound+1) * Rnd + lowerbound)
15:
16: End Function
17:
18: ' -------------------------------------------------------------
19:
20: Function GetLongDate (DateToFormat)
21:
22:    GetLongDate = FormatDateTime (DateToFormat,1)
23:
24: End Function
25:
26: ' -------------------------------------------------------------
27:
28: Function GetLongTime (TimeToFormat)
29:
30:    GetLongTime = FormatDateTime (TimeToFormat,3)
31:
32: End Function
33:
34: ' -------------------------------------------------------------
35:
36: </SCRIPT>
```

ANALYSIS The scripting language used by the code in the SCRIPT element is specified in line 1. The remainder of the code defines methods of the scriptlet.

The next section explains how to put together everything that you have covered so far.

5

Putting It All Together: The Utilities Scriptlet

The scriptlet is now ready for use. See Listing 5.11 for the scriptlet's complete source code. Save the scriptlet with the `.sct` extension. You will learn how to register the scriptlet in the next section.

LISTING 5.11. THE SCRIPTLET'S COMPLETE SOURCE CODE.

```
 1: <SCRIPTLET>
 2:
 3: <REGISTRATION
 4:     Description="Utilities Scriptlet"
 5:     ProgID="Scriptlet.Utilities"
 6:     Version="1"
 7:     ClassID="{2b8e29d0-fbbb-11d1-a8d4-00a0cc20afd1}">
 8:
 9: <SCRIPT LANGUAGE="VBScript">
10:
11:    Dim PropertyName1, InternalVariableName
12:
13:    Function Register()
14:      Msgbox "The Scriptlet.Utilities Scriptlet is " & _
15:                   "successfully registered."
16:         End Function
17:
18:         Function Unregister()
19:      Msgbox "The Scriptlet.Utilities Scriptlet is " & _
20:                   "successfully unregistered."
21:    End Function
22:
23: </SCRIPT>
24: </REGISTRATION>
25:
26: <IMPLEMENTS ID=automation TYPE=Automation>
27:    <PROPERTY NAME="UserName"/>
28:    <PROPERTY NAME="AccountBalance" INTERNALNAME="UserAccountBalance"/>
29:    <METHOD NAME="GetRandomNumber"/>
30:    <METHOD
31:       NAME="LongTime"
32:      INTERNALNAME="GetLongTime">
33:    </METHOD>
34:    <METHOD
35:       NAME="LongDate"
36:      INTERNALNAME="GetLongDate">
37:    </METHOD>
38: </IMPLEMENTS>
```

```
39:
40: <SCRIPT LANGUAGE="VBScript">
41:
42: Dim UserName, UserAccountBalance
43:
44: ' Initialize the properties
45: UserName = "Default User"
46: UserAccountBalance = 0
47:
48: ' ----------------------------------------------------------------
49:
50: Function GetRandomNumber (LowerBound,UpperBound)
51:
52:    Randomize ()
53:    GetRandomNumber = Int((upperbound-lowerbound+1) * Rnd + lowerbound)
54:
55: End Function
56:
57: ' ----------------------------------------------------------------
58:
59: Function GetLongDate (DateToFormat)
60:
61:    GetLongDate = FormatDateTime (DateToFormat,1)
62:
63: End Function
64:
65: ' ----------------------------------------------------------------
66:
67: Function GetLongTime (TimeToFormat)
68:
69:    GetLongTime = FormatDateTime (TimeToFormat,3)
70:
71: End Function
72:
73: ' ----------------------------------------------------------------
74:
75: </SCRIPT>
76:
77: </SCRIPTLET>
```

ANALYSIS Lines 3–24 define the scriptlet's REGISTRATION element, which contains information required to register the scriptlet on your computer. The IMPLEMENTS element of the scriptlet is defined in lines 26–38. Lines 40–75 (SCRIPT element) implement the properties and methods of the scriptlet defined in the IMPLEMENTS element.

> **Note**   Use the scriptlet you build today as a model when building your own scriptlets. Be sure to change the Class ID each time you create a different scriptlet, however!

The next section explains how to register the scriptlet file as a COM component.

Registering the Scriptlet File as a COM Component

Before attempting to register a scriptlet, you should have already downloaded and installed scriptlet support for Windows, as outlined in the section "Installing Support for Scriptlets." There are two ways you can register a scriptlet (actually three, if you count the Microsoft Scriptlet Wizard):

1. Locate the scriptlet file in Windows Explorer and select it. Right-click and choose Register. The scriptlet is now registered and ready to use.

2. Open a Windows command-prompt window and issue the following command to register the scriptlet:

   ```
   regsvr32 C:\PathOfScriptlet\ScriptletFilename.sct
   ```

When the scriptlet is successfully registered, you see the message box shown in Figure 5.3. This message box is generated by the SCRIPT code you added to the scriptlet's REGISTRATION element.

FIGURE 5.3.

The scriptlet is successfully registered.

After the scriptlet is successfully registered, the message box in Figure 5.4 is displayed by RegSvr32 as a confirmation.

FIGURE 5.4.

The confirmation message displayed by RegSvr32.

Now that you have registered your scriptlet file, it's time to use it from within an ASP application. The next section goes over how to use a scriptlet in an ASP application.

Using Scriptlets in ASP Applications

After you create a scriptlet, you can use it from within any ASP application by instantiating it with the `CreateObject` function if you use VBScript or the new `ActiveXObject` function if you use JScript. The ASP application in Listing 5.11 illustrates how to instantiate and use the scriptlet you just built. Refer to Figure 5.5 for the output of the ASP application.

FIGURE 5.5.

Output of the ASP application.

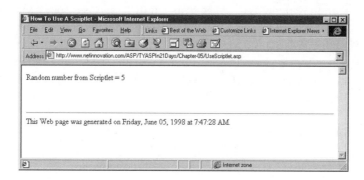

LISTING 5.11. INSTANTIATING AND USING THE SCRIPTLET.

```
 1: <!DOCTYPE HTML PUBLIC "-//W3C//DTD HTML 3.2 Final//EN">
 2:
 3: <HTML>
 4: <HEAD>
 5:     <TITLE>How To Use A Scriptlet</TITLE>
 6: </HEAD>
 7: <BODY>
 8:
 9: <%
10:   Set UtilitiesScriptlet = CreateObject ("Scriptlet.Utilities")
11:         Response.Write "Random number from Scriptlet = " & _
12:             UtilitiesScriptlet.GetRandomNumber(1,10)
13: %>
14:
15: <P> </P>
16: <HR>
17:
18: This Web page was generated on
19: <%= UtilitiesScriptlet.LongDate(Date) %> at
20: <%= UtilitiesScriptlet.LongTime(Time) %>.
21:
22: </BODY>
23: </HTML>
```

5

ANALYSIS An instance of the scriptlet is created in line 10 by using the `CreateObject()` function. Lines 11, 12, 19, and 20 demonstrate how to use the scriptlet's methods.

Using the Microsoft Scriptlet Wizard

Now that you know how to create a scriptlet by yourself, it's time to explore how the Microsoft Scriptlet Wizard can help you with this task. You can invoke the Microsoft Scriptlet Wizard from the Windows Start menu by choosing Programs, Microsoft Server Scriptlets, Microsoft Scriptlet Wizard. You then see the dialog box shown in Figure 5.6. Use it to supply general information about the scriptlet you are creating, such as the name, filename, prog ID, version, and location of the scriptlet file you are creating. When you're done, click the Next button.

FIGURE 5.6.

The Microsoft Scriptlet Wizard gets general information about the scriptlet.

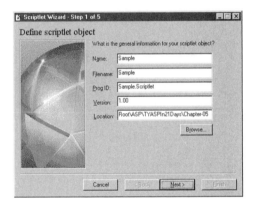

The next step is specifying characteristics of the scriptlet, using the dialog box in Figure 5.7. Select the options for creating a server scriptlet that uses VBScript. Click the Next button to continue.

FIGURE 5.7.

Characteristics of the scriptlet are specified.

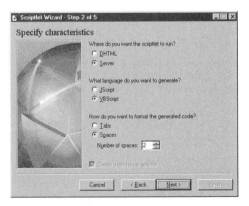

Use the dialog box in Figure 5.8 to define properties of the scriptlet. As you can see, the
Microsoft Scriptlet Wizard makes it a breeze to add properties to a scriptlet. Click the
Next button to continue.

FIGURE 5.8.

*Defining properties of
the scriptlet.*

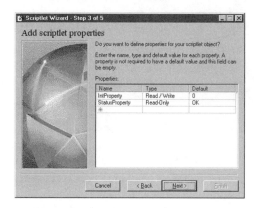

Use the dialog box in Figure 5.9 to define methods of the scriptlet. Of course, you have
to type in the methods' actual code. However, Microsoft Scriptlet Wizard makes your
task easier by creating a skeleton scriptlet that is waiting for you to add code.

FIGURE 5.9.

*Defining methods of
the scriptlet.*

5

The Microsoft Scriptlet Wizard now has all the information it needs to create a scriptlet
for you. It shows a summary of the settings you selected for the scriptlet (see Figure
5.10). Go over the summary of information displayed, and click the Finish button.

FIGURE 5.10.

Summary of settings for the scriptlet.

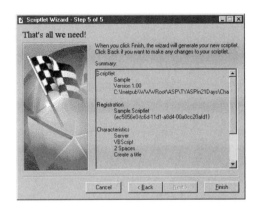

The Microsoft Scriptlet Wizard creates a scriptlet and displays the message box shown in Figure 5.11. All you have to do now is add your code to the scriptlet.

FIGURE 5.11.

The scriptlet is successfully created.

Refer to Listing 5.13 for the code created by the Microsoft Scriptlet Wizard.

LISTING 5.13. CODE CREATED BY THE MICROSOFT SCRIPTLET WIZARD.

```
 1: <SCRIPTLET>
 2:
 3: <REGISTRATION
 4:   Description="Sample"
 5:   ProgID="Sample.Scriptlet"
 6:   Version="1.00"
 7:   ClassID="{ec5856e0-fc6d-11d1-a8d4-00a0cc20afd1}"
 8: >
 9: </REGISTRATION>
10:
11: <IMPLEMENTS id=Automation type=Automation>
12:   <property name=IntProperty>
13:     <get/>
14:     <put/>
15:   </property>
16:   <property name=StatusProperty>
17:     <get/>
18:   </property>
19:   <method name=GetNumber>
20:   </method>
```

```
21:    <method name=GetString>
22:    </method>
23: </IMPLEMENTS>
24:
25: <SCRIPT language=VBScript>
26:
27: dim IntProperty
28: IntProperty = 0
29: dim StatusProperty
30: StatusProperty = "OK"
31:
32: function get_IntProperty()
33:    get_IntProperty = IntProperty
34: end function
35:
36: function put_IntProperty(newValue)
37:    IntProperty = newValue
38: end function
39:
40: function get_StatusProperty()
41:    get_StatusProperty = StatusProperty
42: end function
43:
44: function GetNumber()
45:    GetNumber = "Temporary Value"
46: end function
47:
48: function GetString()
49:    GetString = "Temporary Value"
50: end function
51:
52: </SCRIPT>
53: </SCRIPTLET>
```

5

ANALYSIS A Class ID is automatically generated for your scriptlet in line 7. Notice how you need to add code to the functions defined in lines 44–46 and 48–50.

Where to Go for Additional Information About Scriptlets

There are many resources on the Internet you can use to learn more about scriptlets and other Web scripting technologies. Visit and bookmark the URLs mentioned in the following sections so you can keep up-to-date with the latest scripting technologies.

Microsoft Scripting Technologies Web Site

The Microsoft Scripting Technologies Web site is a great place to start for learning all about scripting technologies. Topics covered include VBScript, JScript, scriptlets, remote scripting, Windows Scripting Host, and script debugging. I strongly recommend that you make it a point to keep an eye on the following URL:

```
http://www.microsoft.com/scripting/
```

Microsoft's Scriptlet Web Site

Visit the following Web page on Microsoft's Web site for additional information about scriptlets:

```
http://www.microsoft.com/msdn/sdk/inetsdk/help/scriptlets/scrlt.htm
```

Newsgroups About Scripting

Microsoft has established the newsgroups in Table 5.3 to discuss issues and questions about scripting. You can access these newsgroups by pointing your favorite newsgroup reading application to `msnews.microsoft.com`.

TABLE 5.3. NEWSGROUPS ABOUT SCRIPTING.

Purpose of Newsgroup	Newsgroup Name
Remote Scripting	`microsoft.public.scripting.remote`
VBScript	`microsoft.public.scripting.vbscript`
JScript	`microsoft.public.scripting.jscript`
Microsoft Scripting Host	`microsoft.public.scripting.wsh`
Scriptlets	`microsoft.public.scripting.scriptlets`

Summary

Scriptlets are self-contained code components you build with a familiar scripting language, such as VBScript, JavaScript, or any other scripting language that supports the Microsoft ActiveX Scripting Interfaces. At the time of this writing, you can use over half a dozen scripting languages to build scriptlets. They are an evolving technology you can expect to see incorporated into future Microsoft applications and technologies.

Q&A

Q **When I can use subroutines in an ASP file with server-side includes, why should I bother with scriptlets?**

A Scriptlets allow the developer to write commonly used ASP subroutines only once in the form of a scriptlet. When the subroutines are needed, the developer just needs to instantiate the scriptlet once to use its subroutines anywhere in the scriptlet. This method saves time because the developer does not need to copy and paste a certain subroutine into every ASP page. Scriptlets are ideal for packing subroutines and functions you commonly use into small, efficient COM components.

Q **What happens if you do not call the `Randomize()` function before requesting random numbers?**

A If you do not seed the random number generator with the `Randomize()` function, the "random" numbers you get will be the same each time.

Q **Why should I go to the trouble of implementing `Register()` and `Unregister()` functions in the `REGISTRATION` element of a scriptlet?**

A When you register a scriptlet, it is convenient if the scriptlet can let you know whether it was successfully registered on the computer. This is the purpose of the `Register()` and `Unregister()` functions.

Workshop

The quiz questions and exercises are provided for your further understanding. Please refer to Appendix A, "Answers to Questions," for the answers to the quiz questions; answers to the exercises are on the MCP Web site.

5

Quiz

1. Name three languages you can use to build scriptlets.
2. Name two ways in which you can register a scriptlet as a COM component.
3. Scriptlets end with what file extension?
4. How can you instantiate a scriptlet from within an ASP application if you use VBScript or JScript?
5. Why is it recommended that you do not have a Class ID value automatically assigned by the scriptlet registration program each time the scriptlet is registered?
6. What is ECMAScript?
7. Name two applications that support DHTML scriptlets.

8. Are VBScript and JScript the only two languages you can use to build scriptlets?

9. What is the purpose of the IMPLEMENTS element of a scriptlet definition?

10. What is the purpose of the SCRIPT element?

Exercises

1. Create a scriptlet with two properties. The first one, CurrentStatus, is a read-only property with a default value of "Ready". The second one, MessageToDisplay, is a read-write property with a default value of "Hello World".

2. Browse the Microsoft scriptlets newsgroup to learn what's new and how other people are using scriptlets.

3. Build your own scriptlet containing code from functions and subroutines you have previously written.

DAY 6

Getting Information About HTTP Requests with the Request Object

You have already used the Request object to get data entered by users in an HTML form. Today, you cover the Request object in more detail and learn how its methods, collections, and properties can be used to build Web applications. Today you cover the following:

- Use ASP objects in ASP applications.
- Access the values of server variables.
- Find the values of HTML form data entry fields.
- Examine variables in the HTTP QueryString.
- Find the values of client-side cookies.

Using the `Request` Object

When users connect to a Web server and request a document that is an ASP application, certain information about that transaction is available to the ASP application through the `Request` object. It's important that you become familiar with the `Request` object because you will be using it extensively in the ASP applications you build. Almost all the interaction that takes place between the Web browser and your ASP application is funneled through the `Request` object, which has the following applications:

- Determining which Web browser is used
- Getting data in an HTML form
- Determining values of cookies
- Finding out information about the Web server software
- Determining the IP address of the Web browser

You do not have to do anything special before using the `Request` object. Here is its syntax:

`Request.[collection¦property¦method]`

Table 6.1 lists the collections of the `Request` object.

NEW TERM   A *collection* is an object containing an assortment of values of a certain object. For example, the `Form` collection of the `Request` object contains data entered in an HTML form.

TABLE 6.1. COLLECTIONS OF THE `Request` OBJECT.

Collection Name	Purpose
Cookies	Can be used to get the value of a client-side cookie.
Form	Used to get the values of HTML form variables that are submitted to an ASP application with the POST method.
QueryString	Used to get the values of HTML form variables that are submitted to an ASP application with the GET method.
ServerVariables	Used to get the values of server variables with information about the current HTTP transaction.

Accessing the Values of Form Variables

It is very easy to access the value of an HTML form variable by using the `Request` object. Figure 6.1 illustrates how HTML form data can be submitted to an ASP application.

Figure 6.1.

How HTML form data is processed.

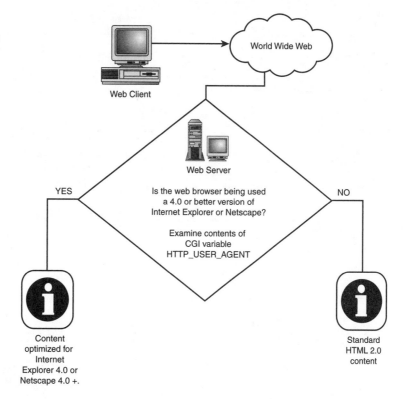

In the ancient days of Web application development (which translates to about two years ago), Web application developers had to go to the trouble of parsing complex strings to get values of HTML form variables. Thanks to the Request object, all you have to do is examine either the Request.Form or Request.QueryString collection to determine the value of an HTML form variable. Both of these collections support the methods Count and Item().

Count returns the number of elements currently in the collection. For example, if a form contains three data entry fields and a submit button, Request.Form.Count or Request.QueryString.Count will return 4, depending on how the form is submitted to the ASP application.

6

Note

You might wonder why Request.Form.Count would return the number 4 for a form containing only three data entry fields. That's because the form's submit button is also considered a data entry field.

The Item() method is used to get the value of a form data entry field. For example, the following ASP statements both return the value of the HTML data entry field "ZipCode". The ASP statement you use depends on the submit method of the HTML form.

```
Request.QueryString.Item("ZipCode")
Request.Form.Item("ZipCode")
```

 Note You'll see that both the QueryString and the Form collections are used with the Request object. You use QueryString when the form was submitted with GET, and you should use Form when the form is submitted with PUT.

Accessing Data Sent with the POST Method

When getting data from forms, most often you use the POST method and the Form collection of the Request object. The POST method is a more elegant way of submitting data from an HTML form to an ASP application because the data in the HTML form is not added to the URL of the ASP application defined in the form's ACTION argument. The following syntax is used to get values of the Request.Form collection:

```
Request.Form(element)[(index)¦.Count]
```

The placeholder *element* simply refers to the name of an HTML form data entry field whose value you want to examine. For example, the following ASP statement displays the value of the HTML form variable "UserName".

```
<%= Request.Form("UserName") %>
```

 Note Use the POST method to submit data from an HTML form to your ASP application. Avoid using the GET method unless you have a special reason because the GET method imposes a restriction of about 2044 bytes on the length of data.

If an element has more than one data value, those data values can be accessed by using the *index* placeholder, which can take any integer value between 1 and the number of elements in the data field. You can get the total number of elements in the data field by using Request.Form(*element*).Count. The following statement returns the number of data values for the HTML form variable called "UserSelections":

```
Request.Form("UserSelections").Count
```

Tip   Use `Request.Form(element).Count` to determine if the user has selected more than one item in a drop-down selection list that allows selecting multiple items. Use the name of the drop-down selection list variable in place of `element`.

If a form element, such as a multiselect list box, passes multiple items, you can access each item by its index. For example, `request.form("colors")(1)` would access the first item in the Colors list box.

Accessing Values in an HTTP Query String

When an HTML form is submitted to an ASP application by using the GET method, the form's data is actually added to the end of the URL of the ASP application.

Caution   Do not use the GET method if you expect the data entered by the user to exceed about 1,000 characters. Using the GET method to get large amounts of data via an HTML form could cause undesired results.

The ASP application in Listing 6.1 demonstrates how to use the `Request.QueryString` collection.

LISTING 6.1. USING THE `Request.QueryString` COLLECTION.

```
 1: <%@ LANGUAGE=VBScript %>
 2: <HTML>
 3: <HEAD>
 4:
 5: <TITLE>Get Method Demo</TITLE>
 6: </HEAD>
 7: <BODY>
 8:
 9: <P><STRONG><FONT face="Comic Sans MS" size=5
10: style="BACKGROUND-COLOR: #adff2f">Get Method
11: Demo</FONT></STRONG></P>
12: <%
13:    If Request.QueryString.Count = 0 Then
14: %>
15:
16: <P>This ASP application demonstrates how to submit data to
17: an ASP application using the GET method.</P>
```

6

continues

LISTING 6.1. CONTINUED

```
18:
19: <P><FORM method=get action=GetMethodDemo.asp
20:   id=DataEntryForm name=DataEntryForm>
21: Please enter your name <INPUT id=UserName name=UserName ><BR>
22: Please enter the date
23: <INPUT value="<%= Date %>"
24:   id=UserDate name=UserDate><BR>
25: <BR>
26: <INPUT type=submit value="Submit Form" id=SubmitButton
27:   name=SubmitButton>
28:
29: </FORM></P>
30: <%
31:   Else %>
32: <P><FONT style="BACKGROUND-COLOR: #ffffe0"> <FONT
33:   style="BACKGROUND-COLOR: #f0e68c">Thanks for filling in the HTML
34:   form!You entered the following data:</FONT></FONT></P>
35:
36: You filled in a total of <%= Request.QueryString.Count %> data
37: entry fields:<BR><BR>
38:
39: <%
40: For Each FormItem in Request.QueryString
41:   Response.Write FormItem & " = " & _
42:     Request.QueryString.Item(FormItem) & "<BR>"
43: Next
44: %>
45:
46: <%
47:   End If
48: %>
49:
50: <P><HR></P>
51:
52: <P>This Web page was generated on <%= Date %> at <%= Time %>.<BR>
53: <A href="getMethodDemo.asp">Restart this application</A>.</P>
54: </BODY>
55: </HTML>
```

ANALYSIS   When the ASP application is executed, line 13 checks whether the HTML data
            entry form has been filled in. If it has not, the If statement executes lines 13–29
to display the data entry form shown in Figure 6.2.

After the data entry form is submitted to the ASP application, the Else clause defined in
lines 32–47 is executed. Refer to Figure 6.3 and notice how the data entered by the user
is actually made part of the URL of the ASP application. A For...Next loop is used in
lines 40–43 to display the data of the form variables.

FIGURE 6.2.

The form is filled in.

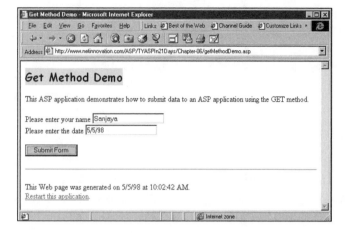

FIGURE 6.3.

Information in the HTML form is processed by the ASP application.

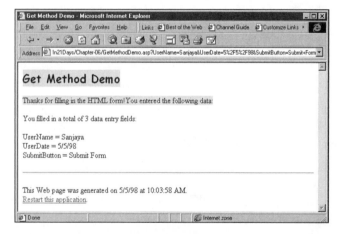

Do	Don't
DO use the POST method instead.	**DON'T** use the GET method to send large amounts of data to your ASP application.

6

Accessing Server Variables

Each time an ASP application is executed, the Web server creates environment variables that contain information about the server, the browser, and how the ASP application is being invoked. This section discusses useful server variables that can be accessed by ASP scripts. By accessing these variables, ASP scripts get useful information about the current

HTTP transaction. After you read the following discussion about environment variables, you learn how to find their values from an ASP application.

> **Tip**
>
> When accessing environment variables or supplying them to ASP scripts, use all uppercase letters. ASP responds to lowercase environment variables; however, it is good practice to use uppercase to help differentiate server variables.

Accessing Server Variables from ASP Applications

ASP applications can easily access server variables by using the `ServerVariables()` method of the `Request` object. Here is the syntax of this method:

```
Request.ServerVariables("NameOfServerVariableName")
```

 Server variables are special variables available to applications executed on the Web server. They are instrumental in getting additional information about an HTTP transaction, such as the IP address of the user, the IP address of the Web server, and so on. *Server variables* and *CGI variables* refer to the same thing.

NameOfServerVariableName can be replaced with any of the CGI variables discussed in the following section. For example, the following command can be used to determine the value of the `SERVER_SOFTWARE` variable:

```
Request.ServerVariables ("SERVER_SOFTWARE")
```

> **Caution**
>
> Depending on how the ASP script is invoked, some environment variables are not available in some cases.

Listing 6.1 demonstrated how an ASP application can display all the available server variable values. The application in Listing 6.2 simply uses the `Request.ServerVariables()` method to display the values of server variables. See Figure 6.4 for the output of the ASP script in Listing 6.2.

LISTING 6.2. ACCESSING SERVER VARIABLES FROM ASP APPLICATIONS.

```
1: <%@ LANGUAGE="VBSCRIPT" %>
2: <!DOCTYPE HTML PUBLIC "-//IETF//DTD HTML//EN">
3: <html>
4:
```

```
 5: <head>
 6: <meta http-equiv="Content-Type"
 7: content="text/html; charset=iso-8859-1">
 8: <title>Accessing Values of Server Variables</title>
 9: </head>
10:
11: <body bgcolor="#FFFFFF">
12:
13: <p><font color="#FF0000" face="Comic Sans MS"><Strong>
14: Server Variables can be used to get information about the
15: current HTTP session.
16: </Strong></font></p>
17:
18: <div align="left">
19:
20: <table border="4" width="400">
21:     <tr>
22:         <td width="100" bgcolor="#000000"><font color="#FFFFFF">
23:         <strong>Server Variable</strong></font></td>
24:         <td bgcolor="#000000"><font color="#FFFFFF">
25:         <strong>Value of Server Variable</strong></font></td>
26:     </tr>
27: <%
28:       Dim LoopCount
29:       LoopCount = 0
30:
31:       For Each ServerVariable In Request.ServerVariables
32:       LoopCount = LoopCount + 1
33:       If LoopCount Mod 2 = 0 Then
34: %>
35:         <TR><td bgcolor="#FFDDBB">
36:           <%= ServerVariable %>
37:         </td>
38:         <td bgcolor="#FFDDBB">
39:           <%= Request.ServerVariables(ServerVariable) %>
40:         </td></TR>
41: <%      Else %>
42:         <TR><td bgcolor="#E3FFB0">
43:           <%= ServerVariable %>
44:         </td>
45:         <td bgcolor="#E3FFB0">
46:           <%= Request.ServerVariables(ServerVariable) %>
47:         </td></TR>
48: <%      End If
49:         Next %>
50: </table>
51: </div>
52:
53: <hr>
54:
```

6

continues

LISTING 6.2. CONTINUED

```
55: <p>
56: This Web page was generated on <%= Date %> at <%= Time %>.
57: </p>
58: </body>
59: </html>
```

ANALYSIS The For...Each...Next loop defined in lines 31–49 of Listing 6.2 displays the values of the server variables by using Request.ServerVariables() method. The application does not need to know the names of server variables in advance. The For...Each loop defined in line 31 uses the ServerVariables collection of the Request object to iterate through all the available server variables. Notice how the LoopCount variable is used inside the loop to create a table with alternating background colors (see the table in Figure 6.4). To look at the complete list of server variables, execute the ASP application in the directory \Chapter-06\ServerVariables.asp.

FIGURE 6.4.

Output of the ASP application in Listing 6.2.

Server Variables Available to ASP Applications

This section examines several server variables that are useful when developing ASP applications. Refer to Table 6.2 to find out which server variables are covered in today's lesson.

TABLE 6.2. SERVER VARIABLES COVERED TODAY.

Name of Server Variable	Purpose
CONTENT_TYPE	MIME content type of data
HTTP_ACCEPT	MIME types supported by the Web browser
GATEWAY_INTERFACE	CGI revision number supported by the Web server
HTTP_USER_AGENT	Web browser used to call the ASP script
PATH_INFO	Options passed to ASP script
PATH_TRANSLATED	Absolute pathname of ASP script
QUERY_STRING	Input passed to ASP application
REMOTE_ADDR	IP address of Web browser
REMOTE_HOST	DNS lookup of client's IP address (if the Web server is configured to automatically do DNS lookups)
REQUEST_METHOD	Method used to call ASP application
SCRIPT_NAME	ASP script name in relation to the Web server's document root directory
SERVER_NAME	Web server's domain name
SERVER_PORT	Port of the Web server
SERVER_PROTOCOL	The HTTP version supported by the Web server
SERVER_SOFTWARE	Determine the name of the Web server software

MIME Content Type of Data (CONTENT_TYPE)

MIME content types are used to label types of objects (HTML files, Microsoft Word files, GIF files, and so on). The MIME content type for data being submitted to the ASP script is stored in CONTENT_TYPE. For example, if data is submitted to an ASP script by using the GET method, CONTENT_TYPE contains the value application/x-www-form-urlencoded. This is because responses to the form are encoded according to URL specifications.

MIME Types Supported by Web Browser (HTTP_ACCEPT)

Web clients can handle different MIME types, which are described in the HTTP_ACCEPT variable. MIME types accepted by the Web client calling the ASP application appear as a list separated by commas. This list takes the format type/subtype, type/subtype. For example, if the Web client supports GIF and JPEG image types, the HTTP_ACCEPT variable contains the items image/gif, image/jpeg.

6

CGI Revision Number (GATEWAY_INTERFACE)

The CGI specification revision number is stored in the GATEWAY_INTERFACE environment variable. The format of this variable is CGI/*revision*. By examining this variable, an ASP application can determine what version of CGI the Web server is using. This variable is particularly useful if your ASP application uses newer CGI specifications and you need to verify that the Web server supports the new CGI specification. For example, the CGI 1.1 specification supports HTTP Keep Alive, a feature that allows the connection between the Web server and Web browser to remain open for a certain time period after an HTTP transaction has been completed. This feature enhances the performance of subsequent HTTP requests. Another feature of CGI is the ability to send files from the Web browser to the Web server. If an ASP script uses a special feature supported by a certain version of CGI, the ASP script can check the CGI version used by the Web server before attempting to use that feature.

Web Browser Used (HTTP_USER_AGENT)

By examining this value, the Web browser being used by the client can be determined. For example, if Internet Explorer 4.01 is being used on a Windows NT computer, the HTTP_USER_AGENT variable contains the value Mozilla/4.0 (compatible; MSIE 4.01; Windows NT). The general format of this variable is *software/version library/ version*.

> **Tip**
>
> The Web Browser Capabilities component can be used to determine specific features of a Web browser. Day 9, "Using ActiveX Components Built for ASP," covers the Web Browser Capabilities component.
>
> Although you can use the HTTP_USER_AGENT variable to determine which Web browser is being used, it does not tell you much about the browser's capabilities (such as whether it supports tables, Java, dynamic HTML, and so forth). This is where the Web Browser Capabilities component comes in handy. You can use it to find out exactly what features are supported by the Web browser whose identity you determine with the HTTP_USER_AGENT variable.

Options Passed to ASP Script (PATH_INFO)

The PATH_INFO variable is generally used to pass options/input to an ASP program. These options follow the script's URL. Clients can invoke ASP scripts with additional information after the URL of the ASP script. PATH_INFO always contains the string that was used to call the ASP script after the name of the ASP script. For example, PATH_INFO has the value /These/Are/The/Arguments if the ASP script FunWithNT.ASP is called with the URL http://your_server.your_domain/cgi-bin/ FunWithNT.ASP/These/Are/The/Arguments.

Absolute Pathname of ASP Script (PATH_TRANSLATED)

If the ASP script needs to know its absolute pathname, it can get this information from the PATH_TRANSLATED variable. For example, if the ASP script being invoked is HelloNTWorld.ASP, the ASP script is physically located at H:\www\http\ ns-home\root\cgi-bin, and the ASP script is accessed with the URL

http://your_server.your_domain/root/cgi-bin/HelloNTWorld.ASP

then PATH_TRANSLATED contains this value:

H:\www\http\ns-home\root\cgi-bin\HelloNTWorld.ASP

If the ASP program needs to save or access any temporary files in its home directory, the ASP program can examine the PATH_TRANSLATED variable to determine its absolute location.

Input Passed to ASP Application (QUERY_STRING)

You might have noticed that when you submit certain forms, a string of characters appears after a question mark, followed by the URL name of the script being called. This string of characters is referred to as the *query string*, and contains everything after the question mark. When an ASP script is called with the GET method, QUERY_STRING typically contains variables and their values as entered by the person who filled in the form. QUERY_STRING is sometimes used by search engines to examine the input when a form is submitted for a keyword search. For example, if an ASP application is executed using the URL

http://www.server.com/cgi-bin/application.asp?WindowsNT=Fun

then QUERY_STRING contains the string WindowsNT=Fun.

IP Address of Client (REMOTE_ADDR)

The IP address of the client that called the ASP program is stored in the REMOTE_ADDR environment variable. For security reasons, the value of this variable should never be used for user authentication purposes. It's not hard to trick your Web server into believing a client is connecting from a false IP address. Refer to Day 18, "Building in Security," for information on authenticating users.

DNS Lookup of Client's IP Address (REMOTE_HOST)

If the Web server performs a DNS lookup of the client's IP address and finds its alias, the REMOTE_HOST variable contains that alias. Some Web servers allow DNS lookups to be turned on or off. If you plan to use this variable to find the IP address alias of clients, be

6

sure the DNS lookup option is turned on. The Web server can find the IP address alias of most, but not all, clients. If the Web server cannot find a cient's IP address alias, the REMOTE_HOST variable is not assigned the client's DNS alias value; it just contains the client's IP address. This value should never be used for user authentication purposes.

Method Used to Call an ASP Application (REQUEST_METHOD)

A client can call an ASP script in a number of ways; the method used is stored in the REQUEST_METHOD variable. This variable can have a value such as HEAD, POST, GET, or PUT.

Script Name in Relation to Document Root (SCRIPT_NAME)

All files on a Web server are usually referenced in relation to their document root directory. SCRIPT_NAME contains the virtual pathname of the script called in relation to the document root directory. For example, if the document root directory is c:\www\http\ns-home\root, all ASP scripts are stored in c:\www\http\ns-home\root\cgi-bin\, and if the ASP script HelloNTWorld.asp is called, the SCRIPT_NAME variable contains the value \cgi-bin\HelloNTWorld.asp. The advantage of this variable is that it allows the ASP script to refer to itself. This is handy if, somewhere in the output, the script's URL needs to be made into a hypertext link.

Web Server Domain Name (SERVER_NAME)

The domain name of the Web server that invoked the ASP script is stored in SERVER_NAME. This domain name can be an IP address or DNS alias. The SERVER_NAME variable can be used by ASP applications to construct self-referring URLs with the Web server name.

Port of Web Server (SERVER_PORT)

Typically, Web servers listen to HTTP requests on port 80. However, a Web server can listen to any port that's not in use by another application. An ASP program can determine at what port the Web server is handling HTTP requests by looking at the value of the SERVER_PORT environment variable. When you display self-referencing hypertext links at runtime by examining the contents of SERVER_NAME, be sure to append the port number of the Web server (typically port 80) by concatenating it with the value of SERVER_PORT.

Web Server's HTTP Version (SERVER_PROTOCOL)

Web servers speak the Hypertext Transport Protocol (HTTP) language. You can determine which version of HTTP the Web server is using by examining the SERVER_PROTOCOL environment variable, which contains the name and revision data of the protocol being used. This information is in the format *protocol/revision*. For example, if the server speaks HTTP 1.0, this variable has the value HTTP/1.0.

Name of Web Server (SERVER_SOFTWARE)

The name of the Web server that invoked the ASP script is stored in the SERVER_SOFTWARE environment variable, which is in the format *name/version*. If an ASP script is designed to use special capabilities of a Web server (such as IIS), the ASP script can determine what Web server is being used by examining this variable before those special capabilities are used.

Accessing Values of Client-Side Cookies

Cookies can be used to store data on the user's computer for future reference. The Cookies collection of the Request object can be used to get the values of cookies stored in the user's computer. Cookies are set by using the Response object; you learn how to do this in Day 7, "Customizing HTTP Responses with the Response Object."

Note

> Although today you are shown how to use the Cookies collection, this topic is covered in more detail in Day 13, "Retaining Information Between Sessions Using Cookies." You should already be familiar with the Form and QueryString collections, which were covered in Day 3, "Interacting with Your Users."

This is the syntax of the Cookies collection, for getting the values of cookies:

```
Request.Cookies(NameOfCookie)[SubKey]
```

To get the value of the cookie LastVisit, you would use the ASP statement Request.Cookies("LastVisit"). Cookies can have some keys. The statement Request.Cookies("LastVisit").HasKeys can be used to determine if the cookie LastVisit has any subkeys (such as LastVisitTime, LastVisitDate, and so forth).

Summary

Today you learned that the Request object can be used to get information about the current HTTP transaction. By accessing properties, methods, and collections of the Request object, you can get data in HTML forms, cookies, server-side variables, client-side certificates, and more.

6

Q&A

Q Isn't ASP a replacement for CGI?

A Yes and no. It depends on how you define CGI. The CGI specification is actually very useful. However, ASP offers Web developers a more streamlined and easier environment for creating Web applications.

Q Which method is recommended for submitting data from HTML forms to an ASP script?

A The POST method is recommended for submitting data from HTML forms to an ASP script. The GET method creates a QueryString of information appended to the URL and has a size limitation of about 2044 bytes. You have the potential to lose data using the GET method if the user submits a form with too much data.

Q How would you determine if the user has selected more than one item in a drop-down selection list that allows selecting multiple items?

A Use Request.Form(element).Count to determine if the user has selected more than one item in a drop-down selection list.

Q If the GET method is used to submit data in an HTML form to an ASP script, is there a limit placed on the size of HTML form data?

A Yes. Do not use the GET method if you expect data entered by the user to exceed about 1,000 characters. Using the GET method to get large amounts of data via an HTML form could cause undesired results, such as data being truncated.

Workshop

The quiz questions and exercises are provided for your further understanding. Please refer to Appendix A, "Answers to Questions," for the answers.

Quiz

1. An HTML form contains a drop-down list, called "CoursesSelected," that allows the user to select multiple items. How would you determine how many items are selected by the user?

2. Why shouldn't you use the GET method with long data entry forms?

3. How can you get the physical path of an ASP application?

4. What ASP statement do you use to access the server variable SERVER_SOFTWARE?

5. Which method must a form use so that you can examine the values of form variables by using the Request.Form collection?

6. How do you access the HTML form variable "UserID" if the form is submitted to an ASP application with the POST method?

Exercises

1. Modify the ASP application in Listing 6.2 to display only server variables that have values (that is, the program does not display server variables with empty values).

2. Go over values returned by the ASP application you just modified in Exercise 1. How do these values relate to your Web server and the ASP application?

3. Write an ASP script that displays the IP address of the Web browser.

4. Write an ASP script that displays the domain name of the Web server.

5. Write an ASP script that displays the full pathname of the ASP script.

6

DAY **7**

Responding to Requests with the Response Object

by Steve Elfanbaum

In previous days, you learned how to extract information from forms and from the query string within the URL. In today's lesson, you learn to use the Response object to dynamically create HTML content for your Internet audience. Today you will cover the following:

- Learn about the collections in the Response object.
- Discover how to save information as cookies on a client machine.
- Explore the Response object's many properties used to control how a page is returned to the browser.
- Understand the methods available in the Response object to write information returned within the HTML header.
- Control buffering and redirect the browser to alternative URLs.

Learning About the Response Object

Traditional Web development involves creating static pages that are returned to a client browser when a specific URL is requested. Using Active Server Pages, you dynamically build pages that are unique to each client request. The Response object is used to create these dynamic pages. Using the Response object, you can add and alter HTTP headers, dynamically build page bodies, and automatically redirect your clients to alternative pages. The Response object is also used to write cookies to the client machine.

Note

> The Hypertext Transfer Protocol, better known as HTTP, is a communication protocol that defines standard messages consisting of requests from a client to a server and responses from a server to a client. Message headers, which are broken up into general headers, request headers, and response headers, help the client and server determine the nature of the data being sent or received in the message body. The order in which the header fields are received is not important, only that all HTTP headers are sent before the first byte of content data is sent.
>
> General header fields include information about page caching, date, and connection information. Request headers allow the client browser to pass information about the request and about the client itself to the server for use in processing a request. Response headers are used to notify the client of the outcome of the request.

As you learned in previous days, there are two parts to each server response from a browser request. The first is the HTTP headers that give the client information about the page he or she is going to receive. After the HTTP headers are sent, the message body (HTML code) is sent. The Response object allows you to create and modify both parts of your dynamically delivered page.

In the following sections, you learn about how the Response object can be used to create both parts of the response to your client requests. The first sections explore HTTP headers and how the Response object can create and modify them. Cookies, which are just a specific type of HTTP header, are also covered. Subsequent sections show you how to create dynamic content within the message body.

Managing HTTP Headers Using the Response Object

A number of properties and methods are available in the Response object that allow you to write HTTP headers to the HTTP data stream. Many of the properties set a specific value for an HTTP header record. The properties for the Response object that relate to HTTP headers are covered in the next few sections. These properties are as follows:

- CacheControl
- Charset
- ContentType
- Expires
- ExpiresAbsolute
- IsClientConnected
- Status
- Redirect
- AddHeader

Setting the CacheControl Property

Many Internet users connect to the Internet through a proxy server. By default, the Active Server Page returned from a request is not cached by the proxy server. If you want the page to be cached when a proxy server is used, you set the CacheControl property to Public as follows:

```
Response.CacheControl = Public
```

Understanding the CharSet and ContentType Properties

The Content-Type HTTP header is used to notify the client what type of data is returned within the message body. The Content-Type header is defined as

```
Content-Type = "Content-Type"
```

Common content types are shown in the following list.

Common HTTP Content Types

Text/html

Image/GIF

Image/JPEG

Application/x-cdf

Application/x-www-form-encoded

7

The `ContentType` property of the `Response` object allows you to set the `Content-Type` header in your ASP script. To set the `Content-Type` header, use the following command:

```
Response.ContentType = strContentType
```

In this line, `strContentType` is a valid content type. By default, ASP provides the text/html content header. If you want to add additional content types, you can use the `Response.ContentType` property as follows:

```
Response.ContentType = "Image/GIF"
```

To set the character set, you can use the `Reponse.Charset` property. The IANA Character Set registry defines all valid character sets. To set the character set to `iso-latin-2`, for example, add the following to your script:

```
Response.Charset = "iso-latin-2"
```

Examining Page Expiration

When a client requests a page on your server, the page is delivered to the browser where it is placed in the browser's cache and then displayed on the screen. If the browser can fulfill a page request using a local cached copy, by default it uses the cached version.

For most dynamic and transactional Web sites, the information in any given page changes from day to day and possibly from minute to minute (such as a stock price page). Using the `Response` object, you can set an expiration date for your pages so that the browser knows when the cached copy has expired.

There are two ways to set page expiration using the `Response` object. The first is by setting the `Expires` property. This property, invoked as shown:

```
Response.Expires numberMinutesFromNow
```

allows you to set the number of minutes after which the page will expire. The second property you can use in your ASP scripts is the `ExpiresAbsolute` property. This property, used as shown here, can set the expiration to the specified date and time:

```
Response.ExpiresAbsolute = DateandTime
```

Both of these properties set an HTTP header called `Expires`. The `Expires` header is passed back to the browser to notify it of the page expiration date. Within the HTML stream, the `Expires` header looks like this:

```
Expires: Thu, 07 May 1998 16:27:44 GMT
```

Determining Whether a Client Is Still Connected

Your Active Server Pages applications can perform a number of operations on behalf of your clients. These operations can include lengthy database queries or report requests to generate summaries from multiple systems. If the activities the Active Server Page performs are done in multiple steps, each of which can take time and processing power, you can check to see if the user is still connected before proceeding to the next step.

You can determine whether a client is still connected by accessing the IsClientConnected property of the Response object. This read-only property returns true or false. Listing 7.1 shows an example of using the IsClientConnected property.

LISTING 7.1. DETERMINING IF A CLIENT IS STILL CONNECTED (LISTING7_1.ASP).

```
 1: <HTML>
 2: <HEAD><TITLE>Report Summary</TITLE></HEAD>
 3: <BODY>
 4: <%
 5:    If queryMainframe() Then
 6:       'ensure client is still connected
 7:       If Not Response.IsClientConnected Then
 8:          'End processing of the page
 9:          Response.End
10:       End If
11:       If queryMidRange() Then
12:          If Not Response.IsClientConnected Then
13:             'End processing of the page
14:             Response.End
15:          End If
16:       End If
17:    End If
18: %>
19: </BODY>
20: </HTML>
```

ANALYSIS The first part of the report summary page retrieves information from a mainframe within the function queryMainframe() on line 5. If the mainframe query is successful (which might have taken a minute or two), you then check, on line 7, to see whether the client is still connected. You don't want to continue processing the report if the client has disconnected. If the client did disconnect, the page will end, as shown on line 9.

7

Caution Checking to see whether a client is still connected is really available only with HTTP 1.1. If a user is still using an older version of IIS that does not support HTTP 1.1 or later, this method doesn't work.

Using the Status Property

For each page request, the server sets a status code within the returned HTTP headers. The status code notifies the browser as to the outcome of the last transaction. To set the status line returned by the server, you set the Response object's Status property:

```
Response.Status = PageStatus
```

In this line, *PageStatus* is the status text, which consists of a three-digit status code followed by a space, and then a description of the status code. Common status codes defined in the HTTP standard are shown in Table 7.1.

TABLE 7.1. COMMON HTTP STATUS CODES.

Status Code	Description
100	Continue
101	Switching Protocols
200	OK
201	Created
202	Accepted
203	Non-Authoritative Information
204	No Content
300	Multiple Choices
301	Moved Permanently
303	Moved Temporarily
304	Not Modified
305	Use Proxy
400	Bad Request
401	Unauthorized
403	Forbidden
500	Internal Server Error
501	Not Implemented
503	Service Unavailable
505	HTTP Version Not Supported

Redirecting Users to an Alternative Page

In some situations, it is extremely useful to be able to easily redirect your users to an alternative page, instead of the one they requested. If you are requiring a user ID and password to gain access to parts of your site, for example, you might redirect users to the login page when they request an item that is in the "members" area. Redirection is also useful when you are updating a public page in your production environment. You can easily add a redirect to your current page notifying the user that it is currently unavailable. Then, when the update is complete, you can remove the redirect.

The status codes in the 3xx group pertain to redirecting a user. The Response object has a method that sets up the appropriate HTTP headers to prompt the browser to redirect to a new location. This is the syntax for the redirection method:

```
Response.Redirect NewUrl
```

NewUrl is the URL to redirect the browser to.

Listing 7.2 shows the code for a simple password entry form that calls the code in Listing 7.3 to validate the password. If the password entered is correct, the user is taken to the page shown in Listing 7.4. The code redirects the user back to the login page if the password he or she entered on the form is not valid.

In this example, the password has been hard-coded so you can run the code on your system. If this code were in production, you could store the password in the Registry or store it in a database and query for the password when the page is requested.

LISTING 7.2. THE PASSWORD ENTRY PAGE (LISTING7_2.ASP).

```
 1: <HTML>
 2: <HEAD><TITLE>Password Entry</TITLE></HEAD>
 3: <BODY>
 4:    <!-- If this page is being viewed because of a
 5:         failed verification, the LID query string
 6:         variable will be set and we want to display
 7:         an appropriate notification message
 8:    -->
 9:    <% If Request.QueryString("LID") Then %>
10:        <STRONG>You have entered an invalid password.
11:               Please try again.</STRONG><P>
12:    <% End If %>
13:    <FORM METHOD=POST ACTION=LISTING7_2.ASP>
14:        Please Enter the Password: <INPUT TYPE=PASSWORD
           ➥NAME=EF_PASSWORD>
15:        <P><INPUT TYPE=SUBMIT VALUE=Verify>
16:    </FORM>
17: </BODY>
18: </HTML>
```

7

The page presented in Listing 7.2 posts the form data to the Listing 7.3 page that then verifies the password and redirects the user based on the password verification outcome.

LISTING 7.3. THE PASSWORD VERIFICATION SCRIPT (LISTING7_3.ASP).

```
1: <% Response.Buffer=True%>
2: <%
3:    If UCase(Request.Form("EF_PASSWORD")) = "PASSWORD" Then
4:        Response.Redirect "LISTING7_4.ASP"
5:    Else
6:        Response.Redirect "LISTING7_2.ASP?LID=1"
7:    End If
8: %>
```

ANALYSIS Listing 7.3 verifies the entry in the password field using the If statement in line 3. If the correct password is entered, the user is redirected to the welcome page (line 4). If an invalid password is entered, the user is redirected to the password entry page and a query string field is sent so that an error notification is displayed (line 6).

Caution

It is important that you avoid using the Redirect method after any content (such as HTML tags) is sent to the browser. Remember that the Redirect method sets specific records within the HTTP header stream, and that after any data is sent to the client, no additional header information can be sent. If you attempt to call the Redirect method after the server has sent information back to the client, you will generate an error.

Finally, in Listing 7.4, there is a simple HTML welcome page that the user sees after successful password verification from Listing 7.3.

LISTING 7.4. THE WELCOME PAGE (LISTING7_4.HTM).

```
1: <HTML>
2: <HEAD><TITLE>Welcome Verified User</TITLE></HEAD>
3: <BODY>
4: <H2>Welcome!</H2>
5: <p>You have been authenticated on our system!
6: </BODY>
7: </HTML>
```

Investigating the HTTP Headers Created by the `Redirect` Method

The `Response.Redirect` method invoked when the user has entered an invalid password creates the following HTTP headers:

```
HTTP/1.1 302 Object moved
Server: Microsoft-IIS/4.0
Date: Tue, 21 Apr 1998 03:51:27 GMT
Location: LISTING7_1.ASP?LID=1
Connection: Keep-Alive
Content-Length: 141
Content-Type: text/html
Cache-control: private
```

It also automatically generates this page content:

```
<head><title>Object moved</title></head>
<body><h1>Object Moved</h1>This object may be found
<a HREF="LISTING7_1.ASP?LID=1">here</a>.</body>
```

Many of the older browsers still active on the Internet do not automatically redirect the user when the redirection headers are received. In those cases, the user can navigate to the correct page simply by selecting the `<A>here</A>` link. The HTTP standards specify another case in which a browser would not automatically redirect the user. In the specification, it states that a browser should redirect the user without interaction only if the method used in the second request is `GET` or `HEAD`.

The ability to automatically generate the HTTP headers and associated content to redirect a browser to an alternative page is one of the most powerful methods in the `Response` object.

Dynamically Adding HTTP Headers

Up to now, you have seen how many of the `Response` object's properties and methods actually generate HTTP headers to return to the client. The `Response` object also provides a method to allow you to write any HTTP response header you want to the HTML stream returned to the client.

The Syntax for the `AddHeader` Method

The following code shows the syntax for the `AddHeader` method of the `Response` object:

```
Response.AddHeader Name, Value
```

Name is the name of the header you want to add and *Value* is the header value.

When you invoke the `AddHeader` method, a new header is added to any that are already in the buffer. If you add a header that already exists, it is not replaced. The duplicate header is added.

7

A listing of standard response and message body headers are shown in Table 7.2. You can also add your own custom headers, but you must be sure that the application requesting the page can decipher them to be of any use.

TABLE 7.2. RESPONSE AND CONTENT HEADERS.

Header Type	Header
Age	Response
Location	Response
Proxy-Authenticate	Response
Public	Response
Retry-After	Response
Server	Response
Vary	Response
Warning	Response
WWW-Authenticate	Response
Allow	Content
Content-Base	Content
Content-Encoding	Content
Content-Language	Content
Content-Length	Content
Content-Location	Content
Content-MD5	Content
Content-Range	Content
Content-Type	Content
Etag	Content
Expires	Content
Last-Modified	Content
Extension-header	Content

If you want to add the `Last-Modified` header tag to the HTML stream, for example, add the following line to your script:

```
Response.AddHeader "Last-Modified", FormatDateTime(strFileDate,
➥vbLongDate)
```

Remember that just like all the other header functions you have seen today, buffering must be set to On, or all `Response.AddHeader` statements must precede the first content information sent to the client.

Managing the HTTP Message Body with the Response Object

Now you are ready to start crafting the page your client will ultimately see. The `Response` object has several properties and methods you will use to dynamically create the content that is returned from the page request. These properties and methods include:

- `Buffer`
- `Clear`
- `Flush`
- `End`
- `Write`

Page Buffering

HTTP is a stateless protocol, meaning that between requests for specific server resources (a page, an image), no connection is maintained between the client and the server. Interactions between a browser and a server involve multiple request/response pairs. The HTTP protocol requires that all headers must be sent before any message body (content) data. Therefore, if you want to create, add, modify, or remove any HTTP header information from a server response, it must be done *before* the first byte of data is returned to the browser.

Page buffering within your ASP pages is determined by the `Response.Buffer` property. The `Buffer` property can have one of two values, `true` or `false`. If the property is set to `true`, all scripts in the current page execute before the first byte of data is written to the client. By default, buffering is set to `false` and data is written as it is made available by the server.

The default page buffering property is set in the IIS Metabase under the key `MD_ASP_BUFFERINGON`. The Metabase is an in-memory datastore (think of a *datastore* as an in-memory table) specifically built for IIS, allowing fast access to configuration data. The `Response.Buffer` property overrides the default ASP buffering value for any page in which it is used. You can access the default `ASPBufferingOn` property via the IIS Administration Objects interface.

7

See the IIS documentation on Microsoft's Web site at www.microsoft.com for more information about the Metabase and the IIS Administration Objects.

Managing Page Buffering

Many of the properties and methods of the Response object are used to set HTTP response headers in the HTML stream. If page buffering is not on, any attempt to use these Response object properties to write headers after the initial <HTML> tag generates an error because all response headers must be written before any message body data is sent.

There are three methods available in the Response object that let you control, after page buffering has been turned on, when the buffer is sent to the client.

Using the Response.Clear Method

The Clear method of the Response object erases any buffered output in the message body. The Clear method does not erase any previously set response headers. It is often used when an error occurs during the execution of a page. In Listing 7.5, you can see how the Clear method can be effectively used to manage the message body buffer.

LISTING 7.5. USING THE RESPONSE.CLEAR METHOD.

```
 1:   <% Response.Buffer=True %>
 2:   <HTML>
 3:   <HEAD><TITLE>Testing Results</TITLE></HEAD>
 4:   <BODY>
 5:   <H2>Record Results</H2><P>
 6:   <% If Len(Request.QueryString("UID")) Then %>
 7:      <table border=1>
 8:         <tr><th>Test Pass</th><th>Result</th>
 9:         <tr><td>1</td><td>Passed</td></tr>
10:         <tr><td>2</td><td>Failed</td></tr>
11:      </table>
12:   <% Else
13:         Response.Clear %>
14:         <H2>Error</H2><P>
15:         You must enter a valid Id.
16:   <% End If %>
17:   </BODY></HTML>
```

ANALYSIS In Listing 7.5, the script is going to generate the HTML to display results records for testing runs if a user ID is entered on the URL query string. If the user ID is not found, an error message is sent back to the client. On lines 7 through 11, the script is writing the text, Record Results, to the message body. If the user ID is not entered, the script clears that heading by using the `Response.Clear` method in line 13 to erase the message body. Be sure to note that setting the `Response.Buffer` property to `True` in line 1 has turned page buffering on. If the page had not been buffered, when the `Response.Clear` line was executed, the following ASP error would have been generated:

```
Record Results
Response object error 'ASP 0159 : 80004005'
Buffering Off
/tysasp/day7/listing7_1.asp, line 11
Buffering must be on.
```

Dynamically Returning Buffered Output

You can dynamically send all buffered output back to the browser while still processing the page by using the `Flush` method of the `Response` object. The `Flush` method takes no parameters and is called as follows:

```
Response.Flush
```

In Listing 7.6, you build on the previous example to integrate returning information to the client while the script is still processing.

LISTING 7.6. ADDING THE RESPONSE.FLUSH METHOD.

```
1:  <% If Len(Request.QueryString("EF_ID")) Then %>
2:      <!-- The User ID has been entered; let the client view the
3:          heading while the report is generated -->
4:      <table border=1>
5:          <!-- Database Query code would go here -->
6:      </table>
7:      Response.Flush
8:  <% Else %>
```

ANALYSIS Imagine that the code that executes to generate the report records is going across a WAN to query a SQL Server database in another location. This process will take a few seconds. By calling `Response.Flush` on line 7, the heading `Report Results` is returned to the client right away, and as the results records are available, they are sent as well. Although this seems like a minor point, from the users' perspective, the header being returned lets them know their request has been received and is being processed.

Ending ASP Page Processing

Sometimes during page processing, when a condition is met you want to immediately end processing the script. These situations could include an error condition or some type

7

of notification. To end processing an ASP page, use the End method of the Response object, invoked by calling

```
Response.End
```

This command immediately stops all script execution. If page buffering has been turned on for the page, it flushes the buffer before ending processing.

Understanding HTTP Responses

The first data items passed back to a browser after page requests are the HTTP response headers. These headers, like the request headers, contain a wealth of information required for the browser to be able to display the returned page property. Typical HTTP response headers include information such as the server type and the date. The following is an example of an HTTP header response:

```
Server: Microsoft-IIS/4.0
Date: Mon, 20 Apr 1998 01:56:43 GMT
Connection: Keep-Alive
Content-Length: 49232
Content-Type: text/html
Expires: Mon, 20 Apr 1998 02:20:43 GMT
expires=Tue, 20-Apr-1999 01:56:42 GMT; path=/
Set-Cookie: ELFMISC=CITYCODE=MO%5FSt%5FLouis; expires=Tue, 20-Apr-1999
➡01:56:42 GMT; path=/
Cache-control: private
```

IIS supplies many of these headers automatically for you. To dynamically set, modify, and send your own HTTP headers, you use the properties and methods of the Response object.

 To view the complete specification for the HTTP protocol and HTTP headers, check out the World Wide Web Consortium site at http://www.w3.org.

Sending Information to the Browser

You have been learning about HTTP headers and page buffering. You are now going to learn how to write data to the HTTP message body by using the Response object.

There are two ways you can write textual information to the client: explicitly or implicitly. The first method involves using the Response.Write method, and the second is performed by using a special tag in your ASP scripts.

Writing Text Using the `Response.Write` Method

The `Write` method allows you to add textual data to the HTML data stream. Here is its syntax:

```
Response.Write variant
```

The *variant* variable parameter is evaluated as a string and sent along with the body content data. If page buffering is turned on, all data is cached until the script ends or the `Flush` or `End` method is invoked. Listing 7.7 shows an example of using the `Response.Write` method to return information to the client. In this listing, the browser provides three variables on the query string—PRIN, RATE, and YEARS—that are used to calculate the total of all payment on a YEARS long loan.

LISTING 7.7. WRITING DATA WITH THE RESPONSE.WRITE METHOD.

```
 1: <HTML>
 2: <HEAD><TITLE>Mortgage Amount Financed</TITLE></HEAD>
 3: <BODY>
 4: <%
 5:     Dim lPrincipal, dRate, lYears
 6:
 7:     lPrincipal = Request.QueryString("PRIN")
 8:     dRate      = Request.QueryString("RATE")
 9:     lYears     = Request.QueryString("YEARS")
10:
11:     Response.Write "Total Amount Financed based upon a Principal of "
        ➥& lPrincipal
12:     Response.Write "<BR>and an Interest Rate of " & dRate & " over "
        ➥& lYears
13:     Response.Write " will be <P>" & lPrincipal * ( 1 + dRate * lYears)
14: %>
15: </BODY>
16: </HTML>
```

For the following URL

```
http://{YourServerName}/{path}/Listing7_7.asp?prin=100000&rate=
➥.085&years=5
```

the page shown in Listing 7.7 would produce the following output:

```
Total Amount Financed based upon a Principal of 100000
and an Interest Rate of .085 over 5 will be
142500
```

7

Writing Text Using <%= and %> Inline Evaluation

Another method of writing text back to the requesting client is to allow ASP to dynamically evaluate variables as they occur within your scripts. Special tags are used to notify ASP that there is a variable that needs to be converted to its textual equivalent and returned to the client. If you have a variable called `strName` that holds a user's name, you can return that name within your script by adding the following code:

```
Welcome back <%=strName%>, glad you could make it.
```

This code causes ASP to evaluate `strName` and actually return `Steve`, `Joe`, or whatever value is in the `strName` variable. It is equivalent to the following code:

```
Welcome back <% Response.Write strName %>, glad you could make it.
```

To demonstrate how you can use this implicit `Response.Write` functionality in your scripts, Listing 7.8 takes the previous Listing 7.7 code and reworks it to use the new tag syntax.

LISTING 7.8. WRITING DATA USING IMPLICIT WRITES.

```
 1: <HTML>
 2: <HEAD><TITLE>Mortgage Amount Financed</TITLE></HEAD>
 3: <BODY>
 4: <%
 5:    Dim lPrincipal, dRate, lYears
 6:
 7:    lPrincipal = Request.QueryString("PRIN")
 8:    dRate      = Request.QueryString("RATE")
 9:    lYears     = Request.QueryString("YEARS")
10: %>
11: </BODY>
12: Total Amount Financed based upon a Principal of <%=lPrincipal%> <BR>
13: and an Interest Rate of <%=dRate%>  over <%=lYears%>
14: will be <P> <%=lPrincipal * ( 1 + dRate * lYears) %>
15: </BODY>
16: </HTML>
```

ANALYSIS The output for Listing 7.7 and Listing 7.8 is identical. They are two different methods of performing similar tasks. In the case of Listing 7.8, the <%= and %> inline evaluators are used in lines 12, 13, and 14. As you continue to develop ASP application, you will get a feel for which method to use when.

Writing Binary Data to the HTML Stream

If you need to write binary data to the HTML stream, you can use the `BinaryWrite` method of the `Response` object. It is useful for custom applications that use HTTP as their communication protocol. You call the `BinaryWrite` method as shown here:

```
Response.BinaryWrite binaryData
```

In this line, *binaryData* is a variant containing binary data.

Logging Information to the Web Server Log

When you install Microsoft's Internet Information Server, the default settings enable logging of all page requests. The log files are found, by default, in the \WinNt\System32\ LogFiles directory and are generated daily. By using the Internet Service Manager, you can specify several options for logging site activity.

The default daily log stores the access time, IP address, request type, page requested, and HTTP status of the request, as shown here:

```
#Software: Microsoft Internet Information Server 4.0
#Version: 1.0
#Date: 1998-04-22 17:21:08
#Fields: time c-ip cs-method cs-uri-stem cs-uri-query sc-status
17:18:16 127.0.0.1 POST /TysAsp/_vti_bin/_vti_aut/author.dll 200
17:18:27 127.0.0.1 GET /tysasp/day7/listing7_2a.asp 200
```

With ASP and the `Response` object, you can add additional text to be associated with a page's log entry. You use the `AppendToLog` method of the `Response` object to add this additional text. Here is its syntax:

```
Response.AppendToLog TextToAppend
```

For this method to execute correctly, you must select the URI Query option on the Extended Logging Properties page. Here are the steps you take to enable the URI Query option:

1. Start the Internet Service Manager.
2. Navigate to the default Web site, or the Web site that contains the page you want to log from.
3. Open the Properties dialog box by choosing Properties from the Sites Context menu. You can also choose Properties from the Action menu.
4. Click the Properties button in the Enable Logging frame on the Web Site tab to display the Extended Logging Properties dialog box.

7

5. Select the Extended Properties tab and then select the URI Query check box.

You can now log additional text to the log record for a page that your users have requested. Listing 7.9 shows how you can integrate logging in one of your scripts.

LISTING 7.9. APPENDING RECORDS TO THE SERVER LOG.

```
1: <HTML>
2: <HEAD><TITLE>AppendToLog</TITLE></HEAD>
3: <BODY>
4:    <H2> Welcome Back!</H2><P>
5:     We have really missed you.
6:    <% Response.AppendToLog "Another Visitor Returned" %>
7: </BODY></HTML>
```

ANALYSIS After the page executes line 6, the log file then contains the following record:

```
18:17:35 127.0.0.1 GET /tysasp/day7/listing7_2a.asp
➥Another+Visitor+Returned 200
```

Storing Information on the Client's System Using Cookies

NEW TERM A *cookie*, or more formally, a "Persistent Client HTTP Cookie," is a small file located on the client machine that contains information the server requests the client browser to store locally. Different browsers store the cookie files in different locations (for examples, Internet Explorer running on Windows NT stores cookies in a folder called \winnt\cookies{user profile}\cookies), but each cookie has a standard format for storing information. The cookies are written to the HTTP header stream and processed by the client's browser as it reads the page. Most of the today's browsers allow the client to be notified before a cookie is written, or turn off cookies altogether.

To use the persistent cookie data, you need to perform two tasks. First, you need a mechanism to send and store the cookie on the client's machine. Second, you need a method to retrieve and read the cookie that was previously stored. To write cookies, you use the Response object. For subsequent reads of cookie information, you use the Request object.

Tip

In today's security-conscious society, matters of privacy are foremost in many Internet users' thoughts. By being sensitive to your users' concerns, you can create a better sense of community. As a rule, if you are storing information using cookies, be sure to notify your users before they are written. You might also provide a link to a "Statement of Privacy" that your site sub-scribes to. These simple pre-emptive strikes can make your users much more comfortable as they interact with your site.

Understanding Cookie Structures

Before you get too far into how to use cookies, you need to be sure you understand that cookies are just records that are sent as part of the request and response HTTP headers.

Cookies come in many forms, from the simple to the complex. The most basic cookie has a name and an associated value. More complex cookies have additional attributes associated with them. Cookies can also have multiple keyed entries, creating a "cookie dictionary" on the client's machine. To write cookies, you interact with the `Cookies` col-lection of the `Response` object.

Interacting with the `Cookies` Collection

As mentioned, you create cookies on a client machine by using the `Cookies` collection of the `Response` object. The following code shows the syntax for accessing the `Cookies` col-lection:

```
Response.Cookies(cookie)[(key)¦.attribute = value.
```

In this code, *cookie* is the name of the cookie to write, *key* is an optional *key* parameter that specifies the key, and *attribute* is a variable that can have one of the following values:

Domain	An optional attribute that restricts the cookie being returned to only this domain.
Expires	A required date parameter that specifies the cookie's expiration. After this date, the cookie is removed from the client's system. If no date is specified, the cookie is removed at the end of the session.
Path	An optional attribute that, like the domain, restricts the cookie being returned only when the path is matched.
Secure	An optional attribute that requires the connection between the client and the server to be secure before the cookie is written.

7

Understanding Cookie Attributes

If a client's browser accepts cookies, any server can write cookies to the client's machine. To make sure you receive the cookie you want, there needs to be a mechanism to ensure that the client sends the correct cookie along with its page request.

In the earlier application, you wanted to be able to find out the last time the client connected to the site, so you will create a cookie called `LastAccess`. Now, many other sites the user visits might also keep track of the last visit and will likely want to write a cookie, quite possibly called `LastAccess`. You can see the problem. If both sites were using the same cookie, one site would always be getting the wrong last-accessed date.

To make sure the "Last Access" cookie problem doesn't happen, you set the `Domain` attribute to ensure that the `LastAccess` cookie for your domain is returned when the client requests a page from your site. You can also set the `Path` attribute, which restricts the cookie to a page within a particular virtual directory on the site.

Baking Your First Cookie

The first cookie you need to store is the last time users viewed the page. With this cookie, you can let them know the last time they viewed the page. For example, you could display messages such as "Welcome back! You've been gone for quite a while!" or "Hey, didn't we just see you yesterday? Pretty great site, isn't it?" or "You might want to check out our new…." I think you get the idea!

To create the cookie, you use the `Cookies` collection of the `Response` object as follows:

```
Response.Cookies("LastAccess") = FormatDateTime(now, vbDateLong)
Response.Cookies("LastAccess").Expires = #August 15, 1999#
```

These statements create a cookie on the client called `LastAccess` and put the current date and time stamp into the cookie.

 Caution

> Remember that cookies are written to the HTTP header. After the header has been returned to the client, you cannot add additional header information. Be sure to buffer the HTTP information by specifying `<% Response.Buffer=True %>` at the top of your ASP page or place all `Response.Cookies` commands before the first content data is written, when you are going to write cookies to the client.

To retrieve the cookie, you access the `Cookies` collection of the `Request` object:

```
StrLastAccess = Request.Cookies("LastAccess")
```

Setting Cookie Attributes

You assign cookie attributes to make sure you receive the correct cookie along with the client page requests. In the previous section, you can ensure that you receive the correct `LastAccess` cookie by assigning values to that cookie's attributes as shown in Listing 7.10.

LISTING 7.10. SETTING COOKIE ATTRIBUTES.

```
 1: <%
 2:    Response.Cookies("LastAccess") = FormatDateTime(now, vbDateLong)
 3:    Response.Cookies("LastAccess").Domain = "localhost"
 4:    Response.Cookies("LastAccess").Path = "/tysasp/day7"
 5:    Response.Cookies("LastAccess").Expires = #Aug 27, 1998#
 6: %>
 7: <HTML>
 8: <HEAD><TITLE>Your Page</TITLE></HEAD>
 9: <BODY>
10: Welcome Back.  Your last page access was
    ➥<%=Request.Cookies("LastAccess")%>
11: </BODY>
12: </HTML>
```

ANALYSIS Listing 7.10 creates an HTTP cookie header that is sent to the browser formatted as follows:

```
Set-Cookie: LastAccess=4%2F22%2F98+3%3A02%3A59+PM; expires=Thu,
➥27-Aug-1998 05:00:00 GMT;
            domain=localhost; path=/
```

This cookie is formatted and sent in lines 2 to 5. Line 10 displays the "Welcome Back..." message. Included in this message is information on the last access the user had. This information is obtained by using the `Request.Cookies` method, also in line 10.

Cookies with Keys: A New Recipe

In addition to the simple cookie discussed in the previous section, cookies can also be dictionary objects—meaning that they can have keys. Just as you might use a keyed collection to store set information, you can also use keyed cookies to store related sets within the same cookie.

If you don't remember, this is the syntax for the cookie command:

```
Response.Cookies(cookie)[(key)¦.attribute = value.
```

Let's say you want to store a user's preferences for colors on his or her main page. You can create a keyed cookie named `colors` and create keys for each of the color selections

7

(background, buttons, and so forth). Listing 7.11 shows setting up a dictionary cookie to handle a user's color preferences.

LISTING 7.11. USING COOKIES WITH KEYS.

```
 1: <%
 2:     Response.Cookies("color") ("background") =
         ⮕Request.Form("BackgroundColor")
 3:     Response.Cookies("color") ("buttonbar") =
         ⮕Request.Form("ButtonBarColor")
 4:     Response.Cookies("color") ("anchors") = Request.Form("AnchorColor")
 5:     Response.Cookies("LastAccess").Expires = "April 16, 1999"
 6:     Response.Cookies("LastAccess").Domain = "elf.com"
 7:     Response.Cookies("LastAccess").Path = "/tysasp/day7"
 8:     Response.Cookies("LastAccess").Expires = #Aug 27, 1998#
 9:     Response.Redirect "YourPage.Asp"
10: %>
```

ANALYSIS The script shown in Listing 7.11 accepts input from a personalization form and creates a keyed cookie that is returned to the client. Notice that line 9 redirects the user to the personalized page. The cookies, which are sent along with the redirection (302 Object Moved) HTTP headers, are written and returned to the server with the redirect page request.

Understanding the `Response.Cookies` Collection

Often you want to set the attributes of all the cookies in the response header to a particular value. This is easy to do if you remember that cookies are a *collection* and can be iterated through.

The code in Listing 7.12 shows how you can set the cookie attributes for all cookies you have written to the HTTP response headers.

LISTING 7.12. SETTING COOKIE ATTRIBUTES.

```
1: <%
2:     Dim Cookie
3:     For each Cookie in Response.Cookies
4:         Response.Cookies(Cookie).Expires = "July 12, 1998"
5:         Response.Cookies(Cookie).Domain = "elf.com"
6:         Response.Cookies(Cookie).Path = "/tysasp"
7:     Next
8: %>
```

Line 3 starts a For...Next loop that loops through each cookie that has been created. Lines 4, 5, and 6 simply print out response information.

Retrieving Cookie Values

Cookies are written to the HTTP response headers using the Response object and are read from the HTTP request headers using the Request object. Cookies are a collection within the Request object and can be iterated through the same way you would iterate through any VBA collection, using a For...Each loop. The code in Listing 7.13 shows how you can iterate through all the cookies sent from a client browser.

LISTING 7.13. RETRIEVING COOKIES FROM THE HTTP REQUEST HEADER.

```
 1: <HTML>
 2: <HEAD><TITLE>Cookie Values Sent from Browser</TITLE></HEAD>
 3: <%
 4:    Dim cookie, cookieKey
 5:    'Walk the cookies collection
 6:    For Each cookie in Request.Cookies
 7:       If cookie.HasKeys Then
 8:          Response.Write cookie & "<br>"
 9:          For Each cookieKey in Request.Cookies(cookie)
10:             Response.Write "   " & cookieKey & " = " &
                ➥Request.Cookies(cookie)(key) & "<br>"
11:          Next
12:          Response.Write "<p>"
13:       Else
14:          Response.Write cookie & " = " & Request.Cookies(cookie) &
                ➥"<p>"
15:       End If
16:    Next
17: %>
18: <BODY></BODY>
19: </HTML>
```

 Notice that if the cookie is a dictionary (cookie.HasKeys = True), then lines 9–11 will iterate through each of the keys in the cookie dictionary and line 10 will output the values.

Summary

You have covered quite a bit of information today. You should give yourself a big pat on the back for staying with it. The capabilities of the Response object are many and varied, and can give you a host of tools to use as you create your ASP applications.

7

Q&A

Q **How big can a cookie be?**

A You should try to keep cookies as small as possible. Not all browsers can read cookies that are larger than 4KB (4,096 bytes).

Q **Should I rely on cookies for storing personalized information?**

A No. Always include code that allows your Web page or site to work without cookies. Many people disable cookies to prevent information from being written to their computer. You should include code in your Web page that provides a backup if cookies are not supported.

Workshop

The quiz questions and exercises are provided for your further understanding. Please refer to Appendix A, "Answers to Questions," for the answers to the quiz questions; the answers to the exercises are on the MCP Web site.

Quiz

1. What will be the outcome of the following code?

```
<HTML><BODY>
<% Response.Redirect "NewPage.asp"%>
</BODY></HTML>
```

2. How can you fix the code in the previous example?

3. How do you delete a cookie?

4. What type of cookie would you use to store a user's favorite football teams?

5. Show two different ways to write the value of the variable userName to the client's browser from an Active Server Page.

Exercises

1. Create an ASP script that redirects a user based on a REDIR=URL parameter in the request's QueryString.

2. For each request to the previous script, add a comment to the server log.

WEEK 1

In Review

In your first week, you have covered the fundamental topics
of Active Server Pages. In Day 1, "Getting Started with
Active Server Pages," you learned the basics of using ASP to
implement Web projects. ASP can be used to easily add a
new level of interactivity to your Web site. Traditional server-
side application development environments are not optimized
for developing interactive Web applications and producing
information formatted in HTML. You are now aware of ASP's
unique features and capabilities and how you can use them to
develop interactive Web applications.

You discovered the structure and core components of an ASP
application on your second day, "Web Development with
Active Server Pages." You should now understand the structure of an ASP application, which is composed of server-side
includes (optional), HTML code, script delimiters, script
code, ActiveX components, and ASP objects (optional).
Server-side includes can be used to easily insert text from
other files into ASP applications. They can also be used to
call VBScript subroutines in another file. Components and
objects are really the foundation of ASP because they allow
you to interact with other objects on the server and process
information. You now have a good understanding of what
objects and components are all about. The global.asa file is
instrumental in carrying out actions at critical stages of the
life of a session or application and also defines resources that
can be used by other ASP applications. Loops can be used to
perform repetitive tasks within ASP applications. It is easy to
add intelligence to ASP applications by using conditional
statements for flow control. You can easily store and access
data by using the Dictionary object and an integer or string
index value.

1

2

3

4

5

6

7

By default, the HTTP protocol is a stateless protocol and does not retain any information between HTTP sessions, which makes things a bit complicated for Web application developers. However, ASP gives Web application developers two powerful tools that can be used to retain information between HTTP sessions: the `Session` object and methods for manipulating cookies.

You learned how to build effective Web user interfaces that use HTML forms, input and message boxes, ActiveX controls, and Java on Day 3, "Interacting with Your Users." Nearly all Web applications interact with users to get and display information, so you learned how to use HTML, message boxes, input boxes, ActiveX controls, and HTML form elements to interact with users browsing your Web site. Use ActiveX controls to interact with users when you are certain they use a Web browser that supports ActiveX; ActiveX controls offer additional control over attributes of data entry objects.

On Day 4, "Building and Processing Web Forms," you learned how to process the information you retrieve through Web forms. Data validation is an important aspect of building an ASP application, and you should always validate information entered by users before processing it. ASP applications can easily validate virtually any type of data, including numbers, dates, and time values, as well as strings. Consider using client-side scripting to complement server-side data validation to make your user interfaces more efficient and user-friendly. Text streams can be manipulated in ASP applications through the use of the Text Stream component, which allows you to create files on the server as well as read them later.

You learned how to build your own scriptlets and use them in ASP applications on your fifth day, "Using Scriptlets to Componentize ASP Code." Scriptlets are self-contained code components you build with a familiar scripting language, such as VBScript, JavaScript, or any other scripting language that supports the Microsoft ActiveX Scripting Interfaces. At the time of this writing, you can use over half a dozen scripting languages to build scriptlets. Scriptlets is an evolving technology that you can expect to see incorporated into future Microsoft applications and technologies.

Day 6, "Getting Information About HTTP Requests with the `Request` Object," shows you how to use the `Request` object to get information about an HTTP transaction. By accessing properties, methods, and collections of the `Request` object, you can get data in HTML forms, cookies, server-side variables, and client-side certificates. You should spend the time to thoroughly understand the `Request` object because you will use it often.

On the last day of your first week, "Responding to Client Requests with the `Response` Object," you learned how to customize HTTP responses (including cookies and URL redirects) sent to Web browsers with the `Response` object.

WEEK 2

At a Glance

On Day 8, "Processing Web Data with the Server, Session, and Application Objects," you master how and when to use the Server, Application, and Session objects to process Web data. ASP ships with several built-in ActiveX components. By learning how to make the best use of these components, you can build powerful ASP applications in very little time. On Day 9, "Using ActiveX Components Built for ASP," you learn how to determine capabilities of the Web browser, rotate advertisements, send e-mail, conduct online elections, insert Web counters, and much more! Most ASP applications make use of databases, so you learn the basics of developing typical Web database applications, including how to use SQL statements for data access, on Day 10, "Programming Web Databases." You build your first ASP-based database application in that day's lesson! ActiveX Data Objects (ADO) allows you to build powerful Web database applications. Day 11, "Building Database Applications Using ActiveX Data Objects," helps you master all the features of ADO, including understanding the significance of recordsets, ADO objects, collections, field traversing, and more! ASP is well suited for building Web database applications. Day 12, "Database Development Illustrated: Building a User Registration System," shows you how to build a fully functional Web database application. You can easily build your own Web database applications by reusing the code presented on that day. Cookies are instrumental in retaining information between HTTP sessions. Learn how to set and retrieve cookies, including the difference between persistent and in-memory cookies, on Day 13, "Retaining Information Between Sessions Using

Cookies." By the end of Day 13, you will have mastered using them. On Day 14, "Developing a User Personalization System with Cookies," you learn how to use cookies to build a user personalization system. Web database application development is also revisited on Day 14.

DAY **8**

Processing Web Data with the Server, Session, and Application Objects

by Duncan Mackenzie

ASP revolves around objects. On previous days, you learned about the Request and Response objects and how they allow you to interact with the user. Today, you cover the following:

- Learn to use the Server object.
- Maintain state with the Session object.
- Use the Application object.
- Work with Microsoft Transaction Server in ASP.

Using the `Server` Object

The `Server` object is one of the five built-in (or *intrinsic*, as they are often called) objects in ASP. You have already seen the first two, `Request` and `Response`, which deal with interactions between the client (browser) and the server. `Server` objects, as well as the next two discussed—`Session` and `Application` objects—work only on the server. This is not to say they have nothing to do with the client, but their properties and methods set values and perform actions only at the back end.

The `Server` object gives you access to some of the features and settings of the Web server you are running under. The methods exposed by this object are as follows:

- `CreateObject()`
- `HTMLEncode()`
- `URLEncode()`
- `MapPath()`

It also exposes the property `ScriptTimeOut`.

These items are discussed individually to help you understand how and when you would use them.

The `CreateObject()` Method

If you have programmed in Visual Basic before, you probably have some idea what this function does. If not, don't worry; this section explains it. The `CreateObject()` call allows you access to external objects. You have already seen, in previous days, that you can use objects in your pages, but you have been using only the internal, or intrinsic, ASP objects. Those objects were created for you. You didn't have to do anything to use them except type their name, as in this example:

```
Response.Write "<P>Test</P>".
```

External objects are libraries of code, generally stored in a DLL (`*.dll`) file, an abbreviation that stands for *dynamic linked library*. You can find these libraries through third parties (either bought or given), you can get some from Microsoft, and you can also create your own.

How they work and what is involved in creating your own is beyond the scope of this chapter, but you do not need to know these things to use these libraries in your pages. All you need to know is that each one has a unique identifying string, known as its *Class ID*. It is this value you use, with the `CreateObject()` call, to gain access to the library. When you use this method, it creates an instance of that library and places it into a variable for you. The following piece of code creates an instance of the external library whose Class ID is `Validate.clsValidate` and places it into the `objValidate` variable:

```
Set objValidate = Server.CreateObject("Validate.clsValidate")
```

> **Note**
>
> An *instance* is an in-memory copy of an object. External objects exist so that a set of functions can be stored in one place (a DLL), but accessed by many different programs. If each program used the DLL directly, it would run into conflicts, such as more than one program trying to set the same property. Instead, each program receives an instance of the library, each having its own memory and executing independently of the others. Instancing allows every program to behave as though it is the only one using that library.

Notice the `Set` keyword in front of the `objValidate` variable. Normally, when assigning a value to a variable, this keyword is not required. `Set`, used only when dealing with objects, tells the application that more than just a value is being placed into this variable. If this keyword is omitted, an error results.

After you have an instance of the object, you can use its properties and methods just as you can with one of the built-in ASP objects. Exactly what you can do with the object is different for each external library, so you need to consult the documentation supplied by the object's creator. The `CreateObject()` method is used extensively in tomorrow's lesson, and the rest of the book, so you will have plenty of opportunity to become familiar with it.

The `HTMLEncode()` Method

The `HTMLEncode()` method is more of a general ASP utility function than one associated with the `Server` object itself. Its purpose is simple—to take a string and format it to correctly display on a Web page. In the following example, you have created an ASP-based online discussion room where users can enter any text they want. A user has typed in this string:

```
Hi there! My name is "Fred", <grin>, what's yours?
```

You have retrieved this text from the `Request.Form` collection and saved it into a database. When you want to display that text to another user, for instance, you could do so in this manner:

```
<p><%=UserComment%></p>
```

Assuming `UserComment` is a variable holding the previous text, this statement produces the following HTML text at runtime:

```
<p>Hi there! My name is "Fred", <grin>, what's yours?</p>
```

This text appears to be exactly what you wanted. It has been placed directly into your page, but it does not produce the correct result when viewed. A Web browser displaying this page produces the result with missing text, as shown in Figure 8.1.

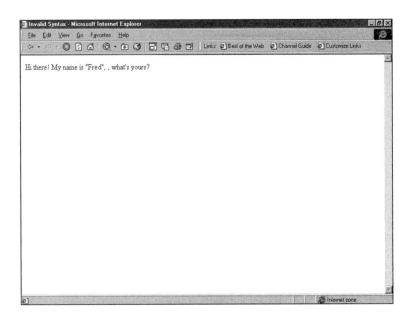

This omission of text occurs because browsers are designed to understand HTML, not straight text, and HTML treats certain characters as special. Those characters, such as the greater-than and less-than symbols, are not displayed correctly if included as part of your page's text. The HTMLEncode() function is "smart," so it knows which characters HTML doesn't like and replaces them with the special codes used to represent those values. Table 8.1 lists some of those characters and their corresponding HTML codes.

TABLE 8.1. SPECIAL HTML CHARACTER CODES.

Character	HTML Code
" (quote)	&quot;
< (less than)	&lt;
> (greater than)	&gt;
(space)	

Many CGI programmers have created code routines to convert these characters into the appropriate codes and, sadly, so have many ASP programmers. You do not need to, however; simply wrap any text that has the possibility of containing a special character within a Server.HTMLEncode call and take the rest of the week off. The preceding sample code can be redone as follows to display the comment:

```
<p><%=Server.HTMLEncode(UserComment)%></p>
```

When run, the code produces this result:

```
<p>Hi there! My name is &quot;Fred&quot;, &lt;grin&gt;, what's yours?</p>
```

This code would be displayed correctly in any browser.

This method is designed for display text that is unknown until runtime. Text from forms or a database could contain these characters and should always be run through this function, to guarantee that it is displayed as intended. If you are attempting to display static text, such as a page heading, then you shouldn't use this function, even if the heading contains special characters. Instead of causing the server to perform the translation every time the page is executed, convert the text once and put it in your page with the proper codes already in place. This doesn't mean you have to convert the text yourself; most HTML editors can perform this translation for you. Simply typing the original text from the example into FrontPage produces the correctly encoded text.

If you are not using an editor, or do not have one available, the following two listings can be used to create a simple utility to do the encoding for you. The first page, Listing 8.1, consists of a simple HTML form with a large text entry area, and a submit button labeled "Convert." The second page, Listing 8.2, is the target of the first page's form, and just takes whatever you have entered and converts it by using the HTMLEncode() function. The displayed result will be your text, appearing exactly as you entered it, but viewing the source reveals the HTML code required. Using the encoded text in your own page is as simple as copying and pasting that source text.

LISTING 8.1. A SIMPLE HTML FORM PROVIDES THE ENTRY POINT FOR A CONVERSION UTILITY.

```
1: <html>
2: <head>
3: <title>Conversion Utility</title>
4: </head>
5:
6: <body bgcolor="#FFFFFF">
7:
8: <p> </p>
9:
```

continues

LISTING **8.1.** CONTINUED

```
10: <form method="POST" action="Convert.asp" name="ConversionUtility">
11:   <p><textarea rows="5" name="txtOriginal" cols="40"></textarea></p>
12:   <div align="left">
13:     <p><input type="submit" value="Convert" name="cmdSubmit"></p>
14:   </div>
15: </form>
16: </body>
17: </html>
```

LISTING **8.2.** AN ASP SCRIPT, THE TARGET OF THE PREVIOUS FORM, CONVERTS ENTERED TEXT INTO PROPERLY ENCODED HTML.

```
 1: <html>
 2:
 3: <head>
 4: <title>Conversion Results</title>
 5: </head>
 6:
 7: <body>
 8: <p><%=Server.HTMLEncode(Request.Form("txtOriginal"))%></p>
 9: </body>
10: </html>
```

ANALYSIS The code in Listing 8.1 displays an HTML form that allows users to enter text they want to have converted. Listing 8.2 performs the actual conversion. The file consists mostly of HTML header information (lines 1–7) and really contains only one line of actual scripting code. Line 8 executes the Server.HTMLEncode() method, displaying the converted text.

The URLEncode() Method

This method is very similar to the previous one, HTMLEncode(), but it has a slightly different purpose and uses a slightly different encoding scheme.

URLEncode() is designed to convert text so that it can be used as part of an HTTP URL. URLs (Universal Resource Locators), like HTML, have certain characters that they treat differently, such as /, \, &, ?, and spaces. To use these characters as part of a URL, because a query parameter or Web page name contains them, could create an error.

 Note

Using special characters, such as spaces, in a URL might not always generate an error because some browsers (such as Microsoft Internet Explorer) con-

> vert those characters to the proper codes before trying to navigate to the location.

The URLEncode() method converts those characters into the corresponding special codes that Web browsers and servers understand. One common example of this conversion is the space character. If a space exists in a URL, either in a parameter or the path itself, it should be replaced with %20 to be correctly interpreted. The method itself is simple to use, taking only one argument (the string to be converted) and returning the result. Listing 8.3 demonstrates how you could modify the utility provided for HTMLEncode() to work with this encoding function instead.

LISTING 8.3. THE URLEncode() VERSION OF THE ASP SCRIPT FROM THE PREVIOUS CONVERSION UTILITY.

```
 1: <html>
 2:
 3: <head>
 4: <title>Conversion Results</title>
 5: </head>
 6:
 7: <body>
 8: <p><%=Server.URLEncode(Request.Form("txtOriginal"))%></p>
 9: </body>
10: </html>
```

ANALYSIS As with the other encoding function, you should use this method only with dynamic URLs, and perform the conversion ahead of time for static information. With the modified code shown in Listing 8.3, you can use the conversion utility to produce your static URLs if needed. Line 8 is, once again, the only scripting code in this listing, and it simply executes the URLEncode() method to display the properly converted text.

The MapPath() Method

When dealing with Web sites, file paths are not always what they appear to be. The file pointed to by http://www.myserver.com/default.asp might have a physical path on the server of C:\InetPub\wwwroot\default.asp, but the page located at http://www.myserver.com/software/default.asp could be stored on the server at D:\webfiles\main\software\default.asp or any other path. It is not always possible to determine the location of a file from the URL used to access it.

Web servers, unlike word processors or other traditional applications, never allow the browser to access a Web site's physical file system directly. The browser simply asks the Web server for the file and then accepts whatever it is given. This allows the Web server a large degree of freedom in how its files are stored and exposed to clients. Requests for a particular path can be redirected to another location easily, and two different URLs could even point to the same file, all without the browser having any knowledge of what is going on. In IIS, file requests are based on *virtual roots*. A virtual root is a directory in a Web site where a logical (URL based) location in the Web does not necessarily correspond to its physical location as it relates to the root of the site. Using the IIS interface, site administrators can point that directory to any path they want, even one that exists on another server. What this creates is the equivalent of two file systems—one visible to the server's Web clients, and the other physically present on the server itself.

Note

> IIS is not the only Web server that supports the concept of virtual roots. Personal Web Server (PWS) functions in the same manner. In fact, most Web servers available today (including Netscape, Apache, and others) allow some form of directory mapping.

To the Web site developer, the difference is usually unimportant. All paths in Web pages are referred to in terms of the client, using whatever virtual directories exist. Certain things in ASP scripts, however, could require you to know or find the physical location of a file when you have only its Web path. Perhaps you are using a third-party component (through the `Server.CreateObject()` method) that zips files. The component needs the physical path for the files to be supplied. To translate from the virtual or logical file system seen by the client to the physical path on the server, you can use the `Server.MapPath()` method. It accepts the virtual path as an argument and returns the corresponding physical location, making it easy to use.

Caution

> The `Server.MapPath()` method returns the corresponding physical path to any Web path you pass to it, regardless of whether the path is valid. If you used `http://www.myserver.com/thefile.asp` as an argument, then it would return a result of what that file's path *would* be if it existed directly under the site's root (such as `C:\InetPub\wwwroot\thefile.asp`), even if the file did not exist. This result is not a bug. The method is designed this way to allow you to determine the path at which to create a file or directory, if needed.

The "." (current directory) and ".." (parent directory) path shortcuts do not work with this method, but you can determine the path of the site's root directory by calling MapPath() with a single slash (/ or \) as the argument. Here's a quick example:

```
<%
    Response.Write "<H2 align='center'>"
    Response.Write "The root path of this web site is: "
    Response.Write "<br>"
    Response.Write Server.MapPath("\")
    Response.Write "</H2>"
%>
```

Note

> If you need only the physical path of the current file (the currently executing script), you do not need to use this method. That information is available to you directly through the PATH_INFO member of the Request.ServerVariables collection and can be accessed simply as <%=Request.ServerVariables("PATH_INFO")%>. This method is the preferred one, if it fits your needs, because it places no additional load on your server.

Setting the ScriptTimeOut Value

When a client requests an Active Server Page, that page's script has to execute before the page can be returned to the browser. How long this process takes can depend on several factors, including how busy the Web server is and what the code in that page is doing. To prevent infinite loops or overly long-running ASP code from holding up client requests, the Web server uses a timeout value. Scripts that execute for any period longer than that value are stopped, and an error message is returned to the client (see Figure 8.2). Listing 8.4 contains ASP code that never finishes executing (it contains an example of an infinite loop), so it causes a timeout error on any Web server.

LISTING 8.4. THIS ASP SCRIPT NEVER STOPS EXECUTING UNTIL A TIMEOUT IS GENERATED BY THE SERVER.

```
1: <html>
2: <head>
3: <title>Endless Loop</title>
4: </head>
5: <body>
6: <p>Start Loop</p>
7: <%
8:     Do While 2 > 1
9:     Loop
```

continues

LISTING 8.4. CONTINUED

```
10: %>
11: <p>End Loop</p>
12: </body>
13: </html>
```

FIGURE 8.2.

The infinite loop in this page caused a Script timed out *error after 90 seconds of execution.*

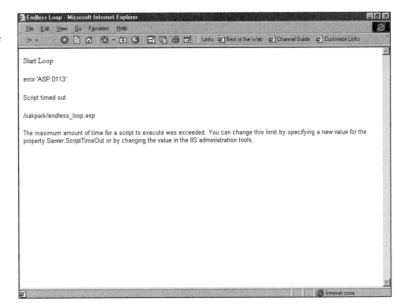

ANALYSIS In Listing 8.4, lines 7 and 8 create an infinite loop by using a continuation condition that will never be false (2 > 1). This condition is not advisable in a final system, but it allows the simulation of an infinite loop, which is generally caused by a programming error.

Setting the Value for the Time Out

The default timeout value for ScriptTimeOut is 90 seconds, which should be enough for most scripts, but it can be changed. In Internet Information Server (IIS) version 4.0, you can change it in the Application Configuration window, shown in Figure 8.3, and set the value for an entire Web site or by directory. You might need to increase this value to stop a timeout from occurring during the execution of some vital, but time-consuming, script, such as the payment stage of an online ordering system. Making this change through IIS is likely more than you need, as it applies that value to every script executed. Because most scripts execute well within the 90-second default value, you generally have only one or two places where this value needs to be increased. The Server.ScriptTimeOut property exists for that reason, allowing you to specify a different timeout value that affects only the currently executing script. You can easily do this in any of your pages; just set the property value to the desired number (in seconds). The following example shows setting the timeout value to 200 seconds, which should allow for almost anything to be started and finished on the server:

```
Server.ScriptTimeOut = 200
```

FIGURE 8.3.

The IIS 4.0 interface for changing the ASP ScriptTimeOut *value.*

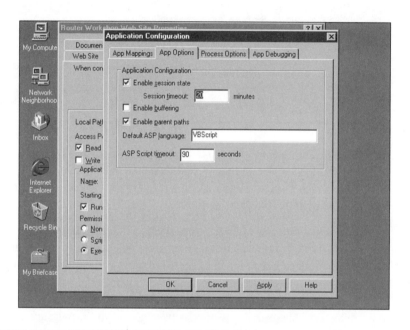

Note

You can set this timeout property to any value you want, but only values greater than the one set through the IIS interface will take effect. If the current timeout value is 90 seconds, and you set the ScriptTimeOut property to 50, the script will still run for 90 seconds before stopping. If, on the other hand, you set the value to 150, it will be used as the timeout value for that script.

Retrieving the Value of the Time Out

In addition to setting the value of the ScriptTimeOut property, you can also retrieve it. Doing so allows you to base the increase on the original value, if you want. Listing 8.5 shows an example of this method.

LISTING 8.5. BASING THE INCREASED TIMEOUT VALUE ON THE CURRENT SETTING.

```
 1: <html>
 2: <head>
 3: <title>ScriptTimeOut Example</title>
 4: </head>
 5: <body>
 6: <%
 7: Dim iTimeout
 8: iTimeout = Server.ScriptTimeOut
 9:
10: Server.ScriptTimeOut = iTimeout + 40
11:
12: 'Do complex processing
13: %>
14: </body>
15: </html>
```

ANALYSIS   The code in Listing 8.5 retrieves the value of the `ScriptTimeOut` property into the variable `iTimeout`, and then uses that value in line 10 to set the same property to a higher value. This allows the script to always increase the timeout value, regardless of what its current value is.

The actual timeout, when IIS stops the execution of the script, occurs only during the script itself. This means that if an external object is causing the long execution time, IIS can't terminate execution until control returns to the script (the line after the external object call). If you are using a third-party component, you probably can't do anything about this problem, but if you build your own components, you should make sure any potentially long-running processes have their own timeout functionality.

The Session Object

A requirement of computer programs, regardless of the medium they are created in, is a way of maintaining state. As a user moves from one section of the application to another, you need to keep track of certain user-specific information. ASP enables this task through the `Session` object, which can store objects and information for the life of an individual's visit to your Web site.

How the Session Object Works

For the `Session` object to function correctly, it is necessary to determine when a person's visit to the site starts and ends. You do this by using a *cookie*, a value stored on the client's machine that can be retrieved later. This particular cookie identifies an ASP Session ID, which the server then uses to maintain a set of information about that user.

When a request for an Active Server Page comes into the server, it first looks at this ID value. If the ID isn't there, it considers this request to be the start of a visit. In other words, this is the first time (recently) that this person has come to this site. The visit ends when no requests (for ASP files) from that user have been received for a certain amount of time. This time period is 20 minutes by default, but can be changed, as you'll see later in this section.

Session Events

When a session, or visit, begins or ends, an event occurs. Using the global.asa file, you can create event procedures that run in response to these events. To create these procedures, add a text file named global.asa to the root of your Web application. Place the following code into that file:

```
<SCRIPT LANGUAGE=VBScript RUNAT=Server>

SUB Session_OnStart

END SUB

</SCRIPT>

<SCRIPT LANGUAGE=VBScript RUNAT=Server>

SUB Session_OnEnd

END SUB

</SCRIPT>
```

Now whatever code you place into these procedures will execute at the start or end of every visit.

Storing Information in the Session Object

The benefit of the Session object is that you can place information into it and retrieve that information at any point during the user's visit. This feature is implemented by using a collection similar to the Request and Response objects you learned about on previous days. Values are placed into the collection through simple assignment statements. Retrieving the value is done in exactly the same fashion as the previous collections you have seen. A sample of both these operations (setting and retrieving values) is shown in Listing 8.6, which is designed to increment a value every time the page is requested by that user.

LISTING 8.6. EVERY TIME YOU REFRESH THIS PAGE, THE NUMBER DISPLAYED INCREASES BY ONE.

```
 1: <html>
 2: <head>
 3: <title>Sample</title>
 4: </head>
 5: <body>
 6: <%
 7:     Session("Counter") = CInt(Session("Counter")) + 1
 8: %>
 9: <p>The current number is: <%=Session("Counter")%> </p>
10: </body>
11: </html>
```

ANALYSIS In Listing 8.6, line 7 increments the value of Session("Counter") by one, a simple process with a little twist. The first time this page is called, Session("Counter") is equal to an empty string, not zero, as you might expect. VBScript would happily convert that value for you when line 7 is executed, but it is good practice to force your own conversion by using a function such as CInt, which converts variables into integer values. Now that the value has been incremented, line 9 displays it along with a caption.

Create and run this page a few times, noticing how the number is increased by one each time. To demonstrate the end of one session and the creation of a new one, close your browser (all open browser windows must be closed) and then reopen this page. The value should start at the beginning again. The ASP Session ID cookie does not remain on the machine after the browser is closed. When you reopen the browser and request the page again, a new session is created; therefore, the value of Session("Counter"), and the rest of the Session object's collection, is equal to empty or undefined.

The Session object, like the rest of VBScript, deals only with variants, allowing it to store almost any type of value. It is even possible to place arrays and objects into this collection. If you do place such items into the Session object, you must first assign them to a variable before you work with their values. Accessing the items directly from within the Session object is not allowed. Listing 8.7 shows an example of placing an array into the Session object and an example of how *not* to access the elements of that array. Listing 8.8 demonstrates the correct two-step procedure.

LISTING 8.7. THE INCORRECT WAY TO WORK WITH AN ARRAY STORED IN THE SESSION OBJECT.

```
1: <html>
2: <head>
3: <title>Array Sample</title>
4: <body>
```

```
 5: <%
 6: Dim X(10)
 7:     X(1)="John"
 8:     X(2)="Donald"
 9: Session("Names") = X
10: Session("Names")(3) = "Jack"
11: %>
12: </body>
13: </html>
```

ANALYSIS   In Listing 8.7, line 6 creates an array that is then populated with two names in lines 7 and 8. This array is then stored in the Session object in line 9, where it is accessible to every page. Up to this point, this is a good demonstration of how you can store a complex data structure, such as an array, into the Session object. The mistake is in how the array is referenced after it has been placed into the collection. Line 10 attempts to directly access one of the array's subscripts, which is not allowed. You must always copy the array into a local variable before you can retrieve or modify its contents.

LISTING 8.8. TO USE AN ARRAY FROM THE SESSION COLLECTION, YOU MUST ASSIGN IT TO A VARIABLE.

```
 1: <html>
 2: <head>
 3: <title>Array Sample</title>
 4: <body>
 5: <%
 6:
 7: Y = Session("Names")
 8: Y(3)="Jack"
 9: Session("Names") = Y
10:
11: %>
12: </body>
13: </html>
```

ANALYSIS   Listing 8.8 shows the correct method of working with arrays and the Session object. Before any values can be modified, the array must be placed into a local variable, as in line 7. After it's placed into Y, you can modify values as desired through a simple assignment statement, as shown in line 8. Notice that the array Y is placed back into the collection in line 9. This procedure is required or your changes don't take effect. Y is a copy of the array stored in Session("Names"), not the original.

The Session ID

Each session that's created gets a new ASP Session ID, a unique value, of the form
316758066 that is not repeated. You can get this value through the Session.SessionID
property, but it can't be changed because it is read-only. It generally has value only
because it uniquely identifies a session. This value is different for every visit to your Web
site (but not for every user because the same user could visit more than once). This
means you could use it as a key into a database, to store information that is not well suited for the Session object or information that must exist after the session has expired.

Modifying the Session Timeout

Earlier you learned how ASP defines a session—one person's visit to the Web site—by
using a cookie known as the Session ID and a timeout value. The timeout, a certain number of minutes, determines how long after the user's last request the session should be
kept alive. The default is 20 minutes, so as long as the user requests something from the
site at least every 20 minutes, the session, and all its associated information, is maintained.

Note   If the server's World Wide Web publishing service is stopped (if the server is
shut down, for instance), then all sessions are abandoned and all their information is lost.

This interval can be modified in two main ways: through the IIS interface (see Figure
8.4) or through scripting code itself. It is usually modified through the interface, as an
administrative task. Sessions use system resources, and reducing the timeout interval
reduces the overall number that are open at any one time. Conversely, increasing this
value allows for a longer period between requests, but places a greater burden on the
server.

Caution   Remember that many sessions can be open at one time. A popular site with
10 visitors per minute has, on average (assuming a session timeout of 20
minutes), at least 200 sessions open at all times. This value will increase
depending on the amount of time usually spent actually browsing the site.

The memory requirements of each session depend on what you use the Session object
for. If you do not use it at all, it still uses some resources to track the Session ID. If, on
the other hand, you use it to store many variables or objects, each session could use a

great deal of resources. The effect of sessions on resources is why the timeout value is generally modified through the interface; it is an administrative issue.

FIGURE 8.4.

Using the IIS 4.0 interface to modify the session timeout value.

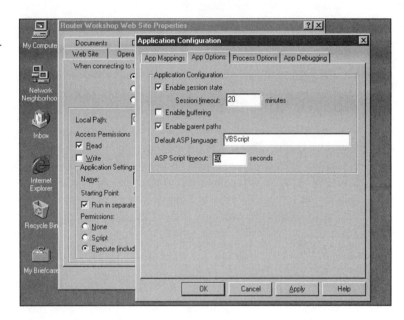

The syntax of modifying or retrieving the timeout value is a simple assignment statement, as shown in the following code, but how and why you would want to do this is more complex.

```
<p>The Session Timeout is <%=Session.Timeout%></p>
<%
    Session.Timeout = 50
%>
```

Changing the Session.Timeout property affects only the current session; it has no lasting effect. If you were to place the code <%Session.Timeout = 50%> into the Session_OnStart procedure in your global.asa file, it would affect every single session. If that is what you need to do, it is much more efficient to simply modify the interval value through the IIS interface. Setting this property through code should be reserved for more dynamic uses. You just learned that increasing or decreasing this value can have an effect on system resources, which provides the following example of a use for this property.

Suppose you needed to reduce the load on your Web server during peak periods (after 5 p.m., in this case), but didn't want to affect the site's behavior during the rest of the day.

You could get this result by placing the following code in your `Session_OnStart` procedure:

```
If Time > "5:00 PM" Then
    Session.Timeout = 5
End If
```

This code has the effect of keeping the timeout at 5 minutes during your peak period, but leaving it set to the default timeout at all other times.

Abandoning the Session

Sessions expire when there has not been a request in however many minutes are set in `Session.Timeout`, but this is not the only way a session can end. For instance, if the Web server stops for any reason, all the sessions end. You can also force a session to end in your ASP script. Calling the `Session.Abandon` method causes the session to expire at that moment. It can be used as a logoff from the site, allowing the user to explicitly choose to be finished with your Web application.

You have now seen how to use the `Session` object to share information throughout one user's visit to your Web site, but what about sharing information among all users of your site? This is where the `Application` object comes in, working at a higher level than the `Session` object.

The `Application` Object

The `Application` object has much in common with the `Session` object. Both exist so the developer has a way of maintaining *state*, a place to store information and have it persist for more than the life of one page. Both have a start and an end; in fact, event procedures for `Application_OnStart` and `Application_OnEnd` are also placed into your `global.asa` file, as shown in Listing 8.9.

LISTING 8.9. ADDING THESE PROCEDURES TO YOUR GLOBAL.ASA FILE ALLOWS YOU TO RUN CODE AT THE START AND END OF YOUR WEB APPLICATION.

```
 1: <SCRIPT LANGUAGE=VBScript RUNAT=Server>
 2:
 3: SUB Application_OnStart
 4:     ' This script executes when
 5:     ' the first user comes to the site.
 6:
 7: END SUB
 8:
 9: </SCRIPT>
10:
```

8

```
11: <SCRIPT LANGUAGE=VBScript RUNAT=Server>
12:
13: SUB Application_OnEnd
14:
15:     ' This script executes when
16:     ' the server shuts down or
17:     ' when global.asa changes.
18:
19: END SUB
20:
21: </SCRIPT>
```

ANALYSIS In Listing 8.9, the global.asa file, you have two separate event procedures, one for when your application begins and one for when it ends. The OnStart event procedure (lines 3–7) is called when the first (since it last stopped executing) Active Server Page file is requested from this Web application, but many different events can cause the second procedure to be called. The OnEnd event (lines 13–19) is called when the Web application shuts down, which can happen when the entire Web server is closed or if the contents of the global.asa file are changed. Modifying the global.asa file (adding a blank line, for instance) is a quick shortcut for causing your Web application to restart.

The difference between the Session object and the Application object is scope. A session exists for the duration of one individual visit to the site, but the Application object persists from the first request in a site until that site stops operating. That means you use the objects for different purposes. Information can be maintained in the Application object that is used across all the site's sessions. A simple example, shown in Listing 8.10, is tracking the number of sessions created on a Web server since it started running, which could be done with the following code placed into the Application_OnStart and Session_OnStart procedures in your global.asa file.

LISTING 8.10. A SIMPLE APPLICATION TO TRACK THE NUMBER OF SESSIONS.

```
 1:    SUB Application_OnStart
 2:
 3:        Application("Counter") = 0
 4:
 5:    END SUB
 6:
 7:    SUB Session_OnStart
 8:
 9:        Application.Lock
10:        Application("Counter") = Application("Counter") + 1
11:        Application.Unlock
12:
13:    END SUB
```

> **Note**
>
> Modifying the `global.asa` file resets the application, all its information, and all the currently open sessions.

ANALYSIS The code in the `Application_OnStart` procedure (lines 1–5) just initializes the collection item for later use. Similar to the `Session` object, as well as the `Request` and `Response` objects, it is a straightforward process to retrieve and modify collection items. The `Session_OnStart` procedure contains something new, however: the `Lock` method in line 9 and the `Unlock` methods of the `Application` object in line 11.

Avoiding Conflict

The `Application` object, unlike any other ASP object, contains values that can be modified by multiple users. That means it is possible for conflicts to occur. Take the previous example: If two sessions started at the same time, then they could both execute the line that increments `Application("Counter")`. This duplication could result in false or corrupted data being stored in this object.

The `Lock` and `Unlock` methods prevent this type of problem from occurring. A call to `Application.Lock` does not return until it gets an exclusive hold on the `Application` object. Other attempts to issue that same command do not return until the session that locked the object calls `Application.Unlock`. Therefore, if you bracket all interactions with the `Application` object with calls to `Lock` and `Unlock`, only one session can work with those values at a time.

However, these calls bring their own problems. It is important to minimize the time the `Application` object is locked because all other sessions requiring its use will be stalled. If you must perform a series of operations between two uses of the `Application` object, use multiple `Lock` and `Unlock` pairs to ensure the shortest possible locking time.

The concept of shared access to an object is not limited to the `Application` object; similar conflicts and other problems occur whenever multiple users access an object. The `Lock` and `Unlock` methods work well for the `Application` object, but they are not available for any other type of shared objects, so a different method of providing shared access must be found. Microsoft Transaction Server (MTS) offers this type of resource sharing, as well as many other useful features, to your ASP application.

Microsoft Transaction Server (MTS)

To explain how MTS can work with your server-side script, you need to understand what it is and why it is so useful. The concept of a transaction is not new; it has existed in

8

computers for a long time, mostly in databases. A *transaction* is the idea that a series of actions should be grouped and that if any one of those actions cannot be completed, all the actions in the group (that have executed so far) should be undone. This grouping of actions was necessary in computer programs. Consider the following example...

You go down to the bank and request a transfer. You want to move $2,000.00 from your account here to an account in Switzerland. The clerk pushes some buttons on the computer and the amount is debited from your account. The bank's systems then attempt to wire that money to the account in Switzerland, but the transaction fails. The debit to your account is removed, and you are told that the transfer could not go through.

Looking at this example from a computer's viewpoint, you can see the following steps in the simplified version of a bank transfer:

1. Money is removed from one account.
2. Money is added to another account.

If either of these steps fails, for whatever reason, the other must be undone. In other systems, it might be acceptable if the first step was not undone, but not when money is involved. Almost every task in a banking system works like this, but really involves hundreds of individual steps, not just two.

Writing code intelligent enough to back out of the operation from any point would be difficult and probably take more time than the transfer code itself. This is where transactions came in. Database systems gained a few new commands—one to mark the start of a transaction, one to mark the end, and one to undo (roll back) the entire thing. Applying this new concept to the previous example, you would start a transaction right before the first step and end it immediately after the last one. After each individual command, you would check whether it has succeeded and roll back the transaction if it has not. This procedure works great. The systems can never be left in an incorrect state; either the money transfers successfully, or nothing happens at all. No code is required to undo the previous steps. Simply wrap every set of related actions into a transaction.

This transaction process was, until recently, a function of the database system only. If, as part of a single transaction, you wanted to connect to three different databases, or call a component that could also perform operations on data, you could not wrap a transaction around it all. This limitation became more and more of a problem as systems became component based and multiple; heterogeneous databases were often present.

Microsoft Transaction Server (MTS) moves the concept of a transaction up a level, allowing it to encompass the actions of components, not just databases. DLLs and other types of objects can be placed under the control of MTS and can then participate in these transactions. The other key benefit and purpose of MTS is to act as an object-request broker (ORB); allowing it to manage all the instances and shared resources of your components can greatly increase efficiency and performance.

Note

> This discussion, designed to give you an overview of the topic, is an oversimplification of MTS, which is a very complex product. For more information on MTS, see *Roger Jennings' Database Workshop: Microsoft Transaction Server 2.0* by Sams Publishing, November 1997 (ISBN: 0-672-311305).

Because IIS and ASP are both component-based, they use MTS to manage many of their objects. Your pages can also take advantage of the benefits of transactions by using the `ObjectContext` object and a few simple commands.

The @ `Transaction` Statement

You have already seen the @ `Language` statement, used at the start of your script to indicate the default scripting language for that page. The @ `Transaction` statement is another setting of that type, which must be placed on the first line of the page.

Note

> If you need to use both the `Language` and `Transaction` statements, they must both be the first line of the page. To do so, you can actually combine the two statements into one, like this:
>
> ```
> <%@ Language=VBScript Transaction=Required%>
> ```

The `Transaction` statement controls whether the page's script is run as a transaction, one that ends when the page does. Table 8.2 lists transaction settings and their meanings.

TABLE 8.2. TRANSACTION SETTINGS.

Settings	Meaning
Required	The page must run in a transaction.
Requires_new	The page must run in a transaction, but must create a new one just for this page.
Supported	The page will use a transaction, if one already exists.
Not_Supported	The page will not create or use a transaction.

In general, you use only `Required`; not specifying anything is the same as `Not_Supported`, and those two settings are enough for the needs of Active Server Pages.

After you have specified that your page should work within a transaction, you can use the two methods and two events of the `ObjectContext` object supplied by MTS.

 Note

> The `ObjectContext` object actually has more features than described here, but only the ones discussed are available through ASP. The object's full functionality is available through Visual Basic or Visual C++ components written to run under MTS.

The `SetComplete` and `SetAbort` Methods

The `SetComplete` method is used to tell MTS whether a transaction has finished successfully; `SetAbort` tells MTS whether a transaction has failed in some way. Listing 8.11 gives you an example of how these two methods are used in your scripts.

LISTING **8.11.** MTS METHODS USED IN ASP SCRIPTS.

```
 1: <%@ Transaction=Required%>
 2: <html>
 3: <head>
 4: <title>Order Processing</title>
 5: </head>
 6: <body>
 7: <%
 8: Set objOrder=Server.CreateObject(Order.clsNewOrder")
 9: ObjOrder.StartNewOrder
10: Set objAddress=Server.CreateObject("Validate.clsAddress")
11: objAddress.Name = Request.Form("Name")
12: objAddress.Street = Request.Form("Street")
13: objAddress.City = Request.Form("City")
14: objAddress.State = Request.Form("State")
15: objAddress.ZipCode = Request.Form("ZipCode")
16: objAddress.Email = Request.Form("Email")
17: If objAddress.Valid Then
18:     ObjectContext.SetComplete
19:     Response.Write "<p>Your Address was accepted, thank you.</p>"
20: Else
21:     ObjectContext.SetAbort
22:     Response.Write "<p>Your address was not valid.</p>"
23: End If
24: %>
```

ANALYSIS In Listing 8.11, the @ `Transaction` line is used in line 1 to tell MTS that this page requires a transaction; in line 8, the script creates an instance of the `clsNewOrder` object. This object is now participating in the same transaction as the ASP

script, so any actions performed when its `StartNewOrder` method is called (line 9) could
be rolled back if the entire transaction was aborted. The next section of the page (lines
10–16) create another object instance and then set a series of that object's properties.
After the properties are set, the value of the `Valid` property (line 17) is used to determine
whether the entire transaction should be considered successful or rolled back (lines 18
or 21).

The `If` statement in line 17 also controls what message is displayed to the user: either a
thank you (line 19) or an error message (line 22). If the code didn't contain any reference
to MTS at all, the same message would be displayed, so you might argue that MTS was-
n't even necessary. Under MTS, however, a lot more is happening than what is immediately apparent. Actions that had been performed by the `objOrder` and `objValidate` components would also be undone when `SetAbort` was called, something that regular scripting would find difficult, if not impossible, to accomplish.

It is also possible that the address would have been valid (`objAddress.Valid` is true), but
that `SetAbort` would be called from within `objOrder`, not the page. `ObjectContext` and
all its methods are also available to all the components in the transaction, so that they can
also abort a transaction if an error is encountered. If this were to happen, nothing would
be shown to the user, which might suggest that the operation was successful when it was
not. For this reason, to allow your script to react to your transaction aborting from any
source, two events are provided.

The `OnTransactionCommit` and `OnTransactionAbort` Events

The `OnTransactionCommit` and `OnTransactionAbort` events are used when you are
working with a transaction and want to run code based on the result of that transaction,
regardless of how it ends. If any component calls `SetAbort`, then the entire transaction is
undone and the `OnTransactionAbort` event is called, allowing you to display a failure
message and perform any other processing you want. The successful completion of the
transaction causes the `OnTransactionCommit` event to occur, but the transaction is not
considered to have completed successfully until all the components involved have completed without calling `SetAbort`. One component, or your page, simply calling
`SetComplete` does not cause the successful conclusion of the transaction; it is simply
informing MTS that it has completed successfully (so far).

> **Caution**
>
> Unfortunately, aborting a transaction does not undo everything. The most notable exception, from the view of an ASP programmer, is that it doesn't undo changes made to the contents of the session collection. Use the `OnTransactionAbort` event to undo whatever changes you made to those values.

The code in Listing 8.12 demonstrates the proper syntax for adding these two events to your code.

LISTING 8.12. THE `OnTransactionCommit` AND `OnTransactionAbort` EVENT PROCEDURES.

```
 1: <SCRIPT LANGUAGE=VBScript RUNAT=Server>
 2:
 3: SUB OnTransactionCommit()
 4:
 5: Response.Write "<h3>"
 6: Response.Write "Order Taken Successfully"
 7: Response.Write "</h3>"
 8:
 9: END SUB
10:
11: SUB OnTransactionAbort()
12:
13: Response.Write "<h3>"
14: Response.Write "Order Processing Failed"
15: Response.Write "<br>"
16: Response.Write "Please Try Again.</h3>"
17:
18: END SUB
19:
20: </SCRIPT>
```

ANALYSIS In Listing 8.12, the `OnTransactionCommit` event procedure (lines 3–9) reacts to the successful completion of all parts of the transaction by displaying a nice little message. This message, unlike the one in the previous example, is shown only if all components and script involved in the transaction complete successfully. Similarily, the `OnTransactionAbort` event (lines 11–18) is called if any component or scripting code calls the `ObjectContext.SetAbort` method, regardless of when or where this occurs.

Overall, when used properly, Microsoft Transaction Server makes your Active Server Pages suitable for use with important multi-step processes (such as sales orders). In such systems, it is essential that any process that fails before successfully completing be completely and easily reversed, regardless of where in the system the failure occurs.

Summary

ASP is based on objects; without them, it would not be possible to do almost anything. Each of the objects introduced in today's lesson provides useful functionality for your pages, but only if you use it. The `Server` object's `CreateObject()` method will quickly become indispensable to you; if you are going to use any external objects in your code, it is the only way to access them. The `Session` and `Application` objects allow your Web site to maintain information beyond the life of one page, or even one visit. Their associated events in the `global.asa` file are also quite useful, giving you the ability to execute code whenever a person arrives at your site, regardless of the page he or she is visiting.

The final object discussed introduced you to the world of Microsoft Transaction Server (MTS), which is quickly becoming an essential part of distributed application development. If you plan on building an efficient, reliable system, you need to use the `ObjectContext` object it provides.

Overall, there is a great deal of functionality offered through just the built-in objects of ASP. When you consider the external objects available through `CreateObject()`, the possibilities are endless.

Q&A

Q When would I use the `Server.HTMLEncode()` method?

A This method, along with `Server.URLEncode()` is useful for processing dynamic text, such as from forms or databases. You cannot process that text ahead of time.

Q Why must you minimize the time between `Application.Lock` and `Application.Unlock`?

A No other sessions (users) can use the `Application` object between these two statements. Large amounts of code placed in that location could cause long delays for other users of the Web site.

Q My users don't like cookies, but ASP uses them. Can I turn them off?

A Yes. The cookies are used to give your pages the `Session` object's functionality. If you are willing to not use the `Session` object and its collection, then you can place the following line at the beginning of your page to disable it:

```
<%@ EnableSessionState=False%>
```

This statement is another one like `@ Transaction` and `@ Language`, so it must be the first line of your code to function correctly.

Q I want an object to be available to all my users. Does it matter whether I put it into the `Application` or `Session` object?

A   Yes and no. Placing it in either object will make it available to all your users. The difference, however, is memory usage. If you create an object and add it to the Session object's collection, you are creating a copy in memory for every single active session. Placing it in the Application object, on the other hand, makes it available to everyone, but only a single copy is required.

Workshop

The quiz questions and exercises are provided for your further understanding. Please refer to Appendix A, "Answers to Questions," for the answers.

Quiz

1. What object and method is used to gain access to external objects?
2. What is the default timeout of a session?
3. What category of software originated the concept of transactions?
4. Name two things that can cause a user's session to end.
5. What does %20 mean if it is part of a Web page's URL?

Exercises

1. Write code that doubles the current session's timeout value.
2. Build an @ statement to go at the top of your page that makes the page require a transaction and use VBScript as its default scripting language.
3. Write code to take the physical path to the Web site's root, prepare it for display on a Web page, and then store that value in the Application object.
4. Rewrite the following code to minimize the time the Application object is locked.

```
<%
Dim iAverageSpeed
Dim i
Application.Lock
iAverageSpeed = Application("AverageSpeed")

For i = 1 to 20
iAverageSpeed = iAverageSpeed + Session("User Speed Test " & i)
iAverageSpeed = iAverageSpeed / 2
Next i

Application("AverageSpeed") = iAverageSpeed
Application.Unlock
%>
```

WEEK 2

DAY 9

Using ActiveX Components Built for ASP

by Steve Elfanbaum

You've seen in the previous chapter how ASP provides objects that can be used to enhance the user experience. Today, you learn how to further improve that experience with objects that conform to Microsoft's ActiveX standard. These objects allow you to supply information taken from a database, change the page each time it's refreshed, and even customize the page to work differently based on the type of browser being used. Moreover, these operations work whether or not the user's browser supports ActiveX objects because the Web server does all the work. Today, you cover the following:

- Discover how to use ASP ActiveX components.
- Learn how to use the Ad Rotator and Content Rotator components to offer dynamic page content.
- Understand the Browser Capabilities component and how you can create content for specific browser clients.

- Access data from databases using the Data Access component.
- Use the Tools component to perform a variety of programming tasks.

How to Use ASP ActiveX Components

You'll find that using an ActiveX component in your ASP document is just as easy as using the built-in ASP objects you learned about yesterday. After the object has been installed and registered on the Web server, there are essentially two steps to the process.

First, create an instance of the component and assign it to a variable. To create an instance, you can use the ASP Server.CreateObject() command, passing the registered name of the object, or PROGID, as shown in the following code line. (The PROGID should be available in the accompanying documentation for the ActiveX object.) To assign the object to a variable, use the variable assignment command for the scripting language being used:

```
Set MyObject = Server.CreateObject("PROGID")
```

Next, use the object's properties and methods to perform the function you want. Now that the object has been created and is available to the script in your page, you can use the properties and methods supported by the object to make it work for you, as shown here:

```
MyObject.SomeProperty = aValue
```

You can also display a property's value, as shown in this example, within the ASP tags:

```
<% =MyObject.SomeProperty %>
<% MyObject.DoSomethingCool "With", "These", "Parameters" %>
```

Note

> Keep in mind that to use ActiveX components with ASP scripting, they *cannot* have any graphical elements. Many handy controls and "widgets" for use in Windows development are now available as ActiveX components. Such components have a graphical element or user interface to them. They might be useful for Web development if the client's browser supports ActiveX technology, but these kinds of components cannot be used within ASP scripting. None of the objects you explore in today's lesson has a user interface; they are strictly encapsulated programs that perform a specific function.

Downloading and Installing ActiveX Components

The ActiveX objects that come with the Active Server Pages installation have already been downloaded and registered on your PC during the product installation.

If you want to download and install additional components, it is a straightforward process. Most of the time, the component is downloaded as part of a package or a setup EXE file. If this is the case, the setup program will most likely register the component for you. It is then ready for use.

If the component is downloaded as a set of files with no setup program, you can register it on your system by using the REGSVR32.EXE command. Typing REGSVR32 with no parameters displays a message box that explains the command's usage. The following is a typical command line used to register the object contained in myactvex.dll:

```
REGSVR32 C:\OBJECTS\MYACTVEX.DLL
```

After this operation is finished, the object is registered and ready for use in your ASP script.

Rotating Advertisements for Increased Information Exposure

Advertising is big business on the Web, and has been shown the most effective way to make money on the Internet. In many cases, free services offered on the Web, such as search engines, news and sports sites, and electronic magazines are free because they can make money by placing advertisements on their sites.

If one ad can generate income, then 10 or 100 ads can generate enough to make the time and money spent setting up a world-class Web site worthwhile. Here is the problem: How can you display as many different advertisements as possible without coming up with some goofy schemes, such as having each page in your site associated with different ads?

The answer is, of course, the Ad Rotator ActiveX component. This component selects an advertisement for your page each time the user refreshes or loads the page for the first time. In addition, the ads and their locations are listed in a text file that can be changed on-the-fly to add or remove advertisements without changing the HTML or ASP code on the page.

The call for the Ad Rotator component can be placed anywhere on your Web page that you would like to place an ad. (In fact, you aren't limited to the number of ads on a page—you just place the code wherever you want an ad to appear.)

 Caution | All advertisements to be rotated in an area must be exactly the same size.

The Rotator Schedule File

The first step is to create a *rotator schedule file* that the component uses to determine which ad to display. This file has two sections. The first gives the component information about all the advertising images and is made up of four parameters, all of which are optional:

- REDIRECT
- WIDTH
- HEIGHT
- BORDER

The REDIRECT Parameter

The REDIRECT parameter specifies what page the user's browser will access if he or she clicks on the ad. Here is the format:

```
[REDIRECT URL]
```

If this parameter is used, the page specified should be a *redirection file* (see the section "The Redirection File (Optional)"). If this parameter is not specified, the default is to send the user directly to the URL attached to the ad. The redirection URL can be a complete address, such as http://www.MySite.com/handleAds.asp, or an address relative to the current location of the page calling the component, such as handleAds.asp.

The WIDTH Parameter

The WIDTH parameter specifies the width, in pixels, for the ad images in this list. The default is 440 pixels. This is the format:

```
[WIDTH numWidth]
```

The HEIGHT Parameter

The HEIGHT parameter specifies the height, in pixels, for the ad images in this list. The default is 60 pixels. Here's the format:

```
[HEIGHT numHeight]
```

The BORDER Parameter

The BORDER parameter specifies the thickness, in pixels, for the hyperlink border around the image. If you don't want a border at all, specify 0. The default is 1 pixel. This is the format:

```
[BORDER numBorder]
```

The Ad Listings

After the component information for the ads comes information on each ad listing. You should place an asterisk on a line by itself to denote the beginning of the ad listing.

For each advertisement to be rotated in this position, supply the following four pieces of information, shown in Table 9.1.

TABLE 9.1. THE AD INFORMATION.

Parameter	Description
AdURL	The location of the advertising image to be displayed.
AdHomePageURL	The location where users should be directed if they click on the advertisement shown. This is usually the advertiser's home page, but it could be any Web address.
Text	The text displayed in the ad area before the image has been loaded, or if the browser used does not support images.
Impressions	A number that denotes the weight this advertisement should be given when the component is determining which ad to show.

When the impression number is combined with the impression numbers from the other ads in the list, the component can calculate the percentage of times the user sees this ad compared to the other ads in the list. For example, if the impression value for the Microsoft Visual Coffee Maker is 5, and the sum of all impression values in this rotator schedule file is 100, the Microsoft ad will be visible 5% of the time. However, if ads are removed from the list until the sum is only 20, the Microsoft ad will appear 25% of the time.

The parameters in Table 9.1 should be specified for each ad to appear in the prescribed location, and the parameters should follow each other, one on each line, with no blank lines in between.

Listing 9.1 presents a sample rotator schedule file that is used to rotate four ads for other Web sites, in a 500×80 pixel area, with no hyperlink border.

LISTING 9.1. AN AD ROTATOR FILE.

```
 1:   REDIRECT /asp/adHandler.asp
 2:   WIDTH 500
 3:   HEIGHT 80
 4:   BORDER 0
 5:   *
 6:   http://www.superauction.com/ads/latest_ad.gif
 7:   http://www.superaction.com
 8:   Get it cheap at SuperAuction!
 9:   25
10:   http://www.mysite.comn/ad_gifs/totally_games.gif
11:   http://www.totallygames.com
12:   Bored?  Tired of surfing?  Get some action on Totally Games!
13:   30
14:   http://www.megasearch.net/adlist/todaysad.gif
15:   http://www.megasearch.net/scripts/clicked_in.asp
16:   Find what you need at MegaSearch
17:   20
18:   http://www.spatulacity.com/gifs/bestbuy.gif
19:   http://www.spatulacity.com
20:   Click here for name-brand spatulas at a fraction of retail cost!
21:   25
```

ANALYSIS Listing 9.1 presents an Ad Rotator file in the format described previously. The first four parameters describe the overall ads. The separator asterisk is in line 5, followed by descriptions for four ads. You can see *AdURL* parameters in lines 6, 10, 14, and 18. Lines 7, 11, 15, and 19 have *adHomePageURL* parameters. Lines 8, 12, 16, and 20 have the text that's while waiting for each corresponding image to load. Finally, lines 9, 13, 17, and 21 have the impressions. The first ad in lines 6 through 9 has an impression of 25. Because this value is out of 100 (25+30+20+25), it is displayed 25% of the time. The second ad is displayed 30% of the time.

The Redirection File (Optional)

If you want to log advertisement activity by recording each time an ad is clicked, the next step is to create the redirection file, which is accessed whenever a user clicks on the displayed advertisement. The URL of this page should have been specified in the REDI-RECT parameter of the rotator schedule file. When the hyperlink goes to your redirection file page, the URL of the Web page for the advertiser is passed in. The main job of the redirection page is to redirect the browser to the advertiser's site, using an ASP Response.Redirect() command, like this:

```
Response.Redirect(Request.QueryString("url"))
```

This redirection command automatically writes an entry to the Web server's log file, describing when and where the redirection occurred.

However, if you would like to take this opportunity to update a count for that advertiser, or save some information on users' browsers about where they were when they clicked on the ad, this is the time to do it. Just add the necessary ASP scripting on this page and perform those actions before executing the redirection command.

Incorporating the Ad Rotator

You've created the rotator schedule file to tell the control where the images are and when to show them. You've created the redirection file to log the response to the advertisements. You are now ready to incorporate the advertisements into your Web page.

First, create an instance of the object by placing the following command somewhere in your script before you want the advertisement to appear:

```
Set ad = Server.CreateObject("MSWC.AdRotator")
```

Then, place the following script code wherever on the page that you want the ad to appear, specifying which rotator schedule file to use:

```
<%= ad.GetAdvertisement("/path/rotatorSchedule.txt") %>
```

That's it! When the user accesses the Web page where this script appears, the GetAdvertisement call is then replaced with the following HTML code:

```
<A HREF="/asp/adHandler.asp?http://www.superauction.com">
<IMG SRC="http://www.superauction.com/latest_ads.gif"
ALT="Get it cheap at SuperAuction!"
WIDTH=500 HEIGHT=80 BORDER=0></A>
```

Each time the page is refreshed, the HTML code is regenerated, using the information from the next scheduled advertisement. The image is a hyperlink, so when the user clicks on the image, the redirection page is loaded and executed by the server.

Rotating Web Site Contents

The Content Rotator component allows you to easily replace entire sections of HTML every time a user loads or refreshes your page. This component could have a variety of uses:

- Provide a "Tip/Quote of the Day," randomly selected from a list.
- Show announcements about upcoming events or changes.
- Have a featured sponsor/book/software write-up that can be easily changed from day to day.
- Provide a rotating e-mail address that is displayed so the same technician does not have to receive all the correspondence.

9

This component also uses a schedule file so you can easily adjust the content and control the prioritization of which items are shown.

 Note

> The Content Rotator component is not installed automatically with IIS and ASP. You need to either download it from the Microsoft Web site at `http://www.microsoft.com/iis/` or install the IIS Resource Kit on your Web server.
>
> After you install the component, you need to register it from the command prompt as explained in the earlier section, "Downloading and Installing ActiveX Components." For more information, consult the README file that comes with the documentation for the component.
>
> The components included with the IIS Resource Kit are automatically registered, so you can begin using them immediately.

Using the Content Rotator Component

The Content Rotator component works much like the Ad Rotator component, in that there is a driver file (called a content schedule file) that contains the information needed to show each rotating item. After this file is created, you're ready to use the component in your ASP script.

The Content Schedule File

The content schedule file, unlike the rotator schedule file, has no header information. There can be as many rotating entries as you want, each using the following syntax:

```
%% [#weight] [//Comments]
ContentString
```

Listing 9.2 presents a sample content schedule file.

LISTING 9.2. A SAMPLE CONTENT SCHEDULE FILE.

```
 1:  %% #2 // This is the first entry.
 2:  <H2>Quote for the Day:</H2></P>
 3:  "I'm not a vegetarian because I love animals,
 4:      I'm a vegetarian because I hate plants."</P>
 5:  <I>- A. Whitney Brown</I>
 6:  %% // This entry has a weight of 1.
 7:  %% // It also has a second line of comments.
 8:  <IMG SRC="/images/dancing_vegetables.gif">
 9:  %% #3
10:  Vegetable Site of the Day: <A HREF="http://www.secretgarden.com">
11:      The Secret Garden Seed Store</A>
12:  If You Don't Like The Content, Come Back In Five Minutes…
```

ANALYSIS Each entry begins with %% at the beginning of the line. You can see this in lines 1, 6, 7, and 9. After that delimiter, the weight to be considered when picking an entry can be specified, preceded by a pound sign (#). The *weight* value is used in the same way as in the Ad Rotator component. The percentage of occurrences of the entry is equal to the ratio of that entry's weight to the combined weight values of all entries. The *weight* value is optional, and, if left blank (as in lines 6 and 7), the default is 1. A zero weight means that the entry is never shown.

After the *weight* value, comments that describe the entry can be entered after the // delimiter. If more than one line is needed, each line must begin with %% //, followed by the remaining comments. Lines 6 and 7 in Listing 9.2 contain comments.

On the next line after the entry header, enter the content to be displayed. This content can be any HTML code that could be placed into a Web page, including text, images, sounds, and hyperlinks. The entry can be as many lines as you want because the entries are delimited by the %% symbol at the beginning of the line.

Adding Dynamic Content to Your Web Site

Now you're ready to put dynamic, randomly selected content into your Web site. All it takes is two lines of ASP scripting. The first line creates an instance of the object and assigns it to a variable of your choosing, using a now-familiar statement:

```
Set myContentRotator = Server.CreateObject("MSWC.ContentRotator")
```

Then you need to place the following statement wherever you would like your randomly selected HTML to appear:

```
<% =myContentRotator.ChooseContent("ContentSchedule.txt") %>
```

Notice the equal sign in front of the function call. That's important because the ChooseContent() method returns the HTML for you to use. Therefore, calling it without the equal sign will work, but no content will be displayed.

Tip

The Content Rotator component has another method, GetAllContent(), which serves a useful purpose: It displays all the entries in the content schedule file one after the other, separated by lines. This method allows you to make sure all the content snippets you have placed in your file are actually displayed the way you expect. Here's what the call looks like:

```
<% =myContentRotator.GetAllContent("ContentSchedule.txt") %>
```

Note that, unlike the ChooseContent() method, this function displays the content to the page without having to use the equal sign.

Optimizing Content for Various Web Browsers

One of the most attractive features of publishing content on the World Wide Web is that what is published is available to so many people, regardless of operating system or type of computer, as long as they have a browser that can interpret HTML. However, as the medium has advanced and corporations have needed a competitive advantage to distinguish their browser from that of another company, features have been added and components (or plug-ins) have been introduced.

This is great for the end user, but hard on the Web site author. Now the decision must be made whether to support features that are available on some browsers, but not others. Furthermore, what happens if a user with an unsupported browser pulls up the site's pages anyway? How can the page be smart enough to support all browsers and still use the coolest, latest features for the browsers that can handle them?

That's where the Browser Capabilities component comes in. Using this component, the author can determine which features are supported and which aren't available. Then the Web page can be customized to fit the capabilities of the browser being used, and the user of an unsupported or outdated browser can be informed of what he or she is missing.

 Note

> Every time a browser connects to any Web server, the browser automatically sends a User Agent HTTP header—a string that specifies the browser and its version number. The Browser Capabilities component compares this header to entries in the browscap.ini file.
>
> If it finds a match, the BrowserType object assumes the properties and the property values of the browser listing that matched the User Agent header. If no match is found, the object assumes the properties of the "Default Browser" entry.
>
> For more information about the User Agent HTTP header, refer to the HTTP specification available at http://www.w3.org/.

Using the Browser Capabilities Component

The Browser Capabilities component consists of a set of methods and a driver file. However, this time the driver file has already been started for you, and a copy of it should already be on your computer. This means you can use the component right away without creating a file first, and you can update the driver file later to add browser properties and to support new browsers or new versions.

To use the Browser Capabilities component in your ASP script, first create an instance of the object:

```
Set myBrowserType = Server.CreateObject("MSWC.BrowserType")
```

After the object is created, the browser's properties are accessible as properties of the object and can be used for display, comparison, or any other needed use. Listing 9.3 shows how the Browser Capabilities component is used within your ASP code.

LISTING 9.3. DETERMINING WHETHER A CLIENT SUPPORTS TABLES (LISTING9_3.ASP).

```
1:  The browser you are using is: <%= myBrowserType.browser%>
2:  version <%= myBrowserType.version%>. </P>
3:  Your browser
4:    <% if (myBrowserType.tables = TRUE) then %>
5:    supports
6:  <% else %>
7:    does not support
8:  <% end if %>
9:    tables.
```

ANALYSIS Listing 9.3 assumes that you have used the CreateObject() method of the Server object to create a browser object called myBrowserType, as shown earlier in this section. After this has been done, you can use the methods of the Browser Capabilities component. Line 1 uses the browser method to get the type of browser your user is using. Line 2 gets the version of the browser by using the version method. In line 4, a check is done to see whether the user's browser supports tables. If the tables method returns TRUE, then you know tables are supported and line 5 prints a message saying "supports". If tables are not supported, then line 7 prints a message saying "does not support". Instead of messages, it could just as easily have been HTML code that uses, or doesn't use, tables.

A list of some of the browser properties provided with the default browser file is shown in Table 9.2.

TABLE 9.2. BROWSER CAPABILITIES PROPERTY LIST.

Property	Description
ActiveXControls	Whether the browser supports ActiveX controls.
Backgroundsounds	Whether the browser supports background sounds.
Beta	Whether the browser is in a beta-testing phase.
Browser	The name of the browser.
Cookies	Whether the browser supports cookies.
Frames	Whether the browser supports frames.
Javaapplets	Whether the browser supports Java applets.
Javascript	Whether the browser supports client-side JavaScript.
Majorver	Number before the first decimal in the version number.
Minorver	Number after the first decimal in the version number.
Platform	In which operating system the browser will run.
Tables	Whether the browser supports tables.
Vbscript	Whether the browser supports client-side VBScript.
Version	The complete version number of the browser in use.
Win16	Whether the browser will run in a 16-bit Windows OS.

The `browscap.ini` File

The file that the Browser Capabilities component uses to determine what kind of browser is being used is the `browscap.ini` file. Each browser has its own section in the file, and the entry headers match the User Agent HTTP header sent by the browser.

The `browscap.ini` file supplied with Active Server Pages contains entries for most known browsers, plus a default entry that is applied if the browser in use does not have an entry in the file. You should need to update this file only in the following cases:

- A browser that is not specifically named is being used to load your site.
- A version of a browser is created that supports a new feature you would like to support on your site.
- You want to add a browser property of your own that isn't currently defined.

If you would like to enhance or change the file yourself, here is the syntax used:

```
[; comments]
[HTTPUserAgentHeader]
[parent = browserDefinition]
[property1 = value1]
...
```

```
[propertyN = valueN]
[Default Browser Capability Settings]
[defaultProperty1 = defaultValue1]
...
[defaultPropertyN = defaultValueN]
```

The *comments* section allows the user to describe in plain English which browser the entry defines because the User Agent HTTP headers can be rather cryptic at times. The *HTTPUserAgentHeader* parameter is the exact character string sent by the browser and is used to match the browser to a browscap.ini entry.

The *browserDefinition* parameter listed after the parent property allows you to build on a previous browser definition. If a new version of a browser adds only one or two features, you can greatly abbreviate the entry for the new browser by supplying the old browser's header as the parent name. Then you can supplement the definition with the new properties that have changed in that version.

The next set of lines describes the properties of the browser. You can use any property name you want, as long as it begins with a letter and is no longer than 255 characters. The values given for each property are assumed to be strings, unless you put a # in front to specify an integer, or use the Boolean values TRUE and FALSE. You can specify as many property and values pairs for a browser as you want.

Tip

Make sure you are consistent with the way you spell property names for different browser entries, or the Browser Capabilities component will read them as different properties. Remember that the properties of a browser are what you define them to be.

The last section defines what property values are used if the browser is not specifically named in the file. These property values follow the same rules as the values for specifically defined browsers, but the entry header must be defined exactly as in the previous code listing. If no default browser section is defined, and the user is using a browser that is not defined in the file, all properties for that browser are defined as the string UNKNOWN.

Linking Web Pages with the Content Linking Component

In many cases, Web sites have supplemented or replaced written material in corporations and consumer media. However, one complaint about the World Wide Web, and hypertext in general, has always been that all sense of "order" is lost. Users are free to click on any link they like, and the order in which the material is absorbed is not necessarily the order intended by the author. This flexibility is great when the reader wants to go at his or her own pace, but it also means that an important topic or point could be missed.

This problem is alleviated by including "Next" and "Previous" links that guide the user through a series of pages in the order intended by the author, while still providing the ability to wander off on a tangent and come back later. Adding this capability to a set of Web pages isn't difficult...until you need to maintain it. Adding a page in the middle of the series requires changes to three pages (the previous page, the page being added, and the next page), or four pages if a table of contents needs to be maintained. You can imagine the effort required in changing the page order!

Fortunately, the Content Linking component gives you an easy way to link pages in a site and maintain that linkage in the future. A driver file lists a description of each page and its URL in the order desired, and the inclusion of a couple of lines of ASP scripting on each page provides maintenance-free hyperlinks that always point to the next and previous documents in the prescribed series.

As a bonus, you can easily use this functionality to create a self-generating table of contents, so users can easily jump into the middle of the series without having to plod through pages that are not of interest.

Using a Content Linking List

The first step in using the Content Linking component is to create a Content Linking List file. This file names the pages to be used, in order, along with an optional description and comment.

Each page entry is contained on one line and delimited by tabs with the following syntax:

```
Web-page-URL [ text-description [ comment]]
```

The `Web-page-URL` is the filename of the next page in the list. This file must be a file on the current site being accessed; in other words, this URL should not begin with `http://` or `//` or `\\`. It can be accompanied by a relative pathname.

The optional `text-description` describes what content the page contains, and is the information the user sees in the table of contents.

The optional `comment` is for the use of anyone reading the file; it is not shown by the Content Linking component.

Here is a sample Content Linking List file:

```
overvw.htm     Overview: How To Make A Fried Egg Sandwich
step1.htm      Step 1: Preparing The Frying Pan
step2.htm      Step 2: Cooking The Eggs
step3.htm      Step 3: Choosing And Applying Condiments
step4.htm      Step 4: Putting The Sandwich Together
index.htm      Table of Contents        Returns the user to the home page
```

After the Content Linking List file has been created and is available on a Web server virtual path, you can use the Content Linking component in an ASP script.

Here's how you create an instance of the object:

```
<% Set PageLinker = Server.CreateObject ("MSWC.NextLink") %>
```

Then you can use four methods to create links to the adjacent pages in the list, each of which takes the path and name of the Content Linking List file as the only parameter:

GetListCount	Returns the total number of pages in the list
GetListIndex	Returns the index of the current page
GetPreviousURL	Returns the URL of the previous page, if there is one
GetNextURL	Returns the URL of the next page, if there is one

Using these methods, you can create a code snippet like the one in Listing 9.4 that can be used on each page in the list, without ever needing to be changed.

LISTING 9.4. DYNAMIC CONTENT ROTATION.

```
1:    <% If (PageLinker.GetListIndex ("pageorder.txt") > 1) Then %>
2:    <a href=" <%= PageLinker.GetPreviousURL ("pageorder.txt") %> ">
3:    Previous Page</a>
4:    <% End If %>
5:    <% If (PageLinker.GetListIndex ("pageorder.txt") <
      ➡PageLinker.GetListCount ("pageorder.txt")) Then %>
6:    <a href=" <%=PageLinker.GetNextURL ("pageorder.txt") %> ">Next
      ➡Page</a>
7:    <% End If %>
```

ANALYSIS This code uses the pageorder.txt file to determine whether there are next and previous pages. If there is a previous page, then lines 2 and 3 provide a link to it. Line 1 checks for a previous page by simply checking whether the current page has an index greater than 1. The URL for the previous page is obtained from the pageorder.txt file, using the GetPreviousURL() method in line 2. A similar process is used in lines 5 and 6 to set up a link for the next page. Line 5 checks whether the current page is less than—before—the last item in the list. If so, then the next page link is set up in line 6.

Dynamically Building a Table of Contents

Now that your pages are linked together, you can also take advantage of the Content Linking List file and a few more methods in the Content Linking component and create a table of contents on-the-fly.

Here are the other methods you need to know to build the table of contents (each of which takes the Content Linking List filename and an index number as parameters):

GetNthURL()   Gets the URL of the item with the specified index number

GetNthDescription()   Gets the description of the item with the specified index number

Using these methods, you can access any URL and description in the list just by knowing the index of the item. Therefore, it is a simple matter to create a loop and make a list of all the items in the linking file, as shown in Listing 9.5.

LISTING 9.5. CREATING A DYNAMIC TABLE OF CONTENTS.

```
1: <% Set PageLinker = Server.CreateObject ("MSWC.NextLink") %>
2: <% count = PageLinker.GetListCount ("pageorder.txt") %>
3: <% I = 1 %>
4: <% Do While (I <= count) %>
5: <a href=" <%= PageLinker.GetNthURL ("pageorder.txt", I) %> ">
6: <%= PageLinker.GetNthDescription ("pageorder.txt", I) %> </a><BR>
7: <% I = (I + 1) %>
8: <% Loop %>
```

ANALYSIS Listing 9.5 simply loops through the pageorder.txt file using a Do While...Loop command in lines 4–8. During each loop, the GetNthURL() method is used to get the URL value of each index value. Line 6 then uses the GetNthDescription() method to print the description of the URL value obtained in line 5. Line 7 increments the counter before the loop reiterates.

Checking for Access Rights with the Permission Checker Component

The Internet can be a dangerous place for your data to be exposed. The horror stories are numerous, and damage caused by sensitive information falling into the wrong hands has cost many corporations (not to mention governments) millions of dollars. Even on an intranet, where your users can generally be trusted, not every member of the organization is meant to see certain documents that need to be shared.

Microsoft Windows NT implements an easy-to-use and proven security system, but that system is not directly available to Web scripts. Fortunately, Microsoft has made an ActiveX component available that allows file access checking through Active Server Pages. With the Permission Checker component, the script can determine—by using a single method, `HasAccess()`—whether the current user has permission to open a file.

Caution   The Permission Checker is supported only on Windows NT.

9

Note   The Permission Checker component is not installed automatically with IIS and ASP. You need to either download it from the Microsoft Web site at `http://www.microsoft.com/iis/` or install the IIS Resource Kit on your Web server.

After you install the component, you need to register it from the command prompt as explained in the earlier section, "Downloading and Installing ActiveX Components." For more information, consult the README file that comes with the documentation for the component.

Applications of the Permission Checker Component

Internet Information Server implements three levels of security for individual Web pages:

Anonymous Access   Allows users to access pages without specifically identi-
                            fying themselves; all anonymous users use the same ID
                            for access to files.

Basic Access   Allows restrictions to be placed on files so that only cer-
                            tain defined lists of users are given access. The user is
                            asked to give a user name and password whenever a
                            restricted file is encountered; this method works with all
                            browsers, but is not completely secure because the user
                            name and password given can be intercepted.

Windows NT Access   Similar to Basic access, but much more secure; requires
                            Internet Explorer browser.

Most documents are probably intended for viewing by all Web users, but for those sensitive items, having some level of restricted access can be very useful. Windows NT access is the most restrictive and safest over the Internet, but the users viewing the document must have an Internet Explorer browser until this kind of access is implemented on all browsers.

For intranet applications, Basic access is probably enough. Even though it is susceptible to interception, it is unlikely that a hacker could break in to the local network and intercept a user name and password entry for a particular file. This solution removes the Internet Explorer–only restriction while keeping unwanted eyes off sensitive material.

> **Caution**
>
> Basic access performs no encoding or encryption when the user name and password are sent to the server. This limitation makes it susceptible. NT Challenge/Response offers encoding, which makes it a bit more secure, but not something to rely on.

> **Note**
>
> To learn more about security for your Web server, consult the Internet Information Server documentation. You can use the Microsoft Management Console to control all aspects of security on your site.
>
> For individual files accessible from the server, consult the Windows NT Server documentation. You can control access to individual files (as long as you have access to them) by right-clicking on the file and choosing Properties, Security, Permissions.

Using the `HasAccess()` Method

After the desired level of security has been set up on your Web server, using the Permission Checker component to make sure the client has access to any particular file is a simple matter. Simply create an instance of the object, as usual, and then use the component's `HasAccess()` method, passing in a filename, to determine whether the Web user has access to a particular file.

IIS and Windows NT take care of asking for the login ID and password from the user, if necessary. This should be necessary only in the following situation:

- The Web site is not using an anonymous login ID for all Web access, and
- The user has not already provided a valid login, and
- The filename passed to `HasAccess()` is not a file that is available to everyone (in other words, it has a specific Access Control List that names which users can use the file).

The code in Listing 9.6 shows how the object can be used in an ASP script.

LISTING 9.6. USING THE PERMISSION CHECKER COMPONENT.

```
1: <%
2:    ' Create Permission Checker Object
3:    Set permCheck =
4:        Server.CreateObject("IISSample.PermissionChecker")
5: %>
6: <%  If permCheck.HasAccess("\data\secret_file.txt") Then %>
7:          <A HREF="\data\secret_file.txt>Click here
8:          to read the secret file.</A>.
9: <%  Else %>
10:         You don't have access rights to the secret file.
11: <%  End If %>
```

ANALYSIS Listing 9.6 is pretty straightforward. Lines 3 and 4 create an object called `permCheck` by using the Permission Checker component. The `HasAccess()` method of this object is then used in line 6 to determine whether the current user has permission to read the `secret_file.txt` file. If so, users see a message with a link (lines 7 and 8); otherwise, they see a message saying they don't have rights to the file (line 10).

A Presidential Election on the Web: ASP Style!

Wouldn't it be great to be able to hold a presidential election via the Web? No long lines, screaming kids, annoying exit pollsters…just sitting at the computer, placing your vote. Well, good news! Thanks to Microsoft Active Server Pages and the Voting component, you'll be able to place your next vote for president from the comfort of your own home!

Well, probably not. However, if you have a need to get consensus from your Web users, the Voting component makes setting it up and displaying results a snap. This kind of polling has become very popular on Web sites lately, especially news sites that want to get the pulse of their readers on a topic. However, it could also be useful in an office environment for planning an activity, getting an idea of how employees feel about a new company policy, or soliciting opinions on a new intranet design.

This component is different from the ones introduced earlier today because it uses a Microsoft Access database to record responses. When the component is installed, a new data source is created for a voting database, and you should be able to use your favorite ODBC query utility to examine results. Creating new "elections" is easy, and you can show users how others have voted immediately after any vote is submitted.

Note

> The Voting component is not installed automatically with IIS and ASP. You need to get the Microsoft Personalization System (MPS), which, at the time of this writing, is bundled with the Microsoft Site Server. Along with the Voting component, you get all the tools and documentation you need to set up a Web site that is personalized for each user.
>
> When you install the MPS, the Voting component is automatically registered. In addition, the Voting database is installed, and the ODBC data source pointing to the Microsoft Access version of the Voting database is set up for you, so you can begin making use of the system immediately.
>
> If you want to use a different database management system (DBMS) to store your voting results, you can find instructions on running the appropriate SQL table creation queries and setting up the ODBC data source with the MPS documentation.

Using the Voting Component

The Voting component considers each vote to be a "ballot" that could have two or more possible answers, or values. Therefore, it can handle yes/no questions ("Do you think our team could benefit from the services of a technical writer?") as well as multiple choice ("Where should we have our holiday party?": "Hilton," "Marriott," "Office cafeteria"). Each answer is stored in the Voting database, and can optionally be stored with the voter's identity to keep people from voting more than once.

The Voting component automatically creates the appropriate records in the Voting database for you each time a new question is submitted. If you want to create a ballot, you need only create a Web page to ask the questions and interact with the Voting database. The first time a user submits a ballot, the ballot and all supporting data is created in the Voting database.

There are four basic methods used for counting and displaying votes:

`Open()`	Opens the Voting database for use in the script.
`SetBallotName()`	Specifies on which ballot the vote should be counted.
`Submit()`	Processes the user's vote.
`GetVote()`	Displays voting results in an HTML table.

The code in Listing 9.7 is an example of how a vote would be recorded. Imagine that in our technocentric society, we've decided to elect a president who has had success in implementing technology to lead us into the twenty-first century. The choices are down to three candidates: Bill Gates of the Microsoft Party, Scott McNealy of the Sun Party, and Larry Ellison of the Oracle Party. Your job is to design the Web site that America will use to place its votes. The first page just needs to ask for whom the user will vote and submit that answer to the vote-processing page.

LISTING 9.7. THE FORM TO GET THE USER'S VOTE.

```
1:  <form action="storeVote.asp" method="post">
2:  Place your vote for President of the United States:
3:  <input type=radio name=pres_vote value="Bill">Bill Gates
4:  <input type=radio name=pres_vote value="Scott">Scott McNealy
5:  <input type=radio name=pres_vote value="Larry">Larry Ellison
6:  <input type=submit value="Vote">
7:  </form>
```

ANALYSIS As you can see, the code in Listing 9.7 is a simple form containing radio buttons for each candidate (lines 3–5) as well as a command button on line 6. When the user clicks the submit button, the vote-processing ASP page (storeVote.asp in Listing 9.8) is called, which stores the user's vote and shows him or her how the candidates are doing so far.

LISTING 9.8. SAVING THE USER'S VOTE (STOREVOTE.ASP).

```
1:  <% set myVote = Server.CreateObject("MPS.Vote") %>
2:  <% REM Open the vote database, passing in the ODBC data source name
    ➥and
3:    the user ID and password needed to log in to the database %>
4:  <% if myVote.Open("vote", "guest", ") = TRUE then %>
5:  <% myVote.SetBallotName("US President") %>
6:  <% voteresult = myVote.Submit("US President", Request("pres_vote")) %>
7:   <% = myVote.GetVote("US President") %> <p>
8:  <% else %>
9:  The Voting component is not set up correctly.
10: <% end if %>
```

ANALYSIS This listing uses the Voting component. Notice how the commands are used here. The Open() method used on line 4 must always be called first. It opens the Voting database for use, so you must pass in the data source name, as defined in ODBC, and the login ID and password needed to log into the database and insert and update records. Next, the SetBallotName() method must be called, as shown on line 5. This function creates the ballot if it doesn't already exist, and sets the component to store or retrieve information for that ballot.

After the database is prepared, you can either submit new votes or display the current results. To submit a vote, the `Submit()` method is used on line 6, passing in the name of the ballot and the choice the user has selected (this example accomplished this by using the value passed in through the form). To display all votes for this ballot in a table, the `GetVote()` method is called on line 7 and the results are included with the HTML sent to the browser. Now the user can immediately see how others have voted on the same ballot.

There are many possibilities for how this component could be used:

- With client-side VBScript or JavaScript, you could have a self-refreshing page that displayed up-to-the-minute vote results.
- Using the capabilities of the Voting component and the Microsoft Personalization System, you can make sure each user votes only once, and you can display the number of people who have cast votes.
- You can customize the voting results to compare the number of votes cast for a certain choice to the total votes and give a percentage for each choice.

For further information on capturing user identity for restricted voting and for customizing voting results, consult the information about the Voting component included with the MPS documentation.

Accessing Databases Through Your Web Page

Having a Web page that rotates images or content is wonderful, but to have truly dynamic and useful Web pages, you need a database. Long, long ago, when Web development was in its infancy (circa 1995), creating Web pages that read from databases was a difficult task. Most Web servers were on UNIX platforms, and reading from databases usually meant writing scripting code and using database programming interfaces (database APIs) specific to a particular manufacturer. Now, reading from and writing to a database is greatly simplified with the use of ODBC drivers and the ActiveX Database Access component.

The Database Access component allows SQL queries to be submitted through ASP scripting to any ODBC-compliant database. After the database has been defined in the ODBC Manager, the developer need only submit the data source name to the component and let the querying begin!

There are several steps to follow in accessing an ODBC database through an ASP script. Day 10, "Programming Web Databases," is devoted to using this component for database access. On Day 10, you learn to display information from an ODBC database in a Web page. This is an incredibly powerful tool, especially for the corporate intranet. Imagine the search capabilities now available to anyone in the company with a Web browser! Without needing to install any applications or ODBC drivers, users can specify search criteria on any database that is accessible through ODBC on the Web server. Creating a site that would accomplish this task can be done with the steps outlined in tomorrow's lesson.

Adding a Page Counter to a Web Page

As Neilsen ratings are to television programs, so are page hit counts to Web sites. If advertising is the easiest way to make money on the Web, then as a Web site creator, you need to know how many people are looking at your pages. If the number of hits to your site is significant, your advertisers will know they are getting their money's worth and will want to continue advertising on your site.

Knowing the number of hits per page is also important for determining the following:

- What kinds of information your customers are looking for
- How your users navigate the site
- How changes affect traffic to your site

The Page Counter component keeps up with all of this information, enables you to brag about your popularity by displaying the count on your page, and even saves the latest results to a text file every once in a while in case the server crashes. As usual, you barely have to lift a finger to have all this information available.

Note

The Page Counter component is another component that is not installed automatically when you install IIS and ASP. You need to either download it from the Microsoft Web site at http://www.microsoft.com/iis/ or install the IIS Resource Kit on your Web server.

After you install the component, you need to register it from the command prompt, as explained in the earlier section "Downloading and Installing ActiveX Components." For more information, consult the README file that comes with the documentation for the component.

Using the Page Counter Component

As with all the other ASP components that have been discussed today, using the Page Counter is ridiculously easy. However, there are a few things behind the scenes that you should know about.

The Page Counter component uses an internal *Central Management* object to keep up with count totals for all pages on the server. At regular intervals, this object saves all information to a text file so that no counts are lost because of power loss or system failure. The text file where the backup information is saved is called the *Hit Count Data File*. You can decide the name and location of this file, but by default the file is saved in the Windows directory and called `hitcnt.cnt`. Editing this file is not recommended—the Central Management object automatically reads this file after an unexpected shutdown to update its totals. Interfering with the file's format could cause loss of data. You'll need to update the Windows Registry if you want to change the location or name of this file, so read the documentation accompanying the component carefully before doing so. You've heard the warning a hundred times, but it's worth repeating: Altering the Windows Registry can render your system inoperable, so make sure you know what you're doing.

The Page Counter component uses three methods:

`Hits()`	Displays the number of hits for a Web page. The default is the current page, but you can pass in a path and filename to get totals for another page on the server.
`PageHit()`	Increments the hit count for the current page.
`Reset()`	Resets the hit count for a page to zero. The default is the current page, but you can pass in a path and filename to reset the count for another page on the server.

The rest is simple. On each page where you want a count to be implemented, you can place the following script:

```
<% Set pgCount = Server.CreateObject("MSWC.PageCounter") %>
<% pgCount.PageHit %>
You are visitor number <% =pgCount.Hits %> to this site.
```

Using the Tools Component

Finally, we come to a component made up of several miscellaneous functions that have been wrapped in a single package called the Tools component. These methods allow you to add a new level of sophistication to your Web site by enabling you to do the following:

- Create random numbers.
- Process an HTML page with scripting included and place the processed HTML in the middle of another Web page.
- Check for the existence of a file.

Note

> The Tools component is not installed automatically when you install IIS and ASP. To use it, you need to install the IIS Resource Kit on your Web server. The object is registered automatically by the installation, so you can begin using the object immediately.

9

Creating Random Numbers

If you want to give your site the ability to play a game involving random events, lead your user through an ever-changing adventure, or even just display a random sampling of data from a database, you need the ability to generate random numbers. The Tools component contains a method, Random, that generates a random number between –32768 and 32767, which is the range of a Visual Basic integer.

What if you just need a number between 1 and 10? You can use the Abs() function, which gives the absolute value of a number, to generate a positive integer. You can also use the Mod operator, which gives the remainder after one integer is divided by another, to limit the range of values. The code in Listing 9.9 shows how these functions can be applied with some arithmetic to produce the values you need.

LISTING 9.9. GENERATING RANDOM NUMBERS.

```
1:  <% Set Tools = Server.CreateObject("MSWC.Tools") %>
2:  Here is a random integer: <% =Tools.Random %> <P>
3:  Here is a random positive integer: <% =Abs( Tools.Random ) %> <P>
4:  Here is a random positive integer between 0 and 9:
5:     <% =(Abs(Tools.Random) Mod 10) %> <P>
6:  Finally, here is a random positive integer between 1 and 10:
7:     <% =((Abs(Tools.Random) Mod 10) + 1) %>
```

ANALYSIS This code should be easy to follow. In line 1, you are creating a Tools object called Tools. It is then used in the rest of the listing to get random numbers by calling the Random method. The Abs() function is then used in lines 3, 5, and 7 to cause the number to be a positive value. In lines 5 and 7, the Mod operator is used to limit the range of values selected. In the case of lines 5 and 7, Mod 10 is used. If you want a different range of numbers, you can simply change the value. For example, Mod 100 will give you 100 possible values.

> **Note**   You should note that Abs() is a VBScript function and Mod is a VBScript operator.

Processing Web Forms

ProcessForm is an unusual method that can have some impressive results. ProcessForm can create one HTML document from another, on-the-fly in the middle of an ASP script. If the form being read (the template form) has ASP scripting in it, that scripting is retained. Whenever the form created by ProcessForm is retrieved, that scripting is run as usual.

The template form can also contain ASP scripting that can be executed as the form is being processed. If you enclose ASP scripting inside the delimiters <%% and %%>, that script is executed before the template form is inserted into the output form.

If the output file specified does not exist, ProcessForm creates a new output file that is the processed template file. If the output form already exists, it is overwritten. An example should help clarify how ProcessForm works. The template for the code is in Listing 9.10.

LISTING 9.10. TEMPLATE FILE (TEMPLATE.HTM).

```
 1: <HTML>
 2: <BODY>
 3: This is text that has been inserted. <P>
 4: <%
 5: Response.Write("This is ASP script processed in the output file. <P>")
  ➥%>
 6: <%%
 7: Response.Write("This is ASP script processed by the ProcessForm
  ➥method.<P>")
 8: %%>
 9: </BODY>
10: </HTML>
```

ANALYSIS   This listing should look like standard ASP with only a minor exception. As you can see, line 7 is enclosed between the <%% and %%> tags (on lines 6 and 8, respectively).

The ASP script with the ProcessForm method is shown in Listing 9.11.

LISTING 9.11. PROCESSING THE FORM.

```
1:  <% Set Tools = Server.CreateObject("MSWC.Tools") %>
2:  <% Tools.ProcessForm "output.asp", "template.htm" %>
```

ANALYSIS When the ProcessForm method is executed in line 2 of Listing 9.11, the resulting output is a new HTML file, as shown in Listing 9.12.

LISTING 9.12. THE PROCESSED FILE RETURNED TO THE CLIENT.

```
1:  <HTML>
2:  <BODY>
3:  This is text that has been inserted. <P>
4:  <%
5:  Response.Write("This is ASP script processed in the output file. <P>")
    ➡%>
6:  This is ASP script processed by the ProcessForm method.<P>
7:  </BODY>
8:  </HTML>
```

ANALYSIS Notice how line 6 appears as standard HTML text in the ASP file after line 7 of the template form (Listing 9.10) is processed. This is because the <%% and %%> delimiters tell the ProcessForm method to process the commands while the new form is being generated. Using the ProcessForm method in this manner means that your Web site can create new pages and links as the user is loading other pages, which could be a very powerful feature.

Checking File Existence

If you want to avoid broken links to other files on your site, you can verify the file's existence before you allow the link to be displayed on the page. This procedure could also be useful for checking on driver files that are needed to run some components or for code snippets that are supposed to be included in the document.

The method to check for file existence is called FileExists(). It returns TRUE or FALSE and accepts as its parameter the name of a file with a relative pathname (because the file must be on your own site to use the method). Here's a quick example:

```
<%If Tools.FileExists("link.gif") then %>
<A HREF="http://www.clickme.com/"><IMG SRC="link.gif"></A>
<% End If %>
```

Where to Download Additional ASP Components

The best source of components for Active Server Pages is Microsoft's Web site, `http://www.microsoft.com/iis/`. Along with the components from today's lesson, many other handy components that can be used in ASP scripts are available and ready for use.

To see the list of ASP components available, go to the download section and narrow the search to Internet Information Server downloads. You'll see a list of components that all come with reasonably extensive documentation, along with some other IIS utilities that might come in handy.

As Active Server Pages gains acceptance, there will be more components available. Try doing an Internet search on "Active Server Pages" every once in a while and see what comes up. You might find that one killer component that will save your company millions and get you promoted to CIO! If not, perhaps you'll at least save yourself some time and frustration.

Summary

In today's lesson, you have seen a multitude of ActiveX components that can be used to enhance your Web site with minimal effort. Here's a review of the components covered and what they do:

- **Ad Rotator**: Rotates advertising images in the same spot on a page.
- **Content Rotator**: Rotates HTML content in the same spot on a page.
- **Browser Capabilities**: Allows you to customize your page based on what browser is being used.
- **Content Linker**: Organizes pages into a sequence that can be easily navigated.
- **Permission Checker**: Verifies that the Web user has access rights to view particular pages or files.
- **Voting**: Allows users of a site to cast votes and view results.
- **Database Access**: Makes ODBC databases available for display and storage through a Web browser.
- **Page Counter**: Records page hits and allows user to view the results.
- **Tools**: Miscellaneous functions, such as generating random numbers, processing Web forms, and checking for file existence.

These functions are the kinds of features seen on major Web sites on the Internet. Remember that these tools are easy to use and fully documented, so take advantage of them to make your Web site sparkle with professionalism. Remember, too, that if these components don't supply the kind of functionality you need, you can either build your own component or find someone who has already built the component you need.

Q&A

Q Do I have to pay any royalties or fees to use these components?

A No, Microsoft offers these components for your free and unlimited use, hoping that you'll realize, by using them, how easy Web development can be with Active Server Pages.

Q Does the user looking at my page that uses an ASP ActiveX component need to have a browser that supports ActiveX technology?

A No, unless you have included an ActiveX object in an HTML tag that is transmitted to the client. If your use of ActiveX objects is confined to ASP scripts, then the user never has any idea that you ever used ActiveX because all the user gets from you is HTML.

Q Does the same go for VBScript?

A Yep, same idea applies. The user's browser never even sees your scripting, so all that matters is what the server can understand.

Workshop

The quiz questions and exercises are provided for your further understanding. Please refer to Appendix A, "Answers to Questions," for the answers to the quiz questions; answers to the exercises are on the MCP Web site.

Quiz

1. True or False: Advertisement images of any size can be cycled on a Web page using the Ad Rotator component. Explain your answer.

2. What does the Browser Capabilities component do if a user loads your page with an undefined browser? How do you define new browsers for the page to recognize?

3. If you decided you wanted to use the Content Rotator component to rotate ads, would it work? What functionality would you lose?

4. Write the calculation you would need to generate a random number between –12 and 49.

5. True or False: The Page Counter component can increment the hit count for a page other than the current page. Explain why this feature is or is not needed.

Exercises

1. Pick an ASP page from a previous day's work and add a Content Rotator component to cycle through a "Thought for the Day" list and a Page Counter component to count the number of hits to the page.

2. Use the Content Linking component to link all the pages from previous exercises, so you can progress through the pages and view your work on each exercise.

3. Using the Page Counter component, add page counters to each of the pages you modified in Exercises 1 and 2.

DAY 10

Programming Web Databases

To truly unleash the potential of ASP, you need to know how to build ASP applications that interface with databases. It's really very easy to build database applications with ASP. As long as you have some basic understanding of a database application, such as Microsoft Access, you will have little trouble understanding today's lesson. Today you cover the following:

- Learn the steps in building a Web database application.
- See how to create a data source name for the database.
- Use SQL statements to manipulate database records.
- Build a guest book application.
- Explore client-side data validation.

Steps in Developing a Typical Web Database Application

The following sections explain the steps involved in developing a Web database application, from designing the actual database to inserting the data in the database with ASP statements. See Figure 10.1 for a flowchart that illustrates the steps for creating a typical Web database application. I suggest you follow all the outlined steps. Although it might take you a bit longer to complete your project, following the steps outlined in Figure 10.1 will ensure that you build a well-thought-out Web application that is less error prone and easier to maintain.

FIGURE 10.1.

Steps for creating a Web database application.

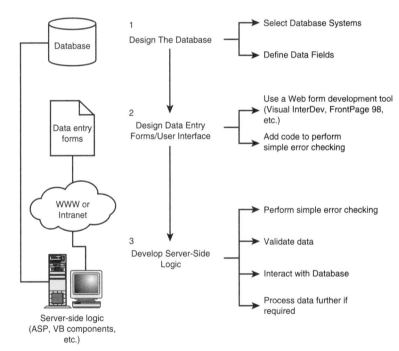

Caution

As long as several users do not access your database application at the same time, you will be fine using a desktop database application, such as Microsoft Access. However, if you are building a Web database application that is simultaneously used by many users, consider a database application such as Microsoft SQL Server, which is scalable to handle thousands of users. Microsoft Access is limited to only 10 concurrent connections.

Designing and Building the Database

The first step in developing a Web database application is designing and creating the actual database. This lesson assumes you are familiar with building a simple database using a product such as Microsoft Access (or a different database application that you may use).

> **Tip**
>
> When building a database, always think about future enhancements and the expandability of the database. For example, if you are building a guest book database, it makes sense to design the database so that it can be used later to store user information in case you plan to add personalization features to your Web site.

When building databases, be sure to establish proper relationships between fields of database tables so you can make sure your database efficiently stores information and ensure data integrity.

In Microsoft Access, you can view and define relationships between fields of database tables by choosing Relationships from the Tools menu. See Figure 10.2 for an example of a database table relationship diagram. In Microsoft Access, you can define a table relationship by dragging a field from a database table and dropping it onto another table with the corresponding data field.

FIGURE 10.2.

Creating proper relationships between relevant database tables is important.

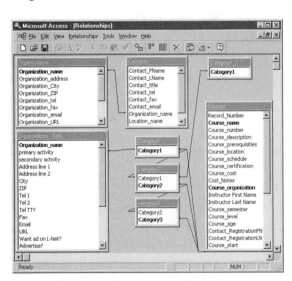

Creating a Data Source Name

After creating a database, you need to create either a file data source name (DSN) or a
system data source name for your database so your ASP application can interact with the
database. Although you can also create a user data source name for a database, this is
discouraged because user data source names are tied to a specific user account. Table
10.1 illustrates the differences between the three types of DSNs you can create.

Table 10.1. TYPES OF DATA SOURCE NAMES.

DSN Type	DSN Description
File DSN	Information about a file DSN is actually stored in a plain text file. A database specified with a file DSN is available to multiple users at the same time. Because the database information is contained in a plain text file, file DSNs can be easily transferred from one server to another server simply by copying the file DSN file. I recommend that you use file DSNs in your Web database applications.
System DSN	Information about a system DSN is contained in the Windows Registry. A database specified with a system DSN is available to multiple users at the same time as long as they are logged onto the same server.
User DSN	Information about a user DSN is contained in the Windows Registry. User DSNs can be accessed only by a certain user with the proper security permissions. Use user DSNs only in high-security Web applications where you need to tightly control who has access to what data. You can, however, always implement security by using either a system DSN or a file DSN and relying on NTFS security permissions. I do not recommend that you use user DSNs unless you have a very good reason for doing so.

Note

The DSNs used by your ASP application must be created on the Web server
that is running the ASP application. If you move your ASP application to a
different Web server, you have to re-create the DSN(s) of your ASP application on the new Web server.

Designing the HTML Forms

It is important that you make your HTML data entry forms user-friendly, which you can
do by implementing proper client-side data validation and making your forms easy to
use. If you're creating forms for general Internet use, try to fit all the data entry fields in
a 640×480 Web browser window. The user should never have to use the horizontal scroll-
bar to use your data entry form. In other words, do not create data entry forms that are
wider than 640 pixels.

> **Note**
>
> Many users still surf the Web with screen resolutions of 640×480, not to mention all those who use devices with limited screen resolutions, such as Web TV and Windows CE.

Although you can certainly use a plain text editor to design your data entry forms, I recommend that you use a WYSIWYG HTML editor (such as Microsoft FrontPage or Visual InterDev) so that you can pay more attention to the form's layout and appearance. Here are some benefits of using a Web form development tool for developing the HTML forms of a Web database application:

- Some Web form development applications also support automatic generation of client-side error checking.
- You don't have to be an expert in HTML. Web form development tools enable you to concentrate on the overall layout of the form instead of the gory details of HTML.
- These tools make it easier to use a table to format data entry controls of the Web form.
- It's easier to make changes to the layout of the HTML form if your data fields change.

Processing Information Submitted by the User

When building database applications, it is very important that you properly detect and handle bad information. Databases are temperamental organisms, especially when they are linked with other databases and applications. It is your responsibility to make sure your ASP applications do not compromise the data integrity of a database. You can easily do that with the help of client-side and server-side data validation. Before inserting data entered by a user into a database, make sure the data is valid and of the correct data type. Data items that you should especially validate include the following:

- Time values
- Date values
- Phone numbers (check for the number of digits)
- Required data fields (make sure they are not empty)

> **Tip**
>
> If you detect invalid data, ask the user for valid data, but don't set up your Web forms so that the user has to re-enter all the data from the beginning. Users don't like to type the same thing twice, although they occasionally make mistakes when filling in Web forms!

Using the Database Access Component

ASP applications interact with databases by using ActiveX Data Objects (ADO). After you create a DSN for a database, it is very easy to use ADO to insert and retrieve database records. Although you start working with ADO today, tomorrow you learn about many of details of ADO. Until then, here are the basic steps for using ADO:

1. Create an instance of the Connection object.
2. Open the connection to the database.
3. Issue SQL commands to your database.
4. Close the data connection.

Step 1: Create an Instance of the Connection Object

The first step for interfacing with a database is creating (or instantiating) an instance of the Connection object. This is done by using the following ASP statement:

```
Set DatabaseConnection = Server.CreateObject("ADODB.Connection")
```

Step 2: Open the Connection to the Database

After the Connection object is instantiated, you need to specify which database you want to work with. This is done by using the Open method and specifying the DSN. The following statement opens the file DSN UserInformationDatabase:

```
DatabaseConnection.Open "FILEDSN=UserInformationDatabase.dsn"
```

> **Caution**
>
> The DSN string should not contain a space after the = sign.

Step 3: Issue SQL Commands to Your Database

NEW TERM After establishing a connection with a database, the Execute method of the Connection object is used to issue *Structured Query Language* (*SQL*, pronounced "se-quel") commands. SQL statements can be used to insert, delete, and retrieve database information. In just a few minutes, you will learn more about SQL.

The syntax of the Execute method of the Connection object is very simple:

```
DatabaseConnection.Execute "<SQLStatementGoesHere>"
```

<SQLStatementGoesHere> is any legal SQL statement. If you need to issue more than one SQL statement, you can do multiple calls to Execute.

Step 4: Close the Data Connection

After you have finished using the database, you should close the database connection. Closing database connections immediately after using the database makes efficient use of your database resources. This is the syntax for closing a database connection:

```
DatabaseConnection.Close
Set DatabaseConnection = Nothing
```

As you can see, to close a database connection, all you have to do is execute the Close method of the database Connection object and then set the database Connection object to Nothing.

Caution

> Always close database connections as soon as you are done using them. Failure to properly close database connections not only wastes system resources, but can also cause the ASP subcomponent to crash and stop parsing any more ASP applications.

Note

> To effectively use databases, you need to understand SQL commands. The next few sections give you some information on using SQL. It is beyond the scope of this book to teach everything about SQL; however, you can check out *Sams Teach Yourself SQL in 21 Days* and *Sams Teach Yourself SQL in 24 Hours* for more information on SQL.

10

Building Database Queries with SQL Statements

It is important that you have a good understanding of SQL when developing Web database applications. A comprehensive overview of all the SQL statements is beyond the scope of this book. However, the next few sections cover some of the more useful SQL statements you need to know to build database applications with ASP. If you are already familiar with SQL, you might want to skip ahead.

The Structure of a SQL Statement

It is important that you understand the structure of a typical SQL statement. Although there are more complex SQL statements, a typical SQL statement is composed of two main parts, illustrated in Figure 10.3.

FIGURE 10.3.

The basic structure of a SQL statement.

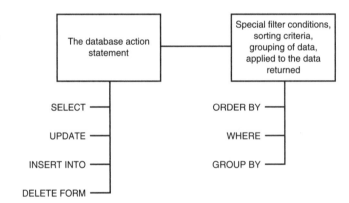

There are a number of SQL commands you will learn about that use this basic structure. They include commands to do the following:

- Retrieve information from a database
- Filter data
- Delete data
- Insert data

Retrieving Information from Databases

After establishing a link to a database, data can then be retrieved by using the SELECT statement to specify which fields you would like to retrieve and from what table. The simplest form of the SELECT statement is to use * to retrieve all the fields from a database

table. For example, the following SQL statement retrieves all the records in the table
UsersTable:

```
SELECT * From UsersTable
```

Instead of getting all the fields in a database table, you can specify which fields you
would like to retrieve. For example, if you would like to retrieve only the fields
FirstName and LastName from the table UsersTable, use the following SQL statement:

```
SELECT FirstName, LastName From UsersTable
```

 Tip

To save system resources, retrieve only the database fields you are actually
going to use. Avoid using SELECT * statements unless you really need to
retrieve all the fields of a database table.

10

Filtering Data

SQL's powerful filtering capabilities can be used to get a recordset that contains only the
fields you need. The WHERE clause is used to specify what records you are interested in.
Its syntax is as follows:

```
WHERE Data-Comparison
```

The following comparison statements can be used with the WHERE clause to filter your
data:

- BETWEEN—Used to compare a given field to a range of values.
- IN—Used to determine if the value of a field equals a value in a given series of
  values.
- LIKE—Compares a data field to an expression containing wildcards.

 Tip

As much as possible, get the database engine to select, filter, and sort the
data for you. You can do that by using SQL statements such as WHERE.

Using a Range of Values for Data Comparison

NEW TERM   Use the BETWEEN command in a SQL statement to get a recordset containing data
between two values. A *recordset* is a collection of data fields of a database.

For example, the following SQL statement returns a recordset containing records whose
FirstName field is between *Q* and *V*:

```
SELECT * FROM Users WHERE FirstName BETWEEN 'Q' AND 'V'
```

You can also use the BETWEEN command with numeric data. The following SQL statement returns a recordset containing records whose TaxRate field is between 5 and 7:

```
SELECT * FROM Customers WHERE TaxRate BETWEEN 5 AND 7
```

Using a Series of Values for Data Comparison

Sometimes it is more convenient to retrieve a recordset of data that exactly matches a given set of data values. Use the IN command for this purpose. For example, if you are interested only in customers who live in Maryland or Pennsylvania, use the following SQL statement:

```
Select * FROM Customers WHERE State IN ('MD','PA')
```

Using Pattern Matching

You can also retrieve a recordset that matches a substring search by using the LIKE command. The following examples illustrate how to select a recordset with SQL's pattern-matching capabilities.

The following SQL statement returns customers whose first name begins with the letter *S*:

```
Select * FROM Customers WHERE FirstName LIKE 'S*'
```

The following SQL statement returns customers whose first name begins with the letter *S* or *M*:

```
Select * FROM Customers WHERE FirstName LIKE '[S,M]*'
```

The following SQL statement returns customers whose first name begins with the letters *Sa*:

```
Select * FROM Customers WHERE FirstName LIKE 'Sa*'
```

The following SQL statement returns customers whose age is between 20 and 29:

```
Select * FROM Customers WHERE Age LIKE '2#'
```

The following SQL statement returns customers whose first name does not begin with the letter *A*, *B*, or *C*:

```
Select * FROM Customers WHERE FirstName LIKE '[!A-C]*'
```

Note | Just a reminder that this section is not a comprehensive discussion of SQL. Rather, it is simply a quick overview to get you started. It is beyond the scope of this book to cover SQL commands in detail.

Data Comparison Operators

You can use the data comparison operators shown in Table 10.2 to filter your data and get a recordset of data.

Table 10.2. DATA COMPARISON OPERATORS.

Operator	Description
=	Equal to
<	Less than
>	Greater than
<=	Less than or equal to
>=	Greater than or equal to
<>	Not equal to

It's easy to use data comparison operators. Simply follow the WHERE clause with a data comparison condition. For example, to get a recordset of users who were added to the database on or after 02/29/1996, use the following SQL statement:

```
SELECT * FROM Users WHERE RecordCreationDate>=#2/29/1996#
```

Note | The pound signs are used to encapsulate date values.

Deleting Data

You can delete data in a database table by using the DELETE SQL statement, which can either delete all the records in a table or selectively delete only certain records. The following SQL statement deletes all the records in the table UserTable:

```
DELETE FROM UserTable
```

Obviously, you rarely want to delete the contents of entire tables. Instead, you use the WHERE clause to specify which records should be deleted. The following SQL statement deletes records in the DelinquentCustomers table with an account balance of 0: table

```
DELETE FROM DelinquentCustomers WHERE AccountBalance='0'
```

Caution
Be careful when using the DELETE statement because if you delete a set of records, you can't recover the ones you deleted unless you are using transaction processing.

Note
Unlike SELECT statements, DELETE statements do not return a recordset of data.

Inserting Data

You can insert data into a database table by using the INSERT SQL statement. Inserting data from an ASP application to a database table is a bit more complex. The best way to understand how to insert data is with an example. Refer to the section "Add User Input to the Database" later today for an example of adding to a database table information entered by users with an HTML form.

Here is the general syntax for the INSERT statement:

```
INSERT INTO <Table Name> (<TableField1>, <TableField2>, <TableField3>)
➥VALUES (<TableFieldValue1>, <TableFieldValue2>, <TableFieldValue3>)
```

<Table Name> is the name of the database where data is inserted. *<TableField1>*, *<TableField2>*, and *<TableField3>* are all fields of the database table. *<TableFieldValue1>*, *<TableFieldValue2>*, and *<TableFieldValue3>* are corresponding values to insert in the fields of the database table.

Note
Microsoft Access was chosen to build the guest book database because it's widely used and easy to use. That does not mean you *have* to use Microsoft Access. As long as you can use your database application to create a system data source name or a file data source name, you won't have any trouble creating the guest book application presented later today.

Also, if you have an ODBC driver that supports your database, you can gain access to the data by using ASP and ADO.

Building a Guest Book

You have learned how to use SQL statements to manipulate information in a database. Now it's time to build a database application with ADO. This section demonstrates how to build a guest book application complete with client-side data validation and a search function.

After reading the next few sections, you should realize that this is no typical guest book application. It is a bit complex, but it also does more. By examining the code of the guest book application, you can build your own Web database applications that add, display, and search database records. The guest book database has been designed with reusability in mind so that the same database can be used for a user registration system as well as a user personalization system.

Here are the steps you follow to create the guest book application:

1. Design the guest book database with proper relationships established between fields of different tables.

2. Create an ODBC DSN for the database.

3. Create the data entry form of the guest book application.

4. Add user's input to the database.

5. View records of the guest book database.

6. Implement a search function for the database.

10

Note
Don't be overly concerned about the length of the guest book application. It uses additional data fields that might not be present in a typical guest book application. These additional database fields are used in Day 12, "Database Development Illustrated: Building a User Registration System," and Day 14, "Developing a User Personalization System with Cookies," to extend the capabilities of the guest book application in today's lesson.

Design the Guest Book Database

The guest book database used in today's lesson can be downloaded from the MCP Web site. Before proceeding any further, I suggest you download it and become familiar with its structure and relationships. Keep in mind where you save the database file because you have to specify its location when creating a file DSN. The diagram in Figure 10.4 illustrates the fields and relationships of the guest book database.

FIGURE 10.4.

Relationships of the guest book database.

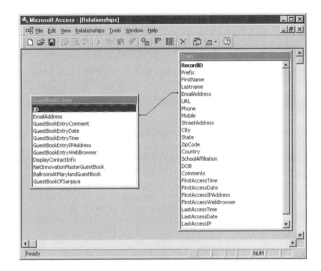

As you see in Figure 10.4, the guest book database consists of two tables. The first table keeps track of individual users. The second table keeps track of guest book entries. The two tables are linked by the user's e-mail address, which is a unique field for each user. Now that you have your database, the next step is creating a DSN for it so that you can access the database from within an ASP application.

Create an ODBC File Data Source Name

As you learned earlier, you need to create a file data source name. The first step in creating a file DSN is to open the Control Panel in Windows or Windows NT. From the Control Panel, click on the ODBC icon.

Tip

You might want to drag and drop the ODBC icon from the Control Panel to your desktop. You can then easily start the ODBC Data Source Administrator without having to open the Control Panel. You will find yourself opening the ODBC Data Source Administrator a lot when you're building Web database applications.

When you execute the ODBC icon, you see the ODBC Data Source Administrator shown in Figure 10.5. Select the File DSN tab to create a file DSN and click the Add button.

FIGURE 10.5.

Select the File DSN tab of the ODBC Data Source Administrator.

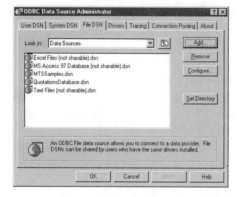

You then see the Create New Data Source dialog box shown in Figure 10.6. Select the Microsoft Access Driver and click the Next button.

10

FIGURE 10.6.

The Create New Data Source dialog box.

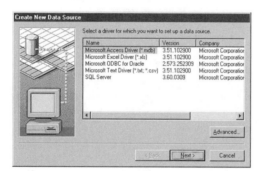

Use the dialog box in Figure 10.7 to give your file DSN a descriptive name. The file DSN given to the guest book database is UserInformationDatabase. When you're done, click the Next button.

> **Tip**
>
> Always give a descriptive name when creating a DSN so you can easily locate and use it, especially when you have dozens of DSNs floating around your hard drives.

FIGURE 10.7.

The file DSN is given a name.

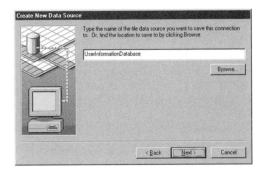

The dialog box in Figure 10.8 displays a summary of the file DSN you are creating. If you want to make any changes, you can use the Back button. If you are happy with the settings you have supplied, click the Finish button.

FIGURE 10.8.

Examine the settings of your file DSN.

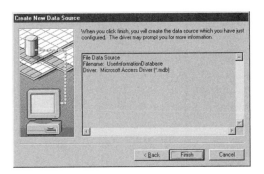

You then see the ODBC Microsoft Access 97 Setup dialog box shown in Figure 10.9. At this point, you have to click the Select button so you can specify the location of the guest book database file.

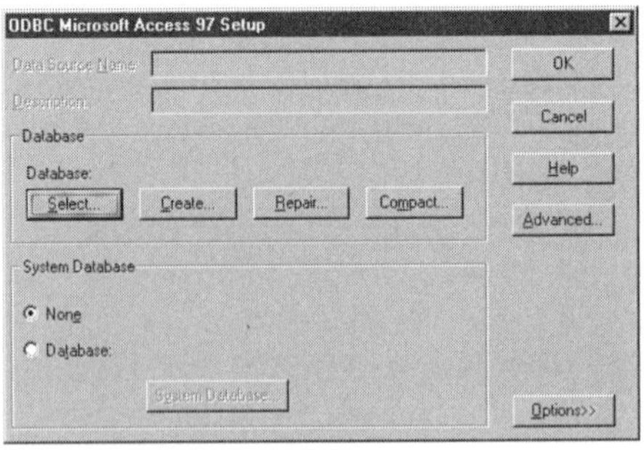

FIGURE 10.9.

The ODBC Microsoft Access 97 Setup dialog box.

The Select Database dialog box in Figure 10.10 is used to specify the location of the guest book database.

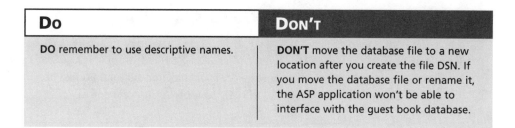

Do	Don't
DO remember to use descriptive names.	**DON'T** move the database file to a new location after you create the file DSN. If you move the database file or rename it, the ASP application won't be able to interface with the guest book database.

Note

If you must rename or move the database file after you create a file DSN for it, first delete the file DSN from the ODBC Data Source Administrator dialog box, then rename or move the database file, and re-create a file DSN as outlined in this section.

10

FIGURE 10.10.

Specify the location of the guest book database file.

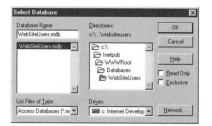

After you specify the location of the database file, the ODBC Data Source Administrator creates a file DSN for it. You then see the UserInformationDatabase file DSN when you examine the File DSN tab of the ODBC Data Source Administrator, as shown in Figure 10.11.

FIGURE 10.11.

A file DSN is created for the guest book database.

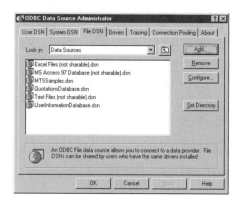

Create the Web Data Entry to Get Input

The guest book's data entry form was created with Microsoft FrontPage 98. I chose
FrontPage because it allows easy layout and creation of HTML forms. It also gives you
the option of automatically adding client-side data validation subroutines that use
JavaScript. Of course, you can use any HTML editor to create your forms.

Note
> Use FrontPage only to design the layout of your HTML forms used for data
> entry. It is not recommended that you use FrontPage for editing ASP appli-
> cations because it sometimes has a tendency to "format" ASP code.

COMPANION **Website** Experiment with the application in Listing 10.1 by downloading the code distribution file for this book from the MCP Web site, copying the file
`Chapter-10/AddGuestBookEntry.asp` to your Web server and executing it with a Web
browser.

See Listing 10.1 for the code of the Web page that gets input from the user. The code in
Listing 10.1 generates the Web page shown in Figure 10.12 so that users can add new
entries to the guest book. If the code looks too complicated, don't worry! You will understand how it works after reading the explanation that follows the code listing.

FIGURE 10.12.

*The guest book entry
form.*

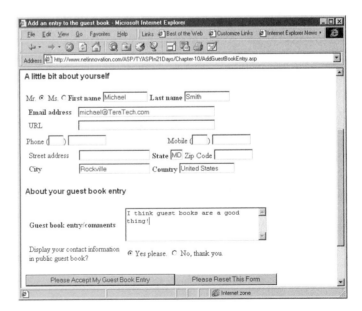

Listing 10.1. THIS WEB PAGE IS USED TO ADD GUEST BOOK ENTRIES FROM USERS.

```
 1: <html>
 2:
 3: <head>
 4: <meta http-equiv="Content-Type"
 5:   content="text/html; charset=iso-8859-1">
 6: <title>Add an entry to the guest book</title>
 7: </head>
 8:
 9: <body>
10:
11: <p align="center"><strong><font face="Comic Sans MS" size="5"
12:   color="#0000FF">Add an entry to the Guest Book</font>
13: </strong></p>
14:
15: <p><font face="Georgia">Thanks so much for taking the time to
16: sign the guest book! Please use the following form to type in
17: your data and submit it. Your guest book data will be immediately
18: inserted to the guest book which is implemented using a Microsoft
19: Access database and Active Server Pages. </font></p>
20: <div align="center"><center>
21:
22: <table border="2" width="450" bordercolor="#000000"
23:   cellspacing="0" cellpadding="3">
24:   <tr>
25:     <td width="100%"><font face="Arial">Please note that only
26:     the data entry fields that are in <strong>BOLD</strong> are
27:     required data entry fields. All other data entry fields are
28:     optional.</font></td>
29:   </tr>
30: </table>
31: </center></div>
32:
33:
34: <!--webbot BOT="GeneratedScript" PREVIEW=" " startspan -->
35: <script Language="JavaScript"><!--
36: function FrontPage_Form1_Validator(theForm)
37: {
38:
39:   if (theForm.FirstName.value == "")
40:   {
41:     alert("Please enter a value for the \"First Name\" field.");
42:     theForm.FirstName.focus();
43:     return (false);
44:   }
45:
46:   if (theForm.FirstName.value.length < 2)
47:   {
48:     alert("Please enter at least 2 characters in the \"First Name\"
      ➡ field.");
```

10

continues

Listing 10.1. CONTINUED

```
49:      theForm.FirstName.focus();
50:      return (false);
51:    }
52:
53:    if (theForm.FirstName.value.length > 30)
54:    {
55:      alert("Please enter at most 30 characters in the \"First Name\"
         ➥ field.");
56:      theForm.FirstName.focus();
57:      return (false);
58:    }
59:
60:    if (theForm.LastName.value == "")
61:    {
62:      alert("Please enter a value for the \"Last Name\" field.");
63:      theForm.LastName.focus();
64:      return (false);
65:    }
66:
67:    if (theForm.LastName.value.length < 2)
68:    {
69:      alert("Please enter at least 2 characters in the \"Last Name\"
         ➥ field.");
70:      theForm.LastName.focus();
71:      return (false);
72:    }
73:
74:    if (theForm.LastName.value.length > 30)
75:    {
76:      alert("Please enter at most 30 characters in the \"Last Name\"
         ➥ field.");
77:      theForm.LastName.focus();
78:      return (false);
79:    }
80:
81:    if (theForm.EmailAddress.value == "")
82:    {
83:      alert("Please enter a value for the \"E-mail Address\" field.");
84:      theForm.EmailAddress.focus();
85:      return (false);
86:    }
87:
88:    if (theForm.EmailAddress.value.length < 7)
89:    {
90:      alert("Please enter at least 7 characters in the \"E-mail
         ➥Address\" field.");
91:      theForm.EmailAddress.focus();
92:      return (false);
93:    }
94:
```

```
95:    if (theForm.EmailAddress.value.length > 49)
96:    {
97:      alert("Please enter at most 49 characters in the \"E-mail
         ➥Address\" field.");
98:      theForm.EmailAddress.focus();
99:      return (false);
100:   }
101:
102:   if (theForm.State.value == "")
103:   {
104:     alert("Please enter a value for the \"Your State\" field.");
105:     theForm.State.focus();
106:     return (false);
107:   }
108:
109:   if (theForm.State.value.length < 2)
110:   {
111:     alert("Please enter at least 2 characters in the \"Your State\"
         ➥ field.");
112:     theForm.State.focus();
113:     return (false);
114:   }
115:
116:   if (theForm.State.value.length > 2)
117:   {
118:     alert("Please enter at most 2 characters in the \"Your State\"
         ➥ field.");
119:     theForm.State.focus();
120:     return (false);
121:   }
122:
123:   if (theForm.City.value == "")
124:   {
125:     alert("Please enter a value for the \"City Name\" field.");
126:     theForm.City.focus();
127:     return (false);
128:   }
129:
130:   if (theForm.City.value.length < 3)
131:   {
132:     alert("Please enter at least 3 characters in the \"City Name\"
         ➥field.");
133:     theForm.City.focus();
134:     return (false);
135:   }
136:
137:   if (theForm.City.value.length > 30)
138:   {
139:     alert("Please enter at most 30 characters in the \"City Name\"
         ➥field.");
140:     theForm.City.focus();
```

10

continues

Listing 10.1. CONTINUED

```
141:     return (false);
142:   }
143:
144:   if (theForm.Country.value == "")
145:   {
146:     alert("Please enter a value for the \"Name of your country\"
         ➥ field.");
147:     theForm.Country.focus();
148:     return (false);
149:   }
150:
151:   if (theForm.Country.value.length < 3)
152:   {
153:     alert("Please enter at least 3 characters in the \"Name of your
         ➥country\" field.");
154:     theForm.Country.focus();
155:     return (false);
156:   }
157:
158:   if (theForm.Country.value.length > 30)
159:   {
160:     alert("Please enter at most 30 characters in the \"Name of your
         ➥country\" field.");
161:     theForm.Country.focus();
162:     return (false);
163:   }
164:
165:   if (theForm.GuestBookEntryComments.value == "")
166:   {
167:     alert("Please enter a value for the \"Your Guest Book Entry
         ➥ (comments)\" field.");
168:     theForm.GuestBookEntryComments.focus();
169:     return (false);
170:   }
171:
172:   if (theForm.GuestBookEntryComments.value.length < 2)
173:   {
174:     alert("Please enter at least 2 characters in the \"Your Guest
         ➥ Book Entry (comments)\" field.");
175:     theForm.GuestBookEntryComments.focus();
176:     return (false);
177:   }
178:   return (true);
179: }
180: //--></script><!--webbot BOT="GeneratedScript" endspan -->
181:
182: <form method="POST" action="InsertGuestBookEntry.asp"
183:   onsubmit="return FrontPage_Form1_Validator(this)"
184:   name="FrontPage_Form1">
```

```
185:    <p><strong><font face="Arial">A little bit about yourself
186:      </font></strong></p>
187:    <div align="left"><table border="0" width="610">
188:      <tr>
189:        <td width="100%" colspan="2">Mr.<input type="radio"
190:        value="Mr" CHECKED name="Prefix"> Ms.<input type="radio"
191:        name="Prefix" value="Ms"><strong>First name</strong>
192:        <!--webbot bot="Validation" S-Display-Name="First Name"
          ➥B-Value-Required="TRUE" I-Minimum-Length="2"
          ➥I-Maximum-Length="30" -->
193:        <input type="text" name="FirstName" size="12" maxlength="30">
194:          <strong>Last name</strong> <!--webbot bot="Validation"
          ➥S-Display-Name="Last Name" B-Value-Required="TRUE" I-Minimum-
          ➥Length="2" I-Maximum-Length="30" -->
195:          <input type="text" name="LastName" size="12"
          ➥maxlength="30"></td>
196:      </tr>
197:      <tr>
198:        <td width="100%" colspan="2"><div align="center"><center>
199:          <table border="0" width="600">
200:          <tr>
201:            <td width="104"><strong>Email address</strong> </td>
202:            <td width="488"><!--webbot bot="Validation"
      ➥S-Display-Name="E-mail Address" B-Value-Required="TRUE"
      ➥I-Minimum-Length="7" I-Maximum-Length="49" -->
203:            <input type="text" name="EmailAddress" size="40"
      ➥ maxlength="49">
204:          </td></tr>
205:          <tr>
206:            <td width="104">URL</td>
207:            <td width="488"><input type="text" name="URL" size="40"
208:            maxlength="49"></td>
209:          </tr>
210:        </table>
211:        </center></div></td>
212:      </tr>
213:      <tr>
214:        <td width="50%">Phone (<input type="text" name="PhoneAreaCode"
215:        size="3" maxlength="3">)
216:        <input type="text" name="PhoneNumber" size="10" maxlength="12">
217:        </td><td width="50%">
218:        Mobile (<input type="text" name="MobileAreaCode"
219:        size="3" maxlength="3">) <input type="text"
          ➥name="MobilePhoneNumber"
220:        size="10" maxlength="12"></td>
221:      </tr>
222:      <tr>
223:        <td width="100%" colspan="2"><div align="center"><center>
224:          <table border="0" width="600">
225:          <tr>
226:            <td width="105">Street address</td>
```

continues

Listing 10.1. CONTINUED

```
227:            <td width="487"><input type="text" name="StreetAddress"
228:            size="20" maxlength="49"> <strong>State</strong>
229:            <!--webbot bot="Validation" S-Display-Name="Your State"
                ➡B-Value-Required="TRUE" I-Minimum-Length="2"
                ➡I-Maximum-Length="2" -->
230:            <input type="text" name="State" size="2" maxlength="2">
231:            Zip Code <input type="text" name="ZipCode" size="10"
232:            maxlength="10"> </td>
233:          </tr>
234:          <tr>
235:            <td width="105"><strong>City</strong> </td>
236:            <td width="487"><!--webbot bot="Validation"
                ➡S-Display-Name="City Name" B-Value-Required="TRUE"
                ➡ I-Minimum-Length="3" I-Maximum-Length="30" -->
237:            <input type="text" name="City" size="20" maxlength="30">
238:            <strong>Country</strong>
239:            <!--webbot bot="Validation" S-Display-Name="Name of
                ➡your country" B-Value-Required="TRUE"
                ➡I-Minimum-Length="3" I-Maximum-Length="30" -->
240:            <input type="text" name="Country" size="15"
241:            value="United States" maxlength="30"></td>
242:          </tr>
243:        </table>
244:        </center></div></td>
245:      </tr>
246:    </table>
247:    </div><p><font face="Arial"><strong>About your guest book entry
248:      </strong></font></p>
249:    <div align="left"><table border="0" width="610">
250:      <tr>
251:        <td width="100%"><div align="center"><center><table border="0"
252:        width="600">
253:          <tr>
254:            <td width="205"><strong>Guest book entry/comments</strong>
                ➡</td>
255:            <td width="387"><!--webbot bot="Validation"
                ➡S-Display-Name="Your Guest Book Entry (comments)"
                ➡ B-Value-Required="TRUE" I-Minimum-Length="2" -->
256:            <textarea rows="4" name="GuestBookEntryComments"
257:            cols="35"></textarea></td>
258:          </tr>
259:          <tr>
260:            <td width="205">Display your contact information in public
261:            guest book?</td>
262:            <td width="387"><input type="radio" value="True"
263:            checked name="DisplayContactInfo">Yes please.
264:            <input type="radio" name="DisplayContactInfo"
                ➡value="False">
265:            No, thank you.</td>
```

```
266:         </tr>
267:       </table>
268:       </center></div></td>
269:     </tr>
270:   </table>
271:   </div><p><input type="submit" value="Please Accept My Guest Book
        ➥ Entry"
272:   name="SubmitButton"><input type="reset" value="Please Reset This
        ➥ Form"
273:   name="B2"></p>
274: </form>
275:
276: <p> </p>
277: <hr>
278: This Web page was generated on <%= Date %> at <%= Time %>.<br>
279: <a HREF="Default.asp">Return to guest book's main menu</a>.
280: </body>
281: </html>
```

ANALYSIS   The Activer Server Page in Listing 10.1 displays an HTML form used by users to add new records to the guest book database. The JavaScript code in lines 34–180 validates data entered by the user. If invalid data is detected, a dialog box, similar to the one shown in Figure 10.13, is displayed. After the user enters valid data, the data is submitted to an ASP application to be processed. The remainder of the code displays the HTML form used for data entry.

FIGURE 10.13.

Invalid input is detected on the client side.

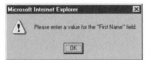

Add User Input to the Database

The Active Server Page in Listing 10.2 inserts new records to the guest book database. After a new record is added to the guest book, the Web page shown in Figure 10.14 is displayed so that the user knows the process was completed.

Tip

Whenever possible, design your ASP applications with a personal touch. Notice how the Web page in Figure 10.14 personally thanks the user for the guest book entry.

FIGURE **10.14.**

*A new record is added
to the guest book.*

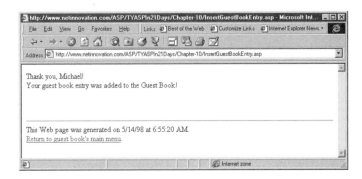

Experiment with the application in Listing 10.2 by downloading the code distribution file for this book from the MCP Web site, copying the file Chapter-
10/InsertGuestBookEntry.asp to your Web server and executing it with a Web browser.

Listing 10.2. THIS ASP APPLICATION INSERTS THE USER'S GUEST BOOK ENTRY TO THE GUEST BOOK
DATABASE.

```
 1: <%@ LANGUAGE=VBScript %>
 2: <HTML>
 3: <HEAD>
 4: <META NAME="GENERATOR" Content="Microsoft Visual Studio 6.0">
 5: </HEAD>
 6: <BODY title="Your guest book entry was processed">
 7:
 8: <%
 9:
10: ' ########## Begin Subroutine ##########
11:
12: Sub AddGuestBookEntry
13:
14:    Dim SQLDataInsertionString
15:    Dim CommandObject
16:
17:    ' Create an instance of the Command object.
18:    Set CommandObject= Server.CreateObject("ADODB.Command")
19:
20:    ' The ActiveConnection property is used to connect the Command
       ➡Object
21:    ' to the Connection Object.
22:    Set CommandObject.ActiveConnection = DatabaseConnection
23:
24:    ' The SQL string that inserts the guest book data about the
25:    ' user is created.
26:    SQLDataInsertionString = "INSERT INTO GuestBookEntries (" & _
```

```
27:      "EmailAddress,GuestBookEntryComment," & _
28:      "GuestBookEntryDate,GuestBookEntryTime,GuestBookEntryIPAddress," & _
29:      "GuestBookEntryWebBrowser,DisplayContactInfo) " & _
30:      "VALUES (?,?,?,?,?,?,?)"
31:
32:    ' The SQL statement that actually inserts the data is defined
33:    CommandObject.CommandText = SQLDataInsertionString
34:
35:    ' The prepared or pre-compiled SQL statement defined in the
36:    ' CommandText property is saved.
37:    CommandObject.Prepared = True
38:
39:    ' The parameters of the SQL string are defined below.
40:    CommandObject.Parameters.Append _
41:       CommandObject.CreateParameter("EmailAddress",200, ,255)
42:    CommandObject.Parameters.Append _
43:       CommandObject.CreateParameter("GuestBookEntryComment",200, ,255)
44:    CommandObject.Parameters.Append _
45:       CommandObject.CreateParameter("GuestBookEntryDate",200, ,255)
46:    CommandObject.Parameters.Append _
47:       CommandObject.CreateParameter("GuestBookEntryTime",200, ,255)
48:    CommandObject.Parameters.Append _
49:       CommandObject.CreateParameter("GuestBookEntryIPAddress",200,
        ➡,255)
50:    CommandObject.Parameters.Append _
51:       CommandObject.CreateParameter("GuestBookEntryWebBrowser",200,
        ➡,255)
52:    CommandObject.Parameters.Append _
53:       CommandObject.CreateParameter("DisplayContactInfo",200, ,255)
54:
55:  ' Information entered by the user is added to the Guest Book
      ➡database
56:    CommandObject("EmailAddress") = Request.Form.Item("EmailAddress")
57:    CommandObject("GuestBookEntryComment") = _
58:       Request.Form.Item("GuestBookEntryComments")
59:    CommandObject("GuestBookEntryDate") = Date
60:    CommandObject("GuestBookEntryTime") = Time
61:    CommandObject("GuestBookEntryIPAddress") = _
62:      Request.ServerVariables.Item ("REMOTE_ADDR")
63:    CommandObject("GuestBookEntryWebBrowser") = _
64:      Request.ServerVariables.Item ("HTTP_USER_AGENT")
65:    CommandObject("DisplayContactInfo") = _
66:      CBool(Request.Form.Item("DisplayContactInfo"))
67:
68:    CommandObject.Execute
69:
70: End Sub
71:
72: ' ########## End Subroutine ##########
```

10

continues

Listing 10.2. CONTINUED

```
73:
74: ' ########## Begin Subroutine ##########
75:
76: Sub AddUserInformation
77:
78:    Dim SQLDataInsertionString
79:    Dim CommandObject
80:
81:    ' Create an instance of the Command object.
82:    Set CommandObject= Server.CreateObject("ADODB.Command")
83:
84:    ' The ActiveConnection property is used to connect the Command
       ➡Object
85:    ' to the Connection Object.
86:    Set CommandObject.ActiveConnection = DatabaseConnection
87:
88:    ' The SQL string that inserts the guest book data about the
89:    ' user is created.
90:    SQLDataInsertionString = "INSERT INTO Users (Prefix, FirstName," & _
91:      "Lastname, EmailAddress, URL, Phone, Mobile, StreetAddress," & _
92:      "City, State, ZipCode, Country, FirstAccessTime," & _
93:      "FirstAccessDate, FirstAccessIPAddress, FirstAccessWebBrowser," & _
94:      "LastAccessTime, LastAccessDate, LastAccessIP," & _
95:      "LastAccessWebBrowser) VALUES (?,?,?,?,?,?,?,?," & _
96:      "?,?,?,?,?,?,?,?,?,?,?,?)"
97:
98:    ' The SQL statement that actually inserts the data is defined
99:    CommandObject.CommandText = SQLDataInsertionString
100:
101:   ' The prepared or pre-compiled SQL statement defined in the
102:   ' CommandText property is saved.
103:   CommandObject.Prepared = True
104:
105:   ' The parameters of the SQL string are defined below.
106:   CommandObject.Parameters.Append _
107:     CommandObject.CreateParameter("Prefix",200, ,255 )
108:   CommandObject.Parameters.Append _
109:     CommandObject.CreateParameter("FirstName",200, ,255 )
110:   CommandObject.Parameters.Append _
111:     CommandObject.CreateParameter("LastName",200, ,255 )
112:   CommandObject.Parameters.Append _
113:     CommandObject.CreateParameter("EmailAddress",200, ,255 )
114:   CommandObject.Parameters.Append _
115:     CommandObject.CreateParameter("URL",200, ,255 )
116:   CommandObject.Parameters.Append _
117:     CommandObject.CreateParameter("Phone",200, ,255 )
118:   CommandObject.Parameters.Append _
119:     CommandObject.CreateParameter("Mobile",200, ,255 )
```

```
120:    CommandObject.Parameters.Append _
121:      CommandObject.CreateParameter("StreetAddress",200, ,255 )
122:    CommandObject.Parameters.Append _
123:      CommandObject.CreateParameter("City",200, ,255 )
124:    CommandObject.Parameters.Append _
125:      CommandObject.CreateParameter("State",200, ,255 )
126:    CommandObject.Parameters.Append _
127:      CommandObject.CreateParameter("ZipCode",200, ,255 )
128:    CommandObject.Parameters.Append _
129:      CommandObject.CreateParameter("Country",200, ,255 )
130:    CommandObject.Parameters.Append _
131:      CommandObject.CreateParameter("FirstAccessTime",200, ,255 )
132:    CommandObject.Parameters.Append _
133:      CommandObject.CreateParameter("FirstAccessDate",200, ,255 )
134:    CommandObject.Parameters.Append _
135:      CommandObject.CreateParameter("FirstAccessIPAddress",200, ,255 )
136:    CommandObject.Parameters.Append _
137:      CommandObject.CreateParameter("FirstAccessWebBrowser",200, ,255 )
138:    CommandObject.Parameters.Append _
139:      CommandObject.CreateParameter("LastAccessTime",200, ,255 )
140:    CommandObject.Parameters.Append _
141:      CommandObject.CreateParameter("LastAccessDate",200, ,255 )
142:    CommandObject.Parameters.Append _
143:      CommandObject.CreateParameter("LastAccessIPAddress",200, ,255 )
144:    CommandObject.Parameters.Append _
145:      CommandObject.CreateParameter("LastAccessWebBrowser",200, ,255 )
146:
147:    ' Information entered by the user is added to the Guest Book
        ➥database
148:    CommandObject("Prefix") = Request.Form.Item("Prefix")
149:    CommandObject("FirstName") = Request.Form.Item("FirstName")
150:    CommandObject("LastName") = Request.Form.Item("LastName")
151:    CommandObject("EmailAddress") = Request.Form.Item("EmailAddress")
152:    CommandObject("URL") = Request.Form.Item("URL")
153:    CommandObject("Phone") = "(" & Request.Form.Item("PhoneAreaCode")
        ➥& _
154:      ") " & Request.Form.Item("PhoneNumber")
155:    CommandObject("Mobile") = "(" &
        ➥Request.Form.Item("MobileAreaCode") _
156:      & ") " & Request.Form.Item("MobilePhoneNumber")
157:    CommandObject("StreetAddress") =
        ➥Request.Form.Item("StreetAddress")
158:    CommandObject("City") = Request.Form.Item("City")
159:    CommandObject("State") = Request.Form.Item("State")
160:    CommandObject("ZipCode") = Request.Form.Item("ZipCode")
161:    CommandObject("Country") = Request.Form.Item("Country")
162:    CommandObject("FirstAccessTime") = Time
163:    CommandObject("FirstAccessDate") = Date
164:    CommandObject("FirstAccessIPAddress") = _
165:      Request.ServerVariables.Item ("REMOTE_ADDR")
```

10

continues

Listing 10.2. CONTINUED

```
166:      CommandObject("FirstAccessWebBrowser") = _
167:        Request.ServerVariables.Item ("HTTP_USER_AGENT")
168:      CommandObject("LastAccessTime") = Time
169:      CommandObject("LastAccessDate") = Date
170:      CommandObject("LastAccessIPAddress") = _
171:        Request.ServerVariables.Item ("REMOTE_ADDR")
172:      CommandObject("LastAccessWebBrowser") = _
173:        Request.ServerVariables.Item ("HTTP_USER_AGENT")
174:
175:      CommandObject.Execute
176:
177: End Sub
178:
179: ' ########## End Subroutine ##########
180:
181: If Request.Form.Count <= 0 Then
182:    Response.Write ("I am sorry but you did not fill in the Form.")
183: Else
184:
185:      ' Create an instance of the Connection Object
186:      Set DatabaseConnection = Server.CreateObject("ADODB.Connection")
187:
188:      ' Open a connection to the Guest Book File DSN
189:      ' Before the following statement can execute properly, you have to
190:      ' create a File DSN for the Guest Book database as outlined in the
191:      ' book.
192:      DatabaseConnection.Open   "FILEDSN=UserInformationDatabase.dsn"
193:
194:      Call AddUserInformation
195:      Call AddGuestBookEntry
196:      DatabaseConnection.Close
197:
198:      Response.Write ("Thank you,
         ➥"&Request.Form.Item("FirstName")&"!<BR>")
199:      Response.Write ("Your guest book entry was added to the Guest
         ➥Book!")
200:
201: End If
202: %>
203: <P> </P>
204: <HR>
205: This Web page was generated on <%= Date %> at <%= Time %>.<BR>
206: <A HREF=Default.asp>Return to guest book's main menu</A>.
207: </BODY>
208: </HTML>
```

Execution of the code in Listing 10.2 begins at line 181. The `If...Then` statement in line 181 first determines if the form has been filled in. If it has not, an error message is displayed for the user. If the user has filled in the form, the `Else` clause defined in lines 183–201 is executed. Line 186 creates an instance of the ADO `Connection` object. Line 192 opens the file DSN you created for the guest book database earlier.

Line 194 calls the procedure `AddUserInformation`, which adds user information to the guest book database's `Users` table. This procedure was defined in lines 76–177. Line 195 calls the procedure `AddGuestBookEntry`, which adds the guest book entry corresponding to the user to the guest book database's `GuestBookEntries` table. This procedure was defined in lines 12–70. Because both these procedures function the same way, you need to examine only the procedure that adds user information to the `Users` table. Line 82 creates an instance of the ADO `Command` object. The SQL statement that inserts the data is created in lines 90–96 and the SQL statement is executed in line 175. Lines 106–145 create parameters of the record that will be inserted in the database. Lines 148–173 get the user's information and assign it to the new database record.

View Records of the Guest Book Database

The ASP code that displays the records of the guest book database is given in Listing 10.3. The Active Server Page in Listing 10.3 generates the Web page shown in Figure 10.15. Notice how the e-mail address is displayed only for users who have given you permission, through the HTML form, to include their contact information.

FIGURE 10.15.

Entries of the guest book database.

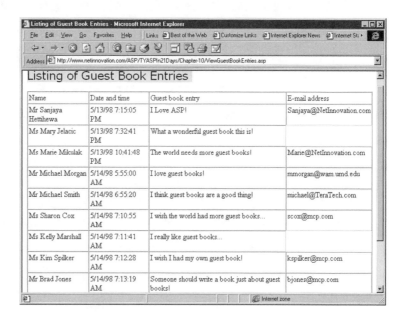

Name	Date and time	Guest book entry	E-mail address
Mr Sanjaya Hetthhewa	5/13/98 7:15:05 PM	I Love ASP!	Sanjaya@NetInnovation.com
Ms Mary Jelacic	5/13/98 7:32:41 PM	What a wonderful guest book this is!	
Ms Marie Mikulak	5/13/98 10:41:48 PM	The world needs more guest books!	Marie@NetInnovation.com
Mr Michael Morgan	5/14/98 5:55:00 AM	I love guest books!	mmorgan@wam.umd.edu
Mr Michael Smith	5/14/98 6:55:20 AM	I think guest books are a good thing!	michael@TeraTech.com
Ms Sharon Cox	5/14/98 7:10:55 AM	I wish the world had more guest books...	scox@mcp.com
Ms Kelly Marshall	5/14/98 7:11:41 AM	I really like guest books...	
Ms Kim Spilker	5/14/98 7:12:28 AM	I wish I had my own guest book!	kspilker@mcp.com
Mr Brad Jones	5/14/98 7:13:19 AM	Someone should write a book just about guest books!	bjones@mcp.com

COMPANION **Web site** Experiment with the application in Listing 10.3 by downloading the code distribution file for this book from the MCP Web site, copying the file Chapter-10/ViewGuestBookEntries.asp to your Web server and executing it with a Web browser.

LISTING 10.3. THIS ASP APPLICATION DISPLAYS ALL THE RECORDS IN THE GUEST BOOK DATABASE.

```
 1: <html>
 2:
 3: <head>
 4: <meta http-equiv="Content-Type" content="text/html; charset=iso-8859-
    ➥1">
 5: <title>Listing of Guest Book Entries</title>
 6: </head>
 7:
 8: <BODY>
 9: <P><FONT face=Verdana size=5 style="BACKGROUND-COLOR: #fafad2"><FONT
10: style="BACKGROUND-COLOR: #98fb98">Listing of Guest Book
11: Entries
12: </FONT></FONT></P>
13: <P> </P>
14: <%
15:
16:     Dim SQLString
17:
18:     ' Create an instance of the Connection Object
19:     Set DatabaseConnection = Server.CreateObject("ADODB.Connection")
20:
21:     ' Open a connection to the Guest Book File DSN
22:     ' Before the following statement can execute properly, you have to
23:     ' create a File DSN for the Guest Book database as outlined in the
24:     ' book.
25:     DatabaseConnection.Open  "FILEDSN=UserInformationDatabase.dsn"
26:
27:     ' Create an Instance of the Recordset object
28:     Set UserRecordset = Server.CreateObject("ADODB.Recordset")
29:
30:     ' The Open method of the Recordset Object is used to retrieve
31:     ' data from the Guest Book database.
32:     SQLString = "SELECT Users.Prefix, Users.FirstName, " & _
33:       "Users.LastName, GuestBook.EmailAddress, " & _
34:       "GuestBook.GuestBookEntryDate, GuestBook.GuestBookEntryTime, " & _
35:       "GuestBook.GuestBookEntryComment, " & _
36:       "GuestBook.DisplayContactInfo   FROM Users As Users, " & _
37:       "GuestBookEntries AS GuestBook, Users RIGHT JOIN GuestBook ON " & _
38:       "Users.EmailAddress=GuestBook.EmailAddress"
39:
40:     UserRecordset.Open SQLString, DatabaseConnection
```

```
41:
42:    Set objUserPrefix     = UserRecordset("Prefix")
43:    Set objUserFirstName  = UserRecordset("FirstName")
44:    Set objUserLastName   = UserRecordset("LastName")
45:    Set objUserEmail      = UserRecordset("EmailADdress")
46:    Set objUserAccessDate = UserRecordset("GuestBookEntryDate")
47:    Set objUserAccessTime = UserRecordset("GuestBookEntryTime")
48:    Set objUserComment    = UserRecordset("GuestBookEntryComment")
49:    Set objUserPublic     = UserRecordset("DisplayContactInfo")
50:
51: %>
52:    <Table BORDER=1 cellspacing=0 cellpadding=2>
53:    <TR><TD>Name</TD><TD>Date and time</TD><TD>Guest book entry</TD>
54:    <TD>E-mail address</TD></TR>
55: <%
56:
57:    Do Until UserRecordset.EOF
58:      Response.Write "<TR VALIGN=TOP><TD>" & objUserPrefix & " " & _
59:        objUserFirstName & " " & objUserLastName & "</TD><TD>" & _
60:        objUserAccessDate & " " & objUserAccessTime & "</TD><TD>" & _
61:        objUserComment & "</TD>"
62:      If  objUserPublic="True" Then
63:        Response.Write "<TD>" & objUserEmail & "</TD>"
64:      End If
65:      Response.Write "</TR>"
66:    UserRecordset.MoveNext
67:    Loop
68:
69:    DatabaseConnection.Close
70: %>
71:
72:    </TABLE>
73:
74: <P> </P>
75: <HR>
76: This Web page was generated on
77: <%= Date %> at <%= Time %>.<BR>
78: <A href="Default.asp">Return to guest book's main menu</A>.
79: </BODY>
80: </html>
```

ANALYSIS Line 18 creates an instance of the Connection object and line 25 opens the file DSN created earlier. Line 28 creates an instance of the Recordset object, which is instrumental in retrieving and iterating through records in a database. The SQL statement in lines 32–38 defines the SQL statement that retrieved data from the guest book database. Line 40 executes the SQL statement to retrieve all the guest book records. Lines 42–49 create a reference to the fields of the Recordset object opened in line 40. The Do Until...Loop in defined in lines 57–67 displays the records of the guest book database.

10

You probably noticed the following already. The SQL statement defined in lines 32–38 is rather sophisticated. You might remember that the guest book data is actually spread between two tables. So how would you retrieve data from multiple tables using only one SQL statement? The answer is simple. You join the two tables together. Notice how line 36 creates a `RIGHT JOIN` and line 38 defines the relationship between the two tables (see Figure 10.4 if you do not quite remember the structure of the two tables and the relationship between them).

Note

Using a `RIGHT JOIN` is a relatively complex database topic. However, it is an important part of developing Web database applications. Very few databases have just one table, and most databases are relational databases with data scattered across multiple tables. By using the application presented today as a model, you can develop applications that use multiple tables for retrieving data.

Note

If the concept of joining tables is new to you, you should look for more information from books on using SQL, such as *Sams Teach Yourself SQL in 21 Days*.

Implement a Search Function

The ASP code in Listing 10.4 demonstrates how to implement a search function so that users can search records in a database for a given string. When the search application in Listing 10.4 is first invoked, users see the Web page in Figure 10.16. The Web page in Figure 10.16 initiates a search for guest book entries made by users from Indianapolis (where the friendly people who publish this book live).

FIGURE 10.16.

The ASP application in Listing 10.4 allows the guest book database to be searched using various search criteria.

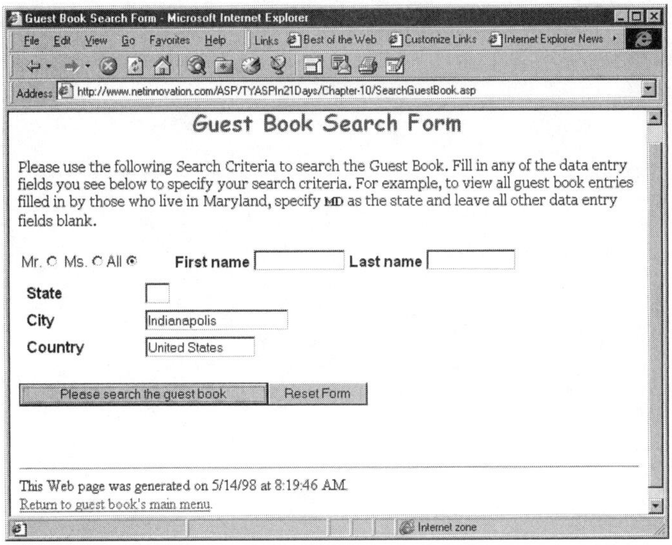

10

After a user fills in the Web page in Figure 10.16 and submits it, the Web page shown in Figure 10.17 displays the records of the guest book database that match the user's search criteria.

FIGURE 10.17.

Displaying the records of the guest book database that match the user's search criteria.

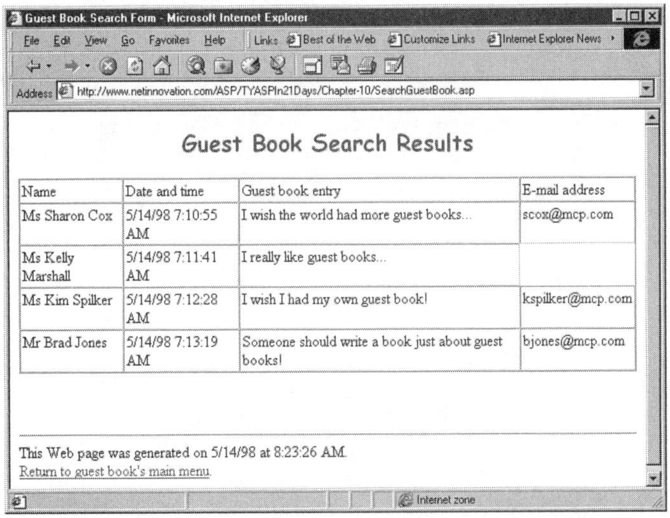

COMPANION **Web site** Experiment with the application in Listing 10.4 by downloading the code distribution file for this book from the MCP Web site, copying the file `Chapter-10/SearchGuestBook.asp` to your Web server and executing it with a Web browser.

LISTING 10.4. THIS ASP APPLICATION ALLOWS THE USER TO SEARCH FOR SPECIFIC RECORDS IN THE GUEST BOOK DATABASE.

```
 1: <html>
 2:
 3: <head>
 4: <meta http-equiv="Content-Type"
 5:   content="text/html; charset=iso-8859-1">
 6: <title>Guest Book Search Form</title>
 7: </head>
 8:
 9: <body>
10:
11: <%
12: If Request.Form.Count <= 0 Then
13: %>
14:
15: <p align="center"><font face="Comic Sans MS" size="5"
16: color="#0000FF"><strong>Guest Book Search Form</strong></font></p>
17:
18: <p><font face="Georgia">Please use the following Search Criteria to
19: search the Guest Book. Fill in any of the data entry fields you see
20: below to specify your search criteria. For example, to view all guest
21: book entries filled in by those who live in Maryland, specify </font>
22: <strong>
23: <font face="Courier New">MD</font></strong><font face="Georgia">
24: as the state and leave all other data entry fields blank.</font></p>
25:
26: <form method="POST" action="SearchGuestBook.asp">
27:   <div align="left"><table border="0" width="610">
28:     <tr>
29:       <td width="135" align="left" colspan=1><font face="Arial">Mr.
30:       <input type="radio" value="Mr" name="Prefix" checked> Ms.<input
31:       type="radio" name="Prefix" value="Ms">All<input
32:       type="radio" name="Prefix" value="All"></font></td>
33:       <td align="left"><font face="Arial"><strong>First name</strong>
34:       <input type="text" name="FirstName" size="12"> <strong>Last name
35:       </strong> <input type="text" name="LastName" size="12"></font>
36:     </td></tr>
37:     <tr>
38:     </tr>
39:     <tr>
40:       <td width="100%" colspan="2"><div align="center"><center><table
41:         border="0" width="600">
```

```
42:        <tr>
43:          <td width="116"><strong><font face="Arial">State</font>
44:            </strong></td>
45:          <td width="476">  <input type="text" name="State"
46:            size="2"></td>
47:        </tr>
48:        <tr>
49:          <td width="116"><strong><font face="Arial">City </font>
50:            </strong></td>
51:          <td width="476">  <input type="text" name="City"
52:            size="20"></td>
53:        </tr>
54:        <tr>
55:          <td width="116"><strong><font face="Arial">Country </font>
56:            </strong></td>
57:          <td width="476">  <input type="text" name="Country"
58:            size="15" value="United States"></td>
59:        </tr>
60:      </table>
61:      </center></div></td>
62:    </tr>
63:  </table>
64: </div><p><input type="submit" value="Please search the guest book"
65:    name="SearchButton"><input type="reset" value="Reset Form"
66:    name="ResetButton"></p>
67: </form>
68:
69: <%
70: Else %>
71:
72: <p align="center"><font face="Comic Sans MS" size="5"
73: color="#0000FF"><strong>Guest Book Search Results</strong></font></p>
74:
75: <%
76:
77:    Dim SQLString
78:
79:    ' This SQL string retrieves all the selected records from the
80:    ' of the Guest Book database
81:    SQLString = "SELECT Users.Prefix, Users.FirstName, " & _
82:      "Users.LastName, GuestBook.EmailAddress, " & _
83:      "GuestBook.GuestBookEntryDate, GuestBook.GuestBookEntryTime, " & _
84:      "GuestBook.GuestBookEntryComment, " & _
85:      "GuestBook.DisplayContactInfo    FROM Users As Users, " & _
86:      "GuestBookEntries AS GuestBook, Users RIGHT JOIN GuestBook ON " & _
87:      "Users.EmailAddress=GuestBook.EmailAddress"
88:
89:    ' These If/Then statements specify additional search criteria
90:    ' if selected by the user.
```

continues

LISTING 10.4. CONTINUED

```
91:
92:      If Not Request.Form.Item("Prefix") = "All" Then
93:        SQLString = SQLString & " WHERE Users.Prefix=" & chr(39) & _
94:          Request.Form.Item("Prefix") & chr(39)
95:      End If
96:
97:      If Not Request.Form.Item("FirstName") = "" Then
98:        SQLString = SQLString & " AND Users.FirstName=" & _
99:          Chr(39) & Request.Form.Item("FirstName") & Chr(39)
100:     End If
101:
102:     If Not Request.Form.Item("LastName") = "" Then
103:       SQLString = SQLString & " AND Users.LastName=" & _
104:         Chr(39) & Request.Form.Item("LastName") & Chr(39)
105:     End If
106:
107:     If Not Request.Form.Item("State") = "" Then
108:       SQLString = SQLString & " AND Users.State=" & _
109:         Chr(39) & Request.Form.Item("State") & Chr(39)
110:     End If
111:
112:     If Not Request.Form.Item("City") = "" Then
113:       SQLString = SQLString & " AND Users.City=" & _
114:         Chr(39) & Request.Form.Item("City") & Chr(39)
115:     End If
116:
117:     If Not Request.Form.Item("Country") = "" Then
118:       SQLString = SQLString & " AND Users.Country=" & _
119:         Chr(39) & Request.Form.Item("Country") & Chr(39)
120:     End If
121:
122: ' Create an instance of the Connection Object
123: Set DatabaseConnection = Server.CreateObject("ADODB.Connection")
124:
125: ' Open a connection to the Guest Book File DSN
126: ' Before the following statement can execute properly, you have to
127: ' create a File DSN for the Guest Book database as outlined in the
128: ' book.
129: DatabaseConnection.Open  "FILEDSN=UserInformationDatabase.dsn"
130:
131: ' Create an Instance of the Recordset object
132: Set UserRecordset = Server.CreateObject("ADODB.Recordset")
133:
134: ' The Open method of the Recordset Object is used to retrieve
135: ' data from the Guest Book database.
136: UserRecordset.Open SQLString, DatabaseConnection
137:
138: Set objUserPrefix    = UserRecordset("Prefix")
139: Set objUserFirstName = UserRecordset("FirstName")
```

```
140:    Set objUserLastName   = UserRecordset("LastName")
141:    Set objUserEmail      = UserRecordset("EmailADdress")
142:    Set objUserAccessDate = UserRecordset("GuestBookEntryDate")
143:    Set objUserAccessTime = UserRecordset("GuestBookEntryTime")
144:    Set objUserComment    = UserRecordset("GuestBookEntryComment")
145:    Set objUserPublic     = UserRecordset("DisplayContactInfo")
146:
147:    If UserRecordset.EOF Then
148: %>
149:
150:    <H1>Sorry. No records match your search criteria.</H1>
151: <%
152:    Else
153: %>
154:    <Table BORDER=1 cellspacing=0 cellpadding=2>
155:    <TR><TD>Name</TD><TD>Date and time</TD><TD>Guest book entry</TD>
156:    <TD>E-mail address</TD></TR>
157: <%
158:
159:    Do Until UserRecordset.EOF
160:      Response.Write "<TR VALIGN=TOP><TD>" & objUserPrefix & " " & _
161:        objUserFirstName & " " & objUserLastName & "</TD><TD>" & _
162:        objUserAccessDate & " " & objUserAccessTime & "</TD><TD>" & _
163:        objUserComment & "</TD>"
164:      If  objUserPublic="True" Then
165:        Response.Write "<TD>" & objUserEmail & "</TD>"
166:      End If
167:      Response.Write "</TR>"
168:    UserRecordset.MoveNext
169:    Loop
170:
171:    DatabaseConnection.Close
172:    Response.Write "</TABLE>"
173:
174: End If
175: End If
176: %>
177:
178: <P> </P>
179: <HR>
180: This Web page was generated on <%= Date %> at <%= Time %>.<BR>
181: <A href="Default.asp">Return to guest book's main menu</A>.
182: </body>
183: </html>
```

ANALYSIS   The If...Then statement in line 12 of Listing 10.4 determines if the form has been filled in. If it has not, the If clause defined in lines 12–67 displays the HTML that allows users to search the database. If the form has been filled in, the Else clause defined in lines 70–175 is executed. Most of the code of the Else clause is very similar to the code that displays all the records of the guest book database. The only difference is the additional WHERE clauses (defined in lines 92–120) of the SQL statement that narrows down records returned by the Recordset object.

Summary

Today turned out to be a bit of a long lesson, but you learned a lot about ASP Web database development. You can now create your own Web database applications that insert, retrieve, and search database records. It is very easy to build Web database applications using ADO. To build a database application, first you have to build the database and create a DSN for it. Afterward, by using the Connection object and ADO, your ASP application can interface with the database and add, delete, modify, and insert database records. Before inserting data to a database, you should always validate the data to make sure it's valid. ADO is covered in more detail in tomorrow's lesson, "Building Database Applications Using ActiveX Data Objects."

Q&A

Q Why should I add client-side data validation to an HTML form when I have already implemented server-side data validation?

A Use client-side data validation to compliment server-side data validation, not to replace it. Client-side data validation adds a more professional touch to your Web forms and makes them more efficient for data entry because a HTTP connection does not have to be established with the Web server to detect a minor error the user might have made.

Q Why must you limit the use of SELECT * statements?

A Never use a SELECT * statement to retrieve all the records in a table (unless this is exactly your intention) and use ASP code to filter the data. Instead, use a SQL statement to filter the data. As much as possible, get the database engine to select, filter, and sort the data for you.

Q Can you use the DELETE statement to delete all the records in a database table?

A Yes. You should be especially careful when using the DELETE statement with wildcards so that you do not inadvertently delete more records than you want!

Q Does deleting all the records in a table automatically delete the database table?

A No. Deleting records in a table does not automatically delete the database table.

Workshop

The quiz questions and exercises are provided for your further understanding. Please refer to Appendix A, "Answers to Questions," for the answers to the quiz questions; answers to the exercises are on the MCP Web site.

Quiz

1. Why should you make sure your Web forms are not wider than 640 pixels?

2. How many connections is Microsoft Access limited to?

3. What type of DSN is recommended?

4. True or False: The DELETE SQL statement returns a recordset of current data after carrying out the DELETE operation.

5. What must you do to transfer an ASP application that uses a DSN to a new Web server?

Exercises

1. Write the ASP statement that instantiates the Connection object for data access.

2. Build a SQL statement that deletes records in the Customers table with an AccountBalance of 50 or more.

3. Build the SQL statement that retrieves a recordset of data containing records with a RecordCreationDate earlier than 1/1/1993.

4. Build a simple database on your own and create a Web application so users can enter and search data. (Hint: Use and modify code from today's lesson to make things easier for yourself.) A good (and useful) database to create would be one that you can use as a phone book. The database can keep track of fields such as first name, last name, e-mail address, phone number, address, birthday, and so forth.

10

DAY 11

Building Database Applications Using ActiveX Data Objects

by Duncan Mackenzie

Yesterday's lesson introduced you to the concept of using databases from Active Server Pages, all based on something called ADO. ADO (or ActiveX Data Objects, as it is never called) is a set of external objects you can access from within your pages, giving them the ability to work with databases. Now that you've seen an example of how you can use them, today's lesson explains each of the ADO objects in much more detail. Today you will cover the following:

- Discover what ADO is.
- Review the ADO Object Model.
- Use ADO to build a user forum application.
- Incorporate the advanced ADO feature, data schemas.

An Introduction to ADO

ADO is a group of objects designed to provide a simple programming interface to databases. Many similar systems have been created in the past, such as DAO (Data Access Objects) and RDO (Remote Data Objects), and have been used extensively by Visual Basic, Visual C++, and Access developers. Microsoft decided that these other systems were too limited in their ability to deal with the many different types of data that exist in the real world, and so created OLE DB. OLE DB is everything that DAO is not—fast, lightweight, and flexible. DAO is an interface to Jet, the database engine behind Microsoft Access, and was not designed to work with other types of data. OLE DB, on the other hand, can work with anything, including data that is not in a traditional tabular format. All these facts mean that OLE DB is the current database tool of choice for programmers, but it has one major flaw that would have prevented it from being widely used: It is extremely complex. To overcome this, Microsoft created ADO, a simple layer over OLE DB that provides an easier programming interface.

With only three main objects and a few supporting collections, ADO is very streamlined. This makes it easy to use and easy to learn, but it is still capable of almost anything people do with databases. ADO's lightweight nature makes it very suitable for use with Active Server Pages, so it has been the only database method used when developing ASP applications. It is also considered the better tool for Visual Basic, and other development environments, but is only now becoming popular outside ASP.

The ADO Object Model

ADO has only six objects and two collections, and of those, only three are main objects you need to understand completely:

- Connection
- Command
- Recordset

Each of these main objects is explained in the following section with a complete list of properties and methods. Examples of their use are provided later as part of the User Forum system. You also saw them briefly in yesterday's lesson.

The Connection Object

As you learned yesterday, every use of a database requires a Connection object. It represents the actual session established with your database. Open() and Close() are usually the only methods of this object used in your ASP scripts. Listing 11.1 shows how the Connection object could be used.

LISTING 11.1. USING THE Connection OBJECT.

```
 1:
 2: <%
 3: Dim Conn 'Our Connection Object
 4:
 5: Set Conn = Server.CreateObject("ADODB.Connection")
 6:
 7: Conn.Open "DSN=WEBSQL;UID=sa;pwd=;"
 8:
 9: 'Any other code goes in here
10:
11: Conn.Close
12: %>
```

ANALYSIS   In the preceding code, a Connection object is created, opened, and then closed through a series of steps. Line 3 declares the variable Conn for use as the Connection object, which is not required, but is considered better programming practice. Line 5 then uses the Server.CreateObject method to create an actual instance of the Connection object, which must happen before any methods or properties of the object can be used. After the object is created, line 7 opens a session with the database, passing the database connection string as a parameter to the Open method. The connection string contains three separate pieces of information—the DSN, the user ID, and the password, all of which can also be supplied separately, as in the following example:

```
Conn.Open "WEBSQL","sa",""
```

Between the call to Open and line 11, which closes the database connection, would be any code that has to work with that connection.

The Connection object contains six methods, listed in Table 11.1.

TABLE 11.1. THE Connection OBJECT'S METHODS.

Method	Description
Open	Creates the database session. Usually the first method called, and definitely the most important.
Close	Closes the session, if one has been opened; generates an error if one has not.
Execute	Runs a SQL statement directly against the database. Useful for performing actions that do not return any records, such as deleting some rows in a table.
BeginTrans	Starts a database transaction. See Day 9, "Using ActiveX Components Built for ASP," for more information on transactions and why they are used.

continues

Method	Description
CommitTrans	One of the two ways to end a database transaction; this one tells the database that the entire operation was successful and all changes should be applied to the data.
RollbackTrans	The other way to end a transaction; this method informs the database that an error has occurred and all database operations since the BeginTrans should be undone.
OpenSchema	This advanced method is rarely used. It returns a recordset whose contents are determined by the method's first argument. The full list of arguments and the corresponding values returned cannot be listed here, but an example is given in the "Working with Database Schemas" section at the end of today's lesson.

The Connection object also contains nine properties; the most common and useful ones are listed in Table 11.2.

TABLE 11.2. THE COMMON AND USEFUL Connection OBJECT PROPERTIES.

Property	Description
ConnectionString	This value contains the information required to establish a database session; can be passed (and usually is) directly to the Open method.
ConnectionTimeout	Determines how long the Open method should wait without receiving a response before generating an error.
CommandTimeout	This value is used to determine how long commands issued against the database session should be allowed to run before a timeout error is generated.
State	This property returns one of two values to indicate whether the database connection is open (1) or closed (0).
Attributes	An advanced property, it returns values to indicate what features the database supports (such as transactions). Not required in simple systems.

Two collections, listed in Table 11.3, can also be accessed through the Connection object.

TABLE 11.3. THE Connection OBJECT COLLECTIONS.

Collection	Description
Errors	This is a collection of Error objects, one for each error generated through this database session.
Properties	Every ADO object supports this collection, which just gives collection-based access to the properties described in Table 11.2.

The Connection object is created and opened first when working with databases, but it is usually not used alone. One or both of the next two objects are generally used to actually manipulate the database. The Command object, discussed next, uses the Connection object through its ActiveConnection property.

The Command Object

The Command object represents one command to issue against a database connection, such as a SQL statement or stored procedure. It is designed to handle the execution of these types of commands better than the Execute method of the Connection object. The Command object has a number of properties, methods, and collections listed in Tables 11.4 through 11.6.

TABLE 11.4. THE Command OBJECT PROPERTIES.

Property	Description
ActiveConnection	Each Command object works against an associated database connection. This property returns or sets the Connection object that this command uses.
CommandText	This property holds the SQL statement or stored procedure to be executed by this object.
CommandTimeout	This property serves the same purpose as the same property in the Connection object.
CommandType	This value tells the data provider the nature of the command text being sent to it. It can have one of many values, but two commonly used ones are Text(1) and Stored Procedure(4).
Prepared	Controls whether a compiled version of the command is generated before it is executed.

TABLE 11.5. THE Command OBJECT METHODS.

Method	Description
CreateParameter	Each Command object has a collection of Parameter objects. This method adds a new parameter to that collection. See the Parameter object in Table 11.6 for more details.
Execute	The main method of this object; it causes the command to be run against the data provider. This method can return a recordset.

11

TABLE 11.6. THE Command OBJECT COLLECTIONS.

Collection	Description
Properties	Like every ADO object, this collection contains all the properties of the Command object and their values.
Parameters	This is a collection of Parameter objects. They correspond to parameters that exist in the SQL statement or stored procedure that this Command object represents.

In general, the Command object is used for working with more complex database actions; simple queries and record manipulation are generally handled through the Recordset object, discussed next.

The Recordset Object

Any group of records—whether it is the result of a query or the entire contents of a table—is represented by a Recordset object. This is the object you will use for almost all your data access, and it's also the most complex. For most situations, though, it is generally used very simply. Listing 11.2 demonstrates a common use of a recordset: retrieving and displaying the results of a query.

LISTING 11.2. USING A RECORDSET AND THE Recordset OBJECT.

```
 1: <%
 2: Dim Conn
 3: Dim RSAuthors
 4: Dim SQL
 5:
 6: Set Conn = Server.CreateObject("ADODB.Connection")
 7: Set RSAuthors = Server.CreateObject("ADODB.Recordset")
 8: Conn.Open "WEBSQL;UID=sa;PWD=;"
 9: SQL = "Select * From Authors"
10: RSAuthors.Open SQL,Conn
11:
12: Do While Not RSAuthors.EOF
13:     Response.Write "<p>" & RSAuthors("Au_lname") & "</p>"
14:     Response.Write vbcrlf
15:     RS.MoveNext
16: Loop
17:
18: RSAuthors.Close
19: Conn.Close
20: %>
```

ANALYSIS In the preceding code, lines 2–4 declare the variables that will be used. Once again, this is not necessary, but is simply good programming practice. Lines 6 and 7 create instances of the Connection object and the Recordset object, respectively, that are used in the rest of the example. The Connection object is then opened in line 8, as it is needed to open the Recordset object later. Line 9 simply stores the desired SQL statement into a variable for use in line 10, where the Recordset object's Open method is called. This method takes two arguments: the SQL statement and the Connection object. After the recordset set is open, lines 12–16 demonstrate the most common method of working with a recordset. A simple loop allows the entire contents of the recordset to be processed. In this case, line 12 contains the loop condition, RSAuthors.EOF, a property that will be true if the current record is past the last record in the recordset. Lines 13 and 14 produce a line of HTML containing the value of the au_lname field of the recordset. Finally, and of extreme importance, is the RSAuthors.MoveNext line, which advances the record pointer and prevents an infinite loop from occurring.

In addition to the few simple properties and methods demonstrated previously, there are many others you should know about that can be useful. Tables 11.7 through 11.9 list the Recordset object's methods, properties, and collections.

TABLE 11.7. THE Recordset OBJECT METHODS.

Method	Description
Open	This is usually the first method you use; it allows you to initialize the object and fill it with the data you have requested. You can specify a Connection object to use for this recordset or connection parameters. If you do not specify a Connection object, a new one is created for every recordset you open.
Close	Usually the last method called; it destroys the data contained in the recordset and allows Open to be called again.
AddNew	Creates a new, empty record.
Update	Saves changes you have made to the current record back to the database.
CancelUpdate	Removes changes made to the current record if Update hasn't been called.
UpdateBatch	Some data providers support recordsets that perform multiple record updates at one time, storing individual changes up until this method is called.
CancelBatch	Cancels pending batch updates. All pending updates are cancelled by default, but you can specify an argument to restrict the cancellation to the current record or records that match a specified filter.

continues

11

TABLE 11.7. CONTINUED

Method	Description
Move	This method allows you to move a certain number of records forward or backward in a recordset. The movement can be in relation to the current record (if no second argument is provided) or to another record in the recordset.
MoveNext	This method moves to the next record in the recordset. An error is generated if you are already at the end of the recordset (the EOF property is true).
MovePrevious	The counterpart of the MoveNext method; it moves you to the record immediately before the current one. An error is generated in this case if you are already at the beginning of the recordset (the BOF property is true).
MoveLast	This method takes you to the very last record in the recordset. It has no effect if you are already there.
MoveFirst	Similar to MoveLast; this method moves you to the very first record, but has no effect if you are already on that record.
NextRecordset	It is possible to issue commands that return more than one recordset. This can occur through a stored procedure, or through using compound command statements, such as this one: `Select ID from Visitor; Select * From ShoppingCart` This method executes the next command in the series and returns the results.
Save	This method takes a filename parameter and saves the current recordset to that file. It can be loaded later by calling the Open method with the filename as its source.
Requery	This method is the equivalent of closing and reopening the recordset; the command is reissued. If more records meet your criteria than before, the new records are now available in the recordset.
Resync	Not to be confused with Requery, this method does not actually reissue the command; it merely compares the data in the records it has with the data on the server and updates the values in the recordset. An optional argument allows you to choose resynchronizing only the current record or only ones that match a certain criteria.
Delete	This method simply deletes the current record.
GetRows	This method returns a two-dimensional variant array, containing field-value pairs. Optional arguments allow you to specify how many records should be retrieved in this manner, and which record the retrieval should start at. By default, all the records from the current one are retrieved.

Clone	This method returns a `Recordset` object containing a copy of the current data.
Supports	This method allows you to determine what functionality is supported by the recordset, such as whether you can add records, move backward, and so forth.

TABLE 11.8. THE Recordset OBJECT PROPERTIES.

Property	Description
EOF	End of File; allows you to check if the current record is past the last record of the recordset. Commonly used to determine when to stop looping through records.
BOF	Beginning of File; similar to `EOF`, but returns true if the current record is past the start of the recordset. If both `EOF` and `BOF` are true, the recordset is empty.
MaxRecords	This property controls how many records are returned as the result of a query. It can be set only before the `Open` method is called, while the record-set is closed.
AbsolutePosition	This property can be used to set or return the current record position in relation to the beginning of file.
PageSize	This property works with the `AbsolutePage` and `PageCount` properties to divide a recordset into logical pages. This property returns or sets the number of records contained in one logical page.
PageCount	This property returns the number of logical pages in a recordset. It is read-only, but changes as the value of `PageSize` is modified.
AbsolutePage	This property indicates which logical page the current record is contained in. It can be set, which moves the current record to the first record in that logical page.
CursorType	This property returns one of several values: `Forward Only` (0), `Keyset` (1), `Dynamic` (2), or `Static` (3). It can be set only when the recordset is closed and is used to determine how the recordset should be opened. It can also be specified as an argument to the `Open` method. A description of each cursor type and its meaning is provided later in today's lesson.
CacheSize	This value controls how many records are retrieved at a time from the data provider. It defaults to one, meaning that only the current record is kept in local memory. If set to a higher value, those records that are cached do not necessarily reflect the true data in the database, but can be refreshed with the `Resync` method.

11

continues

TABLE 11.8. CONTINUED

Property	Description
Recordcount	This property is commonly used, but is not always correct or available. If the recordset does not know how many records it contains, or cannot determine that number, it returns -1 for this property. In general, unless you have already visited all the records (MoveLast), this value is suspect.
Source	This property contains the SQL text to be executed (or the name of a stored procedure), and can be set directly before the recordset is opened or provided as an argument to the Open method.
EditMode	Indicates the state of the current record, and can be one of the following values: None (0), Edit In Progress (1), Add In Progress (2), or Deleted (4).
ActiveConnection	This property is used to set or return the Connection object that this Recordset object uses.
LockType	Indicates what type of lock is placed on records being edited. Can be one of the following values: Read-Only (1), Pessimistic (2), Optimistic (3), or Batch Optimistic (4). An explanation of each of these lock types is provided later in today's lesson.
Bookmark	If the recordset supports bookmarks (which you can check by using the Supports method), you can store the value of this property to a variable. You can then return directly to this record at any time by assigning that saved value back to this property. This value is unique to this recordset. Two identical records in different recordsets might not have the same Bookmark value, but all the records in a Recordset object created with the Clone method will have the same Bookmark value as those in the original.
Filter	This property specifies a criteria to be checked against all the records currently in the recordset. The records that match the criteria become the recordset. Criteria take the form of *fieldname = value*, as in ("VisitorID = 123").
Status	Returns the record's current state with regards to any bulk or batch procedures.
CursorLocation	This value does not apply in ASP because it refers to whether the location is created on the client or the server. ADO through ASP always occurs on the server.
MarshalOptions	As with CursorLocation, this property affects how the recordset is moved between the client and the server and is not used in ASP.

TABLE 11.9. THE Recordset OBJECT COLLECTIONS.

Collection	Description
Properties	As with all ADO objects, this collection contains all the object's properties. Individual values can be retrieved simply, as shown in the statement rsOrder.Properties("Source").
Fields	Contains a group of Field objects, one for each column in the recordset. Useful for enumerating through the columns in a recordset when you do not know their names or positions.

Using ADO to Build a User Forum Application

To illustrate how to use the objects discussed previously, this section walks you through the code behind a complete user forum system. This system uses a Microsoft Access database, but because it connects to its data through ODBC, it could be switched to a different database (such as SQL Server) with only a few minutes' work. This system will be made as plain as possible, with no images or fancy formatting used. This streamlining is done to keep the code simple, not because it isn't required.

Note

The database, and all the ASP code, is available at the MCP Web site, http://www.mcp.com, for this book. Look under Chapter11/UserForum/ and copy all the pages to your Web server along with the Access database.

Introduction to the System

User forums have been around for a long time, longer than the Internet. They began life as *Bulletin Board Services*, or BBSs, as they are more often referred to—places where you could post questions, read other questions, and even receive some answers. They still exist, but have been almost completely replaced by their Internet equivalent, newsgroups. These systems, as shown in Figure 11.1, are almost the same. Users view the messages and create their own using software known as a newsreader, such as Outlook Express.

Note

The newsgroup shown in Figure 11.1 is actually a real one that is very useful for ASP developers. It is located at the newsgroup server msnews.microsoft.com and doesn't require any special user ID or password to participate.

FIGURE 11.1.

Newsgroups are a popular part of the Internet.

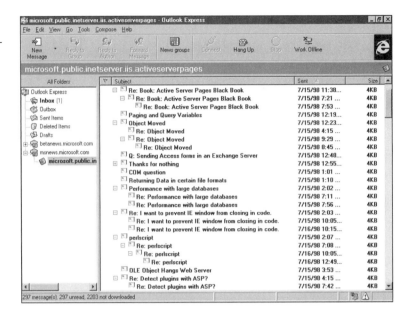

The system you're building in ASP will have to perform the same main functions as existing newsgroups. Listing the functions you need helps design the pages required and the structure of the database:

- Users must be able to create new messages.
- Users must be able to view messages created by themselves and other users.
- Users must be able to reply to messages, and their replies should be shown in relation to the original message.
- Users should be able to delete messages they created, but not able to delete any other user's messages.
- Users must be identified in some manner, so that their messages can be labeled.

These functions translate almost directly into what the system needs to do, but also create a few implied requirements: The system must be able to store messages, and a list of users with their identifying information must be maintained.

The Database

The first step is to create a simple database that meets the requirements described. Only two tables are required: one to hold the list of users, and one to store the messages. The fields and their data types are listed in Tables 11.10 and 11.11.

TABLE 11.10. THE USER TABLE.

Field Name	Field Type	Field Length
ID	AutoNumber	N/A
First Name	Text	30
Last Name	Text	50
Email	Text	50
Last Visit	Date/Time	N/A
UserId	Text	20
Password	Text	20

TABLE 11.11. THE MESSAGE TABLE.

Field Name	Field Type	Field Length
ID	AutoNumber	N/A
User ID	Number	Long
Parent	Number	Long
Subject	Text	50
Date	Date/Time	N/A
Message	Memo	N/A

Note

The newsgroup shown in Figure 11.1 is actually a real one that is very useful for ASP developers. It is located at the newsgroup server `msnews.microsoft.com` and doesn't require any special user ID or password to participate.

To make this database available to your Active Server Pages, you must place it on the Web server and create an ODBC DSN (system or file) that points to its location. The examples assume you have done so and named the DSN "Forum." For more information on setting up a DSN, refer to yesterday's lesson.

Identifying the User

The first step in using the forum application is for the user to login to the system, and should be where your code starts as well. The code in Listing 11.3 creates the login page shown in Figure 11.2.

FIGURE **11.2.**

*Users identify them-
selves through this
login screen.*

LISTING 11.3. THIS HTML PAGE ALLOWS THE USER TO LOGIN TO THE SYSTEM.

```
 1: <html>
 2: <head>
 3: <title>Sign In - User Forum</title>
 4: </head>
 5:
 6: <body bgcolor="#FFFFFF">
 7:
 8: <h1 align="center">User Forum<br>Sign In</h1>
 9:
10: <form action="signin_handler.asp" method="POST" target="_parent">
11:   <div align="center">
12:   <center>
13:     <table border="0">
14:     <tr>
15:       <td><strong>UserId:</strong>
16:       <input type="text" size="20" name="UserName"></td>
17:     </tr>
18:     <tr>
19:       <td><strong>Password*:</strong>
20:       <input type="password" size="20" name="Password"></td>
21:     </tr>
22:     <tr>
23:     </tr>
24:     <tr>
25:       <td>
```

```
26:        <input type="submit" name="Login" value="Login to Member's
           ➥Area">
27:        <input type="reset" name="cmdClear" value="Clear the Sign In
           ➥Form">
28:        </td>
29:      </tr>
30:    </table>
31:    </center>
32: </div>
33: <div align="center">
34: <center>
35:    <h6>*If you have forgotten or misplaced your password,
36:    <a href="forgotpw.asp" target="_parent">click here</a>
37:    .</h6>
38: </center>
39: </div>
40: <div align="center">
41: <center>
42:    <h6><big>New Users, <a href="newuser.asp">click here</a>
43:    .</big></h6>
44: </center>
45: </div>
46: </form>
47: </body>
48: </html>
```

11

ANALYSIS In Listing 11.3, most of the page is straightforward HTML because it is not an Active Server Page. The lines that concern you, as a programmer, are explained here. Line 10, the opening tag of the HTML form on this page, specifies which file will be called to handle the form when the Submit button is clicked. In this case, the handler is signin_handler.asp, which doesn't need a path specified because it resides in the same directory as this form. Lines 16 and 20 represent the input fields for user name and password, respectively. The important detail to note in these lines is the name assigned to these fields because that is how the values are retrieved from the Request.Form collection in the handler page.

The code in Listing 11.2 creates a simple form. The page that accesses the database and actually validates the user's login information is the target of the preceding form (see line 10), signin_handler.asp. Another HTML form, and corresponding ASP script form handlers, also exist for both the New User and Forgot Password links.

The login page handler, presented in Listing 11.4, is where the information supplied in the form must be verified. Based on the validity of the user ID and password supplied, the handler script must also decide how to handle both correct and incorrect logins.

LISTING 11.4. VERIFYING THE USER LOGIN FROM LISTING 11.3.

```
 1: <html>
 2: <head>
 3: <title>User Login</title>
 4: </head>
 5: <body bgcolor="#FFFFFF">
 6: <%
 7: Dim Conn
 8: Dim RSUser
 9: Dim SQL
10:
11: Set Conn=Server.CreateObject("ADODB.Connection")
12: Set RSUser = Server.CreateObject("ADODB.Recordset")
13:
14: Conn.Open "Forum"
15:
16: SQL = "Select * from User Where Userid='" & _
17:          Request.Form("UserName") & "'"
18: RSUser.Open SQL,Conn,1,2
19:
20: If RSUser.EOF Then
21: %>
22: <h2 align="center">User Does Not Exist</h2>
23: <h3 align="center"><%=Request.Form("UserName")%></h3>
24: <h3 align="center"><a href="signin.asp" target="_parent">
    ➥Click to try and login again</a></h3>
25: <p> </p>
26: <h3 align="center">OR</h3>
27: <p> </p>
28: <h3 align="center"><a href="newuser.asp" target="_parent">
    ➥Click here to join</a></h3>
29: <%
30: Else
31:    If RSUser("Password") <> Request.Form("Password") Then
32: %>
33: <h2 align="center">Password is Incorrect for</h2>
34: <h3 align="center"><%=Request.Form("UserName")%></h3>
35: <h3 align="center"><a href="signin.asp" target="_parent">
    ➥Click to try and login again</a></h3>
36: <p> </p>
37: <h3 align="center">OR</h3>
38: <p> </p>
39: <h3 align="center"><a href="forgotpw.asp" target="_parent">
    ➥Click here to have your
40: password emailed to you</a></h3>
41: <%
42:    Else
43:        Session("User") = "Yes"
44:        Session("User_ID") = RSUser("ID")
```

```
45:          Session("UserName") = RSUser("First Name") & " " &
             ➡RSUser("Last Name")
46: %>
47: <h2 align="center">Login Successful</h2>
48: <h3 align="center">Welcome Back <%=RSUser("First Name")%></h3>
49: <h3 align="center">Your last visit was on <%=RSUser("Last
    ➡Visit")%></h3>
50: <h3 align="center">
51: <a href="forum.asp" target="_parent">Click to enter the User Forum</a>
52: </h3>
53: <%
54:          RSUser("Last Visit") = Now
55:          RSUser.Update
56:     End If
57: End If
58:
59: %>
60: </body>
61: </html>
```

ANALYSIS This script attempts to retrieve the database record for the user ID entered (lines 7–18). If this record doesn't exist (line 20), then it is not a valid user ID, and the script displays an appropriate message (lines 22–28). If it does exist, then the next piece of code (lines 31–40) checks whether the password entered is correct for this user ID. If it isn't, another message is displayed. If it is, then code executes to place some values into the Session object (lines 43–45) where they can be used later. A message is then displayed that welcomes the user (lines 47–51). Finally, the Last Visit field of the User table is updated to reflect the current visit, and the page ends.

This code illustrates several ADO functions; each one is explained in more detail in the next few sections.

Opening a Connection

In Listing 11.4, lines 11 and 14 create and then open a connection to the database. A new, closed Connection object is created through the Server.CreateObject method. The Class ID ADODB.Connection is required to tell that method what object you want to create. Then line 14 performs the Open method of that new connection, passing as a parameter the DSN of the database. This first parameter is equivalent to the ConnectionString property of the Connection object and could be specified ahead of time, as shown in this alternative listing:

```
Set Conn=Server.CreateObject("ADODB.Connection")
Conn.ConnectionString = "Forum"
Conn.Open
```

This code is equivalent to the code in the first listing; it performs the same actions, but in separate steps. In this case, the ConnectionString is simply the name of the DSN, but it

11

can also contain other information, such as the user ID and password for accessing the database. If, for instance, your database required a user ID of sa and a blank password, you could use the following ConnectionString:

```
"DSN=Forum;userid=sa;pwd=;"
```

Remember that the Open method also takes two additional parameters (other than just the ConnectionString), the user ID and password. If you want, you can pass those values as separate arguments, as follows:

```
Conn.Open "Forum","sa",""
```

Regardless of which method you use, the Connection object must be created and opened before you can use it.

Creating and Opening a Recordset

In Listing 11.4, lines 12 and 18 create and then open the recordset. The Open method is shown using a series of parameters, SQL, Conn, 1, 2. As with the Connection object's Open method discussed earlier, each of these arguments could also be supplied by setting properties before calling Open. The following code is functionally equivalent to the code used in Listing 11.2:

```
RSUser.Source = SQL
Set RSUser.ActiveConnection = Conn
RSUser.CursorType = 1 'Keyset
RSUser.LockType = 2 'Pessimistic
RSUser.Open
```

You must remember to set these values, through either method, or defaults are used instead. If you do not have a Connection object created and opened, but still want to open the recordset, you can replace the argument of Conn with the actual connection string for your database, producing this:

```
RSUser.Open SQL, "Forum",1,2
```

This method seems to do exactly the same thing, but it does not. Every time a recordset is opened using this method of specifying the connection, a new Connection object is created. The following sample code causes three Connection objects to be created:

```
Set RSSample1 = Server.CreateObject("ADODB.Recordset")
Set RSSample2 = Server.CreateObject("ADODB.Recordset")
Set RSSample3 = Server.CreateObject("ADODB.Recordset")
RSSample1.Open SQL,"Forum",1,2
RSSample2.Open SQL,"Forum",1,2
RSSample3.Open SQL,"Forum",1,2
```

However, this code uses only one Connection object (yet still accomplishes the same result):

```
Set RSSample1 = Server.CreateObject("ADODB.Recordset")
Set RSSample2 = Server.CreateObject("ADODB.Recordset")
Set RSSample3 = Server.CreateObject("ADODB.Recordset")
Set Conn = Server.CreateObject("ADODB.Connection")
Conn.Open "Forum"
RSSample1.Open SQL,Conn,1,2
RSSample2.Open SQL,Conn,1,2
RSSample3.Open SQL,Conn,1,2
```

Using only one `Connection` object reduces the load on the database server to one connection per concurrent execution of this script. This allows for the maximum number of simultaneous connections because one connection per page is the minimum number of connections possible. The next section demonstrates how to determine if the recordset, regardless of how it was created, contains any records.

Checking for an Empty Recordset

Before doing anything with the recordset opened in line 18 of Listing 11.4, the code checks to see if it is empty in line 20. If a recordset is not empty, then its record pointer is on the first record when it is opened, and EOF is false. EOF is true only immediately after opening, if the recordset is empty. If you issue any method of the `Recordset` that attempts to manipulate the current record when the record pointer is not on a valid record (it is at BOF or EOF, for example), an error is generated.

 Note

> Checking for EOF alone is sufficient only if you have just opened the recordset. If the recordset might have been used before your checking, you should check for both BOF and EOF being true.

Retrieving Values from the Recordset

If the recordset is not empty, the code needs to start using the contents of the recordset's fields. The common syntax used to get at those values is this:

```
<RecordsetName>("<Field Name>")
```

This statement can be used to set or retrieve any of the field values. It is actually equivalent to this:

```
RSUser.Fields.Item("UserId").Value
```

This occurs because the `Fields` collection is the default property of the `Recordset` object, the `Item` property is the default for the `Fields` Collection, and the `Value` property is the `Field` object's default, making the two statements exactly the same. This is just good information to know; there is no reason not to use the simpler syntax.

Modifying Values in a Recordset

If you haven't opened a recordset as read-only (see the `CursorType` and `LockType` `Recordset` properties discussed previously), then you can modify the field values with a two-step process. First, you place new values into the fields by using simple assignment statements, as in line 54 of Listing 11.4. Second, you issue the `Update` method. If you modify the values and then close the recordset or move to a new record without calling the `Update` method, the changes are lost. Recordsets from some other data models, such as DAO, require that you use an `Edit` method first, before changing any values, but that method does not exist in ADO, so it generates an error ("Object does not support this method") if used.

Creating a New User

In the previous section, a page was provided for users to login with their user IDs and passwords, but where do those values come from? A page must be provided for new users to register so that they can use the forum. This page is already linked to by the login page as `newuser.asp` and is shown here as Listing 11.5. Figure 11.3 illustrates the New User Registration Form screen created by Listing 11.5.

LISTING 11.5. THIS HTML FORM PROMPTS THE USER FOR NECESSARY INFORMATION TO CREATE A NEW RECORD IN THE USER TABLE (`newuser.asp`).

```
 1: <html>
 2: <head>
 3:
 4: <title>New User Registration Form</title>
 5: </head>
 6:
 7: <body bgcolor="#FFFFFF" text="#000000">
 8:
 9: <h1 align="center">New User Registration Form</h1>
10:
11: <form method="POST" action="createuser.asp">
12:   <div align="center"><center><table border="1">
13:     <tr>
14:       <td><strong>First Name:</strong></td>
15:       <td><input type="text" name="txtFirstName" size="30"></td>
16:     </tr>
17:     <tr>
18:       <td><strong>Last Name:</strong></td>
19:       <td><input type="text" name="txtLastName" size="50"></td>
20:     </tr>
21:     <tr>
22:       <td><strong>Email Address:</strong></td>
23:       <td><input type="text" name="txtEmailAddress" size="50"></td>
```

```
24:      </tr>
25:      <tr>
26:        <td><strong> </strong></td>
27:        <td> </td>
28:      </tr>
29:      <tr>
30:        <td><strong>Userid:</strong></td>
31:        <td><input type="text" name="txtUserID" size="20"></td>
32:      </tr>
33:      <tr>
34:        <td><strong>Password:</strong></td>
35:        <td><input type="password" name="txtPassword" size="20"></td>
36:      </tr>
37:      </table>
38:      </center></div>
39:      <div align="center">
40:      <center>
41:      <p><input type="submit" value="Create New User" name="B1">
42:      <input type="reset" value="Clear All Fields" name="B2"></p>
43:      </center>
44:      </div>
45: </form>
46: </body>
47: </html>
```

11

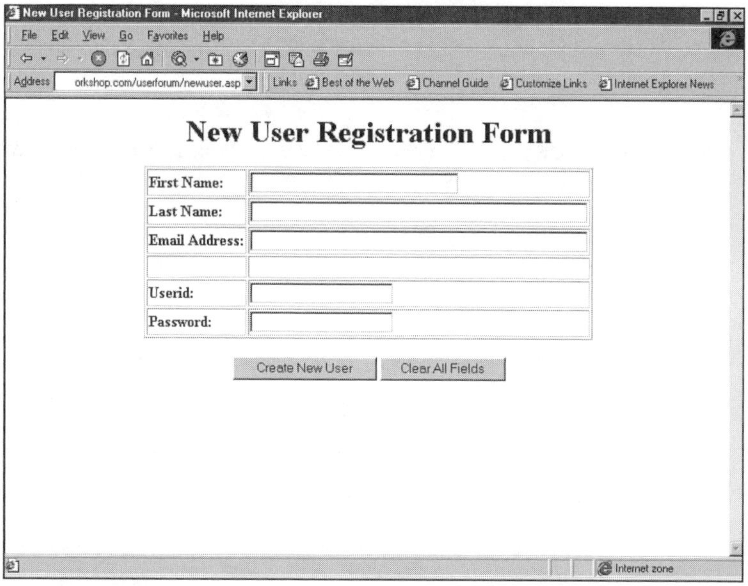

FIGURE 11.3.

The new user registration form allows the user to enter information to be added to the database.

ANALYSIS Listing 11.5 shows the code for an HTML form. The form itself consists mostly of code you should not write yourself. Any HTML editor (FrontPage being the obvious choice, but not the only one) can be used to create the form. In fact, the layout of the form itself is not really important; only the existence and name of the controls on the form have any meaning to the developer. Lines 15, 19, 23, 31, and 35 specify the names of each of the controls, and those names are used in the script that handles the results of this page. The script that handles the results of this form is specified in line 11. This script, named `createuser.asp`, is presented in Listing 11.6.

LISTING 11.6. THIS SCRIPT PROCESSES THE VALUES ENTERED INTO `newuser.asp` AND CREATES A NEW USER IN THE USER TABLE (`createuser.asp`).

```
 1: <html>
 2: <head>
 3: <title>Create New User</title>
 4: </head>
 5:
 6: <body bgcolor="#FFFFFF">
 7: <%
 8: Dim Conn
 9: Dim RSUser
10: Dim SQL
11:
12: Set Conn=Server.CreateObject("ADODB.Connection")
13: Set RSUser = Server.CreateObject("ADODB.Recordset")
14:
15: Conn.Open "Forum"
16:
17: SQL = "Select * from User Where Userid='" & Request.Form("txtUserid")
    ➥& "'"
18:
19: RSUser.Open SQL,Conn,1,2
20:
21: If Not RSUser.EOF Then
22: %>
23:
24: <h2 align="center">User already exists.</h2>
25:
26: <h3 align="center"><%=Request.Form("txtUserId")%></h3>
27:
28: <h3 align="center"><a href="newuser.asp" target="_parent">
29: Click to enter a different userid</a></h3>
30:
31: <p> </p>
32:
33: <h3 align="center">OR</h3>
34:
35: <p> </p>
```

```
36:
37: <h3 align="center"><a href="forgotpw.asp" target="_parent">
38: Click here to have your password emailed to you if you have
39: previously registered using this userid</a></h3>
40: <%
41: Else
42:
43:     RSUser.AddNew
44:     RSUser("First Name") = Request.Form("txtFirstName")
45:     RSUser("Last Name") = Request.Form("txtLastName")
46:     RSUser("Userid") = Request.Form("txtUserid")
47:     RSUser("Password") = Request.Form("txtPassword")
48:     RSUser("Email") = Request.Form("txtEmail")
49:     RSUser("Last Visit") = Now()
50:     RSUser.Update
51: %>
52:
53: <h2 align="center">New User Created</h2>
54:
55: <h3 align="center">
56: Welcome to the User Forum <%=Request.Form("txtFirstName")%>
57: </h3>
58:
59: <h3 align="center">
60: <a href="signin.asp" target="_parent">Click to Sign In</a></h3>
61: <%
62: End If
63: %>
64: </body>
65: </html>
```

ANALYSIS This script performs only a single validation (lines 17–21), checking to see if the user ID entered already exists. Completely blank values would be accepted, but this is enough for the purpose of creating a test ADO system. The concept illustrated in this particular script is adding a new record to a recordset, which is explained in more detail in the following sections.

Adding Records to a Recordset

After Listing 11.4 has determined that the user ID is not already in the database (line 41), it is time to add this user to the table. The recordset must already be open, and must have been opened against the table you want to add records to. In the previous script, the recordset was opened against the User table with a criteria that was not met, by using the SQL statement specified in line 17. Even though no records are returned, the recordset is still pointing at that table, so records added are placed into it. If you need to open a recordset only for adding records, you should specify a criteria in your SQL that no records will be returned, such as this one:

```
Select * From User where 1=2
```

There is no point in using the memory and processor requirements of a full recordset if one is not required.

After you have the recordset, adding the actual record is an easy three-step process:

1. Call the `AddNew` method (line 43).
2. Set the fields equal to the desired values (lines 44–49).
3. Call the `Update` method (line 50).

Notice that you do not need to set the values of the ID field because it is auto-incrementing. Any record-level validation, including index violations, occurs when the `Update` method is called, so that is generally where errors are caused. Errors caused by type or size mismatches for fields occur on the line where that value is set.

Displaying the Forum

The `forum.asp` page presented in Listing 11.7 is the main screen for this system, displaying all messages grouped by conversation. From this screen, the user can click on any single message and view it or add a new message. Figure 11.4 shows the completed page as seen through a browser. The function of replying to messages is available only from the single message screen.

FIGURE 11.4.

The results of forum.asp *show a list of all the messages in the database.*

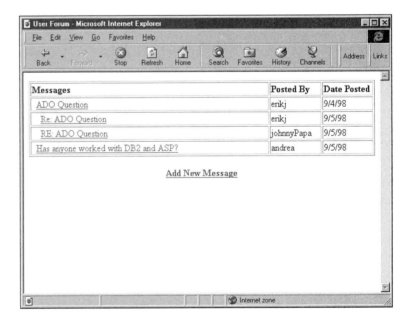

LISTING 11.7. THIS PAGE DISPLAYS ALL THE MESSAGES FROM THE MESSAGE TABLE.

```
 1: <html>
 2: <SCRIPT LANGUAGE=vbscript RUNAT=Server>
 3: Sub DisplayChildMessages(Parent,Level)
 4:
 5:   Dim RSMessages
 6:   Dim SQL
 7:   Dim i
 8:
 9:   Set RSMessages = Server.CreateObject("ADODB.Recordset")
10:
11:   SQL = "SELECT Message.ID, " & _
12:   "Message.Subject, Message.Date, " & _
13:   "User.Userid FROM Message, User " & _
14:   "WHERE Message.[User ID] = User.ID AND " & _
15:   "Message.Parent=" & Parent
16:
17:   RSMessages.Open SQL, Conn,1,2
18:
19:   Do While Not RSMessages.EOF
20:
21:     Response.Write "<tr>"
22:     Response.Write "<td>"
23:
24:     For i = 1 to level
25:       Response.Write "  "
26:     Next
27:
28:     Response.Write "<a href='message.asp?id="
29:     Response.Write RSMessages("ID") & "'>"
30:     Response.Write RSMessages("Subject")
31:     Response.Write "</a>"
32:     Response.Write "</td><td>"
33:     Response.Write RSMessages("Userid")
34:     Response.Write "</td><td>"
35:     Response.Write FormatDateTime(RSMessages("Date"),2)
36:     Response.Write "</tr>"
37:
38:     DisplayChildMessages RSMessages("ID"),Level+1
39:     RSMessages.MoveNext
40:
41: Loop
42:
43: End Sub
44: </SCRIPT>
45:
46: <head>
47: <title>User Forum</title>
48: </head>
```

continues

LISTING **11.7.** CONTINUED

```
49: <body>
50:
51: <table border="1" width="100%">
52:    <tr>
53:       <td width="70%"><strong>Messages</strong></td>
54:       <td width="15%"><strong>Posted By</strong></td>
55:       <td width="15%"><strong>Date Posted</strong></td>
56:    </tr>
57:
58: <%
59:
60: Dim Conn
61: Set Conn = Server.CreateObject("ADODB.Connection")
62:
63: Conn.Open "Forum"
64:
65: DisplayChildMessages 0,1
66:
67: %>
68: </table>
69:
70: <h4 align='center'><a href='newmessage.asp'>Add New Message</a></h4>
71: </body>
72: </html>
```

ANALYSIS   The page in Listing 11.7 works mostly through a *recursive routine*, which means a routine that calls itself. This routine, presented in lines 3–43, is `DisplayChildMessage()`. Only two arguments are used to produce this entire page. The first indicates for what parent message the child messages should be displayed; a zero indicates that the top level of messages, those with no parent, should be displayed. The parent argument is used as part of the SQL statement used to retrieve the messages (see lines 11–15). For each message found under a particular parent message, the function is called again, but with that message's ID value as the parent argument (line 38). This creates a very small piece of code that works for absolutely any number of messages. The second argument is used to control indenting the messages and indicates at what level in the overall tree these messages are displayed.

Recordset Navigation

The subroutine in Listing 11.7 demonstrates the use of a `Recordset` object's navigation methods, as it loops through a recordset and performs a series of actions on each record. Lines 19–41 consist of a loop that is going to execute until the end of the recordset is reached (`EOF`). For every execution of the loop, the MoveNext method of the `Recordset` object is called (line 39), advancing the pointer to the next record in the results. If this command were forgotten, you would have an infinite loop because EOF would never be reached.

Building URLs Based on Database Information

The functionality of clicking on a particular message is implemented simply by building a URL for each message that passes a parameter of the Message ID to a file named message.asp. This is accomplished by using *substitution*, inserting a value from the recordset into the HTML for each link. It is suggested that you keep the URLs simple, passing only an ID or a keyword. The preceding page is completely based on the messages contained in the system's database, but there needs to be a method for getting those messages in there. This method is provided by using the code in Listing 11.8, the newmessage.asp page explained in the next section.

Adding Messages to the System

A simple link was provided in Listing 11.7 (forum.asp) to allow the user to add a new message to the forum. This link in line 70 of Listing 11.7 calls newmessage.asp. This new page allows adding a new top-level message and is also used to add replies to the database. Without the ability to add new messages to the system, no one could post any comments to the system or reply to any posts because both involve creating a new message. Listing 11.8 presents newmessage.asp.

LISTING 11.8. THE PAGE TO CREATE NEW MESSAGES (newmessage.asp).

```
 1: <html>
 2: <head>
 3: <title>Create Message</title>
 4: </head>
 5: <body bgcolor="#FFFFFF" text="#000000">
 6:
 7: <% If Request.QueryString("Type") = "Reply" Then %>
 8: <h1 align="center">Reply To Message</h1>
 9:
10: <form action="addnewmessage.asp?ID=<%=Request.QueryString("ID")%>"
11: method="post" target="_parent">
12: <% Else %>
13:    <div align="center"><center><h1>New Message</h1>
14:    </center></div>
15: </form>
16:
17: <form action="addnewmessage.asp" method="post" target="_parent">
18: <% End If %>
19:    <table border="0">
20:      <tr>
21:         <td>Subject:</td>
```

continues

LISTING **11.8.** CONTINUED

```
22:        <td><input id="txtSubject" name="txtSubject" size="50"
23:        value="<%=Request.QueryString("Subject")%>"></td>
24:      </tr>
25:      <tr>
26:        <td valign="top">Message:</td>
27:        <td><textarea id="txtMessage" name="txtMessage" rows="4"
           ➥cols="50">
28:
29: </textarea></td>
30:      </tr>
31:    </table>
32:    <p><input name="cmdSubmit" type="submit" value="Post">   
33:    <input name="cmdReset" type="reset" value="Clear Form"> </p>
34: </form>
35: </body>
36: </html>
```

ANALYSIS Listing 11.8 creates a simple HTML form, shown in Figure 11.5. It also has a small amount of ASP code to allow this one form to function as the new message page for both adding and replying. Lines 7–18 alter the form's action URL, adding an ID parameter when replying to a message. This parameter, along with the contents of the form itself, are passed on to the form's target (addnewmessage.asp), which is shown in Listing 11.9.

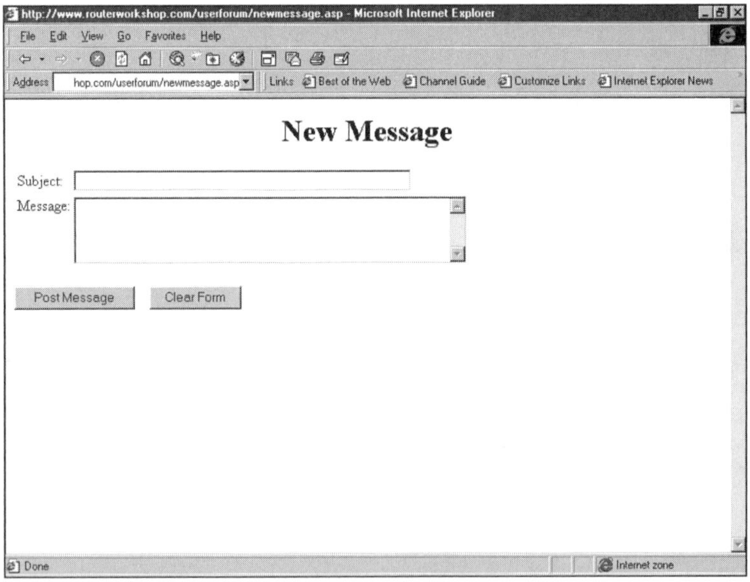

FIGURE 11.5.

This HTML form collects information to create a new forum message.

The script handler receives the results of the form shown in Figure 11.5 and must actually add that information into the database, as explained in the next section.

Processing the New Message Form

Listing 11.9, `addnewmessage.asp`, has to add the new message to the system, behaving slightly differently, depending on whether the message is a reply or a completely new post. Listing 11.9 contains the code used to process the message and adds a new record to the database to do so.

LISTING 11.9. CREATE A NEW MESSAGE OR A REPLY, BASED ON THE VALUES OF THE PARAMETERS (addnewmessage.asp).

```
1: <%@ Language=VBScript %>
2: <html>
3: <%
4: Dim Conn
5: Dim RSAddMessage
6: Dim SQL
7:
8: Set Conn = Server.CreateObject("ADODB.Connection")
9: Set RSAddMessage = Server.CreateObject("ADODB.Recordset")
10:
11: Conn.Open "Forum"
12:
13: SQL = "Select * From Message Where 1=2"
14:
15: RSAddMessage.Open SQL, Conn, 1, 2
16:
17: RSAddMessage.AddNew
18: RSAddMessage("Subject") = Request.Form("txtSubject")
19: RSAddMessage("User ID") = Session("User_ID")
20: RSAddMessage("Date") = Now()
21: IF Request.QueryString("ID") > 0 Then
22:    RSAddMessage("Parent") = Request.QueryString("ID")
23: Else
24:    RSAddMessage("Parent") = 0
25: End If
26:
27: RSAddMessage("Message") = Request.Form("txtMessage")
28: RSAddMessage.Update
29:
30: %>
31:
32: <head>
33: <title>Message Added</title>
34: </head>
35:
36: <body bgcolor="#FFFFFF" text="#000000">
```

continues

LISTING **11.9.** CONTINUED

```
37:
38: <h1 align="center">Your message has been added</h1>
39:
40: <p align="center"><a href="forum.asp">
41: Click here to return to the User Forum</a></p>
42: </body>
43: </html>
```

ANALYSIS   The script of importance in this page is at lines 17–28. A new record is added, its
fields are filled in one at a time, and then, depending on whether it is a reply, the
parent field is set to 0 or the ID of the message being replied to (lines 21–25). After all
the information is in place, the Update (line 28) method is called. It appears in the list on
forum.asp as soon as that page is refreshed.

Most of the functionality of a forum is now in place. The user can login, add messages,
and view a list of messages available, but a few elements are still missing. A major one is
the ability to view a single message. URLs were supplied inside the message list (see
lines 28–29 of Listing 11.7) for this purpose, but no code has been written to handle it
yet. Because this is rather important, it is covered in the next section.

Viewing an Individual Message

Listing 11.10 shows the script to view an individual message. The ADO work in this
page is the same as what you've seen before. Without it, the system doesn't do much.
Listing 11.10 contains the contents of message.asp, a single page used to display any
message needed.

LISTING **11.10.** THIS PAGE DISPLAYS ANY MESSAGE IN THE SYSTEM, BASED ON THE ID PASSED TO IT
(message.asp).

```
 1: <html>
 2: <%
 3: Dim Conn
 4: Dim RSMessage
 5: Dim TheSubject
 6: Dim TheMessage
 7: Dim SQL
 8:
 9: Set Conn = Server.CreateObject("ADODB.Connection")
10: Set RSMessage = Server.CreateObject("ADODB.Recordset")
11:
12: Conn.Open "Forum"
13:
```

```
14: SQL= "SELECT Message.ID, " & _
15: "Message.Subject, Message.Date, Message.Message, " & _
16: "User.Userid, User.[First Name], User.[Last Name] FROM Message, User "
    ➥& _
17: "WHERE Message.[User ID] = User.ID AND " & _
18: "Message ID =" & Request.QueryString("ID")
19:
20: RSMessage.Open SQL, Conn, 1, 2
21:
22: If Not RSMessage.EOF Then
23:
24:   TheSubject = Server.HTMLEncode(RSMessage("Subject"))
25:   TheMessage = Server.HTMLEncode(RSMessage("Message"))
26:   ThePoster = RSMessage("First Name") & " " & RSMessage("Last Name")
27:   QueryString = "Type=Reply&ID=" & RSMessage("ID") & "&Subject=" & _
28:   Server.URLEncode(RSMessage("Subject"))
29:
30: End If
31: %>
32: <head>
33: <title><%=TheSubject%></title>
34: </head>
35:
36: <body>
37:
38: <table border="0" width="100%" cellspacing="4" cellpadding="4">
39:   <tr>
40:     <td width="100%"><strong><font face="Arial">
41:     Subject: <%=TheSubject%></font></strong></td>
42:   </tr>
43:   <tr>
44:     <td width="100%"><strong><font face="Arial"><%=TheMessage%>
45:     </font></strong></td>
46:   </tr>
47:   <tr>
48:     <td width="100%"><strong><font face="Arial">
49:     Posted By: <%=ThePoster%></font></strong></td>
50:   </tr>
51:   <tr>
52:     <td width="100%"><strong><font face="Arial">
53:     <a href="newmessage.asp?<%=QueryString%>">Reply To This
        ➥Message</a>
54: </font></strong></td>
55:   </tr>
56: </table>
57:
58: <p> </p>
59: </body>
60: </html>
```

11

ANALYSIS The display code is simple, producing a readable display of the message (see Figure 11.6), and ensures that no special characters interfere with the message's appearance (lines 24–26). Intermediate variables are used just to simplify the code in the actual page, and are not required. A URL is added in line 53 as the last line in this page's table, one that calls the newmessage.asp page discussed previously. In this case, because you want to reply to this message, a series of parameters are added to the URL. The ID and subject from the current message are both sent, along with a Type parameter used by the newmessage.asp script (see Listing 11.8) to determine how to save the new message.

FIGURE 11.6.

The Message.asp *script displays a single message and allows the user to reply to it.*

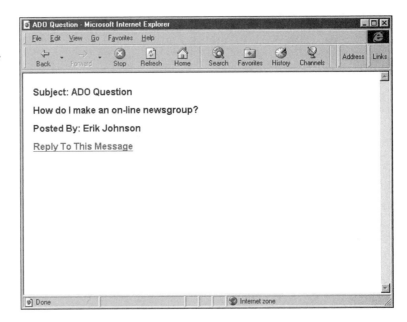

User Forum Conclusion

You have now created the major portions of the forum application. The system is provided almost in its entirety, with the exception of a few minor details that are covered as exercises at the end of today's lesson.

Working with Database Schemas

This section covers an example of a more advanced feature of ADO, the Connection.OpenSchema method.

When working with ADO, or any other database tool, you have to be aware of the database structure before executing any code. Your SQL statements and other commands require table names and other information before they can be written, but what if you want to work with a database where the structure is dynamic—tables and fields are regularly being added, removed, or modified? ADO has several useful features that allow you to retrieve database structure information at runtime. The ability to get a recordset containing all the tables from your database, for instance, could allow the creation of an ad-hoc query engine, without having to hard-code anything. The page shown in Listing 11.11 produces a series of HTML tables, one for each database table accessible through an ODBC DSN. The DSN is shown hard-coded into line 22, but could be obtained from a Request.Form or Request.QueryString parameter.

LISTING 11.11. Sample.asp CREATES A LIST OF ALL THE TABLES IN A DATABASE AND ALL THE FIELDS IN EACH OF THOSE TABLES.

```
 1: <html>
 2:
 3: <head>
 4: <title>Open Schema Example</title>
 5: </head>
 6:
 7: <body>
 8: <%
 9: Dim Conn
10: Dim RSTables
11: Dim RSCurrentTable
12: Dim adSchemaTables
13: Dim Field
14: Dim SQL
15:
16: adSchemaTables = 20
17:
18: Set Conn = Server.CreateObject("ADODB.Connection")
19: Set RSTables = Server.CreateObject("ADODB.Recordset")
20: Set RSCurrentTable = Server.CreateObject("ADODB.Recordset")
21:
22: Conn.Open "Forum"
23:
24: Set RSTables = Conn.OpenSchema(adSchemaTables)
25:
26: RSTables.Filter = "Table_Type='TABLE'"
27:
28:    Do While Not RSTables.EOF
29: %>
30:
31: <h2><%=RSTables("Table_Name")%></h2>
32: <%
33:    SQL = "Select * From [" & RSTables("Table_Name") & "] Where 1=2"
34:
```

continues

LISTING 11.11. CONTINUED

```
35:    RSCurrentTable.Open SQL,Conn,1,2
36:
37:    For Each Field in RSCurrentTable.Fields
38:
39:      Response.Write "<h4>   "
40:      Response.Write Field.Name & "</h4>" & vbcrlf
41:
42:    Next
43:
44:    RSCurrentTable.Close
45:
46:    RSTables.MoveNext
47: Loop
48:
49: RSTables.Close
50: Conn.Close
51: %>
52: </body>
53: </html>
```

ANALYSIS   The code from Sample.asp performs several interesting tricks with ADO. The first is how it obtains the listing of tables, through the OpenSchema() method in line 24. This method takes any one of a large set of possible values as an argument and returns a recordset populated with the results. It is also possible to supply secondary arguments that filter those results in different ways. Many different things can be returned from indexes to constraints, but this example focuses only on returning tables. The value supplied as an argument—20, stored in adSchemaTables—causes the method to return a recordset containing all the tables in the database. Because this includes many system tables that are not useful for most purposes, line 26 applies a filter that limits the recordset to only standard database tables. This filtering could also have been accomplished by using the second argument of the OpenSchema() method.

After the recordset is filtered, the loop (lines 28–47) moves through each record, and then opens a recordset (line 35) based on the table name contained in RSTables. The Fields collection of that Recordset object is then enumerated through to produce a listing of all the columns in this table. This code could be easily modified to suit a variety of purposes, whatever suits your needs.

Summary

ASP's purpose is almost exclusively to bring database information to the Web, and ADO is what you use to accomplish that goal. In addition, ADO is rapidly becoming the database tool of choice for use with many other development environments, including Visual Basic. Today, you have learned about working with databases and ADO by creating the user forum example. Using this example, you explored the Connection, Command, and Recordset objects.

Q&A

Q Why do some of the examples in today's lesson use criteria that always return false (such as Where 1=2)?

A When adding records to a table with the recordset's AddNew method, that recordset needs to be opened against the table. Any query that was based on that table would work for this purpose, but you do not want the query to return records when they are not needed. By using a condition such as 1=2, you know that no records will be added because this condition is guaranteed to be false. The recordset will, however, be opened against the table.

Q When would you use a Recordset's Fields collection?

A The Fields collection allows you to work with all the fields in a table as items in a group. You would use it if you wanted to loop through the collection and perform the same processing for every field.

Q Why can't you use DAO in your ASP script?

A Actually, you can. ADO is not the only database tool you can use; almost anything that is available to Visual Basic can be used within ASP, but most are not well suited to running in a server-side scripting environment. DAO used in an ASP application will function correctly, but have poor performance and place a greater load on your server than ADO.

Q The arguments for the Recordset.Open method can also be specified by setting the Recordset's properties. Which method is better?

A They are both the same. It may theoretically take longer to set the properties individually, but in actual use, it is purely a matter of preference. Setting the properties individually is less common, but more readable.

11

Workshop

The quiz questions and exercises are provided for your further understanding. Please refer to Appendix A, "Answers to Questions," for the answers to the quiz questions; the answers to the exercises are on the MCP Web site.

Quiz

1. Which of the following are methods of the `Recordset` object?

   a.`Open`

   b.`Execute`

   c.`Save`

   d.`Close`

2. Which object exposes the `Parameters` collection?

3. What does the `Properties` collection do?

4. True or False: The `Recordset.Recordcount` property always returns the correct number of records.

5. What two things should you check to see whether a recordset is completely empty?

6. What method of the `Connection` object could you use to run a SQL statement against a database?

7. What does the following line do if `Conn` is a `Connection` object?

   `Conn.Open "DSN=FooBar;uid=Fred;pwd=Apple"`

8. True or False: If you open three recordsets specifying the same connection information each time (instead of using a `Connection` object), they will all use the same connection.

Exercises

1. Add code to the `forum.asp` script so that it forces users to login if they haven't already.

2. The user forum example never provided a way for users to delete their own messages. Add one to the `message.asp` file, making sure that only the user who created a message can delete it.

3. Quiz question 7 contains a call to the `Open` method of a `Connection` object. Rewrite it in two other ways.

DAY 12

Database Development Illustrated: Building a User Registration System

On Day 10, "Programming Web Databases," you were introduced to database application development with ASP and shown how to build an ASP application that allows users to add and search information. Yesterday, you learned all about ADO and how it can be used to build powerful Web database applications. Today, you will be extending the guest book application you built on Day 10 so that it can also be used as a user registration system. At the end of today, you will know how to allow users to search and modify information in a database. Today's lesson covers the following:

- Build reusable Web database applications.
- Keep track of user information in a database between HTTP sessions.
- Learn how to avoid duplication of data in multiple databases.
- Explore how to update database records using SQL.
- Allow users to modify database records.

> You will be concentrating on one application for most of today. By learning how the user registration system works, you can build your own Web database applications that incorporate the same features. The user registration application makes use of a wizard-style user interface to determine whether the application should add a new user to the database or allow the user to modify an existing user information record.

Understanding the User Registration System's Control Structure

The main goal of the user registration system is simple. It allows users to supply information and have that data inserted into a database. The user registration system is integrated with the guest book application developed in Day 10 so that users do not have to re-enter the same information. For example, if a user has already signed the guest book, you already have certain information (such as the user's name, e-mail address, city name, and so forth) about that user in the database. If the user decides to register with the user registration database, the user registration system is designed so that the user does not have to re-enter information that's already been provided.

Refer to Figure 12.1 for the control structure of the user registration system you will build today. As you can see in Figure 12.1, you first get the user's e-mail address. A user's e-mail address is unique to that user and can be used as a basis for determining whether the user is already in the database. If so, the information in the database is displayed so that the user can make modifications to the information and update the database. If the e-mail address is not found in the database, a new record is added to the database after getting additional information from the user.

> When designing the user interface of a Web application, I highly recommend that you use a flowcharting tool to design the control structure. Many times, you want to dive directly into the application's code without giving yourself the time to think about the application and how the data is processed. By designing a flowchart, you can think of special cases you would not have thought of otherwise; this information allows you to build a better application and cut back on development time by spending less time on debugging and making significant changes to your application after you implement it. I highly recommend the Visio application for designing flowcharts.

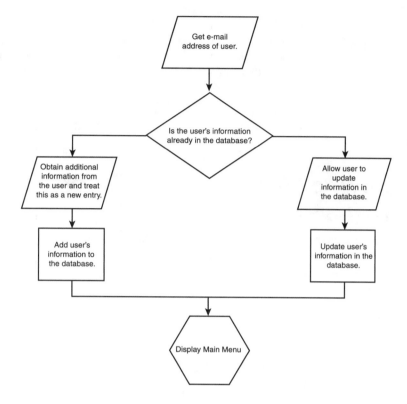

FIGURE 12.1.

The control structure of the user registration system.

Data Reuse Is a Good Thing: Linking to the Guest Book Database

You might remember that the guest book database had several additional fields that were never used. It was designed with reuse in mind, so that the same database can be used to build a user registration system and later a user personalization system for changing the look of a Web site.

Tip

When building Web database applications, always think of future reuse of the information in the database. It is a waste of resources to have multiple databases that duplicate most of the data. Take the time to design your database so that it accommodates future changes and applications.

Note

Proper database design is an important aspect of building Web database applications. Often, developers are so anxious to begin writing the code that they completely overlook the importance of taking the time to design a proper database structure. If at all possible, before writing a single line of code, get together with several other people and carefully go over the structure of your database, taking the time to properly define and identify database relationships, tables, records, default values, and data types.

How to Modify Existing Records in a Database

The highlight of today's lesson is to demonstrate how to develop a Web application that allows users to modify existing data. There are two ways to modify existing records in a database:

- Use the SQL UPDATE method to update selected fields.
- Use the Update method of the Recordset object to modify the values of fields in a database record.

Depending on the nature of your Web application, you should use one of these methods. The next two sections illustrate how to use these methods, outlining the drawbacks and benefits of each one.

Using the SQL UPDATE Method to Update Database Records

Using the SQL UPDATE method to update selected fields is an easy, straightforward procedure. However, there is a downside to using this approach. As you might recall, SQL statements use quotation marks and apostrophes as parameter delimiters. This complicates matters when the data you want to manipulate with a SQL statement might contain quotation marks or apostrophes. For example, a user might enter the following string to a guest book database:

```
I'm happy to use ASP! I often ask myself, "How did I ever get along
➥without ASP?!"
```

If you try to use this message as part of a SQL statement, you are going to run into problems because of the quotation marks and apostrophe. Obviously, the SQL UPDATE method is not suitable for data that might contain quotation marks and apostrophes, so use it only when you are certain your data does not contain these characters.

Do	Don't
DO use the SQL UPDATE method to update records in a database when you are 100% certain your data doesn't contain quotation marks and apostrophes.	**DON'T** use the SQL UPDATE method if your data contains quotations and apostrophes.

The syntax of the SQL UPDATE method is as follows:

```
UPDATE <NameOfTable> Set <Field> = <NewFieldValue> [,<Field> =
➥<NewFieldValue>] [Where <FilterCriteria>]
```

Simply replace the placeholders (italicized and in angle brackets) with the values in Table 12.1.

TABLE 12.1. USING THE SQL UPDATE METHOD.

Placeholder	Value
<NameofTable>	The name of the table containing the records you want to modify.
<Field>	The field you want to modify. Notice how multiple fields can be separated by using commas.
<NewFieldValue>	The new value of the data field. Notice how you can change the values of multiple fields by separating field/value pairs with commas.
<FilterCriteria>	The Where clause can be used to filter which records are modified.

The following examples further illustrate how to use the SQL UPDATE method.

LISTING 12.1. USING THE SQL UPDATE METHOD TO MODIFY DATA.

```
1: ' Sets the value of the Discount field to 25%.
2: UPDATE Customers SET Discount = .25
3: ' Sets the value of the Discount field to 35% if the
4: ' CurrentSales value is over 1,000,000.
5: UPDATE Customers SET Discount = .35 WHERE CurrentSales >= 1000000
6: ' Sets the value of the Discount field to 45% if the
7: ' user has a birthday in the month of May.
8: UPDATE Customers SET Discount = .45 WHERE Birthday
   ➥BETWEEN #05/01/1998# AND #05/31/1998#
```

12

Using the UPDATE Method of the Recordset Object to Modify Database Records

Using the UPDATE method of the Recordset object is a bit more involved. However, by using this method, you no longer have to worry about apostrophes, quotes, and other such anomalies floating all over your data. To use it, first you have to create an instance of the ADODB.Connection object using the ASP statement in Listing 12.2.

LISTING 12.2. CREATING AN INSTANCE OF THE ADOB.Connection OBJECT.

```
1: ' Create an instance of the Connection object
2:   Set DatabaseConnection = Server.CreateObject("ADODB.Connection")
```

The next step is opening a connection to the DSN containing the database table you want to modify with the code in Listing 12.3. You can open a file DSN, a user DSN, or a system DSN.

LISTING 12.3. SPECIFY THE SOURCE OF THE DATA.

```
1:   ' Open a connection to a DSN
2:   DatabaseConnection.Open  "FILEDSN=NameOfFDSN.dsn"
```

Afterward, the ADODB.Recordset object has to be instantiated with the ASP statement in Listing 12.4.

LISTING 12.4. THE ADOB.Recordset OBJECT IS INSTANTIATED.

```
1:   ' Create an instance of the Recordset object
2:   Set UserRecordset = Server.CreateObject("ADODB.Recordset")
```

After this is done, the type of Recordset object to be used is specified. The default Recordset object does not support the Update method. The ASP statements in Listing 12.5 change the type of the recordset so that it can be used not only to traverse data, but also to modify data. To have the Recordset object support the Update method, the following properties of the Recordset object have to be modified:

CursorType   Used to specify the type of cursor used by the recordset.
                            The default CursorType provides a read-only recordset.
                            The value 1 declares a Recordset object with a KeySet
                            cursor that allows data to be updated.

CursorLocation   Specifies the location of the cursor engine. The value 2 specifies that a Recordset object uses server-side cursors.

LockType   Specifies how database records are locked while changes are being made. The value 3 designates the use of Optimistic locking by the Recordset object.

> **Note**
>
> The default CursorType is read-only/forward-only, which is why you can't update a recordset that uses the default CursorType.

LISTING 12.5. THE TYPE OF THE Recordset OBJECT IS CHANGED.

```
1:    ' Change the type of the default recordset.
2:    ' This allows you to update database records.
3:
4:    UserRecordSet.CursorType = 1
5:    UserRecordSet.CursorLocation = 2
6:    UserRecordSet.LockType = 3
```

Last, all you need to do is specify the source of the data with the ASP statements in Listing 12.6.

LISTING 12.6. THE DATA SOURCE IS SPECIFIED.

```
1:  ' The data source is specified.
2:    UserRecordSet.ActiveConnection = DatabaseConnection
3:    UserRecordSet.Source = "TableName"
4:
5:    ' The recordset can now be opened so that
6:    ' the Update method can be used
```

The recordset can now be modified however you want. After it is modified, the Update method of the Recordset object is used to update the changes to the database. The ASP code in Listing 12.7 demonstrates how to change the FirstName field of the recordset to "Tanya" and update the change to the database.

LISTING 12.7. MODIFYING DATA IN A RECORDSET AND UPDATING THE CHANGE TO THE DATABASE.

```
1:    ' The value of the FirstName field is changed
2:    ' to Tanya.
```

continues

12

Listing 12.7. CONTINUED

```
3:    UserRecordset.Fields.Item ("FirstName") = "Tanya"
4:    ' The changes to the recordset are updated to the database.
5:    UserRecordSet.Update
```

> **Caution**
>
> Before attempting to use the Update method, make sure you are on the
> record you're trying to update or modify.

Do
DO use the Update method of the Recordset object to update records in a database when there is a possibility your data will contain quotation marks and apostrophes.

Examining the User Registration System

As mentioned earlier, the highlight of today's lesson is to demonstrate how to put your ASP skills to use by developing a user registration system that is integrated with the guest book application you built two days ago. This section gives you an overview of the user registration system. Afterward, you are shown how the application is implemented with ASP.

 Experiment with the user registration system by downloading the code distribution file for this book from the MCP Web site. You can find it in the directory \Chapter-12\. You must properly create a file DSN for the Microsoft Access database so the user registration system can function correctly on your computer.

You can start experimenting with the user registration system by executing the file default.asp in the \Chapter-12\ folder. You will see the Web page shown in Figure 12.2. For a demonstration of how the user registration system is integrated with the guest book, choose the option to Add a New Guest Book Entry.

Adding a New Guest Book Entry

The Web page shown in Figure 12.3 is used to add new entries to the guest book.

FIGURE 12.2.

*The main menu of the
user registration sys-
tem.*

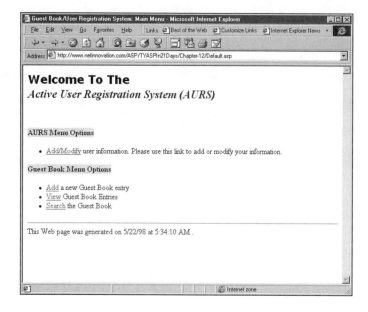

Note

JavaScript is used in the Web page in Figure 12.3 to implement client-side
data validation. Before deploying this application on your Web site, be sure
to add more extensive server-side data validation to maintain the database's
integrity.

FIGURE 12.3.

*A new guest book entry
is added.*

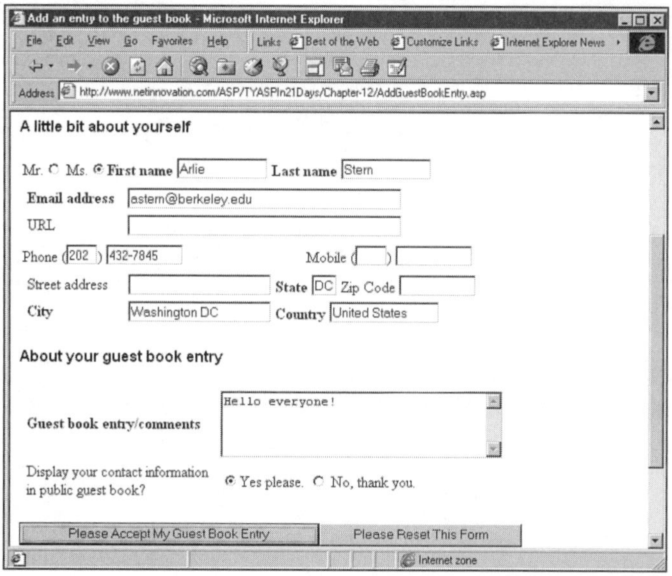

12

After the guest book entry is added to the database, the ASP application displays the Web page shown in Figure 12.4.

FIGURE 12.4.

The new guest book entry is processed.

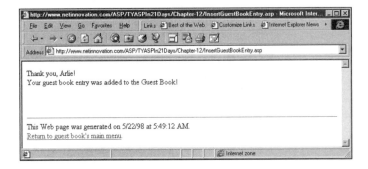

Modifying Records in the Database

As mentioned earlier, the user registration system is integrated with the guest book database. To see how this integration works, choose Add/Modify User Information from the user registration system's main menu (refer back to Figure 12.2). The Web page shown in Figure 12.5 is displayed. Type the e-mail address you specified in Figure 12.3 (remember that it is case sensitive), and click the Submit E-mail Address button.

FIGURE 12.5.

The option to add/modify data is selected.

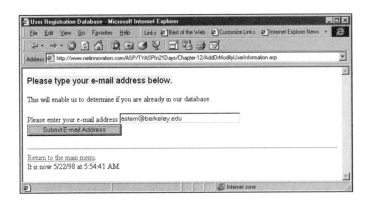

As long as you type the same e-mail address you used in Figure 12.3, you will see the information you supplied in an HTML form, as shown in Figure 12.6.

FIGURE 12.6.

The ASP application finds the existing record for the user.

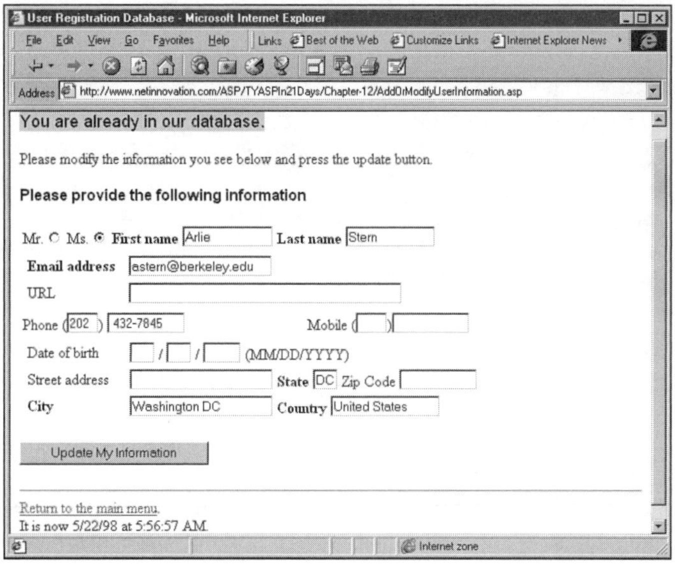

Because the user data is displayed in an HTML form, it can be easily edited. To demonstrate how the data in the recordset in Figure 12.6 can be modified, the user's State and City information is modified in Figure 12.7.

FIGURE 12.7.

The user's record is modified.

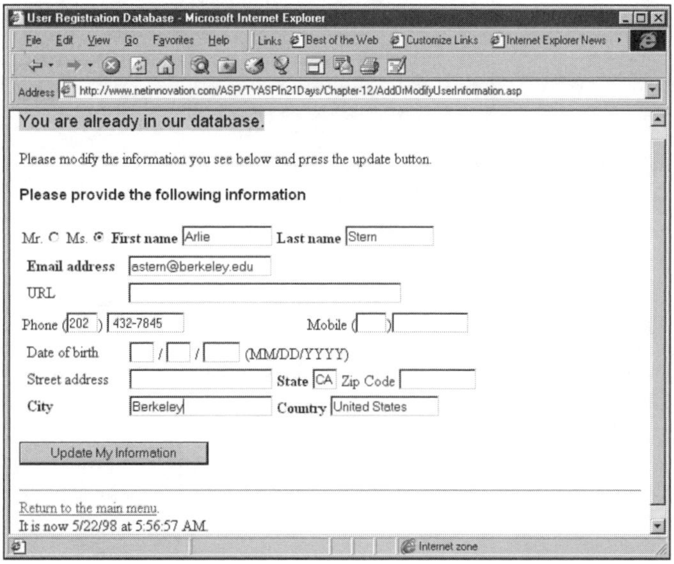

12

Click the Update My Information button to modify the data in the recordset. After the recordset is modified, the Web page in Figure 12.8 is displayed to confirm that the user's record was modified.

FIGURE 12.8.

The modified record is processed by the ASP application.

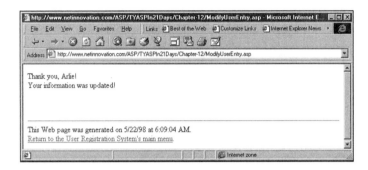

You were just shown how to modify an existing record. But what happens if the user's email address is not in the database? To find out, once again, choose Add/Modify User Information from the main menu (refer back to Figure 12.2). You then see the Web page shown in Figure 12.9. Type an e-mail address you know is not in the database and click the Submit E-mail Address button.

FIGURE 12.9.

A new user chooses the Add/Modify data option.

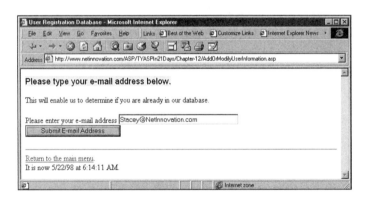

Because the user is not currently in the database, the Web page shown in Figure 12.10 is displayed to get information. After typing in the data, click the Add My Information To The Database button.

FIGURE 12.10.

The ASP application detects the new user and provides a form for adding a new user information record.

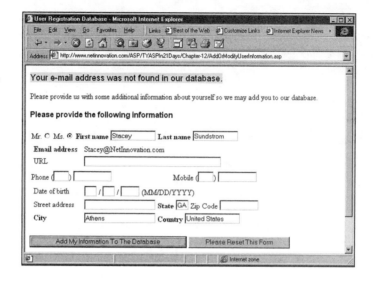

The Web page in Figure 12.11 is displayed to confirm that the new user information is added to the database.

Note

Compare the operation of the user registration system to the flowchart in Figure 12.1. Notice how the program operates exactly as outlined in the flowchart.

FIGURE 12.11.

The new user information record is accepted by the ASP application.

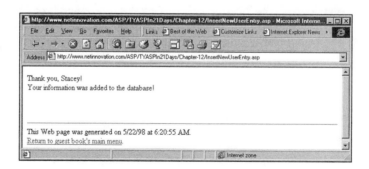

The User Registration Database

You have now added two new records to the Microsoft Access database. Open the database in Microsoft Access, as shown in Figure 12.12, to locate the two records you added. Notice that the City and State information of the first entry has indeed been modified by the ASP application.

FIGURE 12.12.

The Microsoft Access database is updated with user information.

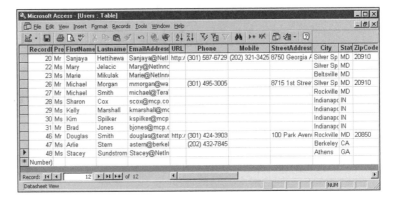

Now that you know how to modify records in a database and have seen the user registration system in action, it's time to use what you learned yesterday about ADO and what you learned today about updating database records. The next section examines how the user registration system, the highlight of today's lesson, uses ADO to modify its records. Before you do anything, you must first get data from the user. The next section shows you how get information from the user, complete with client-side data validation.

Getting Input from the User

The ASP application in Listing 12.8 gets input from the user. The Web pages shown in Figures 12.5, 12.6, 12.9, and 12.10 are generated by the ASP application in Listing 12.8. How are all these different Web pages displayed by the same ASP application? You were already shown how this is done on Day 4, "Building and Processing Web Forms." The ASP application's main code block (executed when the Web page is browsed) consists of a series of If...Then...Else statements, which determine whether the user is a new user or an existing one and display the appropriate Web page. Each Web page is contained in a VBScript subroutine.

Note

To keep the length of the code to an acceptable size, today's user registration system does not use extensive error checking. Error checking is not the emphasis here because you already know how to perform client-side and server-side error checking. The purpose of these code listings is to demonstrate how to build a more complex database application that allows users to modify data they enter into a database.

LISTING 12.8. GET USER INFORMATION FROM THE USER.

```
 1: <%@ LANGUAGE=VBScript %>
 2: <html>
 3: <head>
 4:
 5: <title>User Registration Database</title>
 6: </head>
 7: <body>
 8: <%
 9: Sub GetUserEmailAddress %>
10:
11: <p><font face="Arial" size="4" style="BACKGROUND-COLOR: #ffff99">
12: Please type your e-mail address below.</font></p><p>This
13: will enable us to determine if you are already in our database.</p>
14:
15: <p>
16: <form method="POST" action="AddOrModifyUserInformation.asp"
17:     id="EmailForm" name="EmailForm">
18: Please enter your e-mail address <input type="text"
19:     id="EmailAddress" size="35" name="EmailAddress"><br>
20: <input type="submit" value="Submit E-mail Address"
21:     id="SubmitEmailAddress" name="SubmitEmailAddress">
22: </form>
23: </p>
24: <%
25: End Sub
26:
27: ' =-=-=-=-=-=-=-=-=-=-=-=-=-=-=-=-=-=-=-=-=-=-=-=.
28:
29: Sub GetNewUserInformation %>
30: </font>
31:
32: <p><font face="Arial" size="4" style="BACKGROUND-COLOR: #ccff99">
33: Your e-mail address was not found in our database.</font></p>
34: <p>Please provide us with some additional information about
35: yourself so we can add you to our database.</p>
36:
37:
38: <!--webbot BOT="GeneratedScript" PREVIEW=" " startspan -->
39: <script Language="JavaScript"><!--
40: function FrontPage_Form2_Validator(theForm)
41: {
42:
43:   if (theForm.FirstName.value == "")
44:   {
45:     alert("Please enter a value for the \"First Name\" field.");
46:     theForm.FirstName.focus();
47:     return (false);
48:   }
```

continues

LISTING **12.8.** CONTINUED

```
49:
50:    if (theForm.FirstName.value.length < 2)
51:    {
52:      alert("Please enter at least 2 characters in the
       ➥\"First Name\" field.");
53:      theForm.FirstName.focus();
54:      return (false);
55:    }
56:
57:    if (theForm.FirstName.value.length > 30)
58:    {
59:      alert("Please enter at most 30 characters in the
       ➥\"First Name\" field.");
60:      theForm.FirstName.focus();
61:      return (false);
62:    }
63:
64:    if (theForm.LastName.value == "")
65:    {
66:      alert("Please enter a value for the \"Last Name\" field.");
67:      theForm.LastName.focus();
68:      return (false);
69:    }
70:
71:    if (theForm.LastName.value.length < 2)
72:    {
73:      alert("Please enter at least 2 characters in the
       ➥\"Last Name\" field.");
74:      theForm.LastName.focus();
75:      return (false);
76:    }
77:
78:    if (theForm.LastName.value.length > 30)
79:    {
80:      alert("Please enter at most 30 characters in the
       ➥\"Last Name\" field.");
81:      theForm.LastName.focus();
82:      return (false);
83:    }
84:
85:    if (theForm.State.value == "")
86:    {
87:      alert("Please enter a value for the \"Your State\" field.");
88:      theForm.State.focus();
89:      return (false);
90:    }
91:
92:    if (theForm.State.value.length < 2)
93:    {
```

```
94:      alert("Please enter at least 2 characters in the
         ➥\"Your State\" field.");
95:      theForm.State.focus();
96:      return (false);
97:    }
98:
99:    if (theForm.State.value.length > 2)
100:   {
101:     alert("Please enter at most 2 characters in the
         ➥\"Your State\" field.");
102:     theForm.State.focus();
103:     return (false);
104:   }
105:
106:   if (theForm.City.value == "")
107:   {
108:     alert("Please enter a value for the \"City Name\" field.");
109:     theForm.City.focus();
110:     return (false);
111:   }
112:
113:   if (theForm.City.value.length < 3)
114:   {
115:     alert("Please enter at least 3 characters in the
         ➥\"City Name\" field.");
116:     theForm.City.focus();
117:     return (false);
118:   }
119:
120:   if (theForm.City.value.length > 30)
121:   {
122:     alert("Please enter at most 30 characters in the
         ➥\"City Name\" field.");
123:     theForm.City.focus();
124:     return (false);
125:   }
126:
127:   if (theForm.Country.value == "")
128:   {
129:     alert("Please enter a value for the \"Name of your
         ➥country\" field.");
130:     theForm.Country.focus();
131:     return (false);
132:   }
133:
134:   if (theForm.Country.value.length < 3)
135:   {
136:     alert("Please enter at least 3 characters in the
         ➥\"Name of your country\" field.");
137:     theForm.Country.focus();
```

12

continues

LISTING **12.8.** CONTINUED

```
138:     return (false);
139:   }
140:
141:   if (theForm.Country.value.length > 30)
142:   {
143:     alert("Please enter at most 30 characters in the
         ➥\"Name of your country\" field.");
144:     theForm.Country.focus();
145:     return (false);
146:   }
147:   return (true);
148: }
149: //--></script><!--webbot BOT="GeneratedScript" endspan -->
150: <form method="POST" action="InsertNewUserEntry.asp"
151:     onsubmit="return FrontPage_Form2_Validator(this)"
152:     name="FrontPage_Form2">
153:   <p><strong><font face="Arial">Please provide the following
       ➥information
154:     </font></strong></p>
155:   <div align="left"><table border="0" width="610">
156:     <tr>
157:       <td width="100%" colspan="2">
158:       Mr.<input type="radio" value="Mr" CHECKED name="Prefix">
159:       Ms.<input type="radio" name="Prefix" value="Ms">
160:       <strong>First name</strong>
161:       <!--webbot bot="Validation" S-Display-Name="First Name"
         ➥  B-Value-Required="TRUE" I-Minimum-Length="2" I-Maximum-
         ➥Length="30" -->
162:       <input type="text" name="FirstName" size="12" maxlength="30">
163:         <strong>Last name</strong> <!--webbot bot="Validation"
           ➥S-Display-Name="Last Name" B-Value-Required="TRUE" I-
           ➥Minimum-Length="2"I-Maximum-Length="30" -->
164:         <input type="text" name="LastName" size="12"
           ➥maxlength="30"></td>
165:     </tr>
166:     <tr>
167:       <td width="100%" colspan="2"><div align="center"><center>
168:         <table border="0" width="600">
169:         <tr>
170:           <td width="104"><strong>Email address</strong> </td>
171:           <td width="488">
172:           <input type="hidden" name="EmailAddress" value="
             ➥<%= Request.Form.Item("EmailAddress")%>">
173:             <%= Request.Form.Item("EmailAddress") %>
174:         </td></tr>
175:         <tr>
176:           <td width="104">URL</td>
177:           <td width="488"><input type="text" name="URL"
178:                       size="40" maxlength="49"></td>
```

```
179:            </tr>
180:          </table>
181:          </center></div></td>
182:        </tr>
183:        <tr>
184:          <td width="50%">Phone (<input type="text" name="PhoneAreaCode"
185:                  size="3" maxlength="3">)
186:          <input type="text" name="PhoneNumber" size="10" maxlength="12">
187:          </td><td width="50%">
188:          Mobile (<input type="text" name="MobileAreaCode"
189:                      size="3" maxlength="3">)
190:              <input type="text" name="MobilePhoneNumber" size="10"
191:                    maxlength="12"></td>
192:        </tr>
193:        <tr>
194:          <td width="100%" colspan="2"><div align="center"><center>
195:            <table border="0" width="600">
196:            <tr>
197:              <td width="105">Date of birth</td>
198:              <td width="487">
199:              <input type="text" name="BirthdayMonth" size="2"> /
200:              <input type="text" name="BirthdayDay" size="2"> /
201:              <input type="text" name="BirthdayYear" size="4">
202:              (MM/DD/YYYY)</td>
203:            </tr>
204:            <tr>
205:              <td width="105">Street address</td>
206:              <td width="487"><input type="text" name="StreetAddress"
207:                      size="20" maxlength="49"><strong>State</strong>
208:              <!--webbot bot="Validation" S-Display-Name="Your State"
              ➡B-Value-Required="TRUE" I-Minimum-Length="2" I-Maximum-
              ➡Length="2" -->
209:              <input type="text" name="State" size="2" maxlength="2">
210:              Zip Code <input type="text" name="ZipCode" size="10"
211:                                      maxlength="10"> </td>
212:            </tr>
213:            <tr>
214:              <td width="105"><strong>City</strong> </td>
215:              <td width="487"><!--webbot bot="Validation" S-Display-Name=
              ➡"City Name" B-Value-Required="TRUE" I-Minimum-Length="3"
              ➡I-Maximum-Length="30" -->
216:                <input type="text" name="City" size="20" maxlength="30">
217:                <strong>Country</strong>
218:                <!--webbot bot="Validation" S-Display-Name=
              ➡"Name of your country" B-Value-Required="TRUE" I-
              ➡Minimum-Length="3"I-Maximum-Length="30" -->
219:                <input type="text" name="Country" size="15"
220:                        value="United States" maxlength="30"></td>
221:            </tr>
222:          </table>
```

continues

LISTING **12.8.** CONTINUED

```
223:        </center></div></td>
224:      </tr>
225:    </table>
226:    </div>
227:    </table>
228:    </div><p>
229:      <input type="submit" value="Add My Information To The Database"
230:        name="SubmitButton">
231:      <input type="reset" value="Please Reset This Form" name="B2"></p>
232: </form>
233:
234: <%
235: End Sub
236:
237: ' =-=-=-=-=-=-=-=-=-=-=-=-=-=-=-=-=-=-=-=-=-=-=-=-=-=-
238:
239: Sub UpdateUserInformation %>
240: </font>
241:
242: <p><font face="Arial" size="4" style="BACKGROUND-COLOR: #ffcc99">
243: You are already in our database.</font></p><p>
244: Please modify the information you see below and press the
245: update button.</p>
246:
247:
248: <!--webbot BOT="GeneratedScript" PREVIEW=" " startspan -->
     ➥<script Language="JavaScript"><!--
249: function FrontPage_Form3_Validator(theForm)
250: {
251:
252:   if (theForm.FirstName.value == "")
253:   {
254:     alert("Please enter a value for the \"First Name\" field.");
255:     theForm.FirstName.focus();
256:     return (false);
257:   }
258:
259:   if (theForm.FirstName.value.length < 2)
260:   {
261:     alert("Please enter at least 2 characters in the
           ➥\"First Name\" field.");
262:     theForm.FirstName.focus();
263:     return (false);
264:   }
265:
266:   if (theForm.FirstName.value.length > 30)
267:   {
268:     alert("Please enter at most 30 characters in the
           ➥\"First Name\" field.");
```

```
269:      theForm.FirstName.focus();
270:      return (false);
271:    }
272:
273:    if (theForm.LastName.value == "")
274:    {
275:      alert("Please enter a value for the \"Last Name\" field.");
276:      theForm.LastName.focus();
277:      return (false);
278:    }
279:
280:    if (theForm.LastName.value.length < 2)
281:    {
282:      alert("Please enter at least 2 characters in the
          ➥\"Last Name\" field.");
283:      theForm.LastName.focus();
284:      return (false);
285:    }
286:
287:    if (theForm.LastName.value.length > 30)
288:    {
289:      alert("Please enter at most 30 characters in the
          ➥\"Last Name\" field.");
290:      theForm.LastName.focus();
291:      return (false);
292:    }
293:
294:    if (theForm.EmailAddress.value == "")
295:    {
296:      alert("Please enter a value for the \"E-mail Address\" field.");
297:      theForm.EmailAddress.focus();
298:      return (false);
299:    }
300:
301:    if (theForm.EmailAddress.value.length < 7)
302:    {
303:      alert("Please enter at least 7 characters in the
          ➥\"E-mail Address\" field.");
304:      theForm.EmailAddress.focus();
305:      return (false);
306:    }
307:
308:    if (theForm.EmailAddress.value.length > 49)
309:    {
310:      alert("Please enter at most 49 characters in the \"E-mail
          ➥Address\" field.");
311:      theForm.EmailAddress.focus();
312:      return (false);
313:    }
314:
```

12

continues

LISTING 12.8. CONTINUED

```
315:    if (theForm.State.value == "")
316:    {
317:      alert("Please enter a value for the \"Your State\" field.");
318:      theForm.State.focus();
319:      return (false);
320:    }
321:
322:    if (theForm.State.value.length < 2)
323:    {
324:      alert("Please enter at least 2 characters in the \"Your
          ➥State\" field.");
325:      theForm.State.focus();
326:      return (false);
327:    }
328:
329:    if (theForm.State.value.length > 2)
330:    {
331:      alert("Please enter at most 2 characters in the \"Your
          ➥State\" field.");
332:      theForm.State.focus();
333:      return (false);
334:    }
335:
336:    if (theForm.City.value == "")
337:    {
338:      alert("Please enter a value for the \"City Name\" field.");
339:      theForm.City.focus();
340:      return (false);
341:    }
342:
343:    if (theForm.City.value.length < 3)
344:    {
345:      alert("Please enter at least 3 characters in the \"City
          ➥Name\" field.");
346:      theForm.City.focus();
347:      return (false);
348:    }
349:
350:    if (theForm.City.value.length > 30)
351:    {
352:      alert("Please enter at most 30 characters in the \"City
          ➥Name\" field.");
353:      theForm.City.focus();
354:      return (false);
355:    }
356:
357:    if (theForm.Country.value == "")
358:    {
359:      alert("Please enter a value for the \"Name of your country\"
          ➥field.");
```

```
360:    theForm.Country.focus();
361:    return (false);
362:  }
363:
364:  if (theForm.Country.value.length < 3)
365:  {
366:    alert("Please enter at least 3 characters in the \"Name of your
        ➥country\" field.");
367:    theForm.Country.focus();
368:    return (false);
369:  }
370:
371:  if (theForm.Country.value.length > 30)
372:  {
373:    alert("Please enter at most 30 characters in the \"Name of your
        ➥country\" field.");
374:    theForm.Country.focus();
375:    return (false);
376:  }
377:  return (true);
378: }
379: //--></script><!--webbot BOT="GeneratedScript" endspan -->
380: <form method="POST" action="ModifyUserEntry.asp"
381:    onsubmit="return FrontPage_Form3_Validator(this)"
382:    name="FrontPage_Form3">
383:  <p><strong><font face="Arial">Please provide the following
     ➥information
384:    </font></strong></p>
385:  <div align="left"><table border="0" width="610">
386:    <tr>
387:      <td width="100%" colspan="2">
388:      <% If UserRecordset("Prefix")="Mr" Then %>
389:        Mr.<input type="radio" value="Mr" CHECKED name="Prefix">
390:        Ms.<input type="radio" name="Prefix" value="Ms">
391:      <% Else %>
392:        Mr.<input type="radio" value="Mr" name="Prefix">
393:        Ms.<input type="radio" CHECKED name="Prefix" value="Ms">
394:      <% End If %>
395:      <strong>First name</strong>
396:      <!--webbot bot="Validation" S-Display-Name="First Name"
        ➥B-Value-Required="TRUE" I-Minimum-Length="2" I-Maximum-
        ➥Length="30" -->
397:      <input type="text" name="FirstName" size="12" maxlength="30"
        ➥value="<%= UserRecordset("FirstName")%>">
398:        <strong>Last name</strong> <!--webbot bot="Validation"
        ➥S-Display-Name="Last Name" B-Value-Required="TRUE" I-
        ➥Minimum-Length="2"I-Maximum-Length="30" -->
399:        <input type="text" name="LastName" size="12" maxlength="30"
        ➥value="<%= UserRecordset("LastName")%>"></td>
400:    </tr>
```

12

continues

LISTING 12.8. CONTINUED

```
401:    <tr>
402:      <td width="100%" colspan="2"><div align="center"><center>
403:        <table border="0" width="600">
404:        <tr>
405:          <td width="104"><strong>Email address</strong> </td>
406:          <td width="488"><!--webbot bot="Validation"
            ➥S-Display-Name="E-mail Address" B-Value-Required="TRUE"
            ➥I-Minimum-Length="7" I-Maximum-Length="49" -->
407:          <input type="text" name="EmailAddress" value="<%=
            ➥UserRecordset("EmailAddress")%>">
408:        </td></tr>
409:        <tr>
410:          <td width="104">URL</td>
411:          <td width="488"><input type="text" name="URL"
            ➥value="<%= UserRecordset("URL")%>" size="40"
            ➥maxlength="49"></td>
412:        </tr>
413:        </table>
414:      </center></div></td>
415:    </tr>
416:    <tr>
417:      <td width="50%">Phone (<input type="text" name=
            ➥"PhoneAreaCode" size="3" maxlength="3" value="<%= Mid
            ➥(UserRecordset("Phone"),2,3) %>">)
418:      <input type="text" name="PhoneNumber" size="10" value="
            ➥<%= Mid (UserRecordset("Phone"),6)%>" maxlength="12">
419:      </td><td width="50%">
420:      Mobile (<input type="text" name="MobileAreaCode" size="3"
            ➥value="<%= Mid (UserRecordset("Mobile"),2,3) %>"
            ➥maxlength="3">)
            ➥<input type="text" name="MobilePhoneNumber" value="
            ➥<%= Mid (UserRecordset("Mobile"),6)%>" size="10" maxlength=
            ➥"12"></td>
421:    </tr>
422:    <tr>
423:      <td width="100%" colspan="2"><div align="center"><center>
424:        <table border="0" width="600">
425:        <tr>
426:          <td width="105">Date of birth</td>
427:          <td width="487">
428:          <input type="text" name="BirthdayMonth" size="2"
            ➥value="<%= Month(UserRecordset("DOB"))%>"> /
429:          <input type="text" name="BirthdayDay" size="2"
            ➥value="<%= Day(UserRecordset("DOB"))%>"> /
430:          <input type="text" name="BirthdayYear"
            ➥size="4" value="<%= Year(UserRecordset("DOB"))%>">
431:          (MM/DD/YYYY)</td>
432:        </tr>
```

```
433:        <tr>
434:          <td width="105">Street address</td>
435:          <td width="487"><input type="text" name="StreetAddress"
             ➥value="<%= UserRecordset("StreetAddress")%>" size="20"
             ➥maxlength="49"> <strong>State</strong>
436:          <!--webbot bot="Validation" S-Display-Name="Your State"
             ➥B-Value-Required="TRUE" I-Minimum-Length="2" I-Maximum-
             ➥Length="2" -->
437:          <input type="text" name="State" size="2" maxlength="2"
             ➥value="<%= UserRecordset("State")%>">
438:          Zip Code <input type="text" name="ZipCode" size="10"
             ➥value="<%= UserRecordset("ZipCode")%>"
             ➥maxlength="10"></td>
439:        </tr>
440:        <tr>
441:          <td width="105"><strong>City</strong> </td>
442:          <td width="487"><!--webbot bot="Validation" S-Display-Name=
             ➥"City Name" B-Value-Required="TRUE" I-Minimum-Length="3"
             ➥I-Maximum-Length="30" -->
443:            <input type="text" name="City" size="20" maxlength="30"
             ➥value="<%= UserRecordset("City")%>">
444:            <strong>Country</strong>
445:            <!--webbot bot="Validation" S-Display-Name="Name of your
             ➥country"  B-Value-Required="TRUE" I-Minimum-Length="3"
             ➥I-Maximum-Length="30" -->
446:            <input type="text" name="Country" size="15"
             ➥value="<%= UserRecordset("Country")%>"
             ➥maxlength="30"></td>
447:        </tr>
448:      </table>
449:      </center></div></td>
450:    </tr>
451: </table>
452: </div>
453: </table>
454: </div><p>
455:    <input type="hidden" name="RecordID" value="<%=
             ➥UserRecordset("RecordID")%>">
456:    <input type="submit" value="Update My Information"
             ➥name="SubmitButton"></p>
457: </form>
458:
459: <%
460: End Sub
461:
462: ' =-=-=-=-=-=-=-=-=-=-=-=-=-=-=-=-=-=-=-=-=-=-=-=-=-=-=-=.
463: ' Main Program Block
464: ' =-=-=-=-=-=-=-=-=-=-=-=-=-=-=-=-=-=-=-=-=-=-=-=-=-=-=-=.
465:
466:    Dim SQLString
```

continues

LISTING **12.8.** CONTINUED

```
467:
468:
469:    If Request.Form.Item("EmailAddress") = "" Then
470:      Call GetUserEmailAddress
471:    Else
472:
473:    ' This SQL string retrieves all the selected records from the
474:    ' Users table of the user registration database
475:    SQLString = "SELECT RecordID, Prefix, FirstName, Lastname, " & _
476:      "EmailAddress, URL, Phone, Mobile, StreetAddress, City, " & _
477:      "State, ZipCode, Country, DOB " & _
478:      "FROM Users WHERE EmailAddress=" & chr(39) & _
479:      Request.Form.Item("EmailAddress") & chr(39)
480:
481:    ' Create an instance of the Connection object
482:    Set DatabaseConnection = Server.CreateObject("ADODB.Connection")
483:
484:    ' Open a connection to the guest book file DSN
485:    ' Before the following statement can execute properly, you have to
486:    ' create a file DSN for the guest book database as outlined in the
487:    ' book.
488:    DatabaseConnection.Open  "FILEDSN=UserInformationDatabase.dsn"
489:
490:    ' Create an instance of the Recordset object
491:    Set UserRecordset = Server.CreateObject("ADODB.Recordset")
492:
493:    ' The Open method of the Recordset object is used to retrieve
494:    ' data from the guest book database.
495:    UserRecordset.Open SQLString, DatabaseConnection
496:
497:    If UserRecordset.EOF Then
498:      Call GetNewUserInformation
499:    Else
500:      Call UpdateUserInformation
501:    End If
502:
503:    ' Always release resources after you are done using them.
504:    ' Always close your database connections after you are done using
505:    ' them.
506:      UserRecordset.Close
507:      DatabaseConnection.Close
508:
509:    End If
510:
511: %>
512:
513: <hr>
514: <a href="Default.asp">Return to the main menu</a>.<br>
515: It is now <%= Date %> at <%= Time %>.
516:
```

```
517: </body>
518: </html>
```

ANALYSIS The VBScript subroutine defined in lines 9–25 displays a Web page used initially to get the user's e-mail address. After an e-mail address is obtained, the VBScript subroutine defined in lines 29–235 is used to get a new user information record if the user's e-mail address is not found in the database. This subroutine simply displays an HTML form with client-side data validation.

> **Note** See the client-side data validation subroutines in action by leaving out a required data field when adding a new user information record.

If a user record already exists with the e-mail address supplied by the user, the VBScript subroutine defined in lines 239–460 is displayed. This VBScript subroutine is similar to the one that gets a new user information record. The only difference is that the VBScript subroutine defined in lines 239–460 uses a `Recordset` object to display information you already have about the user. The information is displayed as default HTML form field values. The main program block defined in lines 462–511 is really the heart of the ASP application in Listing 12.8. The `If` statement in line 469 gets the user's e-mail address if the user has not yet supplied it. After an e-mail address is obtained from the user, the SQL statement in lines 475–479 is used to determine if the e-mail address is already in the database. If it is not, the `If` statement in line 497 uses the `GetNewUserInformation` subroutine to display a form for adding a new user information record. The `Else` statement in line 500 uses the `UpdateUserInformation` subroutine to display a form for modifying an existing database record.

Adding a New User Record to the Database

If the user's e-mail address is not in the database, the `GetNewUserInformation` subroutine in Listing 12.8 displays a form that can be used to add a new user information record. The new user information form is submitted to the ASP application in Listing 12.9, which in turn adds the new user information to the database.

LISTING 12.9. ADDING A NEW USER TO THE DATABASE.

```
1: <%@ LANGUAGE=VBScript %>
2: <HTML>
```

continues

LISTING **12.9.** CONTINUED

```
 3: <HEAD><TITLE>Your personal information was processed</TITLE>
 4: <META NAME="GENERATOR" Content="Microsoft Visual Studio 6.0">
 5: </HEAD>
 6: <BODY>
 7:
 8: <%
 9:
10: ' ########## Begin Subroutine ##########
11:
12: Sub AddNewUserInformation
13:
14:   Dim SQLDataInsertionString
15:   Dim CommandObject
16:
17:   ' Create an instance of the Command object.
18:   Set CommandObject= Server.CreateObject("ADODB.Command")
19:
20:   ' The ActiveConnection property is used to connect the Command
      ➥object
21:   ' to the Connection object.
22:   Set CommandObject.ActiveConnection = DatabaseConnection
23:
24:   ' The SQL string that inserts the guest book data about the
25:   ' user is created.
26:   SQLDataInsertionString = "INSERT INTO Users (Prefix,
      ➥FirstName," & _
27:     "Lastname, EmailAddress, URL, Phone, Mobile, StreetAddress," & _
28:     "City, State, ZipCode, Country, DOB, FirstAccessTime," & _
29:     "FirstAccessDate, FirstAccessIPAddress,
      ➥FirstAccessWebBrowser," & _
30:     "LastAccessTime, LastAccessDate, LastAccessIPAddress," & _
31:     "LastAccessWebBrowser) VALUES (?,?,?,?,?,?,?,?," & _
32:     "?,?,?,?,?,?,?,?,?,?,?,?,?)"
33:
34:   ' The SQL statement that actually inserts the data is defined
35:   CommandObject.CommandText = SQLDataInsertionString
36:
37:   ' The prepared or pre-compiled SQL statement defined in the
38:   ' CommandText property is saved.
39:   CommandObject.Prepared = True
40:
41:   ' The parameters of the SQL string are defined below.
42:   CommandObject.Parameters.Append _
43:     CommandObject.CreateParameter("Prefix",200, ,255 )
44:   CommandObject.Parameters.Append _
45:     CommandObject.CreateParameter("FirstName",200, ,255 )
46:   CommandObject.Parameters.Append _
47:     CommandObject.CreateParameter("LastName",200, ,255 )
48:   CommandObject.Parameters.Append _
49:     CommandObject.CreateParameter("EmailAddress",200, ,255 )
```

```
50:   CommandObject.Parameters.Append _
51:     CommandObject.CreateParameter("URL",200, ,255 )
52:   CommandObject.Parameters.Append _
53:     CommandObject.CreateParameter("Phone",200, ,255 )
54:   CommandObject.Parameters.Append _
55:     CommandObject.CreateParameter("Mobile",200, ,255 )
56:   CommandObject.Parameters.Append _
57:     CommandObject.CreateParameter("StreetAddress",200, ,255 )
58:   CommandObject.Parameters.Append _
59:     CommandObject.CreateParameter("City",200, ,255 )
60:   CommandObject.Parameters.Append _
61:     CommandObject.CreateParameter("State",200, ,255 )
62:   CommandObject.Parameters.Append _
63:     CommandObject.CreateParameter("ZipCode",200, ,255 )
64:   CommandObject.Parameters.Append _
65:     CommandObject.CreateParameter("Country",200, ,255 )
66:   CommandObject.Parameters.Append _
67:     CommandObject.CreateParameter("DOB",200, ,255 )
68:   CommandObject.Parameters.Append _
69:     CommandObject.CreateParameter("FirstAccessTime",200, ,255 )
70:   CommandObject.Parameters.Append _
71:     CommandObject.CreateParameter("FirstAccessDate",200, ,255 )
72:   CommandObject.Parameters.Append _
73:     CommandObject.CreateParameter("FirstAccessIPAddress",200, ,255 )
74:   CommandObject.Parameters.Append _
75:     CommandObject.CreateParameter("FirstAccessWebBrowser",200,
        ➥,255 )
76:   CommandObject.Parameters.Append _
77:     CommandObject.CreateParameter("LastAccessTime",200, ,255 )
78:   CommandObject.Parameters.Append _
79:     CommandObject.CreateParameter("LastAccessDate",200, ,255 )
80:   CommandObject.Parameters.Append _
81:     CommandObject.CreateParameter("LastAccessIPAddress",200, ,255 )
82:   CommandObject.Parameters.Append _
83:     CommandObject.CreateParameter("LastAccessWebBrowser",200, ,255 )
84:
85:   ' Information entered by the user is added to the guest book
      ➥database
86:   CommandObject("Prefix") = Request.Form.Item("Prefix")
87:   CommandObject("FirstName") = Request.Form.Item("FirstName")
88:   CommandObject("LastName") = Request.Form.Item("LastName")
89:   CommandObject("EmailAddress") = Request.Form.Item("EmailAddress")
90:   CommandObject("URL") = Request.Form.Item("URL")
91:
92:   If IsNumeric (Request.Form.Item("PhoneAreaCode")) Then
93:     CommandObject("Phone") = "(" &
        ➥Request.Form.Item("PhoneAreaCode") & _
94:       ") " & Request.Form.Item("PhoneNumber")
95:   Else
96:     CommandObject("Phone") = Request.Form.Item("PhoneNumber")
97:   End If
```

12

continues

LISTING 12.9. CONTINUED

```
 98:     If IsNumeric (Request.Form.Item("MobileAreaCode")) Then
 99:        CommandObject("Mobile") = "(" &
           ➥Request.Form.Item("MobileAreaCode") _
100:        & ") " & Request.Form.Item("MobilePhoneNumber")
101:     Else
102:        CommandObject("Mobile") = Request.Form.Item("MobilePhoneNumber")
103:     End If
104:
105:     CommandObject("StreetAddress") =
           ➥Request.Form.Item("StreetAddress")
106:     CommandObject("City") = Request.Form.Item("City")
107:     CommandObject("State") = Request.Form.Item("State")
108:     CommandObject("ZipCode") = Request.Form.Item("ZipCode")
109:     CommandObject("Country") = Request.Form.Item("Country")
110:
111:      If IsDate(Request.Form.Item("BirthdayMonth") & _
112:       "/" & Request.Form.Item("BirthdayDay")  & "/" & _
113:         Request.Form.Item("BirthdayYear") ) = True Then
114:          CommandObject ("DOB") = _
115:            Request.Form.Item("BirthdayMonth") & "/"  & _
116:              Request.Form.Item("BirthdayDay")  & "/" & _
117:              Request.Form.Item("BirthdayYear")
118:      Else
119:        CommandObject ("DOB") = ""
120:      End If
121:
122:     CommandObject("FirstAccessTime") = Time
123:     CommandObject("FirstAccessDate") = Date
124:     CommandObject("FirstAccessIPAddress") = _
125:       Request.ServerVariables.Item ("REMOTE_ADDR")
126:     CommandObject("FirstAccessWebBrowser") = _
127:       Request.ServerVariables.Item ("HTTP_USER_AGENT")
128:     CommandObject("LastAccessTime") = Time
129:     CommandObject("LastAccessDate") = Date
130:     CommandObject("LastAccessIPAddress") = _
131:       Request.ServerVariables.Item ("REMOTE_ADDR")
132:     CommandObject("LastAccessWebBrowser") = _
133:       Request.ServerVariables.Item ("HTTP_USER_AGENT")
134:
135:     CommandObject.Execute
136:
137: End Sub
138:
139: ' ########## End Subroutine ##########
140:
141: If Request.Form.Count <= 0 Then
142:   Response.Write ("I am sorry but you did not fill in the Form.")
143: Else
144:
145:    ' Create an instance of the Connection object
```

```
146:    Set DatabaseConnection = Server.CreateObject("ADODB.Connection")
147:
148:    ' Open a connection to the guest book file DSN
149:    ' Before the following statement can execute properly, you have to
150:    ' create a file DSN for the guest book database as outlined in the
151:    ' book.
152:    DatabaseConnection.Open  "FILEDSN=UserInformationDatabase.dsn"
153:
154:    Call AddNewUserInformation
155:    DatabaseConnection.Close
156:
157:    Response.Write ("Thank you,
          ➥"&Request.Form.Item("FirstName")&"!<BR>")
158:    Response.Write ("Your information was added to the database!")
159:
160: End If
161: %>
162: <P> </P>
163: <HR>
164: This Web page was generated on <%= Date %> at <%= Time %>.<BR>
165: <A HREF=Default.asp>Return to guest book's main menu</A>.
166: </BODY>
167: </HTML>
```

ANALYSIS   The AddNewUserInformation subroutine defined in lines 12–137 adds a new user information record to the database. Line 18 creates an instance of the ADO Command object. Line 22 connects the Command object to the DatabaseConnection object instantiated in line 146 before the AddNewUserInformation subroutine is invoked. The SQL string in lines 26–32 inserts the new user record to the database with the aid of the Command object. Lines 42–83 create parameters for inserting the user's information to the database. The Command object is used so that if the user's data contains apostrophes, quotation marks, or other reserved SQL characters, they will not cause any problems. Lines 86–133 add the user's data to the Command object's parameters. Line 135 executes the SQL query that actually inserts the user's data to the database. The main code block of the ASP application starts at line 141. If the user has not filled in the form, an error message is displayed in line 142. Otherwise, lines 144–160 instantiate a database connection, call the AddNewUserInformation subroutine to add the user's information to the database, and display a message that the data has been inserted into the database.

Modifying Existing User Data

The ASP application in Listing 12.10 is used to modify existing database records. Use the code as a model when building your own ASP applications that need to modify existing database records.

The user registration database uses the e-mail address of users to control modifications to database records. To enhance security, you might want to use a password along with the user's e-mail address before allowing users to look up and modify information. This prevents unauthorized users from gaining access to sensitive information. Remember, it is your responsibility to maintain the confidentiality of information your users provide.

LISTING 12.10. MODIFYING USER INFORMATION AND UPDATING THE CHANGES TO THE DATABASE.

```
 1: <%@ LANGUAGE=VBScript %>
 2: <HTML>
 3: <HEAD title="Your personal information was processed">
 4: <META NAME="GENERATOR" Content="Microsoft Visual Studio 6.0">
 5: </HEAD>
 6: <BODY>
 7:
 8: <%
 9:
10: ' ########## Begin Subroutine ##########
11:
12: Sub ModifyUserInformation
13:
14:    Dim SQLString, DatabaseConnection, UserRecordSet
15:
16:    ' Create an instance of the Connection object
17:    Set DatabaseConnection = Server.CreateObject("ADODB.Connection")
18:
19:    ' Open a connection to the guest book file DSN
20:    ' Before the following statement can execute properly, you have to
21:    ' create a file DSN for the guest book database as outlined in the
22:    ' book.
23:    DatabaseConnection.Open  "FILEDSN=UserInformationDatabase.dsn"
24:
25:    ' Create an instance of the Recordset object
26:    Set UserRecordset = Server.CreateObject("ADODB.Recordset")
27:
28:    ' Retrieve the recordset containing the user's data.
29:    ' Notice how the recordset is opened so that you can use the
30:    ' Update method of the Recordset object to modify the user's
31:    ' data.
32:
33:    UserRecordSet.CursorType = 1
34:    UserRecordSet.CursorLocation = 2
35:    UserRecordSet.LockType = 3
36:    UserRecordSet.ActiveConnection = DatabaseConnection
37:    UserRecordSet.Source = "Users"
38:    UserRecordSet.Filter = "RecordID = " &
     ➥Request.Form.Item("RecordID")
```

```
39:
40:    ' The Open method of the Recordset object is used to retrieve
41:    ' data from the user registration database.
42:
43:    UserRecordset.Open
44:
45:    If UserRecordset.EOF Then
46:       Response.Write ("<H1>Your record was not found.</H1>")
47:    Else
48:
49:       UserRecordset.Fields.Item ("Prefix") = _
50:          Request.Form.Item("Prefix")
51:       UserRecordset.Fields.Item ("FirstName") = _
52:          Request.Form.Item("FirstName")
53:       UserRecordset.Fields.Item ("Lastname") = _
54:          Request.Form.Item("Lastname")
55:       UserRecordset.Fields.Item ("EmailAddress") = _
56:          Request.Form.Item("EmailAddress")
57:       UserRecordset.Fields.Item ("URL") = _
58:          Request.Form.Item("URL")
59:
60:       If IsNumeric (Request.Form.Item("PhoneAreaCode")) Then
61:          UserRecordset.Fields.Item ("Phone")  = "(" & _
62:          Request.Form.Item("PhoneAreaCode") & _
63:          ") " & Request.Form.Item("PhoneNumber")
64:       Else
65:          UserRecordset.Fields.Item ("Phone")  = _
66:             Request.Form.Item("PhoneNumber")
67:       End If
68:       If IsNumeric (Request.Form.Item("MobileAreaCode")) Then
69:          UserRecordset.Fields.Item ("Mobile") = "(" & _
70:             Request.Form.Item("MobileAreaCode") _
71:             & ") " & Request.Form.Item("MobilePhoneNumber")
72:       Else
73:          UserRecordset.Fields.Item ("Mobile") = _
74:             Request.Form.Item("MobilePhoneNumber")
75:       End If
76:
77:       UserRecordset.Fields.Item ("StreetAddress") = _
78:          Request.Form.Item("StreetAddress")
79:       UserRecordset.Fields.Item ("City") = _
80:          Request.Form.Item("City")
81:       UserRecordset.Fields.Item ("State") = _
82:          Request.Form.Item("State")
83:       UserRecordset.Fields.Item ("ZipCode") = _
84:          Request.Form.Item("ZipCode")
85:       UserRecordset.Fields.Item ("Country") = _
86:          Request.Form.Item("Country")
87:       If IsDate(Request.Form.Item("BirthdayMonth") & _
88:          "/" & Request.Form.Item("BirthdayDay")  & "/" & _
```

12

continues

LISTING 12.10. CONTINUED

```
 89:          Request.Form.Item("BirthdayYear") ) = True Then
 90:          UserRecordset.Fields.Item ("DOB") = _
 91:            Request.Form.Item("BirthdayMonth") & "/"  & _
 92:            Request.Form.Item("BirthdayDay")  & "/" & _
 93:            Request.Form.Item("BirthdayYear")
 94:        End If
 95:        UserRecordset.Fields.Item ("LastAccessDate") = Date
 96:        UserRecordset.Fields.Item ("LastAccessTime") = Time
 97:        UserRecordset.Fields.Item ("LastAccessIPAddress") = _
 98:          Request.ServerVariables.Item ("REMOTE_ADDR")
 99:        UserRecordset.Fields.Item ("LastAccessWebBrowser") = _
100:          Request.ServerVariables.Item ("HTTP_USER_AGENT")
101:
102:        UserRecordSet.Update
103:
104:        Response.Write ("Thank you, " & Request.Form.Item("FirstName") _
105:          & "!<BR>")
106:        Response.Write ("Your information was updated!")
107:
108:      End If
109:
110:      ' Database connections should always be closed after they are used.
111:      UserRecordSet.Close
112:      DatabaseConnection.Close
113:
114: End Sub
115:
116: ' ########## End Subroutine ##########
117:
118: If Request.Form.Count <= 0 Then
119:    Response.Write ("I am sorry but you did not fill in the Form.")
120: Else
121:    Call ModifyUserInformation
122: End If
123:
124: %>
125: <P> </P>
126: <HR>
127: This Web page was generated on <%= Date %> at <%= Time %>.<BR>
128: <A HREF=Default.asp>Return to the User Registration System's
     ➥main menu</A>.
129: </BODY>
130: </HTML>
```

ANALYSIS   The ASP subroutine defined in lines 12–114 modifies the fields of an existing database record. Line 17 creates an instance of the ADO `Connection` object, and line 23 opens the user information database. The `Recordset` object instantiated in line 26 is used to modify the user's database record. Lines 33–38 modify the default settings of the `Recordset` object so that it can be used to update a database record. Line 43 opens the `Recordset` object. If the user's record is found, lines 49–100 replace the values of the recordset's fields with the values entered by the user. After all the fields are modified, the `Update` method of the `Recordset` object is called in line 102 to update the changes to the database. As shown in lines 111 and 112, always close your database and `Recordset` objects when they are no longer needed.

Applications of the User Registration System

The user registration system you built today can be modified and used as a model when building your own database applications. Here are a few practical applications of the user registration system:

- Online user survey
- Online voting application
- Get information about users visiting your Web site
- Get contact information from your customers
- Keep customer information up-to-date by allowing customers to modify their own information

Remember, however, that in the interest of saving trees, the user registration application does not use extensive error checking. It is up to you to add more error checking.

12

Summary

When building complex Web applications, get into the habit of first creating a flowchart that outlines the application's control flow of the application. This method makes the task of developing the application more straightforward and less error prone—saving you both time and frustration.

There are two primary methods of updating records in a database. You can use the SQL `UPDATE` statement or the `Update` method of the `Recordset` object. The SQL `UPDATE` statement is suitable for fields that do not contain quotes or apostrophes. Before using the `Update` method of the `Recordset` object, you must open the `Recordset` object so that it supports data updating. The default settings of the `Recordset` object do not support the `Update` method.

Q&A

Q **When should I use a wizard-style user interface to get data from the user?**

A Use a wizard-style user interface when you need to get different information from the user based on a certain condition. For example, based on the user's shipping address, an online shopping cart application can display a standard local shipping form for those who live in the United States and an international shipping form for those who live in, say, Sri Lanka.

Q **What must you do after using a `Recordset` or ADO `Connection` object?**

A You should always close the `Recordset` and ADO `Connection` objects after using them. Failure to do so can result in IIS refusing to parse ASP applications after database connection resources are depleted. If you use Microsoft Access, it is limited to only 10 database connections. Failing to close the `Recordset` or ADO `Connection` objects makes this situation even worse because database connections can remain open until the user session expires if you do not explicitly close them.

Q **How can I modify information in a database record?**

A The SQL `UPDATE` method and the `Update` method of the `Recordset` object can be used to modify information in a database record.

Workshop

The quiz questions and exercises are provided for your further understanding. Please refer to Appendix A, "Answers to Questions," for the answers to the quiz questions; the answers to the exercises are on the MCP Web site.

Quiz

1. Why is it a good idea to design a flowchart that outlines the control structure of a Web application before actually building the Web application?

2. Which SQL statement modifies existing data in a database?

3. How do you close `Recordset` and ADO `Connection` objects so that the resources used by these objects are returned to your system?

4. Is the SQL `UPDATE` method suitable for updating the value of a numeric field? Why?

5. Which ASP statements open a recordset so that the `Update` method can be used to modify the recordset data?

Exercises

1. Write the SQL statement to add an extra 10 percent to the price of all the `RetailPrice` fields in the table `SpecialOrderItems`.

2. Incorporate the user registration system with the home page of your Web site. Use the user information database to personally greet registered users with their names. (Hint: Use a cookie to keep track of registered users.)

12

DAY **13**

Retaining Information Between Sessions Using Cookies

A lot of Web sites use cookies, and most likely you will eventually want to use them, too. On Day 6, "Getting Information About HTTP Requests with the `Request` Object," and Day 7, "Responding to Client Requests with the `Response` Object," you were briefly introduced to cookies. Today, you cover the following:

- Understand the purpose of cookies.
- Learn to create cookies and maintain them on the client side.
- Explore different applications of cookies.
- Determine the drawbacks of cookies.
- Address Web browser compatibility issues.
- Use cookies in ASP applications.

Using Cookies

 Cookies are defined as small packets of information used to store persistent state information on the user's computer. These packets of information are just a few bytes in size and have expiration dates associated with them. After the specified expiration date, the cookie is deleted.

Although you might not have noticed it, cookies are nothing new to you. Your ASP applications have already made use of them. As a matter of fact, the ASP environment is a cookie-based technology. ASP uses cookies internally to maintain state between HTTP sessions. You already know how to retain information between HTTP sessions. In Day 4, "Building and Processing Web Forms," you first learned how to use the Session object to temporarily store user information between HTTP sessions. The Session object was covered in more detail in Day 8, "Processing Web Data with the Server, Session, and Application Objects." The Session object stores information between HTTP sessions on the server, but cookie information is usually stored on the client side.

> **Note**
>
> The applications presented in today's lesson make use of cookies. Please make sure you have enabled cookies in your Web browser before proceeding any further. If you are unsure about how to do that, chances are you don't have to worry about it because cookies are enabled by default. Unless you changed the default setting, cookies are enabled on your Web browser.

Understanding the Purpose of Cookies

HTTP is a stateless protocol. Although this feature makes HTTP efficient for distributing information, it makes it harder for Web applications to track client sessions and remember certain information between each one. Therefore, cookies have been implemented to address this limitation of HTTP.

When a Web server receives an HTTP request, it fulfills it and terminates the connection between the Web server and the Web client. No information about the HTTP transaction is retained for future reference. This is a major obstacle for Web applications, such as online shopping cart applications, that need to remember certain information between connections. Figure 13.1 shows an example of a typical HTTP transaction. Notice how no information about the HTTP transaction is retained after the HTTP connection between the Web server and the Web client is broken.

FIGURE 13.1.

A typical HTTP transaction that does not use cookies.

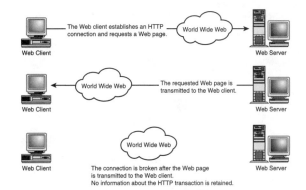

Figure 13.2 demonstrates how a cookie is used to retain information about an HTTP transaction. The cookie, `Repeat=Yes`, can be created by an ASP application. A server- or client-side application can examine the cookie to determine whether the Web client is a repeat visitor.

FIGURE 13.2.

An HTTP transaction that uses cookies to remember certain information between sessions.

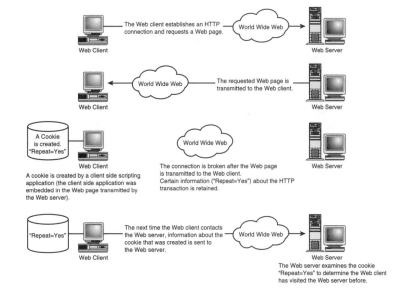

13

Cookies can be used to develop sophisticated Web applications that remember certain pieces of information between HTTP sessions. Figure 13.3 shows an example of how cookies can be used to make it easier for users to get information they need. Users visit the MovieLink Web page to find out about movies playing in different areas of the U.S.; to learn about movies playing in their area, users simply supply their zip code. Because it is a hassle for users to type their zip code each time they want to find out which movies are playing in their area, a cookie containing the user's zip code can be created and stored in the user's computer. Notice how the MovieLink Web page remembers my zip code (20910) and city (Silver Spring).

FIGURE 13.3.

Cookies can be used to avoid asking the same question ("What's your zip code?") each time a user visits your Web page.

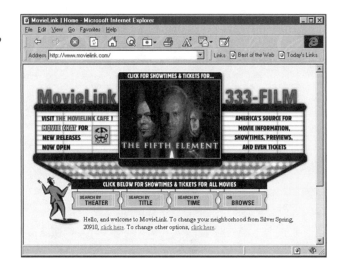

Are Cookies Evil?

Contrary to many people's beliefs, cookies are not evil. They are used by millions of Web surfers and do not pose a security threat to the user's computer. When a cookie is created, a small package of information is created in the user's computer. The information created by cookies is very limited and governed by a series of restrictions outlined in the following section. These restrictions effectively make sure cookies are not abused by Web application developers.

Tip

> Cookies should not be used to store large amounts of data. This is not the purpose for which they are intended. If you have to store large amounts of data, store it in a server-side database and create a cookie that contains only a reference to the database record.

Restrictions and Limitations When Creating Cookies

When creating cookies, it is important that you understand the restrictions and limitations. Restrictions have been set up to make sure cookies are not abused and are used for the purpose for which they are designed—to store limited information on the client side to maintain state. When creating and using cookies, keep in mind the following restrictions:

- Web browsers are required to maintain a total of only 300 cookies.
- Only 4KB of data are allowed for each cookie. Cookies with more than 4KB of data should be trimmed to 4KB. Generally, avoid creating cookies larger than 1KB.
- Only 20 cookies are allowed for each Web server.

Note   When the 300 total cookies limit is reached, the Web browser can delete the oldest cookie in the cookie collection.

Caution   A bug in Internet Explorer 3.0 might cause cookies larger than 1KB to be improperly processed.

Applications for Cookies

There are many practical applications for cookies. Examples of information that can be retained between HTTP sessions with the aid of cookies include the following:

- Information about an online transaction: Items in a shopping cart, time spent shopping, shopping cart expiration time/date
- Personal information: User's name, geographic location (country, state/province, zip code), time zone, and account number (if applicable)
- Personal preferences: Preferred background color/bitmap, background music (be sure to include the option of no background music if you implement a cookie for this purpose), preferred typeface for the text of Web pages (font name, point size, color)

Later in this chapter, the "Using Cookies in ASP Applications" section demonstrates how cookies are used in an actual ASP application to retain information between HTTP transactions. First, however, you will explore some of the applications for cookies to see how they can be used to develop sophisticated Web applications.

13

Online Shopping Carts

The Internet is being used more and more to conduct business transactions. Online shopping carts use cookies to keep track of items selected by the customer from a product catalog (see Figure 13.4).

FIGURE 13.4.

An online product catalog linked to an online shopping cart.

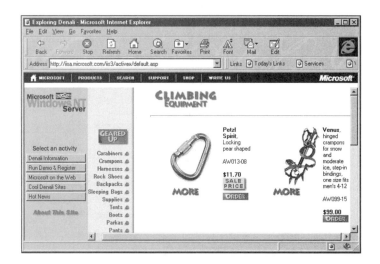

A cookie is updated each time an item is selected by the user. When the user finishes shopping, the online shopping cart application examines cookie information created as a result of the customer selecting items for purchase. The customer can pay for the selected items after they are verified, as shown in Figure 13.5.

FIGURE 13.5.

An online shopping cart application keeps track of items selected for purchase by the customer.

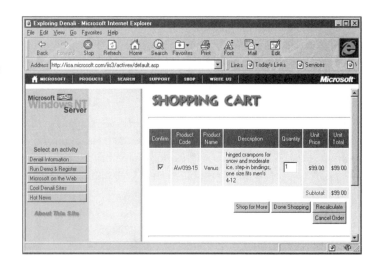

Customized Web Pages

Customized Web pages can be dynamically created to provide personalized content to users browsing a Web site. They enhance the experience of browsing by presenting the information the user is most likely interested in. The MSNBC home page is shown in Figure 13.6. Notice how it offers the option of personalizing the page.

COMPANION **Web site** Visit the Microsoft Network home page and the MSNBC home page to explore how personalized Web pages are dynamically created by the Web server with the aid of cookies:

http://www.msn.com/

and

http://www.msnbc.com/

FIGURE 13.6.

The home page of MSNBC.

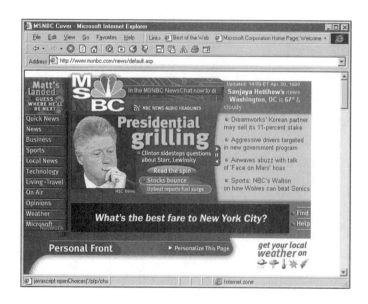

Customization categories in the MSNBC home page are shown in Figure 13.7.

Drawbacks of Using Cookies

Although client-side cookies are powerful tools for developing sophisticated Web applications, there are a number of drawbacks associated with using them. It is important that you consider the following drawbacks before you deploy Web applications that rely on cookies to accurately identify and authenticate users:

- Cookies can be lost.
- Cookies can be changed by users.
- Cookies can be copied.
- Cookies can be stolen.
- Cookies can be disabled.
- Not all browsers support cookies.

FIGURE 13.7.

Customization categories in the MSNBC home page.

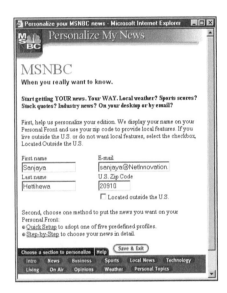

Cookies Can Be Lost

Cookie files can be corrupted, deleted, or overwritten when you install a new version of a Web browser (this problem could be caused by a badly written setup application). When using cookies, be prepared for a user to lose the file used to store cookies.

> **Caution**   Never depend on cookies to store valuable or irreplaceable information. Such information should always be stored in a server-side database. Because cookie information is stored in the user's hard drive, it can easily be lost.

One solution to lost cookies is to store all cookie information (user name, e-mail address, preferences) in a server-side database. Only a reference to the data stored in the server-side database is contained in the client-side cookie (such as the record number). When this method is implemented, users can simply provide their e-mail addresses and passwords to restore the cookie containing the reference to the server-side database. This solution ensures that a user does not have to re-enter all the information in case a cookie is lost.

Cookies Can Be Changed by Users

Technically inclined users might be able to figure out how to change the information stored in a cookie. Never assume cookie information is authentic. If you are using a cookie to determine relatively unimportant information, such as the last time a user visited a Web page, it is okay to rely on the cookie's value. However, it is not a good idea to rely on its value to determine critical or important information, such as a user's account balance. Have you ever wished you could reset the balance of your credit cards by editing a file on your computer? If credit card companies used client-side cookies to store account balances, you would be able to make that wish a reality!

As a rule of thumb, use cookies to store non-confidential information. If you need to store confidential information for future reference, store it in a server-side database, and assign an identification code and password to users. Store the identification code in a client-side cookie and ask users for their passwords before allowing them to perform a transaction (say, buy a laptop computer) using the information stored in your database.

Cookies Can Be Copied

Cookies are not universally unique, even if you create a universally unique cookie for each HTTP transaction. It is possible for two computers to have the exact same cookie information. Never use cookies to store information that's unique to the user's computer (screen resolution, color depth, operating system, and so on). For one thing, after the cookie is created, the user might decide to change any of these items.

Cookies Can Be Stolen

As discussed in the previous section, cookie information can be copied with or without the consent or knowledge of the cookie file's owner. Web browsers store cookie information in a file. Someone could easily copy this file and move it to another computer and then have access to another user's cookies. Although the chances of this happening are very slim, it is a possibility that you should consider.

13

Caution You should never authenticate a user based only on the value of a cookie. Use a password to verify the user's identity.

Cookies Can Be Disabled

Cookies are wonderful for helping maintain state between Web client sessions. However, you should be aware that some users might have cookies turned off in the Web browser. It has been my experience, however, that only the most paranoid of people and companies do this. Almost all users who visit your Web site will have cookies turned on (the default setting). If your application depends on cookies, it's best that you educate your users on the benefits of allowing cookies. If your application does not depend on cookies, but uses them to give repeat visitors a richer experience (such as displaying their local weather information), design your ASP application so that if the Web browser supports cookies, it uses them. On the other hand, if cookies are not allowed, your application simply does not display any customized information.

Web Browser Compatibility Issues

Both Internet Explorer and Netscape Navigator support client-side persistent cookies. Although Internet Explorer and Netscape Navigator account for over 95 percent of all Web browsers used to navigate the Internet, some users might be using other Web browsers that do not support cookies. When designing Web pages, be sure to take all Web browsers into consideration. Always provide a URL that can be used by even a technologically challenged Web browser to access the information.

Where Cookies Are Stored by Web Browsers

Cookies created by Internet Explorer can be found in the following directories, listed in Table 13.1, based on the version of Internet Explorer you use.

TABLE 13.1. INTERNET EXPLORER COOKIE DIRECTORIES.

Version of Internet Explorer	Location of Cookies
Internet Explorer 1.5 for Windows NT	`%systemroot%\cookie.jar`
Internet Explorer 2.0	`\Program Files\Plus!\Microsoft Internet\ cookies.txt`
Internet Explorer 3.0 (Win NT)	`%systemroot%\COOKIES\<username>@ <sitename>.txt`
Internet Explorer 3.0 (Win 95)	`\Windows\Cookies\ <username>@<site name>.txt`
Internet Explorer 3.0 (WFWG/NT 3.51)	The file `Emcookie.dat` in the Internet Explorer installation directory
Internet Explorer 4.0 (Win NT)	`%systemroot%\Profiles\<UserName>\Cookies <username>@<sitename>.txt`

Netscape Communicator stores cookies in the text file `bookmark.htm` in the Netscape Communicator application settings directory.

Using Cookies in ASP Applications

There are two main kinds of cookies: in-memory cookies and persistent cookies. An *in-memory cookie* goes away when the user shuts the browser down. A *persistent cookie* resides on the hard drive and is retrieved later.

It is easy to use cookies in ASP applications. Applications manipulate cookies by using the `Response` and `Request` objects of Active Server Pages.

Before you can use a cookie, it needs to be created. The code for creating a cookie should be placed at the beginning of the ASP file. You need to generate the cookies before any HTML text is sent to the browser.

The `Response` object is used to create and set cookie values. The `Request` object retrieves cookie values stored in the user's computer. The following syntax illustrates how the `Response` object is used to create a cookie and set its attributes:

```
Response.Cookies (NameOfCookie) = ValueOfCookie
```

`NameOfCookie` is the name of the cookie you want to be created. If `NameOfCookie` already exists, then the existing cookie's value is replaced with the new value, which is `ValueOfCookie`. For example, if you use the following line of code, you will create a cookie named `TimeZone` with the value `Eastern`:

```
Response.Cookies("TimeZone") = "Eastern"
```

Setting Attributes of Cookies

Cookies can contain attributes such as when they expire and to which domains they are sent. A cookie's attributes can be changed by using the following syntax:

```
Response.Cookies(NameOfCookie).CookieAttribute = ValueOfCookieAttribute
```

`NameOfCookie` is the name of the cookie whose attribute is about to be changed. `CookieAttribute` is the attribute to be changed. The possible types of `CookieAttribute` are described in Table 13.2. `ValueOfCookieAttribute` is the value of the cookie attribute.

13

TABLE 13.2. COOKIE ATTRIBUTES.

Name	Description of the Attribute
Expires	Used to specify when the cookie expires. It is a write-only attribute.
Domain	Used to specify to which domains the cookie is sent. It is a write-only attribute.
Path	Used to specify requests originating from the path to which the cookie is sent. The default path is the path of the ASP application. It is a write-only attribute.
Secure	Used to specify whether the cookie is secure. It is a write-only attribute.
HasKeys	Used to specify whether the cookie has keys. It is a read-only attribute.

> **Note**
>
> Remember, the Response object sets or writes values to the client and the Request object retrieves values.

The following ASP statements create a cookie named TimeZone, assign it the value Eastern, and set it to expire on February 29, 2000:

```
Response.Cookies("TimeZone") = "Eastern"
Response.Cookies("TimeZone").Expires = "February 29, 2000"
```

If you create a cookie without specifying an expiration date, you are creating an in-memory cookie. If you want to have the cookie information available to you at a future date, you should create a persistent cookie by specifying an expiration date.

Retrieving the Values of Cookies

The Request object is used to retrieve the value of a cookie created during a previous Web session. The following ASP statement retrieves the value of the cookie named *NameOfCookie*:

```
Request.Cookies(NameOfCookie)
```

Working with SubKeys

 Subkeys are instrumental in organizing the cookies you create into logical categories. A *subkey* is simply a value used to locate information. Say you want to create a cookie to keep track of three vehicles the user would like to have. Instead of creating three different cookies, it makes more sense to use one cookie (FavoriteVehicle) with three keys (SUV, Car, Convertible), as shown in the following code:

```
Response.Cookies("FavoriteVehicle")("SUV") = "Lexus LX 470"
Response.Cookies("FavoriteVehicle")("Car") = " Mercedes-Benz S600 Sedan"
Response.Cookies("FavoriteVehicle")("Convertible") = "Mercedes-Benz SL600"
```

Caution   If you assign a value to a cookie with keys without specifying a key, the cookie's keys are deleted.

Before you try to access the value of a cookie subkey, use the `HasKeys` attribute, as shown in the following example, to determine whether the cookie has a subkey:

```
Request.Cookies(NameOfCookie).HasKeys
```

If the result is `TRUE`, the cookie has subkeys; if the result is `FALSE`, the cookie does not have subkeys.

You can find the value of a cookie subkey by using the following syntax:

```
Request.Cookies(NameOfCookie)(NameOfSubKey)
```

Deleting a Cookie

Now that you know all about cookies and how to create them, you should know how to delete them. You delete a cookie by setting its expiration date to one that has already elapsed. The following ASP statement illustrates how to delete the cookie `MyCookie` by setting its expiration date to `February 29, 1976`:

```
Response.Cookie("MyCookie").Expires = #February 29, 1976#
```

 Note   The user's computer must have the correct date to delete a cookie successfully.

Cookies in Use

The best way to understand cookies is to see them in action. The ASP application in Listing 13.1 demonstrates how to use the `Response` and `Request` objects to remember information between HTTP sessions by using cookies. Client-side in-memory cookies are used to keep track of when and how many times the user has invoked the ASP application. The Web page in Figure 13.8 is displayed the first time a user invokes the ASP application.

13

LISTING 13.1. USING COOKIES TO REMEMBER INFORMATION BETWEEN HTTP SESSIONS.

```
 1: <%@ LANGUAGE="VBSCRIPT" %>
 2:
 3: <% LastAccessTime = Request.Cookies ("LastTime") %>
 4: <% LastAccessDate = Request.Cookies ("LastDate") %>
 5:
 6: <%
 7: If (Request.Cookies ("NumVisits")="") Then
 8:   Response.Cookies ("NumVisits") = 0
 9: Else
10:   Response.Cookies ("NumVisits") = Request.Cookies ("NumVisits") + 1
11: End If
12: %>
13:
14: <% Response.Cookies ("LastDate") = Date %>
15: <% Response.Cookies ("LastTime") = Time %>
16:
17: <!DOCTYPE HTML PUBLIC "-//IETF//DTD HTML//EN">
18: <html>
19:
20: <head>
21: <meta http-equiv="Content-Type"
22: content="text/html; charset=iso-8859-1">
23:
24: <title>Using Cookies In ASP Applications</title>
25: </head>
26:
27: <body bgcolor="#FDFFA4">
28:
29: <p><font size="4" face="Arial"><STRONG>
30: Welcome to the dynamic and personalized world of ASP
31: application development with client-side persistent cookies!
32: </STRONG></font></p>
33:
34: <p>When you access this Web page, three cookies are created. The
35: first cookie counts the number of times you have visited this Web
36: page. The other two cookies are used to determine the date and
37: time you last visited this Web page.</p>
38: <div align="center"><center>
39:
40: <table border="4" width="300">
41:     <tr>
42:         <td>
43:         <CENTER>
44:         <% IF (Request.Cookies ("NumVisits")=0) THEN %>
45:
46:         <font color="#0000FF" face="Comic Sans MS">
47:         Welcome!<br>
48:         This is the first time you are visiting this Web page!
49:         </font><br>
```

```
50:
51:          <% ELSE %>
52:
53:          <p><font color="#400000" size="4"><strong>
54:          Thanks for visiting this Web page again! You have
55:          visited this Web page a total of
56:          <%= Request.Cookies ("NumVisits") %> time(s).
57:          </strong></font></p>
58:
59:          <% END IF %>
60:          </CENTER>
61:          </td>
62:       </tr>
63: </table>
64: </center></div>
65:
66: <hr>
67:
68: <p>
69: <font color="#FF0000" size="4" face="Comic Sans MS"><strong>
70:
71: The Current time is <%= Time %> on <%= Date %> <BR>
72:
73: <% IF (Request.Cookies ("NumVisits")>0) THEN %>
74:
75:    You last accessed this Web page
76:    at <%= LastAccessTime %>
77:    on <%= LastAccessDate %>
78:
79: <% END IF %>
80: </strong></font>
81:
82: <HR>
83:
84: <A HREF="DeleteCookies.asp">
85: Select this link to delete all cookies created for this page</A>
86:
87: </p>
88: </body>
89: </html>
```

13

ANALYSIS Lines 3 and 4 examine the values of the cookies LastTime and LastDate. The If...Then...Else statement defined in lines 7–11 checks whether the user has visited the Web page before. If he or she has, the counter that keeps track of the number of visits is incremented and sent back to the Web browser as a cookie. If the user hasn't visited the Web page before, a counter is created (with the initial value of 0) to keep track of the number of times the user visits the Web page. The remainder of the Web page uses the cookies created in lines 3–15 to display information about the user's previous visits to the same Web page.

FIGURE 13.8.

This page appears the first time the ASP application in Listing 13.1 is invoked.

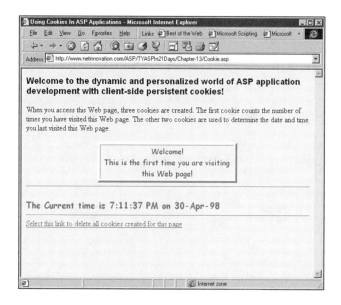

When the ASP application in Listing 13.1 is invoked a second time by the same user, the Web page shown in Figure 13.9 is displayed.

FIGURE 13.9.

This page appears after the ASP application in Listing 13.1 is loaded a second time by the same user.

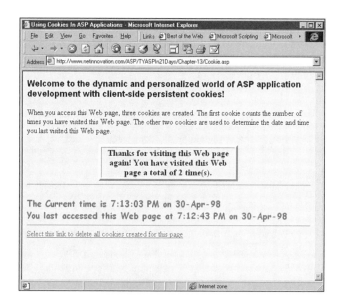

The hyperlink defined in lines 84–85 of Listing 13.1 points to the ASP application in Listing 13.2.

LISTING 13.2. THE ASP APPLICATION THAT DELETES COOKIES CREATED BY THE ASP APPLICATION IN LISTING 13.1.

```
 1: <%@ LANGUAGE="VBSCRIPT" %>
 2:
 3: <% Response.Cookies ("NumVisits").Expires = "January 1, 1997" %>
 4: <% Response.Cookies ("LastDate").Expires = "January 1, 1997" %>
 5: <% Response.Cookies ("LastTime").Expires = "January 1, 1997" %>
 6:
 7: <HTML>
 8: <HEAD>
 9:
10: <META HTTP-EQUIV="Content-Type" content="text/html; charset=iso-8859-
    ➥1">
11: <TITLE>Cookies Are Deleted</TITLE>
12: </HEAD>
13: <BODY BGCOLOR="FFFFFF">
14:
15: <H1>Cookies Are Deleted</H1>
16:
17: <A HREF="Cookie.asp">
18: Click here to start over</A>
19:
20: </BODY>
21: </HTML>
```

ANALYSIS Lines 3–5 of the ASP application in Listing 13.2 delete cookies created by the ASP application in Listing 13.1. Notice how the cookies are deleted through the use of the Response object's Expire attribute by specifying an expiration date that has already passed.

Note

> The cookies created in this example are in-memory cookies. Because no expiration date was specified, the cookie information is not written to the user's hard drive.

13

 Visit the following Web page for additional information about client-side persistent cookies and how they are used to retain information between HTTP sessions:

http://home.netscape.com/newsref/std/cookie_spec.html

Summary

Cookies can be used to develop sophisticated Web applications that remember information between HTTP sessions. When a cookie is created, certain information is stored in the user's computer for future reference. When the Web client contacts the Web server responsible for creating the cookie, the information stored in the user's computer (in the form of a cookie) is sent to the Web server. This information can be used by either a client- or server-side Web application to implement sophisticated Web applications, such as shopping carts and personalized Web pages. For additional information about developing ASP applications that use cookies, refer to Day 14, "Developing a User Personalization System with Cookies."

Q&A

Q Are cookies harmful to the user's computer?

A Contrary to a deluded belief, cookies are not harmful to the user's computer. Cookies are actually helpful to the user because they enable Web application developers to make it easier for users to surf the Internet! What concerns most people about cookies is that they are written transparently to the user's machine, unless the user chooses the option to be warned before accepting them. It also concerns people that persisted cookies don't automatically go away when you leave a Web page.

Q Why are there all kinds of restrictions about cookies?

A These restrictions have been set up to make sure Web application developers do not abuse cookies and to make sure cookies do not pose any harm to the user's computer, such as taking over all the user's hard drive space!

Workshop

The quiz questions and exercises are provided for your further understanding. Please refer to Appendix A, "Answers to Questions," for the answers to the quiz questions; the answers to the exercises are on the MCP Web site.

Quiz

1. What is the limit on the total number of cookies?

2. Is there a limit to the number of cookies that can be created by a server?

3. Which ASP object is used to create a cookie?

4. Which ASP object is used to retrieve the value of a cookie?

5. What is the ASP statement used to delete a cookie named EMailAddress?

6. What is the ASP statement that creates a cookie named TimeZone with the value Eastern?

7. What ASP statement deletes a cookie by the name of DatabaseID?

8. Why shouldn't you store large amounts of data in cookies?

Exercises

1. Create an ASP application that uses the InputBox() function to get the user's name and store it in a cookie. When the user visits the same ASP application in the future, the cookie created earlier is used to personally greet the user. Design the ASP application so that if the Web browser does not support the VBScript InputBox() function, an HTML form is used instead.

2. Create an ASP application used to delete the cookies created in Exercise 1. Link the application to the ASP application in Exercise 1 so that a user can reset the ASP application by deleting the cookies.

3. Create an ASP application that allows the user to customize the text and background color of the Web page. (Hint: Cookies are used to remember the text and background color information.)

4. Create an ASP application used to delete the cookies created in Exercise 3. Link the application to the ASP application in Exercise 3 so that a user can reset the ASP application by deleting the cookies.

13

DAY 14

Developing a User Personalization System with Cookies

Today, you learn how to use tips and techniques presented over the past two weeks to build a User Personalization System (UPS). Many Web sites now offer users custom information. At the end of today, you will be able incorporate personalization features into your Web site. The UPS allows users to select custom information to be displayed in a Web page. Today you cover the following topics:

- Use multiple database connections.
- Allow users to select custom information.
- Store user personalization information in a database.
- Use a cookie to access the UPS database.
- Retrieve and modify database information.
- Apply advanced ADO techniques.
- Display custom information to users.

Goals of the User Personalization System

The UPS you build today is an extension of the User Registration System you built on Day 12, "Database Development Illustrated: Building a User Registration System." See Figure 14.1 for the flowchart of the UPS you are building today.

FIGURE 14.1.

The flowchart of the User Personalization System.

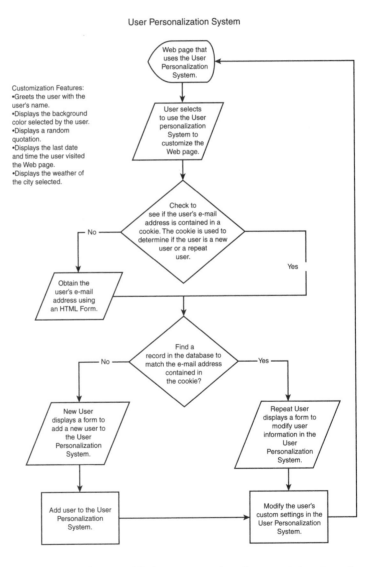

The UPS checks whether a user has specified custom settings by examining the value of a cookie. If the cookie is found, its value is used to access and display custom information selected by the user. If the cookie is not found, the UPS gets the user's e-mail address and searches the database. If the user's e-mail address is found in the database, it is assumed the user is using a new computer and a cookie is created on the new computer to access the user's personal settings found in the database. If the user's e-mail address is not found, a new user record is added to the database.

Note   Before deploying the UPS on a production Web site, you might want to extend it further and add error checking to data entry forms. Data entry forms already incorporate some level of error checking. However, it is recommended that you add additional error checking before using the UPS on your Web site. You might also want to password-protect database records.

Platform Compatibility Issues

The UPS is compatible across multiple Web browsers. As long as the Web browser supports cookies, it can be used to personalize a Web page (or an entire Web site). Virtually all Web browsers, including Internet Explorer, Mosaic, and Netscape Navigator, support cookies.

Note   The UPS you build today is cross-browser compatible. In addition to HTML support, support for cookies is the only additional Web browser feature used by the UPS, and practically all Web browsers support cookies.

Linking with the User Registration System

Instead of building a new database from scratch for the UPS, it makes sense to modify the database you used in Day 12 to store personalization information. All you need to do is add an additional table called PersonalSettings to the database in Day 12, as shown in Figure 14.2. The table has six data fields; Table 14.1 explains the purpose of each one.

TABLE 14.1. DATA FIELDS OF THE UPS.

Data Field Name	Purpose of Data Field
ID	Primary key of the UPS.
UserRecordID	The corresponding primary key of the Users table. This key is for accessing the user's personal information.
BackgroundColor	Background color selected by the user.

continues

14

TABLE 14.1. CONTINUED

Data Field Name	Purpose of Data Field
ForegroundColor	Foreground color selected by the user.
WeatherOfCity	Indicates the weather of the city the user has chosen to display.
RandomQuotation	Indicates whether the user has selected to display a random quotation.

FIGURE 14.2.

A new table is created.

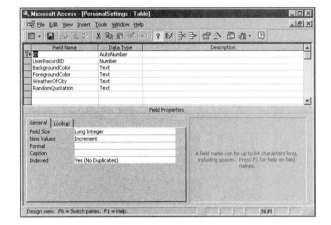

Refer to Figure 14.3 for the relationships of the UPS database. Notice how the UserRecordID field of the PersonalSettings table is linked to the RecordID field of the Users table.

FIGURE 14.3.

Relationships of the database.

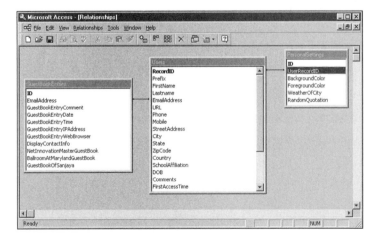

> **Note**
>
> Before attempting to execute the code from today's tutorial, you must create the two file DSNs listed here. Both database files are included in the code distribution file for this book.
>
> - Create the file DSN `UserInformationDatabase` for the database file `WebSIteUsers.mdb`.
> - Create the file DSN `QuotationsDatabase` for the database file `Quotes.mdb`.

The User Personalization System in Action

Before delving into the code of the UPS, it helps to understand how the UPS functions. You can then better understand how the code works when it is presented. Refer to Figure 14.4 for the UPS's default Web page, which is displayed when no information about the user is available in the UPS database.

FIGURE 14.4.

The Web page before it is customized.

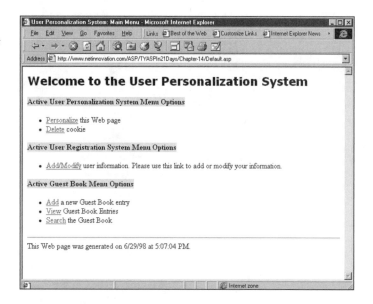

A user can select the "Personalize this Web page" hyperlink to customize the Web page in Figure 14.4. A cookie containing the user's e-mail address is used to determine whether the user has used the UPS before. If a cookie with the user's e-mail address is not found, the Web page shown in Figure 14.5 is displayed to get the user's e-mail address. The user types his or her e-mail address and clicks the Submit button.

14

FIGURE 14.5.

Getting the user's email address.

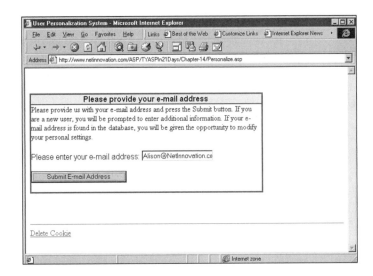

After the user submits the e-mail address, the UPS checks to see if the user is in the UPS database by searching the database for the e-mail address. If the e-mail address is not found, the Web form shown in Figure 14.6 is displayed to get information about the user.

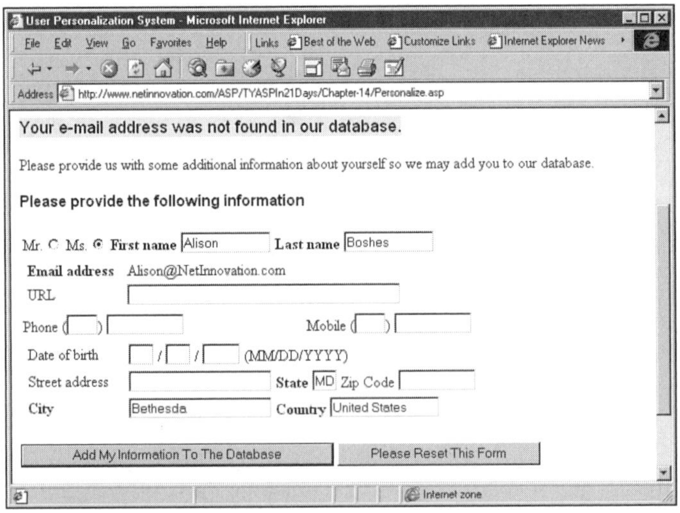

FIGURE 14.6.

A new user is added to the database.

After getting information about the user, the Web page in Figure 14.7 is used to specify the user's preferred background and text color. The user can change these colors later by choosing to personalize the default Web page.

FIGURE 14.7.

The background and text colors are specified.

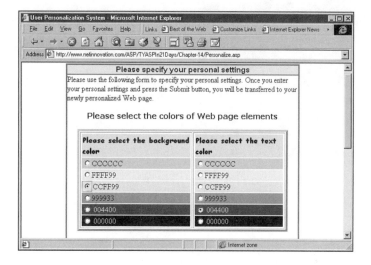

The user can also select to display custom information, such as a city's weather and a random quotation. The Web page in Figure 14.8 tells the UPS to display the weather in Redmond along with a random quotation.

FIGURE 14.8.

The user selects custom information to be displayed.

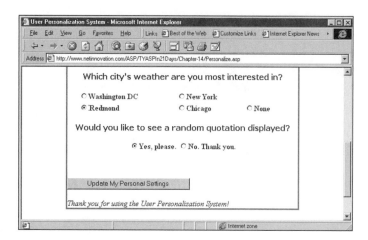

After the user specifies custom information to be displayed, the UPS updates the user's settings in the database and displays the Web page shown in Figure 14.9 to confirm the update. The information entered by the user is now saved in the UPS database.

14

FIGURE **14.9.**

*The user's personal
settings have been
updated.*

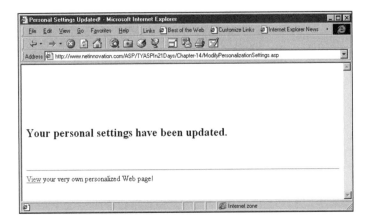

Select the "View your very own personalized Web page" hyperlink to view the Web page
in Figure 14.4 with custom information selected by the user. As you can see in Figure
14.10, the Web page is customized with the text and background colors selected by the
user along with a random quotation and the current weather in Redmond (yes, it still
rains in Redmond!). Notice how the Web page now personally greets the user with her
name.

FIGURE **14.10.**

*The Web page is
customized with infor-
mation selected by the
user.*

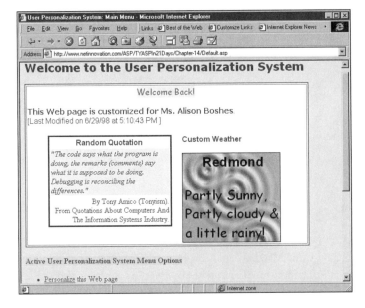

Modifying Custom Settings

The same hyperlink originally selected to customize the Web page in Figure 14.4 can be used to modify the custom settings selected by the user. Select the "Personalize this Web page" hyperlink to display the Web page shown in Figure 14.11. Notice how the user no longer needs to re-enter her e-mail address. The UPS already knows the user's e-mail address with the aid of a cookie, and the database is searched for the user's e-mail address. Information about the user that's already in the database is displayed so that the user can review and modify the information.

FIGURE 14.11.

Information stored in the UPS can be modi-fied.

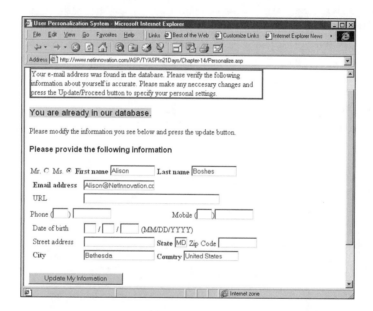

After the user reviews her information and clicks the Update My Information button, she can modify additional information to be displayed, as shown in Figure 14.12. The user decides to have a random quotation displayed without displaying weather information.

Figure 14.13 shows the newly customized Web page generated by the UPS. Notice how a random quotation is displayed while not displaying any weather information.

Now that you know how the UPS functions to display custom information to the user, it's time to understand how the ASP code works. Some of it is a bit complex. However, the code gives you many practical applications of tips and techniques presented over the past two weeks, so by the end of today's lesson, you will be able to use the code from this tutorial to customize your own Web site!

14

FIGURE 14.12.

The user decides not to display weather information.

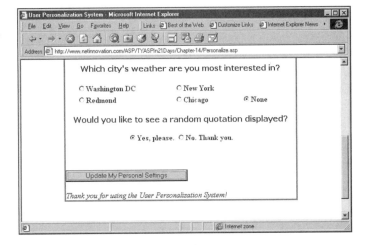

FIGURE 14.13.

The newly customized Web page.

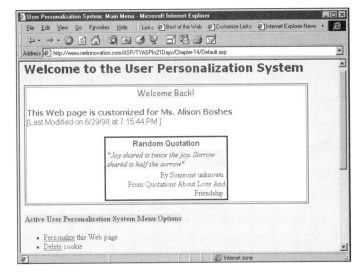

Note

The UPS application consists of three ASP files. When code listings are presented, the ASP file from which the code is derived is given inside parentheses next to the code listing's caption. This has been done to make it easier for you to determine from which ASP file a code listing is derived.

Displaying Personalized Information

The Web page default.asp in Listing 14.1 uses the UPS database to display custom information to users. This section explores how an ASP application can use the UPS database to display custom information to the user. The user's information is stored in two tables of the database. As you will soon discover, all the ASP application has to do is establish a connection to the database and retrieve the user's information from the database with the aid of a SQL statement.

LISTING 14.1. THE DEFAULT WEB PAGE OF THE USER PERSONALIZATION SYSTEM (default.asp).

```
1: <%@ LANGUAGE=VBScript %>
2: <% Option Explicit
3:
4: Sub DisplayRandomQuotation ()
5:
6:    Dim strDSN, strSQL, QuotationsDatabase,
   ➥QuotationsDatabaseConnection
7:
8:    'Establish a connection with data source.
9:    strDSN  = "FILEDSN=QuotationsDatabase.dsn"
10:   Set QuotationsDatabaseConnection = _
11:      Server.CreateObject("ADODB.Connection")
12:   QuotationsDatabaseConnection.Open strDSN
13:
14:   'Instantiate a Recordset object.
15:   Set QuotationsDatabase = Server.CreateObject("ADODB.Recordset")
16:
17:   ' Seed the random number generator.
18:   Randomize ()
19:
20:   'Open a recordset using the Open method
21:   'and use the connection established by the Connection object.
22:
23:   strSQL = "SELECT TOP 1 QuotationsTable.QuoteID, " & _
24:     "QuotationsTable.Quote, QuotationsTable.QuoteAuthor, " & _
25:     "QuotationsTable.QuoteCategory FROM QuotationsTable " & _
26:     "WHERE QuotationsTable.QuoteID=" & Int((186)*Rnd()+1)
27:
28:   QuotationsDatabase.Open  strSQL, QuotationsDatabaseConnection %>
29:
30:   <table align=center border="2" width="250"
31:   bordercolor="#000080" cellpadding="0" cellspacing="0">
32:   <tr>
33:     <td width="260"><table width="260">
34:       <tr>
35:         <td align="center"><strong><font face="Arial">
36:           Random Quotation</font></strong></td>
```

14

continues

LISTING 14.1. CONTINUED

```
37:        </tr>
38:        <tr>
39:         <td bgcolor=#ffff99><i>"<%= QuotationsDatabase("Quote")%>"
40:          </i></td>
41:        </tr>
42:        <tr>
43:         <td align="right">
44:         By <%= QuotationsDatabase("QuoteAuthor") %>.<BR>
45:         From <%= QuotationsDatabase("QuoteCategory") %>.
46:         </td>
47:        </tr>
48:       </table>
49:      </td>
50:    </tr>
51:    </table>
52: <%
53:      QuotationsDatabase.Close
54:      Set QuotationsDatabase = Nothing
55:      QuotationsDatabaseConnection.Close
56:      Set QuotationsDatabaseConnection = Nothing
57:
58:    End Sub
59:
60:    Dim SQLString, DatabaseConnection, UserRecordset
61:
62:    ' Create an instance of the Connection object.
63:    Set DatabaseConnection = Server.CreateObject("ADODB.Connection")
64:
65:    ' Open a connection to the UPS file DSN.
66:    ' Before the following statement can execute properly, you have to
67:    ' create a file DSN for the UPS database.
68:    DatabaseConnection.Open  "FILEDSN=UserInformationDatabase.dsn"
69:
70:    ' Create an Instance of the Recordset object.
71:    Set UserRecordset = Server.CreateObject("ADODB.Recordset")
72:
73:    ' The Open method of the Recordset object is used to retrieve
74:    ' data from the database.
75:    SQLString = "SELECT Users.Prefix, Users.FirstName, " & _
76:      "Users.LastName, Users.LastAccessDate, Users.LastAccessTime, " & _
77:      "Users.EmailAddress, PersonalSettings.BackgroundColor, " & _
78:      "PersonalSettings.ForegroundColor, " & _
79:      "PersonalSettings.WeatherOfCity, " & _
80:      "PersonalSettings.RandomQuotation FROM Users As Users, " & _
81:      "PersonalSettings AS PersonalSettings, Users " & _
82:      "RIGHT JOIN PersonalSettings ON " & _
83:      "Users.RecordID=PersonalSettings.UserRecordID " & _
84:      "WHERE Users.EmailAddress=" & chr(39) & _
85:      Request.Cookies("UserEmailAddress") & chr(39)
```

```
 86:
 87:    UserRecordset.Open SQLString, DatabaseConnection
 88: %>
 89:
 90: <HTML>
 91: <HEAD>
 92:    <TITLE>User Personalization System: Main Menu</TITLE>
 93: </HEAD>
 94: <% If Not UserRecordset.EOF Then %>
 95:    <BODY bgcolor="#<%= UserRecordset("BackgroundColor") %>"
 96:          text="#<%= UserRecordset("ForegroundColor") %>">
 97: <% Else %>
 98:    <BODY bgcolor="#FFFFFF">
 99: <% End If %>
100:
101: <P><FONT face=Verdana size=5><STRONG> Welcome to the User
102:    Personalization System </STRONG></FONT></P>
103: <%
104:    If Not UserRecordset.EOF Then %>
105:      <TABLE width=610  border=2 bordercolor=#ff3300 bgcolor=FFFFFF>
106:        <TR><TD><P><CENTER><FONT face="Comic Sans MS"
107:          size=4 color=#ff0000 style="BACKGROUND-COLOR: #ffff99">
108:          Welcome Back!</FONT></CENTER><BR>
109:          <FONT face=Verdana><STRONG>This Web page is customized for
110:      <% Response.Write UserRecordset("Prefix") & ". "
111:          Response.Write UserRecordset("FirstName") &  " "
112:          Response.Write UserRecordset("LastName") %></STRONG></FONT>.
113:      <BR>[<FONT face=Arial>Last Modified on
114:      <% Response.Write UserRecordset("LastAccessDate") &  " at "
115:          Response.Write UserRecordset("LastAccessTime") %>
116:      ]</FONT></P>
117:      <TABLE align=center border=0 cellPadding=1 cellSpacing=1
118:          width=550><TR>
119:      <% If UserRecordset("RandomQuotation") = "True" Then %>
120:        <TD vAlign=top><P>
121:          <% DisplayRandomQuotation () %>
122:        </P></TD>
123:      <% End If %>
124:      <% If NOT UserRecordset("WeatherOfCity") = "None" Then %>
125:      <TD vAlign=top><FONT face=Arial><STRONG>Custom
126:        Weather</STRONG></FONT>
127:        <P><IMG SRC="<%=UserRecordset("WeatherOfCity")%>.jpg"></P>
128:      </TD>
129:      <% End If %>
130:      </TR></TABLE>
131:    </TD></TR></TABLE>
132: <%
133:    End If
134:    UserRecordset.Close
135:    Set UserRecordset = Nothing
```

14

continues

LISTING **14.1.** CONTINUED

```
136:    DatabaseConnection.Close
137:    Set DatabaseConnection = Nothing
138: %>
139:
140: <P><strong><font style="BACKGROUND-COLOR: #f0e68c">Active User
141:    Personalization System Menu Options</font></strong></P>
142: <ul>
143:    <li><A href="Personalize.asp">Personalize</A> this Web page</li>
144:    <li><A HREF="DeleteCookie.asp">Delete</A> cookie</li>
145: </ul>
146: <P><STRONG><FONT style="BACKGROUND-COLOR: #f0e68c">Active User
147: Registration System Menu Options</FONT></STRONG></P>
148: <UL>
149:    <LI><A href="AddOrModifyUserInformation.asp">Add/Modify</A>
150:    user information. Please use this link to add or modify your
151:    information.</LI></UL>
152: <P><STRONG><FONT style="BACKGROUND-COLOR: #f0e68c">Active Guest
153:    Book Menu Options</FONT></STRONG></P>
154: <UL>
155:    <LI><A href="AddGuestBookEntry.asp">Add</A>
156:    a new Guest Book entry
157:    <LI><A href="ViewGuestBookEntries.asp">View</A>
158:    Guest Book Entries
159:    <LI><A href="SearchGuestBook.asp">Search</A>
160:    the Guest Book</LI></UL>
161: <HR>
162: This Web page was generated on
163: <%= Date %> at <%= Time %>.
164:
165: <P> </P>
166:
167: </BODY>
168: </HTML>
```

ANALYSIS   The subroutine defined in lines 4–58 retrieves a random quotation from the quotations database and displays it. Line 6 defines the variables used to retrieve and display a random quotation. The file DSN created for the quotations database is specified in line 9. Lines 10 and 11 create an instance of the ADO Connection object, and line 12 opens a connection to the file DSN specified in line 9. A recordset is used to retrieve data from the quotations database. Line 15 instantiates the ADO Recordset object. Pay attention to line 18 because it is important when generating random numbers. Before getting a random number, you should seed the random number generator, as shown in line 18. The SQL statement that actually retrieves a random quotation is specified in lines 23–26. The SQL statement depends on the QuoteID field being a unique integer number between 1 and 186 for each of the 186 quotations in the quotations database.

Caution
If you modify or delete quotations, keep in mind that the QuoteID field should be contiguous between 1 and the number of quotations. For example, if you delete the quotation with the QuoteID 23, you should replace the deleted quotation with another quotation, or the SQL statement will fail if it tries to retrieve the quotation with the QuoteID 23.

Line 28 opens the quotations database and retrieves a random quotation using the SQL statement generated in lines 23–26. Lines 30–51 simply format and display the random quotation. After using a database, you should *always* close the Recordset and Connection objects used to access the database and set them to Nothing, as shown in lines 53–56. The subroutine that retrieves and displays a random quotation ends in line 58. The subroutine is called only if the user has selected to display a random quotation.

The main execution block of the ASP application begins in line 60, where the variables used to access the UPS database are defined. Lines 62–71 should already look quite familiar to you.

Lines 75–85 define the SQL statement that determines whether the user is in the UPS database. Lines 75–81 specify the fields to retrieve from the database. The fields are spread across two database tables. To retrieve fields from multiple tables using a single SQL statement, the common fields of the multiple tables need to be specified with a SQL JOIN statement, as shown in lines 81–83. Line 83 specifies that the RecordID field of the Users table should equal the UserRecordID field of the PersonalSettings table. The WHERE clause of the SQL statement in lines 84 and 85 uses the user's e-mail address stored in the cookie UserEmailAddress to retrieve the user's information (if the user's information is available in the database) from the UPS database.

The value of UserRecordset.EOF is used to determine whether the user's information is found in the database. The If...Then...Else statement in lines 94–99 uses the value of UserRecordset.EOF to specify custom background and text colors for the Web page if the user's information is found in the database. Otherwise, a default background color is used. Lines 105–116 personally greet the user with her name and display the last time the user modified her information. The If statement defined in line 119 checks whether the user has selected to display a random quotation, and if so, displays a random quotation by using the DisplayRandomQuotation () subroutine. The If statement in line 124 displays the weather of the city selected by the user.

The next section demonstrates how to add user information to the database.

14

How to Add User Information to the Database

If a user is not already in the database, a form is displayed to get information about the user. The subroutine in Listing 14.2 displays a form to get information about a new user and also performs limited client-side error checking to make sure the data is valid.

LISTING **14.2.** THIS SUBROUTINE DISPLAYS A FORM TO ADD A NEW USER TO THE DATABASE (`personalize.asp`).

```
 1: <%
 2: ' *****
 3: ' Begin Subroutine GetNewUserInformation (UserEmailAddress)
 4: ' *****
 5: %><% Sub GetNewUserInformation (UserEmailAddress)%>
 6:
 7: <div align="center"><center>
 8: <table border="2" cellpadding="0" cellspacing="0"
 9:   width="500" bordercolor="#800000">
10:     <tr>
11:        <td align="center" bgcolor="#FFFF00"><font face="Arial">
12:          <strong>Please provide us with some information about
13:          yourself</strong></font></td>
14:     </tr>
15:     <tr>
16:        <td width="100%">Please provide us with some information
17:        about yourself so we may add you to our database. Once
18:        you press the Submit button, you will be able to specify
19:        your personal settings.<p> </p>
20:        </td>
21:     </tr>
22: </table>
23: </center></div>
24:
25: <p><font face="Arial" size="4" style="BACKGROUND-COLOR: #ccff99">
26: Your e-mail address was not found in our database.</font></p>
27: <p>Please provide us with some additional information about
28: yourself so we may add you to our database.</p>
29:
30:
31:
32: <!--webbot BOT="GeneratedScript" PREVIEW=" " startspan -->
33: <script Language="JavaScript"><!--
34: function FrontPage_Form3_Validator(theForm)
35: {
36:
37:    if (theForm.FirstName.value == "")
38:    {
39:      alert("Please enter a value for the \"First Name\" field.");
40:      theForm.FirstName.focus();
```

```
41:      return (false);
42:    }
43:
44:    if (theForm.FirstName.value.length < 2)
45:    {
46:      alert("Please enter at least 2 characters in the \"First Name\
         ➡" field.");
47:      theForm.FirstName.focus();
48:      return (false);
49:    }
50:
51:    if (theForm.FirstName.value.length > 30)
52:    {
53:      alert("Please enter at most 30 characters in
         ➡the \"First Name\" field.");
54:      theForm.FirstName.focus();
55:      return (false);
56:    }
57:
58:    if (theForm.LastName.value == "")
59:    {
60:      alert("Please enter a value for the \"Last Name\" field.");
61:      theForm.LastName.focus();
62:      return (false);
63:    }
64:
65:    if (theForm.LastName.value.length < 2)
66:    {
67:      alert("Please enter at least 2 characters in
         ➡the \"Last Name\" field.");
68:      theForm.LastName.focus();
69:      return (false);
70:    }
71:
72:    if (theForm.LastName.value.length > 30)
73:    {
74:      alert("Please enter at most 30 characters in
         ➡the \"Last Name\" field.");
75:      theForm.LastName.focus();
76:      return (false);
77:    }
78:
79:    if (theForm.State.value == "")
80:    {
81:      alert("Please enter a value for the \"Your State\" field.");
82:      theForm.State.focus();
83:      return (false);
84:    }
85:
86:    if (theForm.State.value.length < 2)
```

14

continues

LISTING 14.2. CONTINUED

```
 87:    {
 88:      alert("Please enter at least 2 characters in
        ➥the \"Your State\" field.");
 89:      theForm.State.focus();
 90:      return (false);
 91:    }
 92:
 93:    if (theForm.State.value.length > 2)
 94:    {
 95:      alert("Please enter at most 2 characters in
        ➥the \"Your State\" field.");
 96:      theForm.State.focus();
 97:      return (false);
 98:    }
 99:
100:    if (theForm.City.value == "")
101:    {
102:      alert("Please enter a value for the \"City Name\" field.");
103:      theForm.City.focus();
104:      return (false);
105:    }
106:
107:    if (theForm.City.value.length < 3)
108:    {
109:      alert("Please enter at least 3 characters in
        ➥the \"City Name\" field.");
110:      theForm.City.focus();
111:      return (false);
112:    }
113:
114:    if (theForm.City.value.length > 30)
115:    {
116:      alert("Please enter at most 30 characters in
        ➥the \"City Name\" field.");
117:      theForm.City.focus();
118:      return (false);
119:    }
120:
121:    if (theForm.Country.value == "")
122:    {
123:      alert("Please enter a value for the \"Name of
        ➥your country\" field.");
124:      theForm.Country.focus();
125:      return (false);
126:    }
127:
128:    if (theForm.Country.value.length < 3)
129:    {
130:      alert("Please enter at least 3 characters in the \"Name
        ➥of your country\" field.");
```

```
131:      theForm.Country.focus();
132:      return (false);
133:    }
134:
135:    if (theForm.Country.value.length > 30)
136:    {
137:      alert("Please enter at most 30 characters in the \"Name
          ➥of your country\" field.");
138:      theForm.Country.focus();
139:      return (false);
140:    }
141:    return (true);
142: }
143: //--></script><!--webbot BOT="GeneratedScript" endspan -->
144: <form method="POST" action="Personalize.asp"
145:    onsubmit="return FrontPage_Form3_Validator(this)"
146:    name="FrontPage_Form3">
147:    <p><strong><font face="Arial">Please provide the following
148:    information</font></strong></p>
149:    <div align="left"><table border="0" width="610">
150:      <tr>
151:        <td width="100%" colspan="2">
152:        Mr.<input type="radio" value="Mr" CHECKED name="Prefix">
153:        Ms.<input type="radio" name="Prefix" value="Ms">
154:        <strong>First name</strong>
155:        <!--webbot bot="Validation" S-Display-Name="First Name"
          ➥B-Value-Required="TRUE"

156: I-Minimum-Length="2" I-Maximum-Length="30" -->
157:        <input type="text" name="FirstName" size="12" maxlength="30">
158:          <strong>Last name</strong> <!--webbot bot="Validation"
          ➥S-Display-Name="Last Name"
159: B-Value-Required="TRUE" I-Minimum-Length="2" I-Maximum-Length="30" -->
160:        <input type="text" name="LastName" size="12"
161:          maxlength="30"></td>
162:      </tr>
163:      <tr>
164:        <td width="100%" colspan="2"><div align="center"><center>
165:        <table border="0" width="600">
166:        <tr>
167:          <td width="104"><strong>Email address</strong> </td>
168:          <td width="488">
169:          <input type="hidden" name="EmailAddress"
170:            value="<%= UserEmailAddress %>"> <%= UserEmailAddress %>
171:        </td></tr>
172:        <tr>
173:          <td width="104">URL</td>
174:          <td width="488"><input type="text" name="URL" size="
175:            40" maxlength="49"></td>
176:        </tr>
177:      </table>
```

14

continues

LISTING 14.2. CONTINUED

```
178:        </center></div></td>
179:      </tr>
180:      <tr>
181:        <td width="50%">Phone (<input type="text"
182:          name="PhoneAreaCode" size="3" maxlength="3">)
183:        <input type="text" name="PhoneNumber" size="10"
184:          maxlength="12">
185:        </td><td width="50%">
186:        Mobile (<input type="text" name="MobileAreaCode" size="3"
187:          maxlength="3">)
188:            <input type="text" name="MobilePhoneNumber" size="10"
189:              maxlength="12"></td>
190:      </tr>
191:      <tr>
192:        <td width="100%" colspan="2"><div align="center"><center>
193:          <table border="0" width="600">
194:          <tr>
195:            <td width="105">Date of birth</td>
196:            <td width="487">
197:            <input type="text" name="BirthdayMonth" size="2"> /
198:            <input type="text" name="BirthdayDay" size="2"> /
199:            <input type="text" name="BirthdayYear" size="4">
200:            (MM/DD/YYYY)</td>
201:          </tr>
202:          <tr>
203:            <td width="105">Street address</td>
204:            <td width="487"><input type="text"
205:              name="StreetAddress" size="20" maxlength="49">
206:            <strong>State</strong>
207:            <!--webbot bot="Validation" S-Display-Name="Your
                ➥State" B-Value-Required="TRUE"
208: I-Minimum-Length="2" I-Maximum-Length="2" -->
209:            <input type="text" name="State" size="2" maxlength="2">
210:            Zip Code <input type="text" name="ZipCode" size="10"
211:              maxlength="10"> </td>
212:          </tr>
213:          <tr>
214:            <td width="105"><strong>City</strong> </td>
215:            <td width="487"><!--webbot bot="Validation"
                ➥S-Display-Name="City Name" B-Value-Required="TRUE"
216: I-Minimum-Length="3" I-Maximum-Length="30" -->
217:              <input type="text" name="City" size="20" maxlength="30">
218:              <strong>Country</strong>
219:              <!--webbot bot="Validation" S-Display-Name="Name
                ➥of your country" B-Value-Required="TRUE"
220: I-Minimum-Length="3" I-Maximum-Length="30" -->
221:              <input type="text" name="Country" size="15"
222:                value="United States" maxlength="30"></td>
223:          </tr>
```

```
224:        </table>
225:        </center></div></td>
226:      </tr>
227:    </table>
228:    </div>
229:    </table>
230:    </div><p>
231:      <input type="hidden" name="CurrentStep"
232:        value="NewUserInformation">
233:      <input type="submit" value="Add My Information To The Database"
234:        name="SubmitButton">
235:      <input type="reset" value="Please Reset This Form" name="B2"></p>
236: </form>
237:
238: <% End Sub %>
```

ANALYSIS The `GetNewUserInformation(UserEmailAddress)` subroutine does not contain any complex ASP code. The user's e-mail address that has already been obtained by an HTML form is passed into the subroutine as a parameter, as shown in line 5. Lines 32–143 consists of client-side JavaScript code that performs limited error checking to ensure the data is valid. The HTML form that gets information about the user is defined in lines 144–236. Notice how the user's e-mail address passed into the subroutine is used as a hidden HTML form field in lines 169–170.

When a new user types in information about herself and clicks the Submit button, that information is processed by the `InsertNewUserInformation()` subroutine in Listing 14.3. The `InsertNewUserInformation()` subroutine adds a new user to the UPS database.

 Note

> The client-side JavaScript code you see in code listings is generated automatically by FrontPage to add client-side error checking to Web forms.

LISTING 14.3. THE `InsertNewUserInformation()` SUBROUTINE ADDS A NEW USER TO THE DATABASE (`personalize.asp`).

```
1: <%
2: ' *****
3: ' Begin subroutine.
4: ' *****
5: %><% Sub InsertNewUserInformation ()
6:
```

continues

14

LISTING 14.3. CONTINUED

```
 7:   Dim SQLString, DatabaseConnection
 8:   Dim CommandObject, RecordID, UserRecordset
 9:
10:   ' Create an instance of the Connection object.
11:   Set DatabaseConnection = Server.CreateObject("ADODB.Connection")
12:
13:   ' Open a connection to the UPS file DSN.
14:   ' Before the following statement can execute properly, you have to
15:   ' create a file DSN for the UPS database.
16:   DatabaseConnection.Open  "FILEDSN=UserInformationDatabase.dsn"
17:
18:
19:   ' Create an instance of the Command object.
20:   Set CommandObject= Server.CreateObject("ADODB.Command")
21:
22:   ' The ActiveConnection property is used to connect the Command
      ➥object
23:   ' to the Connection object.
24:   Set CommandObject.ActiveConnection = DatabaseConnection
25:
26:   ' The SQL string that inserts the user's data into the
27:   ' UPS database.
28:   SQLString = "INSERT INTO Users (Prefix, FirstName," & _
29:     "Lastname, EmailAddress, URL, Phone, Mobile, StreetAddress," & _
30:     "City, State, ZipCode, Country, DOB, FirstAccessTime," & _
31:     "FirstAccessDate, FirstAccessIPAddress, FirstAccessWebBrowser," & _
32:     "LastAccessTime, LastAccessDate, LastAccessIP," & _
33:     "LastAccessWebBrowser) VALUES (?,?,?,?,?,?,?,?," & _
34:     "?,?,?,?,?,?,?,?,?,?,?,?,?)"
35:
36:   ' The SQL statement that actually inserts the data is defined.
37:   CommandObject.CommandText = SQLString
38:
39:   ' The prepared or pre-compiled SQL statement defined in the
40:   ' CommandText property is saved.
41:   CommandObject.Prepared = True
42:
43:   ' The parameters of the SQL string are defined below.
44:   CommandObject.Parameters.Append _
45:     CommandObject.CreateParameter("Prefix",200, ,255 )
46:   CommandObject.Parameters.Append _
47:     CommandObject.CreateParameter("FirstName",200, ,255 )
48:   CommandObject.Parameters.Append _
49:     CommandObject.CreateParameter("LastName",200, ,255 )
50:   CommandObject.Parameters.Append _
51:     CommandObject.CreateParameter("EmailAddress",200, ,255 )
52:   CommandObject.Parameters.Append _
53:     CommandObject.CreateParameter("URL",200, ,255 )
54:   CommandObject.Parameters.Append _
```

```
55:     CommandObject.CreateParameter("Phone",200, ,255 )
56: CommandObject.Parameters.Append _
57:     CommandObject.CreateParameter("Mobile",200, ,255 )
58: CommandObject.Parameters.Append _
59:     CommandObject.CreateParameter("StreetAddress",200, ,255 )
60: CommandObject.Parameters.Append _
61:     CommandObject.CreateParameter("City",200, ,255 )
62: CommandObject.Parameters.Append _
63:     CommandObject.CreateParameter("State",200, ,255 )
64: CommandObject.Parameters.Append _
65:     CommandObject.CreateParameter("ZipCode",200, ,255 )
66: CommandObject.Parameters.Append _
67:     CommandObject.CreateParameter("Country",200, ,255 )
68: CommandObject.Parameters.Append _
69:     CommandObject.CreateParameter("DOB",200, ,255 )
70: CommandObject.Parameters.Append _
71:     CommandObject.CreateParameter("FirstAccessTime",200, ,255 )
72: CommandObject.Parameters.Append _
73:     CommandObject.CreateParameter("FirstAccessDate",200, ,255 )
74: CommandObject.Parameters.Append _
75:     CommandObject.CreateParameter("FirstAccessIPAddress",200, ,255 )
76: CommandObject.Parameters.Append _
77:     CommandObject.CreateParameter("FirstAccessWebBrowser",200, ,255 )
78: CommandObject.Parameters.Append _
79:     CommandObject.CreateParameter("LastAccessTime",200, ,255 )
80: CommandObject.Parameters.Append _
81:     CommandObject.CreateParameter("LastAccessDate",200, ,255 )
82: CommandObject.Parameters.Append _
83:     CommandObject.CreateParameter("LastAccessIPAddress",200, ,255 )
84: CommandObject.Parameters.Append _
85:     CommandObject.CreateParameter("LastAccessWebBrowser",200, ,255 )
86:
87:  ' Information entered by the user is added to the database.
88: CommandObject("Prefix") = Request.Form.Item("Prefix")
89: CommandObject("FirstName") = Request.Form.Item("FirstName")
90: CommandObject("LastName") = Request.Form.Item("LastName")
91: CommandObject("EmailAddress") = Request.Form.Item("EmailAddress")
92: CommandObject("URL") = Request.Form.Item("URL")
93:
94:   If IsNumeric (Request.Form.Item("PhoneAreaCode")) Then
95:     CommandObject("Phone") = "(" & _
96:       Request.Form.Item("PhoneAreaCode") & _
97:       ") " & Request.Form.Item("PhoneNumber")
98:   Else
99:     CommandObject("Phone") = Request.Form.Item("PhoneNumber")
100:   End If
101:   If IsNumeric (Request.Form.Item("MobileAreaCode")) Then
102:     CommandObject("Mobile") = "(" & _
103:       Request.Form.Item("MobileAreaCode") _
104:       & ") " & Request.Form.Item("MobilePhoneNumber")
```

14

continues

LISTING **14.3.** CONTINUED

```
105:    Else
106:      CommandObject("Mobile") = Request.Form.Item("MobilePhoneNumber")
107:    End If
108:
109:    CommandObject("StreetAddress") = Request.Form.Item("StreetAddress")
110:    CommandObject("City") = Request.Form.Item("City")
111:    CommandObject("State") = Request.Form.Item("State")
112:    CommandObject("ZipCode") = Request.Form.Item("ZipCode")
113:    CommandObject("Country") = Request.Form.Item("Country")
114:
115:      If IsDate(Request.Form.Item("BirthdayMonth") & _
116:        "/" & Request.Form.Item("BirthdayDay")  & "/" & _
117:          Request.Form.Item("BirthdayYear") ) = True Then
118:          CommandObject ("DOB") = _
119:            Request.Form.Item("BirthdayMonth") & "/"  & _
120:              Request.Form.Item("BirthdayDay")  & "/" & _
121:              Request.Form.Item("BirthdayYear")
122:      Else
123:        CommandObject ("DOB") = ""
124:      End If
125:
126:    CommandObject("FirstAccessTime") = Time
127:    CommandObject("FirstAccessDate") = Date
128:    CommandObject("FirstAccessIPAddress") = _
129:      Request.ServerVariables.Item ("REMOTE_ADDR")
130:    CommandObject("FirstAccessWebBrowser") = _
131:      Request.ServerVariables.Item ("HTTP_USER_AGENT")
132:    CommandObject("LastAccessTime") = Time
133:    CommandObject("LastAccessDate") = Date
134:    CommandObject("LastAccessIPAddress") = _
135:      Request.ServerVariables.Item ("REMOTE_ADDR")
136:    CommandObject("LastAccessWebBrowser") = _
137:      Request.ServerVariables.Item ("HTTP_USER_AGENT")
138:
139:    CommandObject.Execute ()
140:
141:    'Instantiate a Recordset object.
142:    Set UserRecordset = Server.CreateObject("ADODB.Recordset")
143:
144:    'Open a recordset using the Open method
145:    'and use the connection established by the Connection object.
146:
147:    SQLString ="SELECT Users.RecordID, Users.EmailAddress " & _
148:      "FROM Users " & _
149:      "WHERE Users.EmailAddress=" & Chr(39) & _
150:      Request.Form.Item("EmailAddress") & Chr(39)
151:
152:    UserRecordset.Open  SQLString, DatabaseConnection
```

```
153:    RecordID = UserRecordset("RecordID")
154:
155:    DatabaseConnection.Close
156:    Set DatabaseConnection = Nothing
157:
158:    ModifyPersonalSettings Request.Form.Item("EmailAddress"), RecordID
159:
160: End Sub
161: %>
```

ANALYSIS Lines 7 and 8 define variables used to add a new user to the database. The ASP statements in lines 10–24 should be nothing new to you. They instantiate and initialize ADO objects required to access the database. The SQL string that inserts the user's data is defined in lines 28–34. The VALUES statement in lines 33 and 34 allows apostrophes and other miscellaneous characters (ones that can sabotage a SQL statement) as part of data entered by the user. Lines 43–85 create the parameters used to add a new record to the database. The values of the parameters are specified in lines 87–137. Notice how the Request.Form.Item() method is used to retrieve data entered by the user. Line 139 uses the Command object's Execute() method to add the user's information to the database's Users table. The ASP statements in lines 141–156 get the RecordID of the new data record inserted into the database. The RecordID value is passed to the ModifyPersonalSettings() subroutine in line 158 so that the user's settings (in the PersonalSettings table) can be properly inserted into the database to reference the user's information (in the Users table).

The next section examines how to modify information about an existing user in the database.

How to Modify User Information in the Database

An existing user in the database is given the opportunity to review and modify his or her personal information that's already in the database. The ASP code in Listing 14.4 shows a form containing information about the user that's already in the database. The user can either accept the information in the form or make any necessary modifications and submit the form. After the form is submitted, the user can specify personalization settings.

LISTING 14.4. THE FOLLOWING ASP SUBROUTINE IS USED TO REVIEW AND UPDATE INFORMATION ABOUT AN EXISTING USER (personalize.asp).

```
1: <%
2: ' *****
3: ' Begin subroutine ReviewUserInformation (UserRecordset).
4: ' *****
```

14

continues

LISTING **14.4.** CONTINUED

```
 5: %><% Sub ReviewUserInformation (UserRecordset) %>
 6:
 7: <table border="2" cellpadding="0" cellspacing="0" width="500"
 8:   bordercolor="#800000">
 9:     <tr>
10:       <td align="center" bgcolor="#FFFF00"><font face="Arial">
11:       <strong>Please review your information</strong></font></td>
12:     </tr>
13:     <tr>
14:         <td width="100%">Your e-mail address was found in the
15:         database. Please verify that the following information about
16:         yourself is accurate. Please make any necessary changes
17:         and press the Update/Proceed button to specify your
18:         personal settings.
19:         </td>
20:     </tr>
21: </table>
22:
23: <p><font face="Arial" size="4" style="BACKGROUND-COLOR: #ffcc99">
24: You are already in our database.</font></p><p>
25: Please modify the information you see below and press the
26: update button.</p>
27:
28:
29: <!--webbot BOT="GeneratedScript" PREVIEW=" " startspan
    �español--><script Language="JavaScript"><!--
30: function FrontPage_Form2_Validator(theForm)
31: {
32:
33:   if (theForm.FirstName.value == "")
34:   {
35:     alert("Please enter a value for the \"First Name\" field.");
36:     theForm.FirstName.focus();
37:     return (false);
38:   }
39:
40:   if (theForm.FirstName.value.length < 2)
41:   {
42:     alert("Please enter at least 2 characters in
          �español the \"First Name\" field.");
43:     theForm.FirstName.focus();
44:     return (false);
45:   }
46:
47:   if (theForm.FirstName.value.length > 30)
48:   {
49:     alert("Please enter at most 30 characters in
          �español the \"First Name\" field.");
50:     theForm.FirstName.focus();
```

```
51:     return (false);
52:   }
53:
54:   if (theForm.LastName.value == "")
55:   {
56:     alert("Please enter a value for the \"Last Name\" field.");
57:     theForm.LastName.focus();
58:     return (false);
59:   }
60:
61:   if (theForm.LastName.value.length < 2)
62:   {
63:     alert("Please enter at least 2 characters in
       ➡the \"Last Name\" field.");
64:     theForm.LastName.focus();
65:     return (false);
66:   }
67:
68:   if (theForm.LastName.value.length > 30)
69:   {
70:     alert("Please enter at most 30 characters in
       ➡the \"Last Name\" field.");
71:     theForm.LastName.focus();
72:     return (false);
73:   }
74:
75:   if (theForm.EmailAddress.value == "")
76:   {
77:     alert("Please enter a value for the \"E-mail Address\" field.");
78:     theForm.EmailAddress.focus();
79:     return (false);
80:   }
81:
82:   if (theForm.EmailAddress.value.length < 7)
83:   {
84:     alert("Please enter at least 7 characters in
       ➡the \"E-mail Address\" field.");
85:     theForm.EmailAddress.focus();
86:     return (false);
87:   }
88:
89:   if (theForm.EmailAddress.value.length > 49)
90:   {
91:     alert("Please enter at most 49 characters in
       ➡the \"E-mail Address\" field.");
92:     theForm.EmailAddress.focus();
93:     return (false);
94:   }
95:
96:   if (theForm.State.value == "")
```

14

continues

LISTING **14.4.** CONTINUED

```
 97:   {
 98:     alert("Please enter a value for the \"Your State\" field.");
 99:     theForm.State.focus();
100:     return (false);
101:   }
102:
103:   if (theForm.State.value.length < 2)
104:   {
105:     alert("Please enter at least 2 characters in
        ➥the \"Your State\" field.");
106:     theForm.State.focus();
107:     return (false);
108:   }
109:
110:   if (theForm.State.value.length > 2)
111:   {
112:     alert("Please enter at most 2 characters in
        ➥the \"Your State\" field.");
113:     theForm.State.focus();
114:     return (false);
115:   }
116:
117:   if (theForm.City.value == "")
118:   {
119:     alert("Please enter a value for the \"City Name\" field.");
120:     theForm.City.focus();
121:     return (false);
122:   }
123:
124:   if (theForm.City.value.length < 3)
125:   {
126:     alert("Please enter at least 3 characters in
        ➥the \"City Name\" field.");
127:     theForm.City.focus();
128:     return (false);
129:   }
130:
131:   if (theForm.City.value.length > 30)
132:   {
133:     alert("Please enter at most 30 characters in
        ➥the \"City Name\" field.");
134:     theForm.City.focus();
135:     return (false);
136:   }
137:
138:   if (theForm.Country.value == "")
139:   {
140:     alert("Please enter a value for the \"Name of
        ➥your country\" field.");
```

```
141:     theForm.Country.focus();
142:     return (false);
143:   }
144:
145:   if (theForm.Country.value.length < 3)
146:   {
147:     alert("Please enter at least 3 characters in the \"Name
         ➡of your country\" field.");
148:     theForm.Country.focus();
149:     return (false);
150:   }
151:
152:   if (theForm.Country.value.length > 30)
153:   {
154:     alert("Please enter at most 30 characters in the \"Name
         ➡of your country\" field.");
155:     theForm.Country.focus();
156:     return (false);
157:   }
158:   return (true);
159: }
160: //--></script><!--webbot BOT="GeneratedScript" endspan -->
161:   <form method="POST" action="Personalize.asp"
162:     onsubmit="return FrontPage_Form2_Validator(this)"
163:     name="FrontPage_Form2">
164:   <p><strong><font face="Arial">Please provide the following
165:     information </font></strong></p>
166:   <div align="left"><table border="0" width="610">
167:     <tr>
168:       <td width="100%" colspan="2">
169:       <% If UserRecordset("Prefix")="Mr" Then %>
170:         Mr.<input type="radio" value="Mr" CHECKED name="Prefix">
171:         Ms.<input type="radio" name="Prefix" value="Ms">
172:       <% Else %>
173:         Mr.<input type="radio" value="Mr" name="Prefix">
174:         Ms.<input type="radio" CHECKED name="Prefix" value="Ms">
175:       <% End If %>
176:       <strong>First name</strong>
177:       <!--webbot bot="Validation" S-Display-Name="First Name"
         ➡B-Value-Required="TRUE"
178: I-Minimum-Length="2" I-Maximum-Length="30" -->
179:       <input type="text" name="FirstName" size="12" maxlength="30"
180:         value="<%= UserRecordset("FirstName")%>">
181:       <strong>Last name</strong> <!--webbot bot="Validation"
         ➡S-Display-Name="Last Name"
182: B-Value-Required="TRUE" I-Minimum-Length="2" I-Maximum-Length="30" -->
183:       <input type="text" name="LastName" size="12" maxlength="30"
184:           value="<%= UserRecordset("LastName")%>"></td>
185:     </tr>
186:     <tr>
```

14

continues

LISTING 14.4. CONTINUED

```
187:        <td width="100%" colspan="2"><div align="center"><center>
188:          <table border="0" width="600">
189:          <tr>
190:            <td width="104"><strong>Email address</strong> </td>
191:            <td width="488"><!--webbot bot="Validation"
               ➥S-Display-Name="E-mail Address"
192: B-Value-Required="TRUE" I-Minimum-Length="7" I-Maximum-Length="49" -->
193:            <input type="text" name="EmailAddress"
194:              value="<%= UserRecordset("EmailAddress")%>">
195:          </td></tr>
196:          <tr>
197:            <td width="104">URL</td>
198:            <td width="488"><input type="text" name="URL"
199:              value="<%= UserRecordset("URL")%>" size="40"
200:            maxlength="49"></td>
201:          </tr>
202:          </table>
203:          </center></div></td>
204:        </tr>
205:        <tr>
206:          <td width="50%">Phone (<input type="text"
207:            name="PhoneAreaCode" size="3" maxlength="3"
208:            value="<%= Mid (UserRecordset("Phone"),2,3) %>">)
209:          <input type="text" name="PhoneNumber" size="10"
210:            value="<%= Mid (UserRecordset("Phone"),6)%>" maxlength="12">
211:          </td><td width="50%">
212:          Mobile (<input type="text" name="MobileAreaCode" size="3"
213:            value="<%= Mid (UserRecordset("Mobile"),2,3) %>"
214:            maxlength="3">)<input type="text" name="MobilePhoneNumber"
215:            value="<%= Mid (UserRecordset("Mobile"),6)%>" size="10"
216:            maxlength="12"></td>
217:        </tr>
218:        <tr>
219:          <td width="100%" colspan="2"><div align="center"><center>
220:            <table border="0" width="600">
221:            <tr>
222:            <td width="105">Date of birth</td>
223:            <td width="487">
224:            <% On Error Resume Next %>
225:            <input type="text" name="BirthdayMonth"
226:              size="2" value="<%= Month(UserRecordset("DOB"))%>"> /
227:            <input type="text" name="BirthdayDay" size="2"
228:              value="<%= Day(UserRecordset("DOB"))%>"> /
229:            <input type="text" name="BirthdayYear"
230:              size="4" value="<%= Year(UserRecordset("DOB"))%>">
231:            (MM/DD/YYYY)</td>
232:          </tr>
233:          <tr>
234:            <td width="105">Street address</td>
```

```
235:              <td width="487"><input type="text" name="StreetAddress"
236:                value="<%= UserRecordset("StreetAddress")%>" size="20"
237:                maxlength="49"> <strong>State</strong>
238:              <!--webbot bot="Validation" S-Display-Name="Your
              ➥State" B-Value-Required="TRUE"
239: I-Minimum-Length="2" I-Maximum-Length="2" -->
240:              <input type="text" name="State" size="2" maxlength="2"
241:                value="<%= UserRecordset("State")%>">
242:              Zip Code <input type="text" name="ZipCode" size="10"
243:                value="<%= UserRecordset("ZipCode")%>"
              ➥maxlength="10"></td>
244:          </tr>
245:          <tr>
246:            <td width="105"><strong>City</strong> </td>
247:            <td width="487"><!--webbot bot="Validation"
            ➥S-Display-Name="City Name" B-Value-Required="TRUE"

248: I-Minimum-Length="3" I-Maximum-Length="30" -->
249:                <input type="text" name="City" size="20"
250:                  maxlength="30" value="<%= UserRecordset("City")%>">
251:                <strong>Country</strong>
252:                <!--webbot bot="Validation" S-Display-Name="Name
                ➥of your country" B-Value-Required="TRUE"
253: I-Minimum-Length="3" I-Maximum-Length="30" -->
254:                <input type="text" name="Country" size="15"
255:                  value="<%= UserRecordset("Country")%>"
256:                  maxlength="30"></td>
257:          </tr>
258:        </table>
259:        </center></div></td>
260:      </tr>
261:    </table>
262:  </div>
263:  </table>
264:  </div><p>
265:    <input type="hidden" name="CurrentStep"
266:      value="UpdateUserInformation">
267:    <input type="hidden" name="RecordID"
268:      value="<%= UserRecordset("RecordID")%>">
269:    <input type="submit"
270:      value="Update My Information" name="SubmitButton"></p>
271: </form>
272: </center></div>
273: <% End Sub %>
```

14

ANALYSIS A recordset containing existing information about the user is passed into the subroutine with the variable UserRecordset, as shown in line 5. This subroutine displays a form with information about the user already in the database. Lines 29–160 contain the client-side JavaScript code that performs limited client-side error checking.

The ASP code in lines 164–264 displays an HTML form containing information about the user already in the database. The hidden form variable defined in lines 265 and 266 is very important. It indicates that the information in the form should be used to modify an existing database record, not to insert a new database record. The hidden form variable RecordID, defined in lines 267 and 268, specifies the RecordID of the user's record. This information is used when adding personal settings to the PersonalSettings table so that its records refer to the correct user in the Users table.

The UpdateUserInformation() subroutine, in Listing 14.5, makes modifications specified by the user to an existing record in the database.

LISTING **14.5.** UPDATES USER INFORMATION IN THE UPS DATABASE (Personalize.asp).

```
 1: <%
 2: ' *****
 3: ' Begin subroutine UpdateUserInformation().
 4: ' *****
 5: %><% Sub UpdateUserInformation ()
 6:
 7:    Dim SQLString, DatabaseConnection, UserRecordSet, RecordID
 8:
 9:    ' Create an instance of the Connection object.
10:    Set DatabaseConnection = Server.CreateObject("ADODB.Connection")
11:
12:    ' Open a connection to the UPS file DSN.
13:    ' Before the following statement can execute properly, you have to
14:    ' create a file DSN for the UPS database as outlined in the
15:    ' book.
16:    DatabaseConnection.Open  "FILEDSN=UserInformationDatabase.dsn"
17:
18:    ' Create an instance of the Recordset object.
19:    Set UserRecordset = Server.CreateObject("ADODB.Recordset")
20:
21:    ' Retrieve the recordset containing the user's data.
22:    ' Notice how the recordset is opened so that you can use the
23:    ' Update method of the Recordset object to modify the user's
24:    ' data.
25:
26:    UserRecordSet.CursorType = 1
27:    UserRecordSet.CursorLocation = 2
28:    UserRecordSet.LockType = 3
29:    UserRecordSet.ActiveConnection = DatabaseConnection
30:    UserRecordSet.Source = "Users"
31:    UserRecordSet.Filter = "RecordID = " &
       ➥Request.Form.Item("RecordID")
32:
33:    ' The Open method of the Recordset object is used to retrieve
34:    ' data from the user registration database.
```

```
35:
36:   UserRecordset.Open
37:
38:   If UserRecordset.EOF Then
39:     Response.Write ("<H1>Your record was not found.</H1>")
40:   Else
41:
42:     UserRecordset.Fields.Item ("Prefix") = _
43:       Request.Form.Item("Prefix")
44:     UserRecordset.Fields.Item ("FirstName") = _
45:       Request.Form.Item("FirstName")
46:     UserRecordset.Fields.Item ("Lastname") = _
47:       Request.Form.Item("Lastname")
48:     UserRecordset.Fields.Item ("EmailAddress") = _
49:       Request.Form.Item("EmailAddress")
50:     UserRecordset.Fields.Item ("URL") = _
51:       Request.Form.Item("URL")
52:
53:     If IsNumeric (Request.Form.Item("PhoneAreaCode")) Then
54:       UserRecordset.Fields.Item ("Phone")  = "(" & _
55:        Request.Form.Item("PhoneAreaCode") & _
56:        ") " & Request.Form.Item("PhoneNumber")
57:     Else
58:       UserRecordset.Fields.Item ("Phone")  = _
59:         Request.Form.Item("PhoneNumber")
60:     End If
61:     If IsNumeric (Request.Form.Item("MobileAreaCode")) Then
62:       UserRecordset.Fields.Item ("Mobile") = "(" & _
63:         Request.Form.Item("MobileAreaCode") _
64:         & ") " & Request.Form.Item("MobilePhoneNumber")
65:     Else
66:       UserRecordset.Fields.Item ("Mobile") = _
67:         Request.Form.Item("MobilePhoneNumber")
68:     End If
69:
70:     UserRecordset.Fields.Item ("StreetAddress") = _
71:       Request.Form.Item("StreetAddress")
72:     UserRecordset.Fields.Item ("City") = _
73:       Request.Form.Item("City")
74:     UserRecordset.Fields.Item ("State") = _
75:       Request.Form.Item("State")
76:     UserRecordset.Fields.Item ("ZipCode") = _
77:       Request.Form.Item("ZipCode")
78:     UserRecordset.Fields.Item ("Country") = _
79:       Request.Form.Item("Country")
80:     If IsDate(Request.Form.Item("BirthdayMonth") & _
81:       "/" & Request.Form.Item("BirthdayDay")  & "/" & _
82:       Request.Form.Item("BirthdayYear") ) = True Then
83:       UserRecordset.Fields.Item ("DOB") = _
84:         Request.Form.Item("BirthdayMonth") & "/"  & _
```

14

continues

LISTING 14.5. CONTINUED

```
85:            Request.Form.Item("BirthdayDay")  & "/" & _
86:            Request.Form.Item("BirthdayYear")
87:     End If
88:     UserRecordset.Fields.Item ("LastAccessDate") = Date
89:     UserRecordset.Fields.Item ("LastAccessTime") = Time
90:     UserRecordset.Fields.Item ("LastAccessIP") = _
91:       Request.ServerVariables.Item ("REMOTE_ADDR")
92:     UserRecordset.Fields.Item ("LastAccessWebBrowser") = _
93:       Request.ServerVariables.Item ("HTTP_USER_AGENT")
94:
95:     UserRecordSet.Update
96:     RecordID = UserRecordset.Fields.Item ("RecordID")
97:
98:    End If
99:
100:    ' Database connections should ALWAYS be closed after they are used.
101:    UserRecordSet.Close
102:    Set UserRecordSet = Nothing
103:    DatabaseConnection.Close
104:    Set DatabaseConnection = Nothing
105:
106:    ModifyPersonalSettings Request.Form.Item("EmailAddress"),RecordID
107:
108: End Sub
109: %>
```

ANALYSIS   Lines 26–31 specify properties of the Recordset object before using the Open() method in line 36 to access the database. The following list describes the purpose of each of the properties set in those lines. For additional information about the ADO properties, please refer to Day 11, "Building Database Applications Using ActiveX Data Objects."

Property	Description
CursorType	The CursorType property indicates the type of cursor used by the recordset. It specifies how records of the database are browsed. A value of 1 specifies a keyset cursor.
CursorLocation	A value of 2 for the CursorLocation property specifies using a server-side cursor.
LockType	This property specifies how records are locked while being edited. A value of 3 means using optimistic locking, which locks records only when the Update() method is called.

ActiveConnection	Specifies the ADO `Connection` object used to connect to the database. In this case, the `DatabaseConnection` object is used.
Source	Specifies the table where data is obtained. In this case, the data is retrieved from the `Users` table.
Filter	Used to filter only the records you are interested in. The value `"RecordID = " &` `Request.Form.Item("RecordID")` retrieves the record whose `RecordID` field is equal to the value of `Request.Form.Item("RecordID")`.

Note

For a list of ADO constants that can be used in ASP applications, refer to the file `\Program Files\Common Files\System\ADO\adovbs.inc`. You can use ADO constants (`adLockReadOnly`, `adLockPessimistic`, `adLockOptimistic`, and so forth) in your ASP files by including this file using server-side includes.

You can easily include the ADO constant definitions file by copying it to the Includes directory of your Web server's document root directory (create the Includes directory if it does not exist) and using the following statement at the beginning of the ASP file:

```
<!--#Include virtual ="/Includes/adovbs.inc " -->
```

The `If` statement in line 38 checks to see if there's a record whose `RecordID` field is equal to the value of `Request.Form.Item("RecordID")`. If a record is found, the `Else` clause replaces the existing values of the database record with values entered by the user. Line 95 uses the `Update()` method to update the changes to the database. Line 106 calls the `ModifyPersonalSettings ()` subroutine, which displays a form that allows the user to select personal settings.

The next section examines how a user's personal settings are stored in the UPS database.

How to Modify Personalization Settings

The ASP code in Listing 14.6 displays a form used to get custom information to display. The subroutine in Listing 14.6 is called after a user information record is either added or modified.

14

LISTING 14.6. THE FOLLOWING ASP CODE DISPLAYS THE FORM USED TO SELECT CUSTOM INFORMATION TO BE DISPLAYED (personalize.asp).

```
 1: <%
 2: ' *****
 3: ' Begin subroutine DisplayPersonalizationForm().
 4: ' *****
 5: %> <% Sub ModifyPersonalSettings (UserEmailAddress,RecordID) %>
 6:
 7: <table border="2" cellpadding="0" cellspacing="0"
 8:   align="center" width="500" bordercolor="#008000">
 9:     <tr>
10:         <td align="center" bgcolor="#FFFF00"><font face="Arial">
11:         <strong>Please specify your personal settings</strong>
12:         </font></td>
13:     </tr>
14:     <tr>
15:         <td width="100%">Please use the following form to specify
16:         your personal settings. Once you enter your personal
17:         settings and press the Submit button, you will be
18:         transferred to your newly personalized Web page.
19:         <form ACTION="ModifyPersonalizationSettings.asp"
20:           METHOD="POST" NAME="DataForm">
21:         <% DisplayPersonalizationSettings () %>
22:           <input type="hidden" name="RecordID"
23:             value="<%= RecordID %>">
24:           <input type="hidden" name="UserEmailAddress"
25:             value="<%= UserEmailAddress %>">
26:           <input TYPE="Submit" VALUE="Update My Personal Settings"
27:             name="SubmitPersonalizationSettings">
28:         </form>
29:         <p><em>Thank you for using the User Personalization
30:         System!</em></p>
31:         </td>
32:     </tr>
33: </table>
34:
35: <% End Sub %>
```

ANALYSIS Most of the subroutine consists of standard HTML statements. Line 21 calls the DisplayPersonalizationSettings() subroutine, which displays personalization settings the user can select, including background and text colors, a random quotation, and the weather of a predefined city. Refer to Listing 14.7 for the code of the DisplayPersonalizationSettings() subroutine.

LISTING 14.7. DISPLAYS PERSONALIZATION SETTINGS (personalize.asp).

```
1: <%
2: ' *****
3: ' Begin subroutine.
4: ' *****
5: %> <% Sub DisplayPersonalizationSettings %>
6:
7:     <div align="center"><center>
8:     <p><font face="Verdana"><strong>Please select the colors
9:     of Web page elements</strong></font></p>
10:
11:     <table border="4" width="450">
12:     <tr><td><table>
13:     <tr><td BGCOLOR="99FF99">
14:     <font face="Comic Sans MS">
15:     <strong>Please select the background color</strong>
16:     </font></td></tr>
17:     <tr><td BGCOLOR="CCCCCC">
18:     <input TYPE="RADIO" NAME="Background" VALUE="CCCCCC">CCCCCC
19:     </td></tr>
20:     <tr><td BGCOLOR="FFFF99">
21:     <input TYPE="RADIO" NAME="Background" VALUE="FFFF99" CHECKED>FFFF99
22:     </td></tr>
23:     <tr><td BGCOLOR="CCFF99">
24:     <input TYPE="RADIO" NAME="Background" VALUE="CCFF99">CCFF99
25:     </td></tr>
26:     <tr><td BGCOLOR="999933">
27:     <input TYPE="RADIO" NAME="Background" VALUE="999933">999933
28:     </td></tr>
29:     <tr><td BGCOLOR="004400">
30:     <input TYPE="RADIO" NAME="Background" VALUE="004400">
31:     <font COLOR="FFFFFF">004400</font>
32:     </td></tr>
33:     <tr><td BGCOLOR="000000">
34:     <input TYPE="RADIO" NAME="Background" VALUE="000000">
35:     <font COLOR="FFFFFF">000000</font>
36:     </td></tr>
37:     </table></td>
38:     <td><table>
39:     <tr><td BGCOLOR="99FF99">
40:     <font face="Comic Sans MS">
41:     <strong>Please select the text color</strong>
42:     </font>
43:     </td></tr>
44:     <tr><td BGCOLOR="CCCCCC">
45:     <input TYPE="RADIO" NAME="Text" VALUE="CCCCCC" CHECKED>CCCCCC
46:     </td></tr>
47:     <tr><td BGCOLOR="FFFF99">
48:     <input TYPE="RADIO" NAME="Text" VALUE="FFFF99">FFFF99
```

14

continues

LISTING 14.7. CONTINUED

```
49:    </td></tr>
50:    <tr><td BGCOLOR="CCFF99">
51:    <input TYPE="RADIO" NAME="Text" VALUE="CCFF99">CCFF99
52:    </td></tr>
53:    <tr><td BGCOLOR="999933">
54:    <input TYPE="RADIO" NAME="Text" VALUE="999933">999933
55:    </td></tr>
56:    <tr><td BGCOLOR="004400">
57:    <input TYPE="RADIO" NAME="Text" VALUE="004400" CHECKED>
58:    <font COLOR="FFFFFF">004400</font>
59:    </td></tr>
60:    <tr><td BGCOLOR="000000">
61:    <input TYPE="RADIO" NAME="Text" VALUE="000000">
62:    <font COLOR="FFFFFF">000000</font>
63:    </td></tr>
64:    </table>
65:    </td></tr></table>
66:
67:    <p><font face="Verdana"><strong>Which city's weather are you
68:    most interested in?</strong></font></p>
69:
70:    <table width="450">
71:      <tr><td>
72:        <input TYPE="RADIO" NAME="City" CHECKED VALUE="WashingtonDC">
73:        <b>Washington DC</b>
74:      </td><td>
75:        <input TYPE="RADIO" NAME="City" VALUE="NewYork"><b>New York</b>
76:      </td></tr>
77:      <tr><td>
78:        <input TYPE="RADIO" NAME="City" VALUE="Redmond"><b>Redmond</b>
79:      </td><td>
80:        <input TYPE="RADIO" NAME="City" VALUE="Chicago"><b>Chicago</b>
81:      </td><td>
82:        <input TYPE="RADIO" NAME="City" VALUE="None"><b>None</b>
83:      </td></tr>
84:    </table>
85:
86:    <p><font face="Verdana"><strong>Would you like to see a random
87:    quotation displayed?</strong></font></p>
88:      <input TYPE="RADIO" NAME="Quotation" CHECKED
89:        VALUE="True"><b>Yes, please.</b>
90:      <input TYPE="RADIO" NAME="Quotation"
91:        VALUE="False"><b>No. Thank you.</b>
92:    <p> </p></center></div>
93:
94: <%
95: End Sub
96: %>
```

ANALYSIS The entire subroutine consists of standard HTML statements that should be familiar to you. After the user selects custom information and clicks the Submit button, that information is processed by the ASP application `ModifyPersonalizationSettings.asp` (see Listing 14.8).

LISTING 14.8. THE FOLLOWING ASP CODE INSERTS OR MODIFIES PERSONAL SETTINGS IN THE UPS DATABASE (`ModifyPersonalizationSettings.asp`).

```
 1: <%@ Language=VBScript %>
 2: <% Option Explicit %>
 3: <HTML>
 4: <HEAD>
 5:
 6: <%
 7: ' *****
 8: ' Begin subroutine InsertNewRecord(UserEmailAddress,RecordID).
 9: ' *****
10: %> <% Sub InsertNewRecord (UserRecordID)
11:
12:    Dim SQLDataInsertionString
13:
14:    ' The SQL string that inserts the personal settings
15:    ' of the user into the UPS database is created.
16:    SQLDataInsertionString = "INSERT INTO PersonalSettings (" & _
17:      "UserRecordID,BackgroundColor," & _
18:      "ForegroundColor,WeatherOfCity,RandomQuotation) " & _
19:      "VALUES (" & UserRecordID & ", " & Chr(39) & _
20:      Request.Form.Item("Background") & Chr(39) & ", " & _
21:      Chr(39) & Request.Form.Item("Text") & Chr(39) & "," & _
22:      Chr(39) & Request.Form.Item("City") & Chr(39) & ", " & _
23:      Request.Form.Item("Quotation") & ")"
24:
25:    DatabaseConnection.Execute SQLDataInsertionString
26:
27: End Sub %>
28:
29:
30: <TITLE>Personal Settings Updated!</TITLE>
31: </HEAD>
32: <BODY>
33: <P> </P>
34: <%
35:    Dim DatabaseConnection, UserRecordset, RecordID
36:
37:    RecordID = Request.Form.Item ("RecordID")
38:
39:    ' Create an instance of the Connection object.
40:    Set DatabaseConnection = Server.CreateObject("ADODB.Connection")
```

14

continues

LISTING 14.8. CONTINUED

```
41:
42:   ' Open a connection to the UPS file DSN.
43:   ' Before the following statement can execute properly, you have to
44:   ' create a file DSN for the user information database.
45:   DatabaseConnection.Open  "FILEDSN=UserInformationDatabase.dsn"
46:
47:   'Instantiate a Recordset object.
48:   Set UserRecordset = Server.CreateObject("ADODB.Recordset")
49:
50:   ' Retrieve the recordset containing the user's data.
51:   ' Notice how the recordset is opened so that you can use the
52:   ' Update method of the Recordset object to modify the user's
53:   ' data.
54:
55:   UserRecordSet.CursorType = 1
56:   UserRecordSet.CursorLocation = 2
57:   UserRecordSet.LockType = 3
58:   UserRecordSet.ActiveConnection = DatabaseConnection
59:   UserRecordSet.Source = "PersonalSettings"
60:   UserRecordSet.Filter = "UserRecordID = " & RecordID
61:
62:   'Open a recordset by using the Open method
63:   'and use the connection established by the Connection object.
64:
65:   UserRecordset.Open
66:
67:   If UserRecordset.EOF Then
68:     UserRecordset.Close
69:     Set UserRecordset = Nothing
70:     InsertNewRecord (RecordID)
71:   Else
72:     UserRecordset("BackgroundColor") = Request.Form.Item("Background")
73:     UserRecordset("ForegroundColor") = Request.Form.Item("Text")
74:     UserRecordset("WeatherOfCity") = Request.Form.Item("City")
75:     UserRecordset("RandomQuotation") = Request.Form.Item("Quotation")
76:     UserRecordset.Update
77:     UserRecordset.Close
78:     Set UserRecordset = Nothing
79:   End If
80:
81:   DatabaseConnection.Close
82:   Set DatabaseConnection = Nothing
83: %>
84: <H2>Your personal settings have been updated.</H2>
85: <P> </P>
86: <HR>
87: <A HREF="Default.asp">View</A> your very own personalized Web page!
88:
89: </BODY>
90: </HTML>
```

ANALYSIS The main execution block begins at line 35. Line 37 gets the `RecordID` passed from the Personalization form in Listing 14.6. You use this value to filter on the user's `RecordID` field. The `If` statement in line 67 checks to see if the user's personal settings are already in the UPS database. If they aren't, line 70 calls the `InsertNewRecord()` subroutine to insert a new record into the `PersonalSettings` table. If a record is found, the `Else` clause defined in lines 72–78 modifies the user's personal settings already in the database.

You already know that a cookie is used to keep track of the user's e-mail address. The next section shows you how to use ASP code to delete the cookie containing the user's e-mail address.

How to Reset the Cookie

Listing 14.9 shows the code for `DeleteCookie.asp`. The ASP application in this listing deletes the cookie used to keep track of a user's e-mail address. When using cookies, it is a good idea to always give users a way to reset the cookie if needed. A cookie can be deleted by setting its expiration date to a date that has already elapsed.

LISTING 14.9. THE ASP CODE THAT DELETES THE COOKIE IS USED TO KEEP TRACK OF A USER'S E-MAIL ADDRESS (`DeleteCookie.asp`).

```
 1: <%@ Language=VBScript %>
 2: <%
 3:    ' The cookie is deleted by using the Response
 4:    ' object (the expiration date is set to a date that has elapsed).
 5:    Response.Cookies("UserEmailAddress").Expires = _
 6:       "February 29, 1996"
 7: %>
 8: <HTML>
 9: <HEAD>
10:
11: <TITLE>Cookie Deleted</TITLE>
12: </HEAD>
13: <BODY>
14: <H1>Cookie Deleted</H1>
15: <H3>Personal Settings For Your Computer Have Been Reset</H3>
16: <P>
17: <A HREF="Default.asp">Return</A> to main menu.
18: </P>
19: </BODY>
20: </HTML>
```

14

Lines 5 and 6 delete the cookie (UserEmailAddress) used to keep track of the user's e-mail address by setting its expiration date to a date that has already elapsed (February 29, 1996).

> **Caution**
>
> You can use the Request object to get the value of a cookie anywhere in an ASP application. However, when using the Response object to set the value of a cookie, you should do so before any HTML text is sent to the Web browser.

Examining User Information in the Database

All the information about the user, including the user's personalization settings, is stored in two tables, shown in Figure 14.14, of the UPS database. Experiment with the UPS by adding more users and examining how they are added to the UPS database. Notice how the UserRecordID 76 of the PersonalSettings table corresponds with the RecordID 76 of the Users table.

FIGURE 14.14.

User information is stored in the database.

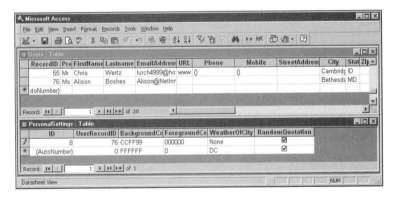

> **Tip**
>
> After adding new data, you might need to reopen the database table to view the data.

The Complete Source Code of
`personalize.asp`

Earlier, we explained how the main subroutines in the file personalize.asp function, so most of the subroutines in Listing 14.10 should be familiar to you. The complete source code of the ASP application `personalize.asp`, which is the heart of the UPS application, is given in Listing 14.10 for your reference.

LISTING 14.10. THE COMPLETE SOURCE CODE OF `personalize.asp`.

```
 1: <%
 2:    Option Explicit
 3:
 4:    ' Get the user's e-mail address if it has been provided
 5:    ' via an HTML form. A cookie is used to store the user's
 6:    ' e-mail address for future reference.
 7:    If Request.Form.Item("FormStep") = "GetEmailAddress" Then
 8:      If NOT Request.Form.Item("UserEmailAddress") = "" Then
 9:        Response.Cookies("UserEmailAddress") = _
10:          Request.Form.Item("UserEmailAddress")
11:        Response.Cookies("UserEmailAddress").Expires = _
12:          "February 29, 2000"
13:      End If
14:    End If
15: %>
16: <!DOCTYPE HTML PUBLIC "-//W3C//DTD HTML 3.2 Final//EN">
17: <html>
18: <head>
19:     <title>User Personalization System</title>
20: </head>
21:
22: <body>
23:
24: <%
25: ' *****
26: ' Begin subroutine GetUserEmailAddress().
27: ' *****
28: %><% Sub GetUserEmailAddress () %>
29:
30: <p> </p>
31: <table border="2" cellpadding="0" cellspacing="0" width="500"
32:    bgcolor="#FFFFFF" bordercolor="#0000FF">
33:      <tr>
34:        <td align="center" bgcolor="#FFFF00"><font face="Arial">
35:        <strong>Please provide your e-mail
           ➥address</strong></font></td>
36:      </tr>
37:      <tr>
38:         <form method="POST" action="Personalize.asp">
39:         <td width="100%"><p>Please provide us with your e-mail
40:         address and press the Submit button. If you are a new
41:         user, you will be prompted to enter additional
42:         information. If your e-mail address is found in the
43:         database, you will be given the opportunity to modify
```

14

continues

LISTING **14.10.** CONTINUED

```
44:          your personal settings.</p><p><font face="Arial">
45:          Please enter your e-mail address:
46:          <input type="UserEmailAddress" id="UserEmailAddress"
47:            name="UserEmailAddress"></font><p>
48:          <input type="hidden" name="FormStep"
49:            Value="GetEmailAddress">
50:          <input type="submit" value="Submit E-mail Address"
51:            id="EmailAddressSubmit" name="EmailAddressSubmit">
52:          </form>
53:          </td>
54:      </tr>
55: </table>
56: </center></div>
57: <% End Sub %>
58:
59: <%
60: ' *****
61: ' Begin Subroutine ReviewUserInformation (UserRecordset)
62: ' *****
63: %><% Sub ReviewUserInformation (UserRecordset) %>
64:
65: <table border="2" cellpadding="0" cellspacing="0" width="500"
66:   bordercolor="#800000">
67:    <tr>
68:      <td align="center" bgcolor="#FFFF00"><font face="Arial">
69:      <strong>Please review your information</strong></font></td>
70:    </tr>
71:    <tr>
72:        <td width="100%">Your e-mail address was found in the
73:        database. Please verify the following information about
74:        yourself is accurate. Please make any neccesary changes
75:        and press the Update/Proceed button to specify your
76:        personal settings.
77:        </td>
78:    </tr>
79: </table>
80:
81: <p><font face="Arial" size="4" style="BACKGROUND-COLOR: #ffcc99">
82: You are already in our database.</font></p><p>
83: Please modify the information you see below and press the
84: update button.</p>
85:
86:
87: <!--webbot BOT="GeneratedScript" PREVIEW=" " startspan -->
    ➡<script Language="JavaScript"><!--
88: function FrontPage_Form2_Validator(theForm)
89: {
90:
91:   if (theForm.FirstName.value == "")
```

```
 92:   {
 93:     alert("Please enter a value for the \"First Name\" field.");
 94:     theForm.FirstName.focus();
 95:     return (false);
 96:   }
 97:
 98:   if (theForm.FirstName.value.length < 2)
 99:   {
100:     alert("Please enter at least 2 characters in
       ➥the \"First Name\" field.");
101:     theForm.FirstName.focus();
102:     return (false);
103:   }
104:
105:   if (theForm.FirstName.value.length > 30)
106:   {
107:     alert("Please enter at most 30 characters in
       ➥the \"First Name\" field.");
108:     theForm.FirstName.focus();
109:     return (false);
110:   }
111:
112:   if (theForm.LastName.value == "")
113:   {
114:     alert("Please enter a value for the \"Last Name\" field.");
115:     theForm.LastName.focus();
116:     return (false);
117:   }
118:
119:   if (theForm.LastName.value.length < 2)
120:   {
121:     alert("Please enter at least 2 characters in
       ➥the \"Last Name\" field.");
122:     theForm.LastName.focus();
123:     return (false);
124:   }
125:
126:   if (theForm.LastName.value.length > 30)
127:   {
128:     alert("Please enter at most 30 characters in
       ➥the \"Last Name\" field.");
129:     theForm.LastName.focus();
130:     return (false);
131:   }
132:
133:   if (theForm.EmailAddress.value == "")
134:   {
135:     alert("Please enter a value for the \"E-mail Address\" field.");
136:     theForm.EmailAddress.focus();
137:     return (false);
```

14

continues

LISTING 14.10. CONTINUED

```
138:    }
139:
140:    if (theForm.EmailAddress.value.length < 7)
141:    {
142:      alert("Please enter at least 7 characters in
           ➥the \"E-mail Address\" field.");
143:      theForm.EmailAddress.focus();
144:      return (false);
145:    }
146:
147:    if (theForm.EmailAddress.value.length > 49)
148:    {
149:      alert("Please enter at most 49 characters in
           ➥the \"E-mail Address\" field.");
150:      theForm.EmailAddress.focus();
151:      return (false);
152:    }
153:
154:    if (theForm.State.value == "")
155:    {
156:      alert("Please enter a value for the \"Your State\" field.");
157:      theForm.State.focus();
158:      return (false);
159:    }
160:
161:    if (theForm.State.value.length < 2)
162:    {
163:      alert("Please enter at least 2 characters in
           ➥the \"Your State\" field.");
164:      theForm.State.focus();
165:      return (false);
166:    }
167:
168:    if (theForm.State.value.length > 2)
169:    {
170:      alert("Please enter at most 2 characters in
           ➥the \"Your State\" field.");
171:      theForm.State.focus();
172:      return (false);
173:    }
174:
175:    if (theForm.City.value == "")
176:    {
177:      alert("Please enter a value for the \"City Name\" field.");
178:      theForm.City.focus();
179:      return (false);
180:    }
181:
182:    if (theForm.City.value.length < 3)
```

```
183:    {
184:      alert("Please enter at least 3 characters in
          ➡the \"City Name\" field.");
185:      theForm.City.focus();
186:      return (false);
187:    }
188:
189:    if (theForm.City.value.length > 30)
190:    {
191:      alert("Please enter at most 30 characters in
          ➡the \"City Name\" field.");
192:      theForm.City.focus();
193:      return (false);
194:    }
195:
196:    if (theForm.Country.value == "")
197:    {
198:      alert("Please enter a value for the \"Name of your
          ➡country\" field.");
199:      theForm.Country.focus();
200:      return (false);
201:    }
202:
203:    if (theForm.Country.value.length < 3)
204:    {
205:      alert("Please enter at least 3 characters in
          ➡the \"Name of your country\" field.");
206:      theForm.Country.focus();
207:      return (false);
208:    }
209:
210:    if (theForm.Country.value.length > 30)
211:    {
212:      alert("Please enter at most 30 characters in
          ➡the \"Name of your country\" field.");
213:      theForm.Country.focus();
214:      return (false);
215:    }
216:    return (true);
217:  }
218: //--></script><!--webbot BOT="GeneratedScript" endspan -->
219:  <form method="POST" action="Personalize.asp"
220:    onsubmit="return FrontPage_Form2_Validator(this)"
221:    name="FrontPage_Form2">
222: <p><strong><font face="Arial">Please provide the following
223:    information </font></strong></p>
224: <div align="left"><table border="0" width="610">
225:    <tr>
226:      <td width="100%" colspan="2">
227:      <% If UserRecordset("Prefix")="Mr" Then %>
```

14

continues

LISTING **14.10.** CONTINUED

```
228:         Mr.<input type="radio" value="Mr" CHECKED name="Prefix">
229:         Ms.<input type="radio" name="Prefix" value="Ms">
230:         <% Else %>
231:         Mr.<input type="radio" value="Mr" name="Prefix">
232:         Ms.<input type="radio" CHECKED name="Prefix" value="Ms">
233:         <% End If %>
234:         <strong>First name</strong>
235:         <!--webbot bot="Validation" S-Display-Name="First Name"
        ➡B-Value-Required="TRUE" I-Minimum-Length="2"
        ➡I-Maximum-Length="30" -->
236:         <input type="text" name="FirstName" size="12" maxlength="30"
237:          value="<%= UserRecordset("FirstName")%>">
238:         <strong>Last name</strong> <!--webbot bot="Validation"
        ➡S-Display-Name="Last Name" B-Value-Required="TRUE"
        ➡I-Minimum-Length="2" I-Maximum-Length="30" -->
239:         <input type="text" name="LastName" size="12" maxlength="30"
240:             value="<%= UserRecordset("LastName")%>"></td>
241:     </tr>
242:     <tr>
243:       <td width="100%" colspan="2"><div align="center"><center>
244:         <table border="0" width="600">
245:         <tr>
246:           <td width="104"><strong>Email address</strong> </td>
247:           <td width="488"><!--webbot bot="Validation"
        ➡S-Display-Name="E-mail Address" B-Value-Required="TRUE"
        ➡I-Minimum-Length="7" I-Maximum-Length="49" -->
248:           <input type="text" name="EmailAddress"
249:             value="<%= UserRecordset("EmailAddress")%>">
250:         </td></tr>
251:         <tr>
252:           <td width="104">URL</td>
253:           <td width="488"><input type="text" name="URL"
254:             value="<%= UserRecordset("URL")%>" size="40"
255:             maxlength="49"></td>
256:         </tr>
257:         </table>
258:       </center></div></td>
259:     </tr>
260:     <tr>
261:       <td width="50%">Phone (<input type="text"
262:         name="PhoneAreaCode" size="3" maxlength="3"
263:         value="<%= Mid (UserRecordset("Phone"),2,3) %>">)
264:       <input type="text" name="PhoneNumber" size="10"
265:         value="<%= Mid (UserRecordset("Phone"),6)%>" maxlength="12">
266:       </td><td width="50%">
267:       Mobile (<input type="text" name="MobileAreaCode" size="3"
268:         value="<%= Mid (UserRecordset("Mobile"),2,3) %>"
269:         maxlength="3">)<input type="text" name="MobilePhoneNumber"
270:         value="<%= Mid (UserRecordset("Mobile"),6)%>" size="10"
```

```
271:          maxlength="12"></td>
272:      </tr>
273:      <tr>
274:        <td width="100%" colspan="2"><div align="center"><center>
275:          <table border="0" width="600">
276:          <tr>
277:            <td width="105">Date of birth</td>
278:            <td width="487">
279:            <% On Error Resume Next %>
280:            <input type="text" name="BirthdayMonth"
281:              size="2" value="<%= Month(UserRecordset("DOB"))%>"> /
282:            <input type="text" name="BirthdayDay" size="2"
283:              value="<%= Day(UserRecordset("DOB"))%>"> /
284:            <input type="text" name="BirthdayYear"
285:              size="4" value="<%= Year(UserRecordset("DOB"))%>">
286:            (MM/DD/YYYY)</td>
287:          </tr>
288:          <tr>
289:            <td width="105">Street address</td>
290:            <td width="487"><input type="text" name="StreetAddress"
291:              value="<%= UserRecordset("StreetAddress")%>" size="20"
292:              maxlength="49"> <strong>State</strong>
293:            <!--webbot bot="Validation" S-Display-Name="Your State"
            ➥B-Value-Required="TRUE" I-Minimum-Length="2"
            ➥I-Maximum-Length="2" -->
294:            <input type="text" name="State" size="2" maxlength="2"
295:              value="<%= UserRecordset("State")%>">
296:            Zip Code <input type="text" name="ZipCode" size="10"
297:              value="<%= UserRecordset("ZipCode")%>"
            ➥maxlength="10"></td>
298:          </tr>
299:          <tr>
300:            <td width="105"><strong>City</strong> </td>
301:            <td width="487"><!--webbot bot="Validation"
            ➥S-Display-Name="City Name" B-Value-Required="TRUE"
            ➥I-Minimum-Length="3" I-Maximum-Length="30" -->
302:            <input type="text" name="City" size="20"
303:              maxlength="30" value="<%= UserRecordset("City")%>">
304:            <strong>Country</strong>
305:            <!--webbot bot="Validation" S-Display-Name="Name
            ➥of your country" B-Value-Required="TRUE"
            ➥I-Minimum-Length="3" I-Maximum-Length="30" -->
306:            <input type="text" name="Country" size="15"
307:              value="<%= UserRecordset("Country")%>"
308:              maxlength="30"></td>
309:          </tr>
310:          </table>
311:        </center></div></td>
312:      </tr>
313:    </table>
```

14

continues

LISTING **14.10.** CONTINUED

```
314:    </div>
315:    </table>
316:    </div><p>
317:      <input type="hidden" name="CurrentStep"
318:        value="UpdateUserInformation">
319:      <input type="hidden" name="RecordID"
320:        value="<%= UserRecordset("RecordID")%>">
321:      <input type="submit"
322:        value="Update My Information" name="SubmitButton"></p>
323: </form>
324: </center></div>
325: <% End Sub %>
326:
327: <%
328: ' *****
329: ' Begin subroutine GetNewUserInformation(UserEmailAddress).
330: ' *****
331: %><% Sub GetNewUserInformation (UserEmailAddress)%>
332:
333: <div align="center"><center>
334: <table border="2" cellpadding="0" cellspacing="0"
335:   width="500" bordercolor="#800000">
336:     <tr>
337:        <td align="center" bgcolor="#FFFF00"><font face="Arial">
338:          <strong>Please provide us with some information about
339:          yourself</strong></font></td>
340:     </tr>
341:     <tr>
342:        <td width="100%">Please provide us with some information
343:        about yourself so we may add you to our database. Once
344:        you press the Submit button, you will be able to specify
345:        your personal settings.<p> </p>
346:        </td>
347:     </tr>
348: </table>
349: </center></div>
350:
351: <p><font face="Arial" size="4" style="BACKGROUND-COLOR: #ccff99">
352: Your e-mail address was not found in our database.</font></p>
353: <p>Please provide us with some additional information about
354: yourself so we may add you to our database.</p>
355:
356:
357:
358: <!--webbot BOT="GeneratedScript" PREVIEW=" " startspan -->
359: <script Language="JavaScript"><!--
360: function FrontPage_Form3_Validator(theForm)
361: {
362:
```

```
363:    if (theForm.FirstName.value == "")
364:    {
365:      alert("Please enter a value for the \"First Name\" field.");
366:      theForm.FirstName.focus();
367:      return (false);
368:    }
369:
370:    if (theForm.FirstName.value.length < 2)
371:    {
372:      alert("Please enter at least 2 characters in
           ➡the \"First Name\" field.");
373:      theForm.FirstName.focus();
374:      return (false);
375:    }
376:
377:    if (theForm.FirstName.value.length > 30)
378:    {
379:      alert("Please enter at most 30 characters in
           ➡the \"First Name\" field.");
380:      theForm.FirstName.focus();
381:      return (false);
382:    }
383:
384:    if (theForm.LastName.value == "")
385:    {
386:      alert("Please enter a value for the \"Last Name\" field.");
387:      theForm.LastName.focus();
388:      return (false);
389:    }
390:
391:    if (theForm.LastName.value.length < 2)
392:    {
393:      alert("Please enter at least 2 characters in
           ➡the \"Last Name\" field.");
394:      theForm.LastName.focus();
395:      return (false);
396:    }
397:
398:    if (theForm.LastName.value.length > 30)
399:    {
400:      alert("Please enter at most 30 characters in
           ➡the \"Last Name\" field.");
401:      theForm.LastName.focus();
402:      return (false);
403:    }
404:
405:    if (theForm.State.value == "")
406:    {
407:      alert("Please enter a value for the \"Your State\" field.");
408:      theForm.State.focus();
```

14

continues

LISTING 14.10. CONTINUED

```
409:       return (false);
410:    }
411:
412:    if (theForm.State.value.length < 2)
413:    {
414:      alert("Please enter at least 2 characters in
          ➡the \"Your State\" field.");
415:      theForm.State.focus();
416:      return (false);
417:    }
418:
419:    if (theForm.State.value.length > 2)
420:    {
421:      alert("Please enter at most 2 characters in
          ➡the \"Your State\" field.");
422:      theForm.State.focus();
423:      return (false);
424:    }
425:
426:    if (theForm.City.value == "")
427:    {
428:      alert("Please enter a value for the \"City Name\" field.");
429:      theForm.City.focus();
430:      return (false);
431:    }
432:
433:    if (theForm.City.value.length < 3)
434:    {
435:      alert("Please enter at least 3 characters in the
          ➡\"City Name\" field.");
436:      theForm.City.focus();
437:      return (false);
438:    }
439:
440:    if (theForm.City.value.length > 30)
441:    {
442:      alert("Please enter at most 30 characters in
          ➡the \"City Name\" field.");
443:      theForm.City.focus();
444:      return (false);
445:    }
446:
447:    if (theForm.Country.value == "")
448:    {
449:      alert("Please enter a value for the \"Name of your
          ➡country\" field.");
450:      theForm.Country.focus();
451:      return (false);
452:    }
```

```
453:
454:   if (theForm.Country.value.length < 3)
455:   {
456:     alert("Please enter at least 3 characters in the \"Name
         ➥of your country\" field.");
457:     theForm.Country.focus();
458:     return (false);
459:   }
460:
461:   if (theForm.Country.value.length > 30)
462:   {
463:     alert("Please enter at most 30 characters in the \"Name
         ➥of your country\" field.");
464:     theForm.Country.focus();
465:     return (false);
466:   }
467:   return (true);
468: }
469: //--></script><!--webbot BOT="GeneratedScript" endspan -->
470: <form method="POST" action="Personalize.asp"
471:   onsubmit="return FrontPage_Form3_Validator(this)"
472:   name="FrontPage_Form3">
473:   <p><strong><font face="Arial">Please provide the following
474:   information</font></strong></p>
475:   <div align="left"><table border="0" width="610">
476:     <tr>
477:       <td width="100%" colspan="2">
478:       Mr.<input type="radio" value="Mr" CHECKED name="Prefix">
479:       Ms.<input type="radio" name="Prefix" value="Ms">
480:       <strong>First name</strong>
481:       <!--webbot bot="Validation" S-Display-Name="First Name"
           ➥B-Value-Required="TRUE" I-Minimum-Length="2"
           ➥I-Maximum-Length="30" -->
482:       <input type="text" name="FirstName" size="12" maxlength="30">
483:         <strong>Last name</strong> <!--webbot bot="Validation"
           ➥S-Display-Name="Last Name" B-Value-Required="TRUE"
           ➥I-Minimum-Length="2" I-Maximum-Length="30" -->
484:         <input type="text" name="LastName" size="12"
485:           maxlength="30"></td>
486:     </tr>
487:     <tr>
488:       <td width="100%" colspan="2"><div align="center"><center>
489:         <table border="0" width="600">
490:         <tr>
491:           <td width="104"><strong>Email address</strong> </td>
492:           <td width="488">
493:           <input type="hidden" name="EmailAddress"
494:             value="<%= UserEmailAddress %>"> <%= UserEmailAddress %>
495:         </td></tr>
496:         <tr>
```

LISTING 14.10. CONTINUED

```
497:             <td width="104">URL</td>
498:             <td width="488"><input type="text" name="URL" size="
499:             40" maxlength="49"></td>
500:         </tr>
501:       </table>
502:       </center></div></td>
503:     </tr>
504:     <tr>
505:       <td width="50%">Phone (<input type="text"
506:       name="PhoneAreaCode" size="3" maxlength="3">)
507:       <input type="text" name="PhoneNumber" size="10"
508:       maxlength="12">
509:       </td><td width="50%">
510:       Mobile (<input type="text" name="MobileAreaCode" size="3"
511:       maxlength="3">)
512:           <input type="text" name="MobilePhoneNumber" size="10"
513:             maxlength="12"></td>
514:     </tr>
515:     <tr>
516:       <td width="100%" colspan="2"><div align="center"><center>
517:         <table border="0" width="600">
518:         <tr>
519:           <td width="105">Date of birth</td>
520:           <td width="487">
521:           <input type="text" name="BirthdayMonth" size="2"> /
522:           <input type="text" name="BirthdayDay" size="2"> /
523:           <input type="text" name="BirthdayYear" size="4">
524:           (MM/DD/YYYY)</td>
525:         </tr>
526:         <tr>
527:           <td width="105">Street address</td>
528:           <td width="487"><input type="text"
529:             name="StreetAddress" size="20" maxlength="49">
530:           <strong>State</strong>
531:           <!--webbot bot="Validation" S-Display-Name="Your
            ➥State" B-Value-Required="TRUE" I-Minimum-Length="2"
            ➥I-Maximum-Length="2" -->
532:           <input type="text" name="State" size="2" maxlength="2">
533:           Zip Code <input type="text" name="ZipCode" size="10"
534:             maxlength="10"> </td>
535:         </tr>
536:         <tr>
537:           <td width="105"><strong>City</strong> </td>
538:           <td width="487"><!--webbot bot="Validation"
            ➥S-Display-Name="City Name" B-Value-Required="TRUE"
            ➥I-Minimum-Length="3" I-Maximum-Length="30" -->
539:           <input type="text" name="City" size="20" maxlength="30">
540:           <strong>Country</strong>
541:           <!--webbot bot="Validation" S-Display-Name="Name
```

```
                        ➥of your country" B-Value-Required="TRUE" I-Minimum
                        ➥Length="3" I-Maximum-Length="30" -->
542:                    <input type="text" name="Country" size="15"
543:                      value="United States" maxlength="30"></td>
544:                </tr>
545:              </table>
546:              </center></div></td>
547:            </tr>
548:          </table>
549:          </div>
550:        </table>
551:      </div><p>
552:        <input type="hidden" name="CurrentStep"
553:          value="NewUserInformation">
554:        <input type="submit" value="Add My Information To The Database"
555:          name="SubmitButton">
556:        <input type="reset" value="Please Reset This Form"
          ➥name="B2"></p>
557: </form>
558:
559: <% End Sub %>
560:
561: <%
562: ' *****
563: ' Begin subroutine ProcessEmailAddress(UserEmailAddress).
564: ' *****
565: %> <% Sub ProcessEmailAddress (UserEmailAddress)
566:
567:    Dim SQLString, DatabaseConnection, UserRecordset
568:
569:    ' This SQL string retrieves all the selected records from the
570:    ' Users table of the user registration database.
571:    SQLString = "SELECT RecordID, Prefix, FirstName, Lastname, " & _
572:      "EmailAddress, URL, Phone, Mobile, StreetAddress, City, " & _
573:      "State, ZipCode, Country, DOB " & _
574:      "FROM Users WHERE EmailAddress=" & chr(39) & _
575:      UserEmailAddress & chr(39)
576:
577:    ' Create an instance of the Connection object.
578:    Set DatabaseConnection = Server.CreateObject("ADODB.Connection")
579:
580:    ' Open a connection to the UPS file DSN.
581:    ' Before the following statement can execute properly, you have to
582:    ' create a file DSN for the UPS database as outlined in the
583:    ' book.
584:    DatabaseConnection.Open  "FILEDSN=UserInformationDatabase.dsn"
585:
586:    ' Create an instance of the Recordset object.
587:    Set UserRecordset = Server.CreateObject("ADODB.Recordset")
588:
```

14

continues

LISTING 14.10. CONTINUED

```
589:    ' The Open method of the Recordset object is used to retrieve
590:    ' data from the UPS database.
591:    UserRecordset.Open SQLString, DatabaseConnection
592:
593:    If UserRecordset.EOF Then
594:      Call GetNewUserInformation (UserEmailAddress)
595:    Else
596:      Call ReviewUserInformation (UserRecordSet)
597:    End If
598:
599:    ' Always release resources after you are done using them.
600:    ' Always close your database connections after you are done using
601:    ' them.
602:    UserRecordSet.Close
603:    Set UserRecordSet = Nothing
604:    DatabaseConnection.Close
605:    Set DatabaseConnection = Nothing
606:
607: End Sub
608: %>
609:
610: <%
611: ' *****
612: ' Begin subroutine.
613: ' *****
614: %> <% Sub DisplayPersonalizationSettings %>
615:
616:    <div align="center"><center>
617:    <p><font face="Verdana"><strong>Please select the colors
618:    of Web page elements</strong></font></p>
619:
620:    <table border="4" width="450">
621:    <tr><td><table>
622:    <tr><td BGCOLOR="99FF99">
623:    <font face="Comic Sans MS">
624:    <strong>Please select the background color</strong>
625:    </font></td></tr>
626:    <tr><td BGCOLOR="CCCCCC">
627:    <input TYPE="RADIO" NAME="Background" VALUE="CCCCCC">CCCCCC
628:    </td></tr>
629:    <tr><td BGCOLOR="FFFF99">
630:    <input TYPE="RADIO" NAME="Background" VALUE="FFFF99"
       ➥CHECKED>FFFF99
631:    </td></tr>
632:    <tr><td BGCOLOR="CCFF99">
633:    <input TYPE="RADIO" NAME="Background" VALUE="CCFF99">CCFF99
634:    </td></tr>
635:    <tr><td BGCOLOR="999933">
```

```
636:   <input TYPE="RADIO" NAME="Background" VALUE="999933">999933
637:   </td></tr>
638:   <tr><td BGCOLOR="004400">
639:   <input TYPE="RADIO" NAME="Background" VALUE="004400">
640:   <font COLOR="FFFFFF">004400</font>
641:   </td></tr>
642:   <tr><td BGCOLOR="000000">
643:   <input TYPE="RADIO" NAME="Background" VALUE="000000">
644:   <font COLOR="FFFFFF">000000</font>
645:   </td></tr>
646:   </table></td>
647:   <td><table>
648:   <tr><td BGCOLOR="99FF99">
649:   <font face="Comic Sans MS">
650:   <strong>Please select the text color</strong>
651:   </font>
652:   </td></tr>
653:   <tr><td BGCOLOR="CCCCCC">
654:   <input TYPE="RADIO" NAME="Text" VALUE="CCCCCC" CHECKED>CCCCCC
655:   </td></tr>
656:   <tr><td BGCOLOR="FFFF99">
657:   <input TYPE="RADIO" NAME="Text" VALUE="FFFF99">FFFF99
658:   </td></tr>
659:   <tr><td BGCOLOR="CCFF99">
660:   <input TYPE="RADIO" NAME="Text" VALUE="CCFF99">CCFF99
661:   </td></tr>
662:   <tr><td BGCOLOR="999933">
663:   <input TYPE="RADIO" NAME="Text" VALUE="999933">999933
664:   </td></tr>
665:   <tr><td BGCOLOR="004400">
666:   <input TYPE="RADIO" NAME="Text" VALUE="004400" CHECKED>
667:   <font COLOR="FFFFFF">004400</font>
668:   </td></tr>
669:   <tr><td BGCOLOR="000000">
670:   <input TYPE="RADIO" NAME="Text" VALUE="000000">
671:   <font COLOR="FFFFFF">000000</font>
672:   </td></tr>
673:   </table>
674:   </td></tr></table>
675:
676:   <p><font face="Verdana"><strong>Which city's weather are you
677:   most interested in?</strong></font></p>
678:
679:   <table width="450">
680:     <tr><td>
681:       <input TYPE="RADIO" NAME="City" CHECKED VALUE="WashingtonDC">
682:       <b>Washington DC</b>
683:     </td><td>
684:       <input TYPE="RADIO" NAME="City" VALUE="NewYork"><b>New
       ➡York</b>
```

14

continues

LISTING 14.10. CONTINUED

```
685:    </td></tr>
686:    <tr><td>
687:     <input TYPE="RADIO" NAME="City" VALUE="Redmond"><b>Redmond</b>
688:    </td><td>
689:     <input TYPE="RADIO" NAME="City" VALUE="Chicago"><b>Chicago</b>
690:    </td><td>
691:     <input TYPE="RADIO" NAME="City" VALUE="None"><b>None</b>
692:    </td></tr>
693:    </table>
694:
695:    <p><font face="Verdana"><strong>Would you like to see a random
696:    quotation displayed?</strong></font></p>
697:     <input TYPE="RADIO" NAME="Quotation" CHECKED
698:        VALUE="True"><b>Yes, please.</b>
699:     <input TYPE="RADIO" NAME="Quotation"
700:        VALUE="False"><b>No. Thank you.</b>
701:    <p> </p></center></div>
702:
703: <%
704: End Sub
705: %>
706:
707:
708: <%
709: ' *****
710: ' Begin subroutine DisplayPersonalizationForm().
711: ' *****
712: %> <% Sub ModifyPersonalSettings (UserEmailAddress,RecordID) %>
713:
714: <table border="2" cellpadding="0" cellspacing="0"
715:    align="center" width="500" bordercolor="#008000">
716:     <tr>
717:        <td align="center" bgcolor="#FFFF00"><font face="Arial">
718:        <strong>Please specify your personal settings</strong>
719:        </font></td>
720:     </tr>
721:     <tr>
722:        <td width="100%">Please use the following form to specify
723:        your personal settings. Once you enter your personal
724:        settings and press the Submit button, you will be
725:        transferred to your newly personalized Web page.
726:        <form ACTION="ModifyPersonalizationSettings.asp"
727:          METHOD="POST" NAME="DataForm">
728:        <% DisplayPersonalizationSettings () %>
729:         <input type="hidden" name="RecordID"
730:           value="<%= RecordID %>">
731:         <input type="hidden" name="UserEmailAddress"
732:           value="<%= UserEmailAddress %>">
733:         <input TYPE="Submit" VALUE="Update My Personal Settings"
```

```
734:                    name="SubmitPersonalizationSettings">
735:          </form>
736:            <p><em>Thank you for using the User Personalization
737:            System!</em></p>
738:          </td>
739:        </tr>
740: </table>
741:
742: <% End Sub %>
743:
744:
745: <%
746: ' *****
747: ' Begin subroutine UpdateUserInformation().
748: ' *****
749: %><% Sub UpdateUserInformation ()
750:
751:    Dim SQLString, DatabaseConnection, UserRecordSet, RecordID
752:
753:    ' Create an instance of the Connection object.
754:    Set DatabaseConnection = Server.CreateObject("ADODB.Connection")
755:
756:    ' Open a connection to the UPS file DSN.
757:    ' Before the following statement can execute properly, you have to
758:    ' create a file DSN for the UPS database as outlined in the
759:    ' book.
760:    DatabaseConnection.Open  "FILEDSN=UserInformationDatabase.dsn"
761:
762:    ' Create an instance of the Recordset object.
763:    Set UserRecordset = Server.CreateObject("ADODB.Recordset")
764:
765:    ' Retrieve the recordset containing the user's data.
766:    ' Notice how the recordset is opened so that you can use the
767:    ' Update method of the Recordset object to modify the user's
768:    ' data.
769:
770:    UserRecordSet.CursorType = 1
771:    UserRecordSet.CursorLocation = 2
772:    UserRecordSet.LockType = 3
773:    UserRecordSet.ActiveConnection = DatabaseConnection
774:    UserRecordSet.Source = "Users"
775:    UserRecordSet.Filter = "RecordID = " &
       ➥Request.Form.Item("RecordID")
776:
777:    ' The Open method of the Recordset object is used to retrieve
778:    ' data from the user registration database.
779:
780:    UserRecordset.Open
781:
782:    If UserRecordset.EOF Then
```

14

continues

LISTING 14.10. CONTINUED

```
783:     Response.Write ("<H1>Your record was not found.</H1>")
784:   Else
785:
786:     UserRecordset.Fields.Item ("Prefix") = _
787:       Request.Form.Item("Prefix")
788:     UserRecordset.Fields.Item ("FirstName") = _
789:       Request.Form.Item("FirstName")
790:     UserRecordset.Fields.Item ("Lastname") = _
791:       Request.Form.Item("Lastname")
792:     UserRecordset.Fields.Item ("EmailAddress") = _
793:       Request.Form.Item("EmailAddress")
794:     UserRecordset.Fields.Item ("URL") = _
795:       Request.Form.Item("URL")
796:
797:     If IsNumeric (Request.Form.Item("PhoneAreaCode")) Then
798:       UserRecordset.Fields.Item ("Phone")  = "(" & _
799:        Request.Form.Item("PhoneAreaCode") & _
800:        ") " & Request.Form.Item("PhoneNumber")
801:     Else
802:       UserRecordset.Fields.Item ("Phone")  = _
803:         Request.Form.Item("PhoneNumber")
804:     End If
805:     If IsNumeric (Request.Form.Item("MobileAreaCode")) Then
806:       UserRecordset.Fields.Item ("Mobile") = "(" & _
807:         Request.Form.Item("MobileAreaCode") _
808:         & ") " & Request.Form.Item("MobilePhoneNumber")
809:     Else
810:       UserRecordset.Fields.Item ("Mobile") = _
811:         Request.Form.Item("MobilePhoneNumber")
812:     End If
813:
814:     UserRecordset.Fields.Item ("StreetAddress") = _
815:       Request.Form.Item("StreetAddress")
816:     UserRecordset.Fields.Item ("City") = _
817:       Request.Form.Item("City")
818:     UserRecordset.Fields.Item ("State") = _
819:       Request.Form.Item("State")
820:     UserRecordset.Fields.Item ("ZipCode") = _
821:       Request.Form.Item("ZipCode")
822:     UserRecordset.Fields.Item ("Country") = _
823:       Request.Form.Item("Country")
824:     If IsDate(Request.Form.Item("BirthdayMonth") & _
825:       "/" & Request.Form.Item("BirthdayDay")  & "/" & _
826:       Request.Form.Item("BirthdayYear") ) = True Then
827:       UserRecordset.Fields.Item ("DOB") = _
828:         Request.Form.Item("BirthdayMonth") & "/"  & _
829:         Request.Form.Item("BirthdayDay")  & "/" & _
830:         Request.Form.Item("BirthdayYear")
831:     End If
```

```
832:        UserRecordset.Fields.Item ("LastAccessDate") = Date
833:        UserRecordset.Fields.Item ("LastAccessTime") = Time
834:        UserRecordset.Fields.Item ("LastAccessIP") = _
835:          Request.ServerVariables.Item ("REMOTE_ADDR")
836:        UserRecordset.Fields.Item ("LastAccessWebBrowser") = _
837:          Request.ServerVariables.Item ("HTTP_USER_AGENT")
838:
839:        UserRecordSet.Update
840:        RecordID = UserRecordset.Fields.Item ("RecordID")
841:
842:    End If
843:
844:    ' Database connections should ALWAYS be closed after they are
            ➥used.
845:    UserRecordSet.Close
846:    Set UserRecordSet = Nothing
847:    DatabaseConnection.Close
848:    Set DatabaseConnection = Nothing
849:
850:    ModifyPersonalSettings Request.Form.Item("EmailAddress"),RecordID
851:
852: End Sub
853: %>
854:
855:
856: <%
857: ' *****
858: ' Begin subroutine.
859: ' *****
860: %><% Sub InsertNewUserInformation ()
861:
862:    Dim SQLString, DatabaseConnection
863:    Dim CommandObject, RecordID, UserRecordset
864:
865:    ' Create an instance of the Connection object.
866:    Set DatabaseConnection = Server.CreateObject("ADODB.Connection")
867:
868:    ' Open a connection to the UPS file DSN.
869:    ' Before the following statement can execute properly, you have to
870:    ' create a file DSN for the user information database.
871:    DatabaseConnection.Open  "FILEDSN=UserInformationDatabase.dsn"
872:
873:
874:    ' Create an instance of the Command object.
875:    Set CommandObject= Server.CreateObject("ADODB.Command")
876:
877:    ' The ActiveConnection property is used to connect the Command
878:    ' object to the Connection object.
879:    Set CommandObject.ActiveConnection = DatabaseConnection
880:
```

14

continues

LISTING 14.10. CONTINUED

```
881:    ' The SQL string that inserts data about the
882:    ' user is created.
883:    SQLString = "INSERT INTO Users (Prefix, FirstName," & _
884:      "Lastname, EmailAddress, URL, Phone, Mobile, StreetAddress," & _
885:      "City, State, ZipCode, Country, DOB, FirstAccessTime," & _
886:      "FirstAccessDate, FirstAccessIPAddress,
        ➡FirstAccessWebBrowser," & _
887:      "LastAccessTime, LastAccessDate, LastAccessIP," & _
888:      "LastAccessWebBrowser) VALUES (?,?,?,?,?,?,?,?," & _
889:      "?,?,?,?,?,?,?,?,?,?,?,?,?)"
890:
891:    ' The SQL statement that actually inserts the data is defined.
892:    CommandObject.CommandText = SQLString
893:
894:    ' The prepared or pre-compiled SQL statement defined in the
895:    ' CommandText property is saved.
896:    CommandObject.Prepared = True
897:
898:    ' The parameters of the SQL string are defined below.
899:    CommandObject.Parameters.Append _
900:      CommandObject.CreateParameter("Prefix",200, ,255 )
901:    CommandObject.Parameters.Append _
902:      CommandObject.CreateParameter("FirstName",200, ,255 )
903:    CommandObject.Parameters.Append _
904:      CommandObject.CreateParameter("LastName",200, ,255 )
905:    CommandObject.Parameters.Append _
906:      CommandObject.CreateParameter("EmailAddress",200, ,255 )
907:    CommandObject.Parameters.Append _
908:      CommandObject.CreateParameter("URL",200, ,255 )
909:    CommandObject.Parameters.Append _
910:      CommandObject.CreateParameter("Phone",200, ,255 )
911:    CommandObject.Parameters.Append _
912:      CommandObject.CreateParameter("Mobile",200, ,255 )
913:    CommandObject.Parameters.Append _
914:      CommandObject.CreateParameter("StreetAddress",200, ,255 )
915:    CommandObject.Parameters.Append _
916:      CommandObject.CreateParameter("City",200, ,255 )
917:    CommandObject.Parameters.Append _
918:      CommandObject.CreateParameter("State",200, ,255 )
919:    CommandObject.Parameters.Append _
920:      CommandObject.CreateParameter("ZipCode",200, ,255 )
921:    CommandObject.Parameters.Append _
922:      CommandObject.CreateParameter("Country",200, ,255 )
923:    CommandObject.Parameters.Append _
924:      CommandObject.CreateParameter("DOB",200, ,255 )
925:    CommandObject.Parameters.Append _
926:      CommandObject.CreateParameter("FirstAccessTime",200, ,255 )
927:    CommandObject.Parameters.Append _
928:      CommandObject.CreateParameter("FirstAccessDate",200, ,255 )
```

```
929:   CommandObject.Parameters.Append _
930:     CommandObject.CreateParameter("FirstAccessIPAddress",200, ,255 )
931:   CommandObject.Parameters.Append _
932:     CommandObject.CreateParameter("FirstAccessWebBrowser",200, ,255 )
933:   CommandObject.Parameters.Append _
934:     CommandObject.CreateParameter("LastAccessTime",200, ,255 )
935:   CommandObject.Parameters.Append _
936:     CommandObject.CreateParameter("LastAccessDate",200, ,255 )
937:   CommandObject.Parameters.Append _
938:     CommandObject.CreateParameter("LastAccessIPAddress",200, ,255 )
939:   CommandObject.Parameters.Append _
940:     CommandObject.CreateParameter("LastAccessWebBrowser",200, ,255 )
941:
942:   ' Information entered by the user is added to the database.
943:   CommandObject("Prefix") = Request.Form.Item("Prefix")
944:   CommandObject("FirstName") = Request.Form.Item("FirstName")
945:   CommandObject("LastName") = Request.Form.Item("LastName")
946:   CommandObject("EmailAddress") = Request.Form.Item("EmailAddress")
947:   CommandObject("URL") = Request.Form.Item("URL")
948:
949:   If IsNumeric (Request.Form.Item("PhoneAreaCode")) Then
950:     CommandObject("Phone") = "(" & _
951:       Request.Form.Item("PhoneAreaCode") & _
952:       ") " & Request.Form.Item("PhoneNumber")
953:   Else
954:     CommandObject("Phone") = Request.Form.Item("PhoneNumber")
955:   End If
956:   If IsNumeric (Request.Form.Item("MobileAreaCode")) Then
957:     CommandObject("Mobile") = "(" & _
958:       Request.Form.Item("MobileAreaCode") _
959:       & ") " & Request.Form.Item("MobilePhoneNumber")
960:   Else
961:     CommandObject("Mobile") = Request.Form.Item("MobilePhoneNumber")
962:   End If
963:
964:   CommandObject("StreetAddress") = Request.Form.Item("StreetAddress")
965:   CommandObject("City") = Request.Form.Item("City")
966:   CommandObject("State") = Request.Form.Item("State")
967:   CommandObject("ZipCode") = Request.Form.Item("ZipCode")
968:   CommandObject("Country") = Request.Form.Item("Country")
969:
970:   If IsDate(Request.Form.Item("BirthdayMonth") & _
971:     "/" & Request.Form.Item("BirthdayDay") & "/" & _
972:      Request.Form.Item("BirthdayYear") ) = True Then
973:       CommandObject ("DOB") = _
974:         Request.Form.Item("BirthdayMonth") & "/" & _
975:           Request.Form.Item("BirthdayDay") & "/" & _
976:           Request.Form.Item("BirthdayYear")
977:   Else
978:     CommandObject ("DOB") = ""
```

14

continues

LISTING **14.10.** CONTINUED

```
979:      End If
980:
981:      CommandObject("FirstAccessTime") = Time
982:      CommandObject("FirstAccessDate") = Date
983:      CommandObject("FirstAccessIPAddress") = _
984:        Request.ServerVariables.Item ("REMOTE_ADDR")
985:      CommandObject("FirstAccessWebBrowser") = _
986:        Request.ServerVariables.Item ("HTTP_USER_AGENT")
987:      CommandObject("LastAccessTime") = Time
988:      CommandObject("LastAccessDate") = Date
989:      CommandObject("LastAccessIPAddress") = _
990:        Request.ServerVariables.Item ("REMOTE_ADDR")
991:      CommandObject("LastAccessWebBrowser") = _
992:        Request.ServerVariables.Item ("HTTP_USER_AGENT")
993:
994:      CommandObject.Execute
995:
996:      'Instantiate a Recordset object.
997:      Set UserRecordset = Server.CreateObject("ADODB.Recordset")
998:
999:      'Open a recordset using the Open method
1000:     'and use the connection established by the Connection object.
1001:
1002:     SQLString ="SELECT Users.RecordID, Users.EmailAddress " & _
1003:       "FROM Users " & _
1004:       "WHERE Users.EmailAddress=" & Chr(39) & _
1005:       Request.Form.Item("EmailAddress") & Chr(39)
1006:
1007:     UserRecordset.Open  SQLString, DatabaseConnection
1008:     RecordID = UserRecordset("RecordID")
1009:
1010:     DatabaseConnection.Close
1011:     Set DatabaseConnection = Nothing
1012:
1013:     ModifyPersonalSettings Request.Form.Item("EmailAddress"), RecordID
1014:
1015: End Sub
1016: %>
1017:
1018:
1019: <%
1020: ' *****
1021: ' Begin main execution block of program.
1022: ' *****
1023: %><%
1024:
1025:     Dim UserEmailAddress, CurrentStep
1026:
1027:     UserEmailAddress = Request.Cookies("UserEmailAddress")
```

```
1028:    CurrentStep = Request.Form.Item("CurrentStep")
1029:
1030:    If UserEmailAddress = "" Then
1031:      GetUserEmailAddress ()
1032:    Else
1033:      If ((CurrentStep="")OR(CurrentStep="GetEmailAddress")) Then
1034:        ProcessEmailAddress (UserEmailAddress)
1035:      Else
1036:        Select Case CurrentStep
1037:          Case "UpdateUserInformation" : UpdateUserInformation ()
1038:          Case "NewUserInformation" : InsertNewUserInformation ()
1039:        End Select
1040:      End If
1041:    End If
1042:
1043: %>
1044: <p> </p><hr>
1045: <a HREF="DeleteCookie.asp">Delete Cookie</a>
1046: </body>
1047: </html>
```

ANALYSIS The main execution block of the ASP application begins at line 1024. Line 1027 gets the user's e-mail address by examining the value of the cookie UserEmailAddress. Multiple data entry forms are used to get input from the user. Line 1028 determines which form to display next by examining the value of the form field CurrentStep.

The If statement in line 1030 checks to see if the user's e-mail address is stored as a cookie in the user's computer. If the cookie is not found, the GetUserEmailAddress() subroutine is executed to get the user's e-mail address using an HTML form. After getting an e-mail address from the user, the ProcessEmailAddress() subroutine is called.

The ProcessEmailAddress() subroutine defined in line 565 checks to see if a record matching the user's e-mail address is found in the Users table of the UPS database. If a record is found, the ReviewUserInformation() subroutine is called to allow the user to review the information in the database before specifying personal settings. If the user's e-mail address is not found in the Users table, the GetNewUserInformation() subroutine is called in line 594 to get information about the new user to be added to the UPS database. The two subroutines GetNewUserInformation() and ReviewUserInformation() display a form to either add a new user to the database or allow the user to review existing information in the database. Each form defines a different value for the hidden form variable CurrentStep. The value of the CurrentStep variable is used in the Select...Case statement defined in lines 1036–1039 to either add a new record to the Users table or modify an existing record in the Users table. Afterward, the user can select the custom information to be displayed in the default Web page.

14

Summary

A database can be used to implement a User Personalization System and enable users to create their own custom Web pages containing only the information they need. Most Web sites now use a user personalization system to better serve their users. By extending and implementing the UPS presented today, you can easily add personalization features to your own Web site.

Q&A

Q Is the User Personalization System built today compatible across multiple Web browsers?

A Yes. In addition to HTML support, cookie support is the only additional Web browser feature used by the UPS. Virtually all Web browsers, including Internet Explorer, Netscape Navigator, and Mosaic support cookies.

Q What must be done before getting a random number?

A Before getting a random number, you should seed the random number generator.

Q How can you delete a cookie stored in the user's computer?

A A cookie can be deleted by setting its expiration date to a date that has already elapsed.

Q Some users might use security, such as Cookie Crusher, that doesn't allow for cookies. What then?

A If users do not accept cookies, ASP can't keep track of user sessions. ASP is a cookie-based technology, and it uses cookies to track users as they navigate a site. If users don't accept cookies, you can't use the `Session` object to store information about users.

Workshop

The quiz questions and exercises are provided for your further understanding. Please refer to Appendix A, "Answers to Questions," for the answers to the quiz questions; the answers to the exercises are on the MCP Web site.

Quiz

1. What is wrong with the following code listing?

```
<%@ Language=VBScript %>
<HTML>
<HEAD>
```

```
<TITLE>Cookie Deleted</TITLE>
</HEAD>
<BODY>
<H1>Cookie Deleted</H1>
<H3>Personal Settings For Your Computer Have Been Reset</H3>
<%
  ' The cookie is deleted using the Response
  ' object.
  Response.Cookies("UserEmailAddress").Expires = _
    "February 29, 1996"
%>
<P>
<A HREF="Default.asp">Return</A> to main menu.
</P>
</BODY>
</HTML>
```

2. Where can you find a list of ADO constants that can be used in ASP applications along with their corresponding values?

3. What is the purpose of using the ADO recordset LockType Optimistic?

4. How would you include the ADO constant definition file in an ASP application?

5. Can you change the value of a cookie after HTML text has been already sent to the Web browser?

Exercises

1. Come up with a list of at least four improvements for the UPS application.

2. Write ASP code that creates a cookie by the name of Password with the value Top Secret and set its expiration date to February 29, 2000. Add the password field to the database and set its value to the same value as the cookie.

14

WEEK 2

In Review

On Day 8, "Processing Web Data with the Server, Session, and Application Objects," you mastered how and when to use these objects to process Web data. ASP ships with several built-in ActiveX components. By learning how to make the best use of these components, you can build powerful ASP applications in very little time.

On Day 9, "Using ActiveX Components Built for ASP," you learned how to determine capabilities of the Web browser, rotate advertisements, send e-mail, conduct online elections, insert Web counters, and much more!

Most ASP applications make use of databases. You learned the basics of developing typical Web database applications, including how to use SQL statements for data accesson Day 10, "Programming Web Databases." You built your first ASP-based database application in that day's lesson. You can now create your own Web database applications that insert, retrieve, and search database records.

It is easy to build Web database applications using ADO. To build them, first you have to build the database and create a DSN for it. Then, by using the Connection object and ADO, your ASP application can interface with the database and add, delete, modify, search, and insert database records. Before inserting data into a database, you should always validate the data to make sure it is valid.

ADO allows you to build powerful Web database applications. Day 11, "Building Database Applications Using ActiveX Data Objects," helped you master all the features of ADO, including understanding the importance of recordsets, ADO objects, collections, field traversing, and more.

8

9

10

11

12

13

14

Day 12, "Database Development Illustrated: Building a User Registration System," shows you how to build a fully functional Web database application. You can easily build your own Web database applications by reusing the code presented on Day 12. When you're building complex Web applications, get into the habit of first creating a flowchart that outlines the application's control flow. This method makes the task of developing the application more straightforward and less error prone—saving you both time and frustration.Cookies are instrumental in retaining information between HTTP sessions. You learned how to set and retrieve cookies, including the difference between persistent and in-memory cookies, on Day 13, "Retaining Information Between Sessions Using Cookies." Cookies can be used to develop sophisticated Web applications that remember information between HTTP sessions. When a cookie is created, certain information is stored in the user's computer for future reference. When the Web client contacts the Web server responsible for creating the cookie, the information stored in the cookie on the user's computer is sent to the Web server. This information can be used by either a client- or server-side Web application to implement sophisticated Web applications, such as shopping carts and personalized Web pages.

On Day 14, "Developing a User Personalization System with Cookies," you learned how to use cookies to build a user personalization system (UPS). Web database application development was also revisited on Day 14. A database can be used to implement a user personalization system and enable users to create their own custom Web pages containing only the information they need. Most Web sites now have a user personalization system to better serve their users. By extending and implementing the UPS presented on Day 14, you can easily add personalization features to your own Web site.

WEEK 3

At a Glance

ActiveX controls are used to add a rich user interface to ASP applications. You learn how to build an ActiveX control and use it from within an ASP application on Day 15, "Activating Your ASP Applications." Day 16, "Developing a Web Messaging System with TCP/IP Sockets," shows you how to use Visual Basic (VB) along with ASP to create a client/server Web messaging system. You learn the benefits of building multi-tiered Web applications on Day 16, too. With the aid of Visual InterDev 6.0, you can create and manage complex ASP projects. On Day 17, "Building ASP Applications with Visual InterDev 6.0," you learn how features of Visual InterDev 6.0 greatly simplify developing large ASP projects; that day's lesson has many hands-on Visual InterDev exercises. Security is an important, yet often overlooked, aspect of Web application development. Learn how to make your ASP applications more secure on Day 18, "Building in Security." Pay careful attention to the information offered in that day's lesson. On Day 19, "Exploiting ASP: Tips and Advanced Topics," you delve into advanced ASP topics, such as tips for creating effective ASP applications, avoiding memory leaks, using IIS to deploy ASP applications, and ASP registry settings. On Day 20, "Building Custom ASP Components with Visual Basic," you learn how easy it is to build your own custom ASP components with Visual Basic by building a custom Visual Basic component and using it from within an ASP application. Day 21, "Advanced ASP Component Development with Active Automation and the Win32 API," covers how to build more complex ASP components and how to unleash the power of the Win32 API.

15

16

17

18

19

20

21

Activating Your ASP Applications

ActiveX controls can be used to add a new level of interactivity to your Web site. Today, you learn how to use Visual Basic to create your own ActiveX controls and how to use them in ASP applications. You cover the following topics:

- Learn how to add and use ActiveX controls in ASP applications.
- Discover the benefits of using ActiveX controls.
- Use VB to create an ActiveX Calendar control.
- Review ActiveX compatibility issues.
- Address Web browser compatibility issues of ActiveX controls.

Using ActiveX Controls

Before learning how to create your own ActiveX controls, it is important that you understand some of the benefits of using ActiveX controls and how to use them in ASP applications while addressing browser compatibility issues. This section shows their versatility and power by demonstrating how several useful ActiveX controls can be linked to create interactive and useful Web applications.

> **Caution**
>
> At press time, Internet Explorer for Windows NT, 95, and 98 is the only major Web browser that supports ActiveX controls. Microsoft is aggressively porting ActiveX technology components to non-Microsoft platforms, such as the Macintosh and various flavors of UNIX.

ActiveX component developers have created thousands of ActiveX controls that can be used to create server-side and client-side Web applications. Today's lesson doesn't comprehensively cover dozens of ActiveX controls. Instead, you are shown practical uses of ActiveX controls and how they can be used to add a new level of interactivity to your ASP applications. These are some of the benefits of using ActiveX controls:

1. Existing ActiveX controls can be easily migrated to the Internet.
2. ActiveX controls can be easily built using products such as Borland Delphi, Microsoft Visual Basic, and C++.
3. You can use ActiveX controls that are available in Windows and installed as part of Internet Explorer when you are developing Web applications.
4. ActiveX controls are fast.
5. ActiveX controls are lightweight and easily downloaded over the Internet.
6. ActiveX controls provide access to system services such as printing.
7. Several ActiveX controls can be easily linked by using a scripting language such as VBScript to create a complete Web application.

> **Note**
>
> Visit the Microsoft Site Builder Workshop to locate useful ActiveX controls and learn how they can be used to develop compelling Web applications:
> `http://www.microsoft.com/activex/`

Understanding Client-Side and Server-Side ActiveX

There are two different types of ActiveX controls: client-side ActiveX controls and server-side ActiveX controls. Server-side ActiveX controls, also called ActiveX components, can be used to build ASP applications regardless of the Web browser being used because they are executed on the Web server. Client-side ActiveX controls, however, are executed on the user's computer and require a Web browser that supports ActiveX controls.

Inserting ActiveX Controls into ASP Applications

The ActiveX Control Pad simplifies the task of inserting client-side ActiveX controls into ASP applications. You can get a copy of the ActiveX Control Pad from the following URL:

```
http://www.microsoft.com/workshop/misc/cpad/default.asp
```

Additionally, if you have already installed Internet Explorer 4.0 or later on your computer, you can use FrontPage Express (which is installed as part of Internet Explorer) to insert ActiveX controls into ASP applications.

To insert an ActiveX control into an ASP page loaded in FrontPage or FrontPage Express, choose Other Components from the Insert menu, and then choose ActiveX Control. You can then add an ActiveX control to an ASP file. For example, to insert the Microsoft ActiveX Image control, simply select Microsoft ActiveX Image Control from the pull-down list. Many other HTML editors, such as Allaire HomeSite, allow the easy insertion of ActiveX controls.

Using the Microsoft ActiveX Image Control

The Microsoft ActiveX Image control is a versatile control for displaying a variety of images in a Web page. This section demonstrates how to embed the Microsoft ActiveX Image control in an ASP application and allow users to view the weather in a selected city by using the control. The ActiveX Image control is used to display one of the graphics in Figure 15.1 to see the weather of the selected city.

FIGURE 15.1.

Graphics of the weather information Web application.

Web browsers that do not support ActiveX controls are not forgotten, however. The ASP application uses standard HTML to offer the same functionality to users whose Web browsers do not support ActiveX controls. Notice how the ASP application in Listing 15.1 gives users a richer Web browsing experience by using client-side ActiveX controls while offering a standard HTML-based Web page for Web browsers that do not support ActiveX.

LISTING 15.1. USING THE ACTIVEX IMAGE CONTROL.

```
 1: <HTML>
 2:
 3: <HEAD>
 4: <TITLE>Welcome To The Weather Information Page!</TITLE>
 5: </HEAD>
 6:
 7: <BODY BGCOLOR="FFFFFF">
 8:
 9: <%
10:    Dim objBrowserCapabilities
11:
12:    ' Create an instance of the Browser Capabilities component.
13:    Set objBrowserCapabilities =
       ➥Server.CreateObject("MSWC.BrowserType")
14: %>
15:
16: <%
17:    ' The Browser Capabilities component is used to determine if
18:    ' the Web browser supports ActiveX controls.
19:    If (objBrowserCapabilities.ActiveXControls = FALSE) Then
20:    ' Standard HTML is used for Web browsers that do not support
21:    ' ActiveX controls.
22: %>
23:
24: <p><font face="Verdana"><strong>Standard HTML version for Web
25: browsers that do not support ActiveX controls.</strong></font></p>
26:
27: <table align=center border="0" width="400">
28:    <tr>
29:       <td width="100%" bgcolor="#FFFF80">The weather in
30:          <A href="DC.jpg">Washington DC</A></td>
31:    </tr>
32:    <tr>
33:       <td width="100%" bgcolor="#80FF80">The weather in
34:          <A href="NY.jpg">New York</A></td>
35:    </tr>
36:    <tr>
37:       <td width="100%" bgcolor="#FFFF80">The weather in
38:          <A href="Chicago.jpg">Chicago</A></td>
```

15

```
39:    </tr>
40:    <tr>
41:      <td width="100%" bgcolor="#80FF80">The weather in
42:        <A href="Redmond.jpg">Redmond</A></td>
43:    </tr>
44: </table>
45:
46: <%
47:   ' If the Web browser supports ActiveX controls, use the
48:   ' WebBrowserControl ActiveX control.
49:   Else  %>
50:
51: <p><font face="Verdana"><strong>ActiveX version for Web
52: browsers that support ActiveX controls.</strong></font></p>
53:
54: <TABLE>
55: <TR>
56: <TD>
57:     <OBJECT ID="WeatherImage" WIDTH=293 HEIGHT=267
58:      CLASSID="CLSID:D4A97620-8E8F-11CF-93CD-00AA00C08FDF">
59:         <PARAM NAME="BackColor" VALUE="16777215">
60:         <PARAM NAME="BorderStyle" VALUE="0">
61:         <PARAM NAME="SizeMode" VALUE="3">
62:         <PARAM NAME="Size" VALUE="7761;7056">
63:     </OBJECT>
64: </TD>
65: <TD>
66:
67: <SCRIPT LANGUAGE="VBScript">
68: <!--
69: Sub DCButton_Click()
70:   WeatherImage.PicturePath = "DC.jpg"
71: end sub
72: -->
73: </SCRIPT>
74:
75:     <OBJECT ID="DCButton" WIDTH=269 HEIGHT=32
76:      CLASSID="CLSID:D7053240-CE69-11CD-A777-00DD01143C57">
77:         <PARAM NAME="Caption"
78:           VALUE="How is the weather in Washington DC?">
79:         <PARAM NAME="Size" VALUE="7112;846">
80:         <PARAM NAME="FontName" VALUE="Arial">
81:         <PARAM NAME="FontEffects" VALUE="1073741825">
82:         <PARAM NAME="FontHeight" VALUE="200">
83:         <PARAM NAME="FontCharSet" VALUE="0">
84:         <PARAM NAME="FontPitchAndFamily" VALUE="2">
85:         <PARAM NAME="ParagraphAlign" VALUE="3">
86:         <PARAM NAME="FontWeight" VALUE="700">
87:     </OBJECT>
88:
```

continues

LISTING 15.1. CONTINUED

```
 89:    <SCRIPT LANGUAGE="VBScript">
 90: <!--
 91: Sub NYButton_Click()
 92:   WeatherImage.PicturePath = "NY.jpg"
 93: end sub
 94: -->
 95:    </SCRIPT>
 96:
 97:    <OBJECT ID="NYButton" WIDTH=269 HEIGHT=32
 98:     CLASSID="CLSID:D7053240-CE69-11CD-A777-00DD01143C57">
 99:        <PARAM NAME="Caption"
100:          VALUE="How is the weather in New York?">
101:        <PARAM NAME="Size" VALUE="7112;846">
102:        <PARAM NAME="FontName" VALUE="Arial">
103:        <PARAM NAME="FontEffects" VALUE="1073741825">
104:        <PARAM NAME="FontHeight" VALUE="200">
105:        <PARAM NAME="FontCharSet" VALUE="0">
106:        <PARAM NAME="FontPitchAndFamily" VALUE="2">
107:        <PARAM NAME="ParagraphAlign" VALUE="3">
108:        <PARAM NAME="FontWeight" VALUE="700">
109:    </OBJECT>
110:
111:    <SCRIPT LANGUAGE="VBScript">
112: <!--
113: Sub ChicagoButton_Click()
114:   WeatherImage.PicturePath = "Chicago.jpg"
115: end sub
116: -->
117:    </SCRIPT>
118:
119:    <OBJECT ID="ChicagoButton" WIDTH=269 HEIGHT=32
120:     CLASSID="CLSID:D7053240-CE69-11CD-A777-00DD01143C57">
121:        <PARAM NAME="Caption"
122:          VALUE="How is the weather in Chicago?">
123:        <PARAM NAME="Size" VALUE="7112;846">
124:        <PARAM NAME="FontName" VALUE="Arial">
125:        <PARAM NAME="FontEffects" VALUE="1073741825">
126:        <PARAM NAME="FontHeight" VALUE="200">
127:        <PARAM NAME="FontCharSet" VALUE="0">
128:        <PARAM NAME="FontPitchAndFamily" VALUE="2">
129:        <PARAM NAME="ParagraphAlign" VALUE="3">
130:        <PARAM NAME="FontWeight" VALUE="700">
131:    </OBJECT>
132:
133:    <SCRIPT LANGUAGE="VBScript">
134: <!--
135: Sub RedmondButton_Click()
136:   WeatherImage.PicturePath = "Redmond.jpg"
137: end sub
```

15

```
138: -->
139:     </SCRIPT>
140:
141:     <OBJECT ID="RedmondButton" WIDTH=269 HEIGHT=32
142:       CLASSID="CLSID:D7053240-CE69-11CD-A777-00DD01143C57">
143:         <PARAM NAME="Caption"
144:           VALUE="How is the weather in Redmond?">
145:         <PARAM NAME="Size" VALUE="7112;846">
146:         <PARAM NAME="FontName" VALUE="Arial">
147:         <PARAM NAME="FontEffects" VALUE="1073741825">
148:         <PARAM NAME="FontHeight" VALUE="200">
149:         <PARAM NAME="FontCharSet" VALUE="0">
150:         <PARAM NAME="FontPitchAndFamily" VALUE="2">
151:         <PARAM NAME="ParagraphAlign" VALUE="3">
152:         <PARAM NAME="FontWeight" VALUE="700">
153:     </OBJECT>
154: </TD>
155: </TR>
156: </TABLE>
157:
158: <%
159:   End if %>
160:
161: </BODY>
162: </HTML>
```

ANALYSIS Line 13 creates an instance of the Browser Capabilities component, which is used to determine if the Web browser supports ActiveX controls. If it does not, a standard HTML Web page is displayed by the If statement defined in lines 24–44. The Else clause defined in lines 51–156 displays the ActiveX version of the Web page, if the Web browser supports ActiveX controls, by using four ActiveX command buttons and one ActiveX Image control.

 Tip
> For more on the Browser Capabilities component, go back to Day 9, "Using ActiveX Components Built for ASP."

How the Weather Information Web Application Works

When the weather information application is invoked, it looks like the Web page in Figure 15.2. Users choose to view the weather in a certain city by using one of the command buttons on the right-hand side of the page.

FIGURE **15.2.**

The weather informa-tion application.

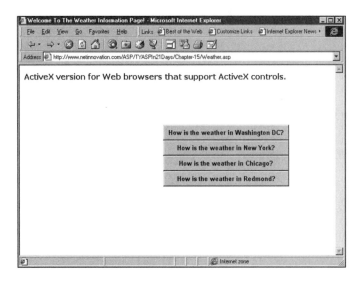

The Washington, D.C., weather information image is displayed when a user clicks the "How is the weather in Washington DC?" button, as shown in Figure 15.3. When the D.C. weather information button is clicked, the VBScript statement in line 70 of Listing 15.1 displays the D.C. weather information graphic.

FIGURE **15.3.**

The weather in Washington, D.C.

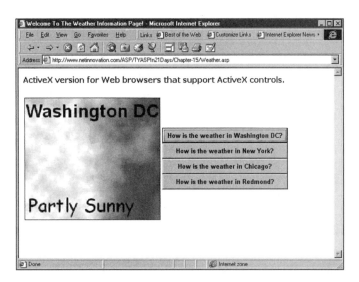

You can easily change the weather information graphic by clicking another command button (without requiring the entire Web page to be reloaded). When a user clicks the

15

"How is the weather in Redmond?" button, the VBScript statement in line 136 of Listing 15.1 displays the Redmond weather information graphic, as shown in Figure 15.4.

FIGURE 15.4.

It still rains in Redmond.

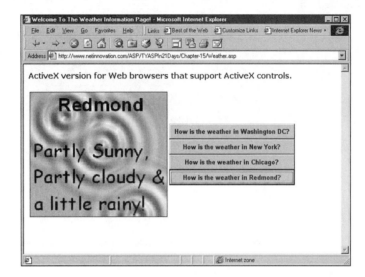

All this is fine if a Web browser that supports ActiveX is being used. What happens if the Web browser does not support ActiveX? Refer to Figure 15.5 for the non-ActiveX version of the same Web application. This Web page is displayed when Netscape Navigator is used to browse the weather information application.

FIGURE 15.5.

Standard HTML version of the weather information application.

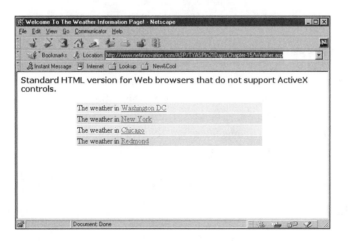

Users can still choose to see the weather of a city. Instead of clicking an ActiveX command button, they can select a hyperlink to view the weather of a city, as shown in
Figure 15.6.

FIGURE 15.6.

*The weather in
Washington, D.C., is
still partly sunny.*

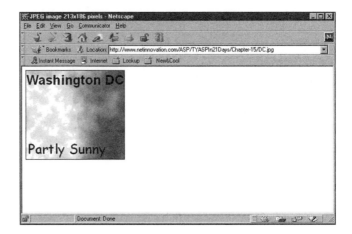

> **Tip**
>
> Always think about Web browser compatibility issues when developing Web
> applications. At a minimum, your Web application should support Netscape
> 2.0. You should consider the Netscape 2.0 Web browser to be the lowest
> common denominator when creating Web applications because practically
> all Web browsers currently in use support, at a minimum, all the features of
> the Netscape 2.0 Web browser.

Creating ActiveX Controls

A thorough overview of building and using ActiveX controls is beyond the scope of this
book. This section illustrates the basics of building an ActiveX control with Visual Basic
by demonstrating how to build an ActiveX Calendar control and use it in an ASP application. Of course, you are shown how to offer the same functionality for users with Web
browsers that do not support ActiveX controls.

> **Note**
>
> This section is based on Visual Basic 6.0.

Developing an ActiveX Calendar Control

Visual Basic can be used to easily create an ActiveX Calendar control. To begin, invoke the Visual Basic compiler. In the dialog box shown in Figure 15.7, select the option to create an ActiveX control.

FIGURE 15.7.

Select the option to create an ActiveX Control.

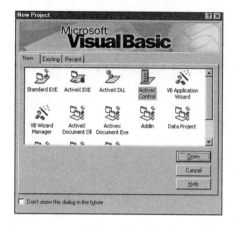

Visual Basic prepares the Integrated Development Environment (IDE) for creating an ActiveX control, as shown in Figure 15.8.

FIGURE 15.8.

The initial project screen.

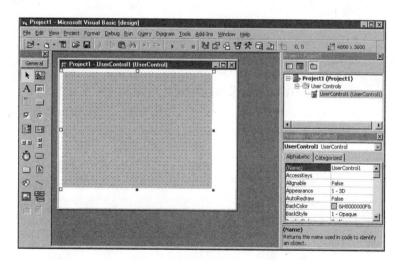

Locate the Project window and highlight the default name given to the project (Project1). Then use the Properties window to change the project name to Calendar. Go back to the Project window and select the default name given to the user control

(UserControl1). Next, use the Properties window to change the default user control name to CalendarControl. The project is now ready for adding controls and code.

The Calendar control has just two different kinds of controls: command buttons and labels. The two command buttons are used to view previous and upcoming months. The label controls are used to label and display the calendar and the date presently selected. After you have finished building the Calendar control, it should look like the user control in Figure 15.9.

FIGURE 15.9.

The ActiveX Calendar control.

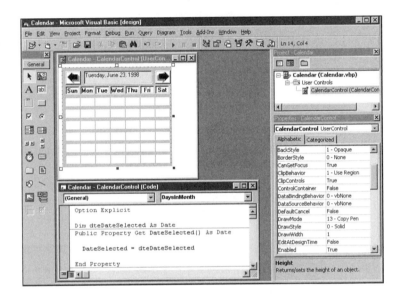

Adding the Two Command Buttons

Add two command buttons to the upper-left corner and the upper-right corner, as shown in Figure 15.9. Notice how the two command buttons have two graphic arrows. Changing the Style property of the command buttons to 1-Graphical creates graphical command buttons, which are assigned graphics by using the Icon property. Refer to Tables 15.1 and 15.2 for the properties of the two command buttons. The command button btnPreviousMonth is used for viewing the previous month, and the command button btnNextMonth is used for viewing the next month. Delete the Caption property string of both command buttons.

TABLE 15.1. PROPERTIES OF THE COMMAND BUTTON `btnPreviousMonth`.

Property	Value
BackColor	&H00FFFFFF&
Height	420
Left	120
MaskColor	&H00FFFFFF&
Picture	"CalendarControl.ctx":0000
Style	1 'Graphical
TabIndex	2
ToolTipText	"Previous Month"
Top	120
Width	500

TABLE 15.2. PROPERTIES OF THE COMMAND BUTTON `btnNextMonth`.

Property	Value
BackColor	&H00FFFFFF&
Height	420
Left	3000
MaskColor	&H00FFFFFF&
Picture	"CalendarControl.ctx":0442
Style	1 'Graphical
TabIndex	1
ToolTipText	"Next Month"
Top	120
Width	500

Adding the Labels

The next step is adding the required label controls. The label in the middle of the two command buttons displays the date selected. Refer to Table 15.3 for the properties of the `lblDateText` label.

TABLE 15.3. PROPERTIES OF THE LABEL `lblDateText`.

Property	Value
BackColor	&H00C0E0FF&
BorderStyle	1 'Fixed Single
Caption	"Tuesday, June 23, 1998"
Height	420
Left	720
TabIndex	0
Top	120
Width	2175

The days of the month have to be labeled from Sunday to Saturday. The labels are displayed with seven labels with the properties defined in Table 15.4. After setting the properties of the first label, you can duplicate the same settings for the other six labels by copying a label to the Clipboard and selecting to create a control array when pasting the copied label.

Tip

Create a control array when adding a series of controls with similar characteristics so you can easily iterate through all the controls by using an index value at runtime to initialize and access values of the controls. Also, it makes it easier to create one control and derive properties of other similar controls from the first one you create.

TABLE 15.4. PROPERTIES OF THE LABELS USED TO MARK THE DAYS OF THE MONTH [`lblWeekdays(0)` - `lblWeekdays(6)`].

Property	Value
Alignment	2 'Center
BackColor	&H00C0FFFF&
BorderStyle	1 'Fixed Single
Caption	"Sun" to "Sat" for each of the labels
Font.Name	"MS Sans Serif"
Font.Size	8.25
Font.Charset	0
Font.Weight	700
Font.Underline	0 'False

Property	Value
Font.Italic	0 'False
Font.Strikethrough	0 'False
Height	255
Index	0
Left	120
TabIndex	3
Top	600
Width	450

All that's left now is to add the label controls used to display the dates of the month, which is very similar to the way the labels used to display the days of the month were added. Create a label with the properties in Table 15.5, copy it to the Clipboard, and paste it to create a control array. A total of 42 labels are used to display all the dates of a month. The indexes of the 42 labels in the control array start from 0 and go up to 41. You need 42 labels to display dates of the month because the Calendar control also displays the last few dates of the previous month as well as the first few dates of the next month.

TABLE 15.5. PROPERTIES OF THE `lblCalendarDates` CONTROL ARRAY.

Property	Value
BackColor	&H00FFFFFF&
Height	255
Index	A value between 0 and 41 for the 42 label controls in the control array
Left	120
TabIndex	10
Top	960
Width	450

You have now finished adding all the controls of the ActiveX Calendar control. All that's required now is adding the code to display the dates of a month.

Adding the Code of the ActiveX Calendar Control

Next, you need to create the main subroutines of the ActiveX Calendar control. The complete source code of the ActiveX Calendar control is given at the end of today's lesson. The `DaysInMonth()` function in Listing 15.2 is used to determine the number of days in a given month.

LISTING **15.2.** DETERMINING THE NUMBER OF DAYS IN A GIVEN MONTH.

```
 1: Public Function DaysInMonth(dteDateToCheck As Date)
 2:
 3:   Dim dteMonthOfDate
 4:
 5:   dteMonthOfDate = Month(dteDateToCheck)
 6:   Select Case dteMonthOfDate
 7:     Case 1, 3, 5, 7, 8, 10, 12
 8:       DaysInMonth = 31
 9:     Case 4, 6, 9, 11
10:       DaysInMonth = 30
11:     Case 2
12:       If (Year(dteDateToCheck) Mod 4) = 0 Then
13:         DaysInMonth = 29
14:       Else
15:         DaysInMonth = 28
16:       End If
17:   End Select
18:
19: End Function
```

ANALYSIS   A date is passed into the function and stored in the variable dteDateToCheck, as shown in line 1. The Select...Case statement defined in lines 6–17 determines the number of days in the month of the given date. The If...Then...Else statement defined in lines 12–16 properly calculates the number of days in February of leap and non-leap years.

The subroutine in Listing 15.3 initializes the ActiveX Calendar control when it is instantiated.

LISTING **15.3.** THE ACTIVEX CALENDAR CONTROL IS INITIALIZED.

```
1: Private Sub UserControl_Initialize()
2:
3:   dteDateSelected = CDate(Month(Date) & "/1/" & Year(Date))
4:   DisplayCalendar (dteDateSelected)
5:
6: End Sub
```

ANALYSIS   By default, the first day of the current month is selected. Line 3 calculates the date of the first day of the current month and assigns it to the variable dteDateSelected. Line 4 calls the DisplayCalendar() subroutine (see Listing 15.4), which displays the dates of the month.

15

Listing 15.4 is the most complex and most important subroutine of the ActiveX Calendar control. The `DisplayCalendar()` subroutine does some tricky date calculations to properly display the dates of the current month, as well as some dates from the previous and next months.

LISTING 15.4. THE CODE THAT DISPLAYS THE CALENDAR.

```
 1: Public Sub DisplayCalendar(dteSelectedDate As Date)
 2:
 3:   Dim IndexCount As Byte
 4:   Dim dteLoopEndDate As Date
 5:   Dim dteFirstDate As Date
 6:
 7:   ' Display the selected date.
 8:   lblDateText.Caption = _
 9:     FormatDateTime(dteDateSelected, vbLongDate)
10:
11:   dteFirstDate = _
12:     CDate(Month(dteSelectedDate) & "/1/" & Year(dteSelectedDate))
13:
14:   ' The following loop displays dates of the previous month.
15:   dteLoopEndDate = _
16:     (Weekday(CDate(Month(dteFirstDate) & "/1/" & _
17:     Year(dteFirstDate))) - 1)
18:   For IndexCount = 0 To dteLoopEndDate
19:     lblCalendarDates(IndexCount).ForeColor = &H80000013
20:     lblCalendarDates(IndexCount).BackColor = &HFFFFFF
21:     lblCalendarDates(IndexCount).Caption = _
22:       Day(DateAdd("d", IndexCount - (dteLoopEndDate), dteFirstDate))
23:   Next
24:
25:   ' The following loop displays dates of the current
26:   ' month.
27:   For IndexCount = (Weekday(dteFirstDate) - 1) To _
28:     DaysInMonth(dteFirstDate) + dteLoopEndDate
29:
30:     ' Display today's date in red.
31:     If Date = DateAdd("d", IndexCount - 1, dteFirstDate) Then
32:       lblCalendarDates(IndexCount).ForeColor = &HFF&
33:     Else
34:       lblCalendarDates(IndexCount).ForeColor = &H80000012
35:     End If
36:
37:     ' Highlight selected date.
38:     If Day(dteSelectedDate) = _
39:       IndexCount - Weekday(dteFirstDate) + 2 Then
40:         lblCalendarDates(IndexCount).BackColor = &HFFFFC0
41:     Else
42:       lblCalendarDates(IndexCount).BackColor = &HFFFFFF
```

continues

LISTING **15.4.** CONTINUED

```
43:      End If
44:
45:         lblCalendarDates(IndexCount).Caption = IndexCount - _
46:            Weekday(dteFirstDate) + 2
47:      Next
48:
49:      ' The following loop displays dates of the next month.
50:      For IndexCount = DaysInMonth(dteFirstDate) + dteLoopEndDate To 41
51:         lblCalendarDates(IndexCount).ForeColor = &H80000013
52:         lblCalendarDates(IndexCount).BackColor = &HFFFFFF
53:         lblCalendarDates(IndexCount).Caption = _
54:            Day(DateAdd("d", IndexCount - dteLoopEndDate, dteFirstDate))
55:      Next
56:
57: End Sub
```

ANALYSIS Line 8 formats and displays the date presently selected. Line 11 calculates the date of the first day of the month and assigns it to the dteFirstDate variable. The calendar displays the ending dates of the previous month, as well as starting dates of the next month. The For...Next loop defined in lines 18–23 display the last few dates of the previous month. The For...Next loop in lines 27–47 displays the dates of the current month. The If...Then...Else statement in lines 31–35 displays today's date in red, and the If...Then...Else statement in lines 38–43 highlights the date presently selected. Finally, the For...Next loop in lines 50–55 displays the first few dates of the next month.

Remember the two command buttons you added to allow the user to browse dates of previous and upcoming months. The subroutine in Listing 15.5 displays dates of the next month and is linked to the Click event of the btnNextMonth button.

LISTING **15.5.** THE CODE THAT DISPLAYS THE DATES OF THE NEXT MONTH.

```
1: Private Sub btnNextMonth_Click()
2:
3:   dteDateSelected = DateAdd("m", 1, dteDateSelected)
4:   DisplayCalendar (dteDateSelected)
5:
6: End Sub
```

ANALYSIS Line 3 adds one month to the date presently selected. Line 4 uses the DisplayCalendar() subroutine to display dates of the next month.

15

The subroutine in Listing 15.6 displays dates of the previous month and is linked to the Click event of the btnPreviousMonth button.

LISTING 15.6. THE CODE THAT DISPLAYS THE DATES OF THE PREVIOUS MONTH.

```
1: Private Sub btnPreviousMonth_Click()
2:
3:   dteDateSelected = DateAdd("m", -1, dteDateSelected)
4:   DisplayCalendar (dteDateSelected)
5:
6: End Sub
```

ANALYSIS Line 3 subtracts one month from the date presently selected. Line 4 uses the DisplayCalendar() subroutine to display dates of the previous month.

The subroutine in Listing 15.7 allows the user to select a date by using the mouse.

LISTING 15.7. THE CODE THAT ALLOWS THE USER TO SELECT A DIFFERENT DATE BY USING THE MOUSE.

```
1: Private Sub lblCalendarDates_Click(Index As Integer)
2:
3:   If (lblCalendarDates(Index).ForeColor = &H80000013) Then
4:     If lblCalendarDates(Index).Caption > 15 Then
5:       dteDateSelected = DateAdd("m", -1, dteDateSelected)
6:     Else
7:       dteDateSelected = DateAdd("m", 1, dteDateSelected)
8:     End If
9:   End If
10:  dteDateSelected = CDate(Month(dteDateSelected) & "/" & _
11:    lblCalendarDates(Index).Caption & "/" & Year(dteDateSelected))
12:  DisplayCalendar (dteDateSelected)
13:
14: End Sub
```

ANALYSIS The If...Then...Else statement in lines 3–9 increments the month of the selected date if the date falls on the next month or decrements the month of the selected date if the date falls on the previous month. Line 10 updates the dteDateSelected variable used to keep track of the date presently selected and calls the DisplayCalendar() subroutine to display the calendar for the date selected.

Using the VB ActiveX Control Interface Wizard

The complete source code of the ActiveX Calendar control is given in Listing 15.8. Some of the code is generated for you by the Visual Basic ActiveX Control Interface Wizard. Use the wizard to simplify the task of adding properties, events, and methods to ActiveX controls you create.

The VB ActiveX Control Interface Wizard creates the required subroutines and variables you can use to implement methods, properties, and events of an ActiveX control.

Before you can use the Visual Basic ActiveX Control Interface Wizard, you need to add it to the Visual Basic Add-Ins menu by choosing Add-In Manager from the Add-Ins menu in the Visual Basic IDE. When the Add-In Manager dialog box appears, select VB 6 ActiveX Ctrl Interface Wizard, as shown in Figure 15.10.

FIGURE 15.10.

Select the VB 6 ActiveX Ctrl Interface Wizard add-in.

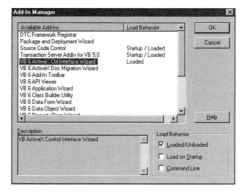

You can now invoke the VB ActiveX Ctrl Interface Wizard by choosing ActiveX Control Interface Wizard from the Add-Ins menu to open the dialog box in Figure 15.11. Click the Next button to continue.

NEW TERM Use the dialog box in Figure 15.12 to select interface members of the Calendar control. *Interface members* are properties, methods, and events that you want your ActiveX control to have. Events, properties, and methods you see under the Available Names column are derived from controls you have already added to the user control. Select the following interface members and click the Next button.

FIGURE 15.11.

The initial dialog box of the ActiveX Control Interface Wizard.

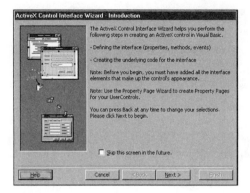

15

AutoRedraw (property)

KeyDown (event)

KeyPress (event)

KeyUp (event)

FIGURE 15.12.

Select interface members of the ActiveX Calendar control.

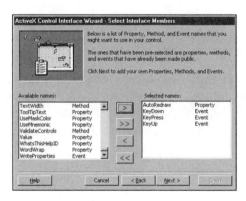

The Create Custom Interface Members dialog box is used to add your own methods, properties, and events to the calendar control. You need to add a new property that can be used to determine the date presently selected. Click the New button to add a new Custom Interface Member. Use the Add Custom Member dialog box (see Figure 15.13) to add a new property by the name of DateSelected.

FIGURE **15.13.**

*A new property is
added to the ActiveX
Calendar control.*

After you add the `DateSelected` property, the new property is displayed in the Create Custom Interface Members dialog box, as shown in Figure 15.14. Click the Next button to continue.

FIGURE **15.14.**

*A new property is
added.*

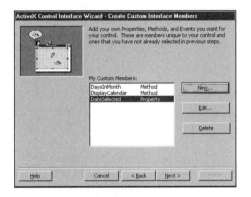

The dialog box in Figure 15.15 is used to map certain interface members to members of constituent controls of the ActiveX control. Map the following interface members (in the Public Name column) to the control UserControl. By doing this, those properties and events are exposed by your ActiveX control. Click the Next button to continue.

AutoRedraw

KeyDown

KeyPress

KeyUp

Attributes of unmapped interface members are specified by using the Set Attributes dialog box shown in Figure 15.16. Select the `DateSelected` property, set its Run Time attribute to Read Only and its Design Time attribute to Not Available.

FIGURE 15.15.

Specifying mapping for interface members.

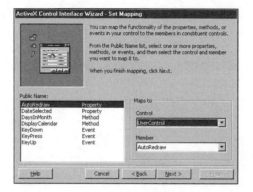

FIGURE 15.16.

Set attributes of unmapped interface members.

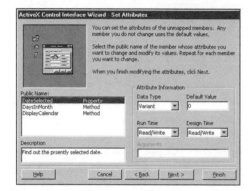

The ActiveX Control Interface Wizard is now ready to create the interface members you specified. You can use the Back button to review your selections or click the Finish button to create the interface members you specified (see Figure 15.17).

FIGURE 15.17.

The last step of the ActiveX Control Interface Wizard.

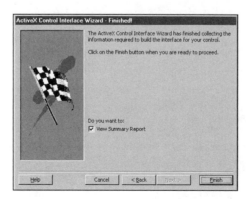

After creating the events, properties, and methods you requested, the ActiveX Control Interface Wizard displays the summary shown in Figure 15.18.

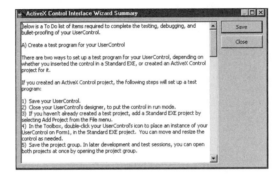

Complete Source Code of the ActiveX Calendar Control

Some of the code generated by the ActiveX Control Interface Wizard needs to be modi-fied to suit your needs. Refer to Listing 15.8 for the complete source code of the ActiveX Calendar control. If you have at least a moderate knowledge of Visual Basic, you will have little trouble understanding the code. Don't worry if the code used to display the calendar looks a bit complicated. The code *is* a bit complicated, but you will understand how it functions as you become a more experienced VB developer. You are fine as long as you have a general idea of how the Visual Basic application in Listing 15.8 displays dates of the month. The ActiveX control you develop in this section can be used to easily add a calendar to your ASP applications.

Listing 15.8. The code of the ActiveX Calendar control.

```
 1: VERSION 5.00
 2: Begin VB.UserControl CalendarControl
 3:    ClientHeight    =    3120
 4:    ClientLeft      =    0
 5:    ClientTop       =    0
 6:    ClientWidth     =    3525
 7:    ScaleHeight     =    3120
 8:    ScaleWidth      =    3525
 9:    Begin VB.CommandButton btnPreviousMonth
10:       BackColor    =    &H00FFFFFF&
11:       Height       =    420
12:       Left         =    120
13:       MaskColor    =    &H00FFFFFF&
14:       Picture      =    "CalendarControl.ctx":0000
```

15

```
15:        Style          =   1  'Graphical
16:        TabIndex       =   2
17:        ToolTipText    =   "Previous Month"
18:        Top            =   120
19:        Width          =   500
20:     End
21:     Begin VB.CommandButton btnNextMonth
22:        BackColor      =   &H00FFFFFF&
23:        Height         =   420
24:        Left           =   3000
25:        MaskColor      =   &H00FFFFFF&
26:        Picture        =   "CalendarControl.ctx":0442
27:        Style          =   1  'Graphical
28:        TabIndex       =   1
29:        ToolTipText    =   "Next Month"
30:        Top            =   120
31:        Width          =   500
32:     End
33:     Begin VB.Label lblCalendarDates
34:        BackColor      =   &H00FFFFFF&
35:        Height         =   255
36:        Index          =   41
37:        Left           =   3000
38:        TabIndex       =   51
39:        Top            =   2760
40:        Width          =   450
41:     End
42:     Begin VB.Label lblCalendarDates
43:        BackColor      =   &H00FFFFFF&
44:        Height         =   255
45:        Index          =   40
46:        Left           =   2520
47:        TabIndex       =   50
48:        Top            =   2760
49:        Width          =   450
50:     End
51:     Begin VB.Label lblCalendarDates
52:        BackColor      =   &H00FFFFFF&
53:        Height         =   255
54:        Index          =   39
55:        Left           =   2040
56:        TabIndex       =   49
57:        Top            =   2760
58:        Width          =   450
59:     End
60:     Begin VB.Label lblCalendarDates
61:        BackColor      =   &H00FFFFFF&
62:        Height         =   255
63:        Index          =   38
64:        Left           =   1560
65:        TabIndex       =   48
```

continues

LISTING 15.8. CONTINUED

```
 66:        Top            =    2760
 67:        Width          =    450
 68:     End
 69:     Begin VB.Label lblCalendarDates
 70:        BackColor      =    &H00FFFFFF&
 71:        Height         =    255
 72:        Index          =    37
 73:        Left           =    1080
 74:        TabIndex       =    47
 75:        Top            =    2760
 76:        Width          =    450
 77:     End
 78:     Begin VB.Label lblCalendarDates
 79:        BackColor      =    &H00FFFFFF&
 80:        Height         =    255
 81:        Index          =    36
 82:        Left           =    600
 83:        TabIndex       =    46
 84:        Top            =    2760
 85:        Width          =    450
 86:     End
 87:     Begin VB.Label lblCalendarDates
 88:        BackColor      =    &H00FFFFFF&
 89:        Height         =    255
 90:        Index          =    35
 91:        Left           =    120
 92:        TabIndex       =    45
 93:        Top            =    2760
 94:        Width          =    450
 95:     End
 96:     Begin VB.Label lblCalendarDates
 97:        BackColor      =    &H00FFFFFF&
 98:        Height         =    255
 99:        Index          =    7
100:        Left           =    120
101:        TabIndex       =    44
102:        Top            =    1320
103:        Width          =    450
104:     End
105:     Begin VB.Label lblCalendarDates
106:        BackColor      =    &H00FFFFFF&
107:        Height         =    255
108:        Index          =    14
109:        Left           =    120
110:        TabIndex       =    43
111:        Top            =    1680
112:        Width          =    450
113:     End
114:     Begin VB.Label lblCalendarDates
```

```
115:            BackColor       =    &H00FFFFFF&
116:            Height          =    255
117:            Index           =    21
118:            Left            =    120
119:            TabIndex        =    42
120:            Top             =    2040
121:            Width           =    450
122:        End
123:        Begin VB.Label lblCalendarDates
124:            BackColor       =    &H00FFFFFF&
125:            Height          =    255
126:            Index           =    8
127:            Left            =    600
128:            TabIndex        =    41
129:            Top             =    1320
130:            Width           =    450
131:        End
132:        Begin VB.Label lblCalendarDates
133:            BackColor       =    &H00FFFFFF&
134:            Height          =    255
135:            Index           =    15
136:            Left            =    600
137:            TabIndex        =    40
138:            Top             =    1680
139:            Width           =    450
140:        End
141:        Begin VB.Label lblCalendarDates
142:            BackColor       =    &H00FFFFFF&
143:            Height          =    255
144:            Index           =    2
145:            Left            =    1080
146:            TabIndex        =    39
147:            Top             =    960
148:            Width           =    450
149:        End
150:        Begin VB.Label lblCalendarDates
151:            BackColor       =    &H00FFFFFF&
152:            Height          =    255
153:            Index           =    3
154:            Left            =    1560
155:            TabIndex        =    38
156:            Top             =    960
157:            Width           =    450
158:        End
159:        Begin VB.Label lblCalendarDates
160:            BackColor       =    &H00FFFFFF&
161:            Height          =    255
162:            Index           =    4
163:            Left            =    2040
164:            TabIndex        =    37
165:            Top             =    960
```

continues

LISTING **15.8.** CONTINUED

```
166:        Width          =     450
167:     End
168:     Begin VB.Label lblCalendarDates
169:        BackColor      =     &H00FFFFFF&
170:        Height         =     255
171:        Index          =     9
172:        Left           =     1080
173:        TabIndex       =     36
174:        Top            =     1320
175:        Width          =     450
176:     End
177:     Begin VB.Label lblCalendarDates
178:        BackColor      =     &H00FFFFFF&
179:        Height         =     255
180:        Index          =     10
181:        Left           =     1560
182:        TabIndex       =     35
183:        Top            =     1320
184:        Width          =     450
185:     End
186:     Begin VB.Label lblCalendarDates
187:        BackColor      =     &H00FFFFFF&
188:        Height         =     255
189:        Index          =     5
190:        Left           =     2520
191:        TabIndex       =     34
192:        Top            =     960
193:        Width          =     450
194:     End
195:     Begin VB.Label lblCalendarDates
196:        BackColor      =     &H80000014&
197:        Height         =     255
198:        Index          =     6
199:        Left           =     3000
200:        TabIndex       =     33
201:        Top            =     960
202:        Width          =     450
203:     End
204:     Begin VB.Label lblCalendarDates
205:        BackColor      =     &H00FFFFFF&
206:        Height         =     255
207:        Index          =     11
208:        Left           =     2040
209:        TabIndex       =     32
210:        Top            =     1320
211:        Width          =     450
212:     End
213:     Begin VB.Label lblCalendarDates
214:        BackColor      =     &H00FFFFFF&
```

15

```
215:            Height           =      255
216:            Index            =      12
217:            Left             =      2520
218:            TabIndex         =      31
219:            Top              =      1320
220:            Width            =      450
221:        End
222:        Begin VB.Label lblCalendarDates
223:            BackColor        =      &H00FFFFFF&
224:            Height           =      255
225:            Index            =      16
226:            Left             =      1080
227:            TabIndex         =      30
228:            Top              =      1680
229:            Width            =      450
230:        End
231:        Begin VB.Label lblCalendarDates
232:            BackColor        =      &H00FFFFFF&
233:            Height           =      255
234:            Index            =      17
235:            Left             =      1560
236:            TabIndex         =      29
237:            Top              =      1680
238:            Width            =      450
239:        End
240:        Begin VB.Label lblCalendarDates
241:            BackColor        =      &H00FFFFFF&
242:            Height           =      255
243:            Index            =      22
244:            Left             =      600
245:            TabIndex         =      28
246:            Top              =      2040
247:            Width            =      450
248:        End
249:        Begin VB.Label lblCalendarDates
250:            BackColor        =      &H00FFFFFF&
251:            Height           =      255
252:            Index            =      23
253:            Left             =      1080
254:            TabIndex         =      27
255:            Top              =      2040
256:            Width            =      450
257:        End
258:        Begin VB.Label lblCalendarDates
259:            BackColor        =      &H00FFFFFF&
260:            Height           =      255
261:            Index            =      24
262:            Left             =      1560
263:            TabIndex         =      26
264:            Top              =      2040
265:            Width            =      450
```

continues

LISTING 15.8. CONTINUED

```
266:    End
267:    Begin VB.Label lblCalendarDates
268:        BackColor       =   &H00FFFFFF&
269:        Height          =   255
270:        Index           =   18
271:        Left            =   2040
272:        TabIndex        =   25
273:        Top             =   1680
274:        Width           =   450
275:    End
276:    Begin VB.Label lblCalendarDates
277:        BackColor       =   &H00FFFFFF&
278:        Height          =   255
279:        Index           =   19
280:        Left            =   2520
281:        TabIndex        =   24
282:        Top             =   1680
283:        Width           =   450
284:    End
285:    Begin VB.Label lblCalendarDates
286:        BackColor       =   &H00FFFFFF&
287:        Height          =   255
288:        Index           =   13
289:        Left            =   3000
290:        TabIndex        =   23
291:        Top             =   1320
292:        Width           =   450
293:    End
294:    Begin VB.Label lblCalendarDates
295:        BackColor       =   &H00FFFFFF&
296:        Height          =   255
297:        Index           =   20
298:        Left            =   3000
299:        TabIndex        =   22
300:        Top             =   1680
301:        Width           =   450
302:    End
303:    Begin VB.Label lblCalendarDates
304:        BackColor       =   &H00FFFFFF&
305:        Height          =   255
306:        Index           =   25
307:        Left            =   2040
308:        TabIndex        =   21
309:        Top             =   2040
310:        Width           =   450
311:    End
312:    Begin VB.Label lblCalendarDates
313:        BackColor       =   &H00FFFFFF&
```

15

```
314:          Height        =      255
315:          Index         =      26
316:          Left          =      2520
317:          TabIndex      =      20
318:          Top           =      2040
319:          Width         =      450
320:       End
321:       Begin VB.Label lblCalendarDates
322:          BackColor     =      &H00FFFFFF&
323:          Height        =      255
324:          Index         =      27
325:          Left          =      3000
326:          TabIndex      =      19
327:          Top           =      2040
328:          Width         =      450
329:       End
330:       Begin VB.Label lblCalendarDates
331:          BackColor     =      &H00FFFFFF&
332:          Height        =      255
333:          Index         =      28
334:          Left          =      120
335:          TabIndex      =      18
336:          Top           =      2400
337:          Width         =      450
338:       End
339:       Begin VB.Label lblCalendarDates
340:          BackColor     =      &H00FFFFFF&
341:          Height        =      255
342:          Index         =      29
343:          Left          =      600
344:          TabIndex      =      17
345:          Top           =      2400
346:          Width         =      450
347:       End
348:       Begin VB.Label lblCalendarDates
349:          BackColor     =      &H00FFFFFF&
350:          Height        =      255
351:          Index         =      30
352:          Left          =      1080
353:          TabIndex      =      16
354:          Top           =      2400
355:          Width         =      450
356:       End
357:       Begin VB.Label lblCalendarDates
358:          BackColor     =      &H00FFFFFF&
359:          Height        =      255
360:          Index         =      31
361:          Left          =      1560
362:          TabIndex      =      15
363:          Top           =      2400
364:          Width         =      450
```

continues

LISTING 15.8. CONTINUED

```
365:    End
366:    Begin VB.Label lblCalendarDates
367:       BackColor       =    &H00FFFFFF&
368:       Height          =    255
369:       Index           =    32
370:       Left            =    2040
371:       TabIndex        =    14
372:       Top             =    2400
373:       Width           =    450
374:    End
375:    Begin VB.Label lblCalendarDates
376:       BackColor       =    &H00FFFFFF&
377:       Height          =    255
378:       Index           =    33
379:       Left            =    2520
380:       TabIndex        =    13
381:       Top             =    2400
382:       Width           =    450
383:    End
384:    Begin VB.Label lblCalendarDates
385:       BackColor       =    &H00FFFFFF&
386:       Height          =    255
387:       Index           =    34
388:       Left            =    3000
389:       TabIndex        =    12
390:       Top             =    2400
391:       Width           =    450
392:    End
393:    Begin VB.Label lblCalendarDates
394:       BackColor       =    &H00FFFFFF&
395:       Height          =    255
396:       Index           =    1
397:       Left            =    600
398:       TabIndex        =    11
399:       Top             =    960
400:       Width           =    450
401:    End
402:    Begin VB.Label lblCalendarDates
403:       BackColor       =    &H00FFFFFF&
404:       Height          =    255
405:       Index           =    0
406:       Left            =    120
407:       TabIndex        =    10
408:       Top             =    960
409:       Width           =    450
410:    End
411:    Begin VB.Label lblWeekdays
412:       Alignment       =    2   'Center
413:       BackColor       =    &H00C0FFFF&
```

15

```
414:        BorderStyle    =   1  'Fixed Single
415:        Caption        =   "Sat"
416:        BeginProperty Font
417:           Name        =   "MS Sans Serif"
418:           Size        =   8.25
419:           Charset     =   0
420:           Weight      =   700
421:           Underline   =   0   'False
422:           Italic      =   0   'False
423:           Strikethrough =  0   'False
424:        EndProperty
425:        Height         =   255
426:        Index          =   6
427:        Left           =   3000
428:        TabIndex       =   9
429:        Top            =   600
430:        Width          =   450
431:     End
432:     Begin VB.Label lblWeekdays
433:        Alignment      =   2  'Center
434:        BackColor      =   &H00C0FFFF&
435:        BorderStyle    =   1  'Fixed Single
436:        Caption        =   "Thu"
437:        BeginProperty Font
438:           Name        =   "MS Sans Serif"
439:           Size        =   8.25
440:           Charset     =   0
441:           Weight      =   700
442:           Underline   =   0   'False
443:           Italic      =   0   'False
444:           Strikethrough =  0   'False
445:        EndProperty
446:        Height         =   255
447:        Index          =   4
448:        Left           =   2040
449:        TabIndex       =   8
450:        Top            =   600
451:        Width          =   450
452:     End
453:     Begin VB.Label lblWeekdays
454:        Alignment      =   2  'Center
455:        BackColor      =   &H00C0FFFF&
456:        BorderStyle    =   1  'Fixed Single
457:        Caption        =   "Fri"
458:        BeginProperty Font
459:           Name        =   "MS Sans Serif"
460:           Size        =   8.25
461:           Charset     =   0
462:           Weight      =   700
463:           Underline   =   0   'False
464:           Italic      =   0   'False
```

continues

LISTING 15.8. CONTINUED

```
465:           Strikethrough   =   0    'False
466:        EndProperty
467:        Height          =   255
468:        Index           =   5
469:        Left            =   2520
470:        TabIndex        =   7
471:        Top             =   600
472:        Width           =   450
473:     End
474:     Begin VB.Label lblWeekdays
475:        Alignment       =   2    'Center
476:        BackColor       =   &H00C0FFFF&
477:        BorderStyle     =   1    'Fixed Single
478:        Caption         =   "Wed"
479:        BeginProperty Font
480:           Name         =   "MS Sans Serif"
481:           Size         =   8.25
482:           Charset      =   0
483:           Weight       =   700
484:           Underline    =   0    'False
485:           Italic       =   0    'False
486:           Strikethrough   =   0    'False
487:        EndProperty
488:        Height          =   255
489:        Index           =   3
490:        Left            =   1560
491:        TabIndex        =   6
492:        Top             =   600
493:        Width           =   450
494:     End
495:     Begin VB.Label lblWeekdays
496:        Alignment       =   2    'Center
497:        BackColor       =   &H00C0FFFF&
498:        BorderStyle     =   1    'Fixed Single
499:        Caption         =   "Tue"
500:        BeginProperty Font
501:           Name         =   "MS Sans Serif"
502:           Size         =   8.25
503:           Charset      =   0
504:           Weight       =   700
505:           Underline    =   0    'False
506:           Italic       =   0    'False
507:           Strikethrough   =   0    'False
508:        EndProperty
509:        Height          =   255
510:        Index           =   2
511:        Left            =   1080
512:        TabIndex        =   5
```

```
513:        Top              =    600
514:        Width            =    450
515:     End
516:     Begin VB.Label lblWeekdays
517:        Alignment        =    2  'Center
518:        BackColor        =    &H00C0FFFF&
519:        BorderStyle      =    1  'Fixed Single
520:        Caption          =    "Mon"
521:        BeginProperty Font
522:           Name          =    "MS Sans Serif"
523:           Size          =    8.25
524:           Charset       =    0
525:           Weight        =    700
526:           Underline     =    0    'False
527:           Italic        =    0    'False
528:           Strikethrough =    0    'False
529:        EndProperty
530:        Height           =    255
531:        Index            =    1
532:        Left             =    600
533:        TabIndex         =    4
534:        Top              =    600
535:        Width            =    450
536:     End
537:     Begin VB.Label lblWeekdays
538:        Alignment        =    2  'Center
539:        BackColor        =    &H00C0FFFF&
540:        BorderStyle      =    1  'Fixed Single
541:        Caption          =    "Sun"
542:        BeginProperty Font
543:           Name          =    "MS Sans Serif"
544:           Size          =    8.25
545:           Charset       =    0
546:           Weight        =    700
547:           Underline     =    0    'False
548:           Italic        =    0    'False
549:           Strikethrough =    0    'False
550:        EndProperty
551:        Height           =    255
552:        Index            =    0
553:        Left             =    120
554:        TabIndex         =    3
555:        Top              =    600
556:        Width            =    450
557:     End
558:     Begin VB.Label lblDateText
559:        BackColor        =    &H00C0E0FF&
560:        BorderStyle      =    1  'Fixed Single
561:        Caption          =    "Tuesday, June 23, 1998"
562:        Height           =    420
563:        Left             =    720
```

continues

LISTING 15.8. CONTINUED

```
564:        TabIndex      =   0
565:        Top           =   120
566:        Width         =   2175
567:     End
568: End
569:
570: Attribute VB_Name = "CalendarControl"
571: Attribute VB_GlobalNameSpace = False
572: Attribute VB_Creatable = True
573: Attribute VB_PredeclaredId = False
574: Attribute VB_Exposed = True
575: Option Explicit
576:
577: Dim dteDateSelected As Date
578:
579: 'Event Declarations:
580: 'MappingInfo=UserControl,UserControl,-1,KeyDown
581: Event KeyDown(KeyCode As Integer, Shift As Integer)
582: 'MappingInfo=UserControl,UserControl,-1,KeyPress
583: Event KeyPress(KeyAscii As Integer)
584: 'MappingInfo=UserControl,UserControl,-1,KeyUp
585: Event KeyUp(KeyCode As Integer, Shift As Integer)
586:
587: Public Function DaysInMonth(dteDateToCheck As Date)
588:
589:    Dim dteMonthOfDate
590:
591:    dteMonthOfDate = Month(dteDateToCheck)
592:    Select Case dteMonthOfDate
593:      Case 1, 3, 5, 7, 8, 10, 12
594:        DaysInMonth = 31
595:      Case 4, 6, 9, 11
596:        DaysInMonth = 30
597:      Case 2
598:        If (Year(dteDateToCheck) Mod 4) = 0 Then
599:           DaysInMonth = 29
600:        Else
601:           DaysInMonth = 28
602:        End If
603:    End Select
604:
605: End Function
606:
607: Public Sub DisplayCalendar(dteSelectedDate As Date)
608:
609:    Dim IndexCount As Byte
610:    Dim dteLoopEndDate As Date
611:    Dim dteFirstDate As Date
612:
```

15

```
613:   ' Display the selected date.
614:   lblDateText.Caption = _
615:     FormatDateTime(dteDateSelected, vbLongDate)
616:
617:   dteFirstDate = _
618:     CDate(Month(dteSelectedDate) & "/1/" & Year(dteSelectedDate))
619:
620:   ' The following loop displays dates of the previous month.
621:   dteLoopEndDate = _
622:     (Weekday(CDate(Month(dteFirstDate) & "/1/" & _
623:     Year(dteFirstDate))) - 1)
624:   For IndexCount = 0 To dteLoopEndDate
625:     lblCalendarDates(IndexCount).ForeColor = &H80000013
626:     lblCalendarDates(IndexCount).BackColor = &HFFFFFF
627:     lblCalendarDates(IndexCount).Caption = _
628:       Day(DateAdd("d", IndexCount - (dteLoopEndDate), dteFirstDate))
629:   Next
630:
631:   ' The following loop displays dates of the current
632:   ' month.
633:   For IndexCount = (Weekday(dteFirstDate) - 1) To _
634:     DaysInMonth(dteFirstDate) + dteLoopEndDate
635:
636:     ' Display today's date in red.
637:     If Date = DateAdd("d", IndexCount - 1, dteFirstDate) Then
638:       lblCalendarDates(IndexCount).ForeColor = &HFF&
639:     Else
640:       lblCalendarDates(IndexCount).ForeColor = &H80000012
641:     End If
642:
643:     ' Highlight selected date.
644:     If Day(dteSelectedDate) = _
645:       IndexCount - Weekday(dteFirstDate) + 2 Then
646:         lblCalendarDates(IndexCount).BackColor = &HFFFFFC0
647:     Else
648:       lblCalendarDates(IndexCount).BackColor = &HFFFFFF
649:     End If
650:
651:     lblCalendarDates(IndexCount).Caption = IndexCount - _
652:       Weekday(dteFirstDate) + 2
653:   Next
654:
655:   ' The following loop displays dates of the next month.
656:   For IndexCount = DaysInMonth(dteFirstDate) + dteLoopEndDate To 41
657:     lblCalendarDates(IndexCount).ForeColor = &H80000013
658:     lblCalendarDates(IndexCount).BackColor = &HFFFFFF
659:     lblCalendarDates(IndexCount).Caption = _
660:       Day(DateAdd("d", IndexCount - dteLoopEndDate, dteFirstDate))
661:   Next
662:
663: End Sub
```

continues

LISTING 15.8. CONTINUED

```
664:
665: ' Advances the calendar one month forward.
666: Private Sub btnNextMonth_Click()
667:
668:    dteDateSelected = DateAdd("m", 1, dteDateSelected)
669:    DisplayCalendar (dteDateSelected)
670:
671: End Sub
672:
673: ' Moves the calendar one month backward.
674: Private Sub btnPreviousMonth_Click()
675:
676:    dteDateSelected = DateAdd("m", -1, dteDateSelected)
677:    DisplayCalendar (dteDateSelected)
678:
679: End Sub
680:
681: ' This subroutine allows the user to select a different
682: ' date.
683: Private Sub lblCalendarDates_Click(Index As Integer)
684:
685:    If (lblCalendarDates(Index).ForeColor = &H80000013) Then
686:      If lblCalendarDates(Index).Caption > 15 Then
687:        dteDateSelected = DateAdd("m", -1, dteDateSelected)
688:      Else
689:        dteDateSelected = DateAdd("m", 1, dteDateSelected)
690:      End If
691:    End If
692:    dteDateSelected = CDate(Month(dteDateSelected) & "/" & _
693:      lblCalendarDates(Index).Caption & "/" & Year(dteDateSelected))
694:    DisplayCalendar (dteDateSelected)
695:
696: End Sub
697:
698: ' This subroutine initializes the calendar with the current
699: ' date.
700: Private Sub UserControl_Initialize()
701:
702:    dteDateSelected = CDate(Month(Date) & "/1/" & Year(Date))
703:    DisplayCalendar (dteDateSelected)
704:
705: End Sub
706: 'WARNING! DO NOT REMOVE OR MODIFY THE FOLLOWING COMMENTED LINES!
707: 'MappingInfo=UserControl,UserControl,-1,AutoRedraw
708: Public Property Get AutoRedraw() As Boolean
709:    AutoRedraw = UserControl.AutoRedraw
710: End Property
711:
```

15

```
712: Public Property Let AutoRedraw(ByVal New_AutoRedraw As Boolean)
713:   UserControl.AutoRedraw() = New_AutoRedraw
714:   PropertyChanged "AutoRedraw"
715: End Property
716:
717: Private Sub UserControl_KeyDown(KeyCode As Integer, Shift As Integer)
718:   RaiseEvent KeyDown(KeyCode, Shift)
719: End Sub
720:
721: Private Sub UserControl_KeyPress(KeyAscii As Integer)
722:   RaiseEvent KeyPress(KeyAscii)
723: End Sub
724:
725: Private Sub UserControl_KeyUp(KeyCode As Integer, Shift As Integer)
726:   RaiseEvent KeyUp(KeyCode, Shift)
727: End Sub
728:
729: 'WARNING! DO NOT REMOVE OR MODIFY THE FOLLOWING COMMENTED LINES!
730: 'MemberInfo=14,0,0,0
731: Public Property Get DateSelected() As Variant
732:   DateSelected = dteDateSelected
733: End Property
734:
735: Public Property Let DateSelected(ByVal New_DateSelected As Variant)
736:
737:   dteDateSelected = New_DateSelected
738:   PropertyChanged "DateSelected"
739:
740: End Property
741:
742: 'Load property values from storage.
743: Private Sub UserControl_ReadProperties(PropBag As PropertyBag)
744:
745:   UserControl.AutoRedraw = PropBag.ReadProperty("AutoRedraw", False)
746:   dteDateSelected = PropBag.ReadProperty("DateSelected")
747:
748: End Sub
749:
750: 'Write property values to storage.
751: Private Sub UserControl_WriteProperties(PropBag As PropertyBag)
752:
753:   Call PropBag.WriteProperty("AutoRedraw", _
754:     UserControl.AutoRedraw, False)
755:   Call PropBag.WriteProperty("DateSelected", dteDateSelected)
756:
757: End Sub
```

Lines 2–568 define the properties of all the constituent controls of the Calendar control. Lines 570–574 specify its attributes. The global variable `dteDateSelected` defined in line 577 is used to keep track of the date presently selected. The subroutines and functions you learned about earlier are declared next.

> **Note**   This is the actual text found in the `CalendarControl.ctl` file, not what appears in the code window in Visual Basic.

Compiling and Deploying the ActiveX Calendar Control

The Calendar control is now fully implemented and ready for use. Choose Make Calendar.ocx from the File menu to compile and register it. You can register the Calendar control on a different machine by issuing the following command at the command prompt:

```
Regsvr32 Calendar.ocx
```

Before the Calendar control can be distributed through the Internet, you need to create a cabinet (`.cab`) file for it by using the VB add-in Package and Deployment Wizard. You should also digitally sign your ActiveX control with Microsoft Authenticode technology.

Using the Calendar ActiveX Control in an ASP Application

Figure 15.19 shows an example of how the Calendar control can be used by an ASP application to interact with users. The Calendar control ensures that the user selects only valid dates.

> **Tip**   When building ASP applications that use ActiveX controls, always use the Browser Capabilities component to offer the same functionality for users whose Web browsers do not support ActiveX.

After a user selects a date and clicks the Submit Selected Date to ASP Application button, the date is submitted by using an HTML form. The ASP application then processes and displays the date selected by the user, as shown in Figure 15.20.

FIGURE 15.19.

The Calendar control is used by an ASP application.

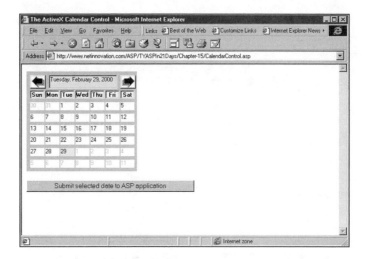

FIGURE 15.20.

The ASP application processes the selected date.

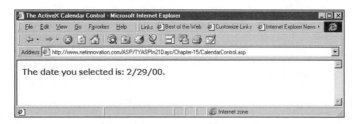

The ASP application is designed so that users whose Web browsers do not support ActiveX controls are not left in the dark. When a Web browser that does not support ActiveX controls is used, the Web page in Figure 15.21 is displayed. Notice that its user interface is not as sophisticated as the one in the ActiveX version shown in Figure 15.19.

FIGURE 15.21.

The non-ActiveX version of the Web page in Figure 15.19.

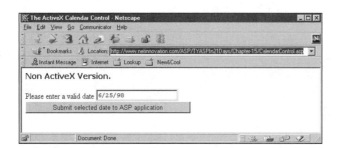

After a user types in a date and submits it, the date is processed and displayed by the ASP application, as shown in Figure 15.22.

FIGURE **15.22.**

*The ASP application
processes the selected
date.*

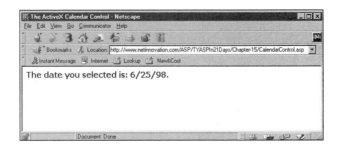

Listing 15.9 shows the complete source code of the ASP application that uses the
Calendar control.

LISTING 15.9. USING THE ACTIVEX CALENDAR CONTROL.

```
 1: <!DOCTYPE HTML PUBLIC "-//W3C//DTD HTML 3.2 Final//EN">
 2:
 3: <SCRIPT language="VBScript">
 4: Sub SubmitButton_OnClick ()
 5:
 6:   DateForm.dteDateSelected.value = Calendar.DateSelected
 7:   DateForm.Submit
 8:
 9: End Sub
10: </SCRIPT>
11:
12: <HTML>
13: <HEAD>
14:     <TITLE>The ActiveX Calendar Control</TITLE>
15: </HEAD>
16:
17: <BODY>
18: <%
19:   If NOT Request.Form ("dteDateSelected") = "" Then %>
20:
21: <p><font face="Verdana"><strong>
22: The date you selected is: <%= Request.Form ("dteDateSelected") %>.
23: </strong></font></p>
24:
25: <% Else
26:
27:   Dim objBrowserCapabilities
28:
29:   ' Create an instance of the Browser Capabilities component.
30:   Set objBrowserCapabilities = Server.CreateObject("MSWC.BrowserType")
31:
32:   ' The Browser Capabilities component is used to determine if
33:   ' the Web browser supports ActiveX controls.
34:   If (objBrowserCapabilities.ActiveXControls = FALSE) Then
```

15

```
35:
36:    ' Standard HTML is used for Web browsers that do not support
37:    ' ActiveX controls.
38: %>
39:
40: <p><font face="Verdana"><strong>
41: Non ActiveX Version.</strong></font></p>
42:
43: <p><form action="CalendarControl.asp"
44:    name=DateForm method="POST">
45: Please enter a valid date
46: <input type="Text" name="dteDateSelected"
47:    value="<%= Date() %>">
48: <input type="Submit" name="SubmitButton"
49:    value="Submit selected date to ASP application">
50: </form></p>
51:
52: <% Else %>
53: <object
54:    id=Calendar name=Calendar
55:    classid="clsid:8FFC84C8-0B43-11D2-A8DE-00A0CC20AFD1">
56: </object>
57:
58: <P>
59: <form action="CalendarControl.asp" name=DateForm method="POST">
60: <input type="Hidden" name="dteDateSelected" value="">
61: <input type="Button" name="SubmitButton"
62:    value="Submit selected date to ASP application">
63: </P>
64: </form>
65:
66: <%
67:    End If
68:    End If
69: %>
70:
71: </BODY>
72: </HTML>
```

ANALYSIS The VBScript subroutine in lines 3–10 is used to copy the date selected by the user to a hidden HTML form variable and submit the form to the ASP application. The If statement in line 19 checks whether the user has entered a date, and if so, processes and displays it. Otherwise, the Else clause of the If statement is executed. Line 30 creates an instance of the Browser Capabilities component. If the Web browser does not support ActiveX controls, the HTML text in lines 43–50 is displayed to allow the user to enter a date using a standard HTML form. If the Web browser supports ActiveX controls, however, the HTML text in lines 53–64 uses an ActiveX control to get a date from the user.

Understanding When to Use ActiveX Controls

Understanding when it's the best time to use ActiveX controls is important. All Web browsers do not support ActiveX controls. At the time of this writing, Internet Explorer is the only major Web browser that supports ActiveX controls. If you are developing an intranet or extranet Web application, and you are sure that virtually all your users have Internet Explorer, you can use ActiveX controls to add a new level of interactivity to your Web application. However, ActiveX controls are not highly suited for developing Internet applications for the general Internet population. Nearly half of Web users use Netscape Navigator, which does not natively support ActiveX controls.

That doesn't mean you can't use ActiveX controls in Internet applications. You were shown how to use ActiveX controls to offer a richer Web browsing experience for Web browsers that support ActiveX controls while making sure those using less sophisticated Web browsers are not forgotten.

Summary

ActiveX controls can be used to create highly interactive Web applications. Because not all Web browsers support ActiveX, you should be aware of Web browser compatibility issues when using ActiveX controls. As demonstrated today, it is possible to use ActiveX controls to add a new level of interactivity to your Web site while making sure your ASP applications are friendly toward Web browsers that do not support ActiveX controls.

Q&A

Q **If you use client-side ActiveX controls, does it mean Web browsers that do not support ActiveX are left in the dark?**

A Not necessarily. As you were shown, the Browser Capabilities component can be used to determine if a Web browser does not support ActiveX and provide a plain-text Web page for such Web browsers.

Q **Are there any Web browser limitations when using server-side ActiveX components?**

A None whatsoever. Server-side ActiveX components are executed on the Web server, so it really does not matter what Web browser is being used.

Q **Why should I go to all this trouble and create ActiveX controls when I know that not all Web browsers on the Internet support them?**

15

A Remember, your goal as a Web developer is to give your readers a rich Web browser experience and make good use of the browser's capabilities. Therefore, you should always take advantage of the browser's capabilities, yet make sure other users are not left out.

Consider the following analogy. Not all TV sets support color, stereo, or surround sound. However, most prime-time TV programs are broadcast with these extra features so that those with TV sets that support them can enjoy the programs more.

Workshop

The quiz questions and exercises are provided for your further understanding. Please refer to Appendix A, "Answers to Questions," for the answers to the quiz questions; the answers to the exercises are on the MCP Web site.

Quiz

1. Name five benefits of using ActiveX controls.

2. What is the benefit of creating a control array when adding a series of controls with similar characteristics?

3. Which ASP statements display the string `"Non ActiveX Version"` for Web browsers that do not support ActiveX controls?

4. Which command-line statement can be used to register the ActiveX control `calendar.ocx` on a remote computer?

5. Describe the purpose of the ActiveX Control Interface Wizard.

6. Do all Web browsers support client-side ActiveX controls?

Exercises

1. The Microsoft Web Browser control can be used to browse objects of the user's computer as well as Web pages on the Internet. Create an ASP application that uses the Microsoft Web Browser control to browse files on the user's computer as well as URLs supplied by the user. (Hint: VBScript on the client side can be used to automate the Microsoft Web Browser control.)

2. Modify the ASP application you created in Exercise 1 to add the same functionality for Web browsers that do not support ActiveX controls (Hint: Use the `Response.Redirect()` method to redirect the Web browser to a new URL.)

3. Add a button to the ASP application created in Exercises 1 and 2 to navigate the user to a predefined URL. The user should be able to navigate to the predefined URL regardless of whether the Web browser supports ActiveX.

DAY 16

Developing a Web Messaging System with TCP/IP Sockets

Today, you will have some fun with Web application development by creating a Web messaging system (WMS) that uses TCP/IP sockets. Users browsing a Web site can send instant messages to any computer on the Internet by using the WMS. You can incorporate the WMS into your own Web site so that users can provide critical feedback (such as a database not functioning properly) and have that feedback instantly forwarded to either the system administrator's desktop or a help desk. Today you cover the following:

- Understand the three-tier model.
- Understand the benefits of the three-tier model.
- Use TCP/IP sockets for data communication.
- Create the messaging system server using VB.
- Create and use the messaging system client.
- Install TCP/IP sockets support (Winsock) for ASP.

- Connect to hosts on the Internet via sockets.
- Develop an ASP-based client/server Web messaging system.
- Learn how to port the messaging system client to ASP.

Understanding the Three-Tier Model

When developing Web applications that fall into a client/server model, it is important that you understand the three-tier model and how it relates to the Web. By understanding the benefits of the three-tier model, you can create more robust and scalable Web applications that are easy to maintain.

Typically, each tier of the three-tier model is implemented and executed on a different system, although this is not always the case. The three-tier model consists of the following three components:

- User interface
- Programming/business logic
- Database

The complex nature of the Web does not limit you to a preset number of tiers. Web applications are complex organisms and can often span many different computer systems and networks. The client/server's three-tier model sometimes gets gray when the lines that separate the tiers are blurred. There was a time when separate tiers almost always meant that each tier existed on a different computer system, but this is no longer the case. For example, all three tiers of the application you develop today can exist on one, two, or three different computers.

Note Although most traditional applications are limited to three tiers, it is not uncommon for Web applications to have several tiers because of the Internet's distributed and connected nature. Because these applications can have more than three tiers, they are often referred to as *n-tier applications*.

User Interface

In the case of a Web application, the user interface is generally a user's Web browser. The Web browser, which is almost always the client-side portion of an application, is often executed on the user's computer. Web applications have become increasingly complex over the past few years. Although this book does not extensively cover client-side Web application development, you were shown how to spice up your Web pages using

ActiveX, client-side scripting, and Java. The user interface of the WMS application you develop today is HTML form based.

Programming and Business Logic

The middle tier is generally the ASP applications on the Web server. The ASP scripts you write belong in the middle tier and are responsible for processing data retrieved through the user interface by using business objects and databases (that can be implemented on a different computer in large-scale Web applications). The programming logic of the WMS application you develop today consists of the ASP application `SendMessage.asp`, which is in Listing 16.2.

NEW TERM A *business object* can be thought of as a "black box" that performs a certain predefined task. The business object can exist on either the same server as the Web server or a different server. Business objects instantiated by the middle tier make Web applications more robust and scalable. For example, if a Web application needs to validate and charge credit cards, the business objects that perform those tasks can be executed on a different server. As the volume of transactions increases, an additional server can be used to execute the business objects that validate and charge credit cards. Additionally, if the rules for validating a credit card change, you can simply change the business object without touching the rest of the ASP application.

Databases

The third tier, or *back end*, as it is often called, is the database. This tier contains resources used by the programming logic that can be physically located on a different computer, cluster, or network. It consists of components and resources used by the programming logic to process data retrieved through the user interface.

> **Note**
>
> A *cluster* is a collection of computers that share system resources and implement fail-safe operations. A cluster might appear as one large computer to an application, although the cluster can be made up of several computers linked together.

Understanding the Benefits of the Three-Tier Model

The benefits of using the three-tier model are significant even when you're creating a relatively modest Web application. The three-tier model helps you think of your Web application in different layers. Each layer can be easily moved from one computer system to another when the need arises. Here are some benefits of the three-tier model:

- Aids code maintenance
- Promotes robust, scalable Web applications
- Naturally separates business logic from programming logic
- Promotes teamwork by allowing different teams to work on each tier
- Sensitive areas of an application (such as credit card billing and verification) can be protected with additional security

Using TCP/IP Sockets for Data Communication

The application you build today uses TCP/IP sockets. Now that you know the benefits of the three-tier model, it's important that you understand how TCP/IP sockets are used for data communication. Many different computers are connected to the Internet, and they can all communicate with each other because they all support TCP/IP (a communication protocol). Practically all communication takes place on the Internet through TCP/IP. Table 16.1 lists some of the commonly used Internet protocols based on TCP/IP.

TABLE 16.1. COMMONLY USED INTERNET PROTOCOLS.

Name of Protocol	Purpose
HTTP	Web browsing
SMTP/POP/IMAP	E-mail message delivery
IRC	Online chat protocol
FTP	File transfer

Note   A thorough overview of TCP/IP is beyond the scope of this book. The purpose of today's tutorial is to explain how to build an ASP-based messaging system that uses TCP/IP sockets.

The Web Messaging System (WMS) Application

The messaging system you build today allows users browsing a Web site to send messages to any computer on the Internet. When a user types in a message (see Figure 16.1), it is submitted to an ASP application, which establishes a connection with the WMS server by using a TCP/IP socket and transmits the message.

FIGURE 16.1.

Users can send messages to the WMS server application via a Web page.

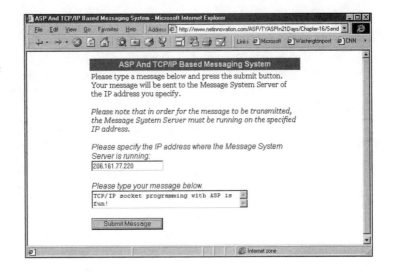

After a message is received by the WMS application, it is displayed in a text box in reverse chronological order, as shown in Figure 16.2. Notice how the message typed by the user is displayed with the date and time the message was received.

FIGURE 16.2.

The WMS server application displays messages sent by users.

Support for TCP/IP sockets is not a built-in feature of ASP. However, several third-party add-ons are available for adding TCP/IP support to ASP. You can download TCP/IP support for ASP by getting the W3 Sockets component from the following Web site:

`http://tech.dimac.net/`

The W3 Sockets component, distributed as a self-installing file, should be installed on the server that runs IIS.

It is important that you understand the three tiers of the WMS application you develop today. The first tier is the application's user interface. For the WMS application, this is the user's Web browser. The next tier consists of the ASP code that runs on the Web server. The ASP code processes the user's input, instantiates the ActiveX component that sends messages, and transmits a message by using the instantiated ActiveX control. The third tier consists of the ActiveX control itself that sends messages using TCP/IP sockets. Although the ActiveX component is instantiated on the same computer as the Web server for the purpose of this exercise, the ActiveX component can be instantiated on a different computer.

Creating the WMS Server with Visual Basic

The WMS server application is simply a Visual Basic application that monitors a certain TCP/IP port for incoming messages. The following steps explain how to create the WMS server application. You can use either Visual Basic 5.0 or 6.0 to develop it. The WMS application runs on the Web server. However, because it is implemented as an ActiveX component, it can be deployed on a computer other than the Web server.

1. Start Visual Basic and select the option to create a new Standard EXE application.

2. Use the Properties window to name the project `MessageSystemServer` and name the default form `ServerForm`.

3. The next step is to add the Microsoft Winsock Control component to the project so the Visual Basic application can use TCP/IP sockets. Choose Components from the Project menu to open the Components dialog box and then select the Controls tab. If you are using Visual Basic 5, select Microsoft Winsock Control 5.0, and if you are using Visual Basic 6.0, select Microsoft Winsock Control 6.0, as shown in Figure 16.3.

FIGURE 16.3.

Add the Microsoft Winsock Control to the VB project.

4. The next step is to add the following four controls to the form ServerForm. Organize them as shown in Figure 16.4.

FIGURE 16.4.

Organize the controls of the WMS server application.

TextBox control—Used to display messages sent by users. Name this control txtMessageList.

Label control—Used to label the TextBox control. Name this control lblMessageList.

Winsock control—Used by the VB application to utilize TCP/IP sockets. Name this control WinsockControl.

CommandButton control—Used to clear the contents of the TextBox control. Name this control cmdClearMsgBuffer.

5. Set the properties of the four controls. Tables 16.2 through 16.5 list the properties for the cmdClearMsgBuffer, WinsockControl, txtMessageList, and lblMessageList controls.

TABLE 16.2. VALUES OF THE cmdClearMsgBuffer CONTROL.

Name of Property	Value
Caption	"Clear Buffer"
Height	375
Left	3360
TabIndex	2
Top	120
Width	1695

16

TABLE 16.3. VALUES OF THE `WinsockControl` CONTROL.

Name of Property	Value
Left	2640
Top	120

TABLE 16.4. VALUES OF THE `txtMessageList` CONTROL.

Name of Property	Value
Height	2295
Left	120
MultiLine	-1 'True
TabIndex	1
Top	720
Width	5055

TABLE 16.5. VALUES OF THE `lblMessageList` CONTROL.

Name of Property	Value
BackStyle	0 'Transparent
Caption	"Messages received are displayed below"
Font Name	"MS Sans Serif"
Font Size	9.75
Height	495
Left	120
TabIndex	0
Top	120
Width	2895

6. Now add the code to open a TCP/IP socket, listen for incoming messages, and display incoming messages. Refer to Listing 16.1 for the complete code of the WMS server application.

7. The last step is to compile the VB application and create an .EXE application by choosing Make from the File menu.

LISTING 16.1. COMPLETE CODE OF THE WMS SERVER APPLICATION.

```
 1: Begin VB.Form ServerForm
 2:    BackColor       =   &H00C0FFFF&
 3:    Caption         =   "Message System Server"
 4:    ClientHeight    =   3330
 5:    ClientLeft      =   60
 6:    ClientTop       =   345
 7:    ClientWidth     =   5310
 8:    LinkTopic       =   "Form1"
 9:    ScaleHeight     =   3330
10:    ScaleWidth      =   5310
11:    StartUpPosition =   3   'Windows Default
12:    Begin VB.CommandButton cmdClearMsgBuffer
13:       Caption      =   "Clear Buffer"
14:       Height       =   375
15:       Left         =   3360
16:       TabIndex     =   2
17:       Top          =   120
18:       Width        =   1695
19:    End
20:    Begin MSWinsockLib.Winsock WinsockControl
21:       Left         =   2640
22:       Top          =   120
23:       _ExtentX     =   741
24:       _ExtentY     =   741
25:       _Version     =   393216
26:    End
27:    Begin VB.TextBox txtMessageList
28:       Height       =   2295
29:       Left         =   120
30:       MultiLine    =   -1   'True
31:       TabIndex     =   1
32:       Top          =   720
33:       Width        =   5055
34:    End
35:    Begin VB.Label lblMessageList
36:       BackStyle    =   0   'Transparent
37:       Caption      =   "Messages received are displayed below"
38:       BeginProperty Font
39:          Name      =   "MS Sans Serif"
40:          Size      =   9.75
41:          Charset   =   0
42:          Weight    =   700
43:          Underline =   0   'False
44:          Italic    =   0   'False
45:          Strikethrough =   0   'False
46:       EndProperty
47:       Height       =   495
```

continues

LISTING 16.1. CONTINUED

```
48:        Left          =    120
49:        TabIndex      =    0
50:        Top           =    120
51:        Width         =    2895
52:     End
53: End
54: Attribute VB_Name = "ServerForm"
55: Attribute VB_GlobalNameSpace = False
56: Attribute VB_Creatable = False
57: Attribute VB_PredeclaredId = True
58: Attribute VB_Exposed = False
59: Option Explicit
60:
61: Private Sub cmdClearMsgBuffer_Click()
62:
63:     txtMessageList.Text = ""
64:
65: End Sub
66:
67: Private Sub Form_Load()
68:
69: ' If another application is using port 5500, you will have
70: ' to select a port number that is not already in use.
71:     WinsockControl.LocalPort = 5500
72:     WinsockControl.Listen
73:
74: End Sub
75:
76: Private Sub WinsockControl_Close()
77:
78:     WinsockControl.Close
79:     WinsockControl.Listen
80:
81: End Sub
82:
83: Private Sub WinsockControl_ConnectionRequest(ByVal requestID As Long)
84:
85:     WinsockControl.Close
86:     WinsockControl.Accept requestID
87:
88: End Sub
89:
90: Private Sub WinsockControl_DataArrival(ByVal bytesTotal As Long)
91:
92:     Dim Message As String
93:
94:     WinsockControl.GetData Message, vbString
95:     txtMessageList.Text = "Message received from " & _
```

```
96:     WinsockControl.RemoteHostIP & " at " & Date & " " & Time &
        ➥vbCrLf & _
97:     Message & vbCrLf & vbCrLf & vbCrLf & txtMessageList.Text
98:
99: End Sub
```

ANALYSIS The subroutines of the WMS server application start at line 60. The subroutine defined in lines 61–65 clears messages displayed in the text box when the command button is clicked. The subroutine in lines 67–74 specifies the TCP/IP port used for listening to incoming messages. After a connection is terminated, the subroutine in lines 76–81 closes the connection and listens for more messages. The subroutine in lines 83–88 accepts connections.

When a message is sent to the WMS server application, that message is processed by the subroutine defined in lines 90–99. Line 94 of the subroutine retrieves the message by using the GetData() method. The message is then displayed with the TextBox control by assigning the message to the Text property of the TextBox, as shown in lines 95–97.

How to Send Messages to the WMS Server

It is very easy to send messages to the WMS server you just built. Simply get a message to send by using an HTML form, use the ASP component installed earlier today, and send the message to the WMS server. You can modify the WMS application and use it for tasks such as keeping system administrators and the help desk informed of special circumstances and errors. Refer to Listing 16.2 for the complete source code of the ASP application that gets messages from users browsing a Web site and sends those messages to the WMS server application.

LISTING 16.2. THIS ASP APPLICATION TRANSMITS MESSAGES ENTERED BY USERS TO THE WMS SERVER APPLICATION.

```
 1: <%@ Language=VBScript %>
 2: <HTML>
 3: <HEAD>
 4:
 5: <TITLE>ASP And TCP/IP Based Messaging System</TITLE>
 6: </HEAD>
 7: <BODY>
 8:
 9: <%
10: If (Request.Form ("Message") = "" ) And _
11:     (Request.Form ("txtHostIPAddress") = "") Then
12: %>
13: <div align="center"><center>
```

continues

LISTING **16.2.** CONTINUED

```
14:
15: <table border="0" cellpadding="3" cellspacing="0" width="450">
16:   <tr>
17:     <td bgcolor="#004080"><p align="center"><font face="Arial"
18:     color="#80FF80"><strong>ASP And TCP/IP Based Messaging System
19:     </strong></font></td>
20:   </tr>
21:   <tr>
22:     <td><font face="Georgia">Please type a message below and press
23:     the Submit button. Your message will be sent to the Message
24:     System Server of the IP address you specify. </font><p><em><font
25:     face="Georgia">Please note that in order for the message to be
26:     transmitted, the Message System Server must be running on the
27:     specified IP address.</font></em></p>
28:
29:     <form method="POST" action="SendMessage.asp">
30:     <p><em><font face="Arial">Please specify the IP address where
31:       the Message System Server is running:</font><br></em>
32:     <input type="text" name="txtHostIPAddress"
33:       size="20" value="127.0.0.1"></p>
34:     <p><em><font face="Arial">Please type your message
      ➥below.</font><br>
35:     <textarea rows="2" name="txtMessage"
      ➥cols="39"></textarea></em></p>
36:     <p><input type="submit" value="Submit Message"
      ➥name="btnSubmit"></p>
37:     </form>
38:     </td>
39:   </tr>
40: </table>
41: </center></div>
42:
43: <%
44: Else
45:
46:   Dim WinsockComponent
47:
48:   ' Creates an instance of the TCP Sockets component.
49:   ' You can download the TCP Sockets component from
50:   ' http://tech.dimac.net/.
51:   Set WinsockComponent = Server.CreateObject("Socket.TCP")
52:
53:   ' If the TCP/IP port 5500 is already in use, you will need to
54:   ' select a different number and recompile the messaging system
55:   ' server VB application.
56:   WinsockComponent.Port = 5500
57:
58:   ' 127.0.0.1 is the address of the local computer.
59:   WinsockComponent.Host = Request.Form ("txtHostIPAddress")
```

```
60:
61:    ' Opens a connection to the specified host and port.
62:    WinsockComponent.Open
63:
64:    ' Transmit the message to the messaging system server.
65:    WinsockComponent.SendLine Request.Form ("txtMessage")
66:
67:    ' Closes the connection.
68:    WinsockComponent.Close %>
69: <P> </P>
70: <table align="center" border="0" cellpadding="3" cellspacing="0"
71:    width="450">
72:    <tr>
73:       <td bgcolor="#004080"><p align="center"><font face="Arial"
74:       color="#80FF80"><strong>ASP And TCP/IP Based Messaging System
75:       </strong></font></td>
76:    </tr>
77:    <tr>
78:       <td><p align="center">
79:          <font face="Comic Sans MS" size="5" color="#FF0000"><strong>
80:          Your message has been sent!</strong></font></p>
81:          <p><font face="Georgia"> </font></td>
82:    </tr>
83: </table>
84: <P> </P>
85: <A HREF="SendMessage.asp">Start over</A>
86: <%
87: End If
88: %>
89: </P>
90:
91: </BODY>
92: </HTML>
```

16

ANALYSIS The If statement in lines 10 and 11 checks whether the user has filled in the form with an IP address and a message. If the user has not completed the form, an HTML form is displayed by the HTML code in lines 13–41. If an IP address and a message are supplied by the user, the Else clause defined in lines 44–87 is executed.

Line 51 creates an instance of the Socket component so that a connection can be established with the WMS server application. The statement in line 56 specifies the remote port used to send the message entered by the user. The IP address of the remote host (entered by the user) is specified in line 59. Please note that the IP address 127.0.0.1 is commonly used to refer to the local computer. Line 62 opens a connection to the remote computer, and line 65 sends the user's message to the remote computer. Line 68 closes the connection, and the remainder of the HTML text displays a message to confirm that the message has been transmitted, as shown in Figure 16.5.

FIGURE 16.5.

The message is successfully transmitted.

Before sending a message using the ASP application, make sure the WMS
server application is running on the IP address specified.

Summary

Computers on the Internet use TCP/IP sockets to communicate with each other and trans-
fer information. By default, ASP does not support the manipulation of TCP/IP sockets.
However, by installing a freely downloadable component from the Internet, you can add
TCP/IP socket support to ASP applications. The ASP application you build today uses
TCP/IP sockets to send messages entered by users browsing the Web site to a VB appli-
cation that runs on any computer on the Internet.

Q&A

Q Why should I care about the three-tier model?

A Although it's sometimes hard to understand the purpose of the three-tier model
when working on simple Web projects, the benefits of using it are significant even
when creating a relatively modest Web application. The three-tier model helps you
think of your Web application in different layers and offers you the flexibility of
moving a layer to a different computer, if the need arises. The three-tier model aids
code maintenance and promotes robust, scalable Web projects.

Q Why should I bother about using TCP/IP?

A TCP/IP is a core Internet protocol, and virtually all Internet applications communicate with each other by using TCP/IP. By knowing how to manipulate TCP/IP
sockets, you can directly communicate with practically any application on the
Internet.

Q What are the benefits of adding Winsock support to ASP?

A By adding Winsock support to ASP, you can easily build ASP applications that manipulate TCP/IP sockets. For example, an ASP application can directly interact with a mail server to validate an e-mail address or send a message using the SMTP protocol.

Q What's the purpose of having business objects run on different servers?

A This method promotes the scalability and availability of an application. For example, a high-traffic Web site might have a dedicated database server, and any database-driven business objects can be executed on the database server to increase scalability and to handle database-driven Web transactions more efficiently.

Workshop

The quiz questions and exercises are provided for your further understanding. Please refer to Appendix A, "Answers to Questions," for the answers to the quiz questions; the answers to the exercises are on the MCP Web site.

Quiz

1. What is a cluster?
2. What are the three elements of the three-tier model?
3. Numerous computers are connected to the Internet. What do all these computers have in common?
4. Name three advantages of using the three-tier model.
5. Does ASP support TCP/IP sockets "out of the box"?

Exercises

1. Add a counter that keeps track of the number of messages received by the messaging system server.

2. Modify the messaging system server application so that the message log can be saved to a local file.

3. The source code of a Visual Basic application (.EXE) that sends messages to the WMS server application is included on the MCP Web site (open the project `MessageSystemClient.vbp` for the code). Convert the application to an ActiveX control. Use the Browser Capabilities component to determine if the user's Web browser supports ActiveX controls. If it does, use the ActiveX control as the user interface of the WMS; otherwise, use an HTML form.

4. Modify the WMS application so that messages sent via the WMS are logged in a database on the server. (Hint: You can use Visual Basic to interact with databases on the server.)

DAY **17**

Building ASP Applications with Visual InterDev 6.0

by Steve Banick

In the past few days you have been digging deeper into ASP development using the essential ASP components. Today, you dig even deeper into ASP development using Microsoft's advanced Web application development environment, Visual InterDev 6.0. Today you will cover the following:

- Discover the benefits of using Visual InterDev.
- Understand the Visual InterDev interface.
- Build ASP applications.
- Manage Web sites.
- Develop ASP applications with Design-Time Controls.
- Develop database applications with ASP.
- Debug ASP applications with Visual InterDev.

Benefits of Using Visual InterDev

Visual InterDev is Microsoft's flagship Web application development tool. Touted as "everything you'll ever need for Web application development," Visual InterDev is tightly integrated with Internet Information Server and ASP. Visual InterDev 6 offers many appealing features that might make you choose it over your average, run-of-the-mill HTML editor. These features include the following:

- A powerful editing environment that combines raw code–level editing and What-You-See-Is-What-You-Get (WYSIWYG) editing.
- Convenient project organization tools and features, including task lists and support for multiple developers.
- Direct integration with Internet Information Server for remote debugging of ASP applications.
- Support for newer Web technologies, including HTML 4.0, Dynamic HTML (DHTML), and Cascading Style Sheets (CSS).
- Design-Time Controls (DTC) that allow you to develop dynamic Web sites, adapting your site for each visitor without requiring extensive programming.
- The Visual Studio environment that gives you a flexible, feature-rich development environment that also directly links with Visual Source Safe for version control.
- Direct database access that allows you to visually create database-based applications without requiring a great deal of code.

Visual InterDev 6 is a large, flexible tool. Microsoft's approach has been to give you, in one box, nearly every tool you need to develop Web applications.

Caution

Visual InterDev is a Microsoft tool that works on Windows 95/98 and Windows NT. If you are using a non-Microsoft development environment or an older version of Windows, you will not be able to use Visual InterDev.

Key Elements of the Visual InterDev User Interface

Visual InterDev is built on the Visual Studio interface, which has developed over many years. The Visual InterDev user interface might seem daunting at first; however, as you work with it, you will discover that the environment has been designed to increase productivity while you're developing applications. The Visual InterDev environment, shown in Figure 17.1, is composed of many different elements. The interface has the traditional interface elements of a menu bar, tool bar, and status bar. It also uses many distinct windows and operating "modes" for development.

FIGURE 17.1.

The Visual InterDev environment is composed of many individual windows and elements.

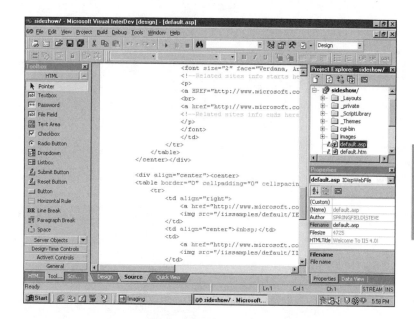

Understanding the Visual InterDev Windows

Visual InterDev is composed of many windows, each of which is targeted to fulfill a specific role for a developer. These windows make up a very powerful and flexible working environment, provided you understand what each window can be used for and how it can help you. Figure 17.2 gives you a labeled look at some of the key Visual InterDev windows.

The next few sections take some time to examine each window in the Visual InterDev environment and explore its purpose. The windows covered include the following:

- The Autos window
- The Call Stack window
- The Document Outline window
- The Find window
- The Immediate window
- The Locals window

- The Output window
- The Properties window
- The Running Documents window
- The Task List window
- The Editor window
- The Threads window
- The Toolbox window
- The Watch window

FIGURE 17.2.

Some of the most frequently used windows in Visual InterDev.

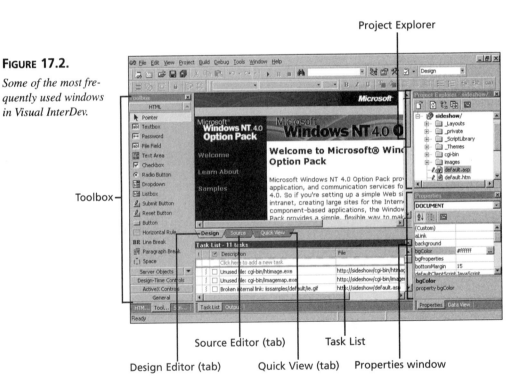

The Autos Window

Visual InterDev has several debugging-related windows, to ease the pain of ASP development. The Autos window is used to display the values of variables that are in the scope of the current line being executed in a procedure. This window, however, is not updated in real-time—it is updated only when the current script is suspended. The Autos window can be used to debug not only scripts, but also SQL stored procedures on a SQL

Server or Oracle database in the Enterprise version of Visual InterDev. Figure 17.3 displays the Autos window in action.

FIGURE 17.3.

The Autos window can be used to display and edit variables during debugging.

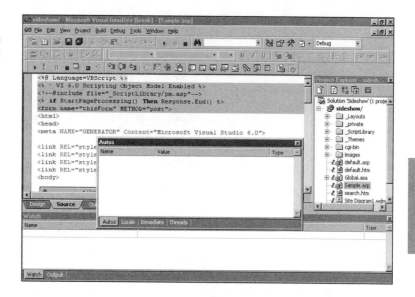

When debugging your code (see "Debugging ASP Applications" later in this chapter), you can use the Autos window to do the following:

- Double-click a variable to edit its value.
- Drag a selected variable to the Immediate window or the Watch window for manipulation.
- Switch between decimal and hex modes.

The Call Stack Window

The Call Stack window is used to display all active procedures for a process. You can use the Call Stack window to change the active thread and to change the contents of the Locals window to the current procedure. The Call Stack window is shown in Figure 17.4.

The Document Outline Window

When you are deep into your code for a page, it is very easy to drop tags and introduce problems with your layout or script. The Document Outline window, typically docked on the left of the Visual InterDev window, represents a hierarchical outline for the current document. As you open documents in Visual InterDev editors, the Document Outline refreshes to display the associated HTML page tags or script blocks. The Document Outline window for an HTML document is shown in Figure 17.5.

FIGURE 17.4.

Updating the Locals window through the Call Stack window makes debugging much easier.

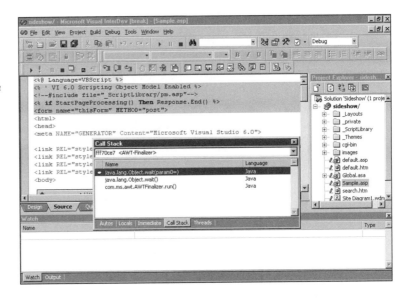

FIGURE 17.5.

The Document Outline window can be used to quickly spot problems with your code.

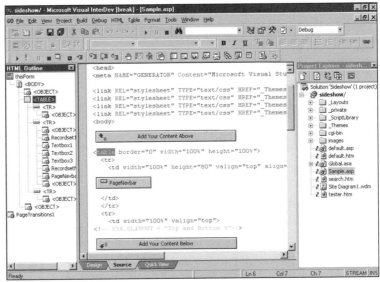

The Document Outline window can also be used to view the structure of your script blocks within a Web page. This window also displays the scripting object model and script blocks for the associated Web page. You can use the Document Outline window to easily identify problems with your code, as well as to quickly jump from element to element. To navigate between elements, simply double-click on the element name in the

Document Outline. Using the Document Outline window for a script block is shown in Figure 17.6.

FIGURE 17.6.

The Document Outline window makes scripting easier by displaying all objects.

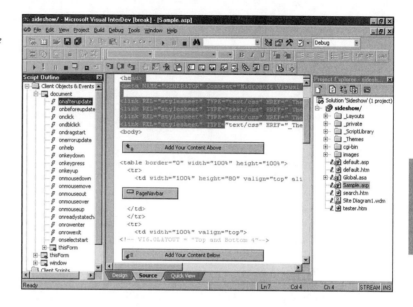

The Find Window

Visual InterDev sports a powerful search and replace facility, making development less taxing. The Find and Replace feature allows you to search for an instance of text and optionally replace it. What makes the Find and Replace stand out are regular expressions.

NEW TERM   A *regular expression* is much like a wildcard in DOS and Windows. Regular expressions let you specify a pattern or sequence to search for—not necessarily the exact text. For example, you could use a regular expression to search for not only the word "Web," but also "Website," "Web site," and "Webs." Regular expressions can even be used to search for sentences, as opposed to simple words.

Figure 17.7 shows you the Find window.

You can use the Find window to locate and/or replace instances of text or code in a single page or throughout your entire project and local drives.

FIGURE 17.7.

The Find window lets you search the current document, the current project, or even an entire directory.

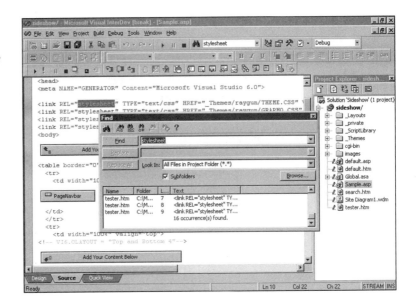

The Immediate Window

The Immediate window is useful for debugging and testing your Web application. This window is used to enter commands and expressions to be evaluated or executed by the development environment. The behavior of the Immediate window depends on the scripting language you are using, such as VBScript or JavaScript. Figure 17.8 shows you the Immediate window.

FIGURE 17.8.

The Immediate window is much like having a command line into your application.

The Locals Window

Used for debugging, the Locals window displays local variables and their values from the current procedure. As your application moves from procedure to procedure, the contents of the Locals window changes to reflect the local variables that are being used. Like the Autos window, you can use the Locals window, shown in Figure 17.9, to modify a variable's value by double-clicking on it.

FIGURE 17.9.

Local variables can be closely monitored through the Locals window.

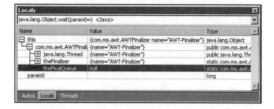

The Output Window

During runtime, the Output window can display status messages as well as debug text and strings generated in your code. Use of the Output window depends on your scripting language and your code. This window, shown in Figure 17.10, can be used to debug your applications by displaying strings generated in your code.

FIGURE 17.10.

The Output window relies on your code and the scripting language to display information.

17

The Project Explorer Window

NEW TERM All work in Visual InterDev is based on a collection of files and information called a *project*. Projects act as a container for your Web application files, including your ASP pages and images. You can also have more than one project open at any given time, creating what is called a *solution*. The Project Explorer is used to organize and manage all the files contained in your project(s). Much like Windows Explorer, the Project Explorer displays a hierarchical tree of the folders and files that make up your Web site. Refer back to Figure 17.2 to see where the Project Explorer window is located.

You can also use the Project Explorer to add files to or remove them from your project and directories. An important concept to understand is that the Project Explorer represents your *Web site* or *Web application*. You can have additional files residing in the same directories as your Web files; however, Visual InterDev does not see them as part of the Web site itself. For Visual InterDev to see a file, it must be part of the project.

The Properties Window

Each element in your project, ranging from a Web page or data connection to the individual HTML tags in a Web page, has *properties*. These properties are used to modify the behavior or attributes of a selected item or element in your project. In the Properties window, you can display and alter the properties of selected items in Visual InterDev. Manipulating properties allows you to precisely control how a particular element appears, behaves, or interacts with other elements. Refer back to Figure 17.2 to see where the Properties window is located.

Each item in your application has different properties, depending on what kind of item it is. For example, images have properties that control their appearance—such as their height, width, and border. A server component, however, has properties that affect its behavior and actions in your application. Modifying and controlling properties is very much at the heart of Web applications and development in Visual InterDev.

The Running Documents Window

When you are working with multiple documents, such as in an HTML frameset, the Running Documents window can be used to display the currently loaded pages. You can also use the Running Documents window, as shown in Figure 17.11, to open a document in an editor window by double-clicking on it.

FIGURE 17.11.

The Running Documents window can be used to keep track of all pages open during a process.

The Task List Window

Managing and developing Web sites can be a tremendous chore, with many individual tasks to complete. Microsoft wisely included the Task List window to allow developers to track development tasks within Visual InterDev. Shown in Figure 17.12, the Task List window is more than a simple "do this, done"–style task manager. The Visual InterDev Task List helps you customize and manage your work with tasks marked with special comments, warnings, and shortcuts generated while you develop.

FIGURE 17.12.

The Task List can automatically add tasks to your list in the event of errors.

You can manually add tasks to the Task List (such as "Update logo before presentation"), as well as track and manage errors in your code that are generated when you are developing or debugging. You can also use the Task List to track comments, errors, and shortcuts for quick location in the Visual InterDev editors. Finally, the Task List can be sorted according to a priority, category, description, file, or line.

The Editor Window

Visual InterDev sports not one, but two, editors in the Editor window. The Design Editor, shown in Figure 17.13, is Visual InterDev's own What-You-See-Is-What-You-Get (WYSIWYG) editor for Web page development. The Source Editor, shown in Figure 17.14, is used to work at the code level for Web page and active scripting development. These two editors can be used with one another by switching back and forth with convenient tabs at the bottom of the Editor window.

FIGURE 17.13.

The Design Editor lets you visually create Web applications without code...

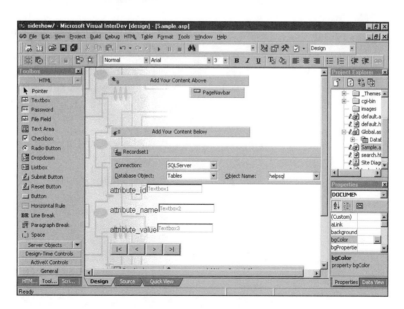

FIGURE 17.14.

*...and the Source
Editor gives you the
ability to work with
raw HTML and script-
ing code.*

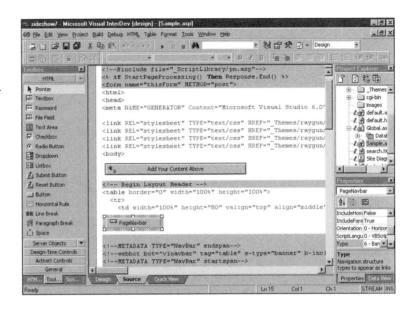

FIGURE 17.14.

*...and the Source
Editor gives you the
ability to work with
raw HTML and script-
ing code.*

These two editors can take advantage of the Document Outline window and the Toolbox
window to create applications quickly. In addition to the Design and Source Editors,
Visual InterDev gives you a handy means of viewing your Web pages as a Web browser
would see them by using Quick View. Quick View, shown in Figure 17.15, is accessed
with a tab at the bottom of the Editor window.

FIGURE 17.15.

*Quick View displays
your pages as a Web
browser would see
them.*

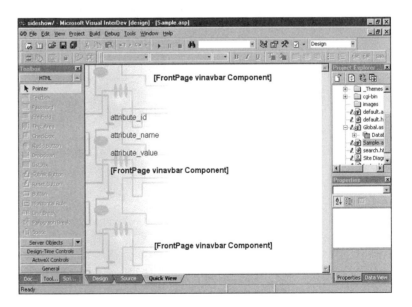

> **Note**
>
> Quick View mode does not process server-side (.asp) scripts. It is intended for viewing the client-side layout and testing client-side scripts.

The Threads Window

The Threads window, familiar to Visual C++ developers, is used to display all the threads for the current process. This window also displays information about each thread, including its state and location. Using this window, you can select a new process or activate individual threads. Threads are used when you have a single process carrying out several consecutive actions—called *multithreading*. Debugging multithreaded applications can be very difficult, hence the Threads window shown in Figure 17.16.

FIGURE 17.16.

The Threads window lets you monitor individual process threads.

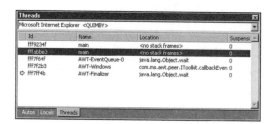

The Toolbox Window

Typically located on the left side of the Visual InterDev window, the Toolbox is used as a tools palette for Web application development. Individual components, HTML elements, controls, and code snippets can be added to the Toolbox for convenient access. You can then drag and drop any item from the Toolbox onto your Web page by using either the Source or Design Editors. For example, you could use the Toolbox to house a server component for file access and incorporate it into your Web page by dragging and dropping it into the Editor. Refer back to Figure 17.2 to see where the Toolbox window is located.

You can customize the Toolbox by creating separate tabs to contain specific items. For example, you could use one tab to house frequently used ActiveX objects, and another could be used to hold common HTML code chunks.

The Watch Window

The Watch window is a powerful tool for debugging. By using it for displaying the values of selected variables or expressions, you can closely monitor the progress of your application. This window, updated whenever execution has stopped, lets you edit variables by double-clicking on their values. You can also use this window to drag individual variables into the Immediate window for manipulation. The Watch window is shown in Figure 17.17.

FIGURE 17.17.

The Watch window is your means of monitoring the progress of variables and expressions in your Web applications.

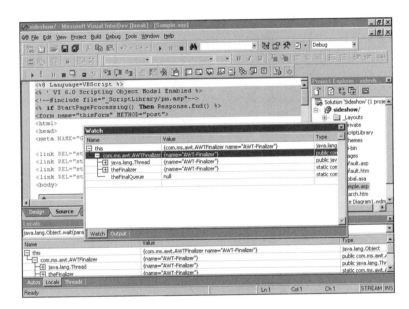

Building ASP Applications

With a basic understanding of the Visual InterDev interface under your belt, it's time to dig into ASP development using this tool. The fundamentals of creating ASP applications remain the same as what you have learned in previous days; Visual InterDev is intended to make that job easier, as opposed to different. Visual InterDev piggybacks on Internet Information Server and Active Server Pages to create a powerful development and debugging environment.

Note

You should be using Internet Information Server 4.0 or higher to take advantage of all the features of Visual InterDev 6. Previous versions (namely IIS 3.0) *will* function; however, you won't be able to take advantage of advanced features, such as server-side debugging.

Using Visual InterDev with Personal Web Server might cause some limitations. For example, Personal Web Server on NT Workstation has full debugging capabilities; however, on Windows 95/98, it does not.

Before proceeding, make sure your Web server is properly configured and that you have access to create new Web sites.

Creating a "Solution" with a Project

NEW TERM In Visual InterDev parlance, your workspace is referred to as a *solution*. Solutions act as a global container for all projects related to your Web application. You might have multiple projects per solution for a variety of reasons, such as:

- Your Web site is split into several different sub-Webs on the Web server to restrict access.

- Your Web site uses a separate database connection (see "Developing Database Applications with Visual InterDev" later today).

- You can develop on multiple servers at the same time, with each project pointing to an individual server.

- Your Web site has several distinct sections that have been organized to isolate code.

A solution is created by Visual InterDev when you first begin a project. Each subsequent project you choose to add to the solution becomes accessible to the solution.

 Your sub-Webs do not have to be part of the same solution to function or to access files from one another. Although you might choose to use separate projects that never meet, you should consider creating one solution for Web site management.

To create a new project—and, in turn, a new solution—follow these steps:

1. Open Visual InterDev 6, if it is not already open.

2. If the New Project dialog box appears, skip ahead to Step 3. Otherwise, choose New Project from the File menu.

3. With the New Project dialog box open, as shown in Figure 17.18, click on the Visual InterDev Projects folder in the left pane.

17

Figure 17.18.

The New Project window is used to create not only Web projects, but also database projects.

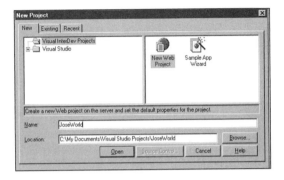

4. Select New Web Project from the icons in the right pane of the dialog box.

5. Enter a name for your new Web project in the Name text box. This is the name you use to refer to your project—it need not be the same as your Web site name.

6. If you want to store your project's local files in a specific location, change the path in the Location text box.

7. Click the Open button.

These steps instruct Visual InterDev to create a new project, initiating a new solution. After the solution has been created, Visual InterDev proceeds by contacting the Web server by displaying the Web Project Wizard, as shown in Figure 17.19.

Figure 17.19.

The Web Project Wizard automates the process of creating a new Web application.

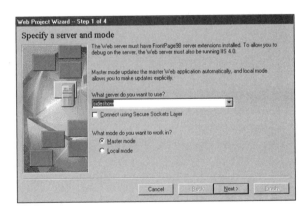

With the first page of the wizard open, continue with these steps:

1. Specify the host name of your Web server in the "What server do you want to use?" text box. In the drop-down list beside the text box, you'll see the servers that Visual InterDev has previously communicated with.

2. If your Web server uses secure connections with Secure Sockets Layer (SSL), select the Connect Using Secure Sockets Layer check box.

3. Click the Next button to proceed. This instructs Visual InterDev to communicate with the specified Web server.

4. Page 2 of the wizard, shown in Figure 17.20, appears. Select the Create a New Web Application radio button.

FIGURE 17.20.

You can choose to create a new Web application or open an existing one on the Web server.

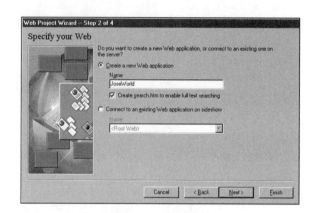

17

5. Click the Finish button to instruct Visual InterDev to create your new Web application.

Note

Creating a new Web application might take some time, depending on the speed of your connection and your Web server. When creating a new Web application, Visual InterDev might inform you that the ASP script library is not on the Web server. You should choose to add the script library to your Web application for proper operation.

With your Web application freshly created, you are given a clean Visual InterDev project and solution to begin development, as shown in Figure 17.21.

Adding ASP Files to a Project

When you first create a project, it is merely an empty shell, waiting for you to fill it with pages and content. You can create new pages to be added to the project, or choose to add existing pages to the project. Today, you will work with creating new pages for use in your project. To create a new ASP page to be added to your project, follow these steps:

1. With your new project open, right-click on your project in the Project Explorer.
2. From the context menu that pops up, choose Add, Active Server Page to open the Add Item dialog box, shown in Figure 17.22.

FIGURE 17.21.

Your new project is ready for you to populate it with information.

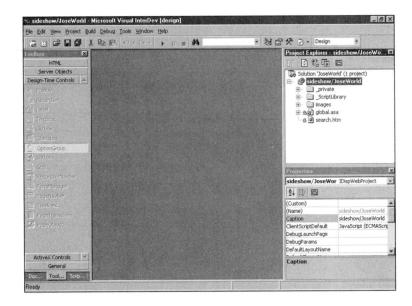

FIGURE 17.22.

Using the Add Item dialog box, you can create ASP pages, conventional static pages, text files, and style sheets.

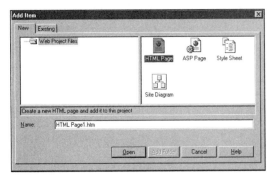

3. Select the ASP Page icon from the left pane.
4. Enter a name for your new ASP page in the Name text box.

5. Click the Open button. This creates a new ASP page (called "New ASP Page" with a number) in your project and opens it in the Source Editor.

> **Tip**
>
> You can use the Add Item dialog box to add existing files by selecting the Existing tab. This lets you locate a file on your local file system or LAN to be added to the Web project.

With your new ASP page created and added to your project, you're ready to get down to work. Using the Design and Source Editors, you can alternate between WYSIWYG page design and source-level ASP programming. Both editors are easy to use and sport helpful features, including:

- Word processor–like functionality in the Design Editor.
- IntelliSense statement completion for scripting in the Source Editor.
- Drag and drop of data connections, controls, and HTML elements from the Toolbox and Project Explorer.

17

> **Tip**
>
> Take some time experimenting in both editors. As you gain more experience with the Visual InterDev environment, you can tailor these editors around your work habits. You will find yourself rapidly switching between the two editors to create attractive and effective Web applications.

Saving ASP Pages

After you have finished your ASP development, you're ready to save your work. To save your file, choose Save from the File menu. You can opt to save the file under a different name by choosing Save As from the File menu. Although saving your page itself is a simple matter, the implications of saving your page are greater. When you are working with a live Web site, saving your pages could have a drastic impact on your site. Visitors might experience transition problems when your page has been saved or potentially experience bugs that have slipped through the debugging process.

Working in Master and Local Modes

To give you more development flexibility, Visual InterDev offers you two methods of operation:

- Master Mode
- Local Mode

Understanding Master Mode

Master Mode is your traditional method of working with a Web server. When you are working in Master Mode, all changes you make to your Web pages take effect directly on the Web server. If this is a production Web server, you might introduce problems as you develop and debug. Master Mode can become particularly troublesome when you are working with multiple developers—developer A might overwrite developer B's changes. Very little is available in terms of features for versioning or protecting individual changes.

Understanding Local Mode

Visual InterDev offers a unique *developer isolation* mode, called Local Mode. Local Mode enables developers to work with a unique local copy of the Web project. All changes to the Web files are made using the local copies, instead of updating the master Web project. After all changes are made, they can be merged into the master Web project. This method lets you safely develop with local copies, debug them completely, and then deploy them on the public Web server.

Determining the Best Mode to Use

Which mode you use depends entirely on your situation. Both Local Mode and Master Mode have their advantages and disadvantages. You should consider using Master Mode in the following situations:

- You are working on a development server that is not used by end users.
- Your code has passed the debugging stage and is ready for prime time.
- You are a lone developer working on the application.

You should consider using Local Mode in these situations:

- You are working on a production Web server that is used by end users.
- Your code is new and requires debugging.
- You are working with multiple developers on the application.

Switching Modes

You can choose the development mode when you first create your Web application. You can also switch modes as you work, allowing you to update your Web server with all the changes made in Local Mode. To switch modes in your project, follow these steps:

1. Right-click on your project name in the Project Explorer window.

2. From the context menu, choose Working Mode, Local or choose Working Mode, Master, depending on the mode you want to switch to.

If you choose to move to Master Mode after having worked in Local Mode, you see a prompt indicating that the master Web server will be updated with any modified files. Click the Yes button to update your Web server and switch modes.

Previewing ASP Applications

When you are ready to test your ASP application, you can preview your application pages in a Web browser. Before previewing, you must specify a start page for your application. This page is used by the Web server as the beginning of your Web application (it is often named `default.asp`). To specify a start page, follow these steps:

1. Right-click on your start page in the Project Explorer.

2. From the context menu, choose Set as Start Page.

With a start page defined, you can easily preview your application in an external Web browser by clicking the Play button in the toolbar. You can also choose Start from the Debug menu.

 Note

> You can also preview your pages by right-clicking on them and choosing View in Browser. This opens your page in a Web browser without entering debugging mode.

Using the Toolbox

The Toolbox, as explained earlier, acts as your tool palette during Web application development. When you run Visual InterDev for the first time, you get a simple yet effective Toolbox with four individual tabs. Switching between these tabs, described in Table 17.1, is simply a matter of clicking on the tab's title.

17

TABLE 17.1. THE TOOLBOX TABS.

Tab	Description
HTML	The first Toolbox tab provides the core HTML elements that you would incorporate into a Web page: form fields, horizontal lines, line breaks, paragraph breaks, horizontal rules, spaces, and labels.
Server Objects	Server components for Internet Information Server are located in the second tab. They include ADO (Active Data Objects) connections, file system controls, and access to the common server-side objects.
Design-Time Controls	As explained in the section "Developing ASP Applications with Design-Time Controls," the Design-Time Controls in this tab let you quickly add interactivity to your Web applications.
ActiveX Controls	Commonly used ActiveX controls, such as Microsoft Wallet and assorted multimedia controls, are located in this tab.
General	A generic empty tab.

You can think of Toolbox tabs as individual *drawers* in a toolbox, used to hold specific tools and information to organize your development.

Using Drag and Drop

Although the elements in the Toolbox tabs can differ, their use is the same. To incorporate an item from a Toolbox tab, drag the item from the Toolbox tab into the Editor window. You can typically drag and drop items into either the Design or Source Editor, although this isn't necessarily always true.

After an element or object has been added to your page, you might need to alter its properties by selecting it and using the Properties window. When you incorporate some components, Visual InterDev automatically inserts its required script blocks. You will probably still need to customize this code and insert your own code to take advantage of the component.

Customizing Your Own Toolbox Tab

Changing the contents of the Toolbox couldn't be much easier than it already is. Visual InterDev lets you not only customize the existing Toolbox tabs, but also lets you create your own tabs. Toolbox tabs can contain the following:

- Server components
- ActiveX controls

- Design-Time Controls
- Code snippets

To create your own Toolbox tab, follow these three simple steps:

1. Right-click on the Toolbox window.

2. From the context menu, choose Add Tab. This creates a new tab in the Toolbox that immediately requires you to enter a name.

3. Enter the name for your new tab. For example, if you plan on using this tab to hold your code snippets, name it Snippets.

> **Note**
>
> A code *snippet* shouldn't be confused with a *scriptlet*. A snippet is a selected piece of code from one of your Web pages that you plan on reusing. Visual InterDev calls code snippets *HTML fragments*. A *scriptlet* is code contained in its own file that can be used by any page, requiring you to update only one scriptlet file when you need to make changes.

17

Adding to your tab is also very simple. To add a code snippet to your tab, follow these instructions:

1. With the Source Editor open, select the code you want to use as a snippet. For example, perhaps you have a commonly used block of text that is added to every page.

2. Drag the selected block into your Toolbox tab. This adds a new item to the Toolbox named "HTML Fragment."

3. Right-click on the new HTML Fragment item.

4. From the context menu, choose Rename Item.

5. Enter a new name for your snippet/fragment in the Toolbox tab.

> **Caution**
>
> HTML Fragments and code snippets are a convenient means of reusing common code. Keep in mind, however, that updating your Toolbox item does not update pages that have used it in the past. You need to go back to each page and make those changes, if necessary. Perhaps you could use the Find and Replace feature in such cases.

To add an ActiveX control or Design-Time Control to your Toolbox tab, follow these steps:

1. Select your Toolbox tab.

2. Right-click on the Toolbox and choose Customize Toolbox from the context menu to open the Customize Toolbox dialog box, as shown in Figure 17.23.

FIGURE 17.23.

The Customize Toolbox dialog box lets you quickly personalize your Toolbox tabs.

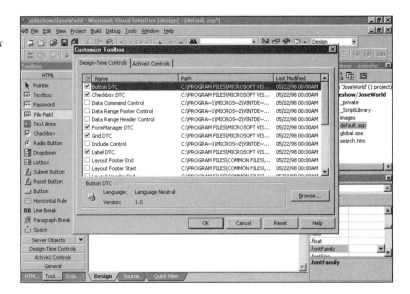

3. The first tab displayed is the Design-Time Controls tab. If you are adding an ActiveX Control, click on the ActiveX Controls tab at the top of the dialog box.

4. Locate the control in the list of available controls. Items with their check boxes selected are currently in your Toolbox.

5. Select the check box for your new control to add it to the Toolbox.

6. If you are unable to locate your control in the list, click the Browse button to use an Explorer window to locate the control.

7. Click the OK button to save your changes and add the selected items to the Toolbox.

Tip

You can just as easily remove controls from your Toolbox by deselecting their check boxes in the Customize Toolbox dialog box.

Using the Object Browser

When you are working with ActiveX controls, it is often difficult to determine their available methods and properties. The Object Browser, shown in Figure 17.24, is used to display an object's classes, methods, properties, and events (among other things). You can use this information to determine how to use individual controls in your code.

FIGURE 17.24.

The Object Browser is often a necessity when working with components.

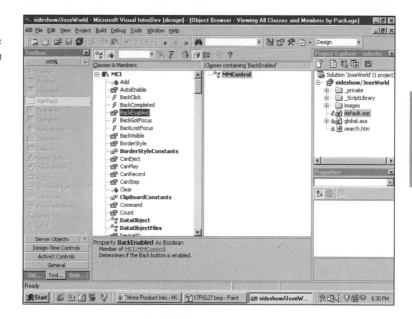

Selecting Packages and Libraries

To use the Object Browser, you must select the package or library (a control) to view. You can select multiple objects and use the Object Browser to sort them according to their type and group. The Object Browser also displays all members of individual classes, for easy reference. To select a package or library to view, follow these instructions:

1. Open the Object Browser by choosing View, Other Windows, Object Browser.

2. Click the Current Packages/Libraries button on the Object Browser toolbar (fifth button).

3. Click the Select Current Packages/Libraries button on the Object Browser toolbar. This opens the Select Packages/Libraries dialog box shown in Figure 17.25.

FIGURE 17.25.

The Select Packages/Libraries dialog box displays the currently selected controls in a hierarchical list.

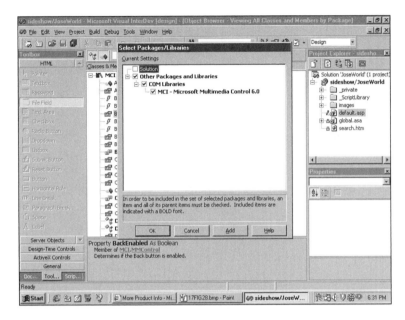

4. Click the Add button to open the Add New Packages/Libraries dialog box shown in Figure 17.26.

FIGURE 17.26.

Selecting controls for the Object Browser is much like adding controls to the Toolbox.

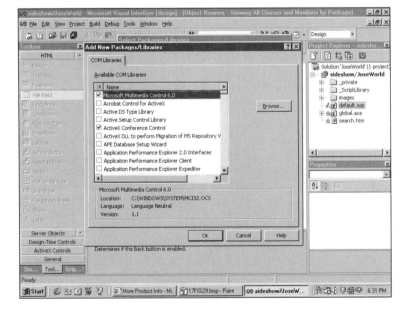

5. From the list of available controls, select the check box for each control you want to view. If the control is not listed, click the Browse button to open an Explorer window for locating the control.

6. Click the OK button to return to the Select Packages/Libraries dialog box.

7. Click OK to return to the Object Browser.

Browsing Individual Objects

After a control has been selected for display, it appears in the left pane of the Object Browser. You can sort this display according to the class type (classes, enums, methods, properties, events, and constants) and access types (public and private). The Object Browser displays each object as a hierarchical list that can be expanded and selected. When an item is selected in the left pane, the Object Browser's right pane updates to display the members of that item. By selecting a member in the left pane, the bottom pane of the Object Browser updates to display a description of the member (see Figure 17.27).

FIGURE 17.27.

As you expand items and select members, the Object Browser updates to display the pertinent information.

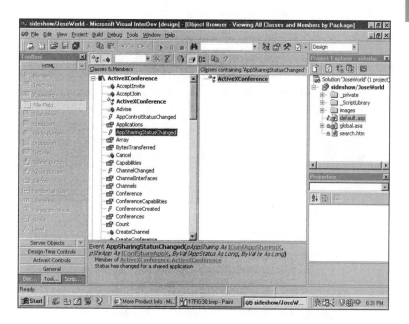

Tip

You can use the Object Browser to search for a control's events and properties, instead of relying on the control's documentation. Well-designed controls give you a clear idea of their behaviors through the available methods, events, and properties.

Managing Web Sites with Visual InterDev

The chore of managing a Web site can often be more difficult than its actual development. Maintaining consistency throughout the site, ensuring that all pages are functioning correctly and are accessible by all users, and avoiding the infamous dead link—all are aspects of site management that most people would like to avoid. Visual InterDev offers several features for managing your Web site in its simplest form, including site-wide navigation control and link management.

 Note

> Visual InterDev's site-management features are not a replacement for more specialized site managers. Instead, they make the simple management of your site after development easier. If you are looking for more advanced site-management features, such as complex logging, you should look to another solution, such as Microsoft Site Server.

Using Site Diagrams

Have you ever looked at a Web site like an organizational chart? Web sites can be represented in a manner much like organizational charts, illustrating each page's relation to other pages, the navigational links, and even their prominence. Visual InterDev's Site Diagrams feature is exactly that—an organizational chart for your Web site that allows you to visually map your site's layout and structure. You can also directly control site-wide navigation and add new pages to the mix. A sample site diagram is shown in Figure 17.28.

To create a site diagram for your Web application, follow these instructions:

1. Right-click on your project name in the Project Explorer window.
2. From the context menu, choose Add, Site Diagram to open the Add Item dialog box, previously shown in Figure 17.22, with the Site Diagram icon selected.
3. Enter a name for your site diagram in the Name text box and click OK. A new, blank site diagram is created for you, as shown in Figure 17.29.
4. To begin the site diagram, select the pages you want to add to it from the Project Explorer. Drag each page's icon onto the site diagram.
5. To add your Web site's home page, click the Add Home Page button (third button from the left) on the Site Diagram toolbar. Your home page is added to the diagram with a small "Home" icon.

FIGURE 17.28.

Site diagrams are essential for creating coherent Web sites.

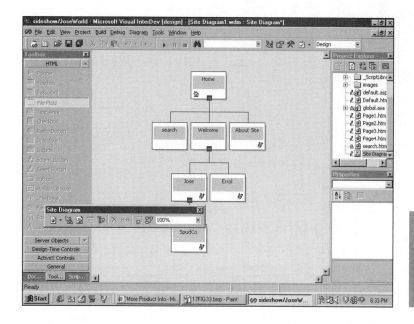

6. To add a page to the global navigation of your site, select it in the site diagram and click the Add to Global Navigation Bar button (fourth button from the left) on the Site Diagram toolbar.

FIGURE 17.29.

Your new site diagram is ready to be filled in.

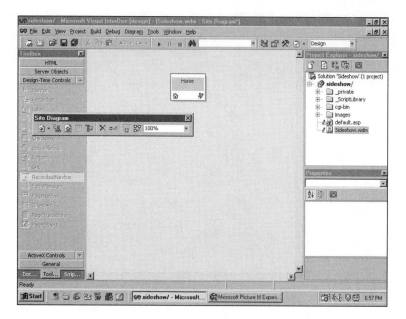

7. To link pages, drag a page in the site diagram close to the page you want to link to. A visible line appears to connect the two pages.

8. When you are satisfied with your site diagram, save your changes by choosing Save from the File menu.

Tip

You can use site diagrams to add new pages or existing pages to your site through the Site Diagram toolbar. You can also remove pages from your site or diagram with the same toolbar. Experiment with site diagrams and practice manipulating their sizes and orientation.

Using Link View and Verification Tools

Visual InterDev sports a useful pair of management tools for hyperlinks in your Web site. The first tool, the Broken Links Report, scans your entire Web project for broken links and unused files. Each identified item is then added to your Task List for correction—a very convenient feature for tracking what you have to fix. The second tool, Link View, allows you to view your entire site's hyperlinks (to other pages, images, resources, and even other Web sites) in a graphical manner. Using this view, you can then get a big picture of your Web site and spot broken links or potential problems. The Link View window is shown in Figure 17.30.

FIGURE 17.30.

Link View gives you the big picture of your Web site; you can even use it to view the links on other Web sites.

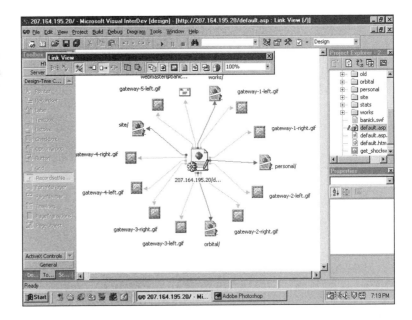

To carry out a Broken Links Report on your Web project, follow these steps:

1. Select your Web project in the Project Explorer.

2. From the menu bar, choose View, Broken Links Report. A status dialog box appears, indicating that it is carrying out the broken link check. Each item that it finds is added to the Output window.

3. After the check is finished, the Output window prints the message Broken links report complete. All items have been added to the task list. Open the Task List by choosing View, Other Windows, Task List.

4. To open the offending Web page in an Editor, double-click on its name in the Task List.

5. As you correct your broken links, select the check box beside the task to mark it as complete.

To enter Link View, follow these steps:

1. Select a page you want to use as your Link View starting point from the Project Explorer. This is typically your start page or home page.

2. From the menu bar, choose View, View Links. This displays the Link View window beginning with your selected page, extending out to all items it is hyperlinked to.

3. Click the Change Diagram Layout button in the Link View toolbar (third button from the left).

4. Using the Link View toolbar, you can filter Link View to display only certain types of links, inbound or outbound links, as well as repeated links. To view links in a more manageable form, click the Change Diagram Layout button in the toolbar.

17

Tip

You can use Link View to spot broken links by their red color and broken icon. This tool can also be extended to looking at broken links on remote Web sites that you have linked to.

Note

You can view inbound links only from within your own Web project. You can't see links from other Web sites to your own.

Developing ASP Applications with Design-Time Controls

Adding interactivity and logic to your Web site can often mean many hours of development and frustration. Even the simplest of ASP applications requires care and attention when developing and debugging. To shorten development time, Microsoft has provided a feature known as *Design-Time Controls* in Visual InterDev 6.

What Are Design-Time Controls?

NEW TERM A *Design-Time Control* (DTC) is a data-bound control used to quickly add functionality to your Web site. It lets you create sophisticated functionality by dragging and dropping a control onto your page and setting a few properties, instead of coding a lot of functionality on your own. DTCs are built to take advantage of the new Visual InterDev scripting object model.

Design-Time Controls Included with Visual InterDev

Visual InterDev 6 includes several useful Design-Time Controls (with the ability to add more as you find them). The standard DTCs included with Visual InterDev give you the ability to create database applications, intelligent forms, multimedia transitions, and timelines. These controls, located in the Design-Time Controls tab of the Toolbox, include the following:

- *Button*—Creates a form Button script object, which creates an intrinsic HTML button.
- *Checkbox*—Creates a form Checkbox script object, which creates an intrinsic HTML check box that can be bound to data.
- *FormManager*—Used to create event-driven forms with Browse, Edit, and Insert modes. This control is used to manipulate the script objects of other controls associated with the form (such as a Listbox control).
- *Grid*—Creates a grid object at design time that generates the appropriate HTML for a data-bound grid at runtime.
- *Label*—Creates a Label script object, which creates a data-bound string of text (bracketed by the <SPAN> tag).
- *Listbox*—Creates a form Listbox script object, which creates an intrinsic HTML list box that can be bound to data.
- *OptionGroup*—Creates a form OptionGroup script object, which then creates a set of intrinsic HTML radio buttons that can be bound to data.

- *PageNavbar*—Creates a navigation bar object at design time that generates the required HTML for navigational bars at runtime. The navigational bar is controlled through site diagrams.

- *PageObject*—A script object used to access an ASP page as an object. This exposes the scriptable methods and properties of an ASP page.

- *PageTransitions*—Used to control how pages visually replace one another when a page is entered or exited.

- *Recordset*—Creates a Recordset script object, which enables you to access data from a page. The Recordset control acts as a data source when binding data-bound .

- *RecordsetNavbar*—Creates a RecordsetNavbar script object, which creates a set of HTML buttons for moving through a recordset. The RecordsetNavbar is capable of updating records in a recordset.

- *Textbox*—Creates a form Textbox script object, which creates an intrinsic HTML <INPUT> tag or <TEXTAREA> tag that can be bound to data.

- *Timelines*—Used to control when events in your Web page occur. You can specify single or multiple timeline objects to determine when actions take place.

Using a Visual InterDev Design-Time Control

For almost all Design-Time Controls, the intent is to be able to drag and drop the control into your page (via the Source or Design Editors) and alter a few properties. DTCs are built for rapid development, without requiring a great deal of care and attention to code. Let's take an example of inserting a PageTransitions DTC into one of your Web pages. Follow these steps:

1. Open a Web page in the Design or Source Editor.
2. Select the Design-Time Controls tab in the Toolbox.
3. Drag the PageTransitions control onto your page with the Editor.
4. Right-click on the PageTransitions control and choose Properties from the context menu to open the Page Transitions Properties dialog box, shown in Figure 17.31.
5. From the Page Enter panel, select a transition type from the Transition drop-down list.
6. From the Page Exit panel, select a transition type from the Transition drop-down list. (Tip: Choose a different transition than you did for the Page Enter panel.)
7. Click the OK button to close the dialog box.
8. Test your new transition by opening your page in a Web browser and then moving to another page.

17

FIGURE 17.31.

The Page Transition Properties dialog box applies a transition to the page while it loads or unloads in the browser window.

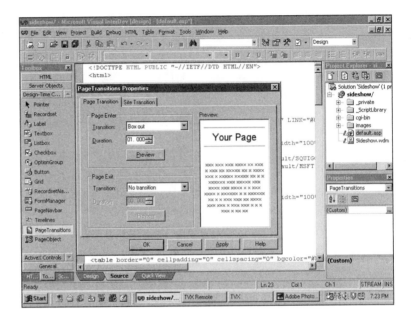

Caution | The PageTransitions Design-Time Control does not work in Netscape. It relies on the Internet Explorer document object model.

Tip | You can use the PageTransitions DTC for a site transition effect, not just for individual pages.

Using Themes and Layouts to Create Professional-Looking ASP Applications

NEW TERM   Creating a visually consistent Web site can often be a chore, especially when you
           are trying to concentrate on the underlying functionality. Visual InterDev *themes*
let you apply a particular look to your entire Web site or even individual Web pages.
Layouts, on the other hand, are used to determine how the page controls—such as navigational controls and banners—are presented in your pages. Figures 17.32 and 17.33 display the same Web page content; however, the page shown in Figure 17.33 has a theme applied.

FIGURE 17.32.

This page has no theme applied...

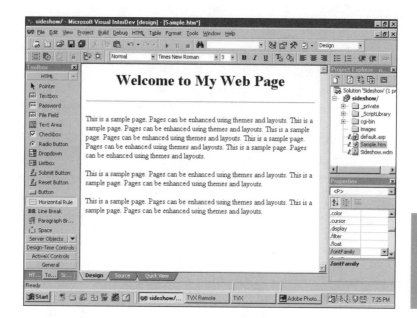

FIGURE 17.33.

...but this page has a theme applied!

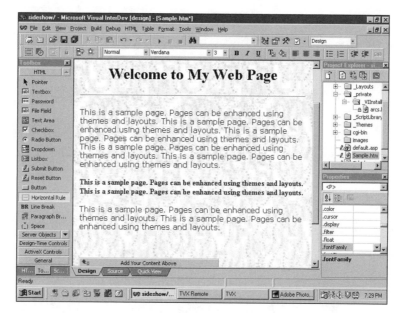

> **Note**
>
> The application of CSS (Cascading Style Sheets), although it is a standard set by the World Wide Web Consortium (W3C), doesn't always implement nicely across both sets of browsers. You should check your work in multiple browsers to verify compatibility.

17

To apply a theme to a Web page or your entire site, follow these steps:

1. Right-click on either your Web project or a single page (to apply a theme to only one page) and choose Apply Theme and Layout from the context menu.

2. The Apply Theme and Layout dialog box, shown in Figure 17.34, lets you define your theme. From the Theme tab, select the Apply Theme radio button.

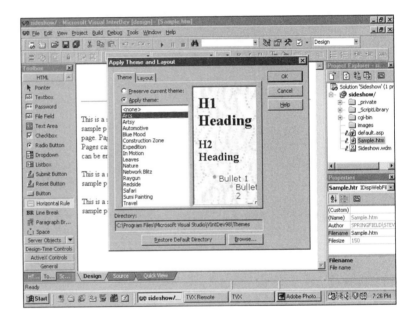

3. Each theme that Visual InterDev has installed is listed in the left pane. When you select a theme, it is previewed in the right pane. Choose a theme you want to use for your site or page.

Tip

You can browse for additional themes on your computer by clicking the Browse button. You might also be able to install additional themes using the Visual InterDev Setup program.

4. To apply a layout, click the Layout tab, shown in Figure 17.35.

5. Select the Apply Layout and Theme radio button.

6. From the list of available layouts, select one to see a preview of it in the right pane.

7. When you have found a layout and theme you are satisfied with, click the OK button to apply your changes.

FIGURE 17.35.

A preview of each lay-out gives you an idea of what it will look like.

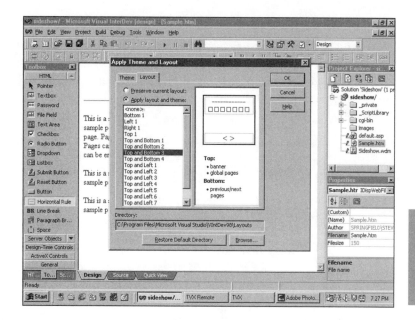

Developing Database Applications with Visual InterDev

At the heart of the most powerful Web applications are databases. In the past, developing database-driven Web applications required a great deal of effort and time. Thanks to Visual InterDev's data environment and Design-Time Controls, the development of database applications is made considerably easier.

Establishing a Database Connection

Before you can use a database in your Web application, you must create a connection. Creating a database connection in Visual InterDev is easy to do; just follow these steps:

1. Right-click on your Web project in the Project Explorer and choose Add Data Connection from the context menu to open the Select Data Source dialog box.

2. Select the ODBC Data Source Name (DSN) from the dialog box, or create a new one. For more information on creating a data source name, refer back to Day 10, "Programming Web Databases."

3. Click the OK button. Your data connection is created in the Project Explorer.

Querying the Database

With a database connection established, you are ready to use the data source in your application. Interaction with the database take place in the form of *data commands*. Data commands are typically queries to a table or a view, but can also be stored procedures, synonyms, or raw SQL code. To query the database, create a data command to your data source by following these steps:

1. Right-click on your project in the Project Explorer and choose Add Data Command from the context menu. This opens the Command Properties dialog box, shown in Figure 17.36.

FIGURE 17.36.

The Command Properties dialog box is used to select the database object used in data commands.

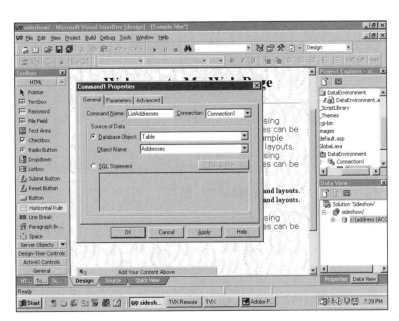

2. Specify a name for your data command in the Command Name text box. This is the name Visual InterDev will use to identify this command.

3. Select the database connection from the Connection drop-down list. This is particularly important if your project uses more than one database connection.

4. Choose Table or View from the Database Object drop-down list. This selection defines the type of database object this data command will use.

5. Select a specific table or view from the Object Name drop-down list. This choice defines the actual database object to be used by the data command.

6. Click the OK button to create the database connection.

> **Tip**
>
> You can use the Command Properties dialog box to specify parameters for your data command, including recordset management and command time-outs.

To complete a quick query of the data connection, double-click on the data command in the Project Explorer. Figure 17.37 shows a sample result.

FIGURE 17.37.

You can quickly query the database to confirm the presence of data.

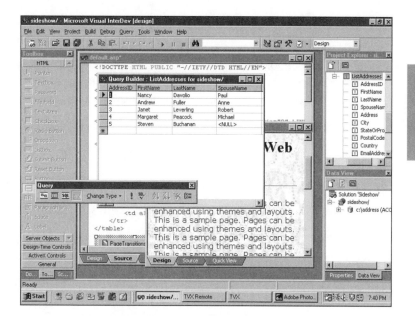

Displaying Records in the Database

Querying your database in Visual InterDev is one thing—displaying records in a Web page is another. Visual InterDev's Design-Time Controls are data-bound controls, provided so that you can easily create database applications to display records. To display records in your Web page, follow these steps:

1. Open an ASP page in the Source or Design Editor.
2. Select the Design-Time Controls tab in the Toolbox.
3. Drag a Recordset DTC onto your Web page.
4. Choose the data Connection, Database Object, and Object Name in your Recordset control.

5. Locate the Data Environment folder in the Project Explorer. Expand your data connection and data command to display the individual fields in your command.

6. Drag and drop the individual fields from your data command into your Web page, after the Recordset.

7. Save your changes by choosing Save from the File menu.

View the results by browsing your Web page through an external Web browser.

Debugging ASP Applications

A big part of development is debugging. Before deploying your Web applications, you want to be sure of their stability, reliability, and performance. Visual InterDev provides integrated support for ASP debugging when combined with Internet Information Server 4.0 or higher. Visual InterDev's debugging features include the following:

- Support for breakpoints, break expressions, watch expressions, and code step-through.
- Snapshots of the current state of your application.
- Debugging tools for detecting compilation errors, runtime errors, and logic errors.

| Caution | Debugging with Personal Web Server on NT Workstation works fine, but it does not currently work on Windows 95. |

Before you can begin debugging server-side ASP script, you must enable debugging. You can manually debug your application, or allow Visual InterDev to automatically debug as needed. To enable debugging, follow these steps:

1. Right-click on your project in the Project Explorer and choose Properties from the context menu to open the Property Pages dialog box.

2. Select the Launch tab.

3. Select the option for Automatically Enable ASP Server-Side Script Debugging on Launch.

4. Click OK.

Creating and Using Breakpoints

Breakpoints act as your way of telling Visual InterDev and the Web server to stop what it is doing. You can use them to examine processes, variables, and conditions to determine how your application is behaving. During a breakpoint, you can then make changes, continue the application, or terminate it.

To create a breakpoint, follow these simple steps:

1. Open your ASP page in the Source Editor.

2. Locate the code block that you want to insert the breakpoint for.

3. Click in the column to the left of the code. This inserts the breakpoint as a red stop sign.

You can insert multiple breakpoints throughout your application. As you run your application (by choosing Start from the Debug menu), the Web server and Visual InterDev monitor for breakpoints. As a breakpoint is encountered, your application stops.

| Tip | You can use breakpoints to step through your application's execution. This technique can be invaluable for monitoring how your code behaves. |

17

Using the Three Core Debugging Windows

There are three main windows used during the debugging process: the Immediate window, the Locals window, and the Output window. When your program has entered a break state (typically through a breakpoint), these windows can be used to debug the appearance of your application, the values of variables and expressions, and active procedures.

Let's briefly review the uses for each window again:

- *Immediate window*—This window allows you to change the values of variables so that you can immediately see the effect of your changes. When in break mode, you can also use the Immediate window to evaluate expressions by typing them in.

- *Locals window*—The Locals window displays the values of variables that are local in scope to the current procedure. As your Web application moves from procedure to procedure, this window changes to reflect the applicable variables.

- *Output window*—Status messages at runtime and debugging code can be displayed in the Output window to isolate problems. Also, results from actions taken in the Immediate window are returned in the Output window.

Summary

Visual InterDev is a powerful environment that requires a considerable investment of time to learn. Although the basic features of this tool are easy to grasp, its more powerful (and ultimately more useful) features are more complex. Today you got a brief taste of how Visual InterDev can simplify and extend your ASP development. To fully appreciate Visual InterDev, you should spend some time experimenting with it. You should also consider referring to a more comprehensive resource on this tool, such as Que's *Special Edition Using Visual InterDev 6*.

Q&A

Q Do I have to use Visual InterDev with a Web server, or can I develop locally and upload my code?

A For development, Visual InterDev requires a Web server with Microsoft FrontPage Server Extensions. Included with Visual InterDev is the Windows NT Option Pack for Windows 95/98, Windows NT 4.0 Server, and Windows NT 4.0 Workstation. This option pack includes Internet Information Server and Personal Web Services for your development. After you have finished developing, you can then upload your code to your Web server via FTP or whatever other means your server supports.

Q What databases does Visual InterDev support?

A Visual InterDev can communicate with any ODBC data source; however, to fully appreciate Visual InterDev's integration with database development, you should be using either a Microsoft SQL Server or an Oracle database server.

Q Which should I use for page design: Visual InterDev or Microsoft FrontPage?

A Visual InterDev is targeted for Active Server Pages developers. Although FrontPage's WYSIWYG editor is more mature than Visual InterDev's Design Editor, you should always use Visual InterDev when developing ASP pages. You can use FrontPage to create your pages and then use Visual InterDev to create the underlying code.

Q Can I use different editing tools while still using Visual InterDev to manage my site?

A Yes. Visual InterDev lets you define external editors for different file types, including HTML and ASP pages. You can make your changes in an external editor launched from Visual InterDev and then use Visual InterDev to update your Web site. Right-click on a file in the Project Explorer and choose Open With to define additional editors and use them.

Workshop

The quiz questions and exercises are provided for your further understanding. Please refer to Appendix A, "Answers to Questions," for the answers to the quiz questions; the answers to the exercises are on the MCP Web site.

Quiz

1. Visual InterDev is composed of many windows. Which one is used to organize your Web site files?

2. The Document Outline window can be used to view what two kinds of outlines?

3. When is a solution created?

4. What mode is best to use when working with multiple developers on a live Web site?

5. What purpose does the Object Browser fulfill?

6. How do you add pages to a global navigation bar?

7. What are Design-Time Controls designed to do?

8. Before creating a data command, what must you do?

9. When are the debugging windows (such as the Locals window) updated?

Exercises

1. Experiment with Visual InterDev's Design-Time Controls and database connections by creating an Address Book application bound to a database. This application should be tied to a form that allows users to view and modify contact entries.

2. Work with Visual InterDev's server-side debugging by creating a page that displays random quotes from a text file or a database. Purposefully break the application and then use breakpoints and the debugging facilities to track your application's behavior.

DAY 18

Building in Security

Security is an important aspect of deploying applications on the Internet. Today, you learn ways you can improve the security of a Web site that hosts ASP applications. You will be taking a break from developing ASP applications to explore security issues of publishing information on the Internet. By understanding security considerations that should be taken into account when you're building Internet applications, you can make your ASP applications more secure, thus eliminating a threat to the security of your network or Web server. Today, you cover the following:

- Use NTFS security permissions.
- Learn to limit members of the Administrators group.
- Understand how to monitor security logs.
- Enable auditing.
- Enable Web server access logging.
- Consult Web server access logs to track down suspicious activities.
- Limit access to CGI/ASP directories.
- Discover additional security resources.

Note
Certain topics on security that are discussed today do not apply to you if you are not using Windows NT. If you are setting up a public Web site on the Internet, it is recommended that you use Windows NT Server. It's more secure for Internet applications and allows you to easily implement security and access permissions with NTFS (NT File System) permissions.

Taking Steps to Improve Security

Security is an important aspect of any Internet server. When you publish information on the Internet, you should be aware of security threats and take precautions to guard against them.

Certain security risks are always associated with connecting a server to the Internet. However, this threat to security does not mean you should not set up a server on the Internet. You should simply take whatever precautions necessary to make it harder and more expensive for someone to break into your system. This list of precautions you can take to enhance your Web server's security is discussed in the following sections:

- Disabling the Windows NT Guest account
- Using NTFS security and disk partitions
- Controlling directory browsing
- Understanding potential security holes created by Index Server
- Hiding database files
- Controlling access to CGI/ISAPI/ASP directories
- Enabling auditing (without any help from the IRS)
- Hiding `perl.exe`

Disabling the Windows NT Guest Account

If you have not done so already, disable the Windows NT Guest account because anyone could use it to gain access to your system. If you have an FTP server set up at your site, this account can be especially dangerous because a malicious user could use it to destroy information on your system. You can check the status of your Guest account with User Manager. To launch it, choose Programs, Administrative Tools from the Windows NT Start menu and execute the User Manager application. When User Manager appears, select the Guest account, as shown in Figure 18.1, and press Enter or choose User, Properties from the menu.

FIGURE 18.1.

Monitoring the Guest account with User Manager.

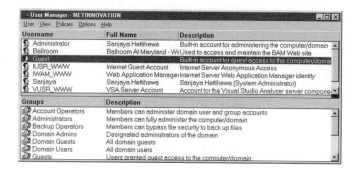

When the User Properties dialog box shown in Figure 18.2 appears, make sure the Account Disabled check box is checked.

FIGURE 18.2.

The User Properties dialog box is used to specify individual user permissions.

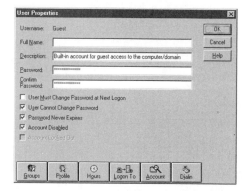

18

Using NTFS Security and Disk Partitions

Devoting an entire disk partition to Internet publishing is recommended if you can afford to do so. This partition should contain not only the FTP and Web server document root directories, but also binary files of Internet services. This setup makes it easier for you to control access to directory structures and manage security. If you follow this advice, you can use NTFS security to restrict access to all other disk partitions.

Note

You can change a FAT partition to NTFS by running Disk Administrator. To run it, choose Programs, Administrative Tools from the Windows Start menu.

Using NTFS partitions exclusively is highly recommended. The following steps explain how to limit access to a directory that is accessible via IIS:

1. In Windows Explorer, select the directory that is a child of your Web server's document root directory.

2. After selecting the directory, choose File, Properties from the menu and select the Security tab. The dialog box shown in Figure 18.3 appears.

FIGURE 18.3.

Specifying security settings for a Web server directory.

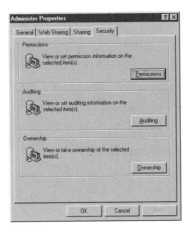

3. Click the Permissions button to specify directory access permissions for users. The dialog box in Figure 18.4 is used to grant and revoke file and directory access permissions to users and user groups. IIS:

FIGURE 18.4.

You can restrict access to files and directories in NTFS partitions by using Windows Explorer.

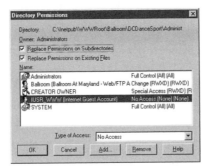

Tip

Select the Replace Permissions on Subdirectories check box in Figure 18.4 to apply specified file and directory access permissions to subdirectories of the selected directory.

As shown in Figure 18.4, access to files and directories in an NTFS partition can be restricted to only certain users and user groups.

DON'T

Don't use FAT partitions to store your Web files. You cannot enforce Windows NT security on FAT partitions.

Controlling Directory Browsing

Directory browsing is a feature that allows a user to type in a URL with a directory name and have the Web server supply a list of all the files and subdirectories in the specified directory.

Depending on the structure and nature of information on your Web site, this feature has advantages as well as disadvantages. If your Web site is an *open* one and you want to share as much information as possible, enable directory browsing. If your Web site contains information that should be accessed in a particular order, however, disable this feature.

Consider the following scenario. You can distribute software with a Web server, and all the applications distributed through the Web server can be in a certain directory. For record-keeping and statistical-analysis purposes, you might have users fill out a form and submit it before they are given permission to download applications. If directory browsing is enabled, a technically inclined user might figure out how to skip registering by typing the name of the directory in which the applications are located and downloading all the applications in that directory without filling in any required registration forms. In this instance, it would not be advantageous for you to enable directory browsing for a certain directory.

The following steps explain how to enable/disable directory browsing with IIS 4.0:

1. Invoke Internet Service Manager by choosing Programs, Windows NT 4 Option Pack, Internet Information Server from the Windows Start menu.
2. When the Microsoft Management Console (MMC) appears, select a directory or site.
3. Choose Action, Properties from the MMC toolbar.
4. Use the Directory Properties dialog box shown in Figure 18.5 to specify whether users can browse the directory. The Directory Browsing Allowed check box in the Content Control section is used to control whether directory browsing is enabled or disabled.

FIGURE **18.5.**

Directory browsing can be enabled or disabled on a per directory/site basis.

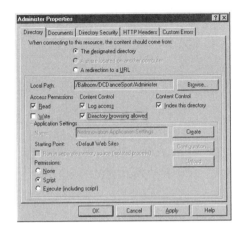

Understand Potential Security Holes Created by Index Server

Most Web sites on the Internet are indexed. Some are indexed via public Web search engines, such as Yahoo!, WebCrawler, AltaVista, and so on, and other Web sites are indexed locally with Web indexing software such as Microsoft Index Server and Excite. Web site indexes are persistent creatures. They look at every nook and cranny of a Web site and index everything they can find. This persistence can potentially compromise the security of a Web server and expose unintended parts of the site to the entire world.

Never store databases and log files (including those generated by your ASP applications) in the document root directory of a Web server because their contents could be unintentionally exposed to users browsing a Web site with a search engine. By using a special robot file, you can control which files on your Web site are indexed by search engines. To learn more about robot files, visit the following Web page:

```
http://www.yahoo.com/Computers_and_Internet/Internet/World_Wide_Web/Search
ing_
➡_the_Web/Robots__Spiders__etc__Documentation/
```

Hide Those Databases

Never store databases anywhere in the document root directory of your Web server. Doing so allows anyone knowing the correct URL to download your entire database! When creating an ODBC DSN for a database, always store your database in a directory that is not accessible through IIS. If you must store the database in the the Web server's document root directory, be sure to secure the database with NTFS security.

Controlling Access to CGI/ISAPI/ASP Directories

Controlling access to the CGI, ISAPI, and Active Server Pages directories of your Web server is very important. Only trusted users should have access to these directories. Any user who has access to a CGI directory of the Web server can easily execute programs on the server by using a Web browser. For this reason, never allow just any user to have access to the CGI directory through FTP, which uses clear-text user names and passwords. Someone who has access to part of your local network or the part of the Internet over which the authentication data is transmitted can monitor FTP transactions with a simple protocol analyzer. A protocol analyzer can be used to get user names and passwords of those authorized to access your system. An unauthorized user, possibly with malicious intent, can then access your system through FTP by pretending to be an authorized user and execute any application on your system by copying it to the CGI directory.

Auditing Your Web Server (Without Any Help from the IRS)

Use resource-auditing capabilities of Windows NT to monitor critical resources of your Internet server. From the User Manager's main menu, choose Policies, Audit. The Audit Policy dialog box that appears can be used to turn on auditing (see Figure 18.6).

18

FIGURE 18.6.

You can audit system resources with User Manager.

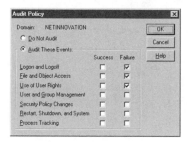

After you enable auditing with User Manager, select a directory from Windows Explorer and then choose File, Properties from the menu. When the Administer Properties dialog box appears (refer to Figure 18.3), select the Security tab and click the Auditing button. The Directory Auditing dialog box, shown in Figure 18.7, appears. Use the options in this dialog box to audit critical areas of your Internet server.

FIGURE **18.7.**

The Directory Auditing dialog box.

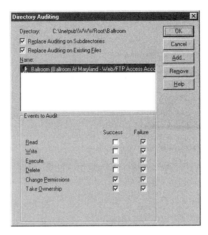

You can use the Event Detail dialog box shown in Figure 18.8 to monitor possible breaches of security. To open the Event Detail dialog box, select an event from the Windows NT Event Viewer. The event in this figure was logged as a result of an unsuccessful login attempt.

FIGURE **18.8.**

Unsuccessful login attempt recorded.

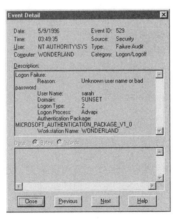

Warning

Do not get carried away and audit too many activities; otherwise, you'll clutter your event log. When the event log becomes cluttered, it makes it almost impossible for you to locate critical information. Auditing too many events can also slow down your system. Nonetheless, at the very least, I recommend that you audit access failures.

Keep Your Perl Safe: Hide `perl.exe`

Perl is a powerful language you can use for a variety of purposes. It is especially suitable for creating CGI and, of course, ASP applications to process user input. However, do not place `perl.exe` in a directory within the Web server's document root directory. A malicious user could use `perl.exe` to execute commands on your Web server. Instead of placing `perl.exe` in a directory of your Web server, you should create a CGI extension mapping and place `perl.exe` in a directory that's not accessible through your Web server.

Note

An extension mapping is automatically created when you install Perl 5.0 or higher. Refer to IIS documentation for more information about creating CGI extension mappings.

DON'T

DON'T place `perl.exe` in a directory within your Web server's document root directory.

18

Allowing FTP Access to Your Web Site

You can use the File Transfer Protocol (FTP) to allow users to upload contents to your Web site, but take the time to make sure your users are aware that anything they upload to the Web server through FTP can be viewed by someone eavesdropping on the network connection. If users upload sensitive material to your server through FTP, make them use a powerful data encryption mechanism, such as Pretty Good Privacy (PGP). Visit the following Web site for information about PGP:

```
http://www.yahoo.com/Computers_and_Internet/Security_and_Encryption/
➥PGP___Pretty_Good_Privacy/
```

Monitoring for Security Violations

After enabling auditing, it is important that either you or a system administrator keep a close eye on the Web server's security log files. This enables you to detect and take action when unusual and potentially harmful activity is detected in a log file. The next two sections explain how to monitor your server for security violations.

Monitoring Event Viewer

You should periodically (at least once every few days) monitor Event Viewer entries to detect suspicious activities. Figure 18.9 shows a typical Event Viewer listing. The event log contains valuable information that should be monitored.

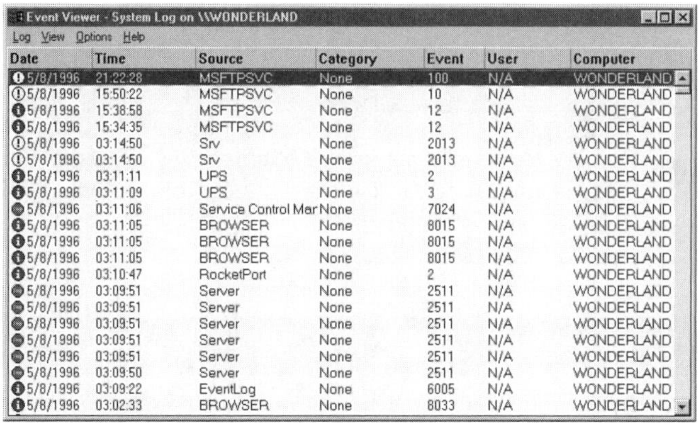

FIGURE 18.9.

An Event Viewer listing.

You can get additional information about events displayed in Event Viewer by selecting an event and double-clicking it. The dialog box shown in Figure 18.10 is invoked by double-clicking the event selected in Figure 18.9.

FIGURE 18.10.

Detailed information about an event displayed in Event Viewer.

Monitoring Access Log Files

If you detect suspicious activity in Event Viewer, you can get additional information by consulting the access log files. Log files can be several megabytes, so manually examining them is not a very good idea. If you detect repeated suspicious activity, however, you can use the access log file to get additional information. If several messages similar to the one shown in Figure 18.10 appear in the event log, you can use the access log file to get information such as the IP address of the user who tried to access the system. Figure 18.11 demonstrates how the access log file can be used to find detailed information about the event in Figure 18.10. In this example, the time and date of the event are used as indexes to locate the corresponding access log file entry. Refer to your Web or FTP documentation and configuration settings for the location of the access log file.

Note The default location of the IIS log files is \WINNT\system32\LogFiles\.

FIGURE 18.11.

You can use access log files to get detailed information about suspicious activities.

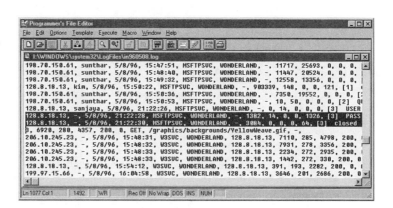

18

Publishing Sensitive Information

Sensitive information should never be distributed through a Web server unless the data is encrypted before it is transmitted. Although you can restrict access to parts of a Web site by IP address, users can spoof IP addresses. Therefore, you should never use IP addresses to restrict access to sensitive information. The same goes for basic user authentication. Unless Windows NT challenge/response user authentication is used, someone monitoring connections to your Web server can easily intercept user names and passwords of authorized users and use them to gain unauthorized access to your system.

Enabling Encryption on the Web Server

If you use your Web server to conduct sensitive transactions over the Internet, you should enable encryption on your Web server to make it practically impossible for someone to monitor your Web server traffic. Consult your Web server's documentation for additional information about enabling encryption.

Using Windows NT Challenge/Response User Authentication

If you are hosting your Web site with IIS, you can use Windows NT challenge/response user authentication to ensure that user names and passwords are encrypted before they are transmitted over the Internet. Although doing so improves security, there is a trade-off. At the time of this writing, only Internet Explorer supports Windows NT challenge/response user authentication. Use this method of authentication to improve security if you are certain all your users use Internet Explorer. Note that Windows NT challenge/response user authentication does not encrypt information transmitted through the Internet; it encrypts only user names and passwords.

Simulating Unauthorized Break-ins

You would be wise to test the security of your NT system by trying to gain unauthorized access to it. You can do so with the aid of some administrative tools. ScanNT is one utility for finding weak passwords on NT systems. You can use such a utility to make sure poor passwords chosen by your users do not compromise your system's security by detecting them before a potential breach of security occurs. Find ScanNT at the following URL:

```
http://www.ntsecurity.com/Products/ScanNT/index.html
```

Security Resources

Many Internet security resources are available on the Internet. You should visit the Web sites listed in the following sections to learn more about Internet security and ways of protecting an Internet server against unauthorized access. Monitor these Web sites for the most up-to-date information on Internet security.

The World Wide Web Security FAQ

The World Wide Web Security FAQ has many Internet security resources. Visit this URL to get information about security holes and how to protect your system from unauthorized accesses:

```
http://www.w3.org/Security/Faq/
```

Information Security Web Site

Visit the Information Security Web site for news articles on information data security and Internet Web security:

```
http://www.newspage.com/NEWSPAGE/cgi-bin/walk.cgi/NEWSPAGE/info/d2/d10/
```

Yahoo!'s Internet Security and Encryption Web Page

Yahoo!'s Internet Security and Encryption Web page lists many Internet security Web pages. Visit it at this URL to find the most up-to-date information on Internet security and encryption:

```
http://www.yahoo.com/Computers_and_Internet/Security_and_Encryption/
```

18

NT Web Server Security Issues

The following Web site lists many useful suggestions for securing an NT Web server on the Internet. Visit it to learn about security precautions you can take to prevent unauthorized access to an NT Web server.

```
http://www.telemark.net/~randallg/ntsecure.htm
```

Maximum Security: The Hacker's Guide to Protecting Your Internet Site and Network

For an alternative view of Internet security, check out *Maximum Security: The Hacker's Guide to Protecting Your Internet Site and Network* (published by Sams.net). This book offers comprehensive coverage of security issues on several platforms and offers plenty of resources for additional information.

Summary

You can take steps to protect an NT server on the Internet against unauthorized access. Although setting up an Internet server that is immune to unauthorized access is almost impossible, there are ways to make it harder and, in some cases, prohibitively expensive for someone to gain unauthorized access.

Q&A

Q **Why shouldn't you authenticate users based solely on their IP address?**

A Although you can restrict access to parts of a Web site by IP address, users can spoof IP addresses. Therefore, you should never use IP addresses to restrict access to sensitive information.

Q **Why should you hide Perl from your Web server and instead create an application mapping for the Perl executable file?**

A A user with malicious intent can potentially use `perl.exe` to execute commands on your NT server.

Q **Why should you limit which activities are audited?**

A Auditing too many activities clutters your event log, which makes it practically impossible for you to locate critical information. Auditing too many events can also slow down your system.

Workshop

The quiz questions and exercises are provided for your further understanding. Please refer to Appendix A, "Answers to Questions," for the answers to the quiz questions; the answers to the exercises are on the MCP Web site.

Quiz

1. Which activities should typically be audited?
2. What is the default location of IIS log files?
3. Why should you disable the Windows NT Guest account?
4. Name the two main drawbacks of using Windows NT challenge/response for user authentication.
5. Are there any drawbacks in auditing too many activities?

Exercises

1. Visit your favorite Web search engine and search for ASP, Windows NT, and IIS security Web pages to discover new and informative Web sites about security. Bookmark informative Web pages you find so you can visit them later.
2. Create a directory on your Web server, disable directory browsing, and modify its access permissions so that only users in the Administrators group can access that directory.
3. Use Event Viewer to examine whether there have been any recent security violations on your Web server.

Day 19

Exploiting ASP: Tips and Advanced Topics

You are nearing the end of your 21-day tutorial. Although you have covered quite an exhaustive list of topics related to ASP over the past 18 days, there are several important ASP topics that don't really belong in one of the previous days. Nevertheless, these topics are important to ASP and understanding them will make you a better ASP developer. The purpose of today's lesson is to give you some useful tips and techniques for deploying ASP applications on the Internet and exploiting ASP to the fullest. Today, you cover the following topics:

- Learn tips for creating effective ASP applications.
- Analyze the use of ASP applications.
- Understand when and how to use ASP2HTML to create static Web pages from dynamic ASP applications.
- Convert IDC applications to ASP applications.
- Stress-test an ASP application.
- Isolate unstable IIS processes.
- Review ASP registry settings.

> **Note**
>
> Today's lesson is a how-to tutorial as well as a reference guide. The section on ASP Registry settings in particular is more of a reference guide, but also discusses their importance and their applications.

Tips for Creating Effective ASP Applications

You should now be quite familiar with building ASP applications. ASP applications are different from traditional applications built with languages such as C++, Visual Basic, Pascal and so forth. ASP is a technology developed with the primary focus of making it easier to build Web applications. Along with this focus come some special considerations you should be aware of when building your own ASP applications. The following sections explore ways you can make your ASP applications more scalable, efficient, and robust. The tips covered include the following:

- What to do when IIS hangs on you.
- Where to store small values between sessions.
- How to skip past runtime errors.
- How to avoid syntax errors in data declarations.
- How to make it easier to reuse code.
- Why you should avoid global variables.
- How to manage key IIS configuration settings with MMC.

What to Do If IIS Hangs

If IIS does hang, and you can't stop the World Wide Web Publishing Service with the Control Panel's Services application, here's what you can do to restart the World Wide Web Publishing Service and avoid having to reboot your server. Use the Windows NT Resource Kit utility Kill.exe to terminate the World Wide Web Publishing Service by issuing the following command:

```
Kill inetinfo
```

Once the inetinfo process is killed, you can restart the World Wide Web Publishing Service with the following command:

```
Net start "World Wide Web Publishing Service"
```

> **Note**
>
> You can buy the Windows NT Resource Kit at any major computer store or bookstore.

Where to Store Small Values

Use the ASP `Session` object whenever you need to store small amounts of data between HTTP sessions, such as a user progressing through a Web-based data entry wizard. If the data entry wizard has three steps, and the user is currently in the third step, the data the user entered in the last two steps can be stored in the `Session` object.

How to Skip Past Runtime Errors Using `On Error Resume Next`

VBScript allows a mechanism for skipping past any runtime errors that might occur in your ASP application. This is a handy feature when you want your ASP application to continue execution, without displaying any error messages, even if the application generates any runtime errors. The syntax is simple; just include the following line of code in your ASP application:

```
On Error Resume Next
```

> **Caution**
>
> Be careful about the scope of the `On Error Resume Next` statement. If you give it global scope by defining it outside a subroutine or function, you can't detect any errors in your ASP application. Always use the `On Error Resume Next` statement inside a subroutine or function.

How to Detect Error Numbers and Descriptions

If an error occurs in your ASP application, it is easy to determine the error number and description by using the `err` object. All you need to do is insert the ASP statement `On Error Resume Next` before the ASP statements and then use the `err` object, as shown in Listing 19.1, to access the error description and number.

LISTING 19.1. DETECTING ERRORS BY USING THE `err` OBJECT.

```
1: On Error Resume Next
2:
3: ' ... ASP statements go here ...
4:
5: If err.number > 0 then
6:   response.write err.number
7:   response.write err.description
8: end if
```

Note

If there are multiple errors, only the most recent error number and description is available in the err object.

How to Avoid Syntax Errors in Data Declarations

If you are a Visual Basic programmer, you probably already understand the virtues of the Option Explicit statement. Visual Basic allows you to declare variables anywhere you like or, should you choose to, not define them at all! That means, by default, you do not have to declare variables before using them. Although this might seem like a great feature at first, it is actually a deceptive one that can lead to applications that are difficult to debug. Consider the application in Listing 19.2. What do you think is its outcome? If you think the outcome is one billion dollars (1,000,000,000), you are mistaken. Observe the program more carefully. See Figure 19.1 for the output of this listing's ASP application.

LISTING 19.2. FAILURE TO USE Option Explicit COULD RESULT IN APPLICATIONS THAT ARE HARD TO DEBUG.

```
 1: <HTML>
 2: <HEAD>
 3:    <TITLE>Does Not Use Option Explicit</TITLE>
 4: </HEAD>
 5:
 6: <BODY>
 7: <%
 8: Dim YourSalary
 9:
10: YourSalary = 1000000000
11: Response.Write "For working so hard, we have decided to increase " & _
12:    "your base salary to $" & CCur(YourSallary) & ".<BR> " & _
13:    "Keep up the great work!"
14:
15: %>
16: </BODY>
17: </HTML>
```

ANALYSIS Do you see why the ASP application produces erroneous output? In line 12, the programmer obviously intended to display the number 1,000,000,000, but this is not what happened.

Modify Listing 19.2 by adding the following before line 1:

```
<% Option Explicit %>
```

FIGURE 19.1.

The ASP application does not produce the correct result.

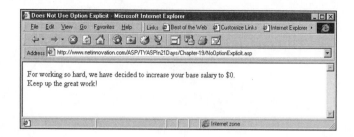

The Option Explicit statement is responsible for making sure you declare variables before using them. Should you, by accident, misspell a variable or forget to declare a variable, the VBScript interpreter points out your mistake so you can easily correct it.

Do

DO use Option Explicit in all your ASP applications and make it a point to declare variables before using them.

As you can see, the failure to use Option Explicit can result in applications that are difficult to debug because no error messages are generated to warn the programmer if a variable is accidentally misspelled because of the Option Explicit statement being left out.

How to Make It Easier to Reuse Code

19

When you're developing ASP applications, you will soon find yourself reusing code subroutines you wrote for previous projects. To make things easier, create a file storing the ASP code subroutines you use most often. The file you create can be used by other ASP applications using server-side includes. You can then easily call the code subroutines without hunting all over your hard drives in search of previous projects you have developed.

Why You Should Avoid Global Variables

It's good programming practice to avoid using global variables. Using global variables can be almost as bad as not using Option Explicit because global variables leave room for hard-to-find bugs. You can easily avoid using global variables in the main code block of your ASP application by encapsulating it in a subroutine, as shown in Listing 19.3, and calling the subroutine from within the main code block.

LISTING 19.3. AVOID USING GLOBAL VARIABLES.

```
 1: <% Option Explicit %>
 2:
 3: <HTML>
 4: <HEAD>
 5:     <TITLE>Use Local Variables</TITLE>
 6: </HEAD>
 7:
 8: <BODY>
 9: <%
10:
11: ' Direct the execution of the ASP application to the Main
12: ' subroutine declared below.
13: Main
14:
15: ' The execution of the ASP code begins in the Main
16: ' subroutine, thanks to the above subroutine call.
17: Sub Main
18:
19:    Dim Greeting
20:    Dim LoopCount
21:
22:    Greeting = "Hi everyone!"
23:    For LoopCount = 1 to 4
24:       Response.Write Greeting & "<BR>"
25:    Next %>
26:
27: <H3>
28: This is the HTML body of the Web page
29: </h3>
30:
31: <%
32:    End Sub
33: %>
34: </BODY>
35: </HTML>
```

ANALYSIS   The ASP application in Listing 19.3 uses local variables instead of global variables. The main code block of the ASP application is enclosed in a subroutine invoked by the subroutine call in line 13.

DON'T

DON'T use global variables in ASP applications unless you absolutely have to.

How to Use Microsoft Management Console

New Term Microsoft Management Console (MMC) offers a powerful, centralized interface for managing and interacting with software components running on a computer. In the future, you can expect to see the Control Panel replaced with the MMC as Microsoft and other software vendors create snap-ins for MMC. An MMC *snap-in* is an application that runs inside MMC and allows the user to interface with another application's configuration settings.

> **Note**
>
> All the server applications that are part of the Windows NT 4.0 option pack use the MMC.

You can use the MMC to administer and manage key IIS configuration settings. To invoke the Microsoft Management Console, from the Start menu, choose Programs, Windows NT 4 Option Pack, Internet Information Server, Internet Service Manager. You then see the dialog box shown in Figure 19.2.

FIGURE 19.2.

The MMC is used to administer and config-ure key IIS features.

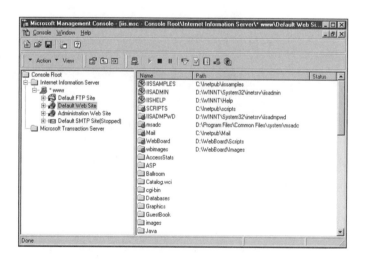

19

Isolating IIS Processes

You can use a feature of IIS to isolate unstable IIS processes so that they don't interfere with other applications executing on the same Web server. Ideally, you should not have to use this feature. However, if you suspect your Web server is not functioning properly because of a rogue application that is unstable, you can have IIS execute that application in its own separate memory space. The following steps explain how to isolate ASP applications in the GuestBook folder of the default Web site.

1. Select the default Web site from MMC.

 Note

> If you have not created any additional Web sites, your Web site will be named "Default Web Site."

2. Open the Default Web Site (by double-clicking on it) and select the GuestBook folder.

3. After the GuestBook folder is highlighted, choose Properties from the Action toolbar. You then see the Directory Properties dialog box shown in Figure 19.3.

FIGURE 19.3.

The Directory Properties dialog box of the selected directory.

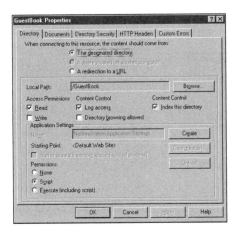

4. Click the Create button to create a new Application Settings profile for the selected directory. The Name text box becomes active so you can supply a name for the Application Settings profile. By selecting the Run In Separate Memory Space (Isolated Process) check box, you can have IIS execute applications in the GuestBook folder in a separate memory space so that if an application in the GuestBook folder crashes, it does not affect other applications running on the Web server.

Managing Log Files

It is important that you have a policy for managing your Web server's log files. Among other information, these files record detailed information about who accesses what from where at what time from your Web server. You can configure how IIS logs Web server access information with the MMC by following these steps:

1. Locate your Web site in MMC. (If you have not created any additional Web servers, simply select Default Web Site.)

2. After highlighting your Web site, choose Properties from the Action toolbar. You then see the Default Web Site Properties dialog box shown in Figure 19.4.

FIGURE 19.4.

The Default Web Site Properties dialog box is used to configure Web server access logging.

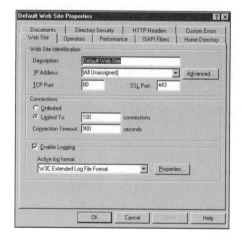

3. Use the Active Log Format drop-down list to select W3C Extended Log File Format. Click the Properties button to configure the logging properties more. The Extended Logging Properties dialog box shown in Figure 19.5 appears.

FIGURE 19.5.

The Extended Logging Properties dialog box is used to configure Web server log files.

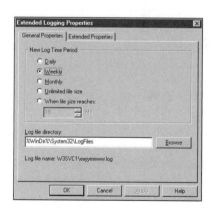

19

4. The General Properties tab of the dialog box in Figure 19.5 is used to specify how often new Web server access log files should be created. You should change the setting in the New Log Time Period section based on how busy your site is.

5. Select the Extended Properties tab to pick which properties you would like to log. As you can see in Figure 19.6, you can choose to log over 20 different fields of data per each HTTP transaction. I recommend that you select to log the data items shown in Figure 19.6.

Tip

The User Agent data field can be used to determine which percentage of users visiting your Web site use Internet Explorer, Netscape Navigator, or another Web browser.

FIGURE 19.6.

The Extended Properties tab is used to select data items to log.

Note

The default locations of IIS log files is %WinDir%\System32\LogFiles.

Analyzing Use of ASP Applications

There are many tools available for analyzing log files generated by Web servers. By analyzing your files, you can determine which resources of your Web server are used and who is visiting your Web site at what time. Depending on the software used to analyze the Web server's access log files, you can even determine from which locality (see Figure 19.7) people are visiting your Web site.

I highly recommend WebTrends for analyzing your Web server's log files. At the time this book was published, you could download an evaluation version of WebTrends from the following URL:

```
http://www.webtrends.com/
```

FIGURE 19.7.

WebTrends can be used to comprehensively analyze a Web server's log file.

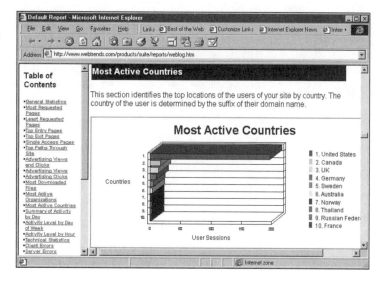

Stress-Testing an ASP Application

Stess-testing an ASP application before putting it on the Web is always a good idea, especially if you expect a Web application to get a lot of use. Say that because you are now an ASP expert, TeachYourselfBookSeller.com has hired you to develop an online storefront for them using Active Server Pages so that they can sell all their 2.5 million books (and order 2.5 million more books). Needless to say, you have to make sure the ASP application you develop for them scales well so they can sell all of their 2.5 million books.

19

 Caution   *Never* stress-test a Web server without getting permission from the Web server's system administrator.

Your ASP applications seems to work wonderfully on your Pentium laptop, but you are not entirely sure how well your application scales. Is there a way to find out just how much your application can take? You bet! You can use InetLoad, a utility developed by Microsoft, to determine how well an ASP application scales. At the time this book was written, you could download InetLoad free of charge from the following URL:

```
http://www.microsoft.com/msdownload/
```

After downloading the InetLoad application distribution file, execute it to install it. After it is installed, you can invoke InetLoad by choosing Programs, Internet Benchmarking from the Windows Start menu. The following steps demonstrate how to use InetLoad to stress-test an ASP application.

 Note

Run InetLoad from a Windows NT PC other than the Web server you are testing.

1. After installing InetLoad on a remote computer, the next step is creating a command script that InetLoad uses to access the Web server. The command script you will be using is very simple. In fact, it contains only one line of text:

   ```
   GET <FIXED>url:/Sanjaya/Quotes/Default.asp
   ```

   Save the command script and give it a filename extension of .txt. The command script file used in this exercise is called StressTest.txt and contains only one line of text. The GET command instructs InetLoad to retrieve the URL (/Sanjaya/Quotes/Default.asp) specified.

2. After saving the command script, choose New from the File menu to create a new stress-test configuration. Next, as shown in Figure 19.8, type in the IP address of the Web server you are testing. Use the Number of Users field to specify the number of simultaneous users you are simulating. For this test, you can simulate 30 concurrent users. You can conduct the stress test for 1 minute. Specify the filename of the command script file created earlier, as shown in the dialog box. You are now ready to run the stress test, but there is one last thing you should do.

3. Run Performance Monitor on the Web server you are testing so that you can monitor how well the Web server scales. Add ASP performance counters such as Requests Queued, Requests Executing, and Request Wait Time so you can monitor how your ASP application handles the extra load.

4. You are now ready to begin the stress test! While keeping an eye on Performance Monitor, go to your second computer that is running InetLoad and click the Run Test button (yes, it helps if the two computers are close by!).

5. Observe the numbers being displayed in InetLoad (Figure 19.9) and how the Performance Monitor (Figure 19.10) counter values are increasing while InetLoad performs the stress test.

FIGURE 19.8.

InetLoad is configured for stress testing an ASP application.

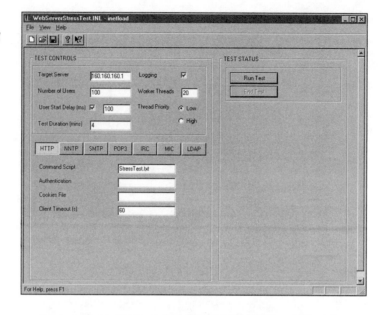

FIGURE 19.9.

InetLoad displays statistics of stress tests.

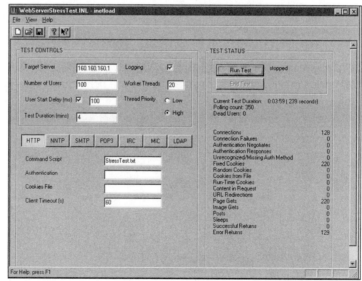

19

FIGURE 19.10.

Performance Monitor graphs the stress imposed by InetLoad on the ASP application.

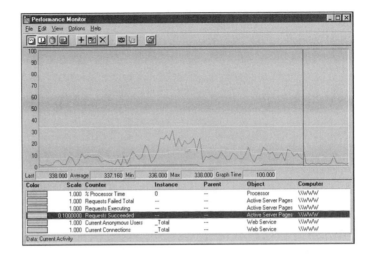

> **Note**   Refer to InetLoad's online documentation (`inetload.doc`) for a more thorough overview of its features and options.

Analyzing Results of the Stress Test

When examining the results of the stress test, pay particular attention to the CPU utilization of the Web server. If it reaches around 80 percent, it is an indication that you need to fine-tune your ASP application or upgrade your hardware. Also, pay attention to Performance Monitor graphs. Ideally, you should see a smooth curve as the ASP application handles increasingly more users.

While running the stress test, access your ASP application with a Web browser. You can then experience firsthand how your application "feels" to a user under heavy use. If you have to wait a long time for the page to display, or get error messages, you need to fine-tune your ASP application further.

It is a good idea to rerun your stress test, simulating different amounts of users accessing the ASP application. You can then determine how your ASP application behaves under heavy use.

Using ASP2HTM to Create Static HTML Pages

Each time a user visits an ASP page, the page is executed on the server and the results are sent to the user. This feature, however, is not always the most efficient solution for all cases. Sometimes it is more efficient to have an ASP page execute every hour or perhaps even once a day and have the result displayed to users. The best way to do this is with the help of a free utility from Microsoft called ASP2HTM. At the time this book was written, you could download ASP2HTM from the following Web page:

```
http://www.microsoft.com/windows/downloads/default.asp?CustArea=bus&Site=
➥nts&Product=Internet+Information+Server&Category=&x=10&y=16
```

Tip | You can use ASP2HTM to save the runtime costs of ASP.

ASP2HTM is a Java-based component that comes in two flavors. If you use IIS 4.0, you should download the file ASP2HTM2.EXE because it is optimized for IIS 4.0.

- ASP2HTM2.EXE—This version of ASP2HTM requires and is optimized for IIS 4.0.
- ASP2HTM1.EXE—This version of ASP2HTM works with PWS, IIS 3.0, and IIS 4.0.

After you download the application distribution file, execute it. You are then asked for the location of the application files. I recommend the location \InetPub\IISSamples\Components\ASP2HTM so you can easily keep track of all the IIS components you install.

The next step is to download and install the Microsoft Java Virtual Machine (VM) and Software Development Kit (SDK). You can get them from the following URL:

```
http://www.microsoft.com/java
```

Afterward, install ASP2HTM as instructed in the readme.txt file found in the directory \Inetpub\iissamples\Components\ASP2HTM (or the directory you selected to install ASP2HTM). After ASP2HTM is installed on your system, you can use the code in Listing 19.4 to create an HTML file using the output of an ASP application.

LISTING 19.4. HOW TO USE ASP2HTM TO CREATE AN HTML FILE USING AN ASP APPLICATION.

```
1: ' Create an instance of the ASP2HTM component
2: Set HTTP = CreateObject("IISSample.Asp2Htm")
3:
4: ' Specify the URL containing the ASP application
5: HTTP.URL( "http://localhost/Directory/Filename.asp" )
6:
7: ' If the URL is valid, the output of the ASP application is
```

19

continues

LISTING **19.4.** CONTINUED

```
 8: ' saved as an HTML file.
 9: If HTTP.GetData() Then
10:   HTTP.WriteToFile( "c:\inetpub\WWRoot\Directory\Filename.html" )
11: End If
```

 Simply replace the placeholder *http://localhost/Directory/Filename.asp* in line 5 with the URL of the ASP page you want to use to create the HTML page, and replace the placeholder *c:\inetpub\WWRoot\Directory\Filename.html* in line 10 to specify the target filename of the HTML file.

COMPANION **Web site** Visit the following URL for additional information about ASP2HTM:

```
http://backoffice.microsoft.com/downtrial/moreinfo/iissamples/ASP2HTML.asp
```

Converting Internet Database Connector (IDC) Applications

If you are familiar with Windows NT Web development, chances are you are familiar with the Internet Database Connector. You might already have some IDC scripts set up on your Web server. If you have been postponing porting your IDC scripts to Active Server Pages, there is good news. Microsoft has developed an application that can be used to port IDC applications to Active Server Pages.

IDC Conversion Illustrated

The best way to see how to convert IDC applications is with an example. The database application discussed in this section uses the quotations database shown in Figure 9.11. This is a Microsoft Access database used to store quotations.

COMPANION **Web site** You can get a copy of the quotations database by downloading the code distribution file for this book from the MCP Web site. After downloading the code distribution file, look for the file quotations.mdb.

 Tip
> You can easily publish a Microsoft Access 97 (or later) database on the Web by choosing Save As HTML from the File menu.

FIGURE 19.11.

The data fields of the quotations database.

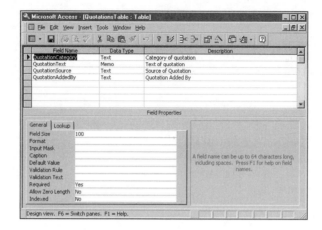

For Active Server Pages to interface with the quotations database, you must create a system or file DSN. For the purposes of applications presented today, a system DSN by the name of `QuotationsDatabase` has been created. You need to set up this DSN on your own system.

Using the IDC for Simple Database Transactions

Before Active Server Pages, databases were primarily published on the Web with IIS using the Internet Database Connector. An example of an IDC application is shown in Listing 19.5. This listing creates the quotations Web page shown in Figure 19.12, which can be used to browse quotations of the Microsoft Access database presented earlier.

FIGURE 9.12.

The quotations form (IDC/HTX version).

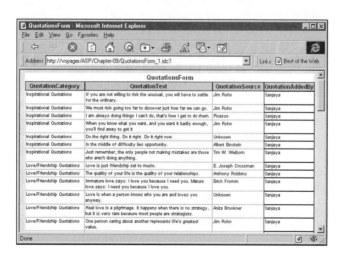

19

LISTING 19.5. THE QUOTATIONS FORM IDC FILE.

```
1: Datasource:QuotationsDatabase
2: Template:QuotationsForm_1.htx
3: SQLStatement:SELECT * FROM [QuotationsTable]
4: Password:
5: Username:
```

ANALYSIS   The IDC file in Listing 19.5 contains a SQL statement in line 3 that extracts data from the QuotationsDatabase DSN. The extracted data is formatted by using the HTML extensions template file (QuotationsForm_1.htx) defined in line 2. This file is presented in Listing 19.6.

LISTING 19.6. THE QUOTATIONS FORM HTML EXTENSIONS FILE.

```
 1: <HTML>
 2:
 3: <TITLE>Quotations Form</TITLE>
 4:
 5: <BODY background = sky.jpg>
 6:
 7: <TABLE BORDER=1 BGCOLOR=#ffffff CELLSPACING=0>
 8: <FONT FACE="Arial" COLOR=#000000>
 9: <CAPTION><B>QuotationsForm</B></CAPTION>
10:
11: <THEAD>
12: <TR>
13: <TH BGCOLOR=#c0c0c0 BORDERCOLOR=#000000 >
14: <FONT SIZE=2 FACE="Arial" COLOR=#000000>
15: QuotationCategory</FONT></TH>
16:
17: <TH BGCOLOR=#c0c0c0 BORDERCOLOR=#000000 >
18: <FONT SIZE=2 FACE="Arial" COLOR=#000000>
19: QuotationText</FONT></TH>
20:
21: <TH BGCOLOR=#c0c0c0 BORDERCOLOR=#000000 >
22: <FONT SIZE=2 FACE="Arial" COLOR=#000000>
23: QuotationSource</FONT></TH>
24:
25: <TH BGCOLOR=#c0c0c0 BORDERCOLOR=#000000 >
26: <FONT SIZE=2 FACE="Arial" COLOR=#000000>
27: QuotationAddedBy</FONT></TH>
28:
29: </TR>
30: </THEAD>
31: <TBODY>
```

```
32: <%BeginDetail%>
33: <TR VALIGN=TOP>
34: <TD BORDERCOLOR=#c0c0c0 ><FONT SIZE=1 FACE="Arial"
    ➥COLOR=#000000><%QuotationCategory%><BR></FONT></TD>
35: <TD BORDERCOLOR=#c0c0c0 ><FONT SIZE=1 FACE="Arial"
    ➥COLOR=#000000><%QuotationText%><BR></FONT></TD>
36: <TD BORDERCOLOR=#c0c0c0 ><FONT SIZE=1 FACE="Arial"
    ➥COLOR=#000000><%QuotationSource%><BR></FONT></TD>
37: <TD BORDERCOLOR=#000000 ><FONT SIZE=1 FACE="Arial"
    ➥COLOR=#000000><%QuotationAddedBy%><BR></FONT></TD>
38:
39: </TR>
40: <%EndDetail%>
41: </TBODY>
42: <TFOOT></TFOOT>
43: </TABLE>
44:
45: </BODY>
46:
47: </HTML>
```

ANALYSIS The extracted data from Listing 9.5 is displayed by the HTML extensions file presented in Listing 19.6. The <%BeginDetail%> and <%EndDetail%> block defined in lines 32–40 displays the information retrieved from the database.

Differences Between the Internet Database Connector and Active Server Pages

There are several differences between the Internet Database Connector and Active Server Pages. The biggest difference is ASP's capability to maintain several database connections to manipulate data. IDC applications are limited to a single database connection at a time. This is a major limitation when you develop Web applications that require several database connections.

Unlike the Internet Database Connector, Active Server Pages support several different scripting languages (JavaScript, VBScript, Perl, and so on); you can use the scripting language you are most familiar with.

Any language that allows the creation of ActiveX controls (such as Visual Basic, Visual C++, or Borland Delphi) can be used to extend Active Server Pages. IDC applications, on the other hand, cannot be extended through the use of other languages.

If an IDC application fails to execute for any reason, a generic error message is displayed to the user. ASP applications can be programmed to display customized, user-friendly error messages that are more helpful to the user.

19

As you can see, Active Server Pages is far better suited for developing Web database applications. The flexibility and features offered by ASP can be used to undertake almost any Web database project.

| Tip | If there are IDC applications on your Web site, convert them to ASP applications. |

The IDC2ASP Conversion Utility

Download the application used to convert IDC scripts to ASP applications by visiting this URL:

```
http://www.microsoft.com/windows/downloads/default.asp?CustArea=bus&Site=
➥nts&Product=Internet+Information+Server&Category=&x=15&y=12
```

After you download the conversion utility, copy it to a temporary directory and execute it. After the IDC/HTX conversion utility is installed, log onto the directory you selected to install the IDC/HTX conversion utility and use the following syntax to convert IDC/HTX files to ASP:

```
IDC2ASP /I<PathToIDCFiles> /O<PathToTheASPDirectory> *.idc
```

For example, the following command was used to convert the IDC/HTX files in Listings 19.4 and 19.5:

```
C:\Program Files\IDC2ASP>IDC2ASP /IE:\Publish\WWW\ASP\Chapter-09
➥/OE:\Publish\WWW\ASP\Chapter-09 *.idc
```

Listing 19.7 shows the ASP file generated by the IDC/HTX utility. The output of the ASP file is identical to that found in Figure 19.12. Unlike the IDC file, the ASP file can be customized with ASP statements and components.

LISTING 19.7. SOURCE CODE OF THE QUOTATIONS WEB PAGE (ASP VERSION OF LISTINGS 19.4 AND 19.5).

```
 1: <%@ LANGUAGE="VBScript" %>
 2: <!--#include file="ADOVBS.inc"-->
 3: <!--#include file="IASUtil.asp"-->
 4:
 5: <%
 6: Set Connection = Server.CreateObject("ADODB.Connection")
 7:
 8: Connection.Open "DSN=QuotationsDatabase; UID=; PWD="
 9:
10: SQLStmt = "SELECT * FROM [QuotationsTable] "
```

```
11:
12: Set RS = Connection.Execute(SQLStmt)
13: %>
14: <HTML>
15:
16: <TITLE>Quotations Form</TITLE>
17:
18: <BODY background = sky.jpg>
19:
20: <TABLE BORDER=1 BGCOLOR=#ffffff CELLSPACING=0>
21: <FONT FACE="Arial" COLOR=#000000>
22: <CAPTION><B>QuotationsForm</B></CAPTION>
23:
24: <THEAD>
25: <TR>
26: <TH BGCOLOR=#c0c0c0 BORDERCOLOR=#000000 >
27: <FONT SIZE=2 FACE="Arial" COLOR=#000000>
28: QuotationCategory</FONT></TH>
29:
30: <TH BGCOLOR=#c0c0c0 BORDERCOLOR=#000000 >
31: <FONT SIZE=2 FACE="Arial" COLOR=#000000>
32: QuotationText</FONT></TH>
33:
34: <TH BGCOLOR=#c0c0c0 BORDERCOLOR=#000000 >
35: <FONT SIZE=2 FACE="Arial" COLOR=#000000>
36: QuotationSource</FONT></TH>
37:
38: <TH BGCOLOR=#c0c0c0 BORDERCOLOR=#000000 >
39: <FONT SIZE=2 FACE="Arial" COLOR=#000000>
40: QuotationAddedBy</FONT></TH>
41:
42: </TR>
43: </THEAD>
44: <TBODY>
45: <%
46:   CurrentRecord = 0
47:   Do While CheckRS(RS)%>
48: <TR VALIGN=TOP>
49: <TD BORDERCOLOR=#c0c0c0 ><FONT SIZE=1 FACE="Arial"
    ➥COLOR=#000000><%= RS("QuotationCategory") %><BR></FONT></TD>
50: <TD BORDERCOLOR=#c0c0c0 ><FONT SIZE=1 FACE="Arial"
    ➥COLOR=#000000><%= RS("QuotationText") %><BR></FONT></TD>
51: <TD BORDERCOLOR=#c0c0c0 ><FONT SIZE=1 FACE="Arial"
    ➥COLOR=#000000><%= RS("QuotationSource") %><BR></FONT></TD>
52: <TD BORDERCOLOR=#000000 ><FONT SIZE=1 FACE="Arial"
    ➥COLOR=#000000><%= RS("QuotationAddedBy") %><BR></FONT></TD>
53:
54: </TR>
55: <%        RS.MoveNext
56:   CurrentRecord = CurrentRecord + 1
```

19

continues

LISTING **19.7.** CONTINUED

```
57:    Loop
58: %>
59: </TBODY>
60: <TFOOT></TFOOT>
61: </TABLE>
62:
63: </BODY>
64:
65: </HTML>
66: <% Connection.Close %>
```

Active Server Pages Registry Settings

You can use the Windows NT Registry to customize different options and features of
Active Server Pages. The following Registry values can be modified by executing the
Windows NT Registry editor, regedt32.exe.

> **Caution**
>
> Be very careful when editing the Windows Registry; never change or delete
> a Windows Registry setting unless you completely understand the ramifica-
> tions of your actions. An improper Registry modification can mean you have
> to reinstall software.

Allowing Session States

By default, Active Server Pages keeps track of user sessions by using a cookie. You can
disable this feature by setting the AllowSessionState Registry value to 0. After this
Registry setting is changed and IIS is restarted, session ID cookies are not sent to Web
browsers. I do not recommend that you modify this Registry value unless you have a
good reason for doing so (for example, if none of your Web browsers allow cookies). You
have to restart IIS if you change this Registry key.

AllowSessionState

Default Value:

1

Data Type:

REG_DWORD

▼ **Registry Key:**

```
HKEY_LOCAL_MACHINE\SYSTEM
\CurrentControlSet
 \Services
  \W3SVC
   \ASP
    \Parameters
```
▲   `\ AllowSessionState`

Buffering ASP Output

Active Server Pages can be configured to buffer output to the browser. By default, buffering is turned off (this is why you had to specify HTTP headers before producing any HTML text). If you set the value of `BufferingOn` to 1, you can specify HTTP headers anywhere in your ASP application. You can also modify this setting with the MMC.

> **Note**   You can use the `Buffer` method of the `Response` object to override this Registry value.

SYNTAX

`BufferingOn`

Default Value:

`0`

Data Type:

`REG_DWORD`

Registry Key:

```
HKEY_LOCAL_MACHINE\SYSTEM
\CurrentControlSet
 \Services
  \W3SVC
   \ASP
    \Parameters
```
▲   `\ BufferingOn`

Specifying the Default Scripting Language

Use the `DefaultScriptLanguage` Registry setting to specify the default scripting language used by ASP applications. You need to restart IIS if you change this Registry setting. You can specify the default scripting language on an ASP application itself or by using the MMC.

19

SYNTAX ▼

DefaultScriptLanguage

Default Value:

VBScript

Data Type:

REG_SZRange

Registry Key:

```
HKEY_LOCAL_MACHINE\SYSTEM
\CurrentControlSet
 \Services
  \W3SVC
   \ASP
    \Parameters
     \DefaultScriptLanguage
```

▲

Allowing Paths Relative to the Current Directory

The EnableParentPaths Registry setting specifies whether Active Server Pages should allow paths relative to the current directory. If this value is set to 0 (false), Active Server Pages cannot access files by using the "..". I recommend that you not change this value unless it poses a specific security risk. You need to restart IIS if you change this setting.

SYNTAX ▼

EnableParentPaths

Default Value:

1

Data Type:

REG_DWORD

Registry Key:

```
HKEY_LOCAL_MACHINE\SYSTEM
\CurrentControlSet
 \Services
  \W3SVC
   \ASP
    \Parameters
     \EnableParentPaths
```

▲

Logging Unsuccessful HTTP Requests

Set the LogErrorRequests Registry setting to 1 to log unsuccessful HTTP requests to the Windows NT event log, and 0 to turn this feature off. Use this Registry setting to detect and log unsuccessful HTTP requests.

SYNTAX ▼

`LogErrorRequests`

Default Value:

1

Data Type:

REG_DWORD

Registry Key:

```
HKEY_LOCAL_MACHINE\SYSTEM
\CurrentControlSet
 \Services
  \W3SVC
   \ASP
    \Parameters
     \LogErrorRequests
```

▲

Specifying the Amount of Memory Available to Active Server Pages

Use the `MemFreeFactor` Registry setting to specify the amount of memory available to Active Server Pages (as a percentage of the used memory list). If you need to use this Registry setting to severely limit the memory available to ASP applications, it's a good indication that your Web server needs more memory. You need to restart IIS if you change this setting.

SYNTAX ▼

`MemFreeFactor`

Default Value:

50

Data Type:

REG_DWORD

Registry Key:

```
HKEY_LOCAL_MACHINE\SYSTEM
\CurrentControlSet
 \Services
  \W3SVC
   \ASP
    \Parameters
     \MemFreeFactor
```

▲

19

Specifying the Minimum Length of the Used Memory List

Use the `MinUsedBlocks` Registry setting to specify the minimum length of the used memory list.

MinUsedBlocks

Default Value:

10

Data Type:

REG_DWORD

Registry Key:

```
HKEY_LOCAL_MACHINE\SYSTEM
\CurrentControlSet
 \Services
  \W3SVC
   \ASP
    \Parameters
     \MinUsedBlocks
```

Specifying the Number of Initial ASP Threads

Specify the number of initial ASP threads using the `NumInitialThreads` Registry value. This value should be less than `ProcessorThreadMax`; otherwise, `ProcessorThreadMax` threads are created. Use this Registry setting if your Web server hosts a high-volume ASP Web site and you always need more than two threads. I do not recommend that you change this Registry setting to a value greater than 10. You need to restart IIS if you change this setting.

NumInitialThreads

Default Value:

2

Data Type:

REG_DWORD

Registry Key:

```
HKEY_LOCAL_MACHINE\SYSTEM
\CurrentControlSet
 \Services
```

▼   \W3SVC
       \ASP
        \Parameters
▲   \NumInitialThreads

Specifying the Maximum Number of ASP Threads

The `ProcessorThreadMax` Registry setting specifies the maximum amount of threads to create for each processor. I recommend that you do not change this value. You need to restart IIS if you change this setting.

SYNTAX

`ProcessorThreadMax`

Default Value:

10

Data Type:

REG_DWORD

Registry Key:

HKEY_LOCAL_MACHINE\SYSTEM
\CurrentControlSet
 \Services
  \W3SVC
   \ASP
    \Parameters
▲   \ProcessorThreadMax

Specifying the Maximum Amount of ASP Requests to Be Handled

The `RequestQueueMax` Registry setting specifies the maximum amount of ASP requests to be handled at any given time. You need to restart IIS if you change this setting.

SYNTAX

`RequestQueueMax`

Default Value:

500

Data Type:

REG_DWORD

Registry Key:

HKEY_LOCAL_MACHINE\SYSTEM
▼ \CurrentControlSet

19

```
\Services
 \W3SVC
  \ASP
   \Parameters
    \RequestQueueMax
```

Specifying the Maximum Number of Scripting Language Engines to Cache

Use the ScriptEngineCacheMax Registry setting to specify the maximum number of scripting language engines to cache. It is rare that you won't have more than 30 scripting languages. Because you are unlikely to exceed this value, I recommend you do not change it unless you have to. You need to restart IIS if you change this setting.

SYNTAX

ScriptEngineCacheMax

Default Value:

30

Data Type:

REG_DWORD

Registry Key:

```
HKEY_LOCAL_MACHINE\SYSTEM
\CurrentControlSet
 \Services
  \W3SVC
   \ASP
    \Parameters
     \ScriptEngineCacheMax
```

Specifying the Script Error Message

Use the ScriptErrorMessage Registry key to specify the error message displayed in the event of an error condition. You might want to include a URL here that can be used to send e-mail about the error condition. The script error message can also be specified with the MMC.

SYNTAX

ScriptErrorMessage

Default Value:

"An error occurred on the server when processing the URL. Please contact the system administrator."

Data Type:

REG_SZ

▼ **Registry Key:**

```
HKEY_LOCAL_MACHINE\SYSTEM
\CurrentControlSet
 \Services
  \W3SVC
   \ASP
    \Parameters
     \ScriptErrorMessage
```
▲

Writing Debug Information to the Web Browser

Set the `ScriptErrorsSentToBrowser` Registry value to 1 if you would like ASP debugging information to be sent to the Web browser. Although I recommend that you set this Registry setting to 1 on a development machine, I recommend that you set this value to 0 on a production server so your users do not see any part of your ASP code (or debugging messages). You can modify this setting with the MMC.

SYNTAX ▼

ScriptErrorsSentToBrowser

Default Value:

1

Data Type:

REG_DWORD

Registry Key:

```
HKEY_LOCAL_MACHINE\SYSTEM
\CurrentControlSet
 \Services
  \W3SVC
   \ASP
    \Parameters
     \ScriptErrorsSentToBrowser
```
▲

19

Specifying the Size of the ASP Script Cache

Use the `ScriptFileCacheSize` Registry setting to specify the size (in bytes) of the ASP script cache. A value of -1 causes all ASP scripts to be cached; a value of 0 causes no ASP scripts to be cached. I strongly discourage you from setting this value to 0 because it adversely affects the performance of Active Server Pages.

SYNTAX ▼

`ScriptFileCacheSize`

Default Value:

-1

Data Type:

REG_DWORD

Registry Key:

```
HKEY_LOCAL_MACHINE\SYSTEM
\CurrentControlSet
 \Services
  \W3SVC
   \ASP
    \Parameters
     \ScriptFileCacheSize
```

▲

Specifying the Amount of Time ASP Scripts Are Kept in Memory Cache

The ScriptFileCacheTTL Registry setting specifies how long an ASP script should remain in memory (Active Server Pages cache). Use a value of 0 to indefinitely cache ASP scripts. You need to restart IIS if you change this setting.

SYNTAX ▼

`ScriptFileCacheTTL`

Default Value:

300

Data Type:

REG_DWORD

Registry Key:

```
HKEY_LOCAL_MACHINE\SYSTEM
\CurrentControlSet
 \Services
  \W3SVC
   \ASP
    \Parameters
     \ScriptFileCacheTTL
```

▲

Specifying the ASP Script Timeout Value

The `ScriptTimeout` setting specifies how long Active Server Pages allow a script to run. If the script does not terminate before the timeout value specified in this Registry value, the script is terminated and an event is written to the event log. You can use the `ScriptTimeout` method of the `Server` object to override this value. The default value (`-1`) allows ASP scripts to run forever. I recommend that you change this Registry setting to a value such as `90` (seconds). You can also set this value by using the MMC.

SYNTAX

`ScriptTimeout`

Default Value:

`90`

Data Type:

`REG_DWORD`

Registry Key:

```
HKEY_LOCAL_MACHINE\SYSTEM
 \CurrentControlSet
  \Services
   \W3SVC
    \ASP
     \Parameters
      \ScriptTimeout
```

Specifying the Amount of Time an ASP Session Object Lasts

The `SessionTimeout` Registry value specifies, in minutes, how long an ASP session object lasts. You might want to increase this value if your users tend to have time intervals greater than 20 minutes between HTTP sessions. For most purposes, the default value should suit you just fine.

SYNTAX

`SessionTimeout`

Default Value:

`20`

Data Type:

`REG_DWORD`

Registry Key:

`HKEY_LOCAL_MACHINE\SYSTEM`

19

```
\CurrentControlSet
 \Services
  \W3SVC
   \ASP
    \Parameters
     \SessionTimeout
```

Tip

If for some reason your users take over 20 minutes to get from one ASP page to another, consider increasing the SessionTimeout value. The opposite is true if your users take less than 20 minutes to get from one ASP page to another.

Tip

Do not use a number less than 10 for the SessionTimeout value. Doing so could make ASP applications that depend on the Session object function improperly.

Note

You can override this Registry value with the Timeout method of the Session object. The timeout value can also be specified by using the MMC.

Specifying ODBC Connection Pooling

The StartConnectionPool Registry setting controls whether ODBC connection pooling is on or off. I do not recommend that you change this value because ODBC connection pooling generally enhances the performance of database-intensive ASP applications. You need to restart IIS if you change this setting.

StartConnectionPool

Default Value:

1

Data Type:

REG_DWORD

Registry Key:

HKEY_LOCAL_MACHINE\SYSTEM
 \CurrentControlSet
  \Services

▼
```
\W3SVC
 \ASP
  \Parameters
   \StartConnectionPool
```
▲

Note

ODBC connection pooling makes the best use of your system resources and enhances system performance. Instead of maintaining ODBC connections for long periods and wasting system resources, ODBC connection pooling can manage the ODBC connections for you and allow your ASP applications to reuse ODBC connections.

DON'T

DON'T keep your database connections open for long periods if you are using ODBC connection pooling. Doing so virtually nullifies the benefits it offers.

DON'T store an ODBC connection in the Session object. This is an inefficient use of system resources and scales very poorly.

Specifying the Number of ASP Requests Handled by an ASP Thread

Use the ThreadCreationThreshold Registry setting to specify the number of ASP requests that can be handled by an ASP thread. If the number of ASP requests handled by the thread pool exceeds the number specified in this Registry setting, a new ASP thread is created (if the size of the thread pool is less than ProcessorThreadMax).

SYNTAX ▼

ThreadCreationThreshold

Default Value:

5

Data Type:

REG_DWORD

Registry Key:

```
HKEY_LOCAL_MACHINE\SYSTEM
\CurrentControlSet
 \Services
  \W3SVC
   \ASP
    \Parameters
     \ThreadCreationThreshold
```
▲

19

Summary

The tips and techniques you learned today can be used to develop more robust and efficient ASP applications. MMC is used to configure and administer IIS. Almost all IIS configuration options can be modified from within the IIS snap-in for MMC. Web server access log files are instrumental in analyzing usage patterns of a Web server.

ASP options and features can be customized through the use of the Windows Registry. Be very careful when editing the Windows NT Registry, however; never change or delete a Registry setting unless you completely understand the ramifications of your actions.

Q&A

Q Why shouldn't you turn off ODBC connection pooling?

A ODBC connection pooling makes the best use of your system resources and enhances system performance. Instead of maintaining ODBC connections for long periods and wasting system resources, ODBC connection pooling can manage the ODBC connections for you and allow your ASP applications to reuse ODBC connections.

Q What is the purpose of the Microsoft Management Console?

A You could think of the Microsoft Management Console as the Control Panel on steroids. MMC offers a more powerful interface for managing and interacting with software components running on a computer. In the future, you can expect to see the Control Panel being replaced with the MMC more and more.

Workshop

The quiz questions and exercises are provided for your further understanding. Please refer to Appendix A, "Answers to Questions," for the answers to the quiz questions; the answers to the exercises are on the MCP Web site.

Quiz

1. How do you invoke the Registry editor?
2. What is the default timeout value for ASP scripts?
3. What is the default timeout value for the ASP Session object?
4. How can you override the SessionTimeout value specified in the Registry?
5. What is the default location of IIS log files?

Exercises

1. Use ASP2HTML to generate an HTML (.html) page from one of your own ASP (.asp) applications.

2. Stress-test one of your own ASP applications as outlined in today's tutorial.

3. Download WebTrends and analyze one of your Web server's log files. Find out the number of ASP page executions for a given week and keep track of this number so you get advance warning when your Web site traffic is increasing and it's time to expand your resources.

19

WEEK 3

DAY 20

Building Custom ASP Components with Visual Basic

On Day 9, "Using ActiveX Components Built for ASP," you learned how to use components available for IIS to develop ASP applications. Today you learn how to develop your own custom ASP components using Visual Basic. Any language that allows creating ActiveX controls can be used to develop custom ASP components, including languages such as Visual C++, Visual J++, and Delphi. Because the syntax of Visual Basic is very similar to VBScript's syntax, Visual Basic is used in today's examples. At the end of the day, you will be able to leverage your VBScript/Visual Basic skills to develop custom ASP components. For those of you who have already used Visual Basic, you will quickly realize how creating a custom ASP component is as straightforward as developing a typical Visual Basic application. Today, you will cover the following:

- Learn the benefits of creating custom ASP components.
- Discover how to create custom ASP components using Visual Basic.

- Transfer custom ASP components you create to other Web servers.
- Use the APILoad utility.
- Call Win32 API functions.
- Send HTML text directly to a Web browser from a custom ASP component.

 Note

> This lesson assumes that you have either Visual Basic 5.0 or Visual Basic 6.0 installed on your computer. As long as you use VB 5.0 or later, the steps outlined in this section can be followed without any problems to create custom ASP components.

Benefits of Developing Custom ASP Components

You might be wondering why you should go to the trouble of creating custom ASP components when you can simply use VBScript, JScript, or another client-side scripting language to write your ASP applications. Some of the benefits of developing custom ASP components include the following:

- Centralized code management
- The black box model
- Access to API functions
- Mix-and-match programming languages
- Security
- Protection of proprietary algorithms
- Ease of alteration
- Ease of distribution

Centralized Code Management

When business logic is implemented as an ASP component, you can centrally manage the business logic code without being concerned about everyone having access to the code's latest revision. Your code is not spread around several Web pages. Instead, only the resulting components are redistributed.

The Black Box Model

ASP components support the *black box model*, which refers to an object that operates in a predictable, consistent manner when proper input is supplied. For example, with a radar detector, the user just needs to know how to turn it on and how to supply the power to use it. The logic required to detect laser and radar from police speed-detection equipment is contained in the radar detector unit, and the user doesn't need o know how the technology works to use the device. Likewise, ASP components hide details of implementation from the user. All the user needs to know to use an ASP component is what the ASP component does and how to provide input. The logic required to process the input is stored in the ASP component.

Access to API Functions

When developing custom ASP components, you can use many Windows API functions to get and process information. The custom ASP component you build later today uses a Windows API function to find system memory resources of the Web server. Custom ASP components give you access not only to the Windows API, but also to additional server resources, such as memory, disk, network, and running processes.

Note
> A thorough overview of the Win 32 API, as well as subtle compatibility issues that might exist between Windows NT, Windows 95, and Windows 98, is beyond the scope of today's tutorial.

Mix-and-Match Programming Languages

Because any language capable of creating an ActiveX control can be used to develop custom ASP components, with Active Server Pages you can make the best use of features of many languages, such as Visual Basic, C++, Java, Delphi, and so on. This is a major benefit of using Active Server Pages; virtually no other Web application development environment, including Allaire Cold Fusion, gives you more freedom in selecting a language for developing custom components.

20

Note
> Many Web developers use Allaire Cold Fusion to build powerful database-driven Web sites. Cold Fusion is based on a markup language that exposes a lot of powerful functionality to the Web developer. However, ASP is better integrated with Windows and offers more flexibility to Web developers.

Security

Windows NT Security can be used to ensure the security of ASP components that contain sensitive information (for example, a database query that requires a secret password). If the database query is implemented using a simple ASP statement, anyone with access to the ASP page (graphic designers, Web page editors, contractors, consultants, temporary employees, and so on) can find out the password. This might not be desirable in some cases, so the database query can be carried out by an ASP component, and Windows NT security can be used to ensure the security of the ASP component.

Protection of Proprietary Algorithms

ASP components protect proprietary algorithms in that implementation details are hidden from the user, such as an application that calculates the cost of a project when certain information is provided. Because of the proprietary nature of the formula used to calculate the cost of the project, the formula can be embedded in an ASP component.

Ease of Alteration

ASP components can be easily modified when business formulas and conditions change. Think of an online storefront implemented with Active Server Pages. Every week, the store puts certain items on sale. The percentage to subtract for the sale is calculated by using a business formula. If the formula is included in each ASP page, any slight change to the formula would require several pages to be updated. On the other hand, if the formula is contained in an ASP component used by the ASP pages, the formula needs to be modified in only one place, making it much easier to update.

Ease of Distribution

ASP components can be easily distributed after they are created. All that's required to use an ASP component after it is developed is to register it on the server. (If the component was developed on the server, Visual Basic automatically registers it for you.) See the section "Distributing ASP Components" to learn more about registering and distributing ASP components.

Benefits of Using Visual Basic

Visual Basic is a powerful, easy-to-use application development environment. Although previous versions of Visual Basic provided an easy-to-use rapid application development environment, there was a trade-off in performance. Since Visual Basic 5.0, Microsoft has increased the performance of Visual Basic by including a native code compiler and an enhanced P-code interpreter. Visual Basic can also be used to easily develop ActiveX controls that can be hosted on Internet Explorer and IIS 4.0, as well as on any application or development tool that supports ActiveX controls, such as Visual C++ and Microsoft Office. Visual Basic includes many useful features that can save you time when developing applications. Visual Basic's speed, access to a rich library of ActiveX controls, and Microsoft sample code make Visual Basic an ideal application development environment for creating custom ASP components.

Developing a Custom ASP Component

Developing a custom ASP component with Visual Basic is easy. The component developed in this section can be used to determine the memory resources of the Web server. The Visual Basic component uses a Win32 API function to get system memory resource information. To begin creating your first custom ASP component, start Visual Basic. From the New Project window, select creating an ActiveX DLL project and click the Open button. You can also get to the New Project window in Visual Basic by choosing File, New Project from the menu bar or pressing Ctrl+N.

Visual Basic creates a project with default project and class names. Before you add code to the Visual Basic application, supply more descriptive project class names. Locate the Project Settings window and replace the default name of the project (Project1) with something more descriptive, such as VBComponent (see Figure 20.1).

FIGURE 20.1.

Give the Visual Basic project a descriptive name.

20

Next, replace the default name of the project class (Class1) with something more descriptive (such as SystemInformation), as shown in Figure 20.2.

Note	The project class name becomes the name of the ASP component referenced by the Active Server Page.

FIGURE 20.2.

Give a descriptive name to the project's default class.

Do	DON'T
DO store all your custom VB components in a separate directory that's not directly accessible through a Web browser.	**DON'T** store custom Visual Basic components you create in the directory structure of your Web server's document root directory. This compromises the security of the Web server and your ASP application because a technically advanced user might figure out how to download your ASP component.

You are now ready to begin writing Visual Basic code. For this example, you are going to use a Windows API function that determines system resources; it's called GlobalMemoryStatus(). To call a Win32 API function from Visual Basic, you need the function prototype and its data structure. Therefore, before you proceed, you need the function prototype and the data structure used by the API function GlobalMemoryStatus(). Fortunately, Visual Basic ships with a utility called APILoad that can be used to easily locate an API function's prototype and data structures. If you use Visual Basic 5.0, find the file apiload.exe in the \Program Files\DevStudio\VB\Winapi\ directory and execute it (assuming you installed Visual Basic in the directory \Program Files\DevStudio\VB\). If you use Visual Basic 6.0, you can find apiload.exe in the \Program Files\Microsoft Visual Studio\Common\Tools\Winapi directory. You will see the application window shown in Figure 20.3.

Note

A mapi32.txt file is also available for using MAPI functions.

FIGURE 20.3.

The API Viewer application can be used to find API function prototypes and data structures.

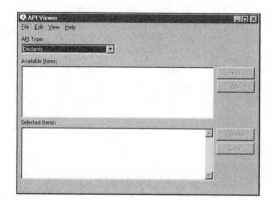

Choose Load Text File from the File menu and select Win32api.txt. The first time you execute apiload.exe, you are prompted to convert to a database. Answer yes to improve the performance of the API Viewer application.

After converting the text file to a database, API Viewer loads information about API functions, types, and constants so you can easily browse items. The Copy button is used to copy the selected items to a Clipboard so you can later paste them to your Visual Basic application. Because you need the declaration for the GlobalMemoryStatus() function, type the string **GlobalMemoryStatus()** into the listbox. After you see the function highlighted, double-click it to see its function definition (see Figure 20.4). Pay particular attention to the data type of the argument of the API function (lpBuffer As MEMORYSTATUS).

FIGURE 20.4.

The function prototype of the GlobalMemoryStatus() function.

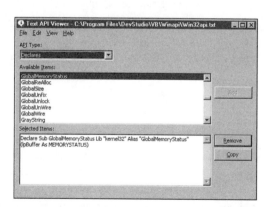

20

To get information from the API function, you must pass it a data structure of MEMORYSTATUS type. Your next task is to locate the data structure definition of MEMORYSTATUS type. Select Types from the API Type list box, and enter the string

MEMORYSTATUS into the Available Items list box. After MEMORYSTATUS is highlighted, double-click it to see its data structure definition, as shown in Figure 20.5.

Note API functions are very useful for interfacing with Windows resources. To use an API function, you have to declare it and the data structure(s) it uses. With the apiload.exe application, you can easily get the declaration used to call an API function along with the data structure(s) it uses.

FIGURE 20.5.

The data structure definition of MEMORYSTATUS.

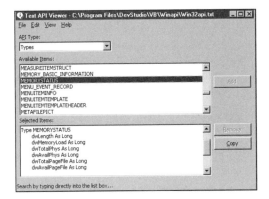

Notice how both the function definition and the data structure definition are in the Selected Items text box. To transfer this information to the Clipboard, click the Copy button. Next, switch back to Visual Basic and double-click the SystemInformation class module. Locate the Declarations module of the SystemInformation class and paste the information from the Clipboard (see Figure 20.6).

Note This is a good time to add comments to the code you pasted from the Clipboard so you can easily identify it at a later time.

Listing 20.1 contains the full source code of the Visual Basic ASP component that can be used to get the memory resource values of the Web server. The next section, "Using Custom ASP Components in ASP Applications," demonstrates how an ASP application can interface with the custom ASP component created in this section.

FIGURE 20.6.

Use the Clipboard to transfer the data structure and function definition information.

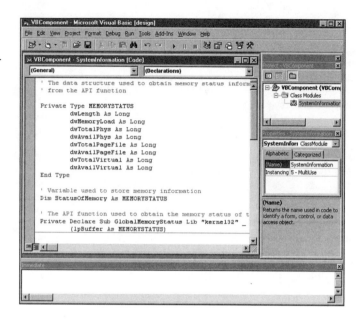

LISTING 20.1. A WIN32 API FUNCTION IS USED TO FIND SYSTEM MEMORY RESOURCE VALUES.

```
 1: ' The data structure used to get memory status information
 2: ' from the API function
 3:
 4: Private Type MEMORYSTATUS
 5:         dwLength As Long
 6:         dwMemoryLoad As Long
 7:         dwTotalPhys As Long
 8:         dwAvailPhys As Long
 9:         dwTotalPageFile As Long
10:         dwAvailPageFile As Long
11:         dwTotalVirtual As Long
12:         dwAvailVirtual As Long
13: End Type
14:
15: ' Variable used to store memory information
16: Dim StatusOfMemory As MEMORYSTATUS
17:
18: ' The API function used to obtain the memory status of the Web server
19: Private Declare Sub GlobalMemoryStatus Lib "kernel32" _
20:         (lpBuffer As MEMORYSTATUS)
21:
22: ' Returns the amount of total physical memory on the Web server
23: Public Function GetTotalPhysicalMemory() As Long
24:    GlobalMemoryStatus StatusOfMemory
25:    GetTotalPhysicalMemory = StatusOfMemory.dwTotalPhys
```

20

continues

LISTING 20.1. CONTINUED

```
26: End Function
27:
28: ' Returns the amount of available physical memory on the Web server
29: Public Function GetAvailablePhysicalMemory() As Long
30:   GlobalMemoryStatus StatusOfMemory
31:   GetAvailablePhysicalMemory = StatusOfMemory.dwAvailPhys
32: End Function
33:
34: ' Returns the amount of total page memory on the Web server
35: Public Function GetTotalPageMemory() As Long
36:   GlobalMemoryStatus StatusOfMemory
37:   GetTotalPageMemory = StatusOfMemory.dwTotalPageFile
38: End Function
39:
40: ' Returns the amount of available page memory on the Web server
41: Public Function GetAvailablePageMemory() As Long
42:   GlobalMemoryStatus StatusOfMemory
43:   GetAvailablePageMemory = StatusOfMemory.dwAvailPageFile
44: End Function
45:
46: ' Returns the amount of total virtual memory on the Web server
47: Public Function GetTotalVirtualMemory() As Long
48:   GlobalMemoryStatus StatusOfMemory
49:   GetTotalVirtualMemory = StatusOfMemory.dwTotalVirtual
50: End Function
51:
52: ' Returns the amount of available virtual memory on the Web server
53: Public Function GetAvailableVirtualMemory() As Long
54:   GlobalMemoryStatus StatusOfMemory
55:   GetAvailableVirtualMemory = StatusOfMemory.dwAvailVirtual
56: End Function
```

ANALYSIS Lines 4–13 define the data structure that gets memory status information using an API function; that function is declared in lines 19 and 20. The subroutines that get information about the memory status are declared in lines 23–56.

You can compile and register your VB component by choosing Make from the File menu. If you have to recompile the component, you must stop the Web server service (using the NT command Net Stop W3SVC) *before* compiling the VB component. It makes things easy if you first build the functionality of your component as a standard EXE application and convert it to an ActiveX DLL after the functionality is fully implemented and debugged. That way, you don't have to go through the inconvenience of stopping and restarting your Web server all the time.

Using Custom ASP Components in ASP Applications

Custom components you create can be used from ASP applications in the same way that components included with Active Server Pages are used. The ASP application in Listing 20.2 demonstrates how to interface with the custom ASP component created in the previous section.

LISTING 20.2. INTERFACING WITH A CUSTOM ASP COMPONENT CREATED WITH VISUAL BASIC.

```
 1: <%@ LANGUAGE="VBSCRIPT" %>
 2:
 3: <HTML>
 4: <HEAD>
 5:
 6:
 7: <TITLE>
 8:   Interfacing With Visual Basic Components
 9: </TITLE>
10: </HEAD>
11:
12: <BODY BGCOLOR=FFFFFF>
13:
14: <H3>
15: This ASP application interfaces with a Visual Basic component
16: to determine the status of memory resources on the server.
17: </H3>
18:
19: <%
20:
21: ' Variable used to instantiate the ASP component
22:    Dim InstanceOfComponent
23:
24: ' Variables used to store memory information
25:
26:    Dim TotalPhysicalMemory
27:    Dim AvailablePhysicalMemory
28:    Dim TotalPageMemory
29:    Dim AvailablePageMemory
30:    Dim TotalVirtualMemory
31:    Dim AvailableVirtualMemory
32:
33:
34: ' Create an instance of the VB ASP component
35:    Set InstanceOfComponent = _
36:      Server.CreateObject ("VBComponent.SystemInformation")
37:
```

20

continues

LISTING **20.2.** CONTINUED

```
38: ' Obtain memory information from the ASP component
39:
40:   TotalPhysicalMemory = _
41:     InstanceOfComponent.GetTotalPhysicalMemory()
42:   AvailablePhysicalMemory = _
43:     InstanceOfComponent.GetAvailablePhysicalMemory()
44:   TotalPageMemory = _
45:     InstanceOfComponent.GetTotalPageMemory()
46:   AvailablePageMemory = _
47:     InstanceOfComponent.GetAvailablePageMemory()
48:   TotalVirtualMemory = _
49:     InstanceOfComponent.GetTotalVirtualMemory()
50:   AvailableVirtualMemory = _
51:     InstanceOfComponent.GetAvailableVirtualMemory()
52:
53: %>
54:
55: <TABLE BORDER=3 >
56: <TR><TD>
57: Total Physical Memory</TD><TD ALIGN=RIGHT>
58: <%= TotalPhysicalMemory %>
59: </TD></TR><TR><TD>
60: Available Physical Memory</TD><TD ALIGN=RIGHT>
61: <%= AvailablePhysicalMemory %>
62: </TD></TR><TR><TD>
63: Total Page Memory</TD><TD ALIGN=RIGHT>
64: <%= TotalPageMemory %>
65: </TD></TR><TR><TD>
66: Available Page Memory</TD><TD ALIGN=RIGHT>
67: <%= AvailablePageMemory %>
68: </TD></TR><TR><TD>
69: Total Virtual Memory</TD><TD ALIGN=RIGHT>
70: <%= TotalVirtualMemory %>
71: </TD></TR><TR><TD>
72: Available Virtual Memory</TD><TD ALIGN=RIGHT>
73: <%= AvailableVirtualMemory %>
74: </TD></TR>
75: </TABLE>
76:
77: <HR>
78:
79: <%= "This Web page was generated on " & Date & " at " & Time & "." %>
80:
81: </BODY>
82: </HTML>
```

ANALYSIS The ASP application first instantiates the custom ASP component with the statement `Set InstanceOfComponent = Server.CreateObject` (`"VBComponent.SystemInformation"`). Afterward, public functions of the ASP component can be called as illustrated in lines 40–51. The output of the ASP application in Listing 20.2 is shown in Figure 20.7.

FIGURE 20.7.

Output of the ASP application in Listing 20.2.

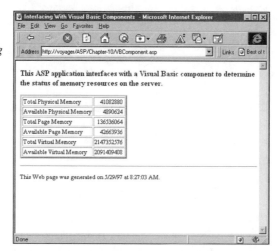

Sending HTML Text to the Web Browser

Instead of sending data to the ASP application each time you need to display information to the user, it would be nice if custom ASP components could send HTML text directly to the Web browser. HTML text can be written directly to the Web browser by referencing the `ScriptingContext` object in the `OnStartPage` method of the ASP component and saving the reference for future use. The `ScriptingContext` object acts as an interface between the ASP component and the Web page generated by the ASP application. Before you can use the `ScriptingContext` object in your Visual Basic application, you must add a reference to the Active Server Pages DLL file (`asp.dll`). Do so by choosing References from the Project menu in Visual Basic. Then select the Microsoft Active Server Pages Object Library check box, as shown in Figure 20.8. After you select the check box, you can send HTML text directly to the Web browser by using the `Write` method of the `Response` object, as demonstrated in Listing 20.3.

20

LISTING 20.3. SENDING HTML TEXT TO THE WEB BROWSER.

```
 1: ' A global variable is used to create a reference to the
 2: ' ScriptingContext object.
 3: Dim MyResponse As Response
 4: Public Function OnStartPage(MyScriptingContext As ScriptingContext)
 5:
 6:    ' A reference is created to the Response object
 7:    Set MyResponse = MyScriptingContext.Response
 8:
 9:    ' The Write method of the Response object is used to
10:    ' send HTML text to the Web browser.
11:    MyResponse.Write "<B>Hello User!</B>"
12:
13: End Function
```

FIGURE 20.8.

Select the Microsoft Active Server Pages 1.0 Object Library check box.

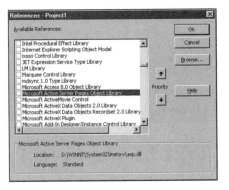

ANALYSIS Line 3 defines the variable used to create a reference to the ScriptingContext object, and the reference is created in line 7. Line 11 uses the reference to the ScriptingContext object to send text directly to the Web browser from within a VB component.

Distributing ASP Components

Custom ASP components need to be registered on your system before they can be used by ASP applications. Visual Basic automatically registers ASP components it creates on your system. For your ASP component to function properly, it must be registered on the Web server (unless the component was developed on that computer).

To register an ASP component, open a command prompt window, change to the directory containing the ASP component file, and type the following command:

REGSVR32 *<ASPComponentFile.dll>*

Replace *<ASPComponentFile.dll>* with the name of the ASP component file. After the component is registered, you see a confirmation message, shown in Figure 20.9.

FIGURE 20.9.

The ASP component was successfully registered.

>
> **Tip**
>
> To make it easier to keep track of your custom ASP components, keep them all in one directory. \Inetpub\iissamples\Components\ is a good location.

>
> **Tip**
>
> I recommend that you install at least a minimal version of Visual Basic on the production Web server. When installing Visual Basic, you are given the option of installing either the full version or a minimal version. The minimal version contains only files that are absolutely necessary for developing Visual Basic applications. This ensures that all the files needed to execute Visual Basic applications are properly installed. As an added incentive, the Visual Basic installation can be used to debug your ASP component if necessary.

Summary

Custom ASP components can be developed by using a variety of application development environments that allow you to create ActiveX controls. Visual Basic can be easily used to develop custom ASP components. Your VBScript skills can be leveraged to develop custom ASP components because Visual Basic is very similar to VBScript. Custom ASP components promote data encapsulation, easy code distribution, security, and centralized code management. When developing large projects, you should create your own custom ASP components to handle those tasks that can be more efficiently and easily carried out by using another application development environment, such as Visual Basic or Visual C++. You can then mix and match the best features of each application development environment.

20

Do not develop overly complicated ASP components. Concentrate on developing well-defined, small, and efficient ASP components that handle a certain task extremely well. You can then efficiently reuse your custom ASP components when you develop future Web applications. Think of ActiveX components as bricks that you use to develop a large structure. If the bricks are too small, the project becomes unnecessarily complicated; if the bricks are too large, you can't design a refined structure.

Q&A

Q I need to display the current date and time on a Web page. Should I create an ASP component to display the time?

A For a task as simple as displaying the current time, I do not recommend that you create an ASP component. You can simply use the ASP statement `<%= " Date & " " & Time & %>`. Consider creating an ASP component when you need to perform a task such as what's outlined in the section "Benefits of Developing Custom ASP Components."

Q I just finished creating an ASP component, and now it has to be moved to my production Web server. How do I register it on my production server?

A Register an ASP component register on another computer by opening a command prompt window, changing to the directory containing the ASP component (the DLL file), and typing the command `REGSVR32 <ASPComponentFile.dll>`. Replace `<ASPComponentFile.dll>` with the name of the ASP component file, and you then see a message confirming that the ASP component was successfully registered.

Q After I made some changes and recompiled my ASP application, Visual Basic informed me that it cannot replace the DLL file. How can I fix this?

A Most likely, the DLL file is being used by the World Wide Web Publishing Service. Temporarily stop the World Wide Web Publishing Service with the command `net stop "World Wide Web Publishing Service"` so Visual Basic can replace the DLL file. Do not forget to restart the World Wide Web Publishing Service, using the command `net start "World Wide Web Publishing Service"`.

Workshop

The quiz questions and exercises are provided for your further understanding. Please refer to Appendix A, "Answers to Questions," for the answers to the quiz questions; the answers to the exercises are on the MCP Web site.

Quiz

1. How can you quickly find out the function prototype and the data structure of an API function?

2. Name three benefits of creating custom ASP components.

3. Which text file should you use to determine the function prototype and the data structures of MAPI functions?

4. Why is it recommended that you keep all your custom ASP components in the same directory?

5. How can a custom ASP component you create using Visual Basic directly send HTML text to the Web browser?

Exercises

1. Transfer the ASP component you created to another IIS 4.0 Web server by properly registering it and calling it from an ASP application.

2. Browse the APILoad application, pick another Win32 API function, and add a Visual Basic subroutine to the ASP component you created today to interface with the Win32 API function.

3. Write a Visual Basic subroutine that directly sends the current date and time to the Web browser.

20

DAY **21**

Advanced ASP Component Development with Active Automation and the Win32 API

Web applications are becoming increasingly complex, and Web developers are often required to build fully functional complex application in a matter of days. Instead of reinventing the wheel every time you build an ASP application, you can mix and match features of other applications already available on your computer. This technique enables you to build your applications more quickly and leverage existing investments for the Internet. Today, you will learn how ASP can access features of other Windows applications and cover the following:

- Explore an introduction to OLE Automation.
- Evaluate ASP component distribution issues.

- Learn how to tap into the power of Microsoft Office from ASP.
- Create an ASP spellchecker component.
- Create an ASP thesaurus component.

Introducing OLE Automation and Leveraging the Power of Microsoft Office

Microsoft Office is a powerful suite of productivity applications. You can use its power to extend the capabilities of your ASP applications by integrating Microsoft Office features with custom ASP components you develop.

You are most likely already familiar with Object Linking and Embedding (OLE) Automation. OLE Automation is not limited to Microsoft applications. It's a framework that allows applications to share features and data with other applications. Refer to Figure 21.1 for an example of OLE at work. Notice how a Visio flowchart is edited in Microsoft Word and how the Microsoft Word menu bar has been transformed into the Visio menu bar.

FIGURE 21.1.

OLE Automation at work.

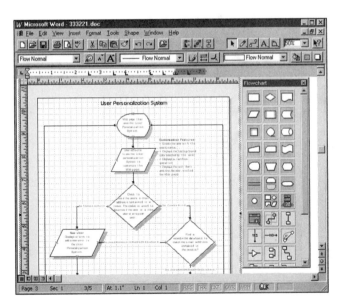

A major benefit of OLE Automation is the ability to mix and match features of different applications, using a language such as Visual Basic, C++, or Perl. For example, after an instance of an application is created, you can use a language such as Visual Basic to interface with the application and use its features that have been made available to other applications.

Note A thorough overview of objects, methods, and properties of Microsoft Word and other applications that support OLE Automation is beyond the scope of this book. The purpose of today's tutorial is to demonstrate how easy it is to build custom ASP components to make use of the features of applications already installed on your computer.

Distribution Issues

Keep in mind that you do not have permission to distribute components of other applications along with your application. If, for example, you develop a custom ASP component that uses a feature of Microsoft Word (such as spellchecking), you do not have permission to distribute Microsoft Word's spellchecking components with your application. However, your application can use Microsoft Word's spellchecking feature as long as the computer that runs your application has Microsoft Word installed.

Note To test and run the spellchecking and thesaurus component you build today, you must have a copy of Microsoft Word installed on your computer and any other computer that runs the component. If you use a word processor other than Microsoft Word, refer to your word processor's documentation to find out if it supports OLE automation, and if so, which methods you should use to access the spellchecking feature.

Using Microsoft Word's Spellchecker and Thesaurus in a Component

Before you develop the ASP component that allows a user to check spelling and look up words for synonyms, it is important that you understand how a simple Visual Basic application using such a component functions. The source code of the application is supplied at the end of this section after a walk-through of how the application functions. Notice how a word is misspelled in Figure 21.2.

21

FIGURE 21.2.

A word is misspelled.

If the word you supply is misspelled, the dialog box shown in Figure 21.3 notifies the user that the word is not correctly spelled.

Note

Microsoft Word's spellchecker has a limited vocabulary. Words can be added by choosing Options from the Tool menu, selecting the Spelling & Grammar tab, clicking the Dictionaries button, selecting the dictionary you want to edit, and clicking the Edit button.

FIGURE 21.3.

The misspelled word is detected by the application.

After you acknowledge the dialog box in Figure 21.3, the application displays a list of suggested words, one at a time, that are similar to the misspelled word (see Figure 21.4).

FIGURE 21.4.

A word similar to the misspelled word is displayed.

A correctly spelled word is typed in the top text box of the application, as shown in Figure 21.5.

FIGURE 21.5.

A correctly spelled word is entered.

If the word you supply is spelled correctly, the dialog box in Figure 21.6 acknowledges that it's correctly spelled.

FIGURE 21.6.

The application acknowledges that the word is correctly spelled.

The bottom text box in the application is used to get a word to search for synonyms. Figure 21.7 initiates a search for the word *Home*.

 Note   You must type a correctly spelled word in the bottom text box in Figure 21.7.

FIGURE 21.7.

Search for synonyms for Home.

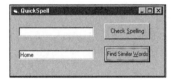

Synonyms have categories used to group similar words. The VB application is designed so that it first displays a synonym category (see Figure 21.8) and then displays all the synonyms in that category. This process is repeated for all the synonym categories.

FIGURE 21.8.

A synonym category is displayed.

After you acknowledge the dialog box in Figure 21.8, all the synonyms in that category are displayed one at a time, as shown in Figure 21.9.

FIGURE 21.9.

All the synonyms in the category in Figure 21.8 are displayed one by one.

21

Refer to Listings 21.1 and 21.2 for the complete source code of the VB application that uses the Microsoft Word spellchecker and thesaurus. The code in Listings 21.1 and 21.2 is slightly modified and used in the ASP component you build later today. If you expected to see pages of Visual Basic code, you will be pleasantly surprised. Notice how just a few lines of code can tap into the power of Microsoft Word and any other application that supports OLE Automation.

> **Tip**
>
> When building an ASP component, it's better to build it first as a Visual Basic EXE application. You can use input boxes and message boxes for data input and output. When the application is running the way you want, you can transfer the code to an ActiveX DLL project you intend to compile to an ASP component. As you will learn, it's a lot easier to debug an EXE project than an ActiveX DLL project.

LISTING 21.1. THE VB APPLICATION THAT USES THE MICROSOFT WORD SPELLCHECKER.

```
 1: Private Sub cmdCheckSpelling_Click()
 2:
 3:   Dim Suggestion
 4:
 5:   Set WordObject = GetObject(, "Word.Application")
 6:
 7:   ' Check to see if the word is spelled correctly
 8:   If WordObject.CheckSpelling(txtWordToCheck, , True) Then
 9:     MsgBox "Correct Spelling"
10:   Else
11:     MsgBox "Incorrect Spelling"
12:     Set sugList = WordObject.GetSpellingSuggestions _
13:         (Word:=txtWordToCheck, SuggestionMode:=wdSpellword)
14:     If sugList.Count = 0 Then
15:         MsgBox "No suggestions."
16:     Else
17:       MsgBox "Press OK for spelling suggestions."
18:       For Each Suggestion In sugList
19:           MsgBox Suggestion.Name
20:         Next Suggestion
21:     End If
22:   End If
23:
24: End Sub
```

ANALYSIS Line 5 creates an instance of the Word Application object if it does not already exist and uses an existing instance of the Word object if one is found. Line 8 uses the CheckSpelling() method of the Word object to determine if the word provided by the user is spelled correctly. If the word is spelled correctly, line 9 displays a message box. If the word is not spelled correctly, the Word object's GetSpellingSuggestions() method is used to locate similarly spelled words. If no similarly spelled words are found, a message box is displayed by line 15 to inform the user. Otherwise, a list of similarly spelled words is displayed, one after the other, by the For Each loop in lines 18–20.

Note

Please note that you can't use the GetObject() method to get a reference to a class created with Visual Basic. To do that, use the CreateObject() function.

Before compiling the code in Listing 21.2, create a project reference to the Microsoft Word 8.0 Object Library.

LISTING 21.2. THE VB APPLICATION THAT USES THE MICROSOFT WORD THESAURUS.

```
 1: Private Sub cmdSearchForSimilarWords_Click()
 2:
 3:   Dim SynonymList, index
 4:
 5:   Set WordObject = GetObject(, "Word.Application")
 6:
 7:   ' Check to see if the word is spelled correctly
 8:   If WordObject.CheckSpelling(TxtWordToSearch, , True) Then
 9:     MsgBox "Correct Spelling"
10:
11:     ' Display synonyms
12:     For Each Meaning In _
13:       WordObject.SynonymInfo(Word:=TxtWordToSearch, _
14:       LanguageID:=wdEnglishUS).MeaningList
15:       MsgBox "Press OK for synonyms with the meaning " _
16:         & Meaning & "."
17:       SynonymList = _
18:         WordObject.SynonymInfo(Word:=TxtWordToSearch, _
19:         LanguageID:=wdEnglishUS).SynonymList(Meaning:=Meaning)
20:       For index = 1 To UBound(SynonymList)
21:         MsgBox SynonymList(index)
22:       Next index
23:     Next
24:
25:   Else
26:     MsgBox "Incorrect Spelling"
27:   End If
28:
29: End Sub
```

ANALYSIS Line 5 creates an instance of the Word Application object if it does not already exist and uses an existing instance of the Word object if one is found. Line 8 uses the CheckSpelling() method of the Word object to determine if the word provided by

21

the user is spelled correctly. If it is, line 9 displays a message box. If the word is not spelled correctly, a message box is displayed by line 26 to inform the user. If the word is spelled correctly, the `For Each` loop in lines 12–23 displays all the synonyms for each meaning of the word. While the `For Each` loop in lines 12–23 iterates through all the meanings of the given word, the `For Next` loop in lines 20–22 displays all the words for each of the meanings. The `SynonymInfo()` method of the Word object returns a list of words that are similar to the `Word:=` argument with the meaning contained in the `Meaning:=` argument.

Building an Online Thesaurus

Now that you know how to use Microsoft Word's spellchecker and thesaurus from Visual Basic, it's time to develop an ASP component that you can use to look up words from ASP applications. Building simple custom ASP components were covered in Day 20, "Building Custom ASP Components with Visual Basic," so you should already be familiar with how to build one. The ASP component you build today uses the `ScriptingContext` object to directly send output to the Web browser.

Creating the VB Project

Start Visual Basic if it is not already running, and then choose File, New. Select the option for creating an ActiveX DLL file.

Locate VB's Project window and highlight Project1(Project1). In the Properties window, change the `Name` property from `Project1` to `TextUtils`. Next, highlight Class1(Class1) under Class Modules in the Project window. Change the `Name` property of `Class1` to `WordUtils`. Your VB application window should look like the VB application window in Figure 21.10.

Creating a Reference to ASP

The next step is to create a reference to Active Server Pages (`asp.dll`) so that the ASP objects that are not native to Visual Basic can be used in your new Visual Basic application. To create a reference to ASP, choose References from the Project menu to open the dialog box shown in Figure 21.11. Select Microsoft Active Server Pages Object Library and click the OK button. Your project now has access to ASP objects.

FIGURE 21.10.

The VB application's project and class are given new names.

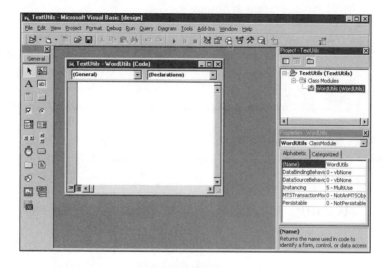

FIGURE 21.11.

Create a reference to the Microsoft Active Server Pages Object Library.

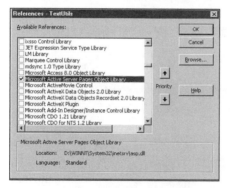

Sending Text Directly to a Browser from an ASP Application

The ASP component you developed yesterday does not directly send text to the Web browser. Instead, it passes a value to an ASP application that in turn sends the value to the Web browser. By saving a reference to the ScriptingContext Object, an ASP component can directly send text to the Web browser using the Write method of the Response object. To save a reference to the ScriptingContext Object, all you have to do is add the subroutine and global variable declaration in Listing 21.3 to your VB application.

21

LISTING 21.3. SAVING A REFERENCE TO THE `ScriptingContext` OBJECT.

```
1: Dim objScriptingContext As ScriptingContext
2:
3: Public Sub OnStartPage(ASPScriptingContext As ScriptingContext)
4:    Set objScriptingContext = ASPScriptingContext
5: End Sub
```

ANALYSIS Line 1 defines the global variable that stores a reference to the `ScriptingContext` object. The subroutine defined in lines 3–5 is executed when a user executes the ASP application that instantiates the VB component.

Creating a Project Reference to Microsoft Word

Because the component you are building uses Microsoft Word objects, you need to create a project reference to Microsoft Word, as shown in Figure 21.12. To do so, choose Reference from Visual Basic's Project menu.

FIGURE 21.12.

Create a project reference to Microsoft Word.

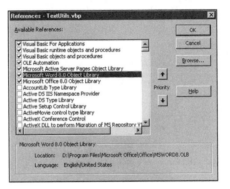

All that's left to do is to create the two methods that allow ASP applications to look up words for synonyms and check spelling. Declaring two subroutines creates the two methods. The two subroutines are made available to ASP applications by preceding the subroutine declaration with the word `Public`.

Using Microsoft Word for Spellchecking

The Visual Basic subroutine you build in this section interfaces with the Microsoft Word spellchecker to check the spelling of words entered by users in a Web form. The Web form in Figure 21.13 gets a word from the user.

FIGURE 21.13.

A misspelled word is submitted to the Online Spellchecker.

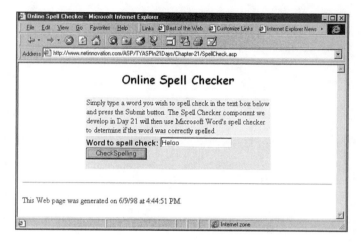

After the word is submitted to the ASP application in Listing 21.5, it uses the Visual Basic subroutine in Listing 21.4 to interface with Microsoft Word's spellchecking component. Listing 21.4 is the code of the subroutine that determines whether a given word is spelled correctly. If it's not, the subroutine displays a list of alternative spelling suggestions, as shown in Figure 21.14.

FIGURE 21.14.

Suggested spellings for the misspelled word.

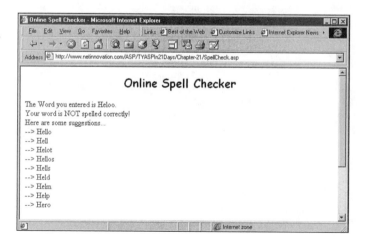

LISTING 21.4. VB CODE OF THE SUBROUTINE THAT CHECKS SPELLING OF WORDS.

```
1: Public Sub CheckSpelling(txtWordToCheck As String)
2:
3:    Dim Suggestion
4:
```

21

continues

LISTING **21.4.** CONTINUED

```
 5:   ' Create an instance of the Word Application
 6:   Set WordObject = CreateObject("Word.Application")
 7:
 8:   ' It is required to add a document to the Word Application
 9:   ' before using the GetSpellingSuggestions() method. This is
10:   ' a workaround for a bug. See Microsoft Knowledge Base
11:   ' Article ID: Q169545 for more details.
12:   WordObject.Documents.Add
13:
14:   objScriptingContext.Response.Write "The Word you entered is " & _
15:     txtWordToCheck & ".<BR>"
16:
17:   ' Check to see if the word is spelled correctly
18:   If WordObject.CheckSpelling(txtWordToCheck, , True) Then
19:     objScriptingContext.Response.Write _
20:       "Your word is spelled correctly!<BR>"
21:   Else
22:     objScriptingContext.Response.Write _
23:       "Your word is NOT spelled correctly!<BR>"
24:     ' Get a list of suggestions for the misspelled word.
25:     Set sugList = WordObject.GetSpellingSuggestions _
26:       (Word:=txtWordToCheck, SuggestionMode:=wdSpellword)
27:     If sugList.Count = 0 Then
28:         objScriptingContext.Response.Write _
29:         "No suggestions. <BR>"
30:     Else
31:       objScriptingContext.Response.Write _
32:         "Here are some suggestions...<BR>"
33:       ' Display all the suggestions for the misspelled word
34:       For Each Suggestion In sugList
35:           objScriptingContext.Response.Write _
36:             "--> " & Suggestion.Name & "<BR>"
37:       Next Suggestion
38:     End If
39:   End If
40:
41:   ' Close the Word document
42:   WordObject.Documents(1).Close
43:   ' Quit the Microsoft Word application
44:   WordObject.Quit
45:
46: End Sub
```

ANALYSIS   Line 6 creates an instance of the Microsoft Word Application object. The state-
            ment in line 12 is required because of a bug in how the
GetSpellingSuggestions() method functions. For that method to return a list of suggestions for a misspelled word, the Word object must contain at least one document.

Line 18 checks to see if the word is spelled correctly. If it is, a message is displayed to the user. If the word is not spelled correctly, line 25 gets a list of alternative spelling suggestions and the For Each loop in lines 34–37 displays them.

The ASP application in Listing 21.5 generates the Web page for users to submit a word to the custom ASP component.

LISTING 21.5. THE ASP APPLICATION INTERFACES WITH THE CUSTOM ASP COMPONENT TO CHECK THE SPELLING OF WORDS ENTERED BY THE USER (spellcheck.asp).

```
 1: <HTML>
 2: <HEAD>
 3:     <TITLE>Online Spell Checker</TITLE>
 4: </HEAD>
 5:
 6: <BODY bgcolor="FFFFFF">
 7: <p align="center"><font face="Comic Sans MS" size="5">
 8: <b>Online Spell Checker</b></font></p>
 9:
10: <% If Request.Form("TextField") = "" Then %>
11:
12: <table border="0" width="400" align="center">
13:    <tr>
14:      <td bgcolor="#FFFFCC">Simply type a word you wish to
15:      spell check in the text box below and press the
16:      Submit button. The Spell Checker component we develop
17:      in Day 21 will then use Microsoft Word's spell
18:      checker to determine if the word was correctly spelled. </td>
19:    </tr>
20:    <tr>
21:      <td bgcolor="#CCFFCC">
22:        <form method="post" action="SpellCheck.asp"
23:             name="SpellCheckForm">
24:         <p><font face="Arial, Helvetica, sans-serif"><b>Word to
25:            spell check:</b></font>
26:            <input type="text" name="textfield">
27:            <br>
28:            <input type="submit" name="submit" value="CheckSpelling">
29:         </p>
30:        </form>
31:
32:      </td>
33:    </tr>
34: </table>
35:
36: <%
37:    Else
38:
```

continues

LISTING 21.5. CONTINUED

```
39:      Set objTextUtils = Server.CreateObject ("TextUtils.WordUtils")
40:      ObjTextUtils.CheckSpelling (Request.Form("TextField"))
41: %>
42: <P> </P>
43: <A HREF="SearchForSynonyms.asp">Return to Synonym data
44: entry form.</A><BR>
45: <A HREF="SpellCheck.asp">Return to Spell Check data
46: entry form.</A><BR>
47: <%
48:    End If
49: %>
50: <BR>
51: <hr>
52: <p>This Web page was generated on <%= Date %> at <%= Time %>. </p>
53: </BODY>
54: </HTML>
```

ANALYSIS Line 10 checks whether the user has supplied a word to check for spelling. If no word is provided, the If clause defined in lines 12–36 is executed. If a word has been provided, line 39 creates an instance of the custom ASP component and line 40 uses the CheckSpelling() method of the custom ASP component to check the spelling of the word submitted by the user.

Using Microsoft Word for Finding Synonyms

The Visual Basic subroutine in Listing 21.6 uses Microsoft Word's thesaurus to find synonyms for words. The Web form in Figure 21.15 gets a word from the user. The ASP application displays synonyms only if a correctly spelled word is entered in the page shown in Figure 21.15.

If the ASP subroutine in Listing 21.6 finds any synonyms, it displays them, as shown in Figure 21.16. Notice how the synonyms are categorized by meaning.

FIGURE 21.15.

Initiating a search for synonyms for Home.

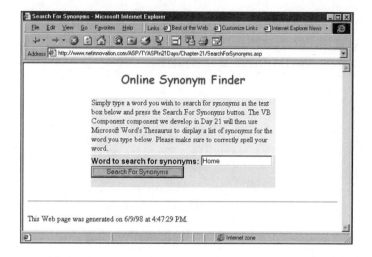

FIGURE 21.16.

A list of synonyms for Home *is displayed by the ASP component.*

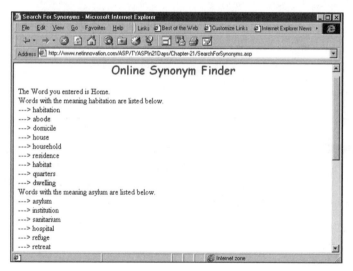

LISTING 21.6. MICROSOFT WORD'S THESAURUS IS USED TO FIND SYNONYMS FOR A GIVEN WORD.

```
1: Public Sub DisplaySynonyms(txtWordToSearch As String)
2:
3:    Dim SynonymList, index
4:
5:    ' Create an instance of the Word Application
6:    Set WordObject = CreateObject("Word.Application")
7:
8:    objScriptingContext.Response.Write "The Word you entered is " & _
9:      txtWordToSearch & ".<BR>"
```

continues

21

LISTING 21.6. CONTINUED

```
10:
11:    ' Check to see if the word is spelled correctly
12:    If WordObject.CheckSpelling(txtWordToSearch, , True) Then
13:
14:      ' Display synonyms
15:      For Each Meaning In _
16:        WordObject.SynonymInfo(Word:=txtWordToSearch, _
17:          LanguageID:=wdEnglishUS).MeaningList
18:        objScriptingContext.Response.Write "Words with the meaning " _
19:          & Meaning & " are listed below.<BR>"
20:        SynonymList = _
21:          WordObject.SynonymInfo(Word:=txtWordToSearch, _
22:          LanguageID:=wdEnglishUS).SynonymList(Meaning:=Meaning)
23:        For index = 1 To UBound(SynonymList)
24:          objScriptingContext.Response.Write _
25:            "---> " & SynonymList(index) & "<BR>"
26:        Next index
27:      Next
28:
29:    Else
30:      objScriptingContext.Response.Write _
31:        "Your word is incorrectly Spelled.<BR>"
32:    End If
33:    WordObject.Quit
34: End Sub
```

> **ANALYSIS** Line 6 creates an instance of the Microsoft Word Application object. Line 12 checks whether the word entered by the user is spelled correctly. If it isn't, line 31 displays a message. Otherwise, the For Each loop defined in lines 15–27 displays synonyms of the given word grouped by synonym meaning.

The ASP application in Listing 21.7 generates the Web page for users to submit a word to the custom ASP component.

LISTING 21.7. THE ASP APPLICATION INTERFACES WITH THE CUSTOM ASP COMPONENT TO DISPLAY SYNONYMS (searchforsynonyms.asp).

```
1: <HTML>
2: <HEAD>
3:     <TITLE>Search For Synonyms</TITLE>
4: </HEAD>
5:
6: <BODY bgcolor="FFFFFF">
7: <p align="center"><font face="Comic Sans MS" size="5">
8:   <b><font color="#0000FF">Online
```

```
 9:    Synonym Finder</font></b></font></p>
10:
11: <% If Request.Form("TextField") = "" Then %>
12:
13: <table border="0" width="400" align="center">
14:   <tr>
15:     <td bgcolor="#FFFFCC">
16:       <p>Simply type a word you wish to search for
17:       synonyms in the text box below and press the
18:       Search For Synonyms button. The VB Component
19:       component we develop in Day 21 will then use
20:       Microsoft Word's Thesaurus to display a list of
21:       synonyms for the word you type below. Please
22:       make sure to correctly spell your word.</p>
23:       </td>
24:   </tr>
25:   <tr>
26:     <td bgcolor="#CCFFCC">
27:       <form method="post" action="SearchForSynonyms.asp"
28:        name="SpellCheckForm">
29:       <p><font face="Arial, Helvetica, sans-serif">
30:          <b>Word to search for synonyms:</b></font>
31:          <input type="text" name="textfield">
32:          <br>
33:          <input type="submit" name="submit"
34:                  value="Search For Synonyms">
35:       </p>
36:       </form>
37:
38:      </td>
39:   </tr>
40: </table>
41: <%
42:   Else
43:     Set objTextUtils = Server.CreateObject ("TextUtils.WordUtils")
44:     ObjTextUtils.DisplaySynonyms (Request.Form("TextField"))
45: %>
46: <P> </P>
47: <A HREF="SearchForSynonyms.asp">Return to Synonym data
48: entry form.</A><BR>
49: <A HREF="SpellCheck.asp">Return to Spell Check data
50: entry form.</A><BR>
51: <%
52:   End If
53: %>
54: <BR>
55: <hr>
56: <p>This Web page was generated on <%= Date %> at <%= Time %>.</p>
57: </BODY>
58: </HTML>
```

21

ANALYSIS Line 11 checks whether the user has supplied a word to check for synonyms. If the user provides no word, a Web form is displayed to get input from the user. Otherwise, line 43 creates an instance of the custom ASP component, and line 44 uses the method `DisplaySynonyms()` to display synonyms for the word.

The Complete Application

For your reference, the complete source code of the Visual Basic component developed today is given in Listing 21.8. As you can see, the component is really not very long. Imagine the amount of code you would have had to write if you were creating a spellchecker and thesaurus from scratch. Thanks to OLE Automation, you can develop applications that leverage your existing investments for the Internet and simplify the task of building complex ASP applications.

LISTING 21.8. COMPLETE SOURCE CODE OF THE ASP COMPONENT.

```
 1: Dim objScriptingContext As ScriptingContext
 2:
 3: Public Sub OnStartPage(ASPScriptingContext As ScriptingContext)
 4:
 5:   ' Save a reference to the ScriptingContext object so you can
 6:   ' directly send text to the Web browser.
 7:   Set objScriptingContext = ASPScriptingContext
 8:
 9: End Sub
10:
11: Public Sub CheckSpelling(txtWordToCheck As String)
12:
13:   Dim Suggestion
14:
15:   ' Create an instance of the Word Application
16:   Set WordObject = CreateObject("Word.Application")
17:
18:   ' It is required to add a document to the Word Application
19:   ' before using the GetSpellingSuggestions method. This is
20:   ' a workaround for a bug. See Microsoft Knowledge Base
21:   ' Article ID: Q169545 for more details.
22:   WordObject.Documents.Add
23:
24:   objScriptingContext.Response.Write "The Word you entered is " & _
25:     txtWordToCheck & ".<BR>"
26:
27:   ' Check to see if the word is spelled correctly
28:   If WordObject.CheckSpelling(txtWordToCheck, , True) Then
29:     objScriptingContext.Response.Write _
30:       "Your word is spelled correctly!<BR>"
```

```
31:    Else
32:      objScriptingContext.Response.Write _
33:        "Your word is NOT spelled correctly!<BR>"
34:      ' Get a list of suggestions for the misspelled word.
35:      Set sugList = WordObject.GetSpellingSuggestions _
36:          (Word:=txtWordToCheck, SuggestionMode:=wdSpellword)
37:      If sugList.Count = 0 Then
38:          objScriptingContext.Response.Write _
39:          "No suggestions. <BR>"
40:      Else
41:        objScriptingContext.Response.Write _
42:          "Here are some suggestions...<BR>"
43:        ' Display all the suggestions for the misspelled word
44:        For Each Suggestion In sugList
45:            objScriptingContext.Response.Write _
46:              "--> " & Suggestion.Name & "<BR>"
47:        Next Suggestion
48:      End If
49:    End If
50:
51:    ' Close the Word document
52:    WordObject.Documents(1).Close
53:    ' Quit the Microsoft Word application
54:    WordObject.Quit
55:
56: End Sub
57:
58: Public Sub DisplaySynonyms(txtWordToSearch As String)
59:
60:    Dim SynonymList, index
61:
62:    ' Create an instance of the Word Application
63:    Set WordObject = CreateObject("Word.Application")
64:
65:    objScriptingContext.Response.Write "The Word you entered is " & _
66:      txtWordToSearch & ".<BR>"
67:
68:    ' Check to see if the word is spelled correctly
69:    If WordObject.CheckSpelling(txtWordToSearch, , True) Then
70:
71:      ' Display synonyms
72:      For Each Meaning In _
73:        WordObject.SynonymInfo(Word:=txtWordToSearch, _
74:          LanguageID:=wdEnglishUS).MeaningList
75:        objScriptingContext.Response.Write "Words with the meaning " _
76:          & Meaning & " are listed below.<BR>"
77:        SynonymList = _
78:          WordObject.SynonymInfo(Word:=txtWordToSearch, _
79:          LanguageID:=wdEnglishUS).SynonymList(Meaning:=Meaning)
80:        For index = 1 To UBound(SynonymList)
```

continues

21

LISTING 21.8. CONTINUED

```
81:            objScriptingContext.Response.Write _
82:              "---> " & SynonymList(index) & "<BR>"
83:         Next index
84:      Next
85:
86:    Else
87:      objScriptingContext.Response.Write _
88:        "Your word is incorrectly Spelled.<BR>"
89:    End If
90:    WordObject.Quit
91: End Sub
```

Summary

OLE is a technology that allows application developers to interact and interface with other Windows applications. Most professional Windows applications support OLE. By building custom ASP components that use it, you can extend your existing software investments to the Internet and build powerful ASP applications in very little time. As you have seen today, with just a few lines of code and a little help from Microsoft Word, you can build an online thesaurus and a spellchecker.

Q&A

Q What is the purpose of the `ScriptingContext` object?

A The `ScriptingContext` object can be used to interface with live ASP objects at runtime. For example, the `ScriptingContext` object can be used to directly send text to the Web browser from a Visual Basic component.

Q What is the purpose of creating a reference to the file `asp.dll`?

A By creating a reference to the file `asp.dll`, ASP objects (that are not native to Visual Basic) can be used in a Visual Basic application.

Q When building a custom ASP component, why is it recommended that you first build the project as a Visual Basic EXE project?

A It's a lot easier to debug an EXE project than an ActiveX DLL project. When building an ASP component, it's better to first build the ASP component as a Visual Basic EXE application. When the application is running the way you want, you can transfer the code to an ActiveX DLL project you intend to compile to an ASP component.

Workshop

The quiz questions and exercises are provided for your further understanding. Please refer to Appendix A, "Answers to Questions," for the answers to the quiz questions; the answers to the exercises are on the MCP Web site.

Quiz

1. Name three languages that can interface with applications that support OLE Automation.

2. True or False: Do you have permission to distribute the spellchecking and thesaurus components of Microsoft Word with your application? Why?

3. Which function is used to create an instance of a class created with Visual Basic?

4. True or False: OLE Automation is a feature exclusive to Microsoft applications.

5. How can a subroutine declared in an ASP component be made available to ASP applications?

6. To create a custom ASP component, what type of VB project should you select to create?

Exercises

1. Register the ASP component created today on another computer.

2. Refer to Microsoft Word's online help to learn about other Word features you can use from Visual Basic by using OLE.

3. Modify the CheckSpelling() subroutine so that if a word is correctly spelled, it automatically displays synonyms for the given word.

21

WEEK 3

15
16
17
18
19
20
21

In Review

ActiveX controls are used to add a rich user interface to ASP applications. How to build an ActiveX control and use it from within an ASP application was covered on Day 15, "Activating Your ASP Applications." ActiveX controls can be used to create highly interactive Web applications. Because not all Web browsers support ActiveX, you should be aware of browser compatibility issues when using ActiveX controls. Day 15 demonstrates that it is possible to use ActiveX controls to add a new level of interactivity to your Web site while making sure your ASP applications are friendly toward Web browsers that do not support ActiveX controls.

Day 16, "Developing a Web Messaging System with TCP/IP Sockets," showed you how to use Visual Basic along with ASP to create a client/server Web messaging system. You also learned the benefits of building multi-tiered Web applications on Day 16. Computers on the Internet use TCP/IP sockets to communicate with each other and transfer information. By default, ASP does not support the manipulation of TCP/IP sockets. However, by installing a freely downloadable component from the Internet, you can add TCP/IP socket support to ASP applications. The ASP application you built uses TCP/IP sockets to send messages entered by users browsing the Web site to a Visual Basic application that can run on any computer on the Internet.

With the aid of Visual InterDev 6.0, you can create and manage complex ASP projects. On Day 17, "Building ASP Applications with Visual InterDev 6.0," you learned how features of Visual InterDev 6.0 greatly simplify the development of large ASP projects.

Security is an important, yet often overlooked, aspect of Web application development. You learned how to make your ASP applications more secure on Day 18, "Building in Security." You can take steps to protect an NT server on the Internet against unauthorized access. Although setting up an Internet server that is immune to unauthorized access is practically impossible, there are ways to make it harder and, in some cases, prohibitively expensive for someone to gain unauthorized access.

On Day 19, "Exploiting ASP: Tips And Advanced Topics," you delved into advanced ASP topics, such as tips for creating effective ASP applications, avoiding memory leaks, using IIS to deploy ASP applications, and the ASP registry settings. Tips and techniques you learned on Day 19 can be used to develop more robust and efficient ASP applications.

On Day 20, "Building Custom ASP Components with Visual Basic," you learned how easy it is to build your own custom ASP components with Visual Basic by building a custom VB component and using it from within an ASP application. Custom ASP components can be developed by using a variety of application development environments that allow creating ActiveX controls. Visual Basic can be easily used to develop custom ASP components, and your VBScript skills can be leveraged to develop these components because Visual Basic is very similar to VBScript. Custom ASP components promote data encapsulation, easy code distribution, security, and centralized code management. When developing large projects, you should create your own custom ASP components to handle those tasks that can be more efficiently and easily carried out in another application development environment, such as Visual Basic, Delphi, or Visual C++. You can then mix and match the best features of each environment. Do not develop overly complicated ASP components, however; concentrate on developing well-defined, small, efficient ASP components that handle a certain task extremely well. You can then efficiently reuse your custom ASP components when you develop future Web applications. Think of ActiveX components as bricks that you use to develop a large structure. If the bricks are too small, the project will become unnecessarily complicated; if the bricks are too large, you will not be able to design a refined structure.

Day 21, "Advanced ASP Component Development with Active Automation and the Win32 API," covers how to build more complex ASP components and how to unleash the power of the Win32 API. OLE Automation is a technology that allows application developers to interact and interface with other Windows applications. Most professional Windows application support OLE Automation. By building custom ASP components that use this technology, you can extend your existing software investments to the Internet and build powerful ASP applications in very little time. On Day 21, you also learned that with just a few lines of code, and a little help from Microsoft Word, you can build an online thesaurus and a spellchecker.

Congratulations! You've successfully completed your three-week tutorial on Active Server Pages!

APPENDIX **A**

Answers to Questions

Answers to Quiz Questions for Day 1

1. You can break down long VBScript statements into several lines with the VBScript code continuation character (_). Generally, you should not allow your VBScript statements to be over 76 characters long to make it easier for you and other people to maintain your code.

2. False. Users see only the HTML code generated by the ASP code. The ASP code is hidden from your Web users.

3. You can add comments to your ASP code by using either the Rem keyword or the apostrophe (') and following it with your comments.

4. False. ASP generates HTML that is readable by almost any Web browser, even Web browsers that run on tiny hand-held devices! It's up to you, the ASP developer, to make sure you use proper HTML that is cross-browser compatible.

5. The Response.Write() statement does the same thing as the <%= %> delimiter.

Answers to Quiz Questions for Day 2

1. Server-side includes (SSI) promote code reuse and make it easy to change a certain formula or subroutine in one place and have the change propagated to all other applications that use the formula or subroutine. SSI also allows you to group similar functions you create in different SSI files.

2. `Application` object, `ObjectContext` object, `Request` object, `Response` object, `Server` object, `Session` object.

3. The `Response` object. `Response.Write()` was used in Day 1 to display HTML text.

4. The `Request` object is used to retrieve information passed to the Web server by the Web browser.

5. Do not constantly make modifications to your `global.asa` file when the server is under heavy load because it might disrupt the activities of your users.

Answers to Quiz Questions for Day 3

1. HTML forms, Java applets, ActiveX controls, message boxes, input boxes.

2. Yes. ActiveX controls can be used to easily add a new level of interactivity to your ASP applications.

3. Whenever a diverse range of Web browsers in a variety of operating systems will be using your Web application, it is best to use HTML forms to interact with your users because HTML forms are supported by all Web browsers.

4. No. You should not use client-side data validation as a substitute for server-side data validation. You still need to validate data on the server by using an ASP subroutine before you process data entered by users. Remember, client-side data validation compliments server-side data validations. It is not a substitute.

5. Do not use the `GET` method to send large amounts of data from HTML forms to the server. In such cases, use the `POST` method instead. The `GET` method is limited to around 2,044 bytes, and the data submitted with it appears as a query string in the Web browser's URL text box.

6. The VBScript subroutine `window_onLoad()` is always executed before the user can manipulate elements of the Web page. Therefore, `MsgBox()` statements should be placed inside the `window_onLoad()` subroutine to ensure the message boxes are displayed as soon as the Web page is loaded. The `onLoad()` JavaScript event handler is executed when the Web page finishes loading.

7. The `alert()` Function is the JavaScript equivalent of the `MsgBox()` function.

Answers to Quiz Questions for Day 4

A

1. The following ASP code creates a text file called `NumVisits.txt` if the file does not already exist:

```
1: Set FileStreamObject = CreateObject("Scripting.FileSystemObject")
2: Set WriteStream = FileStreamObject.CreateTextFile("NumVisits.txt",
↪False)
```

2. A leap year is any year divisible by 4 except for years divisible by 100, unless that year is divisible by 400. For example, 2000 and 2400 are leap years; however, the years 2100, 2200, 2300, and 2500 are not.

3. In Microsoft Windows, the range of dates from January 1, 100 A.D. through December 31, 9999 A.D. are considered valid dates by the `IsDate()` function.

4. Wizard-style user interfaces greatly simplify the process of data entry by guiding the user through complex questions. Another benefit of using wizard-style user interfaces is that they help the user concentrate on one set of questions before moving on to the next set. Also, based on the answers to a previous set of questions, future questions can be customized.

5. The `OpenTextFile()` method of the `FileSystem` object is used to append text.

Answers to Quiz Questions for Day 5

1. You can build scriptlets with the following scripting languages: VBScript, JavaScript/JScript, Perl (PERLScript, PScript), ECMAScript, and Python.

2. A scriptlet can be registered using either the command-line tool `regsvr32.exe` or the Microsoft Scriptlet Wizard.

3. Scriptlets end with the file extension `.sct`.

4. After you create a scriptlet, you can use it from within any ASP application by instantiating it with the `CreateObject` function if you use VBScript or the new `ActiveXObject` function if you use JScript.

5. It is not recommended to have a Class ID automatically assigned to a scriptlet because each time you register the scriptlet, it will then have a different Class ID, complicating the task of maintaining different versions and scriptlet distribution. It is better to have the scriptlet have a unique Class ID across multiple computers.

6. ECMAScript is a standard, general-purpose, cross-platform scripting language based on JScript 2.0 and JavaScript 1.1.

7. Microsoft Visual Basic 6.0 and Microsoft Internet Explorer 4.0.

8. No. You can build scriptlets using any language that supports the Microsoft ActiveX Scripting Interfaces.

9. The `IMPLEMENTS` element is used to define the interface handler as well as properties and methods of a scriptlet.

10. The `SCRIPT` element implements all the functions and properties of the scriptlet.

Answers to Quiz Questions for Day 6

1. You can determine how many items are selected by the user by examining the value of the following ASP statement:

```
Request.Form("CoursesSelected").Count
```

2. The `GET` method is designed to transfer only about 1,000 characters to a server-side application. Using the `GET` method to transfer large amounts of data could cause undesired results.

3. You can find the physical path of an ASP application by using the following ASP statement:

```
Request.ServerVariables (PATH_TRANSLATED)
```

4. The following ASP statement is used to access the server variable SERVER_SOFT-WARE:

```
Request.ServerVariables ("SERVER_SOFTWARE")
```

5. To examine the values of form variables using the `Request.Form` collection, the form must be submitted with the `POST` method.

6. You display the `UserID` HTML form variable by using the following ASP statement:

```
<%= Request.Form("UserID") %>
```

Answers to Quiz Questions for Day 7

1. An error would be generated because the `Redirect` method writes the "302 Object Moved" HTTP response header, and all headers must be written *before* the first content data (in this example, `<HTML>`) is sent to the client.

2. There are two options. First, move the `Redirect` method to the top of the script. Second, you could turn page buffering on by adding the following code to the top of the script:

```
<% Response.Buffer = True %>
```

3. Set the cookie's expiration date attribute to a date that has already passed, as follows:

```
Response.Cookie("FootBallTeams")("GreenBay").Expires = "February 6,
➥1993"
```

4. You would use a dictionary cookie, which allows you to dynamically expand and contract the number of teams within the same keyed cookie.

5. You can use the `Response.Write` object or you can use the inline response:

```
<% Response.Write userName %>
<%= userName %>
```

Answers to Quiz Questions for Day 8

1. `Server.CreateObject`

2. 20 minutes

3. Database software, but financial or banking software is also a good answer.

4. Any two of these answers: The session can time out, your script can call `Session.Abandon`, or the Web server stops operating.

5. In a URL, `%20` represents a space.

Answers to Quiz Questions for Day 9

1. The answer is False. The area in which the ads are rotated must be a constant size. If images of different sizes are given in the Rotator Schedule file, the images will be scaled to fit the defined size.

2. If a "Default Browser" section is in the `browscap.ini` file, it uses the specifications defined in that section. If that section is not present, all property values requested for that browser return the string `"UNKNOWN"`. You can define a new browser type by editing the `browscap.ini` file and creating a section with a header that is an exact string match with the HTTP User Agent header returned from the browser.

3. Yes, it would work. You would lose automatic logging of user responses and automatic redirection, and it would require much more code to be written. However, this is one way around the size limitation described in Question 1.

4. `((Abs(Tools.Random) Mod 61) - 12)`

5. The answer is False. The Page Counter component method `PageHit` takes no parameters, so it always increments the count for the current page. This is needed to prevent artificially high counts from being generated for pages that are not actually loaded.

Answers to Quiz Questions for Day 10

1. Many users still surf the Web with screen resolutions of 640×480 (not to mention all those who use devices with limited screen resolutions, such as Web TV, Windows CE, and certain cars with built-in wireless Internet access). By making sure your Web forms are no wider than 640 pixels, your users can easily enter data regardless of their screen resolutions.

2. Microsoft Access is limited to ten concurrent connections.

3. I recommend that you use file DSNs in your Web database applications. A database specified with a file DSN is available to multiple users at the same time. Because the database information is contained in a plain text file, file DSNs can be easily transferred from one server to another simply by copying the file DSN.

4. False. DELETE does not return a recordset.

5. Please note that the DSNs used by your ASP application must be created on the Web server running the ASP application. If you move your ASP application to a different Web server, you have to re-create the DSN(s) of your ASP application on the new Web server.

Answers to Quiz Questions for Day 11

1. a. Open, c. Save, and d. Close. Execute is not a method of a Recordset; it is a method of the Command and Connection objects.

2. The Command object exposes the Parameters collection, which allows you to provide a stored procedure or SQL statement with values to be used when it executes.

3. The Properties collection exists for every ADO object and gives you a collection-based way of viewing all the properties of the object.

4. False. Unless all the records have been visited (MoveLast), the value might not be correct.

5. You should check both the BOF and EOF properties of the recordset. If both are true, then the recordset is empty.

6. The Execute method will run a SQL statement against a database.

7. It opens a session with the database indicated by the ODBC DSN FooBar, using the user ID Fred and a password of Apple.

8. False. Each recordset will create a separate Connection object for its own use.

Answers to Quiz Questions for Day 12

1. By designing a flowchart, you will be able to think of special cases you would not have thought of otherwise and build a better application and cut back on development time. It is a lot easier to make major changes to an application before any code has been written rather than attempting to coax existing code into doing something it was not designed to do!

2. The UPDATE SQL statement is used to modify existing data in a database.

3. Use the Close method of each object.

4. The SQL UPDATE method is suitable for updating the value of a numeric field because numeric field do not contain apostrophes or quotation marks.

Answers to Quiz Questions for Day 13

1. The limit is 300 cookies.

2. Yes, each server can create only 20 cookies.

3. The Response ASP object is used to create a cookie.

4. The Request ASP object is used to retrieve the value of a cookie.

5. Delete a cookie by setting an expiration date that has already passed. The following statement deletes the cookie named EMailAddress:

   ```
   Response.Cookie("EmailAddress").Expires = "January 1, 1997"
   ```

6. The following ASP statement creates a cookie named TimeZone with the value "Eastern"

   ```
   Response.Cookies("TimeZone") = "Eastern"
   ```

7. The following statement deletes the cookie by the name of DatabaseID by setting its expiration date to a value that has already elapsed:

   ```
   <% Response.Cookies ("DatabaseID").Expires = "January 1, 1997" %>
   ```

8. Cookies can be no larger than about 4K. Storing large amounts of data on the client side is not what cookies are intended for. If you have to store large amounts of data, store it in a server-side database and create a cookie that just contains a reference to the database record.

Answers to Quiz Questions for Day 14

1. The Response object is used to set the value of a cookie after HTML text has been sent to the Web browser. This will cause an error. You should always use the

Response object to set the value of a cookie before any HTML text is sent to the Web browser. `Response.Cookies()` statements should be placed before the `<HTML>` tag.

2. You can find a list of ADO constants that can be used in ASP applications along with their corresponding values at the following location:

`\Program Files\Common Files\System\ADO\adovbs.inc`

3. Optimistic locking locks records only when the `Update()` method of the recordset is called.

4. You can include the ADO constant definitions file easily by copying it to the `Includes` directory of your Web server's document root directory (create the `Includes` directory if it does not exist) and using the following statement at the beginning of the ASP file:

`<!--# virtual ="/Includes/adovbs.inc " -->`

5. No. When using the `Response` object to set the value of a cookie, you should do so before any HTML text is sent to the Web browser.

Answers to Quiz Questions for Day 15

1. The following are some of the benefits of using ActiveX controls:
   - You can leverage existing investments to the Internet.
   - ActiveX controls can be easily built using products such as Borland Delphi, Microsoft Visual Basic, C++, and so on.
   - You have the ability to use ActiveX controls that are available in Windows and installed as part of Internet Explorer.
   - ActiveX controls are fast.
   - ActiveX controls are lightweight and easily downloaded over the Internet.
   - ActiveX controls provide access to system services such as printing.
   - Several ActiveX controls can be easily linked by using a scripting language such as VBScript to create a complete Web application.

2. Create a control array when adding a series of controls with similar characteristics. This enables you to iterate through all the controls very easily by using an index value at runtime to initialize and access values of the controls. Additionally, it makes it easier to create one control and derive properties of other similar controls from the first control you create.

3. The following ASP statements display the string "Non ActiveX Version" for Web browsers that do not support ActiveX controls.

```
<%
   Dim objBrowserCapabilities

   ' Create an instance of the Browser Capabilities component.
   Set objBrowserCapabilities = Server.CreateObject("MSWC.BrowserType")

   ' The Browser Capabilities component is used to determine if
   ' the Web browser supports ActiveX controls.
   If (objBrowserCapabilities.ActiveXControls = FALSE) Then

      ' Standard HTML is used for Web browsers that do not support
      ' ActiveX controls.
%>

<p><font face="Verdana"><strong>Non ActiveX Version.</strong>
</font></p>

<% End If %>
```

4. The following command-line statement can be used to register the ActiveX control calendar.ocx on a remote computer.

```
Regsvr32 Calendar.ocx
```

5. Use the VB ActiveX Control Interface Wizard to simplify the task of adding properties, events, and methods to ActiveX controls you create. The VB ActiveX Control Interface Wizard creates the required subroutines and variables you can use to implement methods, properties, and events of an ActiveX control.

6. No. Mainly, only Internet Explorer supports ActiveX controls at the time of this writing.

Answers to Quiz Questions for Day 16

1. A cluster is a collection of computers that share system resources and implement fail-safe operations. A cluster might appear as one large computer to an application, although the cluster can be made up of several computers that are linked.

2. These are the three components of the three-tier model:

   - User interface
   - Programming logic
   - Business objects and databases

3. All the computers on the Internet support TCP/IP.

4. Here are some of the benefits of the three-tier model:
   - Aids code maintenance
   - Promotes robust, scalable Web applications
   - Naturally separates business logic from programming logic
   - Promotes teamwork by allowing different teams to work on each tier
   - Sensitive areas of an application (such as credit card billing and verification) can be protected with additional security

5. No. However, you can add support for TCP/IP sockets by installing an ASP component that can be downloaded from the Internet.

Answers to Quiz Questions for Day 17

1. The Project Explorer.
2. HTML Outline and Script Outline.
3. When a project is created.
4. Local Mode.
5. The Object Browser allows you to view all methods, properties, events, enums, and constants in a control.
6. Site diagrams.
7. Simplify adding functionality to your Web application without relying on complex code.
8. Create a data connection.
9. When the application is in a break state.

Answers to Quiz Questions for Day 18

1. At the very least, access failures should be audited so you can track down security violations and address them.
2. The default location of the IIS log files is \WINNT\system32\LogFiles\.
3. Anyone can use the Guest account to gain access to your system. If you have an FTP server set up at your site, this account can be especially dangerous because a user with malicious intent could use it to destroy information on your system.

4. Only Internet Explorer supports Windows NT challenge/response user authentication. Use this method of authentication to authenticate users if you are certain all your users use Internet Explorer. The second drawback is that Windows NT challenge/response user authentication does not encrypt information transmitted via the Internet; it encrypts only user names and passwords.

Answers to Quiz Questions for Day 19

1. The default timeout value for ASP scripts is 90 seconds.

2. The default timeout value for the ASP `Session` object is 20 minutes.

3. You can override the `SessionTimeout` value specified in the Registry by using the `Timeout` method of the `Session` object.

4. Registry values can be modified by executing the Windows registry editor located at `C:\<Windows Directory>\system32\regedt32.exe`.

5. The default location of IIS log files is `%WinDir%\System32\LogFiles`.

Answers to Quiz Questions for Day 20

1. Visual Basic ships with a utility that can be used to easily locate the function prototype and the data structures of an API function. The name of this utility is `APILoad.exe`.

2. Here are some of the benefits of creating custom ASP components:
   - Centralized code management
   - The black box model
   - Access to API functions
   - Mix-and-match programming languages
   - Security
   - Protection of proprietary algorithms
   - Ease of alteration
   - Ease of distribution

3. The text file `MAPI32.txt` can be loaded to APILoad to determine function prototype and the data structures of MAPI functions.

4. It is recommended that you keep all your custom ASP components in the same directory to make it easier to keep track of your custom ASP components.

5. HTML text can be written directly to the Web browser by referencing the `ScriptingContext` object in the `OnStartPage` method of the ASP component and saving the reference for future use. The `ScriptingContext` object acts as an interface between the ASP component and the Web page generated by the ASP application.

Answers to Quiz Questions for Day 21

1. Visual Basic, C++, and Perl can interface with applications that support OLE Automation.

2. False. You do *not* have permission to distribute the spellchecking and thesaurus components of Microsoft Word with your applications because those components are part of Microsoft Word.

3. To obtain a reference to a class created with Visual Basic, use the `CreateObject()` function.

4. False. OLE Automation is a feature of Windows that is not limited to Microsoft applications. It's a framework that allows applications from multiple developers to share features and data with other Windows applications.

5. Subroutines defined in an ASP component are made available to ASP applications by preceding the subroutine declaration with the statement `Public`.

6. To create a custom ASP component, you should select the option to create an ActiveX DLL project.

APPENDIX B

Developing ASP Applications with PerlScript

Practical Extraction and Report Language (Perl) is one of the most widely used CGI scripting languages. In this appendix, you learn how to use PerlScript (a version of Perl for Active Server Pages).

Numerous Perl scripts can be found in Internet Perl script archives. By customizing these scripts to suit your needs, you can easily improve your Web site. A comprehensive Perl tutorial is beyond the scope of this book, so the purpose of this appendix is to demonstrate how you can use Perl to develop ASP applications.

Perl for Windows NT is available for the Intel and Alpha platforms.

Benefits of Using Perl to Develop ASP Applications

Many of the best features of C, SED, AWK, and sh (these are the scripting languages most widely used in the UNIX environment) are incorporated into Perl; therefore, you can develop Perl scripts quickly because you don't have to reinvent the wheel for fundamental tasks such as string manipulation. Perl's expression syntax corresponds quite closely to the expression syntax of C programs, which makes Perl very easy to learn if you are already familiar with C.

One of the best things about Perl is its portability. Perl is an interpreted language that is available for several hardware platforms, including PCs, Macs, and different types of UNIX systems. Because of its portability, you can port regular Perl scripts to ASP PerlScripts with very few modifications.

Unlike most scripting languages and utilities, Perl does not impose limits on data size. As long as you have enough system resources, Perl will happily read the contents of a multi-megabyte file into a string. Thanks to the optimizing algorithms built into Perl, scripts written in Perl are robust and fast.

Downloading and Installing PerlScript

COMPANION Web site Before you develop ASP applications with Perl, you must download PerlScript and install it on your system. PerlScript can be freely downloaded from the Internet at `http://www.activestate.com/`. Perl for Windows NT is distributed as three files:

- The Perl for Win32 binary file (available for Intel and Alpha platforms).
- The PerlScript binary file (available for Intel and Alpha platforms). PerlScript requires the Perl for Win32 binary file.
- The Perl ISAPI file (available for Intel and Alpha platforms) can be used to develop ISAPI applications in Perl. Perl for ISAPI requires the Perl for Win32 binary file.

You must download at least the Perl for Win32 and PerlScript binary files to develop ASP applications in Perl. Download the files to a temporary directory.

Installing Perl

After you have downloaded the files, you then need to execute the Perl for Win32 distribution file in the temporary directory where you saved it. When it's launched, you need to acknowledge the dialog box you see first to proceed with the installation. Use the dialog box you see next to specify the target directory for Perl for Win32. Either accept the default path or specify a new path, and make sure the check box to run `PerlW32-install.bat` is checked. This is to ensure that Perl is installed in your system as soon as the distribution file is decompressed.

After the Perl distribution file is decompressed, a Windows NT command window runs the Perl installation script, as shown in Figure B.1. I recommend that you answer yes to all the questions. Perl for Win32 is now installed and ready for use.

Note

At this point, you must log off and log back in for Perl settings to become active.

FIGURE B.1.

Perl for Win32 is installed and ready for use.

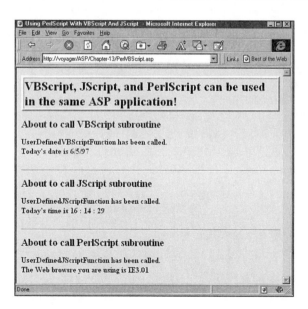

Do not copy any Perl for Win32 executable files (such as `perl.exe`) to a CGI directory of your Web server. This enables a user with malicious intentions to execute Windows NT commands by hacking Perl!

Installing PerlScript

Before you begin developing ASP applications with Perl, you must install PerlScript in the same directory as Perl for Win32. Execute the PerlScript distribution file to begin installing PerlScript. You are asked to specify the target directory for PerlScript. This directory name should be the same as the directory specified when installing Perl for Win32. Make sure the check box to run `PerlScript-install.bat` is checked.

After the PerlScript distribution file is decompressed, a Windows NT command window runs the PerlScript installation script. After the installation script terminates, PerlScript is installed and ready for use.

 After you install PerlScript, log off and log back on for the directory paths to become effective.

Your First Perl Active Server Pages Application

On Day 2, "Web Development with Active Server Pages," you learned how to develop an ASP application using VBScript and JScript at the same time. Now that you have Perl installed on your system, you can also use PerlScript. The ASP application in Listing B.1 demonstrates how to use VBScript, JScript, and PerlScript in the same application. See Figure B.2 for the output of the ASP application in Listing B.1.

LISTING B.1. USING PERL TO DEVELOP ASP APPLICATIONS.

```
1:  <%@ LANGUAGE="VBSCRIPT" %>
2:
3:  <SCRIPT RUNAT=SERVER LANGUAGE=VBSCRIPT>
4:
5:  Sub UserDefinedVBScriptFunction ()
6:
7:    Response.Write("<H3>UserDefinedVBScriptFunction has been
      ➥called.<BR>")
8:    Response.Write("Today's date is " & Date & " </H3>")
```

```
 9:
10: End Sub
11:
12: </SCRIPT>
13:
14: <SCRIPT RUNAT=SERVER LANGUAGE=JSCRIPT>
15:
16: function  UserDefinedJScriptFunction ()
17: {
18:
19:   var DateObject = new Date()
20:   Response.Write("<H3>UserDefinedJScriptFunction has been
    ➥called.<BR>")
21:   Response.Write("Today's time is " + DateObject.getHours() + " : " +
22:                   DateObject.getMinutes() + " : " +
23:                   DateObject.getSeconds() + " </H3>")
24:
25: }
26:
27: </SCRIPT>
28:
29: <SCRIPT RUNAT=SERVER LANGUAGE=PerlScript>
30: sub UserDefinedPerlScriptFunction
31: {
32:
33:   $BrowserCapabilities = $Server->CreateObject("MSWC.BrowserType");
34:
35:   $Response->write
36:     ("<H3>UserDefinedJScriptFunction has been called.<BR>");
37:   $Response->write
38:     ("The Web browsre you are using is ");
39:   $Response->write ($BrowserCapabilities->browser);
40:   $Response->write ($BrowserCapabilities->version);
41:   $Response->write ("</H3>");
42:
43: }
44: </SCRIPT>
45:
46: <HTML>
47: <HEAD>
48:
49:
50: <TITLE>
51:   Using PerlScript With VBScript And JScript
52: </TITLE>
53: </HEAD>
54:
55: <BODY bgcolor="#DBFFBF" link="#0000FF" vlink="#800080">
56:
57: <TABLE BORDER=3><TR><TD>
58: <H1>VBScript, JScript, and PerlScript can be used in
```

continues

```
59: the same ASP application!</H1>
60: </TD></TR></TABLE>
61:
62: <H2>About to call VBScript subroutine</H2>
63: <% Call UserDefinedVBScriptFunction %>
64:
65: <HR>
66:
67: <H2>About to call JScript subroutine</H2>
68: <% Call UserDefinedJScriptFunction %>
69:
70: <HR>
71:
72: <H2>About to call PerlScript subroutine</H2>
73: <% Call UserDefinedPerlScriptFunction %>
74:
75: </BODY>
76: </HTML>
```

ANALYSIS   To use Perl in your ASP applications, simply replace LANGUAGE=VBSCRIPT of
the SCRIPT parameter with LANGUAGE=PerlScript, as shown in line 29 of
Listing B.1.

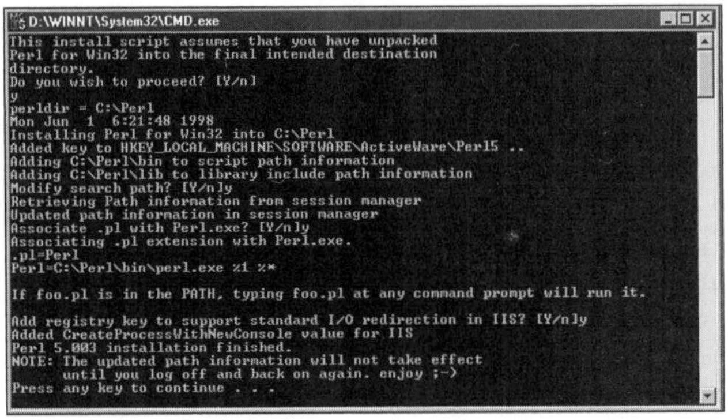

FIGURE B.2.

*VBScript, JScript, and
PerlScript can be used
at the same time.*

Note   To learn more about developing ASP applications with Perl, experiment with
the PerlScript sample applications found in C:\Perl\aspSamples (assuming you
installed Perl in the C:\Perl directory).

Perl Resources on the Internet

 You might want to visit the following URLs for sample Perl scripts and general information about Perl.

Visit Yahoo!'s page about Web programming with Perl scripts at the following URL:

```
http://www.yahoo.com/Computers_and_Internet/Internet/World_Wide_Web/
➡Programming/PERL_Scripts/
```

Check out Yahoo!'s Web page about Internet applications of Perl at the following URL:

```
http://www.yahoo.com/Computers_and_Internet/Languages/PERL/
```

B

APPENDIX C

ASP Resources on the Internet

There are many Active Server Page resources on the Internet. Some of the more useful ones are listed in this appendix for your reference. Browse the following sites to learn more about Active Server Pages.

 Caution

> The Internet is a dynamic medium, which means it is in constant change. The following information was true at the time this book was written; however, some of the sites and other information might have changed.

Microsoft's Internet News Server

If you have any ASP questions, use an Internet newsgroup reading program to connect to Microsoft's Internet news server, `msnews.microsoft.com`. You can then use the `microsoft.public.inetserver.iis.activeserverpages` newsgroup to participate in online discussions about Active Server Pages. I encourage you to monitor this newsgroup at least once a week to find out about innovative uses of ASP and get answers to frequently asked questions.

Active Server Pages Whitepaper

The following site offers an overview of Active Server Pages by discussing what Active Server Pages is and how it is used with Internet Information Server 3.0:

- `http://www.microsoft.com/iis/partners/aspwp.asp`

This site is a good source for learning about ASP's fundamental architecture.

ASP Frequently Asked Questions

The FAQ for ASP is at the following URL:

- `http://www.microsoft.com/iis/guide/aspfaq.asp`

Learn answers to frequently asked questions on ASP. By visiting this Web site, you can identify and avoid mistakes when developing ASP applications and also benefit from the experiences of other ASP developers.

ASP Tips and Troubleshooting

Learn ASP tips and how to avoid common mistakes when developing ASP applications by going to the following site. A troubleshooting guide is also included. ASP development issues related to ADO and security are also covered.

- `http://www.microsoft.com/iis/partners/asp_tips.asp`

The ASP Developer's Site

This is a resource-rich Web page for ASP application developers. Source code, tools, components, tutorials, FAQs, and documentation can be found here:

- `http://www.genusa.com/asp/`

Designing Real-World Applications with Active Server Pages

For useful tips and techniques that can be used to develop real-world applications with Active Server Pages, visit the following Web page:

- http://www.microsoft.com/mind/0397/actservpages.htm

ASP Hole: ASP Resource for Web Professionals

This Web site has been well crafted using ASP to provide dynamic information to users browsing the Web site. Visit this site for ASP primers, books on ASP, ASP mailing lists, and other ASP resources on the Internet.

- http://www.asphole.com/asphole/default.asp

Carl and Gary's Active Server Pages

This site contains links to many ASP-related resources on the Internet. Visit this site to learn how to develop ASP applications. You can find it online at this URL:

- http://www.apexsc.com/vb/asp.html

Ken's Active Server Pages and VBScript Demos

Learn how to develop ASP applications with VBScript by visiting the following Web page:

- http://kencox.corinet.com/kencscripts/index.asp

The Scripting FAQ

Visit this Web page to find answers to common Web-scripting questions and problems:

- http://www.frontpagechat.com/FAQ/Scripts/

C

Microsoft Visual InterDev Web Site

Visit the Microsoft Visual InterDev Web site to learn about Visual InterDev–specific topics. It also contains applications you can download, whitepapers about ASP, and so forth.

- http://www.microsoft.com/vinterdev/

Developing Web Applications for IIS

The development of Active Server Pages, ISAPI applications, CGI applications, and ActiveX components for IIS are discussed in the following Web page:

- http://www.microsoft.com/iis/usingiis/developing/default.htm

Microsoft Universal Data Access

Browse the following Web page for the latest information about Microsoft's strategy for providing access to all types of data: Microsoft Universal Data Access. You will find the latest news about ADO, OLE DB, and ODBC at this Web site.

- http://www.microsoft.com/data/

Integrate ASP with Microsoft Index Server

Microsoft Index Server is the search engine included with IIS. Visit the following site to learn how ASP can be used to build ASP applications that integrate the functionality of Microsoft Index Server.

- http://www.microsoft.com/mind/0697/index.htm

APPENDIX D

Ports Associated with Common Internet Services

Port numbers of some well-known Internet services are listed in Table D.1. These ports are defined in RFC 1060; you can refer to it by visiting the following URL:

`http://www.pmg.lcs.mit.edu/cgi-bin/rfc/view?number=1060`

This site contains a comprehensive listing and discussion of the ports defined in RFC 1060.

TABLE D.1. WELL-KNOWN INTERNET SERVICES' PORT NUMBERS.

Port Number	Service Name	Description
5	RJE	Remote Job Entry
7	ECHO	Echo
9	DISCARD	Discard
11	USERS	Active Users
13	DAYTIME	Daytime
17	QUOTE	Quote of the Day
19	CHARGEN	Character Generator
20	FTP-DATA	File Transfer (Default Data)
21	FTP	File Transfer (Control)
23	TELNET	Telnet
25	SMTP	Simple Mail Transfer Protocol
37	TIME	Time
42	NAMESERVER	Host Name Server
43	NICNAME	Who Is
49	LOGIN	Login Host Protocol
53	DOMAIN	Domain Name Server
67	BOOTPS	Bootstrap Protocol Server
68	BOOTPC	Bootstrap Protocol Client
69	TFTP	Trivial File Transfer
79	FINGER	Finger
80	HTTP	Web HTTP Transactions
93	DCP	Device Control Protocol
101	HOSTNAME	NIC Host Name Server
107	RTELNET	Remote Telnet Service
109	POP2	Post Office Protocol - Version 2
110	POP3	Post Office Protocol - Version 3
113	AUTH	Authentication Service
115	SFTP	Simple File Transfer Protocol
119	NNTP	Network News Transfer Protocol
123	NTP	Network Time Protocol
129	PWDGEN	Password Generator Protocol
130	CISCO-FNA	CISCO FNATIVE

135	LOC-SRV	Location Service
136	PROFILE	PROFILE Naming System
137	NETBIOS-NS	NETBIOS Name Service
138	NETBIOS-DGM	NETBIOS Datagram Service
139	NETBIOS-SSN	NETBIOS Session Service
144	NEWS	NewS
150	SQL-NET	SQL-NET
152	BFTP	Background File Transfer Program
153	SGMP	SGMP
156	SQLSRV	SQL Service
161	SNMP	Simple Network Management Protocol
162	SNMPTRAP	SNMPTRAP
192	OSU-NMS	OSU Network Monitoring System
194	IRC	Internet Relay Chat Protocol
197	DLS	Directory Location Service
1198	DLS-Mon	Directory Location Service Monitor

D

APPENDIX E

Internet Country/ Identification Codes

Listed in Tables E.1 and E.2 are Internet country and identification codes. These codes can be used to analyze an Internet address and determine its origin.

TABLE E.1. COMMON IDENTIFICATION CODES.

COM	U.S. commercial
EDU	U.S. educational
GOV	U.S. government
INT	International
MIL	U.S. military
NET	Network
ORG	Nonprofit organization

continues

TABLE E.1. CONTINUED

ARPA	Old-style ARPAnet
NATO	NATO field

TABLE E.2. COMMON COUNTRY CODES.

AD	Andorra
AE	United Arab Emirates
AF	Afghanistan
AG	Antigua and Barbuda
AI	Anguilla
AL	Albania
AM	Armenia
AN	Netherlands Antilles
AO	Angola
AQ	Antarctica
AR	Argentina
AS	American Samoa
AT	Austria
AU	Australia
AW	Aruba
AZ	Azerbaijan
BA	Bosnia and Herzegovina
BB	Barbados
BD	Bangladesh
BE	Belgium
BF	Burkina Faso
BG	Bulgaria
BH	Bahrain
BI	Burundi
BJ	Benin
BM	Bermuda
BN	Brunei Darussalam
BO	Bolivia

BR	Brazil
BS	Bahamas
BT	Bhutan
BV	Bouvet Island
BW	Botswana
BY	Belarus
BZ	Belize
CA	Canada
CC	Cocos (Keeling) Islands
CF	Central African Republic
CG	Congo
CH	Switzerland
CI	Cote D'Ivoire (Ivory Coast)
CK	Cook Islands
CL	Chile
CM	Cameroon
CN	China
CO	Colombia
CR	Costa Rica
CS	Czechoslovakia (former)
CU	Cuba
CV	Cape Verde
CX	Christmas Island
CY	Cyprus
CZ	Czech Republic
DE	Germany
DJ	Djibouti
DK	Denmark
DM	Dominica
DO	Dominican Republic
DZ	Algeria
EC	Ecuador
EE	Estonia

E

continues

TABLE E.2. CONTINUED

EG	Egypt
EH	Western Sahara
ER	Eritrea
ES	Spain
ET	Ethiopia
FI	Finland
FJ	Fiji
FK	Falkland Islands (Malvinas)
FM	Micronesia
FO	Faroe Islands
FR	France
FX	France, Metropolitan
GA	Gabon
GB	Great Britain (U.K.)
GD	Grenada
GE	Georgia
GF	French Guiana
GH	Ghana
GI	Gibraltar
GL	Greenland
GM	Gambia
GN	Guinea
GP	Guadeloupe
GQ	Equatorial Guinea
GR	Greece
GS	S. Georgia and S. Sandwich Islands
GT	Guatemala
GU	Guam
GW	Guinea-Bissau
GY	Guyana
HK	Hong Kong
HM	Heard and McDonald Islands
HN	Honduras

HR	Croatia (Hrvatska)
HT	Haiti
HU	Hungary
ID	Indonesia
IE	Ireland
IL	Israel
IN	India
IO	British Indian Ocean Territory
IQ	Iraq
IR	Iran
IS	Iceland
IT	Italy
JM	Jamaica
JO	Jordan
JP	Japan
KE	Kenya
KG	Kyrgyzstan
KH	Cambodia
KI	Kiribati
KM	Comoros
KN	Saint Kitts and Nevis
KP	Korea (North)
KR	Korea (South)
KW	Kuwait
KY	Cayman Islands
KZ	Kazakhstan
LA	Laos
LB	Lebanon
LC	Saint Lucia
LI	Liechtenstein
LK	Sri Lanka
LR	Liberia
LS	Lesotho

E

continues

TABLE E.2. CONTINUED

LT	Lithuania
LU	Luxembourg
LV	Latvia
LY	Libya
MA	Morocco
MC	Monaco
MD	Moldova
MG	Madagascar
MH	Marshall Islands
MK	Macedonia
ML	Mali
MM	Myanmar
MN	Mongolia
MO	Macau
MP	Northern Mariana Islands
MQ	Martinique
MR	Mauritania
MS	Montserrat
MT	Malta
MU	Mauritius
MV	Maldives
MW	Malawi
MX	Mexico
MY	Malaysia
MZ	Mozambique
NA	Namibia
NC	New Caledonia
NE	Niger
NF	Norfolk Island
NG	Nigeria
NI	Nicaragua
NL	Netherlands
NO	Norway

NP	Nepal
NR	Nauru
NU	Niue
NZ	New Zealand (Aotearoa)
OM	Oman
PA	Panama
PE	Peru
PF	French Polynesia
PG	Papua New Guinea
PH	Philippines
PK	Pakistan
PL	Poland
PM	St. Pierre and Miquelon
PN	Pitcairn
PR	Puerto Rico
PT	Portugal
PW	Palau
PY	Paraguay
QA	Qatar
RE	Reunion
RO	Romania
RU	Russian Federation
RW	Rwanda
SA	Saudi Arabia
SB	Solomon Islands
SC	Seychelles
SD	Sudan
SE	Sweden
SG	Singapore
SH	St. Helena
SI	Slovenia
SJ	Svalbard and Jan Mayen Islands
SK	Slovak Republic

E

continues

TABLE E.2. CONTINUED

SL	Sierra Leone
SM	San Marino
SN	Senegal
SO	Somalia
SR	Suriname
ST	Sao Tome and Principe
SV	El Salvador
SY	Syria
SZ	Swaziland
TC	Turks and Caicos Islands
TD	Chad
TF	French Southern Territories
TG	Togo
TH	Thailand
TJ	Tajikistan
TK	Tokelau
TM	Turkmenistan
TN	Tunisia
TO	Tonga
TP	East Timor
TR	Turkey
TT	Trinidad and Tobago
TV	Tuvalu
TW	Taiwan
TZ	Tanzania
UA	Ukraine
UG	Uganda
UK	United Kingdom
UM	U.S. Minor Outlying Islands
US	United States
UY	Uruguay
UZ	Uzbekistan
VA	Vatican City State

VC	Saint Vincent and the Grenadines
VE	Venezuela
VG	Virgin Islands (British)
VI	Virgin Islands (U.S.)
VN	Viet Nam
VU	Vanuatu
WF	Wallis and Futuna Islands
WS	Samoa
YE	Yemen
YT	Mayotte
YU	Yugoslavia
ZA	South Africa
ZM	Zambia
ZR	Zaire
ZW	Zimbabwe

E

APPENDIX F

ISO 8859-1 Table

In addition to regular alphanumeric characters, special characters can be added to an HTML document by using the ISO 8859-1 table shown in Table F.1. It is easy to add special characters to an HTML document. For example, if you'd like the copyright symbol © to appear somewhere in an HTML document, just insert © or © where you'd like the © symbol to appear. Note that the semicolon is necessary. An example of how special characters can be used in a Web page is given next. The Web page shown in Figure F.1 was created by using the following HTML code:

```
<HTML>
<HEAD><TITLE>HTML Special character demonstration</TITLE>
</HEAD>
<BODY TEXT="#000000" LINK="#FF0000" VLINK="#808080"
ALINK="#FF0080">

<H1>
Web pages can be
```

```
&#205;     <!-- Í -->
&ntilde;   <!-- ñ -->
t          <!-- t -->
&euml;     <!-- ë -->
r          <!-- r -->
n          <!-- n -->
&acirc;    <!-- â -->
t          <!-- t -->
&iuml;     <!-- ï -->
&ocirc;    <!-- ô -->
&ntilde;   <!-- ñ -->
&agrave;   <!-- à -->
l          <!-- l -->
&iacute;   <!-- í -->
z          <!-- z -->
&euml;     <!-- ë -->
&ETH;      <!-- Ð -->
<BR>
using special HTML character sequences!
</H1>

</BODY>
</HTML>
```

FIGURE F.1.

Web pages can be internationalized by using special HTML character sequences.

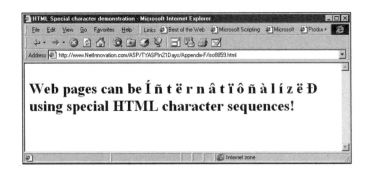

 Visit the following URL for more information about adding special characters to a Web page:

```
http://www.uni-passau.de/%7Eramsch/iso8859-1.html
```

> **Tip**
>
> It is recommended that you use the numeric codes from Table F.1. Character codes are not always equally interpreted by some browsers.

TABLE F.1. THE ISO 8859-1 TABLE OF SPECIAL CHARACTERS.

Decimal	Octal	Hex	Binary	Character	ASCII Name
0	0	0	00000000	^@	NUL
1	01	0x1	00000001	^A	SOH
2	02	0x2	00000010	^B	STX
3	03	0x3	00000011	^C	ETX
4	04	0x4	00000100	^D	EOT
5	05	0x5	00000101	^E	ENQ
6	06	0x6	00000110	^F	ACK
7	07	0x7	00000111	^G	BEL
8	010	0x8	00001000	^H	BS
9	011	0x9	00001001	^I	HT
10	012	0xa	00001010	^J	LF
11	013	0xb	00001011	^K	VT
12	014	0xc	00001100	^L	FF
13	015	0xd	00001101	^M	CR
14	016	0xe	00001110	^N	SO
15	017	0xf	00001111	^O	SI
16	020	0x10	00010000	^P	DLE
17	021	0x11	00010001	^Q	DC1
18	022	0x12	00010010	^R	DC2
19	023	0x13	00010011	^S	DC3
20	024	0x14	00010100	^T	DC4
21	025	0x15	00010101	^U	NAK
22	026	0x16	00010110	^V	SYN
23	027	0x17	00010111	^W	ETB
24	030	0x18	00011000	^X	CAN
25	031	0x19	00011001	^Y	EM
26	032	0x1a	00011010	^Z	SUB
27	033	0x1b	00011011	^esc	ESC
28	034	0x1c	00011100	^\	FS
29	035	0x1d	00011101	^]	GS
30	036	0x1e	00011110	^^	RS
31	037	0x1f	00011111	^_	US

F

continues

TABLE F.1. CONTINUED

Decimal	Octal	Hex	Binary	Character	ASCII Name
32	040	0x20	00100000	space	SP
33	041	0x21	00100001	!	
34	042	0x22	00100010	"	
35	043	0x23	00100011	#	
36	044	0x24	00100100	$	
37	045	0x25	00100101	%	
38	046	0x26	00100110	&	
39	047	0x27	00100111	'	
40	050	0x28	00101000	(	
41	051	0x29	00101001	)	
42	052	0x2a	00101010	*	
43	053	0x2b	00101011	+	
44	054	0x2c	00101100	'	
45	055	0x2d	00101101	-	
46	056	0x2e	00101110	.	
47	057	0x2f	00101111	/	
48	060	0x30	00110000	0	
49	061	0x31	00110001	1	
50	062	0x32	00110010	2	
51	063	0x33	00110011	3	
52	064	0x34	00110100	4	
53	065	0x35	00110101	5	
54	066	0x36	00110110	6	
55	067	0x37	00110111	7	
56	070	0x38	00111000	8	
57	071	0x39	00111001	9	
58	072	0x3a	00111010	:	
59	073	0x3b	00111011	;	
60	074	0x3c	00111100	<	
61	075	0x3d	00111101	=	
62	076	0x3e	00111110	>	
63	077	0x3f	00111111	?	
64	0100	0x40	01000000	@	

Decimal	Octal	Hex	Binary	Character	ASCII Name
65	0101	0x41	01000001	A	
66	0102	0x42	01000010	B	
67	0103	0x43	01000011	C	
68	0104	0x44	01000100	D	
69	0105	0x45	01000101	E	
70	0106	0x46	01000110	F	
71	0107	0x47	01000111	G	
72	0110	0x48	01001000	H	
73	0111	0x49	01001001	I	
74	0112	0x4a	01001010	J	
75	0113	0x4b	01001011	K	
76	0114	0x4c	01001100	L	
77	0115	0x4d	01001101	M	
78	0116	0x4e	01001110	N	
79	0117	0x4f	01001111	O	
80	0120	0x50	01010000	P	
81	0121	0x51	01010001	Q	
82	0122	0x52	01010010	R	
83	0123	0x53	01010011	S	
84	0124	0x54	01010100	T	
85	0125	0x55	01010101	U	
86	0126	0x56	01010110	V	
87	0127	0x57	01010111	W	
88	0130	0x58	01011000	X	
89	0131	0x59	01011001	Y	
90	0132	0x5a	01011010	Z	
91	0133	0x5b	01011011	[	
92	0134	0x5c	01011100	\	
93	0135	0x5d	01011101	]	
94	0136	0x5e	01011110	^	
95	0137	0x5f	01011111	_	
96	0140	0x60	01100000	`	
97	0141	0x61	01100001	a	

F

continues

TABLE F.1. CONTINUED

Decimal	Octal	Hex	Binary	Character	ASCII Name
98	0142	0x62	01100010	b	
99	0143	0x63	01100011	c	
100	0144	0x64	01100100	d	
101	0145	0x65	01100101	e	
102	0146	0x66	01100110	f	
103	0147	0x67	01100111	g	
104	0150	0x68	01101000	h	
105	0151	0x69	01101001	i	
106	0152	0x6a	01101010	j	
107	0153	0x6b	01101011	k	
108	0154	0x6c	01101100	l	
109	0155	0x6d	01101101	m	
110	0156	0x6e	01101110	n	
111	0157	0x6f	01101111	o	
112	0160	0x70	01110000	p	
113	0161	0x71	01110001	q	
114	0162	0x72	01110010	r	
115	0163	0x73	01110011	s	
116	0164	0x74	01110100	t	
117	0165	0x75	01110101	u	
118	0166	0x76	01110110	v	
119	0167	0x77	01110111	w	
120	0170	0x78	01111000	x	
121	0171	0x79	01111001	y	
122	0172	0x7a	01111010	z	
123	0173	0x7b	01111011	{	
124	0174	0x7c	01111100			
125	0175	0x7d	01111101	}	
126	0176	0x7e	01111110	~	
127	0177	0x7f	01111111	del, rubout	

INDEX

client requests, 163-185
**client scriptlets, comparing
to server scriptlets, 120**
**client-side ActiveX controls,
458**
**client-side cookies, value,
159**
client-side scripting, 10, 87
**client/server three-tier
model, 504-506**
clients
connections, 167
IP address, 157
Web browser used, 156
**Close( ) method, Connection
object (ADO), 255,
292-293**
clusters, 505
code
centralized, ASP compo-
nents, 614
reusing, 581
running during scriptlet
registration, 130
Scriptlet Wizard, 140-141
scripting code, session
timeouts, 206
scriptlets
building, 125-127
locating, 125-127
reusing, 124
server-side, 36
code delimiters, 21-23
**Cold Fusion (Allaire), 14,
615**
collections
ADO, 292-301
Command object, 296
Connection object, 294
Cookies, Response object,
182-185
number of elements, 147

Recordset object, 301
Request object, 146
Form, 148
QueryString, 148-150
Response object, Cookies,
181
color, Web forms, 59
**Column property,
TextStream object, 112**
COM components
scriptlet files, 136
scriptlets, 124
command buttons
Calendar control, 468-469
Icon property, 468
Style property, 468
Command object (ADO)
collections, 296
methods, 295
properties, 295
commands
databases (SQL), 255
script, executing on server,
36
Server.CreateObject( ),
instances, 220
SQL databases, 255
**Common Gateway
Interface. *See* CGI**
**comparing IDC and ASP,
595-596**
compatibility, UPS, 387
compiling, 11, 496
components
ASP, 39
Text Stream, 111-112
conditional statements, 47
conditionless protocols, 50
configuration, IIS, 583
**conflicts, Application object,
210**

**Connection object (ADO),
295**
collections, 294
instance, creating, 254,
281
instantiating, 293, 332
methods, 293-294
Close( ), 255, 292-293
Execute, 255
Open( ), 254, 292-293
OpenSchema, 322-324
properties, 294
SQL statements, 293
**connection pooling (ODBC),
Registry setting, 608**
connections
clients, 167
databases
closing, 255
opening, 254
user forum, 307-308
Visual InterDev, 555
constants, type libraries, 40
**Content Linking compo-
nent, Web page linking,
231-234**
**Content Linking List file
(Web page), 232-233**
**Content Rotator (Web
pages), 225-227**
**CONTENT TYPE server
variable, 155**
**ContentType property,
HTTP headers, 165-166**
control structures, 45-49
controls
user registration system,
328
WMS application,
509-510
**conversion utilities, HTML
forms, 195**

M

MapPath( ) method, Server object, 197-199

Master Mode (Visual InterDev), 538

mathematical operations, time/date values, 97

MemFreeFactor Registry setting, 601

memory
availability, Registry setting, 601
resource values, 620-622
used, minimum list length, 602

MEMORYSTATUS data structure, 619

message body (HTTP), writing to, 176-179

message boxes, 72-74

messages
HTTP, Response object, 173
user forum
adding to system, 317-320
displaying, 314-317
URLs, 317
viewing, 320-322
WMS application, 513-515

methods, 11
AddHeader, Response object, 171-173
AppendToLog, Response object, 179-180
calling applications, 158
Clear, Response object, 174-175
Close( ), Connection object, 255, 292-293

Command object, 295

Connection object, 293-294

Count, Request object, 147-148

CreateObject, Server object, 192-193

CreateTextFile, FileSystem object, 111-113

End, Response object, 175

Execute, Connection object, 255

Flush, Response object, 175

GET, Request object, 149

HasAccess( ), 235-237

HTMLEncode( ), Server object, 193-196

Lock, Application object, 210

MapPath( ), Server object, 197-199

Open( ), Connection object (ADO), 254, 292-293

OpenSchema, Connection object, 322-324

OpenTextFile, FileSystem object, 111-115

Page Counter component, 242

POST, Request object, 148-149

Recordset object, 297-299

Redirect, HTTP headers, 171

Request.Form.Item( ), 84

Response object, page buffering, 174

scriptlets, 130-132
implementing, 133
Scriptlet Wizard, 139

Server.MapPath( ), 198

ServerVariables( ), Request object, 152-154

Session.Abandon, 208

SetAbort, MTS, 213-214

SetComplete, MTS, 213-214

StartNewOrder, MTS, 214

TextStream object, 112

Unlock, Application object, 210

Update, Recordset object, 332-333

UPDATE, syntax, 331

URLEncode( ), Server object, 196-197

Write, Response object, 177

Microsoft Internet news server Web page, 675

Microsoft Management Console. *See* MMC

Microsoft Office and OLE automation, 632-633

Microsoft Transaction Server. *See* MTS

Microsoft Visual InterDev Web site, 678

middle-tier, APS application, 505

MIME types, 155

MinUsedBlocks Registry setting, 602

Minute( ) function, 98

MMC (Microsoft Management Console)
IIS, 583-584
log files, 584-586
snap-ins, 583

models, Object model, 38-39

modes, Visual InterDev, 538-539

X-Z

Other Related Titles

Active Server Pages Unleashed
Stephen Walther
0-57521-351-6
$49.99 USA/$70.95 CAN

Special Edition Active Server Pages
Scot Johnson
0-7897-1389-6
$49.99 USA/$70.95 CAN

Special Edition Using Visual InterDev 6
Steve Banick & Michael Morrison
0-7897-1549-X
$39.99 USA/$57.95 CAN

Cold Fusion 4 Web Application Construction Kit
Ben Forta
0-7897-1809-X
$49.99 USA/$71.95 CAN

Sams Teach Yourself HTML 4 in 24 Hours, Second Edition
Dick Oliver
1-57521-366-4
$19.99 USA/$28.95 CAN

Platinum Edition Using HTML 4, XML X, and Java 1.2
Eric Ladd and Jim O'Donnell
0-7897-1759-X
$59.99 USA/$85.95 CAN

Sams Teach Yourself JavaScript
Arman Danesh
1-57521-304-4
$39.99 USA/$56.95 CAN

Net Results: Web Marketing That Works
US Web and Rick Bruner
1-56830-414-5
$29.99 USA/$42.95 CAN

Maximum Security: A Hacker's Guide to Protecting Your Internet Site and Network, Second Edition
Anonymous
0-672-31341-3
$49.99 USA/$71.95 CAN

Sams Teach Yourself Visual InterDev 6 in 21 Days
L. Michael Van Hoozer, Jr.
0-672-31251-4
$34.99 USA/$49.95 CAN

SAMS
www.samspublishing.com